FUNDAMENTALS OF

Contemporary

Business
Communication

Scot Ober

BALL STATE UNIVERSITY

HOUGHTON MIFFLIN COMPANY

BOSTON   NEW YORK

Publisher: Charles Hartford
Associate Sponsoring Editor: Joanne Dauksewicz
Senior Project Editor: Maria Morelli
Editorial Assistant: Lisa M. Goodman
Senior Production/Design Coordinator: Jennifer Meyer Dare
Senior Manufacturing Coordinator: Priscilla Bailey
Marketing Manager: Steven Mikels

Cover Illustration: Bryan Leister

Screen shots reprinted with permission from Microsoft corporation.

Credits continued on page 426.

The model letters provided on authentic company stationery have been included by permission to provide realistic examples of company documents for educational purposes. They do not represent actual business documents created by these companies.

Printed in the U.S.A.

Library of Congress Catalog Card Number: 2002/09655

ISBNs

Instructor's Annotated Edition: 0-618-07375-2

Student's Edition: 0-618-07372-8

123456789—VH—08 07 06 05 04 03

Brief Contents

Contents

iv

CHAPTER ③

Business Sentence Structure 61

Part Two

Developing Your Business Writing Skills 83

CHAPTER ④

Writing with Style: Individual Elements 84

CHAPTER ⑤

Writing with Style: Tone and Process 112

CHAPTER 9

Using Verbs in Business Communication   234

Part Four

Business Report Writing   253

CHAPTER 10

Planning the Business Report and Collecting Data   254

CHAPTER 11

Writing the Business Report   286

CHAPTER 12

Using Pronouns, Adjectives, and Adverbs in Business Communication   322

Part Five
Oral and Employment Communication   343

CHAPTER 13

Business Presentations   344

CHAPTER 14

Employment Communications   371

CHAPTER 15

Mechanics in Business Writing   409

Preface

Students don't have to be convinced of the need for competent communication skills. By the time they enter the business communication class, they know enough about the business environment to appreciate the critical role communication plays in the contemporary organization. They're also aware of the role communication will play in helping them secure an internship or get a job and be successful at work.

To sustain this inherent interest, students need a textbook that is current, fast-paced, and interesting—just like business itself. Thus, a major objective of *Fundamentals of Contemporary Business Communication* is to present comprehensive coverage of real-world concepts in an interesting, lively, and concise manner. The following discussion highlights the features of this complete teaching and learning system:

- Business Communication—In Context
- The 3Ps—Think First; Write Later
- Streamlined Coverage of Essential Topics
- Basic Skills First
- Student Portfolios—For Proof of Competence
- Checkpoints—For Feedback and Reinforcement
- Unprecedented Instructor and Student Support

Business Communication—In Context

Business communication problems in the real world do not occur in a vacuum. Events have happened before the problem and will happen after the problem, affecting its resolution. Thus, in addition to typical end-of-chapter exercises, other learning tools in this text provide more complete long-term situations and provide a "slice-of-life" reality students will actually face at work.

On the Job Each chapter begins with an on-the-job interview with managers from multinational companies (such as 3M), small entrepreneurial companies (such as iVillage), and nonprofit organizations (such as The Wilderness Society). These insider perspectives set the stage for the particular concepts presented in that chapter.

Continuing Text Examples and End-of-Chapter Exercises Continuing examples are often used throughout the chapter in both the text and end-of-chapter exercises. For example, in Chapter 7, students first assume the role of buyer and write a claim letter. Later, they assume the role of seller and answer the same claim letter by writing an adjustment letter. In Chapter 8, students write a persuasive request from a subordinate; and later, they assume the role of superior and turn down a well-written persuasive request.

Such situations are realistic because they give a sense of following a problem through to completion. They are interesting because they provide a continuing thread to the chapters. They also reinforce the concept of audience analysis because students must first assume the role of sender and later the role of receiver for the same communication task.

Real Company Letterheads Full-page models of each major writing task, often on real company letterheads, appear in this text, shown in complete, ready-to-send format, so that students become familiar with the appropriate format for every major type of writing assignment. Each model provides marginal step-by-step composing notes as well as grammar and mechanics notes that point out specific illustrations of the grammar and mechanics rules presented in the business English chapters of the text.

Technology-Centered   Today, if there is one business buzzword, it has to be "technology." And with good reason. Every aspect of contemporary business communication—from determining what information to communicate to processing the information and sharing it—depends on technology. In *Fundamentals* students learn to:

- Compose, format, and manage email.
- Access the Internet and World Wide Web and evaluate the quality of the information they receive.
- Format electronic résumés and search online for a job.
- Give electronic presentations.
- Cite electronic sources such as Web pages, online journals and directories, email, and other Internet sources in business, APA, and MLA formats.

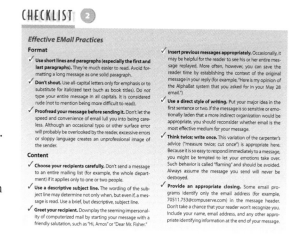

Throughout, the text places minor emphasis on traditional technology (such as word processing) and greater emphasis on newer technologies (such as teleconferencing, videoconferencing, and video and electronic presentations).

The 3Ps—Think First; Write Later

Probably the most important thing this author has learned in his 20-plus years of teaching business communication is the importance of *guiding* the student's practice. And the reason is this: As soon as most students are given a writing assignment, they quickly scan the problem and then immediately begin composing what they think is the final draft—without first planning the best strategy to use.

The result, naturally enough, is the need for extensive revision—based upon instructor feedback, which, of course, requires extensive grading time. The 3Ps (problem, process, product) exercises found in every chapter of *Fundamentals* force students to spend some time planning their strategy before they start to write.

For most business writing tasks, there are only two to three parts that cause students any real problems. Therefore, students should spend most of their time carefully planning these critical elements. If they do, then the other parts will almost write themselves.

Each 3Ps activity begins with a *problem*—a typical business situation that requires some sort of communication task. The *process* questions force students to concentrate on the critical elements of the situation; that is, they must delay their impulse to begin writing until after they've thought through (and solved) these important issues. Better writing skills and less grading time will result. The activity ends with the *product*—the final, ready-to-submit formatted document.

Streamlined Coverage of Essential Topics

As the body of knowledge comprising the theory, research, and practice of business communication has grown, textbooks have expanded to include the new coverage. They have become longer and longer, often making it difficult to cover all the material in a typical course.

Students learn to communicate by communicating—not by just *reading* about communicating. They need a text that presents comprehensive coverage in a concise format—so that they then have sufficient time to practice and refine their craft after each chapter.

Fundamentals is true to its name: it presents the fundamental traditional and emerging topics in business communication in just 10 chapters (as noted later, the other five chapters cover business English essentials), organized as follows:

Part One: COMMUNICATING IN BUSINESS
            1. Understanding Business Communication
            2. Contemporary Issues in Business Communication

Part Two: DEVELOPING YOUR BUSINESS WRITING SKILLS
            4. Writing With Style: Individual Elements
            5. Writing With Style: Tone and Process

Part Three: BASIC CORRESPONDENCE
            7. Routine and Negative Emails, Letters, and Memos
            8. Persuasive Emails, Letters, and Memos

Part Four: BUSINESS REPORT WRITING
            10. Planning the Business Report and Collecting Data
            11. Writing the Business Report

Part Five: ORAL AND EMPLOYMENT COMMUNICATION
            13. Business Presentations
            14. Employment Communications

The business communication portion of *Fundamentals* comprises about 350 pages—half the length of more traditional textbooks. This means students will have more time (both in and out of class) to plan, draft, and revise their documents. Even including the business English chapters, the text still comprises fewer than 500 pages—a third shorter than most traditional texts.

Instructors who need just the business communication portion of the text may contact their Houghton Mifflin sales representative who can arrange to have just these 10 chapters custom-published as a text for their institution. They can even include a more generic title (such as *Contemporary College English*), which may be a more appropriate title for career colleges.

In short, *Fundamentals* provides unmatched flexibility in presenting job-essential coverage of business communication. It is "fat-free"—just like effective business writing itself.

Basic Skills Emphasis

No one can communicate effectively if he or she cannot communicate *correctly.* It is an unfortunate fact of life that many contemporary students today have not had the advantage of the nuts-and-bolts grammar and mechanics instruction that their instructors took for granted in their own prior education. Students *must* learn these basic skills at some point, and the collegiate business communication course is probably their last opportunity.

Every third chapter of *Fundamentals* (five chapters in all) systematically reviews and expands upon basic English skills, organized as follows:

3. **Business Sentence Structure**
   Parts of Speech ■ Parts of a Sentence ■ Patterns of Sentence Organization ■ Functions of Sentences ■ Complexity of Sentences ■ Sentence Errors

6. **Business-Style Punctuation**
   Why Punctuation? ■ Commas ■ Semicolons ■ Colons ■ Periods ■ Parentheses ■ Quotation Marks ■ Italics (or Underlining) ■ Hyphens ■ Apostrophes

9. **Using Verbs in Business Communication**
   Verb Functions and Mood ■ Verb Tenses ■ Principal Parts of Verbs ■ Subject and Verb Agreement

12. **Using Pronouns, Adjectives, and Adverbs in Business Communication**
    Pronouns ■ Adjective or Adverb? ■ Comparison of Adjectives and Adverbs ■ Special Problems with Adjectives and Adverbs

15. **Mechanics in Business Writing**
    Capitalization ■ Number Expression ■ Abbreviations ■ Spelling

These five relatively short chapters concentrate on those aspects of English that occur frequently in on-the-job applications and that cause problems for many students. The chapters have more frequent checkpoints than the other chapters and extensive end-of-chapter exercises to provide plenty of practice opportunities.

Also included on the Instructor's Web site and on the Student CD-ROM (and available through the Houghton Mifflin Faculty Service Center) are 50 handout masters that provide important supplemental reference materials or practice opportunities to help students expand their skills.

In 1992, the U.S. Department of Labor Secretary's Commission on Achieving Necessary Skills (SCANS) issued a report that defined the skills U.S. students and workers need for workplace success. Clearly identified in this report were needed workplace competencies in using resources, acquiring and processing information, developing interpersonal skills, understanding and working with systems, and using technology. Since then, numerous state higher education commissions have required that postsecondary textbooks indicate the extent to which they teach and apply these competencies. The *Instructor's Resource Manual* identifies every SCANS competence taught and applied in *Fundamentals of Contemporary Business Communication.*

Student Portfolios—For Proof of Competence

"When you are in an actual job interview, you do not want to just claim you have a skill. You want to *prove* you have the skill you are claiming."

—Richard Nelson Bolles, author of *What Color Is Your Parachute?*
Practical Guide for Job-Hunters and Career Changers

Students can talk about their competent communication skills all they want, but nothing is as effective as showing the prospective employer actual examples of their work. Unique to *Fundamentals* is a planned progression of seven portfolio projects designed to demonstrate students' communication skills. The seven projects are these:

1. Routine informational message
2. Routine claim
3. Bad-news message
4. Persuasive request
5. Situational business report
6. Videotape of an oral business presentation
7. Résumé, cover letter, and videotape of practice interview

Instructors are encouraged to provide opportunities for revision of each project so that the student's final effort reflects successful attainment of the particular communication skill. To help employers more accurately evaluate the quality of the student's output, the first page of each portfolio project provides the problem (the situation that requires a response), and a process section in which the student describes the strategic thinking that went into the final product, which is then presented in final, ready-to-submit format. Shown below is a sample completed portfolio problem and student solution.

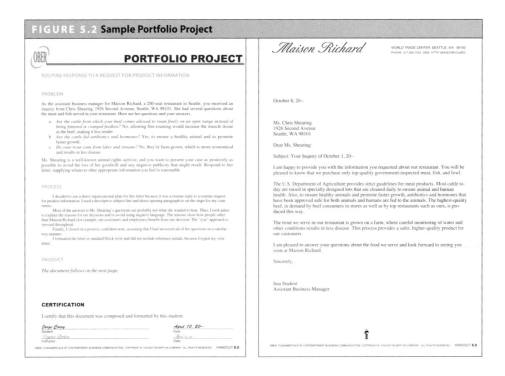

FIGURE 5.2 Sample Portfolio Project

The student portfolio projects, along with the comprehensive instruction on employment communications included in Chapter 14, will go a long way toward ensuring that students will be successful in getting a job.

Checkpoints—For Feedback and Reinforcement

Many students need an opportunity to test their comprehension immediately, rather than waiting for the end-of-chapter problems. *Fundamentals* features frequent checkpoints throughout the chapter that provide immediate feedback and reinforcement of the principles introduced in the previous few pages. Space is provided directly on the page for student responses. These checkpoints are organized according to increasing levels of difficulty.

- *Recall:* Five true/false test items that test the student's retention of the material just presented. An explanation of the false items is provided in the *Instructor's Annotated Edition* of the text.
- *Vocabulary:* Students are asked to define the key terms in their own words. Where appropriate, students are also asked to provide an original example.
- *Comprehension:* Students get to apply their new knowledge in short, focused exercises.
- *Critical Thinking:* This question (for which there is generally no one objective answer) provides students with both an opportunity to think analytically and to compose a short paragraph. Suggestions for evaluating student responses are provided in the *Instructor's Annotated Edition*.

On average, each chapter contains three checkpoints, each about a page long. Reproducible solution sheets are provided on the Instructor Web site for those instructors who wish to use these checkpoints as self-checks and provide the solutions to the students.

Unprecedented Instructor and Student Support

Fundamentals of Contemporary Business Communication provides unprecedented instructor and student support.

Ask Ober   *Fundamentals* takes the concept of communication to a new level. The "Ask Ober" feature (email: **askober@ober.net**) permits and *encourages* direct dialog between you or your students and the textbook author. Whenever you or your students have a question or comment about this text or about the business communication curriculum, *ask Ober.* Add this email address to your own contacts list and include it in your course syllabus. (Please ask students to copy you on their email so that both you and your students receive a personal response from the author.) You and your students have never been so connected.

Instructor's Annotated Edition *Fundamentals* offers an *Instructor's Annotated Edition* of the student text. It provides specific, accessible teaching aids, such as these:

- Answers to Checkpoint Quizzes for quick reference.

- Miniature copies of the PowerPoint slides and handout masters shown in the text margins so that instructors can see immediately what enrichment materials are available for each section of the text.

- Marginal notes that reference related sections in the teaching support package for suggested solutions to text exercises and additional exercises.

- Teaching tips and interesting business examples that offer resources to enrich lectures.

- Marginal notes in the end-of-chapter exercises that identify activities linked to previous or upcoming exercises.

Instructor Web Site   The Instructor Web Site can be accessed via a free password provided to instructors using this text. The site contains a monthly newsletter with additional teaching tips and hot-off-the-press current event items that illustrate business communication concepts and provide detailed lecture and supplemental discussion notes for each chapter, additional application exercises and cases, the PowerPoint slides and handout masters for previewing and downloading, and a forum for exchanging ideas with the author, publisher, and other instructors around the country teaching this course.

Student Web Site   The Student Web site provides students with a one-stop guide to the world of online business communication. Here they can learn more about the Internet, locate business information, get additional help with writing problems, complete enrichment exercises designed to help them get more from the course, take practice chapter tests, and get information about employment communication, available jobs, and employers.

PowerPoint Slides and Transparencies   The PowerPoint program consists of more than 250 slides, including summaries of key concepts, good/bad paired examples, and supplementary information such as answers to selected exercises. For added interest, the examples used in the slides are all different from those used in the text. The slides were all prepared by the author. In addition, 100 of these slides are also available as color transparencies.

Instructor's Resource Manual with Test Bank   The *Instructor's Resource Manual* includes chapter overviews, lecture and discussion notes, and suggested answers to and/or teaching tips for all writing exercises and case problems. The Test Bank contains over 1,000 test items, including multiple-choice, short answer, true-false, revision exercises, and writing items.

HM Testing   This computerized version of the *Test Bank* allows instructors to select, edit, and add questions, or generate randomly selected questions to produce a test master for easy duplication. Online Testing and Gradebook functions allow instructors to administer tests via their local area network or the World Wide Web, set up classes, record grades from tests or assignments, analyze grades, and product class and individual statistics. This program can be used on both PCs and Macintosh computers.

Real Deal Student CD-ROM   Packaged with every text is a student CD-ROM containing study aids for each chapter, copies of the PowerPoint program, student handouts and a wealth of additional practice material, including video quizzes, chapter concept review, and grammar and mechanics reinforcement.

ACKNOWLEDGMENTS

During the development of this text, it has been my great pleasure to work with a dedicated and skillful team of professionals at Houghton Mifflin, and I gratefully salute the major contributions they have made to this text. I specifically acknowledge with deep gratitude the special assistance of Joanne Dauksewicz and Maria Morelli. What a genuine pleasure it has been to work with this talented and dynamic duo.

I also wish to express my sincere appreciation to Duane Miller of Utah Valley State College who prepared the *Instructor's Resource Manual with Test Bank* for this text; and to Marian Wood, consultant and writer extraordinaire, for the many elements she created for this edition.

Finally, I wish to thank the following reviewers for their thoughtful contributions:

Carl Bridges, *Arthur Andersen Consulting*
Annette Briscoe, *Indiana University Southeast*
Mitchel T. Burchfield, *Southwest Texas Junior College*
Janice Burke, *South Suburban College*
Barbara Cameron, *Embry-Riddle Aeronautical University*
G. Jay Christensen, *California State University, Northridge*
Anne Hutta Colvin, *Montgomery County Community College*
Doris L. Cost, *Metropolitan State College of Denver*
L. Ben Crane, *Temple University*
Ava Cross, *Ryerson Polytechnic University*
Terence P. Curran, *Siena College*
Nancy J. Daugherty, *Indiana University-Purdue University, Indianapolis*
Corla Dawson, *Missouri Western State College*
Rosemarie Dittmer, *Northeastern University*
Graham N. Drake, *State University of New York, Geneseo*
Kay Durden, *The University of Tennessee at Martin*
Phillip A. Holcomb, *Angelo State University*
Larry R. Honl, *University of Wisconsin, Eau Claire*
Michelle Kirtley Johnston, *Loyola University*
Alice Kinder, *Virginia Polytechnic Institute and State University*
Richard N. Kleeberg, *Solano Community College*

Patricia Laidler, *Massasoit Community College*
Lowell Lamberton, *Central Oregon Community College*
E. Jay Larson, *Lewis and Clark State College*
Michael Liberman, *East Stroudsburg University*
Julie MacDonald, *Northwestern State University*
Marsha C. Markman, *California Lutheran University*
Diana McKowen, *Indiana University, Bloomington*
Maureen McLaughlin, *Highline Community College*
Sylvia A. Miller, *Cameron University*
Wayne Moore, *Indiana University of Pennsylvania*
Gerald W. Morton, *Auburn University of Montgomery*
James M. O'Donnell, *Huntington College*
Rosemary Olds, *Des Moines Area Community College*
Richard O. Pompian, *Boise State University*
Karen Sterkel Powell, *Colorado State University*
Seamus Reilly, *University of Illinois*
Jeanette Ritzenthaler, *New Hampshire College*
Betty Robbins, *University of Oklahoma*
Joan C. Roderick, *Southwest Texas State University*
Lacye Prewitt Schmidt, *State Technical Institute of Memphis*
Sue Seymour, *Cameron University*
Sherry Sherrill, *Forsyth Technical Community*
John R. Sinton, *Finger Lakes Community College*
Curtis J. Smith, *Finger Lakes Community College*
Dottie Snider, *Eastern Connecticut State University*
Craig E. Stanley, *California State University, Sacramento*
Ted O. Stoddard, *Brigham Young University*
Vincent C. Trofi, *Providence College*
Deborah A. Valentine, *Emory University*
Randall L. Waller, *Baylor University*
Maria W. Warren, *University of West Florida*
Delmar Wilcox, *Western New England College*
Michael R. Wunsch, *Northern Arizona University*
Annette Wyandotte, *Indiana University, Southeast*
Betty Rogers Youngkin, *University of Dayton*

PART ONE
COMMUNICATING IN BUSINESS

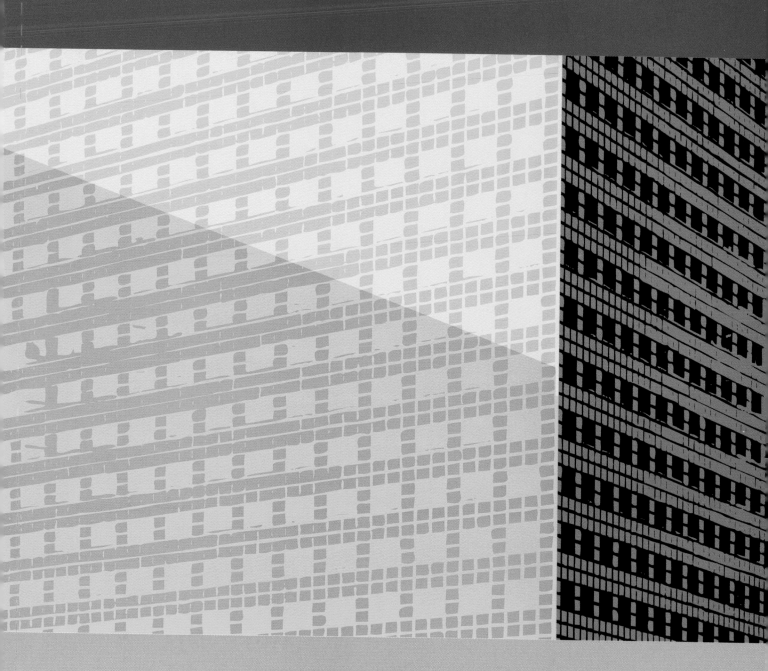

1

Understanding Business Communication

COMMUNICATION OBJECTIVES

After you have finished this chapter, you should be able to:

- Explain the role of communication in the contemporary organization.

- Describe the components of communication.

- Explain the major types of verbal communications.

- Explain the meaning of nonverbal communications.

- Identify the major verbal and nonverbal barriers to communication.

On the Job

DEBRA SANCHEZ FAIR
Vice President, Corporate Communications, Nissan North America, Inc.

Steering communication upward, downward, horizontally, and across business and borders—at full throttle—is part of a race that never ends for Debra Sanchez Fair. As vice president of corporate communications for Nissan North America, she and her 43-person staff drive all communications for the automaker's operations in the United States, Mexico, and Canada.

Fair uses a variety of media to share information within the organization, ranging from email, videoconferencing, and satellite television to more traditional newsletters, meetings, and memos. Before selecting any medium, however, she carefully plans what she wants to achieve. "First, you have to think about your objective, the audiences you are targeting, and your communication strategies," Fair says. "Then you think about the tactics. Every situation or initiative may require a different approach."

To find out whether audiences understand Nissan's messages, at least once a year Fair surveys employees, business leaders, and media representatives. Monitoring this feedback helps Fair and her team analyze audience response and keep Nissan's communication on track in the race that never ends.

Communicating in Organizations

As Debra Sanchez Fair of Nissan North America knows first-hand, effective communication drives successful businesses. Walk through the hallways of any contemporary organization—no matter whether it's a small start-up entrepreneurial firm, a *Fortune* 500 global giant, a state government office, or a not-for-profit organization. What do you see? You see employees:

- Reading documents
- Drafting messages
- Attending meetings
- Conducting interviews
- Talking on the telephone
- Conferring with others
- Reading mail
- Typing on the computer
- Making presentations

In short, you see people *communicating*. An organization is a group of people working together to achieve a common goal. Communication, of course, is a vital part of that process. Indeed, communication must have occurred before a common goal could even be established, because communication is the means by which information is shared, activities are coordinated, and decisions are made.

Understanding how communication works in business and how employees communicate competently within an organization will help you participate more effectively in every aspect of business. Good communication skills are crucial to your success in the organization. Competent writing and speaking skills will help you get hired, perform well, and earn promotions. If you decide to go into business for yourself, having excellent writing and speaking skills will help you obtain venture capital, promote your product, and manage your employees. The same skills will also help you achieve your personal and social goals.

> Communication is necessary if an organization is to achieve its goals.

The Components of Communication

Because communication is such a vital part of the organizational structure, our study of communication begins with an analysis of its components. **Communication** is the process of sending and receiving messages—sometimes through spoken or written words and sometimes through such nonverbal means as facial expressions, gestures, and voice qualities. As illustrated in Figure 1.1 on page 4, the communication model consists of five components: the stimulus, filter, message, medium, and destination. Ideally, the process ends with feedback to the sender, although feedback is not necessary for communication to have taken place.

To illustrate the model, let us follow the case of Dave, a chemist. Several years ago, while working on another project, Dave developed Ultra Light, a flat sheet of luminescent material that serves as a light source. The market for lighting is vast, and Dave was disappointed when his company decided not to manufacture and market this product. As we learn what happened to Dave after this decision, we'll examine the components of communication, one at a time.

> **communication:** The process of sending and receiving verbal and nonverbal messages

Copyright © Houghton Mifflin Company. All rights reserved.

FIGURE 1.1 The Components of Communication

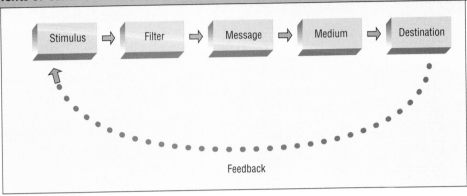

Communication Component	Incident
Dave receives a *stimulus*.	Dave receives a memorandum from his boss.
He *filters* the stimulus.	He interprets the memo to mean that his company has no interest in his invention.
He forms a *message*.	He decides to relay this information to his brother.
He selects a *medium*.	He telephones Marc.
The message reaches its *destination*.	His brother receives the call.
Optional: Marc provides *feedback*.	Marc listens and gives Dave his reaction.

The Stimulus

Step 1: A stimulus creates a need to communicate.

stimulus: An event that creates the need to communicate

For communication to take place, there first must be a **stimulus** (plural: *stimuli*), an event that creates within an individual the need to communicate. This stimulus can be internal or external. An internal stimulus is simply an idea that forms in your mind. External stimuli come to you through your sensory organs—your eyes, ears, nose, mouth, and skin. A stimulus for communicating in business might be any of the following:

- An email message you just read
- A presentation you heard at a staff meeting
- A bit of gossip you heard over lunch
- Your perception that the general manager has been acting preoccupied lately
- The hot air generated by an overworked heating system (or colleague!)

You respond to the stimulus by formulating a message: a *verbal message* (written or spoken words), a *nonverbal message* (nonwritten and nonspoken signals), or some combination of the two. For Dave, the stimulus for communication was a memorandum he received informing him that his company was not interested in developing Ultra Light but would, instead, sell the patent to some other company that *was* interested in bringing this product to market.

An example of communication at work: Dave telephones Marc to discuss Ultra Light.

The Filter

If everyone had the same perception of events, your job of communicating would be easy. That is, you could assume that your view of what happened was accurate and that others would understand your motives and intent. Instead, each person has a *unique* view of reality, based on his or her individual experiences, culture, emotions at the moment, personality, knowledge, socioeconomic status, and a host of other variables. These variables act as a **filter** in shaping everyone's unique impressions of reality.

The memo Dave received simply reinforced what he had come to expect at his company. The company had become successful by focusing on its own long-range objectives and showed little interest in taking advantage of unexpected discoveries such as Ultra Light. Dave had been intimately involved in the research leading to the discovery of Ultra Light and was quite interested in its future. Besides, after so many years in the lab, he was ready for a new challenge. These factors, then, acted as a filter through which Dave interpreted the memo and formulated his response—a phone call to his brother Marc, a marketing manager in Chicago.

Step 2: We interpret the stimulus.

filter: The mental process of interpreting stimuli based on one's knowledge, experience, and viewpoints

The Message

Dave's message to Marc was simple: "Let's form our own company to manufacture and market Ultra Light." The extent to which any communication effort achieves its desired goal depends directly on how well you construct the **message**—that is, the information to be communicated.

Your success depends not only on the purpose and content of the message but also on how skillful you are at communicating, how well you know your **audience** (the person or persons with whom you're communicating), and how much you hold in common with your audience.

As a scientist, Dave did not have an extensive business vocabulary. Nor did he have much practice at oral business presentations and the careful pacing and reinforcement required in such circumstances. In effect, Dave was attempting to make an oral business proposal, but unfortunately without much technique or skill.

Step 3: We formulate a verbal or nonverbal response to the stimulus.

message: The information that is communicated

audience: The person or persons with whom you're communicating

"You're crazy, Dave. You don't know what you're talking about." Marc's initial response made it clear to Dave that his message wasn't getting through. But what Dave lacked in skill, he made up for in knowing his audience (his kid brother) intimately.

"You're chicken, Marc" had always gotten Marc's attention and interest in the past, and it worked again. Dave continued challenging Marc, something he knew his brother couldn't resist, and kept reminding him of their common ground—namely, all the happy adventures they had shared as children and adults.

The Medium

Step 4: We select the medium.

medium: The form of a message

Once the sender has formulated a message, the next step in the process is to transmit that message to the receiver. At this point, the sender must choose the form of message to send, or **medium** (plural: *media*). Oral messages might be transmitted through such media as a staff meeting, personal conference, telephone conversation, voice mail, or informal conversation. Written messages might be transmitted through email, letter, contract, brochure, bulletin-board notice, company newsletter, or an addition to the company's policy and procedures manual. Nonverbal messages might be transmitted through facial expressions, gestures, or body movement. Because Dave is talking with Marc over the phone, his medium is the telephone.

You should be aware, however, that the most commonly used forms of communication may not be the most effective for your purposes. The International Association of Business Communicators recently surveyed nearly 1,000 organizations about their communication practices. As shown in Figure 1.2, the survey revealed that although email was the most frequently used medium of communication, it was not the most effective.[1]

The Destination

Step 5: The message reaches its destination and, if successful, is perceived accurately by the receiver.

The message is transmitted and then enters the sensory environment of the receiver. At this point, control passes from the sender to the receiver. Once the message reaches its destination, there is no guarantee that communication will actually occur. We are constantly bombarded with stimuli, and our sensory organs

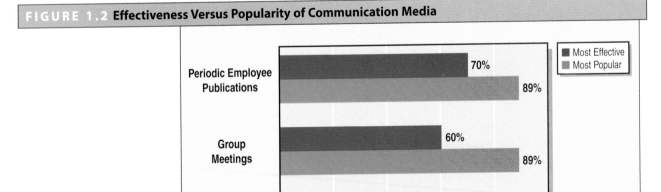

FIGURE 1.2 Effectiveness Versus Popularity of Communication Media

pick up only part of them. Even assuming the receiver *does* perceive your message, you have no assurance that it will be interpreted (filtered) as you intended. Your transmitted message then becomes the source, or stimulus, for the next communication episode, and the process begins anew.

After Dave's enthusiastic, one-hour phone call, Marc promised to consider the venture seriously. Marc's response provided **feedback** (reaction to a message) to Dave on how accurately his own message had been received. Although feedback is not required for communication to occur, it is, of course, helpful. In time, Marc's feedback led to many more versions of the communication process, both written and oral. The brothers' communications ultimately led to their forming a new company to manufacture the Ultra Light product.

feedback: The receiver's reaction or response to a message

The Dynamic Nature of Communication

From our look at the components of communication, you might erroneously infer that communication is a linear, static process—flowing in an orderly fashion from one stage to the next—and that you can easily separate communicators into senders and receivers. In reality, that is not at all the case.

Communication is not a static, linear process.

Two or more people often send and receive messages simultaneously. While you are receiving one message, you may at the same time be sending another message. For example, the look on your face as you are receiving a message may be sending a new message to the sender that you either understand, agree with, or are puzzled by the message being sent. The feedback given in this way may, in turn, prompt the sender to modify his or her intended message.

Thus, artificially "freezing" the action to examine each step of the communication process separately causes us to lose some of the dynamic richness of that process in terms of both its verbal and nonverbal components.

....

RECALL   Write a capital T for *true* or F for *false* before each statement.

1. ____ A verbal message consists only of written words.

2. ____ Email is generally considered to be the most effective form of communication.

3. ____ Every person has a unique view of reality.

4. ____ It is *not* necessary for feedback to occur for communication to take place.

5. ____ The *medium* is the information that is communicated.

CHECKPOINT 1.1

VOCABULARY   Define the following terms in your own words and give an original example of each.

6. Audience:

7. Communication:

8. Feedback:

9. Filter:

10. Medium:

11. Message:

12. Stimulus:

COMPREHENSION   Identify each component each component of communication in the following situation: Eva glanced up just in time to see the pot of pasta begin boiling over. "Oh, no," she yelled. "Now what's the matter?" said Rosario.

13. Stimulus:

14. Filter:

15. Message:

16. Medium:

17. Destination:

18. Feedback:

CRITICAL THINKING

19. Which form of communication (reading, writing, speaking, or listening) do you think is most important in business? Why?

Verbal Communication

It is the ability to communicate by using words that separates humans from the rest of the animal kingdom. Our verbal ability also enables us to learn from the past—to benefit from the experience of others.

Oral Communication

Oral communication is one of the most common functions in business. Consider, for example, how limiting it would be if a manager or staff person could not attend meetings, ask questions of colleagues, make presentations, appraise performance, handle customer complaints, or give instructions.

Oral communication differs from written communication in that it allows more ways to get a message across to others. You can clear up any questions immediately; use nonverbal clues; provide additional information; and use pauses, emphasis, and voice tone to stress certain points.

According to research, the following are the most annoying voice qualities, listed in decreasing order of annoyance:[2]

Whining, complaining, or nagging tone	44%
High-pitched, squeaky voice	16%
Mumbling	11%
Talking very fast	5%
Weak, wimpy voice	4%
Flat, monotonous tone	4%

> Verbal messages are composed of words— either written or spoken.

For oral communication to be effective, a second communication skill— listening—is also required. No matter how well crafted the content and delivery of an oral presentation, it cannot achieve its goal if the intended audience does not have effective listening skills. We'll learn more about listening in Chapter 2.

Written Communication

Writing is more difficult than speaking because you have to get your message correct the first time; you do not have the advantage of immediate feedback and nonverbal clues such as facial expressions to help you achieve your objective. Examples of typical written communication in business include the following:

> Most oral communication is temporary; most written communication is permanent.

- *Email* (see Figure 1.3 on page 10) is a message transmitted electronically over a computer network whose computers are most often connected by cable, telephone lines, or satellites. In the contemporary office, email is replacing traditional memorandums and, in many cases, letters as well.

Jamie Dimon, the 46-year-old CEO of Bank One, meets monthly with Bank Oners to hear problems firsthand. He likes the immediate feedback and use of nonverbal language that direct oral communication provide.

FIGURE 1.3 **Example of Email**

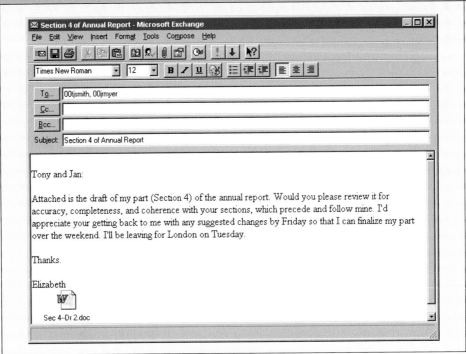

- *Web sites* comprise one or more pages of related information that is posted on the World Wide Web and is accessed via the Internet (the main page of a Web site is called its "home page").
- *Memorandums* are written messages sent to people working in the same organization.
- *Letters* are written messages sent to people outside the organization.
- Other examples of written communications include contracts, sales literature, newsletters, and bulletin-board notices.

Writing is crucial to the modern organization because it serves as the major source of documentation. A speech may make a striking impression, but a written report leaves a permanent record for others to refer to in the future in case memory fails or a dispute arises.

For written messages to achieve their goal, they must, of course, be read. The skill of efficient reading is becoming more important in today's technological society. The abundance of widespread data and word processing, the Internet, and the growth of convenient and economical photocopying and faxing have all created *more* paperwork rather than less.

The typical manager reads about 1 million words every week.[3] As a consequence, information overload is one of the unfortunate by-products of our times (See Spotlight 1—On Technology, on page 11). These and other implications of technology on business communication are discussed throughout this text.

Nonverbal Communication

Not all communication that occurs on the job is spoken, heard, written, or read—that is, verbal. According to management guru Peter Drucker, "The most important thing in communication is to hear what isn't being said."[4]

SPOTLIGHT ① on technology

Overcoming Information Anxiety[5]

People in today's information-laden society are being bombarded by more data than they can absorb. For example, every year the average American reads or completes 3,000 notices or forms, watches 2,463 hours of television, listens to 730 hours of radio, reads 100 newspapers, talks on the telephone 61 hours, reads 36 magazines, buys 20 records, and reads 3 books.

According to Richard Wurman, author of *Information Anxiety 2*, it's a myth that the more choices you have, the more freedom you enjoy. More choices simply produce more anxiety. Thus, as you decrease the number of choices, you decrease the fear of having made the wrong one.

The Black Hole

Information was once sought after and treasured—like a fine wine. Now, it's regarded more like crabgrass, something to be controlled. Trying to process all this information can induce "information anxiety"—apprehension about the ever-widening gap between what we understand and what we think we *should* understand. In other words, information anxiety focuses on the black hole between *data* and *knowledge*.

Wurman believes that "the System" is at fault—too many people are simply putting out too much useless data. In fact, he believes that 99% of the information to which most Americans are exposed each year isn't meaningful or understandable to them.

No One Knows It All

The first step in overcoming information anxiety is to accept that there is much you will never understand. Let your ignorance be an inspiration to learn, not something to conceal. Wurman recommends standing in front of a mirror and practicing, "Could you repeat that?" or "I'm not sure I understand what you're talking about" instead of pretending to understand what you do not.

Other suggestions include separating what you are really interested in from what you merely think you *should* be interested in and minimizing the time you spend reading or watching news that isn't relevant to your life. And, if all else fails, heed Wurman's conclusion: "Most information is useless. Give yourself permission to dismiss it."

A nonverbal message is any message that is not written or spoken. It may accompany a verbal message (smiling as you greet a colleague), or it may occur alone (selecting the back seat when entering the conference room). Nonverbal messages are typically more spontaneous than verbal messages, but that doesn't mean that they are any less important. A classic study by Mehrabian found that only 7% of the meaning communicated by most messages comes from the verbal portion, with the remaining 93% being conveyed nonverbally.[6]

The six most common types of nonverbal communication in business are discussed in the following sections.

> Nonverbal messages are unwritten and unspoken.

Body Movement

By far, the most expressive part of the body is your face—especially your eyes. People tend to be quite consistent in their reading of facial expressions. In fact, many expressions have the same meaning across different cultures. Eye contact and eye movements tell you a lot about a person, although—as we shall see later—maintaining eye contact with the person to whom you're speaking is not perceived as important (or even polite) in some cultures.

> Cultures differ in the importance they attach to eye contact.

Gestures are hand and upper-body movements that add important information to face-to-face interactions. As the game of charades proves, you can communicate quite a bit without using oral or written signals. More typically, gestures are used to help illustrate and reinforce your verbal message.

Body stance (posture, placement of arms and legs, distribution of weight, and the like) is another form of nonverbal communication. For example, leaning slightly toward the person with whom you're communicating would probably be taken as a sign of interest and involvement in the interaction. On the other hand, leaning back with arms folded across the chest might be taken (and intended) as a sign of boredom or defiance.

Physical Appearance

Our culture places great value on physical appearance. Television, newspapers, and magazines are filled with advertisements for personal-care products, and the ads typically feature attractive users of these products. Attractive people tend to be seen as more intelligent, more likable, and more persuasive than unattractive people.

Your appearance is particularly important when you're trying to make a good first impression. Although you may not be able to change some of your physical features, understanding the importance of good grooming and physical appearance can help you to emphasize your strong points. Also, your clothing, jewelry, office and home furnishings, and automobile provide information about your values, taste, heritage, conformity, status, age, sexuality, and group identification.

Voice Qualities

No one speaks in a monotone. To illustrate, read the following sentence aloud, each time emphasizing the italicized word. Note how the meaning changes with each reading.

- *You* were late. (Answers the question "Who was late?")
- You *were* late. (Responds to the other person's denial of being late)
- You were *late*. (Emphasizes just how late the person was)

Your tone of voice can emphasize or subordinate the verbal message—or even contradict it.

Voice qualities such as volume, speed, pitch, tone, and accent carry both intentional and unintentional messages. For example, when you are nervous, you tend to speak faster and at a higher pitch than normal. People who constantly speak too softly risk being interrupted or ignored, whereas people who constantly speak too loudly are often seen as being pushy or insecure.

Time

The meaning we attach to time depends on our status, the specific situation, and our culture.

How do you feel when you're late for an appointment? When others are late? The meaning given to time varies greatly by culture, with Americans and Canadians being much more time conscious than people from South American or Middle Eastern cultures.

Time is related not only to culture but also to one's status within the organization. You would be much less likely to keep a superior waiting for an appointment than you would a subordinate. Time is also situation specific. Although normally you might not worry about being five minutes late for a staff meeting, you would probably arrive early if you were the first presenter.

President George Bush congratulates the nine miners who were rescued in Pennsylvania in July 2002. He enters the "personal" zone (from physical contact to about 18 inches) of one miner to clap him on the back.

Touch

Touch is the first sense we develop, acquired even before birth. Some touches, such as those made by a physician during an examination, are purely physical; others, such as a handshake, are a friendly sign of willingness to communicate; and still others indicate intimacy. Although touching is a very important form of business communication, most people do not know how to use it appropriately and effectively. The person who never touches anyone in a business setting may be seen as cold and standoffish, whereas the person who touches others too frequently may cause the receiver to feel apprehensive and uncomfortable.

Space and Territory

When you are on a crowded elevator, you probably look at the floor indicator, at advertisements, at your feet, or just straight ahead—anywhere but at the person standing beside you. Most people in our culture are uncomfortable in such close proximity to strangers. Psychologists have identified four zones within which people in our culture interact:[7]

1. *Intimate Zone:* From physical contact to about 18 inches is where all your body movements occur; you move in this area throughout the day. This area is normally reserved for close, intimate interactions. Business associates typically enter this space infrequently and only briefly—perhaps to shake hands or pat someone on the back.

2. *Personal Zone:* This zone, extending from 18 inches to about 4 feet, is where conversation with close friends and colleagues takes place. Unlike interaction in the intimate zone, normal talking is frequent in the personal zone. Some, but not a great deal of, business interaction occurs here; for example, business lunches typically occur in this zone.

3. *Social Zone:* From 4 feet to 12 feet, the social zone is where most business exchanges occur. Informal business conferences and staff meetings occur within this space.

4. *Public Zone:* The public zone extends from 12 feet to as far as the eye can see and as far as the ear can hear. It is the most formal zone, and the

Different types of communication occur at different distances.

least significant interactions typically occur here. Because of the great distance, communication in the public zone often goes one way, as from a speaker to a large audience.

Competent communicators recognize their own personal space needs and the needs of others. When communicating with people who prefer more or less space, the competent communicator makes the adjustments necessary to reach his or her objective.

CHECKPOINT 1.2

RECALL   Write a capital T for *true* or F for *false* before each statement.

1. ____ A nonverbal message is any message that is not written.

2. ____ Memorandums are written messages sent to people working in the same organization.

3. ____ Most business interaction occurs in the personal zone—from 18 inches to about 4 feet.

4. ____ Most of the meaning communicated by most messages comes from the nonverbal element of the message.

5. ____ People tend to be quite consistent in their interpretations of facial expressions.

COMPREHENSION

6. What are the four types of verbal communication?

7. What are the six most common types of nonverbal communication?

8. Give an original example of a type of *business* communication that would typically occur in each of the following zones:

   Intimate Zone:

   Personal Zone:

   Social Zone:

   Public Zone:

CRITICAL THINKING

9. If a nonverbal message contradicts a verbal message (for example, if a colleague claimed to like you but left you out of all his or her social interactions), which would you have more faith in—the verbal or nonverbal message? Why?

Barriers to Communication

Considering the complex nature of the communication process, your messages may not always be received exactly as you intended. In fact, sometimes your messages will not be received at all; at other times, they will be received incompletely or inaccurately. Some of the obstacles to effective and efficient communication are verbal; others are nonverbal. As illustrated in Figure 1.4, these barriers can create an impenetrable "brick wall" that makes effective communication impossible.

Verbal Barriers

Verbal barriers are related to what you write or say. They include inadequate knowledge or vocabulary, differences in interpretation, language differences, inappropriate use of expressions, overabstraction and ambiguity, and polarization.

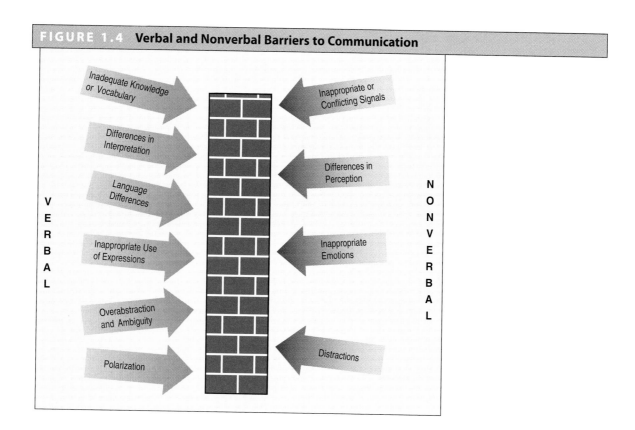

FIGURE 1.4   Verbal and Nonverbal Barriers to Communication

You must know enough about both your topic and your audience to express yourself precisely and appropriately.

Inadequate Knowledge or Vocabulary Before you can even begin to think about how you will communicate an idea, you must first *have* the idea; that is, you must have sufficient knowledge about the topic to know what you want to say. Regardless of your level of technical expertise, developing this knowledge may not be as simple as it sounds. Assume, for example, that your boss has asked you to evaluate the purchase of a new word processing program for your company. You've completed all the necessary research and are now ready to write your report. Or are you?

Have you analyzed your audience? Do you know how much your boss knows about word processing so that you'll know how much background information to include? Do you know how familiar he or she is with word processing terminology? Can you safely use terms like *hanging indent, templates, decimal tabs*, and *styles*, or will you have to define them first?

Do you know whether your boss would prefer to have your conclusions at the beginning of the report, followed by your analysis, or at the end? What tone should the report take? The answers to such questions will be important if you are to achieve your objective in writing the report.

Differences in Interpretation Sometimes senders and receivers attribute different meanings to the same word or attribute the same meaning to different words. When this mismatch happens, miscommunication can occur.

Every word has both a denotative and a connotative meaning. **Denotation** refers to the literal, dictionary meaning of a word. **Connotation** refers to the subjective, emotional meaning that you attach to a word. For example, the denotative meaning of the word *plastic* is "a synthetic material that can be easily molded into different forms." For some people, the word also has a negative connotative meaning—"cheap or artificial substitute."

denotation: The literal meaning of a word

connotation: The subjective, emotional meaning associated with a word

Most interpretation problems occur because of the personal reactions engendered by the connotative meaning of a word. For example, do you have a positive, neutral, or negative reaction to the terms *broad, bad, profit, aggressive, hard-hitting, workaholic, corporate raider, head-hunter, gay, golden parachute*, and *wasted*? Are your reactions likely to be the same as everyone else's? The problem with some terms is not only that people assign different meanings to the term but also that the term itself might cause such an emotional reaction that the receiver is "turned off" to any further communication with the sender.

Language Differences In an ideal world, all managers would know the language of each culture with which they deal. Most of the correspondence between U.S. or Canadian firms and foreign firms is in English; in other cases, the services of a qualified interpreter (for oral communication) or translator (for written communication) may be available. Even with such services, problems can occur. Consider, for example, the following blunders:[8]

- In Brazil, where Portuguese is spoken, a U.S. airline advertised that its Boeing 747s had "rendezvous lounges," without realizing that *rendezvous* in Portuguese implies prostitution.
- In China, Kentucky Fried Chicken's slogan "Finger-lickin' good" was translated "So good you suck your fingers."
- In Puerto Rico, General Motors had difficulties advertising Chevrolet's Nova model because the name sounds like the Spanish phrase *No Va*, which means "It doesn't go."

To ensure that the intended meaning is not lost during translation, legal, technical, and all other important documents should first be translated into the second language and then retranslated into English. Be aware, however, that communication difficulties can arise even among native English speakers. For example, a British advertisement for Electrolux vacuum cleaners displayed the headline "Nothing Sucks Like An Electrolux." Copywriters in the United States and Canada would never use this wording!

Inappropriate Use of Expressions Expressions are groups of words whose intended meanings are different from their literal interpretations. Examples include slag, jargon, and euphemisms.

- **Slang** is an expression, often short-lived, that is identified with a specific group of people. Here, for example, are some slang terms (and their meanings) currently popular on college campuses:[9]

  As If—"In your dreams"
  Bounce—To leave
  Crib—A place of residence
  Homey—A friend, usually male
  My bad—My fault
  Ride—A car
  Stoked—Happy or excited
  Sweet—Generic positive (also *phat* or *tight*)

  Teenagers, construction workers, immigrants, knowledge professionals, and just about every other subgroup you can imagine all have their own sets of slang. Using appropriate slang in everyday speech presents no problem; it conveys precise information and may indicate group membership. Problems arise, however, when the sender uses slang that the receiver doesn't understand. Slang that sends a negative nonverbal message about the sender can also be a source of problems.

- **Jargon** is the technical terminology used within specialized groups; it has sometimes been called "the pros' prose." As with slang, the problem arises not from using jargon—jargon provides a very precise and efficient way of communicating with those familiar with it. Rather, the problem comes either in using jargon with someone who doesn't understand it or in using jargon in an effort to impress others.

- **Euphemisms** are inoffensive expressions used in place of words that may offend or suggest something unpleasant. Sensitive writers and speakers use euphemisms occasionally, especially to describe bodily functions. How many ways, for example, can you think of to say that someone has died?

The use of slang, jargon, and euphemisms is sometimes appropriate and sometimes inappropriate.

slang: An expression, often short-lived, that is identified with a specific group of people

jargon: The technical vocabulary used within specialized groups

euphemism: An inoffensive expression used in place of an expression that may offend or suggest something unpleasant

abstract word: A word that identifies an idea or feeling

concrete word: A word that identifies something that can be seen or touched

The word *transportation* is abstract; the word *automobile* is concrete.

Overabstraction and Ambiguity An **abstract word** identifies an idea or a feeling instead of a concrete object. For example, "communication" is an abstract word, whereas "memorandum" is a **concrete word**, a word that identifies something that can be seen or touched. Abstract words are necessary to communicate about things you cannot see or touch. Unfortunately, communication problems result when you use too many abstract words or when you use too high a level of abstraction. The higher the level of abstraction, the more difficult it is for the receiver to visualize exactly what the sender has in mind. For example, which sentence communicates more information: "I acquired an asset at the store" or "I bought a laser printer at ComputerLand"?

Similar communication problems result from the overuse of ambiguous terms such as *a few, some, several,* and *far away,* which have too broad a meaning for use in much business communication.

Thinking in terms of all or nothing limits our choices.

Polarization At times, some people act as though every situation is divided into two opposite and distinct poles, with no allowance for a middle ground. Of course, some true opposites do exist. You are either male or female, and your company either will or will not make a profit this year. Nevertheless, most aspects of life involve more than two alternatives.

For example, you might assume that a speaker either is telling the truth or is lying. In fact, what the speaker actually says may be true, but by selectively omitting some important information, he or she may be giving an inaccurate impression. Is the speaker telling the truth or not? Most likely, the answer lies somewhere in between. Likewise, you are not necessarily either tall or short, rich or poor, smart or dumb. Competent communicators avoid inappropriate either/or logic, instead making the effort to search for middle-ground words when such language best describes a situation.

Would you consider the examples in the paragraph at the right to be verbal barriers to communication or nonverbal barriers?

Remember that what you do *not* say can also produce barriers to communication. Suppose, for example, that you congratulate only one of the three people who took part in making a company presentation. How would the other two presenters feel—even though you said nothing negative about their performance? Or suppose you tell one of them, "You really did an outstanding job this time." The presenter's natural reaction may be, "What was wrong with my performance last time?"

Nonverbal Barriers

Not all communication problems are related to what you write or say. Some are related to how you act. Nonverbal barriers to communication include inappropriate or conflicting signals, differences in perception, inappropriate emotions, and distractions.

Inappropriate or Conflicting Signals Suppose a well-qualified applicant for an administrative assistant position submits a résumé with a typographical error, or an accountant's personal office is in such disorder that she can't find the papers she needs for a meeting with a client. When verbal and nonverbal signals conflict, the receiver tends to put more faith in the nonverbal signals because nonverbal messages are more difficult to manipulate than verbal messages.

Many nonverbal signals vary from culture to culture. Remember also that the United States itself is a multicultural country: a banker from Boston, an art-shop owner from San Francisco, and a farmer from North Dakota are likely to both use and interpret nonverbal signals in quite different ways. What is appropriate in one context might not be appropriate in another.

Communication competence requires that you communicate nonverbal messages that are consistent with your verbal messages and that are appropriate for the context.

Differences in Perception   Even when they hear the same speech or read the same document, people of different ages, socioeconomic backgrounds, cultures, and so forth often form very different perceptions. We discussed earlier the mental filter by which each communication source is interpreted. Because each person is unique, with unique experiences, knowledge, and viewpoints, each person forms a different opinion about what he or she reads and hears.

Some people tend automatically to believe certain people and to distrust other people. For example, when reading a memo from the company president, one employee may be so intimidated by the president that he or she automatically accepts everything the president says. In contrast, another employee may have such negative feelings about the president that he or she believes nothing the president says.

Inappropriate Emotions   In most cases, a moderate level of emotional involvement intensifies the communication and makes it more personal. However, too much emotional involvement can impose an obstacle to communication. For example, excessive anger can create such an emotionally charged environment that reasonable discussion becomes impossible. Likewise, prejudice (automatically rejecting certain people or ideas), stereotyping (placing individuals into categories), and boredom all hinder effective communication. Such emotions tend to create a blocked mind that is closed to new ideas, rejecting or ignoring information that is contrary to one's prevailing belief.

Distractions   Any environmental or competing element that restricts one's ability to concentrate on the communication task hinders effective communication. Such distractions are called *noise*. Examples of *environmental* noise include poor acoustics, extreme temperature, uncomfortable seating, body odor, poor telephone connections, and illegible photocopies. Examples of *competing* noise include other important business to handle, too many meetings, and too many reports to read.

Competent communicators make the effort to write and speak clearly and consistently and try to avoid or minimize any verbal or nonverbal barriers that might cause misunderstandings.

What's for Dinner?	WORD|wise
Names of actual eateries:	
Aunt Chiladas	*Mexican restaurant*
Boogie Woogie Bagel Boy	*Delicatessen*
Ontrays	*Cafeteria*
Shaky Grounds	*Coffee shop*
Swallows of Cappucino	*Coffee shop*
Thai Food Mary	*Thai restaurant*
The Great Impasta	*Italian restaurant*

It is generally more effective to depend on logic rather than emotions when communicating.

RECALL   Write a capital T for *true* or F for *false* before each statement.

1. ___ Both environmental noise and competing noise are examples of distractions that can present a barrier to effective communication.

2. ___ *Connotation* refers to the literal, dictionary meaning of a word.

3. ___ In most business situations, a moderate level of emotional involvement is desirable.

4. ___ It is generally safe to assume that a speaker or writer is either telling the truth or lying.

5. ___ Just about every subgroup of a population has its own set of slang.

VOCABULARY   Define the following terms in your own words and give an original example of each.

6. Abstract word:

CHECKPOINT 1.3

7. Concrete word:

8. Connotation:

9. Denotation:

10. Euphemism:

11. Jargon:

12. Slang:

COMPREHENSION

13. What are six verbal barriers to communication?

14. What are four nonverbal barriers to communication?

CRITICAL THINKING

15. The text argues against the overuse of ambiguity. Can you think of a business situation in which the use of ambiguity might be effective?

Introducing the 3Ps (Problem, Process, Product)

Every chapter in this text concludes with a 3Ps model designed to illustrate important communication concepts covered in the chapter (see the following section). These short case studies of typical communication assignments include the *problem*, the *process*, and the *product* (the 3Ps). The *problem* defines the situation and discusses the need for a particular communication task. The *process* is a series of questions that provides step-by-step guidance for accomplishing the specific communication task. Finally, the *product* is the result—the finished document.

The 3Ps model provides a practical demonstration of a particular type of communication, shown close up so that you can see the *process* of writing, not just the results. This process helps you focus on one aspect of writing at a time. Use the 3Ps steps regularly in your own writing so that your written communications will be easier to produce and more effective.

Pay particular attention to the questions in the Process section, and ask yourself similar questions as you compose your own messages. Finally, read through the finished document, and note any changes made from the draft sentences composed in the Process section.

The 3Ps model guides you step-by-step through a typical writing assignment by posing and answering relevant questions about each aspect of the message.

Online Help in This Course

Visit the student web site for this text (**http://college.hmco.com**) to find several resources that will help you succeed in this course. See our ACE interactive self-tests to assess your knowledge of chapter content and to review and reinforce basic language arts skills. Here you will also be able to learn more about the Internet, locate business information, get help with writing problems, and learn more about employment communication and available jobs and employers.

Summary

The study of communication is important because communication is such a pervasive part of any organization and because it is so critical for achieving organizational (and personal) goals. In fact, most managers spend the vast majority of their workday in some form of verbal communication.

The communication process begins with a stimulus. On the basis of your unique knowledge, experience, and viewpoints, you filter, or interpret, the stimulus and formulate the message you wish to communicate. The next step is to select a medium of transmission for the message. Finally, the message reaches its destination. If it is successful, the receiver perceives it as a new source for communication and provides appropriate feedback to you.

Verbal communication encompasses both oral (speaking and listening) and written (writing and reading) messages. Common forms of written communication in business include email messages, Web sites, memorandums, letters, and reports. Nonverbal communication includes body movement, physical appearance, voice qualities, time, touch, and space and territory. Cultures differ greatly in terms of how they interpret nonverbal behavior.

Sometimes barriers interfere with effective communication. Verbal barriers include inadequate knowledge or vocabulary, differences in interpretation, language differences, inappropriate use of expressions, overabstraction and ambiguity, and polarization. Nonverbal barriers include inappropriate or conflicting signals, differences in perception, inappropriate emotions, and distractions.

The 3Ps
Problem, Process, Product

Writing Up Research Results

Assume the role of Jason, a quality-control technician for an automobile manufacturer. You are responsible for testing a new airbag design. Your company is eager to install the new airbags in next year's models because two competitors have similar airbags on the market. However, your tests of the new design have not been completely successful. All of the airbags tested inflated on impact, but 10 airbags out of every 100 tested inflated only 60%. These partially inflated airbags would still protect passengers from most of a collision impact, but the passengers might receive more injuries than they would with fully inflated bags.

Before reporting the test results, you tell your supervisor that you would like to run more tests to make sure that the airbags are reliable and safe. But your supervisor explains that the company executives are eager to get the airbags on the market and want the results in a few days. You now feel pressured to certify that the airbags are safe (and indeed, they all inflated—at least partially).[10]

Process

1. What is the problem you are facing?

   I must decide exactly how I will phrase the certification sentence in my report.

2. What would be the ideal solution to this problem?

   I would be given additional time to conduct enough tests to assure myself that the airbags are reliable and safe.

3. Why can't the ideal solution be recommended?

   The company is pressuring me to certify the airbags now because two competitors have already introduced similar airbags.

4. Brainstorm possible certification statements that you might make.

   - All the airbags inflated.

   - None of the airbags failed to inflate.

   - Ninety percent of the airbags inflated fully; the rest inflated only 60%.

5. Now evaluate each alternative in terms of these criteria.

   All the airbags inflated. This statement is true and is a positive statement that will probably satisfy management. However, it overstates the success of the tests and is somewhat misleading in what it omits—that 10% of the airbags inflated only partially. I may be harming potential users by giving them a false sense of security; in addition, I may be leaving the company open to lawsuits resulting from failure of airbags to inflate fully.

None of the airbags failed to inflate. Again, this statment is true but omits important information the consumer needs. In addition, it is a negative statement, which will not please management.

Ninety percent of the airbags inflated fully; the rest inflated only 60%. This statement provides the most accurate assessment of the test results. It emphasizes the positive and does state that some problems exist. The most serious risk with this alternative is that it could delay the release of the new design on the market. If this happens, my job might be at risk. In addition, it doesn't interpret the meaning of the partially inflated airbags.

6. Using what you've discovered about each alternative, construct the certification statement you will include in your report to management.

Product

Results of my testing of the new airbag design indicate that 90% of the

airbags inflate fully on impact; the remaining 10% inflate 60%, which

is sufficient to protect passengers from most of a collision impact.

Looking Ahead

In this chapter, we introduced the process of business communication and the role it plays in the contemporary organization. In the next chapter, we discuss several issues that have a critical impact on business communication—namely, communicating in work teams, communicating in a diverse environment, communication technology, the legal and ethical dimensions of communicating, and appropriate workplace etiquette.

Key Terms

abstract word
audience
communication
concrete word
connotation
denotation
euphemism

feedback
filter
jargon
medium
message
slang
stimulus

Exercises

Communicating in Organizations

1 **Getting to Know You—Part 1**   One of the steps for success in communicating is knowing your audience—and making sure they know you. Write a memo (typed, single-spaced, at least a full page long) introducing yourself to your instructor and to other members of the class. Include such information as the following:

- *Background:* Your grade level, major, extracurricular activities, work experience, and the like.

- *Career Objectives:* What type of position would you like immediately upon graduation? With what type of organization and in what part of the country would you like to work? Where do you expect to be in terms of your profession five years from now?

- *Course Objectives:* Why are you taking this course? What specific skill or skills do you hope to master? What aspects of the course do you expect to find most challenging?

- *Small-Group Experiences:* What experience have you had in working on group projects? What do you see as the advantages and disadvantages of such assignments? What type of group would you find most satisfying to work with?

Include any other information you think would be useful. Edit and proofread your draft before submitting it.

2 **Getting to Know You—Part 2**   Using the memo you prepared in Exercise 1 as a guide (but do not read from it), give a three-minute informal presentation to the class introducing yourself.

3 **Getting a Job**   Scan newspaper ads or go online to find job listings in your preferred field of employment (either entry-level or more experienced positions). Make a copy of at least 10 job vacancies and analyze them for the skill requirements listed. Do any of them include verbal or nonverbal communication skills? Analyze and summarize your findings in a one-page report.

The Components of Communication

4 **Communication on Television**   Use an incident from a recent television program to illustrate each of the five components of the communication process. Discuss any communication barriers that you observed. (Be sure to identify the TV program and describe the incident you're analyzing.)

5 **Synthesizing Information**   Approximately 1,500 words in this chapter were devoted to the discussion of the components of communication. Working in small groups, write a 200- to 250-word abstract (summary) of this discussion. Because this summary is an informational abstract, you may pick up the exact wording of the original discussion when appropriate. Ensure that all important points are covered, your narrative flows smoothly from one topic to another, and your writing is error-free.

6 **Filter**   You are unique—as is every other person in class. List at least 10 ways in which you personally might filter information you receive, based on such factors as your individual experiences, culture, emotions at the moment, personality, knowledge, socioeconomic status, and demographic variables.

Verbal Communication

7 **Workplace Communication Issues**   For this exercise, your instructor will divide you into two-person teams.

a. Exchange email addresses with your partner.
b. Send your partner an email message in which you respond (in complete sentences) to the following two questions:

  1. Do you feel that it is right or wrong for an employer to maintain the right to read any email message sent on company computers?

  2. Do you feel it is acceptable or unacceptable to use a company computer to send a short personal email to a friend once or twice a week?

c. Send a copy of your email message to yourself.
d. When you receive your partner's email message, respond to it by agreeing or disagreeing with his or her position and giving the reason for your position. Again, send a copy of your response to yourself.
e. Print out and submit to your instructor a copy of (1) your original message, (2) your response to your partner's email, and (3) your partner's response to your email.

8 **Email**   Interview at least three full-time employees to learn their experience about email. Ask them such questions as the following:

a. How many emails do you send and receive each week?
b. Do you read all of the ones you receive? If not, why? How do you decide which ones to read and which to skip?
c. How important do you consider the subject line to be on an email?
d. In your opinion, what makes an email effective? Ineffective?

Present your findings in a 200- to 250-word report to your instructor.

Nonverbal Communication

9 **Communicating Without Talking**   Use nonverbal language only to communicate the following messages:

a. surprise
b. anger
c. sorrow
d. puzzlement
e. boredom
f. disinterest

10 **Voice Qualities**   Read a journal article (either print or online) on the effective use of your voice in a business setting. Next, write a one-page typed summary of the article. Proofread your summary for content and language errors and revise as needed. Staple a photocopy of the article to your summary, and submit both to your instructor.

11 **Job Interview**   Assume that you are going on a job interview tomorrow. List at least three positive nonverbal behaviors that you will want to exhibit and at least three negative nonverbal behaviors that you will want to avoid.

Barriers to Communication

12 **Jargon**   Think of a topic with which you are familiar (a sport, computers, an academic subject, or the like).

a. Compose an email message to a colleague who is also an expert on the subject. Include at least six jargon terms that flow easily into the context of your email.
b. Now assume you're sending the same email to someone who is not at all familiar with the topic. Revise your original email to make it appropriate for this reader.
c. Which email is longer? Which is more effective? Why?

13 **Euphemisms**   Working in two-person groups, see how many appropriate terms you can come up with to substitute for the following concepts:

a. dying
b. elderly
c. getting fired
d. having no mobility in your legs
e. going to the bathroom
f. housewife
g. jail

14 **Nonverbal Barriers**   Ling looked up from her computer. "Fortunately, I do all of my writing on the computer—using either word processing software or email. Thus, I don't have to worry about creating any nonverbal barriers." Is Ling correct? Discuss and give examples of nonverbal barriers that might lessen the effectiveness of Ling's written communications.

15 **Verbal and Nonverbal Barriers**   Discuss any communication barriers exhibited in the following situation—and how they might have been avoided.

Erin entered Clarence's office 10 minutes late, finishing up her sandwich as she sat down. "Can I have my girl get you a cup of coffee?" he asked. When she declined, Clarence sat down, propped his feet on the desk, and said "Now, Erin, what seems to be the problem with the new advertising campaign? Will it be effective? I should warn you, by the way, that I have another meeting in 20 minutes." Before Erin could begin, Clarence's phone rang.

2

Contemporary Issues in Business Communication

COMMUNICATION OBJECTIVES

After you have finished this chapter, you should be able to:

- Communicate effectively in small groups.

- Communicate effectively with diverse populations both within the United States and internationally.

- Describe the important technological developments that affect business communication.

- Explain the legal and ethical dimensions of communicating.

- Use a professional demeanor and appropriate behavior to maintain effective working relationships.

On the Job

JAMES RADFORD
Interactive Business
Solutions Manager, 3M

As the architect for the World Wide Web site for 3M, James Radford is at the forefront of the movement toward electronic access and sharing of information, both internally and externally.

Fast and accurate communication is an important priority at 3M, a $14 billion global company with more than 70,000 employees and 60,000 products for sale. "Email has become the communication tool of choice at 3M, replacing volumes of paper and fax documents as well as phone calls and some express courier service," Radford says.

The 3M executive offers this advice for anyone who is looking for data online. "Start by defining the goals and the scope of the search. Then consider the source of the data," he says. "The chance of finding good information improves when you go to recognized sources that have established reputations for highly accurate and current information. Ask questions and verify with a second source before using data from newer or unfamiliar sources."

Contemporary Business Communication Issues

James Radford of 3M is certainly aware of the role technology plays in communicating in the contemporary organization. In fact, because communication is such a pervasive and strategic part of the organization, almost anything that affects the organization and its employees affects the communication function as well. However, four contemporary issues have special implications for business communication:

- *Work teams:* The dynamics of communicating within groups.
- *Diversity:* The effects of cultural differences in the workplace—both within the United States and internationally.
- *Technology:* The effects of automation on communication.
- *Ethics:* The legal and moral implications of communicating in the contemporary business environment.
- *Workplace etiquette:* Appropriate behavior on the job.

Communicating in Work Teams

team A group of individuals who depend on one another to accomplish a common objective.

A **team** is a group of individuals who depend on one another to accomplish a common objective. Teams are often superior to individuals because they can accomplish more work, are more creative, have more information available to them, and offer more interpersonal communication dynamics. A synergy can work to ensure that the group's total output exceeds the sum of the individuals' contributions.

Unfortunately, teams can also waste time, accomplish little work, and create an environment in which interpersonal conflict can rage. As anyone who has ever worked in a group can attest, there is also the danger of *social loafing*, the psychological term for avoiding individual responsibility in a group setting.

If the group is too large, members may begin to form cliques, or subgroups.

Two to seven members seems to be the most appropriate size range for most effective work teams. Small-team research indicates that five is an ideal size for many teams.[1] Smaller teams often do not have enough diversity of skills and

At Samsung Electronics, Chairman Lee Kun Hee uses workgroups, such as this team of creative designers, to launch a "design revolution" so that the Samsung name is no longer a fallback position for those who can't afford a Sony.

interests to function effectively as a team, whereas larger teams may lack healthy team interaction because just a few people may dominate the discussions.

The Variables of Group Communication

Three factors—conflict, conformity, and consensus—greatly affect the efficiency with which a team operates and the amount of enjoyment members derive from it.

Conflict   Conflict is a greatly misunderstood facet of group communication. Many group leaders work diligently to avoid conflict because they think it detracts from a group's goals. They take the attitude that a group experiencing conflict is not running smoothly and is destined to fail.

In fact, conflict is what group meetings are all about. One purpose of collaborating on a project is to ensure that various viewpoints are heard so that agreement as to the most appropriate course of action can emerge. Groups can use conflict productively to generate and test ideas before they are implemented. Rather than indicating that a meeting is disorderly, the presence of conflict indicates that members are actively discussing the issues. If a group does not exhibit conflict by debating ideas or questioning others, there is very little reason for it to exist. The members may as well be working individually.

Conflict, then, is the essence of group interaction. Competent communicators use conflict as a means to determine what is and what is not an acceptable idea or solution. Note, however, that the conflict discussed here involves debate about *issues,* not about *personalities.* Interpersonal conflict can, indeed, have serious negative consequences for work teams.

Debate issues, not personalities.

Conformity   Conformity is agreement with regard to ideas, rules, or principles. Members may be encouraged to disagree about the definition of a problem or possible solutions, but certain fundamental issues—such as how the group should operate—should be agreed to by everyone.

Although group conformity and group cohesiveness are necessary for successful small-group communication, too much cohesiveness can result in **groupthink,** a barrier to communication that results from an overemphasis on unity, which stifles opposing ideas and the free flow of information (see Figure 2.1).[2]

groupthink The communication barrier that results from overemphasizing unity

The pressure to conform can become so great that negative information and contrary opinions are never even brought out into the open and discussed. As a consequence, the group loses the advantage of hearing and considering various

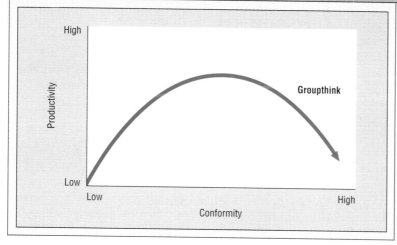

FIGURE 2.1 **Effect of Excessive Conformity on a Group's Productivity**

perspectives. In effective work-team communication, conflicts, different opinions, and questions are considered an inevitable and essential part of the collaborative process.

Consensus   Consensus means reaching a decision that best reflects the thinking of all team members. It entails finding a solution that is acceptable enough that all members can support it (perhaps with reservations) and that no member actively opposes it. Consensus is not necessarily a unanimous vote, or even a majority vote, because in a majority vote only the majority are happy with the end result; people in the minority may have to accept something they don't like at all.

> Consensus does not mean a unanimous or majority vote.

Not every decision, of course, needs to have the support of every member; to push for consensus on every matter would require a tremendous investment of time and energy. The group should decide ahead of time when to push for consensus—for example, when reaching decisions that have a major effect on the direction of the project or the conduct of the team.

Giving Constructive Feedback

> Giving and receiving feedback should be a part of every team's culture.

The single most important skill applied when working through any problem is the ability to give constructive feedback. There are proven methods for giving and receiving criticism that work equally well for giving and receiving praise.[3]

Acknowledge the Need for Feedback   Feedback is vital; it is the only way to find out what needs to be improved and should be an overall part of the team's culture. Your team must agree that giving and receiving feedback is an acceptable part of how you will improve the way you work together. That way, no one will be surprised when he or she receives feedback.

Give Both Positive and Negative Feedback   Many people take good work for granted and give feedback only when problems arise. Unfortunately, this habit is counterproductive. People are far more likely to pay attention to your complaints if they have also received your compliments.

Learn How to Give Feedback   Use these guidelines for compliments as well as for complaints:

1. *Be descriptive.* Relate objectively what you saw or what you heard. Give specific examples—the more recent, the better.
2. *Avoid using labels.* Words such as *undependable, unprofessional, irresponsible,* and *lazy* are labels that we attach to behaviors. Instead, describe the behaviors and drop the labels.
3. *Don't exaggerate.* Be exact. To say, "You're always late for meetings" is probably untrue and therefore unfair.
4. *Speak for yourself.* Don't refer to absent, anonymous people ("A lot of people here don't like it when you. . .").
5. *Use "I" statements.* This point is perhaps the most important guideline. For example, instead of saying, "You are frequently late for meetings," say, "I feel annoyed when you are late for meetings." "I" statements create an adult/peer relationship.

> "I" statements tell specifically how someone's behavior affects you.

Team Writing

The increasing complexity of the workplace makes it difficult for any one person to have either the time or the expertise to be able to identify and solve many of the problems that arise and prepare written responses. Reflecting this trend, team writing is becoming quite prevalent in organizations. (In fact, collaborative communication has always been much more common in organizations than many people realized.)

In addition to the general team-building guidelines discussed in the previous section, writing teams should follow these strategies.

Writing as part of a team is a common task in contemporary organizations.

Assign Tasks and Develop a Schedule

Start by determining the goals of the project and identifying the reader. Determine the components of the project, the research needed, and the date when each aspect needs to be completed. Then divide the tasks equitably, based on each member's needs, interests, expertise, and commitment to the project.

Develop a work schedule—and stick to it.

Meet Regularly

Schedule regular meetings throughout the project to pool ideas, keep track of new developments, assess progress, avoid overlap and omissions, and, if necessary, renegotiate the workload and redefine tasks. As soon as the initial data-gathering phase is complete, confer as a group to develop an outline for the finished project. This outline should show the sequence of major and subordinate topics in the document. Recognize that not all of the information that you collect may need to be included in the report.

Meet frequently to ensure smooth coordination of the project.

Draft the Document

The goal at this stage is not to prepare a finished product but rather to draft all of the content. You have two options:

- Assign parts to different members. Having each member write a different part of the document provides an equitable distribution of the work and may produce a draft more quickly. You must ensure, however, that each member is writing in his or her area of expertise and that all have agreed on such style issues as the degree of formality, direct versus indirect organization, and use of preview and summary.

- Assign one person to draft the entire document. Assigning one member (presumably the most talented writer) to draft the entire document helps guarantee a more consistent writing style and lessens the risk of serious omissions or duplication. You must, however, provide sufficient guidance to the writer and allow ample time for one person to complete the entire writing task.

One common pitfall in team writing is the failure to achieve a single "voice" in the project. Regardless of who prepares each individual part of the report, the final report must look and sound as though it were prepared by one writer. Think of the report as a single document, rather than as a collection of parts. Organize and present the data so that the report comes across as coherent and unified.

Ensure that the final group document "speaks with one voice"—that is, that it is coherent and unified.

Provide Helpful Feedback on Team Writing

Commenting on the writing of peers can be helpful both to you and to the colleague whose writing you're reviewing. As you respond to the writing of others, you practice techniques that will help you react more effectively to your own writing. In addition, realizing that you are not alone with your writing problems and concerns is sometimes comforting.

As a writer, you benefit from the viewpoints of different audiences and from learning what does or doesn't work in your writing. Lastly, in a team environment, peer comments create more active involvement and can help foster a sense of community within the team.

When reviewing a colleague's writing, follow the guidelines presented earlier for providing feedback to team members.

Revise the Draft

Be sure to allow enough time for editing the draft. This task is best accomplished by providing each member with a copy of the draft beforehand (to allow time for reading and annotating). You can then meet as a group to review each section for errors in content, gaps or repetition, and effective writing style.

Do not neglect the final step
of proofreading.

Decide who will be responsible for making the changes to each section, how the document will be formatted, and who will be responsible for proofreading the final document. Typically, one person (preferably not the typist) will be assigned to review the final draft for consistency and correctness in content, style, and format.

CHECKPOINT 2.1

RECALL   Write a capital *T* for true or *F* for false before each statement.

1. ____ A group should strive to reach consensus on every decision.

2. ____ All team members should be involved in revising the draft document.

3. ____ Conflict is always a positive development in group interactions.

4. ____ Effective methods for giving constructive positive feedback are the same as for giving constructive negative feedback.

5. ____ Giving feedback should be an accepted part of every group.

VOCABULARY   Define the following terms in your own words.

6. groupthink:

7. team:

COMPREHENSION

8. List two advantages and two disadvantages of working in teams.

9. Give an example of "good" conflict and an example of "bad" conflict.

10. What are five guidelines for effective team writing?

CRITICAL THINKING

11. What do you think is the one most important attribute of a team member for this course? Why?

Communicating in a Diverse Environment

Paying attention to the needs of others indicates that we recognize and accept diversity. When we talk about diversity, we mean cultural differences not only within the American and Canadian work force but also in the worldwide marketplace.

International business would not be possible without international communication.

Culture encompasses the customary traits, attitudes, and behaviors of a group of people. **Ethnocentrism** is the belief that one's own cultural group is superior to other such groups. Such an attitude hinders communication, understanding, and goodwill between trading partners. An attitude of arrogance is not only counterproductive but also unrealistic, considering that the U.S. population represents less than 5% of the world population.

Diversity will have profound effects on our lives and will pose a growing challenge for workers (see, for example, Spotlight 2, "Internationally Yours"). The following discussion provides useful guidance for communicating with people from different cultures—both internationally as well as domestically. Although it is helpful to be aware of cultural differences, competent communicators recognize that each member of a culture is an individual, with individual needs, perceptions, and experiences, and should be treated as such.

ethnocentrism The belief that one's own cultural group is superior to others

Cultural Differences

Cultures differ widely in the traits they value. Each person interprets events through his or her own mental filter, and that filter is based on the receiver's

Cultures differ not only in their verbal language but also in their nonverbal language.

When Exxon wanted to build a 660-mile pipeline through Chad and Cameroon, the company brought in anthropologist Ellen Brown to explain the process and its impact to the local residents. When she met with a local village chief, she politely left a gift of tea and sugar.

SPOTLIGHT ② across cultures

Internationally Yours

When communicating with international business colleagues and customers, you will often find not only language differences but also other differences.

Phone Numbers

Continental (European) style calls for the use of periods rather than hyphens or parentheses to separate parts of a phone number—for example, 317.555.1086 rather than 317-555-1086 or (317) 555-1086. Dot-style telephone numbers seem to be gaining popularity in the United States, where they are sometimes viewed as more elegant.

Spelling and Word Choice

The British (and current and former British colonies, like Canada) use the spellings *behaviour, centre, theatre, authorise, cheque, labour, legalise, organisation, practise,* and *programme,* among others. Unless your spelling checker uses a British dictionary, it will reject those spellings. The British also use *holiday* instead of *vacation, lift* instead of *elevator,* and *underground* instead of *subway.*

Punctuation

Americans put periods inside closing quotation marks, whereas the British place them outside. Also, British usage calls for single quotation marks where American usage calls for double quotation marks. Thus, Americans would type "I see." The British would type 'I see'. Also, British and Continental style omits periods after *Dr., Mr., Ms.,* and other courtesy titles, as well as after *Jr.* and *Sr.*

Decimals

Americans and the British use a period to indicate a decimal point (1.57%), whereas some other countries (such as France) use a comma instead (1,57%).

Dates

American writers use a month/day/year format (such as June 15, 2004, or 06/15/04). Outside the United States, a day/month/year format is the norm (15 June 2004, or 15-06-04). The influential International Organization for Standardization, a 130-country federation dedicated to global uniformity, has issued ISO 8601, which requires putting the year first, month second, and day last (2004-06-15). Because so many companies seek ISO approval to simplify international trade, this year-month-day style will likely become more prevalent everywhere.

---

unique knowledge, experiences, and viewpoints. For example, the language of time is as different among cultures as is the language of words. Americans, Canadians, Germans, and Japanese are very time conscious and very precise about appointments; Latin American and Arab cultures tend to be more casual about time. For example, if your Mexican host tells you that he or she will meet with you at three o'clock, it's most likely *más o menos* (Spanish for "more or less").

Businesspeople in both Asian and Latin American countries tend to favor long negotiations and slow deliberations. They exchange pleasantries at some length before getting down to business. Likewise, many non-Western cultures use the silent intervals for contemplation, whereas businesspeople from the United States and Canada tend to have little tolerance for silence in business negotiations.

Touching behavior is very culture-specific. Many Asians do not like to be touched, except for a brief handshake in greeting. However, handshakes in much of Europe tend to last much longer than in the United States and Canada, and Europeans tend to shake hands every time they see each other, perhaps several times a day. Germans typically use a firm grip and one shake; Asians typically grasp the other's hand delicately and shake only briefly.

Americans and Canadians are used to wide-open spaces and tend to move about expansively, using hand and arm motions for emphasis. In Japan, which has much smaller living and working spaces, such abrupt and extensive body

When in doubt about how to act, follow the lead of your host.

movements are not typical. Likewise, Americans and Canadians tend to sit face to face, so that they can maintain eye contact, whereas the Chinese and Japanese (to whom eye contact is not so important) tend to sit side by side during negotiations.

Competent communicators become familiar with such role-related behavior and learn the customs regarding the giving (and accepting) of gifts, the exchange of business cards, the degree of formality expected, and the accepted means of entertaining and being entertained.

Strategies for Communicating Across Cultures

When communicating with people from different cultures, use the following strategies.

Maintain Formality Compared to the traditional American and Canadian culture, most other cultures value and respect a much more formal approach to business dealings. Call others by their titles and family names unless specifically asked to do otherwise.

Show Respect Withhold judgment, accepting the premise that attitudes held by an entire culture are probably based on sound reasoning. Listen carefully to what is being communicated, trying to understand the other person's feelings.

Showing respect is probably the easiest strategy to exhibit—and one of the most important.

Communicate Clearly To ensure that your oral and written messages are understood, follow these guidelines:

■ Avoid slang, jargon, and other figures of speech. Expressions such as "They'll eat that up" or "out in left field" are likely to confuse even a fluent English speaker.

■ Be specific and illustrate your points with concrete examples.

■ Provide and solicit feedback, summarize frequently, and encourage questions.

■ Use a variety of media: handouts (distributed before the meeting to allow time for reading), audiovisual aids, models, and the like.

■ Avoid attempts at humor; humor is likely to be lost on your counterpart.

■ Speak plainly and slowly (but not so slowly as to appear condescending), choosing your words carefully.

Value Diversity Those who view diversity among employees as a source of richness and strength for the organization can help bring a wide range of benefits to their organization. Whether you happen to belong to the majority culture or to one of the minority cultures where you work, you will share your work and leisure hours with people different from yourself—people who have values, mannerisms, and speech habits different from your own. This statement is true today, and it will be even truer in the future. The same strategies apply whether the cultural differences exist at home or abroad.

Cultural diversity provides a rich environment for solving problems and for expanding horizons.

A person who is knowledgeable about, and comfortable with, different cultures is a more effective employee because he or she can avoid misunderstandings and tap into the greater variety of viewpoints that a diverse culture provides. In addition, such understanding provides personal satisfaction.

Signs of the Times	WORD|wise
Kansas traffic regulation:	"When two trains approach each other at a crossing, both shall come to a full stop and neither shall start up again until the other has gone."
Newspaper ad:	"Hillside cottage; perfect honeymoon retreat; sleeps three."
Newspaper ad:	"Semi-annual After-Christmas Sale."
Sign at motel swimming pool:	"Pool is open 24 hours. Please do not enter the pool at any other time."
Sign on a school campus:	"No trespassing without permission."

Diversity Within the United States

Perhaps, up to this point, you have been inferring that you must leave the United States and Canada to encounter cultures different from your own. Nothing could be further from the truth. In fact, the term "minority" is becoming something of a misnomer. For example, the white population in the United States is expected to decline from a total of 80% of the population in 1980 to a bare majority (less than 53%) in 2050.[4]

Ethnicity Issues in Communication   As shown in Figure 2.2, the white American population is declining as a percentage of the total population, while Asian and Hispanic populations are increasing. As of the 2000 census, the size of the Hispanic and non-Hispanic black populations were about equal in the United States.[5] Even disregarding international implications, these findings will have major effects on the way Americans conduct business—*and* the way we communicate.

Consider these additional facts from the U.S. Census Bureau:[6]

- There is a 40% chance that two randomly selected North Americans will be of different racial or ethnic backgrounds.
- In 14% of U.S. homes, a language other than English is primarily spoken.
- Of all new entrants into the work force, 43% are people of color and immigrants.
- Women and people of color accounted for 70% of the work force in 2000.

The discussion that follows uses the group terminology of the U.S. Census Bureau: white, black, Hispanic (black or white), and Asian. You should recognize, however, that some white Americans prefer the term "European Americans," some black Americans prefer the term "African Americans," some Hispanic Americans prefer the term "Latinos," and some Asian Americans prefer to be identified by their country of origin—for example, as "Chinese American" or "Indonesian American." Others prefer still other designations.

> Refer to groups of people as they prefer to be referred to.

When communicating about minorities, the first thing we should realize is that what we call ourselves is not a trivial matter. Names matter—a great deal. And the terms used to refer to other groups are not ours to establish. We should follow the self-identity of the group being referred to or the person being communicated with.

FIGURE 2.2 Percentage Distribution of U.S. Population, 1980–2050

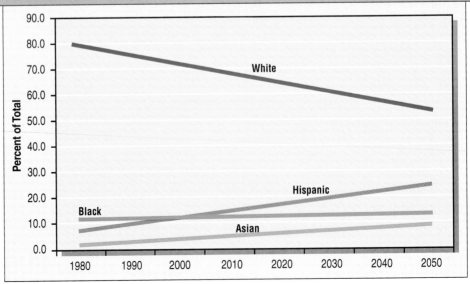

Perhaps the second thing we should realize is that ethnicity is not a characteristic limited to people of color; white Americans are ethnic, too. Every ethnic and racial group in the world—all 6 billion of us—has its own physical and cultural characteristics. Of course, every person within an ethnic group has his or her own individual characteristics as well.

Is it any wonder, then, that communicating about ethnic and racial matters is so hazardous? Yet we have no choice. We must learn to communicate comfortably and honestly with one another. If we use the wrong terminology, make an unwarranted assumption, or present only one side of the story, our readers or listeners will let us know soon enough.

Gender Issues in Communication   Gender roles consist of the learned behavior associated with being male or female. Certain differences typically exist in male/female communication patterns, as shown in Table 2.1.

Recognize that these differences often (but not always) do exist (see Figure 2.3). Competent communicators seek to understand and adapt to these differences. According to Alice Sargeant, author of *The Androgynous Manager,*

Men and women often communicate differently.

> Men and women should learn from one another without abandoning successful traits they already possess. Men can learn to be more collaborative and intuitive, yet remain result-oriented. Women need not give up being nurturing in order to learn to be comfortable with power and conflict.[7]

Communicating with People with Disabilities   Since the Americans with Disabilities Act (ADA) was passed, more physically disabled individuals than ever before have been able to enter the workplace. The act guarantees that people with disabilities who are qualified to perform the essential functions of a job, with or without reasonable accommodation, will not be discriminated against in hiring and promotion in most public and private organizations.

TABLE 2.1

Gender Differences in Communicating

Men	Women
Communicate primarily to preserve independence and status	Communicate primarily to build rapport
Prefer to work out their problems by themselves	Prefer to talk out solutions with another person
Are more likely to be critical of a coworker	Are more likely to compliment a coworker
Tend to interrupt to dominate a conversation or to change the subject	Tend to interrupt to agree with or support what another person is saying
Tend to be more directive	Tend to emphasize politeness
Tend to internalize successes ("That's one of my strengths") and to externalize failures ("We needed more time")	Tend to externalize success ("I was lucky") and to internalize failures ("I'm just not good at that")
Speak differently to other men than they do to women	Speak differently to other women than they do to men

Sources: Jennifer Coates, *Women, Men, and Language,* Longman, New York, 1986; Deborah Tannen, *You Just Don't Understand,* Ballantine, New York, 1990; John Gray, *Men Are from Mars, Women Are from Venus,* HarperCollins, New York, 1992; Patti Hathaway, *Giving and Receiving Feedback,* rev. ed., Crisp Publications, Menlo Park, CA, 1998; Susan Herring, *Making the Net "Work,"* n.d., <http://www.cs.nott.ac.uk/~azq97c/gender.htm> (November 11, 2001); Deborah Tannen, *Talking from 9 to 5,* William Morrow, New York, 1994.

FIGURE 2.3 Goals of Gender Communication

Do you know women and men who defy these gender stereotypes?

Relate versus **Debate**
Rapport versus **Report**
Cooperation versus **Competition**

Making reasonable accommodations for workers with disabilities is a normal part of the contemporary workplace.

Competent communicators go beyond these legal requirements. Depending on the individual situation, some reasonable changes in the way you communicate will be appreciated. For example, when being introduced to someone who uses a wheelchair, bend over slightly to be closer to eye level. If the person is able to extend his or her hand for a handshake, offer your hand. For lengthy conversations, sit down so that you are both eye to eye. People who use wheelchairs may see their wheelchairs as extensions of their personal space, so avoid touching or leaning on their wheelchair.

Most hearing-impaired people use a combination of hearing and lip reading. Face the person to whom you're speaking, and speak a bit slower (but not louder) than usual. It may also be helpful to lower the pitch of your voice. When talking with a person who is blind, deal in words rather than in gestures or glances. As you approach him or her, make your presence known; if in a group, address the person by name so that he or she will know to whom you are talking. Identify yourself and use your normal voice and speed.

Everyone needs help at one time or another. If someone with a disability looks as if he or she needs assistance, ask whether help is wanted and follow the person's wishes. But resist the temptation to take too much care of an individual with a disability. Don't be patronizing.

CHECKPOINT 2.2

RECALL Write a capital *T* for true or *F* for false before each statement.

1. ____ Cultures differ widely in the traits they value.

2. ____ Humor is often an effective way to begin a presentation to an international audience.

3. ____ In the year 2050, whites are expected to still be the largest ethnic group in the United States.

4. ____ Males generally prefer to work out their problems by themselves, whereas females generally prefer to talk out solutions with another person.

5. ____ Most cultures place a similar value on the meaning of time.

VOCABULARY   Define the following term in your own words and give an original example.

6. ethnocentrism:

COMPREHENSION

7. What are four strategies for communicating across cultures?

8. What is the fastest-growing group in the United States?

    The slowest-growing group?

9. When should you offer assistance to a disabled person?

CRITICAL THINKING

10. In your opinion, are men or women generally more effective communicators in business? Why?

··

Communication Technology

Our need for information is insatiable and unrelenting. Today, information is a mass commodity—not a scarce resource. The secret to dealing with this phenomenon is being able to access and make use of that information. As painful as it might be to contemplate, much (if not most) of your education will be obsolete within a few years. You will, therefore, have a lifelong need to update your skills, secure relevant, accurate information, and share that information with others.

To the rescue comes the **Internet**, a worldwide collection of computers in university labs, business offices, and government centers—all interconnected, all filled with massive amounts of information, and all accessible for free (or nearly so) to anyone with an Internet account (which includes almost all college students). The ability to access the information stored in thousands of computers worldwide and to chat with anyone around the globe at any hour of the day bestows tremendous power on anyone who knows how to retrieve, evaluate, and share that information.

Before you can communicate, you must first have something important to communicate. Thus, it makes sense for us to learn how to access and share information now—before we learn about specific communication strategies. The

Contemporary managers need up-to-date information—and they need it now!

Internet A worldwide collection of interconnected computers filled with massive amounts of information, which is accessible anyone with an Internet account

Learn how to secure the information you need—whether it is a phone number, statistic, or research data.

"Didn't you get my e-mail?"

following discussion shows you how to use different forms of technology to communicate more easily, more efficiently, and more effectively.

Accessing Electronic Information

An entire knowledge industry has evolved in which organizations store huge amounts of statistical, financial, and bibliographic information in the memory banks of their mainframe computers or on compact disks and then make this information available to users worldwide for a fee.

electronic database A computer-searchable collection of information on a general subject area

An **electronic database** is a computer-searchable collection of information on a general subject area, such as business, education, or psychology. Electronic databases are fast; you can typically collect more data electronically in one hour than would be possible in an entire day of conventional library research. Such databases are available either on CD-ROM or online via computer network or telephone hookup.

You can conduct a comprehensive search for data without ever leaving your office, via online computer searching.

In addition, electronic databases are typically more current than printed databases, as most are updated weekly or monthly. Also, each contains several years' worth of citations, whereas manual indexes require searching through individual annual volumes and monthly supplements to find the desired information. Finally, electronic databases are extremely flexible. You can use different search terms, combine them, and modify your search at every step.

Much of the information we need is too new to be available in printed form.

Although you may never write another academic report after graduating from college, you *will* continue to need to locate information—for business, political, or personal reasons. Computer-assisted information retrieval has now become so widely available, economical, and easy to use that it has emerged as a powerful tool for helping workers solve problems and make decisions.

The Internet

Chances are that the information you need is stored somewhere on the Internet. You simply have to learn how to access it.

As we noted earlier, the Internet is a vast information system that connects millions of computers worldwide, allowing them to exchange many types of information and to conduct many types of business transactions, such as online banking and shopping. On the Internet, you can send and receive email, transfer files between computers, search for information (our focus here), and participate in discussion groups.

The newest and fastest-growing segment of the Internet, and the resource that is of most interest to us, is the **World Wide Web** (also known as WWW or simply the Web). Web documents, called *pages*, can contain text, graphics, sound, and video, all written in *hypertext*. Hypertext links (highlighted words or images) in the document enable the reader to explore as much or as little of a document as desired. Clicking on a hypertext link instantly opens that document (which may reside on a different computer halfway around the world). Users access this type of information by using a software program known as a Web *browser*, the most popular of which are Microsoft Internet Explorer and Netscape Navigator.

World Wide Web The segment of the Internet that comprises documents containing text, graphics, sounds, and video, as well as electronic links to other documents

Browsing and Searching the Internet

Nobody "owns" the Internet; that is, no one governing authority can make rules and impose order on this vast network. Thus, it should not surprise you that the massive amount of information available on the Internet is not neatly and logically organized for easy search and retrieval.

Fortunately, a variety of search sites are available on the Internet to make accessing resources if not painless, at least more pleasant and productive. These sites fall into two basic categories: directories for browsing the Internet and indexes for searching for specific information.

Browsing the Internet   Web directories are hyperlinked lists of Web sites, hierarchically organized into topical categories and subcategories. Clicking your way through these lists will lead you to Web site links for the subject you're investigating.

When browsing, you can go deeper and deeper into a subject, gradually narrowing your focus.

Use these directories when you need to find common information quickly and easily. If you aren't looking for something specific, try using categories to drill down and narrow your search.

Searching the Internet   Web indexes are massive, computer-generated databases containing information on millions of Web pages. By entering keywords or phrases, you can retrieve lists of Web pages that contain your search term. After your query executes, the Web search site displays the list of hits as a page containing the hyperlinked URLs (Universal Resource Locators, or Internet addresses). To move directly to any particular site, simply click its URL.

The success of your Internet search will depend on how skillfully you choose your keywords (or search terms). Remember that the computer makes a very literal search; it will find exactly what you ask for—and nothing more. If you use the search term "secretaries," most search indexes will not find citations for the words "secretary" or "secretarial." Some indexes have a feature known as *truncation*, which allows you to search for the root of a term. Thus, a search for "secre" would retrieve "secret," "secretarial," "secretaries," "secretary," "secretion," and so on. You would then choose the entries appropriate for your purpose.

Most indexes also allow the use of logical search operators (called Boolean logic) in keywords. The four basic search operators are AND, OR, NOT, and NEAR; as you can see, they are always typed in all capitals. The operators broaden or narrow searches as follows:

Take the time to learn basic Boolean logic. It will save you time and enhance the efficiency of your searches.

Using OR increases the number of sources identified. Using AND, NOT, and NEAR decreases the number of sources identified.

- AND identifies sources that contain both term 1 AND term 2. The use of AND *decreases* the number of hits.

- OR identifies sources that contain either term 1 OR term 2. The use of OR *increases* the number of hits.

- NOT excludes sources that contain the NOT term. The use of NOT *decreases* the number of hits.

■ NEAR identifies sources in which the two terms are within a given distance from each other. The use of NEAR *decreases* the number of hits.

Placing quotation marks around a phrase requires the exact matching of a phrase. As in algebra, the operations inside parentheses are performed first, and most search engines read command lines from left to right. Thus, the search term "heavy metal" would eliminate the flagging of Web sites devoted to metals and ores, whereas "metal" NOT "heavy metal" would find only those sites devoted to metals and ores. As shown in Figure 2.4, Web sites such as America Online (AOL), Yahoo!, and AltaVista can be used for both browsing and searching.

To browse for information, click any of the featured topics. To search for information, type your search term in the Search for: window and then click Search.

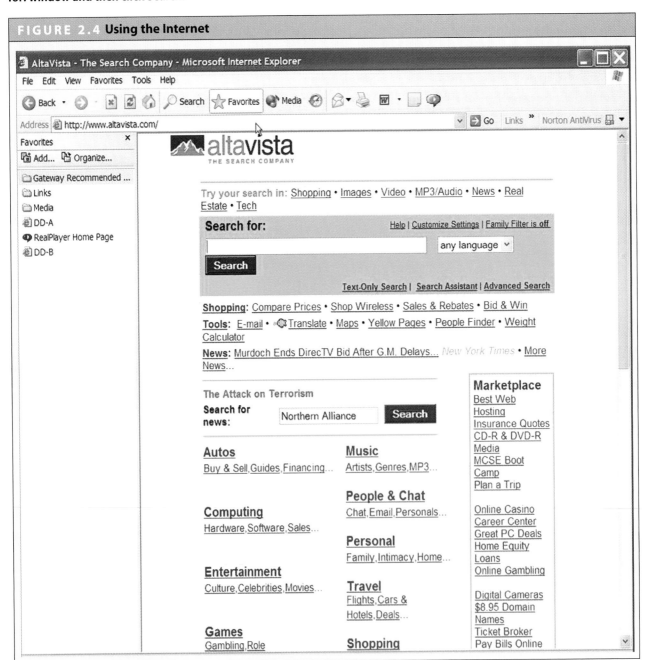

FIGURE 2.4 Using the Internet

Evaluating the Quality of Electronic Information

Anyone with access to the Internet can post almost anything that he or she wants online. No law, regulation, or policy states that the information posted on the Internet must be true, objective, intelligent, or politically correct (recall that no central authority manages the Internet).

The range of informational quality on the Internet is enormous. Information posted by governmental and educational institutions (typically, those sites whose URLs end in ".gov" or ".edu") is most often comprehensive, accurate, and up-to-date. Most pages sponsored by commercial organizations (typically, those sites whose URLs end in ".com") are also of high quality, as long as you recognize the profit incentive behind these pages. Personal home pages and those sponsored by advocacy organizations should be evaluated especially carefully in terms of accuracy, fairness, and breadth and depth of coverage.

Don't believe everything you read!

The consequences of making decisions based on invalid data can range from a minor inconvenience to receiving a failing grade in a class to jeopardizing the financial viability of your organization. You are responsible for the quality of the information you include in your correspondence, reports, and presentations. Avoid accepting something as fact just because you saw it on the Internet. Evaluate your sources critically, using the questions in Checklist 1, "Evaluating the Quality of Internet Resources," as a guide.

Sharing Electronic Information

Technology helps us not only access information but also share it with others. You will often incorporate the information you access electronically into your own

CHECKLIST ①

Evaluating the Quality of Internet Resources

Criterion 1: Authority

✓ Is it clear who sponsors the page and what the sponsor's purpose in maintaining the page is?

✓ Is it clear who wrote the material and what the author's qualifications for writing on this topic are?

Criterion 2: Accuracy

✓ Are the sources for any factual information clearly listed so they can be verified in another source?

✓ Has the sponsor provided a link to outside sources (such as product reviews or reports filed with the SEC) that can be used to verify the sponsor's claims?

✓ Is the information free of grammatical, spelling, and other typographical errors? (These kinds of errors not only indicate a lack of quality control but can actually produce inaccuracies in information.)

✓ Is statistical data in graphs and charts clearly labeled and easy to read?

Criterion 3: Objectivity

✓ For any given piece of information, is the sponsor's motivation for providing it clear?

✓ Is the information content clearly separated from any advertising or opinion content?

✓ Is the point of view of the sponsor presented in a clear manner, with well-supported arguments?

Criterion 4: Currentness

✓ Are there dates on the page to indicate when the page was written, first placed on the Web, and last revised?

✓ Are there any other indications that the material is kept current?

✓ If the material is presented in graphs or charts, is it clearly stated when the data were gathered?

Source: Adapted from Jan Alexander and Marsha Ann Tate, "Evaluating Web Resources," July 25, 2001, http://muse.widener.edu/Wolfgram-Memorial-Library/webevaluation/webeval.htm (February 19, 2002).

electronic communications—correspondence, reports, phone calls, and the like, using a variety of technological innovations.

Email   In email (electronic mail), messages are composed, transmitted, and usually read on computer screens. In recent years, email has replaced the telephone as the preferred medium to communicate in business. In 1997, for the first time more email was sent than letters via the post office.[8] In a recent American Management Association survey, 36% of executives reported that they favor email for most management communication, compared with 26% who preferred the phone. (Surprisingly, one of the less popular alternatives was a face-to-face meeting, favored by only 15% of the executives.[9])

Email has, in fact, become so popular that it can be time-consuming to read and answer. Another problem relates to the fact that email is typically written "on the fly"—composed and sent while keyboarding. As a result, writers sometimes ignore effective writing principles. According to Charles McGoon, email may be

> desensitizing us to egregious grammatical gaffes. . . . Would you write a printed memo to your boss with typos in it? To what earthly purpose? How can someone on the other end of an email message know that you're really an intelligent person?[10]

Always think before you write.

Competent communicators follow the guidelines shown in Checklist 2, "Effective Email Practices," to ensure that their email messages achieve their objectives.

CHECKLIST 2

Effective EMail Practices

Format

✓ **Use short lines and paragraphs (especially the first and last paragraphs).** They're much easier to read. Avoid formatting a long message as one solid paragraph.

✓ **Don't shout.** Use all-capital letters only for emphasis or to substitute for italicized text (such as book titles). Do *not* type your entire message in all capitals. It is considered rude (not to mention being more difficult to read).

✓ **Proofread your message before sending it.** Don't let the speed and convenience of email lull you into being careless. Although an occasional typo or other surface error will probably be overlooked by the reader, excessive errors or sloppy language creates an unprofessional image of the sender.

Content

✓ **Choose your recipients carefully.** Don't send a message to an entire mailing list (for example, the whole department) if it applies only to one or two people.

✓ **Use a descriptive subject line.** The wording of the subject line may determine not only when, but even if, a message is read. Use a brief, but descriptive, subject line.

✓ **Greet your recipient.** Downplay the seeming impersonality of computerized mail by starting your message with a friendly salutation, such as "Hi, Amos" or "Dear Mr. Fisher."

✓ **Insert previous messages appropriately.** Occasionally, it may be helpful for the reader to see his or her entire message replayed. More often, however, you can save the reader time by establishing the context of the original message in your reply (for example, "Here is my opinion of the AlphaBat system that you asked for in your May 28 email.")

✓ **Use a direct style of writing.** Put your major idea in the first sentence or two. If the message is so sensitive or emotionally laden that a more indirect organization would be appropriate, you should reconsider whether email is the most effective medium for your message.

✓ **Think twice; write once.** This variation of the carpenter's advice ("measure twice; cut once") is appropriate here. Because it is so easy to respond immediately to a message, you might be tempted to let your emotions take over. Such behavior is called "flaming" and should be avoided. Always assume the message you send will never be destroyed.

✓ **Provide an appropriate closing.** Some email programs identify only the email address (for example, 70511.753@compuserve.com) in the message header. Don't take a chance that your reader won't recognize you. Include your name, email address, and any other appropriate identifying information at the end of your message.

Fax Communication Fax machines are fast, inexpensive, easy to use, and available worldwide. In addition, personal computers with fax modems allow computer users to send and receive documents through their personal computers, regardless of whether the original sender or the intended recipient has a computer. Follow these guidelines when faxing a document:

- Always use a cover sheet when you send a fax. Include a name, company address, phone number, and fax number for both you and the recipient; the date; the total number of pages; and a brief note explaining why you are sending the fax. If the fax will go outside the company, type the cover sheet so that it will have a professional appearance.

- Ensure that the document to be faxed is legible—that is, that the paper to be faxed is free of smudges and wrinkles and that the font is dark and readable.

- Be courteous. If someone is waiting behind you to fax only one page and you have many pages, let that person go ahead of you. If someone inadvertently leaves an original document behind, return it to him or her—unread.

Telephone Communication There are more than 285 million telephones in the world, 115 million of them in the United States. That number is equivalent to approximately one telephone for every two people in this country.[11] No wonder, then, that communicating effectively by telephone is a critical workplace skill. The caller may equate your telephone demeanor with the attitude of the entire organization. Thus, every time the phone rings, your organization's future is on the line.

Before you pick up the phone to make a call, consider whether you might accomplish your purpose better by writing. If your message is long and complicated, it may be easier for your audience to understand it in writing; in addition, the recipient can refer back to the document when necessary. If you're conveying only simple information, a short email may be more appropriate. If you are conveying bad news, a phone call may soften the blow, whereas a letter may strengthen the force of your message. You should have a clear purpose and understand the effect that the form of your message will have on your audience.

If a telephone call is the most appropriate medium of communication for your message, follow the guidelines shown in Checklist 3, "Effective Telephone Practices."

> Fax communications are widely available around the world.

RECALL Write a capital *T* for true or *F* for false before each statement.

1. ____ Descriptive subject lines should always be used in email messages.

2. ____ If you want a search engine to match a phrase exactly, you should enclose the phrase in parentheses.

3. ____ Information placed on the Internet has generally been screened to ensure that it is accurate and objective.

4. ____ The U.S. government is the central authority for managing the Internet.

5. ____ You should always answer the telephone on the first ring.

VOCABULARY Define the following terms in your own words.

6. electronic database:

CHECKPOINT 2.3

CHECKLIST 3

Effective Telephone Practices

Speaking on the Phone

✓ Sit or stand tall and avoid chewing gum or eating while talking. (If your head is tilted sideways to cradle the phone between your head and shoulder, your throat is strained and the words may sound unclear.)

✓ Greet the caller with a smile—just as you would greet someone in person.

✓ Keep a pad and paper near the phone for note taking.

✓ Answer the phone by the second or third ring.

✓ Identify the company, department, and/or yourself.

✓ Use positive language. Instead of saying, "I don't know," say, "Let me check and call you right back." And then do it.

Using Voice Mail

✓ Before you even call, recognize that you might have to leave a message, so plan your message beforehand.

✓ Be polite and get to the point quickly. Clearly define the purpose of the call and the desired action, and always give your phone number—even if the caller has it on file. Slow down and speak especially clearly when giving your phone number.

✓ Check your messages frequently and return calls promptly.

Using a Cell Phone

✓ Avoid making or answering calls when driving. Your safety (and the safety of others) is more important than the phone message.

✓ Speak clearly and get to the point quickly. Remember that both parties are paying for the call.

✓ Turn off cell phones while in a social environment (for example, during lunch and at the theater) and during meetings. If you are expecting an important call, turn on the vibration mode instead of the ring mode; then politely excuse yourself to a more private area to take the call.

✓ If you get disconnected, redial the party if you initiated the call. Wait for the other party to redial if you received the call.

✓ Do not eavesdrop on phone calls being made by others in public places. Be aware, however, that others may be listening to your call, either intentionally or unintentionally.

7. Internet:

8. World Wide Web:

COMPREHENSION

9. When should you browse the Internet and when should you search the Internet?

10. Compose a search statement that will locate sources of information about hard rock music but not about rocks in general.

11. Assume you're composing an email to your instructor complaining about a recent grade. Compose an effective subject line for this email.

CRITICAL THINKING

12. "I don't have to worry about spelling, typing, or grammar errors in my emails because I have a spelling checker on my computer." Discuss the truth of this statement.

Ethics and Communication

Each of us has a personal code of **ethics,** or rules of conduct, that might go beyond legal rules to tell us how to act when the law is silent. When communicating, we constantly make conscious decisions regarding what information to include and what information to exclude from our messages. For the information that is included, we make conscious decisions about how to phrase the language, how much to emphasize each point, and how to organize the message. Such decisions have legal and ethical dimensions—both for you as the writer and for the organization that you represent.

ethics Rules of conduct that may go beyond legal rules

Oral defamation is slander. Written defamation is libel.

Defamation

Any false and malicious statement that is communicated to others and that injures a person's good name or reputation may constitute *defamation.* Defamation in a temporary form such as in oral communication is called *slander;* defamation in a permanent form such as in writing or on videotape is called *libel.* The three major conditions for defamation to be proved are that the statement be false, be communicated to others, and be harmful to a person's good name or reputation. Thus, telling Joe Smith to his face that he is a liar and a crook does not constitute defamation (slander) unless a third person hears the remarks. In addition, truth is generally an acceptable defense to a charge of defamation.

Invasion of Privacy

Any unreasonable intrusion into the private life of another person or denial of a person's right to be left alone may constitute an invasion of privacy. Thus, using someone's name or photograph in a sales promotion without that person's permission may be an invasion of privacy. Of particular concern today are the vast amounts of employee and customer information being maintained in corporate databases. The proliferation of microcomputers, networks, and electronic mail makes it possible to access large amounts of data about employees and customers very freely.

Various state and federal laws protect the individual's right to privacy. Someone's right to privacy may be violated if his or her records are read by someone who is not authorized to examine them or who has no compelling business reason for examining that information.

Competent communicators ensure that they do not misuse information about others in their communications and that their communications are made available only to people who legitimately need such information.

Fraud and Misrepresentation

A deliberate misrepresentation of the truth for the purpose of inducing someone to give up something of value is called *fraud*. Fraud can occur either when one party makes a deliberately false statement or when one party deliberately conceals some information that he or she is required to reveal.

To be fraudulent, the statements must involve facts. Opinions and persuasive arguments or exaggerated claims about a product do not constitute fraud, even if they turn out to be false. For example, saying that "The Celeste is the only American-made car that comes with leather seats as standard equipment" is a statement of fact, which, if incorrect, might constitute fraud. However, saying that "The Celeste is the most luxurious car in America" is an opinion; even if most car buyers did not agree with the statement, it would still not be considered fraud.

You should also recognize that a statement of opinion, even if it is not fraudulent, might still be unethical. For example, advertising that "The Celeste is the most luxurious car in America" might not be fraudulent; but it would be highly unethical if you did not believe that claim to be true.

Misrepresentation is a false statement that is made innocently with no intent to deceive the other party. If misrepresentation is proved, the contract or agreement may be rescinded. In contrast, if fraud is proved, the contract or agreement may not only be rescinded but the offended party may also collect monetary compensation.

Competent communicators are aware of the relevant laws and ensure that their oral and written messages are accurate, both in terms of what is communicated and in terms of what is left uncommunicated.

Workplace Etiquette

Business etiquette is the practice of polite and appropriate behavior in a business setting. It dictates what behaviors are considered proper and under what circumstances; as a consequence, business etiquette is really concerned with interaction between people—not meaningless ritual.

Each organization has its own rules about what is and is not considered fitting in terms of dress, ways of addressing superiors, importance of punctuality, and the like. In addition, every country and every culture has its own rules. Generally, these rules are not written but rather must be learned informally or through observation. Workers who follow correct business etiquette are more confident and appear more in charge. The higher you advance in your career, the more important such behavior will become.

Business etiquette differs in many ways from social etiquette. The worker who enumerates all of his or her accomplishments to a superior during a performance appraisal is simply being savvy; the worker who does so during a social engagement is being boorish. You must be sensitive to what is appropriate under any given circumstances.

Good manners are good business; they communicate a strong positive message about you as a person. As Mark Twain once observed about etiquette, "Always do right: you will please some people and astonish the rest."

Meeting and Greeting

The important point to remember about making introductions is simply to *make them*. The format you use is less important than the fact that you avoid the awkwardness of requiring two people to introduce themselves.

The basic rule for introductions is to present the lower-ranking person to the higher-ranking person, regardless of age or gender: "Mr. CEO, this is my new assistant." If the people you're introducing are equal in rank, mention the older one first, mention the guest first, or (traditionally) mention the woman first.

The format for an introduction might be like this: "Jacinta, I'd like you to meet Huang Gao. Huang just began working here as a network technician. Huang, this is Jacinta Rios, our office manager." In a social situation, you might just say, "Rosa, this is Charlotte Perkins. Charlotte, Rosa Méndez." The appropriate response to an introduction is, "How do you do, Charlotte?" Regardless of the gender of the two people being introduced, either may initiate the handshake—a gesture of welcome.

Use a person's name in the conversation to help you remember it.

Dining

The restaurant you select for a business meal reflects on both you and your organization. Choose one where the food is of top quality and the service is dependable. In general, the more important your guest, the more exclusive the restaurant. If a maitre d' (headwaiter) seats you and your guest, your guest should precede you to the table. If you're seating yourselves, take the lead in locating an appropriate table. Give your guest the preferred seat, facing the window with an attractive view or facing the dining room if you're seated next to the wall.

Here are some additional tips to follow for a successful and enjoyable business meal:

- The guests wait until the host unfolds the napkin and places it in the lap before doing the same. Do not begin eating until the host takes the first bite of food.

- To signal the server that you're ready to order, close your menu and lay it on the table. To get the server's attention, say "Excuse me" when he or she is nearby, or catch the server's eye and quietly signal for him or her to come to the table, or ask a nearby server to ask yours to come to your table. The host's order is generally taken last.

Treat your server with professional courtesy.

- If you leave the table during the meal, leave your napkin on your chair. At the end of the meal, place the napkin, unfolded, on the table.

- When using silverware, start from the outside. As shown in Figure 2.5, your glass is the one at the right of your place setting. When passing food or condiments, pass to the right, offering items to someone else before you serve yourself.

FIGURE 2.5 Table Setting

Use silverware from the outside and work your way in. Remember: glass to the right; pass to the right.

- Don't put your elbows on the table while eating, although you may do so between courses.
- Place the knife across the top edge of the plate, with the cutting edge toward you, when it is not being used. To signal the waiter that you are through with your plate, place your knife and fork diagonally across the middle of the plate.
- Spoon soup away from you. Avoid salting food before tasting it; if asked to pass the salt or pepper, pass both together.

- The person who issues the invitation is expected to pay the bill. In most parts of the country, the usual tip for standard service is 15% to 20% of the food and bar bill and 10% of the cost of the wine. An appropriate tip for the cloakroom attendant is $.50–$.75 per coat, or $1 in an expensive restaurant. If you use valet parking, tip the attendant $1–$2 after your car is brought to the door.
- Send a thank-you note immediately after the meal. Be sure to write more than a token note, mentioning something special about the decor, the food, the service, the company of the people with whom you dined, or your satisfaction with the business discussed.

Dressing Appropriately

Different positions, different companies, and different parts of the country and world have different dress codes—some stated explicitly in the company manual, others communicated indirectly via corporate culture. In the absence of other information, you should choose well-tailored, clean, conservative clothing for the workplace.

In recent years, dress-down days (like "casual Fridays") have gained popularity in U.S. business. A Gallup poll found that 57% of U.S. companies now allow casual dress at least once a week.[12] The adoption of these casual days has caused some confusion about what exactly is considered appropriate. These guidelines for "business casual" from Levi Strauss & Company should prove helpful:[13]

- Aim for a classic but understated look when selecting casual business wear. Pick clothing that is comfortable yet communicates a professional attitude. Subtle, quality accessories (such as belts, jewelry, and scarves) coordinated with an outfit can show attention to important details.
- Casual does not mean sloppy. Clothing should be clean, pressed or wrinkle-free, and without holes or frayed areas. Like suits and tailored clothing, casual business wear lasts longer and looks better with special care.

- Keep the focus on work. Anything worn to the gym or beach (or to clean the garage) should be left at home. Avoid clothing that is too revealing or tight-fitting. Trendy or "high-fashion" clothing may communicate a whimsical or pretentious attitude that is not suitable for most offices.
- T-shirts or sweatshirts with messages other than the company's logo are probably not a good idea. Keep clothing colors muted and coordinated to help create a professional appearance. Business casual does *not* mean sloppy.
- Pay attention to the fit of your clothing. Pants should break just above the shoe, sleeves should reach the base of the hand and show just a bit of the cuff when a jacket is worn, and shirt collars should button comfortably without pinching or leaving gaps. Also, if a tie is worn, its tip should reach just below the bottom of the belt buckle.
- Shoes matter. Leather shoes are generally preferable, but if athletic shoes are allowed, make sure they are clean, subtle in design, and scuff-free. Leather

shoes look best when polished and in good repair. For most offices, open-toed sandals and beach thongs are not appropriate.

- Take the day's schedule into account when dressing. If a meeting with visitors is on the agenda, dress more traditionally or check whether casual dress might be appropriate.

- When in doubt, leave it out. Casual clothing should make the employee and coworkers work more comfortably. Ask the manager ahead of time if you have any questions.

Around the Office

Many situations occur every day in the typical office that call for common courtesy. The basis for appropriate behavior is always the golden rule: "Treat others as you would like to be treated."

Follow the golden rule in your dealings with others at work.

Drinking Coffee   If a container to pay for the coffee is provided, put in money every time you take a cup; don't force others to treat you to a cup of coffee. Also, take your turn making the coffee and cleaning the pot if that is a task performed by the group. Although in most offices it is acceptable to drink coffee or some other beverage while working, some offices have an unwritten rule against snacking at one's desk. In any event, never eat while talking to someone in person or on the telephone.

Smoking   Some offices have designated smoking areas, and many prohibit smoking anywhere on the premises. If you smoke, follow the rules strictly. Smoking in public anywhere is increasingly considered bad manners, not to mention being a health hazard.

Using the Copier or Fax Machine   If you're using the copier or fax machine for a large job, and someone approaches with a small job, let that person go ahead of you. Also, be sure to refill the paper holder after completing a job, and reset the copier machine counter after using it. (The next user, intending to make one copy, will not appreciate having to wait for—and pay for—100 copies, simply because you failed to reset the counter.)

Nate Moreland manages the sports apparel store run by the Oregon Association of Minority Entrepreneurs. One of the points he stresses to his employees, all young entrepreneurs in the Portland area, is to dress appropriately for the job.

CHECKPOINT 2.4

RECALL Write a capital *T* for true or *F* for false before each statement.

1. ___ Business etiquette is essentially the same as social etiquette.

2. ___ Oral defamation is considered slander, whereas written defamation is considered libel.

3. ___ Stating that your product is the best on the market, even if you do not believe that it is, would not constitute fraud.

4. ___ When introducing a lower-ranking person to a higher-ranking person, you should say the lower-ranking person's name first.

5. ___ When using silverware, you should start from the outside.

VOCABULARY   Define the following terms in your own words.

6. ethics:

7. business etiquette:

COMPREHENSION

8. What is the difference between fraud and misrepresentation?

9. How would you introduce a 21-year-old friend to your business communication instructor?

10. If you're the host for a business luncheon, how much should you tip the server?

CRITICAL THINKING

11. At his company, Silvestre does not have to submit receipts for expenses less than $25. At a conference he attended last week, he skipped the luncheon (which cost $22) to spend more time at the exhibits. Because he was actually working during lunch, he decided to include $15 for lunch on his expense report. What is your reaction?

THE 3Ps
Problem, Process, Product

Evaluating the Quality of Internet Data

Problem

Assume the role of Hoshi Tamura, human resources assistant at your company. You are concerned that one of the data-entry operators at your company has been diagnosed with carpal tunnel syndrome, a neuromuscular disorder of the tendons and tissue in the wrists caused by repeated hand motions. You have been researching the possibility of purchasing speech-recognition software for data-entry operators so that they can dictate their data into a microphone and have it automatically appear on the computer screen, without the need for keyboarding.

You have decided to field-test two speech-recognition programs and to purchase a high-quality microphone. To start your research, you have visited the Internet once again and identified the three sites shown in the accompanying figures. Now you need to evaluate the quality of the information contained in these sites to see whether the information can be used to help you make a decision.

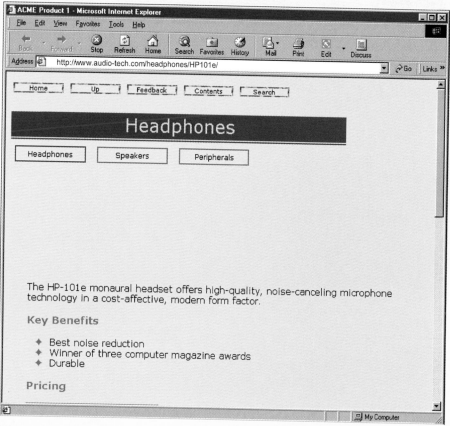

Company Home Page

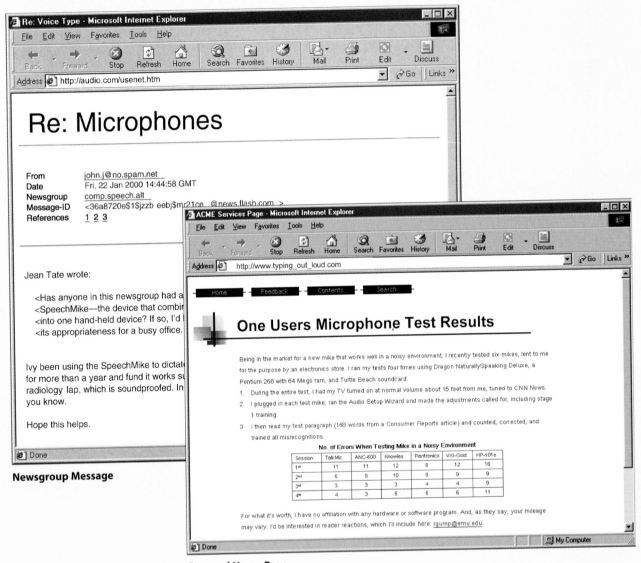

The 3Ps
Problem, Process, Product

Newsgroup Message

Personal Home Page

Process

1. Using the guidelines discussed in Checklist 1 on page 43, evaluate the strengths and weaknesses of the home page of Audio-Tech, a retailer of audio equipment.

   ■ It is clear who sponsors the site.

   ■ The content is free from most grammar and usage errors (note, however, the misspelling of the word "effective" in the first paragraph).

   ■ Because the company is trying to sell its products, the data is probably up to date.

   ■ The site is well designed and easy to read and navigate.

- No evidence is presented to back up the claims of "best noise reduction" and "durable."
- The site provides no links to verify the magazine awards received by the product.

2. Evaluate the strengths and weaknesses of the newsgroup message.

- From the header information, it is easy to identify the sponsor of the site and the date of the message.
- The writer copied enough (and only enough) of the original message to place his comments in perspective.
- Although the information probably represents the writer's objective thinking, it is irrelevant for us because our intended use is in a busy (and noisy) business office.
- The message is full of errors—presumably caused by the speech-recognition software and microphone being used to record the message (which actually contradicts the writer's written message).

3. Evaluate the strengths and weaknesses of the personal home page:

- The site is well designed and easy to read and navigate.
- Although not shown on the screen capture, the site clearly identifies the sponsor, date of the last update, and contact information.
- The content is free from most grammar and usage errors (note, however, the missing apostrophe in the word "users" in the title).
- The content provides specific and helpful details about the test conditions and the results obtained.
- The last paragraph lends credibility to the test results.
- The content doesn't indicate when the test was conducted; thus I don't know whether the hardware and software used are the latest versions.

Product

After conducting my preliminary investigation, I have decided not to purchase either product. The HP-101e microphone was the least accurate of the six mikes tested, and our data-entry operators who have carpal tunnel syndrome may be uncomfortable using a hand-held mike for long periods of data entry. I'll continue researching the issue before making a purchase decision.

Summary

Teams can accomplish more and better-quality work in less time than individuals can if the teams function properly. Otherwise, teams can waste time and cause interpersonal conflicts. Conflict about ideas is a helpful part of the group process, whereas interpersonal conflicts are detrimental. Although placing an appropriate emphasis on consensus and conformity is productive, giving too much deference can lead to groupthink. Group members should acknowledge the need for positive and negative feedback and know how to give productive feedback.

For group-writing projects, team members should develop a work schedule and meet regularly to ensure proper coordination. Either one person can be assigned to write the entire draft, or the parts can be divided among group members. Everyone, however, should be involved in revising the draft.

Cultures differ greatly in terms of how they interpret nonverbal behavior and what importance they attach to group behavior as opposed to individual behavior. Competent communicators maintain formality, show respect, remain flexible, and write and speak clearly when communicating with people of different cultures. Even if you live and work in a small community in the United States, you will be communicating with, and should learn to be comfortable with, people with different ethnic backgrounds, different genders, and different types of disabilities.

Information sources on the Internet include the World Wide Web, which contains pages of text, graphics, sound, and video, with hyperlinks that enable the reader to instantly jump to related topics. This information can be located by using directories for browsing the Internet and indexes for searching for specific information. Because the quality of the information on the Internet varies tremendously, you should critically evaluate the information you receive before deciding whether to use it.

Today, email is the preferred medium for communicating in business. Competent communicators ensure that they use an appropriate format (especially a descriptive subject line) and content for their email messages. They also make appropriate use of other technologies, including fax and telephone communication.

Regardless of the size and type of organization, every business writer faces ethical questions when communicating orally and in writing. Legal questions can arise with regard to defamation, invasion of privacy, and fraud or misrepresentation. In choosing what information to convey, and which words and sentences to use, we inevitably make ethical choices—moral decisions about what is right—even when no question of law is involved.

Business etiquette is a guide to help people behave appropriately in business situations. To be effective in business, you should learn how to make introductions, conduct business lunches, dress appropriately, and maintain good working relationships around the office. Remember: Good manners are good business.

Looking Ahead

No one can communicate effectively if he or she communicates incorrectly. To be successful in business, you need well-developed language arts skills. That is why every third chapter in this text refines your basic skills in a particular area of grammar, usage, and mechanics. Chapter 3 starts us off with a discussion of basic sentence structure in business writing.

Key Terms

business etiquette	groupthink
electronic database	Internet
ethics	team
ethnocentrism	World Wide Web

Exercises

Communicating in Work Teams

1 Dealing with Conflict   Everyone had agreed to have his or her part of the report drafted by the time your team met today. What would be an appropriate response to each of the following incidents at today's meeting?

a. Fred did not have his part ready (although this is the first time he has been late).

b. Rosemary did not have her part ready (the third time this semester she has missed a deadline).

c. Anita not only had her part completed but also had sketched out an attractive design for formatting the final document.

d. Consuelo was 45 minutes late for the meeting because her car had skidded into a ditch as a result of last night's snowstorm.

e. Cheyenne left a message that she would have to miss the meeting because she was working on another report, one due tomorrow.

2 Work-Team Communication   Working in small groups, interview at least three international students or professors, each from a different country. For each country represented, determine the extent of team communications common in business, the extent of technological development, problems with the English language, and the like. Prepare a written report of your findings, proofread, revise as necessary, and submit it to your instructor.

Communicating in a Diverse Environment

3 Meanings Are in People   Locate two foreign-born people from the same country who speak English as a second language. First, ask one of them to translate literally into his or her native language the ad slogans shown below. Then give the foreign-language translation to the second person, and ask that person to retranslate the slogans into English. Compare the original and the retranslated English versions. What are the implications of any discrepancies?

- Twice a day we explain the facts of life (National Public Radio)
- From chips to ships (Hyundai)
- We took a great idea and made it fly (Samsonite)
- Digital has it now (Digital Equipment)
- The heartbeat of America (Chevrolet)
- Satisfy your lust for power and money (NEC)

4 Domestic Intercultural Issues   How would you respond to each of the following situations?

a. Ryan gets angry when several of the people with whom he works talk among themselves in their native language. He suspects they are talking and laughing about him. As a result, Ryan tends to avoid his coworkers and to complain about them to others.

b. Héctor, a slightly built office worker, feels intimidated when talking to his supervisor, a much larger man who is of a different racial background. As a result, Hctor often is unable to negotiate effectively.

c. Darlene is embarrassed when she must talk to Galen, a subordinate who suffered major facial disfigurement from a grenade explosion during the Vietnam War. She doesn't know how to look at him. As a result, Darlene tends to avoid meeting with Galen face to face.

d. Lillian, the only female manager on staff, gets incensed whenever her colleague Gilbert apologizes to her after using profanity during a meeting. First, she tells him that he shouldn't be using profanity at all. Second, if he does, he should not apologize just to her for using it.

e. When Lance arrived as the only male real-estate agent in a small office, it was made clear to him that he would have to get his own coffee and clean up after himself—just like everyone else. Yet, whenever the FedEx truck delivers a heavy carton, the females always ask Lance to lift the package.

5 Diversity   Assume that you are a supervisor in a firm where one-third of the work force is Hispanic, about evenly divided between Mexican Americans and Cuban Americans. All are either U.S. citizens or legal residents. Because both groups have Spanish as their native language, can you assume that both groups have similar cultures? Do some research (including Internet research) on both groups regarding their typical educational backgrounds, political beliefs, job experiences, and the like. Organize your findings into a two-page report (typed, double-spaced).

Communication Technology

6 Internet Sources   Locate and download from the Internet at least one article that will help you resolve the following problems.

a. The removable hard-disk drive you purchased and installed six months ago has just crashed. You need to contact the company (IBM) to determine whether the disk drive is still under warranty and, if so, how you can get it repaired or replaced.

b. Your boss asks you to make a hotel reservation for January 15–18 at a hotel in downtown San Francisco that charges between $200 and $250 per week night.

c. Your company is trying to get ISO 2000 certification so that it can expand its operations into central Europe. You wonder what is involved in securing such certification and what advantages and disadvantages the certification confers.

d. You have just read an article in the *Wall Street Journal* about Auto-by-Tel, an online automobile buying service. You wonder if it would be a profitable company in which to invest your $8,500 Keogh account funds.

e. As part of your term paper in European art history, you need to include a color photograph of the *Mona Lisa*.

f. You've finally finished cramming for tomorrow's accounting exam and are ready to relax for a bit. What movies are on TV tonight?

7 Locating Specific Facts   Your boss has asked you to help determine the feasibility of opening a frozen yogurt store in Akron, Ohio. Answer the following questions, using the latest figures available. Print out the Web pages that support your answers.

a. What are the number of establishments and the total sales last year for TCBY, a frozen yogurt franchise?
b. What is the population of Akron, Ohio? What percentage of this population is between the ages of 18 and 24?
c. What is the per capita income of residents of Akron?
d. What is the address of Everything Yogurt, a frozen yogurt franchise?
e. What is the climate of Akron, Ohio?
f. How many students are enrolled at the University of Akron?
g. What is the market outlook for frozen yogurt stores nationwide?
h. What is the most current journal or newspaper article you can find on this topic?

8 Email Format   Evaluate the following email message against the guidelines provided in Checklist 2 on page 44. Specifically, what would you change to make it more effective? Should this message have been sent as an email message in the first place? Discuss.

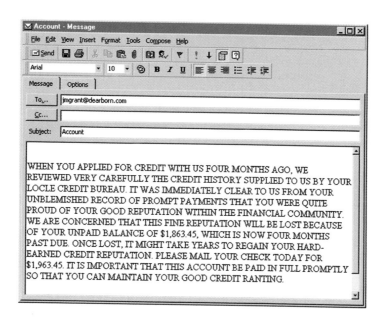

Ethics and Communication

9 Ethics on the Job   You are the office manager of the Natural-Disaster Recovery Team for People Helping People. After testing several new word processing programs, you wrote a memo to your supervisor requesting the purchase of 15 copies of WordXpert so that each member of your office staff would have a copy. You just received your memo back from your supervisor with this handwritten note attached to it:

I'm tired of purchasing software and then not having it do what it says it will do. Let's order one copy of the program first and make copies for all your staff. If in two months everyone is still happy with the program, I'll buy 14 more copies to make us legitimate. After all, we have to be careful with the funds donated to our organization.

How do you respond?

10 Legal Issues   Justin was thinking of hiring Roberta Jordan for an open sales territory. Knowing she had previously worked at Kentron, he called his friend there, Barry Kennedy, to ask about her performance. "She's very smart, but I wouldn't hire her again, Justin," Barry said. "She's a little lazy. Sometimes she wouldn't begin making her calls until late morning or even after lunch. Also, she was sloppy with her paperwork. I assume she's honest, but I never could get her to file receipts for all her expenses. Of course, she was going through a messy divorce then, so maybe that affected her job performance." Justin thanked his friend and notified Roberta that she was not being hired for the job. If Roberta learned of Barry's comments, would she have the basis for a legal suit? If so, what type and on what grounds? How could Barry have reworded his comments to convey the information in a businesslike, ethical manner?

Workplace Etiquette

11 Intercultural Etiquette   For this activity, your instructor will assign you one of the following countries: Canada, Mexico, England, Germany, or Japan. Go online to **www.executiveplanet.com** and follow the links to your country. There you will find abundant information about how to practice professional etiquette in that country. Write a paper entitled "Professional Etiquette in [Your Chosen Country]." Be sure to cover such topics as the following:

a. Entertaining for business success
b. Making appointments
c. Respectfully addressing others
d. Guidelines for business dress
e. Appropriate topics of conversation

12 Introductions   Your instructor will assign you one of the following roles:

a. The 29-year-old female president of your company
b. Your 83-year-old grandmother
c. Your 25-year-old best friend, a female who uses a wheelchair
d. The 60-year-old male clerk in the shipping room, who is originally from Italy
e. Your 7-year-old brother

Standing in a circle, take turns introducing the person on your left to the person on your right (and vice versa).

13 Business Meals   Divide into groups of four, and have each group select who will act as host. Go to a medium-priced restaurant (not a fast-food restaurant) and have a business meal. The "business" you will conduct during the meal is the clarification of appropriate behavior during a business meal; thus, you may freely discuss with one another questions that come up during the meal. Write up the result of your experience.

3

Business Sentence Structure

COMMUNICATION OBJECTIVES

After you have finished this chapter, you should be able to:

- Communicate effectively in small groups.

- Identify the eight parts of speech.

- Identify the parts of a sentence.

- Identify the patterns of sentence organization.

- Identify the four functions of sentences.

- Identify sentences in terms of their complexity.

- Avoid the errors of sentence fragments and run-on sentences.

On the Job

PAUL YU
Director of Information Systems, Recycled Paper Products

Paul Yu, director of information systems at Recycled Paper Products (RPP), had just placed a call to Wallace Schmidt, RPP's president. "Hi, Wally, got a minute?"

"Sure, Paul, what's up?"

"I've been thinking about your plan to install a new data-tracking system for our consumer recycled products, and I've even talked with several of my colleagues in other companies, and the bottom line is, well, I just think we should hold off until we have more information on the system's reliability.

"Who'd you talk to?"

"Just got off the phone with Ray Willard."

"At Overland Products?"

"Yeah, and he says they have not realized the savings they thought they would. That they now wish they'd waited until the second release of the software before purchasing it. And that another company is now pilot-testing a competitive product that looks good."

"Okay, I trust Ray's judgment, so let's hold off for a while, but keep me informed of new developments and let me know how Ray's system finally works out."

"That's great, Wally! And will do. Bye."

Most business communicators would consider the preceding conversation to be an effective business call; after all, Paul accomplished his objective. A second reading of this conversation, however, reveals the presence of numerous sentence fragments and run-on sentences. The point to remember is that what is effective and efficient in oral communication is not always acceptable in business writing. This chapter shows you how to recognize the different elements and types of effective sentences in business writing.

Parts of Speech

Paul Yu, of course, uses words to communicate. Of the hundreds of thousands of words in an unabridged dictionary, each can be classified as one of just eight parts of speech: noun, pronoun, verb, adjective, adverb, preposition, conjunction, or interjection. These eight parts of speech are illustrated in the following sentence:

Interjection	Pronoun	Adverb	Verb	Preposition	Adjective	Noun	Conjunction	Noun

Oh, I eagerly waited for new computers and printers.

Many words can act as different parts of speech, however, depending on how they are used in a sentence. As you learned long ago, a *sentence* is a group of words that contains a subject and predicate and that expresses a complete thought.

Consider, for example, the different parts of speech represented by the word *following:*

We agree to do the following. (*noun*)
I was only following your example. (*verb*)
We met the following day. (*adjective*)
Following his remarks, he sat down. (*preposition*)

All words do not serve more than one function, but many do. This chapter offers a brief introduction to the eight parts of speech. They will be explored in more detail in later chapters. Although you are undoubtedly already familiar with the definitions of most of these terms, each is defined here in case you need a refresher.

Nouns

A **noun** is a word that *names* something, such as a person, place, thing, or idea:

Person:	employee, Ms. Campbell
Place:	office, Chicago
Thing:	animal, computer
Idea:	concentration, impatience, week, typing

The words in italics in the following sentences are nouns.

Samuel promoted his *idea* to the *vice president* on *Wednesday.*
Word processing is just one of the *skills* you'll need as a *temp.*
How much does one *quart* of *water* weigh on our bathroom *scales?*
The animal *doctor* treated that *animal* well in *Houston.*

If you were asked to give an example of a noun, you would probably think of a *concrete noun*, a physical object that you can see, hear, feel, taste, or smell. An *abstract noun*, on the other hand, names a quality or concept rather than something physical. Here are examples of each:

Concrete Noun	*Abstract Noun*
book	success
stapler	patience
computer	skills
dictionary	loyalty

A *common noun*, as its name suggests, is the name of a *general* person, place, thing, or idea. If you want to give the name of a *specific* person, place, thing, or idea, you would use a *proper noun*. Proper nouns are always capitalized.

Margin notes:

You cannot know a word's part of speech until you see it used in a sentence.

noun A word that names something

To determine whether a word is a noun, add "the" in front of the word. If it makes sense, the word is a noun.

Common Noun	Proper Noun
man	Lon Adams
city	Los Angeles
car	Corvette
religion	Judaism

A *singular noun* names one person, place, thing, or idea. A *plural noun* names more than one.

Singular Noun	Plural Noun
Armstrong	Armstrongs
watch	watches
computer	computers
victory	victories

As illustrated here, the spelling of the plural form of a noun typically ends in *-s*, *-es*, or *-ies*. We'll learn the spelling rules in Chapter 15.

Pronouns

A **pronoun** is a word used in place of a noun. Consider the following sentence:

Anna went into *Anna's* kitchen and made *Anna's* favorite dessert because *Anna* was going to a party with *Anna's* friends.

The noun *Anna* is used five times in this awkward sentence. A smoother, less monotonous version of the sentence substitutes pronouns for all but the first *Anna*:

Anna went into *her* kitchen and made *her* favorite dessert because *she* was going to a party with *her* friends.

The words in italics in the following sentences are pronouns. The nouns to which they refer are underlined:

<u>Edmundo</u> thought *he* might get the promotion.
None of the <u>speakers</u> were interesting.
<u>Ms. Kimura</u> forgot to bring *her* slides.
Those were the poorest <u>nations</u>.

pronoun A word used in the place of a noun

The prefix *pro* in pronoun means "for." Thus, a pronoun stands *for* a noun.

Verbs

A **verb** is a word (or group of words) that expresses action or a state of being. The first kind of verb is called an *action verb*; the second kind is known as a *linking verb*. Without a verb, you have no sentence because the verb makes a statement about the subject. Most verbs express action of some sort—either physical or mental—as indicated by the verbs in italics in the following sentences:

Ignacio *planted* his garden while Ann *pulled* weeds.
I *solved* my problems as I *baked* bread.
Ms. Tamura *decided* she should *call* a meeting.

A small (but important) group of verbs do not express action. Instead, they simply link the subject with words that describe it. The most common linking verbs are forms of the verb *to be*, such as *is, am, are, was, were*, and *will*. Other forms of linking verbs involve the senses, such as *feels, looks, smells, sounds*, and *tastes*. The following words in italics are linking verbs (note that verbs can comprise one or more words):

Edna *was* angry because Xun *sounded* impatient.
If Tina *is having* a party, I *should have been* invited.
Ms. Tanaka *had* already *seen* the report.

verb A word that expresses action or a state of being

Is the group of words "Me Tarzan, you Jane" a sentence? What is it lacking?

Remember: No verb, no sentence.

Note in the last sentence the verb is "had seen." "Already" is an adverb.

Adjectives

adjective A word that modifies a noun or pronoun

Articles are a special group of adjectives, including the words *a, an,* and *the.*

Adjectives answer questions about the nouns they modify.

You can make sentences with only nouns or pronouns and verbs (such as "Dogs bark" or "I agree"), but most of the time you'll need to add other parts of speech to make the meaning of the sentence clearer or more complete. An **adjective** is a word that modifies a noun or pronoun. Adjectives answer questions about the nouns or pronouns they describe, such as "how many?", "what kind?", and "which one?" As shown by the words in italics in the following sentences, adjectives may come before or after the nouns or pronouns they modify:

Seventeen applicants took the *typing* test.
The interview was *short,* but *comprehensive.*
She took the *last* plane and landed at a *small Mexican* airport.

Adverbs

adverb A word that modifies a verb, an adjective, or another adverb

An **adverb** is a word that modifies a verb (usually), an adjective, or another adverb. Adverbs often answer the questions "when?", "where?", "how?", or "to what extent?" The words in italics in the following sentences are adverbs:

Please perform the procedure *now.* (*when?*)
Put the papers *here.* (*where?*)
Donald performed *brilliantly.* (*how?*)
I have *almost* finished. (*to what extent?*)
The *exceedingly* expensive car was *very carefully* protected.

In the last sentence, the adverb *exceedingly* modifies the adjective *expensive* (how expensive?) and the adverb *very* modifies the adverb *carefully* (how carefully?). Many (but, by no means, all) adverbs end in *-ly,* for example, *loudly, quickly, really,* and *carefully.* Of course, not all words that end in *-ly* are adverbs; for example, *friendly, stately,* and *ugly* are all adjectives.

Prepositions

preposition A word that shows the relationship between a noun or pronoun and some other word

A **preposition** is a word (such as *to, for, from, of,* and *with*) that shows the relationship between a noun or pronoun and some other word in the sentence. The noun or pronoun that follows the preposition is called the *object* of the preposition, and the entire group of words is called a *prepositional phrase.* In the following sentences, the preposition is shown in italics; the entire prepositional phrase is underlined:

Prepositions always come *before* the noun or pronoun; hence, *pre-position.*

The ceremony occurred *on* the covered bridge.
The ceremony occurred *under* the covered bridge.
Marsha talked *with* Mr. Hines.
Marsha talked *about* Mr. Hines.

Conjunctions

conjunction A word (such as *and* or *or*) that joins words or groups of words

A **conjunction** is a word (such as *and, or,* or *but*) that joins words or groups of words. For example, in the sentence "Jonathan and Vincent are brokers," the conjunction *and* connects the two nouns *Jonathan* and *Vincent.* In the following sentences, the conjunction is shown in italics; the words it joins (conjunction → conjoins) are underlined:

Conceptin *or* Nancy will attend the conference. (*joins two nouns*)
Pancho spoke quietly *and* deliberately. (*joins two adverbs*)
Ms. Duncan tripped *but* caught her balance. (*joins two verbs*)

Interjections

An **interjection** is a word that expresses strong emotions. Interjections are more often used in oral communication than in written communication. If an interjection stands alone, it is followed by an exclamation point. If it is a part of the sentence, it is followed by a comma. You should not be surprised that some words can serve as interjections in some sentences and as other parts of speech in other sentences. In the following sentences, the interjection is shown in italics:

Good! I'm glad to learn that the new employee is competent.

Oh! I didn't mean to startle you.

Oh, I wouldn't say that.

Gosh, that was an exhausting exercise. *Whew!*

interjection A word that expresses strong emotions

Avoid interjections in most business writing. After all, do you really want to sound surprised or angry at a business development?

....

VOCABULARY   Define these terms in your own words and give an original example of each.

1. adjective:

2. adverb:

3. conjunction:

4. interjection:

5. noun:

CHECKPOINT 3.1

6. preposition:

7. pronoun:

8. verb:

COMPREHENSION

9. Label the part of speech for each word in the following paragraph. Use these abbreviations: *adj, adv, conj, interj, n, prep, pron,* and *v.*

   Alas! By the time we arrived from Denver for the business conference in

   October, the trees had already lost some leaves. I was disappointed we

   missed the bright reds and yellows, but I did find many orange or brown

   leaves on the ground. Lee Dye, the conference chair, packed a suitcase and

   left early. Oh, and Richard packed his also, but he will be back shortly.

10. From the paragraph in Exercise 9, provide an example of each of the following terms:
    a. concrete noun:
    b. abstract noun:
    c. common noun:
    d. proper noun:
    e. singular noun:
    f. plural noun:
    g. action verb:
    h. linking verb:

Parts of a Sentence

A sentence must, first of all, make sense by itself; that is, it must contain a complete thought. In addition, there are other required and optional parts of a sentence.

subject The noun or pronoun that does something, has something done to it, or is identified or described

Subjects and Predicates

Every sentence must contain a subject and a predicate. The **subject** of a sentence is the word or group of words that does something, has something done to it, or is identified or described. The **predicate** is the word or group of words that tells what the subject does, what is done to it, or how it is identified or described. In other words, the predicate makes a statement about the subject.

Subject	Predicate
Mr. Sánchez and I *(did something)*	typed the report. *(tells what the subject did)*
The report *(had something done to it)*	was typed by Mr. Sánchez and me. *(tells what was done to the subject)*
Wanda *(is identified)*	was the instigator. *(identifies the subject)*
The reports *(is described)*	were quite long. *(describes the subject)*

predicate The words that tell what the subject does, what is done to it, or how it is identified or described

All of the words that function together as the subject are called the *complete subject*. The noun or pronoun that serves as the essential element of the subject is called the *simple subject*. Similarly, all of the words that function together as the predicate are called the *complete predicate*. The verb that serves as the essential element of the predicate is called the *simple predicate*.

complete subject
The accounting department's slow and unreliable (copier) needed replacing.
                                                simple subject

                complete predicate
Our network (was) down last week for three days.
simple predicate

Most sentences contain a single subject and a single predicate. When two or more nouns or pronouns are linked together, they form a *compound* subject. Similarly, when two or more verbs are linked together, they form a *compound* predicate.

compound subject
Friends and coworkers ‖ applauded.
                single predicate

single subject
Coworkers ‖ stood and applauded.
                compound predicate

Occasionally, the subject of the sentence is implied rather than stated directly. For example, if your superior tells you "Type the report," it is understood that she is telling *you* to type the report. In this case, the subject is the unstated (but understood) *you*.

Optional Sentence Elements

The expression "Phones rang" is a complete sentence. Most sentences in business writing, of course, have more parts than a one-word subject and predicate. This section discusses some additional elements of a sentence.

phrase A group of related words that do not have both a subject and a predicate.

Phrases   A **phrase** is a group of related words that do not have *both* a subject and a predicate. As shown below, phrases can be used as nouns, verbs, adjectives, or adverbs. Each phrase is shown in italics:

Between Thanksgiving and Christmas is our busiest season. (*noun phrase*)

Henderson *will be attending* the national conference. (*verb phrase*)

Lab tests *of many kinds* were then ordered. (*adjectival phrase*)

We will finish the tests *before lunch*. (*adverbial phrase*)

clause A group of related words that contain both a subject and a predicate

Clauses   A **clause** is a group of related words that contain both a subject and a predicate. (A phrase may contain either a subject *or* predicate—but not both.)

Phrase: After the break, we'll continue. (*lacks a subject and predicate*)
Clause: After we take a break, we'll continue.

Phrase: Reading the computer program was difficult. (*contains a subject but no predicate*)
Clause: When I was reading the computer program, I discovered the error.

Phrase: By 2005 Jonathan Stein will have been working for 30 years.
(*contains a predicate but no subject*)
Clause: By 2005 Jonathan Stein will have been working for 30 years.

A sentence with a dependent clause always contains an independent clause as well. (The opposite is not true.)

An *independent* (or *main*) *clause* can stand alone as a complete sentence. Every sentence has at least one independent clause. A *dependent* (or *subordinate*) *clause* does not express a complete thought but is used along with an independent clause to express a related idea. In the following sentences, the independent clauses are underlined and the dependent clauses are italicized:

I quit.

Ms. Méndez entered the sales data into the new accounting system.

Although Sandra tried diligently, she was not able to eliminate the virus.

Sandra tried diligently but was not able to eliminate the virus.

Cindy, *who was hired last week,* was a Rhodes Scholar.

Objects   Recall that a verb is a word that expresses action (an *action verb*) or a state of being (a *linking verb*). Some action verbs require an object to complete the action. For example, you wouldn't say, "The company built," and leave it at that. The listener or reader would say, "Yes, go on. The company built what?"

A **direct object** is a noun or pronoun that receives the action of the verb. It always appears *after* the verb, as illustrated by the italicized words below (the verbs are underlined):

The company <u>built</u> a *warehouse*.

Gene <u>took</u> *notes* at the meeting.

Mr. Menéndez <u>received</u> the *Medal of Honor* for his service in Vietnam.

Ernest <u>thanked</u> *me* for my participation.

direct object A noun or pronoun that receives the action of the verb

To test for the presence of a direct object, repeat the subject and verb and ask "whom" or "what." For example, in the first sentence, "The company built *what?*" or in the last sentence, "Ernest thanked *whom?*" Thus, "warehouse" and "me" are direct objects of the two sentences. Not all action verbs, of course, require an object, as illustrated below:

> Think before you speak.
>
> Janet ate while I wrote.
>
> Who cares?
>
> The eager audience shouted and clapped after the new CEO spoke about the revised retirement plan.

An **indirect object** tells to whom or for whom the action in the verb was done. Although a sentence can have a direct object without having an indirect object, the opposite is not true. A sentence *must* contain a direct object for it to contain an indirect object. The indirect object (a noun or pronoun) always comes *before* the direct object, as illustrated by the italicized indirect objects shown below (the direct objects are underlined):

> I'll bring *Annette* the <u>notes</u>.
>
> My boss promised *me* a <u>raise</u>.
>
> Justine's gives its regular *customers* a <u>discount</u>.
>
> The doctor gave the *patient* a new <u>regimen</u> to follow.

If the first sentence had read "I'll bring the notes *to Annette*," the sentence would not contain an indirect object. Remember that an indirect object always comes *before* the direct object.

Complements Instead of expressing action, linking verbs simply link the subject with words that identify or describe it. The word or words in the predicate that complete the sense of the verb are called the **complement**. (Note the spelling of *complement:* A complement *completes* the sense of the verb.) It may be a noun, pronoun, or adjective. The complement is shown in italics in the following examples:

> Ling is our new *programmer*. (*The noun "programmer" refers to "Ling."*)
>
> The person to contact is *she*. (*The pronoun "she" refers to "person."*)
>
> His harsh assessment was *accurate*. (*The adjective "accurate" modifies "assessment."*)

Margin notes:

To find the direct object, ask who or what the subject and verb did.

indirect object A noun or pronoun that tells to whom or for whom the action in the verb was done

A sentence cannot have an indirect object without also having a direct object.

An indirect object comes before the direct object.

complement A word or phrase that completes the meaning of the verb

---

VOCABULARY Define these terms in your own words and give an original example of each.

1. clause:

2. complement:

CHECKPOINT 3.2

3. direct object:

4. indirect object:

5. phrase:

6. predicate:

7. subject:

COMPREHENSION

8. Underline the complete subject and circle the simple subject in each sentence. Indicate whether the subject is single or compound.

	Single	Compound
a. The only person whose vote counts is Ms. King.		
b. The first page and the last page of the report were missing.		

9. Underline the complete predicate and circle the simple predicate in each sentence. Indicate whether the predicate is single or compound.

	Single	Compound
a. I made a one-hour presentation at the marketing manager's seminar and spoke at the awards dinner as well.		
b. Where in the world is Katmandu located?		

10. Indicate whether each italicized expression is a phrase, an independent clause, or a dependent clause.

	Phrase	Independent Clause	Dependent Clause
a. *Only a few of the remaining personnel* were interested in the proposal.			
b. *If the board of directors wants to sell the subsidiary,* we will do so.			
c. *I know* who the real victims are.			
d. Bruce A. Jacobs, *who wrote the book,* is a newspaper reporter.			
e. Sonia Zapata, *a great amateur singer and dancer,* has volunteered to host the event.			

11. Indicate whether each italicized expression is a direct object, indirect object, or complement.

	Direct Object	Indirect Object	Comple-ment
a.			
b.			
c.			
d.			
e.			
f.			
g.			

a. The session on speech recognition was *the most interesting part of the seminar.*

b. The trees at Overlook Park are *beautiful* in the fall.

c. Jenkins made *a good point* about the annexation issues.

d. In a tall organizational pattern, administrative costs are *higher* because more managers are needed.

e. The employees in the distribution department gave *Inga* a surprise going-away party.

f. Monica demanded *a pay raise* before she would even consider the new assignment.

g. Please hand *me* the contracts to be signed.

Patterns of Sentence Organization

The following four patterns describe how most of the sentences you will encounter in business writing are organized. Learning these common patterns will help you recognize complete sentences and vary the style of your writing.

Subject	*Verb*
I	tried.
Lynn and Gunnar	were fired.

Subject	*Action Verb*	*Direct Object*
Janice	balanced	the books.
Daniela	has made	a fine suggestion.

Subject	*Action Verb*	*Indirect Object*	*Direct Object*
Benjamin	gave	me	the check.
Sears	offered	Monique	a raise.

Subject	*Linking Verb*	*Complement*
Jacobson's	is	our major competitor. *(noun)*
It	could have been	you. *(pronoun)*
All the stores	were	crowded. *(adjective)*

Less common in business writing are sentences in which the verb comes *before* the subject. In each of the following sentences, the subject is shown in italics and the verb is underlined:

Also <u>dissenting</u> <u>was</u> the *vice president*.
Where <u>were</u> *you?*
Why <u>was</u> *Donna* <u>crying?</u>
There <u>was</u> *nothing* left after the party.
Here <u>are</u> the *contracts*.

To locate the subject in sentences in inverted order, rearrange them in normal subject-verb order. For example, the normal order of the first sentence would be "The *vice president* <u>was</u> also <u>dissenting</u>."

Functions of Sentences

Sentences can be classified according to how they express ideas. All sentences in the English language either make a statement, ask a question, give a command, or make an exclamation.

Statements

A *statement* (also called a *declarative* sentence) affirms that something is or is not true. It ends with a period.

> This coming quarter promises to be a most successful one for us.

> Because the network went down, we were not able to prepare the statements on time.

Questions

A *question* (also called an *interrogative* sentence) directly asks whether something is or is not true. It ends with a question mark.

> Has John signed the nondisclosure agreement?

Do not confuse a direct question with an *indirect question*. An indirect question is actually a statement and ends with a period.

Question:	How long will it take?
Indirect question:	My only question is how long it will take.
Indirect question:	Why he was angry was not known.

Similarly, do not confuse a direct question with a polite request. A *polite request* is really a request, suggestion, or command that is put in the form of a question only out of courtesy; it ends with a period. Consider a question to be a polite request if you expect the reader to respond by *acting* rather than by giving you a yes or no answer.

> *Question:* Would you be willing to attend the meeting in my place? (*You expect a yes or no answer.*)

> *Polite Request:* May I have your attention, please. (*You do not expect a yes or no answer. You expect their attention, instead.*)

Commands

A *command* (also called an *imperative* sentence) requests, demands, or forbids something. Because you are speaking directly to the person (or persons), the subject is always *you*, but generally the subject *you* is understood. A command ends with a period.

> Please let me know if I can help. (*requests something*)

> Sign your complete name on the dotted line. (*demands something*)

> Do not cross this line. (*forbids something*)

Exclamations

An *exclamation* (also called an *exclamatory* sentence) expresses strong feeling. It ends with an exclamation point.

> Don't you dare ask her that question!
>
> I couldn't believe it!
>
> I beg your pardon!

Exclamations are rarely used in business writing.

Complexity of Sentences

Sentences are made up of words, phrases, and clauses. Although simple information can be communicated in a short, simple sentence, often the situation calls for more complex sentences. The competent communicator uses variety in sentence complexity to achieve his or her communication goal.

Simple Sentences

A *simple sentence* contains one independent clause and *no* dependent clauses. Although they are generally short, simple sentences can sometimes be long, especially if they contain a compound subject or compound predicate. The sentence is still a simple sentence if it contains only one subject and one predicate (whether simple or compound). All of the following are simple sentences:

> Ms. Banks volunteered.
>
> The spreadsheets and database reports were finally completed and proofread.
>
> The president and two of her vice presidents asked both the sales and marketing departments for their reactions to the addition of generic brands to our product mix in the European and Asian markets.

Remember that an independent clause can stand alone as a complete sentence.

Compound Sentences

A *compound sentence* contains two or more independent clauses and *no* dependent clauses.

> Kenneth typed and I proofread.
>
> Ms. Bennett filed the papers at the courthouse; afterward, she grabbed some lunch.
>
> The on-the-scene officer called for backup, the emergency squad arrived eight minutes later, and the robber was apprehended and taken into custody.

You will learn how to punctuate compound and complex sentences in Chapter 6.

Complex Sentences

A *complex sentence* contains one independent clause and one or more dependent clauses.

> After I left the room, the vote was taken.
>
> The vote was taken after I left the room.
>
> On April 13, Bonnie, who had no experience, received the job offer that she had applied for and hoped to get.

Compound-Complex Sentences

It is not the length of the sentence that determines its complexity but rather the number and types of clauses it contains.

A *compound-complex sentence* contains two or more independent clauses *and* one or more dependent clauses.

> I wanted to write the report myself, but I soon realized that I needed the advice of our legal department. *(two independent clauses and one dependent clause)*

> If I can, I'll do it; if I cannot, I'll ask Dennis to do it. *(two independent clauses and two dependent clauses)*

Sentence Errors

sentence fragment A part of a sentence that is treated as a complete sentence

A **sentence fragment** is a *part* of a sentence that is written and punctuated as if it were a complete sentence. However, it lacks one crucial element—it does not make sense by itself. As shown below, it is easy to revise fragments into complete sentences:

NOT: Lack of proofreading skills, one of the most common weaknesses in office workers.

BUT: Lack of proofreading skills is one of the most common weaknesses in office workers.

NOT: The attorneys, all busy with their clients.

BUT: The attorneys were all busy with their clients.

NOT: After all the lab tests came back negative and the patient was relieved.

BUT: After all the lab tests came back negative, the patient was relieved.

run-on sentence Two or more independent clauses that run together with incorrect punctuation or that would be more effectively stated as separate sentences

A comma splice is one form of a run-on sentence.

A **run-on sentence** is two or more independent clauses (1) that run together without any punctuation between them or with only a comma between them (the latter error is called a *comma splice*) or (2) that would be more effectively stated as separate sentences. Revise run-on sentences by turning them into separate sentences, inserting a semicolon between them (instead of a comma or no punctuation), inserting a comma and a coordinating conjunction (such as *and*, *or*, or *but*), or changing one of the independent clauses into a dependent clause.

NOT: Please sign the contract quickly, Mr. Muñoz is waiting for it.

BUT: Please sign the contract quickly. Mr. Muñoz is waiting for it. (*making into separate sentences*)

OR: Please sign the contract quickly; Mr. Muñoz is waiting for it. (*inserting a semicolon*)

OR: Please sign the contract quickly because Mr. Muñoz is waiting for it. (*creating a dependent clause*)

NOT: Hans is a fast worker he is not very accurate.

BUT: Hans is a fast worker, but he is not very accurate. (*inserting a comma and a coordinating conjunction*)

NOT: I really want this job and if you hire me I promise I'll work hard for you and increase your customer base and also I'll redesign your company's marketing representative orientation program to make it more efficient and more effective.

BUT: I really want this job. If you hire me, I promise I'll work hard for you and increase your customer base. Also, I'll redesign your company's marketing representative orientation program to make it more efficient and more effective. (*making into separate sentences*)

....

VOCABULARY   Define these terms in your own words and give an original example of each.

1. run-on sentence:

2. sentence fragment:

CHECKPOINT 3.3

COMPREHENSION

3. Match these pattern on the left with the example of that pattern on the right by writing the correct letter in the space provided.

Sentence Pattern

a. Subject—Verb

b. Subject—Action Verb—Direct Object

c. Subject—Action Verb—Indirect Object—Direct Object

d. Subject—Linking Verb—Complement

e. Inverted order

Example

___ Consuelo did me a huge favor by agreeing to postpone our negotiating session.

___ I am fine.

___ None of the six managers at the meeting applauded.

___ There is only one way to correct Lin's mistake.

___ The user connected the cable connections on the inside of the computer.

4. Indicate the function of each sentence by writing *S* for statement, *Q* for question, *C* for command, or *E* for exclamation. Also, insert the correct punctuation at the end of each sentence.

   a. ____ As late as the Revolutionary War period, most of the American population lived on farms

   b. ____ I can't believe you actually said that

   c. ____ Would you please take your seats so that we can begin the meeting

   d. ____ Why is Gatorade now being marketed to children

   e. ____ Take your seats, please

   f. ____ Mr. Hunter wanted to know why we were not using his products

   g. ____ Do not begin until instructed to do so

   h. ____ He asked if we would please take our seats

5. Indicate the complexity of each sentence by writing *S* for simple, *CP* for compound, *CX* for complex, or *CC* for compound-complex

   a. ____ Please leave.

   b. ____ After taking a vote, we called the candidates back into the room, and the chairperson announced the results.

   c. ____ Cynthia opened the mail and distributed it.

   d. ____ Who is attending the conference next week, and who is remaining here to mind the store?

   e. ____ On the other hand, when a country exports more than it imports, it is said to have a favorable balance of trade.

   f. ____ Ms. Conti has visited all but two counties in North Carolina in her quest for the Republican nomination for secretary of state.

6. Indicate whether each expression is a complete sentence (*S*), a fragment (*F*), or a run-on sentence (*RO*).

   a. ____ The reason the common stock for General Motors was selling for $37.50 per share being that the company had experienced a long-term work stoppage.

   b. ____ The operators, all busy with their work, did not even notice the disturbance.

   c. ____ A commercial bank is a for-profit organization, it accepts deposits, makes loans, and provides other services.

   d. ____ During the 1980s, a record number of banks failed this trend continued into the early 1990s.

   e. ____ Although I was unhappy with the results and planned to switch my account to another company that took more interest in its customers.

   f. ____ Santiago demanded a pay raise and housing subsidy before he would even consider the new assignment.

Summary

Every word is one of eight parts of speech, depending on how it is used in a sentence:

- *Nouns* name a person, place, thing, or idea.

- *Pronouns* are used in place of a noun.

- *Verbs* express action or a state of being.

- *Adjectives* modify a noun or a pronoun.

- *Adverbs* modify a verb, an adjective, or another adverb.

- *Prepositions* show the relationship between a noun or pronoun and some other word in the sentence.

- *Conjunctions* join words or groups of words.
- *Interjections* express strong emotion.

Every sentence must communicate a complete thought and must contain a subject and a predicate. The subject is the topic of the sentence; the predicate makes a statement about the subject. All of the words that function together make up the complete subject and predicate. The noun or pronoun that serves as the essential element is the simple subject, and the verb that serves as the essential element is the simple predicate. Subjects and predicates may be single or compound.

Phrases do not contain both a subject and a verb and may be used as nouns, verbs, adjectives, or adverbs. Clauses contain both a subject and a verb. An independent clause can stand alone as a complete sentence; a dependent clause cannot stand alone, but rather must be accompanied by an independent clause.

Action verbs sometimes take a direct object, which receives the action of the verb, and an indirect object, which tells to whom or for whom the action in the verb was done. Linking verbs sometimes take a complement, which is a noun, pronoun, or adjective that describes or identifies the subject. The subject-verb-object pattern is the most common pattern of sentence organization in business.

A sentence serves to either make a statement, ask a question, give a command, or make an exclamation. Simple sentences contain one independent clause and no dependent clauses, compound sentences contain two or more independent clauses and no dependent clauses, complex sentences contain one independent clause and one or more dependent clauses, and compound-complex sentences contain two or more independent clauses and one or more dependent clauses.

A sentence fragment is a part of a sentence that is punctuated as if it were a complete sentence. A run-on sentence contains two or more independent clauses that would be more effectively written as a complex or compound sentence or as separate sentences.

Looking Ahead

After studying business sentence structure in this chapter, you should know how to write a *correct* sentence. To be effective in business, however, you must be more than correct. Your sentences must exhibit *style*—that is, you must be able to craft your sentences into an effective communication that will achieve your purpose. You will begin learning to write with style in Chapter 4.

Key Terms

adjective	indirect object	pronoun
adverb	interjection	run-on sentence
clause	noun	sentence fragment
complement	phrase	subject
conjunction	predicate	verb
direct object	preposition	

Exercises

Parts of Speech

1 List the eight parts of speech:

2 Above or below each word in the following sentence, identify its part of speech:

Whew! Mr. Contreras and I quickly asked for more time.

3 List three words that can be used as more than one part of speech; identify the relevant parts of speech.

4 a. Circle all of the nouns in the following sentence.

Dan, accompanied by the Rochester Orchestra, performed his songs on the first anniversary of his greatest success.

b. Write the nouns you circled in the appropriate categories below (some nouns will be used more than once):

abstract:

common:

concrete:

proper:

singular:

plural:

5 Write an appropriate pronoun above each italicized expression in the following paragraph to substitute for the noun.

Give Tony *Tony's* disk to help *Tony and Manual* finish *Tony and Manual's* report. *Tony and Manual* will then give *the report* to Mr. Ellis.

6 Circle all of the verbs in the following paragraphs. Above each verb, indicate whether it is an action verb (*A*) or a linking verb (*L*).

Leo and Bao watched me while I moved the furniture. They were curious because they felt strange in their new offices. When will they get comfortable?

7 Indicate whether an adjective or an adverb answers each of the following questions.

How many?

How?

To what extent?

What kind?

When?

Where?

Which one?

8 In the following sentence, circle all conjunctions and underline all prepositions.

Under the circumstances, Ms. Svoboda and Mr. Woods gave a lesson or two to Teodora about getting along well with others, but he didn't seem to understand.

9 Compose a sentence that contains an interjection that you might properly include in a business letter.

10 Compose a sentence that contains all parts of speech and label each word as to its part of speech.

Parts of Sentences

11 Circle the subject in each of the following sentences (be sure not to circle a prepositional phrase).

a. For that reason, Ms. Cook decided to accept the new job.

b. Your complaint will be thoroughly investigated by the detectives.

c. There are three computers left to be assembled.

d. Four of the employees tested positive.

e. Why was the job not finished on time?

f. The prize was donated by Paola.

g. Across the hall is our new photocopying center.

h. In Leon's view, the real cause was a lack of coordination.

i. Three computers are left to be assembled.

j. Four employees tested positive.

k. Paola donated the prize.

12 Circle all verbs in the following sentences.

a. In October, Quon will have been working here for twenty years.

b. Will she have the support she needs?

c. I could not possibly have guessed the real reason for the delay.

d. That response was open to much interpretation.

e. He seemed hesitant at first but soon lost his shyness.

13 Over each italicized expression, indicate whether the expression is a phrase (*P*) or a clause (*C*).

a. *Because a phrase does not contain both a subject and verb,* it can never serve *as a complete sentence.*

b. I enjoyed *planning the event,* but I *will be taking* a few days off.

c. I moved my desk *against the wall* so that *I would have more room.*

d. *To type accurately* is just as important as *to type rapidly.*

e. We must finish *all of the puzzle* today *because I leave for home tomorrow.*

14 In the following sentences, write *DO* above each direct object, *IO* above each indirect object, and *C* above each complement.

a. I was so angry I had to bite my tongue.

b. Leonard practiced while I rested in bed.

c. The company offered Nina early retirement.

d. The company offered early retirement to Nina.

e. The doctor ordered bed rest for Rhonda because of her chronic fatigue.

f. The manager was so generous he gave me a quick raise.

Patterns of Sentence Organization

15 Compose a sentence in each of the following organizational patterns:

a. Subject-verb:

b. Subject-action verb-direct object:

c. Subject-action verb-indirect object-direct object:

d. Subject-linking verb-complement:

e. Inverted order:

Functions of Sentences

16 In the space provided, write *S* if the sentence is a statement, *Q* if it is a question, *C* if it is a command, or *E* if it is an exclamation. Insert the correct punctuation at the end of each sentence.

a. ____ Alonso wanted to know if I had inspected the warehouse

b. ____ Compare the long-term costs of the two models

c. ____ Hand me the Kyoto file

d. ____ Has Ms. Brooks gotten a flu shot yet

e. ____ I compared the long-term costs of the two models

f. ____ I will ask my server for an extra plate

g. ____ May I please have the Kyoto file

h. ____ Please hand me the Kyoto file

i. ____ The network administrator is working on the problem now

j. ____ When will the question-and-answer session begin

k. ____ Why the chemical didn't work is still a mystery to us

l. ____ Will everyone please have a seat

m. ____ Wow What a surprise announcement

n. ____ What a clever solution you proposed

17 Compose a sentence of each of the following types, inserting the correct punctuation at the end.

a. Statement:

   b. Question:

   c. Polite request:

   d. Command:

   e. Exclamation:

Complexity of Sentences

18 In the space provided, indicate the complexity of each sentence by writing *S* for simple, *CP* for compound, *CX* for complex, or *CC* for compound-complex. Underline each dependent clause in the sentences.

   a. ____ After a delicious dinner, we went to a first-rate movie.

   b. ____ Before we left, Haruko wanted a brief rehearsal.

   c. ____ Both Mr. Cooper and Ms. Dvorak quit their jobs, applied for unemployment benefits, and began out-placement counseling.

   d. ____ Wendy first thought that she could handle the job herself but then found out that she needed extra help.

   e. ____ Haruko wanted a brief rehearsal before we left.

   f. ____ Florence quit.

   g. ____ George began the audit quickly enough; however, he soon found unexpected problems.

   h. ____ Kaori talked while I listened.

   i. ____ The chef planned the menu, the host made out the guest list, and the musician chose the songs for the entertainment.

   j. ____ The package that was sitting unopened on the conference table was not the one that I had been expecting.

   k. ____ The package, which was sitting unopened on the conference table, was not the one that I had been expecting.

   l. ____ While waiting for the verdict to be read, the attorney planned her appeal and the defendant watched the jury.

   m. ____ Why are both the delivery van and the panel truck in the repair shop at the same time?

19 Compose a sentence of each of the following types, inserting the correct punctuation at the end.

   a. Simple:

   b. Compound:

   c. Complex:

   d. Compound-complex:

Sentence Errors

20 Some of the following expressions are sentence fragments, while others are run-on sentences. Put a C next to the correct sentences. Revise the others to make them correct.

a. ____ Gloria modeled the new uniform, everyone applauded.

b. ____ Although I'm very good at figuring out these puzzles.

c. ____ As we entered the elevators to join our colleagues in the third-floor conference room where the meeting had already begun.

d. ____ Because computers had always fascinated him so much and he was good at working with his hands.

e. ____ He has patented five inventions.

f. ____ Ms. Rios explained how to operate the new equipment the demonstration lasted nearly three hours.

g. ____ Shoshana usually finishes in an hour this time she took longer.

h. ____ Since the company purchased a new color printer for the sales department, everyone wants one.

i. ____ Ten minutes after the bank closed for the day.

j. ____ The company purchased a new color printer for the sales department, now everyone wants one.

k. ____ The five inventions that he has patented.

l. ____ Those loose wires are dangerous be careful.

m. ____ To work as safely as possible.

n. ____ Try to work as safely as possible.

PART TWO
DEVELOPING YOUR BUSINESS WRITING SKILLS

Writing with Style: Individual Elements

COMMUNICATION OBJECTIVES

After you have finished this chapter, you should be able to:

- Write clearly.
- Prefer short, simple words.
- Write with vigor.
- Write concisely.
- Prefer positive language.
- Use a variety of sentence types.
- Use active and passive voice appropriately.
- Keep paragraphs unified and coherent.
- Use parallel structure.
- Control paragraph length.

On the Job

MARTHA DURDIN
Vice President of Communications, Bank of Montreal

What is it like to write for an audience of 34,000 employees spread across Canada and the United States, with branch offices located around the world? Communicating with an international audience of employees is only one of the responsibilities handled by Martha Durdin, vice president of communications for Bank of Montreal. Durdin and her staff work with their U.S. and Mexican counterparts to help communicate with shareholders, media representatives, consumers, and businesses across the continent.

Although Durdin's communication responsibilities span highly diverse audiences, each message is planned with the "you" attitude in mind. "It's important to understand your audience and tailor the language and content so it is relevant to your readers," she advises. "Make sure that you are looking at the communication from the reader's viewpoint rather than from your own viewpoint. That prevents you from using language that may not be familiar to your audience."

When the bank's communicators are writing for outside audiences, they are careful to define any industry jargon or acronyms that must be used. "We first spell out terms and show the acronym in parentheses," says Durdin. "Then readers understand what we mean when we use the acronym later in the document." This approach is especially critical in cross-border communications. For example, Canadians talk about *ABMs* (automated banking machines), while Americans talk about *ATMs* (automated teller machines). As a result, Durdin's staff is scrupulous about matching the terminology to the audience and including definitions when needed.

What Do We Mean by *Style?*

After you master the language arts chapters in this book (Chapters 3, 6, 9, 12, and 15), you will know how to express yourself *correctly* in most business writing situations; that is, you will know how to avoid major errors in grammar, spelling, punctuation, and word usage. But a technically correct message may still not achieve its objective. For example, consider the following paragraph:

NOT: During the preceding year just past, Oxford Industries operated at a financial deficit. It closed three plants. It laid off many employees. The company's president was recently named Iowa Small Business Executive of the Year. Oxford is now endeavoring to ascertain the causes of its financial exigency. The company president said that . . .

> Your writing can be error-free and still lack style, but it cannot have style unless it is error-free.

This paragraph has no grammatical, mechanical, or usage errors. But it is not clear, vigorous, or coherent. For example, consider the phrase "preceding year just past." "Preceding" means "just past," so why use both terms? In the second sentence, was closing the three plants the *cause* or the *result* of the financial deficit? What is the point of the sentence about the president? If you were speaking instead of writing, would you really say "endeavoring to ascertain," or would you use simpler language, such as "trying to find out"? Finally, there are no transitions, or bridges, between the sentences; as a result, they don't flow smoothly.

Although the example paragraph is technically correct, it lacks **style**. By style, we mean the way in which an idea is expressed (not its *substance*). Style consists of the particular words that the writer uses and the manner in which those words are combined into sentences, paragraphs, and complete messages.

> **style** The manner in which an idea is expressed

Now compare the first-draft paragraph above with this revised version:

BUT: Last year Oxford Industries lost money and, as a result, closed three plants and laid off 200 employees. Now the company is trying to determine the causes of its problems. In an explanation to stockholders, Oxford's president, who was recently named Iowa Small Business Executive of the Year, said that . . .

The revised version is more direct and readable. It clarifies relationships among the sentences. It uses concise, familiar language. It presents ideas in logical order. In short, it has *style*. Chapters 4 and 5 discuss the principles of effective writing style for business. Apply these principles of style as you write the letters, memos, emails, and reports that are assigned in later chapters and on the job:

Words

1. Write clearly.
2. Prefer short, simple words.
3. Write with vigor.
4. Write concisely.
5. Prefer positive language.

Sentences

6. Use a variety of sentence types.
7. Use active and passive voice appropriately.

Paragraphs

8. Keep paragraphs unified and coherent.
9. Use parallel structure.
10. Control paragraph length.

FIGURE 4.1 Steps to an Effective Message

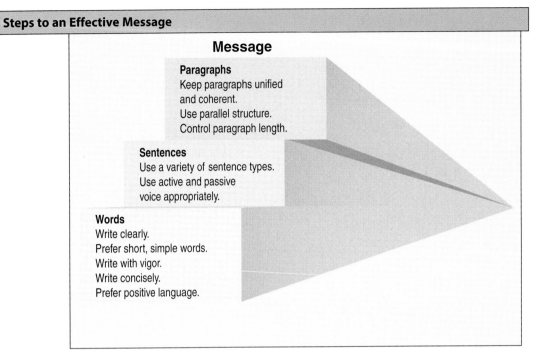

Message

Paragraphs
Keep paragraphs unified
and coherent.
Use parallel structure.
Control paragraph length.

Sentences
Use a variety of sentence types.
Use active and passive
voice appropriately.

Words
Write clearly.
Prefer short, simple words.
Write with vigor.
Write concisely.
Prefer positive language.

Overall Tone

11. Write confidently.
12. Use a courteous and sincere tone.
13. Use appropriate emphasis and subordination.
14. Use nondiscriminatory language.
15. Stress the "you" attitude.

While writing the first draft of a message, you should be more concerned with content than with style. Your major objective should be to get your ideas down in *some* form, without worrying about style and mechanics. (**Mechanics** are elements in communication that show up only in written form—including spelling, punctuation, abbreviations, capitalization, number expression, and word division.)

The more familiar you are with basic stylistic principles, the easier it will be to write your first draft and the less editing you will need to do later. Thus studying these principles first makes your writing process more efficient. You can later return to these principles when revising your writing to make sure that you have followed each guideline.

Principles 1–10 focus on the *parts* of the message (words, sentences, and paragraphs) and are discussed in this chapter (see Figure 4.1). Principles 11–15 focus on the tone of the *whole* message and are discussed in Chapter 5.

mechanics Those elements in communication that show up only in written form—including spelling, punctuation, abbreviations, capitalization, number expression, and word division

Choosing the Right Words

Individual words are our basic units of writing, the bricks with which we build meaningful messages. All writers have access to the same words. The care with which we select and combine words can make the difference between a message that achieves its objective and one that does not. Discussed below and in the following section are five principles of word choice to help you write more effectively.

1. Write Clearly.

The basic guideline for writing, and the one that must be present for the other principles to have meaning, is to write clearly—to write messages the reader can understand, depend on, and act on. You can achieve clarity by making your message accurate and complete, by using familiar words, and by avoiding dangling expressions and unnecessary jargon.

Be Accurate   A writer's credibility is perhaps his or her most important asset, and credibility depends greatly on the accuracy of the message. If by carelessness, lack of preparation, or a desire to manipulate, a writer misleads the reader, the damage is immediate and long-lasting. A reader who has been fooled once may not trust the writer again.

> **How's That Again?**   WORD|wise
>
> "Travel between floors by elevator only in buildings having elevators."
>
> California Department of Food and Agriculture memo
>
> "There will be a regular deacon's meeting next Sunday morning. It will be gin with breakfast at 7:30 a.m."
>
> South Carolina church bulletin notice
>
> "Due to the reorganization, the basement will be on the second floor. Half of the second floor will be on the first floor, but half will remain on the second. First floor will move to the basement. We suggest that you ask for help."
>
> North Dakota State University library sign

Accuracy can take many forms. The most basic is the truthful presentation of facts and figures. But accuracy involves much more. For example, consider the following sentence from a memo to a firm's financial backers:

> The executive committee of Mitchell Financial Services met on Thursday, May 28, to determine how to resolve the distribution fiasco.

Accuracy is the most important attribute in business writing. It involves more than freedom from errors.

Suppose, on checking, the reader learns that May 28 fell on a Wednesday this year—not on a Thursday. Immediately, the reader may suspect everything else in the message. The reader's thinking might be, "If the writer made this error that I *did* catch, how many errors that I *didn't* catch are lurking there?"

Now consider more subtle shades of truth. The sentence implies that the committee met, perhaps in an emergency session, for the *sole* purpose of resolving the distribution fiasco. But suppose this matter was only one of five agenda items being discussed at a regularly scheduled meeting. Is the statement still accurate? Suppose the actual agenda listed the topic as "Recent Distribution Problems." Is *fiasco* the same as *problems?*

The accuracy of a message, then, depends on what is said, how it is said, and what is left unsaid (see, for example, the next section on the importance of completeness). Competent writers assess the ethical dimensions of their writing and use integrity, fairness, and good judgment to make sure their communication is ethical.

Ethical communicators make sure the overall tone of their message is accurate.

Be Complete   Closely related to accuracy is completeness. A message that lacks important information may create inaccurate impressions. A message is complete when it contains all the information the reader needs—no more and no less—to react appropriately.

As a start, answer the five Ws: Tell the reader *who, what, when, where,* and *why.* Leaving out any of this information may either result in decisions based on incomplete information or require extra follow-up correspondence to gather the needed information.

Use Familiar Words   Your message must be understood before someone can act on it. For this reason, you should use words that are familiar both to you (so that you will not misuse the word) and to your readers.

Marilyn vos Savant (identified by the *Guinness Book of World Records* as the smartest person alive) once asked her readers what the following paragraph meant:

Use language that you and your reader understand.

> When promulgating your esoteric cogitations or articulating your superficial sentimentalities and amicable philosophical and psychological observations, beware of platitudinous ponderosity. Let your verbal evaporations have lucidity,

intelligibility, and veracious vivacity without rodomontade or thespian bombast. Sedulously avoid all polysyllabic profundity, pompous propensity, and sophomoric vacuity.[1]

Her translation: Don't use big words!

Long words are sometimes useful in business communication, of course, and should be used when appropriate. The larger your vocabulary and the more you know about your reader, the better equipped you will be to choose and use correctly those words that are familiar to your reader.

Avoid Dangling Expressions   A **dangling expression** is any part of a sentence that doesn't logically fit in with the rest of the sentence. Its relationship with the other parts of the sentence is unclear; it *dangles*. The two most common types of dangling expressions are misplaced modifiers and unclear antecedents. To correct dangling expressions, use one of the following techniques:

- Make the subject of the sentence be the doer of the action expressed in the introductory clause;
- Move the expression closer to the word that it modifies;
- Make sure that the specific word to which a pronoun refers (its *antecedent*) is clear; or
- Otherwise revise the sentence.

> **NOT:** After reading the proposal, a few problems occurred to me. (*As written, the sentence implies that "a few problems" read the proposal.*)
>
> **BUT:** After reading the proposal, I noted a few problems.
>
> **NOT:** Dr. López gave a presentation on the use of drugs in our auditorium. (*Are drugs being used in the auditorium?*)
>
> **BUT:** Dr. López gave a presentation in our auditorium on the use of drugs.
>
> **NOT:** Ming explained the proposal to Lupe, but she was not happy with it. (*Who was not happy—Ming or Lupe?*)
>
> **BUT:** Ming explained the proposal to Lupe, but Lupe was not happy with it.

Avoid Unnecessary Jargon   As discussed in Chapter 1, jargon is technical vocabulary used within a special group. Every field has its own specialized words, and jargon offers a precise and efficient way of communicating with people in the same field. Unfortunately, problems can arise when jargon is used to communicate with someone who does not understand it. For example, to a banker the term *CD* means a "certificate of deposit," but to a stereo buff or computer user it means a "compact disc." Even familiar words can be confusing when given a specialized meaning.

Does the field of business communication have jargon? You bet it does—just look at the Key Terms list at the end of each chapter in this book. The word *jargon* itself might even be considered communication jargon. In this text, such terms are first defined and then used to make communication precise and efficient. Competent writers use specialized vocabulary to communicate with specialists who understand it. They also avoid using it when their readers are not specialists.

2. Prefer Short, Simple Words.

Short and simple words are more likely to be understood, less likely to be misused, and less likely to distract the reader. Literary authors often write to *impress*; they

dangling expression Any part of a sentence that does not logically connect to the rest of the sentence.

Jargon is sometimes appropriate and sometimes inappropriate.

Delilah Winder, owner of four Delilah's Southern Cuisine restaurants in Philadelphia, relies on clearly written directions—from how to prepare the food to how to format the menus—in managing her 100-employee operation.

select words to achieve a specific reader reaction, such as amusement, excitement, or anger. Business writers, on the other hand, write to *express*; they want to achieve *comprehension*. They want their readers to focus on their information, not on how they convey their information. Using short, simple words helps achieve this goal.

> **NOT:** To recapitulate, our utilization of adulterated water precipitated the interminable delays.

> **BUT:** In short, our use of impure water caused the endless delays.

It is true, of course, that often no short, simple word is available to convey the precise shade of meaning you want. For example, there is no one-syllable replacement for *ethnocentrism* (the belief that one's own cultural group is superior), a concept introduced in Chapter 2. Our guideline is not to use *only* short and simple words but to *prefer* short and simple words. (As Mark Twain, who was paid by the word for his writing, noted, "I never write *metropolis* for seven cents because I can get the same price for *city*. I never write *policeman* because I can get the same money for *cop*.")

Here are some examples of needlessly long words, gleaned from various business documents, with their preferred shorter substitutes shown in parentheses:

ascertain (learn)	modification (change)
endeavor (try)	recapitulate (review)
enumerate (list)	substantial (large)
fluctuate (vary)	termination (end)
indispensable (vital)	utilization (use)

You need not strike these long words totally from your vocabulary; any one of them, used in a clear sentence, would be acceptable. The problem is that a writer may tend to fill his or her writing with very long words when simpler ones could be used. Use long words in moderation. Heed the following advice from author Richard Lederer:

> When you speak and write, no law says you have to use big words. Short words are as good as long ones, and short, old words like *sun* and *grass* and *home* are best of all. A lot of small words, more than you might think, can meet your needs with a strength, grace, and charm that large words lack.

Short, simple words are the building blocks of effective business communication.

Big words can make the way dark for those who hear what you say and read what you write. They add fat to your prose. Small words are the ones we seem to have known from birth. They are like the hearth fire that warms the home, and they cast a clear light on big things: night and day, love and hate, war and peace, life and death.

Short words are bright, like sparks that glow in the night; sharp, like the blade of a knife; hot, like salt tears that scald the cheek; quick, like moths that flit from flame to flame; and terse, like the dart and sting of a bee.

If a long word says just what you want, do not fear to use it. But know that our tongue is rich in crisp, brisk, swift, short words. Make them the spine and the heart of what you speak and write. Like fast friends, they will not let you down.[2]

Lederer practices what he preaches. All 223 words in these four paragraphs are one-syllable words! Similarly, 71% of the words in Lincoln's Gettysburg Address (190 out of 267) are only one syllable long.

You've probably heard the advice "Write as you speak." Although not universally true, such advice is close to the mark. Of course, if your conversation is peppered with redundancies, jargon, and clichés, you would not want to put such weaknesses on paper. But typical conversation uses mostly short, simple words—the kind you *do* want to put on paper. Don't assume that the bigger the words, the bigger the intellect. In fact, you need a large vocabulary and a well-developed word sense to select the best word. More often than not, that word is short and simple. Write to express—not to impress.

Write to express—not to impress.

CHECKPOINT 4.1

RECALL   Write a capital T for *true* or F for *false* before each statement.

1. ____   Any word that you use in your writing should be familiar both to you and to all of your readers.

2. ____   Long words should not be used in business writing.

3. ____   The larger your vocabulary, the more likely you will be to use longer and less familiar words.

4. ____   Your communication may be inaccurate even though everything you write is accurate.

5. ____   Writing mechanics are not important in oral communication.

VOCABULARY   Define the following terms in your own words and give an original example of each.

6. dangling expression:

7. style:

8. mechanics:

COMPREHENSION

9. Substitute a shorter, more familiar word for each of the following words.
   a. aggregate:
   b. analogous:
   c. inexhaustible:
   d. perpetuate:

CRITICAL THINKING

10. What is meant by the statement, "Accuracy involves more than the truthfulness of facts and figures"?

3. Write with Vigor.

Vigorous language is specific and concrete. Limp language is filled with clichés, slang, and buzz words. Vigorous writing holds your reader's interest. But if your reader isn't even interested enough to read your message, your writing can't possibly achieve its objective. Another reason for writing with vigor has to do with language itself. Vigorous writing tends to lend vigor to the ideas presented. A good idea looks even better dressed in vigorous language, and a weak idea looks even weaker dressed in limp language.

Use Specific, Concrete Language   Earlier, we discussed the communication barriers created by overabstraction and ambiguity. When possible, choose *specific* words—words that have a definite, unambiguous meaning. Likewise, pick *concrete* words—words that bring a definite picture to your reader's mind.

NOT: The vehicle broke down several times recently.

BUT: The delivery van broke down three times last week.

In the first version, what does the reader imagine when he or she reads the word *vehicle*—a golf cart? automobile? boat? space shuttle? How many times is *several*—two? three? fifteen? The revised version tells precisely what happened.

Sometimes, of course, we do not need such specific information. For example, in "The president answered *several* questions from the audience," the specific number of questions is probably not important. But in most situations, you should watch out for words such as *several, recently, a number of, substantial, a few,* and *a lot of.* You may need to be more exact.

Likewise, use the most concrete word that is appropriate; give the reader a specific mental picture of what you mean; that is, talk in pictures:

NOT: The vice president was bored by the presentation.

BUT: The vice president kept yawning and looking at her watch.

Be sure that your terms convey as much meaning as the reader needs to react appropriately. Watch out for terms such as *emotional meeting* (anger or gratitude?), *bright color* (red or yellow?), *new equipment* (postage meter or cash register?), and *change in price* (increase or decrease?).

Businesses realize the value of using specific, concrete language that paints a picture. You should, too!

Concrete words paint a vivid picture.

Copyright © Houghton Mifflin Company. All rights reserved.

cliché An expression that has become monotonous through overuse

Avoid Clichés, Slang, and Buzz Words   A **cliché** is an expression that has become monotonous through overuse. It lacks freshness and originality and may also send the unintended message that the writer couldn't be bothered to choose language geared specifically to the reader.

> **NOT:** Enclosed please find an application form that you should return at your earliest convenience.

> **BUT:** Please return the enclosed application form before May 15.

Here are some examples of other expressions that have become overused and that therefore sound trite and boring. Avoid them in your writing.

According to our records	It goes without saying that
Company policy requires	Needless to say
Do not hesitate to	Our records indicate that
For your information	Please be advised that
If I can be of further help	Take this opportunity to
If you have any other questions	Under separate cover

Slang is an expression, often short-lived, that is identified with a specific group of people. If you understand each word in an expression but still don't understand what it means in context, chances are you're having trouble with a slang expression. For example, read the following sentence:

> It turns my stomach the way you can break your neck and beat your brains out around here, and they still stab you in the back.

Picture a person finding "Thank you for your recent letter" in all 15 letters he or she read that day. How sincere and original does the statement sound?

To anyone unfamiliar with American slang (a nonnative speaker, perhaps), this sentence might seem to be about the body because it refers to the stomach, neck, brains, and back. The real meaning, of course, is something like this:

> I am really upset that this company ignores hard work and loyalty when making personnel decisions.

Avoid slang in most business writing for several reasons:

- Slang is informal, and much business writing, although not formal, is still *businesslike* and calls for standard word usage.

- Slang is short-lived. An expression used today may not be in use—and thus may not be familiar—in three years, when your letter is retrieved from the files for reference.

- Slang is identified with a specific group of people, and others in the general population may not understand the intended meaning.

For these reasons, avoid such terms as the following in most business writing:

can of worms	pay through the nose
chew out	play up to
go for broke	security blanket
hate one's guts	use your noodle
knock it off	wiped out
once-over	zonked out

buzz word An important-sounding term used mainly to impress people

Clichés and buzz words go in and out of style too quickly to serve as effective components of most written business communication.

A **buzz word** is an important-sounding expression used mainly to impress other people. Because buzz words are so often used by government officials and high-ranking business people—people whose comments are "newsworthy"—these expressions receive much media attention. They become instant clichés and then go out of fashion just as quickly. At either end of their short life span, they cause communication problems. If an expression is currently being used by everyone, it sounds monotonous, lacking originality. If it is no longer being used by anyone, readers may not understand the intended meaning. Here are examples of recent "in" expressions:

Chick Hearn, the legendary announcer for Los Angeles Lakers basketball games who died in 2002, coined such now-famous slang terms as airball (a shot that misses everything) and slam dunk (a shot violently thrust into the basket).

bottom line	paradigm
done deal	parameter
impact (verb)	scenario
interface	user-friendly
no-brainer	vision statement

Be especially careful of turning nouns and other types of words into verbs by adding *-ize*. Such words as *agendize, prioritize, strategize, unionize,* and *operationalize* quickly become tiresome.

4. Write Concisely.

Business people are *busy* people. The information revolution has created more paperwork, giving business people access to more data. Having more data to analyze (but presumably neither being able to read any faster nor having more time in which to read), managers want information presented in the fewest possible words. To achieve conciseness, make every word count. Avoid redundancy, wordy expressions, hidden verbs and nouns, and other space-eaters.

Avoid Redundancy   A **redundancy** is the unnecessary repetition of an idea that has already been expressed or intimated. Eliminating the repetition contributes to conciseness.

> **NOT:** Signing both copies of the lease is a necessary requirement.

> **BUT:** Signing both copies of the lease is necessary.

> **NOT:** Combine the ingredients together.

> **BUT:** Combine the ingredients.

A *requirement* is by definition *necessary,* so only one of the words is needed. Similarly, to *combine* means to bring *together,* so using both words is redundant. Don't confuse redundancy and repetition. Repetition—using the same word more than once—is occasionally effective for emphasis (as we will discuss in the next chapter). Redundancy, however, serves no purpose and should always be avoided.

redundancy The unnecessary repetition of an idea that has already been expressed or intimated

Redundancy and repetition are not the same.

Most redundancies are simply *verbiage—excess* words that consume time and space. Avoid them (see Figure 4.2).

Avoid the following common redundancies (use the words in parentheses instead):

advance planning (planning)   over again (over)
any and all (any *or* all)   past history (history)
basic fundamentals (basics *or* fundamentals)   free gift (gift)
plan ahead (plan)   repeat again (repeat)
but nevertheless (but *or* nevertheless)   sum total (sum *or* total)
each and every (each *or* every)   true facts (facts)

Make every word count.

Avoid Wordy Expressions   Although wordy expressions are not necessarily writing errors (as redundancies are), they do slow the pace of the communication and should be avoided. To solve this problem, try substituting one word for a phrase whenever possible.

NOT: In view of the fact that the model failed twice during the time that we tested it, we are at this point in time searching for other options.

BUT: Because the model failed twice when we tested it, we are now searching for other options.

The original sentence contains 28 words; the revised sentence, 16. Thus, you've "saved" 12 words. Here are examples of other wordy phrases and their preferred one-word substitutes in parentheses:

Use the fewest number of words that will achieve your objective.

are of the opinion that (believe)   in the event that (if)
due to the fact that (because)   pertaining to (about)
for the purpose of (for *or* to)   with regard to (about)

Avoid Hidden Verbs   A hidden verb is a verb that has been changed into a noun form, thereby weakening the action. Verbs are *action* words and should convey the main action in the sentence. They provide interest and forward movement. Consider this example:

NOT: Scott made an announcement that he will give consideration to our request.

BUT: Scott announced that he will consider our request.

FIGURE 4.2 Avoid Unnecessary Words

new beginner   assemble together   connect up
new discovery   combine together   divide up
new fad   cooperate together   eat up
new innovation   gather together   lift up
new progress   mix together   rest up

THE IMPORTANCE OF WRITING WITH CLARITY...

COAT AND TIE REQUIRED

WILEY@NON-SEQUITUR.COM   DIST. BY UNIVERSAL PRESS SYND.   WWW. NON-SEQUITUR.COM

What is the real action? It is not that Carl *made* something or that he will *give* something. The real action is hiding in the nouns: Carl *announced* and will *consider*. These two words, then, should be the main verbs in the sentence. Notice that the revised sentence is much more direct—and four words shorter. Here are some other actions that should be conveyed by verbs instead of being hidden in nouns:

Changing verbs to nouns produces weak, uninteresting sentences.

arrived at the conclusion (concluded)
came to an agreement (agreed)
gave a demonstration of (demonstrated)
gave an explanation of (explained)

has a requirement for (requires)
held a meeting (met)
made a payment (paid)
performed an analysis of (analyzed)

Avoid Hidden Subjects   Like verbs, subjects play a prominent role in a sentence and should stand out. An **expletive** is an expression such as *there is* or *it is* that begins a clause or sentence and for which the pronoun has no antecedent. The subject always follows the expletive. Because the topic of a sentence that begins with an expletive is not immediately clear, you should use such sentences sparingly in business writing. Avoiding expletives also contributes to conciseness.

expletive An expression such as *there is* or *it has been* that begins a clause and for which the pronoun has no antecedent

NOT: There was no indication that it is necessary to invite Zhao. *(11 words)*

BUT: No one indicated that Zhao should be invited. *(8 words)*

Imply or Condense   Sometimes you do not need to explicitly state certain information; you can imply it instead. In other situations, you can use adjectives and adverbs to convey the needed information in a more concise format.

NOT: We have received your recent letter and are happy to provide the data you requested. *(15 words)*

BUT: We are happy to provide the data you recently requested. *(10 words)*

NOT: This brochure, which is available free of charge, will answer your questions. *(12 words)*

BUT: This free brochure will answer your questions. *(7 words)*

A pronoun in an expletive does not stand for any noun.

5. Prefer Positive Language.

Words that create a positive image are more likely to help you achieve your objective than will negative words. For example, you are more likely to persuade someone to do as you ask if you stress the advantages of doing so rather than the disadvantages of *not* doing so. Positive language also builds goodwill for you and your organization and often gives more information than negative language does. Note the differences in tone and amount of information given in the following pairs of sentences:

NOT: The briefcase is not made of cheap imitation leather.

BUT: The briefcase is made of 100% belt leather for years of durable service.

NOT: We cannot ship your merchandise until we receive your check.

BUT: As soon as we receive your check, we will ship your merchandise.

Expressions such as *cannot* and *will not* are not the only ones that convey negative messages. Other words, such as *mistake, damage, failure, refuse,* and *deny,* carry negative connotations and should be avoided when possible.

NOT: Failure to follow the directions may cause the blender to malfunction.

BUT: Following the directions will ensure many years of carefree service from your blender.

NOT: We apologize for this error.

BUT: We appreciate your calling this matter to our attention.

Avoid negative-sounding words.

Some information need only be implied.

In short, stress what *is* true and what *can* be done rather than what is not true and what cannot be done. This is not to say that negative language has no place in business writing. Negative language is strong and emphatic, and sometimes you will want to use it. Unless the situation clearly calls for negative language, however, you are more likely to achieve your objective and to build goodwill for yourself and your organization by stressing the positive.

Because words are the building blocks for your message, choose them with care. Using short, simple words; writing with clarity, vigor, and conciseness; and using positive language will help you construct effective sentences and paragraphs.

CHECKPOINT 4.2

RECALL   Write a capital *T* for true or *F* for false before each statement.

1. ___ "If I can be of further help to you, please do not hesitate to let me know" is an example of a cliché.

2. ___ "Ground zero" and "24/7" are examples of buzz words.

3. ___ Both redundancies and repetition weaken your writing.

4. ___ In the sentence "Giovanni left the report right where it was," the expression "it was" is an expletive.

5. ___ Some information in a typical business document may properly be implied rather than stated directly.

VOCABULARY   Define the following terms in your own words and give an original example of each.

6. buzz word:

7. cliché:

8. expletive:

9. redundancy:

COMPREHENSION

10. Give an original example of each of the following terms:
    a. Buzz word:
    b. Cliché:
    c. Hidden subject:
    d. Hidden verb:
    e. Redundancy:
    f. Slang:

CRITICAL THINKING

11. Describe a business communication situation in which it might be preferable to use *negative* language rather than positive language.

Writing Effective Sentences

A sentence has a subject and predicate and expresses at least one complete thought. Beyond these attributes, however, sentences vary widely in style, length, and effect. They are also very flexible; writers can move sentence parts around, add and delete information, and substitute words to express different ideas and emphasize different points. To build effective sentences, use a variety of sentence types, and use active and passive voice appropriately.

When you're given only 15 minutes to convince venture capitalists to invest $8 million in your small start-up high-tech company, you must make sure every word of your presentation counts. Krishna Subramanian, CEO of Kovair, was successful in her presentation to 300 investors at a Silicon Valley forum.

6. Use a Variety of Sentence Types.

As we learned in Chapter 3, there are four basic sentence types: simple, compound, complex, and compound-complex. All of them are appropriate for business writing.

- Because a simple sentence presents a single idea and is usually short, it is often used for emphasis.
- Because each clause in a compound sentence presents a complete idea, each idea receives *equal* emphasis.
- A complex sentence contains one independent clause and at least one dependent clause. The dependent clause provides additional, but *subordinate*, information related to the independent clause.
- A compound-complex sentence contains *two or more* independent clauses and *one or more* dependent clauses.

Using a variety of sentence patterns and sentence lengths helps keep your writing interesting. Note how simplistic and choppy too many short sentences can be and how boring and difficult too many long sentences can be.

Too Choppy:

Golden Nugget will not purchase the Claridge Hotel. The hotel is 60 years old. The asking price was $110. It was not considered too high. Golden Nugget had wanted some commitments from New Jersey regulators. The regulators were unwilling to provide such commitments. Some observers believe the refusal was not the real reason for the decision. They blame the weak Atlantic City economy for the cancellation. Golden Nugget purchased the Stake House in Las Vegas in 1990. It lost money on that purchase. It does not want to repeat its mistake in Atlantic City. *(Average sentence length = 8 words)*

Too Difficult:

Golden Nugget will not purchase the Claridge Hotel, which is 60 years old, for an asking price of $110 million, which was not considered too high, because the company had wanted some commitments from New Jersey regulators, and the regulators were unwilling to provide such commitments. Some observers believe the refusal was not the real reason for the decision but rather that the weak Atlantic City economy was responsible for the cancellation; and since Golden Nugget purchased the Stake House in Las Vegas in 1990 and lost money on that purchase, it does not want to repeat its mistake in Atlantic City. *(Average sentence length = 50 words)*

The sentences in these paragraphs should be revised to show relationships between ideas more clearly, to keep readers interested, and to improve readability. Use simple sentences for emphasis and variety, compound sentences for coordinate (equal) relationships, and complex sentences for subordinate relationships.

> Use a variety of sentence patterns and lengths.

More Variety:

Golden Nugget will not purchase the 60-year-old Claridge Hotel, even though the $110 million asking price was not considered too high. The company had wanted some commitments from New Jersey regulators, which the regulators were unwilling to provide. However, some observers blame the cancellation on the weak Atlantic City economy. Golden Nugget lost money on its 1990 purchase of the Stake House in Las Vegas, and it does not want to repeat its mistake in Atlantic City. *(Average sentence length = 20 words)*

The first two sentences in the revision are complex, the third sentence is simple, and the last sentence is compound. The lengths of the four sentences range from 12 to 27 words. To write effective sentences, use different sentence patterns and lengths. Most sentences in good business writing range from 16 to 22 words.

7. Use Active and Passive Voice Appropriately.

Voice is the characteristic of a verb that shows whether the subject of the sentence acts or is acted on. In the **active voice**, the subject *performs* the action expressed by the verb. In the **passive voice**, the subject *receives* the action expressed by the verb.

ACTIVE: Inmac offers a full refund on all orders.

PASSIVE: A full refund on all orders is offered by Inmac.

ACTIVE: Shoemacher & Doerr audited the books in 2003.

PASSIVE: The books were audited in 2003 by Shoemacher & Doerr.

> **active voice** The sentence form in which the subject performs the action expressed by the verb
>
> **passive voice** The sentence form in which the subject receives the action expressed by the verb

Passive sentences add some form of the verb *to be* to the main verb, so a passive sentence is always longer than the equivalent active sentence. In the first set of sentences just given, for example, compare *offers* in the active sentence with *is offered by* in the passive sentence.

In active sentences, the subject is the doer of the action; in passive sentences, the subject is the receiver of the action. Because the subject gets more emphasis than other nouns in a sentence, active sentences emphasize the doer and passive sentences emphasize the receiver of the action. In the second set of sentences, either version could be considered correct, depending on whether the writer wanted to emphasize *Shoemacher & Doerr* or *the books*.

Use active sentences most of the time in business writing, just as you unconsciously use active sentences in most of your conversations. Note that verb *voice* (active or passive) has nothing to do with verb *tense*, which shows the time of the action. As the following sentences show, the action in both active and passive sentences can occur in the past, present, or future.

NOT: A very logical argument was presented by Troy. (*Passive voice, past tense*)

BUT: Troy presented a very logical argument. (*Active voice, past tense*)

NOT: An 18% increase will be reported by the eastern region. (*Passive voice, future tense*)

BUT: The eastern region will report an 18% increase. (*Active voice, future tense*)

> *Passive sentences are generally more effective than active sentences for conveying negative information.*

Passive sentences are most appropriate in three circumstances: (1) when you want to emphasize the receiver of the action, (2) when the person doing the action is either unknown or unimportant, or (3) when you want to be tactful in conveying negative information. All of the following sentences are appropriately stated in the passive voice:

Protective legislation was blamed for the drop in imports. *(Emphasizes the receiver of the action)*

Transportation to the construction site will be provided. *(The doer of the action is not important)*

Several complaints have been received regarding the new policy. *(Tactfully conveys negative news)*

Words, sentences, and paragraphs are all building blocks of communication. You have seen how using a variety of sentence types and using active and passive voice appropriately can help make your sentences more effective. Now you are ready to combine these sentences to form logical paragraphs.

Developing Logical Paragraphs

A paragraph is a group of related sentences that focus on one main idea. The main idea is often identified in the first sentence of the paragraph, which is then known as a *topic sentence*. The body of the paragraph supports this main idea by giving more information, analysis, or examples. A paragraph is typically part of a longer message, although one paragraph can contain the entire message, especially in such informal communications as email.

> *Use a new paragraph to signal a change in direction.*

Paragraphs organize the topic into manageable units of information for the reader. Readers need a cue to tell them when they have finished a topic, so that they can pause and refocus their attention on the next topic. To serve this purpose, paragraphs must be unified and coherent, be stated in parallel structure, and be of an appropriate length.

8. Keep Paragraphs Unified and Coherent.

Although closely related, unity and coherence are not the same. A paragraph has *unity* when all its parts work together to develop a single idea consistently and logically. A paragraph has *coherence* when each sentence links smoothly to the sentences before and after it.

Unity   A unified paragraph gives information that is directly related to the topic, presents this information in a logical order, and omits irrelevant details. The following excerpt is a middle paragraph in a memorandum arguing against the proposal that Collins, a baby-food manufacturer, should expand into producing food for adults:

NOT: [1] We cannot focus our attention on both ends of the age spectrum. [2] In a recent survey, two-thirds of the under-35 age group named Collins as the first company that came to mind for the category "baby-food products." [3] For more than 50 years we have spent millions of dollars annually to identify our company as the baby-food company, and market research shows that we have been successful. [4] Last year, we introduced Peas 'N Pears, our most successful baby-food introduction ever. [5] To now seek to position ourselves as a producer of food for adults would simply be incongruous. [6] Our well-defined image in the marketplace would make producing food for adults risky.

Before reading further, rearrange these sentences to make the sequence of ideas more logical.

The paragraph obviously lacks unity. You may decide that the overall topic of the paragraph is Collins's well-defined image as a baby-food producer. So Sentence 6 would be the best topic sentence. You might also decide that Sentence 4 brings in extra information that weakens paragraph unity and should be left out. The most unified paragraph, then, would be Sentences 6, 3, 2, 5, and 1, as shown here:

BUT: Our well-defined image in the marketplace would make producing food for adults risky. For more than 50 years we have spent millions of dollars annually to identify our company as the baby-food company, and market research shows that we have been successful. In a recent survey, two-thirds of the under-35 age group named Collins as the first company that came to mind for the category "baby-food products." To now seek to position ourselves as a producer of food for adults would simply be incongruous. We cannot focus our attention on both ends of the age spectrum.

A topic sentence is especially helpful in a long paragraph. It usually appears at the beginning of a paragraph. This position helps the writer focus on the topic, so the paragraph will have unity. It also lets the reader know immediately what the topic is.

The topic sentence usually goes at the beginning of the paragraph.

Coherence   A coherent paragraph weaves sentences together so that the discussion is integrated. The reader never needs to pause to puzzle out the relationships or reread to get the intended meaning. To achieve coherence,

Coherence is achieved by using transitional words, pronouns, repetition, and parallelism.

- Use transitional words.
- Use pronouns.
- Repeat key words and ideas.
- Use parallel structure.

Transitional words help the reader see relationships between sentences. Such words may be as simple as *first* and other indicators of sequence.

Ten years ago, Collins tried to overcome market resistance to its new line of baby clothes. <u>First</u>, it mounted a multimillion-dollar ad campaign featuring the Mason quintuplets. <u>Next</u>, it sponsored a Collins Baby look-alike contest. <u>Then</u>, it sponsored two network specials featuring Dr. Benjamin Spock. <u>Finally</u>, it brought in the Madison Avenue firm of Morgan & Modine to broaden its image.

The words *first, next, then,* and *finally* clearly signal step-by-step movement. Now note the following logical transitions, aided by connecting words:

I recognize, <u>however</u>, that Collins cannot thrive on baby food alone. <u>To begin with</u>, because we already control 73% of the market, further gains will be difficult. <u>What's more</u>, the current baby boom is slowing. <u>Therefore</u>, we must expand our product line.

Transitional words act as road signs, indicating where the message is headed and letting the reader know what to expect. Here are some commonly used transitional expressions grouped by the relationships they express:

Relationship	*Transitional Expressions*
addition	also, besides, furthermore, in addition, too
cause and effect	as a result, because, consequently, so, therefore, thus
comparison	in the same way, likewise, similarly
contrast	although, but, however, nevertheless, on the other hand, yet
illustration	for example, in other words, to illustrate
sequence	first, second, third, then, next, finally
summary/conclusion	at last, finally, in conclusion, to summarize, therefore

A second way to achieve coherence is to use pronouns. Because a pronoun stands for a word already named, using pronouns ties sentences and ideas together. The pronouns are underlined here:

> If Collins branches out with additional food products, one possibility would be a fruit snack for youngsters. Funny Fruits were tested in Columbus last summer, and <u>they</u> were a big hit. Roger Johnson, national marketing manager, says <u>he</u> hopes to build new food categories into a $200 million business. <u>He</u> is also exploring the possibility of acquiring other established name brands. <u>These</u> acquired brands would let Collins expand faster than if it had to develop a new product of <u>its</u> own.

A third way to achieve coherence is to repeat key words. In a misguided attempt to appear interesting, writers sometimes use different terms for the same idea. For example, a writer may use the words *administrator, manager, supervisor,* and *executive* all to refer to the same person. Such "elegant variation" merely confuses the reader, who has no way of knowing whether the writer is referring to the same concept or to slightly different variations of that concept. Avoid needless repetition, but use purposeful repetition to link ideas and thus promote paragraph coherence. Here is a good example:

> Collins has taken several <u>steps</u> recently to enhance profits and project a stronger leadership position. One of these <u>steps</u> is streamlining operations. Collins's line of children's clothes was <u>unprofitable</u>, so it discontinued the line. Its four produce farms were likewise <u>unprofitable</u>, so it hired an outside professional <u>team</u> to manage them. This <u>team</u> eventually recommended selling the farms.

Ensure paragraph unity by developing only one topic per paragraph and by presenting the information in logical order. Ensure paragraph coherence by using transitional words and pronouns and by repeating key words.

Purposeful repetition aids coherence; avoid needless repetition.

9. Use Parallel Structure.

The term **parallelism** means using similar grammatical structure for similar ideas—that is, matching adjectives with adjectives, nouns with nouns, infinitives with infinitives, and so on. Much widely quoted writing uses parallelism—for example, Julius Caesar's "I came, I saw, I conquered" and Abraham Lincoln's "government of the people, by the people, and for the people." Parallel structure smoothly links ideas and adds a pleasing rhythm to sentences and paragraphs, thereby enhancing coherence.

parallelism Using similar grammatical structure to express similar ideas

> **NOT:** The new dispatcher is competent and a fast worker.
>
> **BUT:** The new dispatcher is competent and fast.

NOT: The new grade of paper is lightweight, nonporous, and it is inexpensive.

BUT: The new grade of paper is lightweight, nonporous, and inexpensive.

NOT: The training program will cover
1. Vacation and sick leaves
2. How to resolve grievances
3. Managing your workstation

BUT: The training program will cover
1. Vacation and sick leaves
2. Grievance resolution
3. Workstation management

NOT: One management consultant recommended either selling the children's furniture division or its conversion into a children's toy division.

BUT: One management consultant recommended either selling the children's furniture division or converting it into a children's toy division.

In the last set of sentences above, note that correlative conjunctions (such as *both/and, either/or,* and *not only/but also)* must be followed by words in parallel form. Be especially careful to use parallel structure in report headings that have equal weight and in numbered or bulleted lists.

10. Control Paragraph Length.

How long should a paragraph of business writing be? As with other considerations, the needs of the reader, rather than the convenience of the writer, should determine the answer to this question. Paragraphs should help the reader by signaling a new idea as well as by providing a physical break. Long blocks of unbroken text look boring and needlessly complex. Also, they may unintentionally obscure an important idea buried in the middle. On the other hand, a series of extremely short paragraphs can weaken coherence by obscuring underlying relationships.

Essentially, there are no fixed rules for paragraph length, and occasionally one- or ten-sentence paragraphs might be effective. However, most paragraphs of good business writers fall into the 60- to 80-word range—long enough for a topic sentence and three or four supporting sentences. Although a single paragraph should never discuss more than one major topic, complex topics may need to be divided into several paragraphs. Your purpose and the needs of your reader should ultimately determine paragraph length.

RECALL Write a capital *T* for true or *F* for false before each statement.

1. ____ For unity, most sentences in a single document should be of the same type.

2. ____ Most active sentences are in the present tense and most passive sentences are in the past tense.

3. ____ It is acceptable to divide a long paragraph into separate paragraphs even if they both discuss the same topic.

4. ____ Parallel structure is required in report headings that have equal weight as well as in numbered and bulleted lists.

5. ____ A series of very short paragraphs enhances readability and comprehension.

CHECKPOINT 4.3

VOCABULARY   Define the following terms in your own words and give an original example of each.

6. active voice:

7. parallelism:

8. passive voice:

COMPREHENSION

9. Write three types of sentences to express the following ideas. For the complex sentence, emphasize the first idea: Mr. Esquibel was given a promotion / Mr. Esquibel was assigned additional responsibilities.

   a. Simple:

   b. Compound:

   c. Complex:

10. Compose an effective compound sentence in which both clauses are in the active voice.

11. Compose a sentence using "either/or" phrases that illustrates parallel structure.

CRITICAL THINKING

12. Assume that today you wrote one email to your boss and another to your best friend. How do you think they might differ in terms of (a) sentence type, (b) coherence and logic, (c) parallel structure, and (d) paragraph length?

Writing a Concise Message

You are Lyn Poe, administrative assistant for the Office and Information Systems Department at Midstate College. You have drafted the following announcement that you intend to post to the university computer network bulletin board (the line numbers are shown for editing purposes only). You now wish to make the announcement as concise as possible—not only to make it more effective but also to have it take up less space (bandwidth) on the computer network.

Administrative Professionals Workshop Scheduled for April 21

Wednesday, April 22, is Administrative Professionals Day, which is	1
a part of the larger observance that is known as Administrative Professionals	2
Week®, which spans April 19–25. Businesses have observed Administrative	3
Professionals Week® or its predecessor annually since 1952 to recognize secre-	4
taries and other administrative professionals, upon whose skills, loyalty, and	5
efficiency the functions of business and government offices depend.	6
In keeping with this occasion, the Office and Information Systems	7
Department of Midstate College makes an announcement of its 11th	8
Annual Administrative Professionals Workshop on Tuesday, April 21,	9
between 8:30 a.m. and 3 p.m. at the New Theatre Restaurant in	10
downtown Portland.	11
Dr. Lee Stafford will begin our workshop by speaking on "How to	12
Manage Conflict, Criticism, and Anger." Stafford motivates and educates	13
people to be the best they can be, but nevertheless he likes to have a	14
good time doing it. His humor-filled presentations are packed with	15
practical information that promotes positive change. He is a licensed	16
psychologist, holds a Ph.D. in motivation, and has more than 30 years of	17
experience in speaking, consulting, and training.	18
Conflict is a hard thing to like. However, whether it involves a	19
client with an overdue bill or an office quarrel with a coworker,	20
conflict is an integral part of the working world. Stafford helps his	21
clients learn that there is value to conflict. He will make a	22
presentation of techniques to handle and give criticism without	23
offense, deal with anger, and respond to hostility from others.	24
Stafford's second presentation is "Life on the High Wire: Balancing	25
Work, Family, and Play." Society has raised the ante on what it takes	26
to be a "normal" human being. There are ever-increasing demands to be,	27
do, and own more and more. Today, for the first time in our history, we	28
talk openly about burnout. Stafford will hold a discussion of the	29
successful balancing of work, family, and play.	30
Our closing session will feature Tom Graves, a professional magician	31
for more than 20 years. Graves was first influenced by watching various	32
magicians and ventriloquists on the *Ed Sullivan Show*. He will give a	33
demonstration of puppetry, mental telepathy, expert close-up magic,	34
comedy, juggling, and balloon-animal sculpture. It would appear that	35
Graves's talents are the most unique in the world. Drawings for free	36
gifts will be held following his performance.	37

38   There is a cost for this all-day workshop in the amount of $125 per

39   participant. For registration or more information, call 555-7821 or visit our

40   Web site at <u>www.workshop.msc.edu</u>.

Process

1. Guideline 4 in this chapter discusses five techniques for writing more concisely. Review your draft. Do you have any redundant phrases that can be eliminated?

    Oops! I see two redundancies: In line 36 I'll change "most unique" to "unique" and in lines 36–37 I'll change "free gifts" to "gifts."

2. Does your document contain any wordy expressions?

    Yes—and I can simply delete both: "It would appear that" in line 35 and "in the amount" in line 38.

3. How about hidden verbs?

    Ouch!—four of them. Here's what I'll do:

    - Line 8: Shorten "makes an announcement of" to "announces."
    - Line 22–23: Shorten "makes a presentation of" to "present."
    - Line 29: Shorten "hold a discussion of" to "discuss."
    - Lines 33–34: Shorten "give a demonstration of" to "demonstrate."

4. Any hidden nouns?

    Actually, my draft contains two hidden nouns, but I want to change only one: In line 38, I'll change "There is a cost for this all-day workshop" to "This all-day workshop costs." In line 27, I want to keep "There are ever-increasing demands to." It sounds natural, and because the announcement contains no other expletive beginnings, I think it's okay.

5. Now reread the draft to see if you can shorten other phrases either by implying them instead of stating them outright or by condensing them.

    The very first sentence contains two—"which is" and "that is"; and I can simply omit both of them.

The 3Ps
Problem, Process, Product

Here is the final version of my announcement, which, incidentally, contains 32 fewer words, making it more concise—and more economical.

Product

ADMINISTRATIVE PROFESSIONALS WORKSHOP SCHEDULED FOR APRIL 21

Wednesday, April 22, is Administrative Professionals Day, part of the larger observance known as Administrative Professionals Week®, which spans April 19–25.

According to the International Association for Administrative Professionals (IAAP), businesses and secretaries have observed this week annually since 1952 to recognize the secretary and other administrative professionals, upon whose skills, loyalty, and efficiency the functions of business and government offices depend.

In keeping with this occasion, the Office and Information Systems Department of Midstate College announces its 11th Annual Administrative Professionals Workshop on Tuesday, April 21, between 8:30 a.m. and 3 p.m. at the New Theatre Restaurant in downtown Portland.

Dr. Lee Stafford will begin our workshop by speaking on "How to Manage Conflict, Criticism, and Anger." Stafford motivates and educates people to be the best they can be, and he likes to have a good time doing it. His humor-filled presentations are packed with practical information that promotes positive change. He is a licensed psychologist, holds a Ph.D. in motivation, and has more than 30 years of experience in speaking, consulting, and training.

Stafford's second presentation is "Life on the High Wire: Balancing Work, Family, and Play." Society has raised the ante on what it takes to be a "normal" human being. There are ever-increasing demands to be, do, and own more and more. Today, for the first time in our history, we talk openly about burnout. Stafford will discuss the successful balancing of work, family, and play.

Our closing session will feature Tom Graves, a professional magician for more than 20 years. Graves was first influenced by watching various magicians and ventriloquists on the *Ed Sullivan Show*. He will demonstrate puppetry, mental telepathy, expert close-up magic, comedy, juggling, and balloon-animal sculpture. Graves's talents are unique. Drawings for gifts will be held following his performance.

The total cost for this all-day workshop is $125 per participant. For registration or to receive more information, call 555-7821 or visit our Web site at www.workshop.msc.edu.

Summary

For business writing to achieve its objectives, it must be clear. Use short, simple, specific, and concrete words; avoid dangling expressions, clichés, slang, buzz words, and unnecessary jargon. Write concisely; avoid redundancies, wordy expressions, and hidden subjects and verbs. Finally, prefer positive language; stress what you can do rather than what you cannot do.

To maintain reader interest, use a variety of sentence types, including simple, compound, complex, and compound-complex sentences. Use active voice to emphasize the doer of the action and passive voice to emphasize the receiver of the action.

Your paragraphs should be unified and coherent. Develop only one topic per paragraph, and use transitional words, pronouns, repetition, and parallelism. Although paragraphs of various lengths are desirable, most should range from 60 to 80 words. To help the reader follow your logic, avoid very long paragraphs and avoid strings of very short paragraphs.

Looking Ahead

In this chapter, we focused on the parts that make up a complete business message—how to choose the right words, how to write effective sentences, and how to develop logical paragraphs. In Chapter 5, we consider how the tone of the overall message can help us achieve our communication goals.

Key Terms

active voice
buzz word
cliché
dangling expression
expletive

mechanics
parallelism
passive voice
redundancy
style

Exercises

Choosing the Right Words

1 Jargon   As anyone who has ever visited a chat room or done online research knows, the Internet has spawned a tremendous number of jargon terms. If necessary, go online to define the following terms:

blog	BTW	IMO	OTOH
bot	distribution list	L8R	ping
bounce	F2F	LOL	post
BRB	flame	lurk	spam

2 Short and Simple Words Revise the following paragraph to incorporate more short and simple words:

> The consultant demonstrated how our aggregate remuneration might be ameliorated by modifications in our propensities to utilize credit for compensating for services. She also endeavored to ascertain which of our characteristics were analogous to those of other entities for which she had fabricated solutions. She recommended we commence to initiate innumerable modifications in our procedures to increase cash flow, which she considers indispensable for facilitating increased corporate health.

3 Specific and Concrete Words Revise the following paragraph to incorporate specific and concrete words:

> In an effort to stimulate sales, Mallmart is lowering prices substantially on its line of consumer items. Sometime soon, it will close most of its stores for several days to provide store personnel time to change prices. Markdowns will range from very little on its line of laundry equipment to a great deal on certain sporting equipment. Mallmart plans to rely on advertising to let people know of these price reductions. In particular, it is considering using a popular television star to publicize the new pricing strategy.

4 Clichés, Slang, and Buzz Words Revise the following paragraph to eliminate clichés, slang, and buzz words:

> At that point in time the corporate brass were under the gun; they decided to bite the bullet and let the chips fall where they may. They hired a head honcho with some street smarts who would be able to interface with the investment community. Financewise, the new top dog couldn't be beat. He was hard as nails and developed a scenario that would have the company back on its feet within six months. Now it was up to the team players to operationalize his plans.

5 Conciseness Revise the following paragraph to make it more concise:

> In spite of the fact that Fox Inc. denied wrongdoing, it agreed to a settlement of the patent suit for a price of $6.3 million. Industry sources were surprised at the outcome because of the fact that the original patent had depreciated in value. In addition to the above, Fox also made an agreement to refrain from the manufacture of similar computers for a period of five years in length. It appears that with the exception of Emerson's new introductions, innovations in workstations will be few in number during the next few years.

6 Positive Language Revise the following paragraph to incorporate more positive language:

> We cannot issue a full refund at this time because you did not enclose a receipt or an authorized estimate. I'm sorry that we will have to delay your reimbursement. We are not like those insurance companies that promise you anything but then disappear when you have a claim. When we receive your receipt or estimate, we will not hold up your check. Our refusal to issue reimbursement without proper supporting evidence means that we do not have to charge you outlandish premiums for your automobile insurance.

7 Wordy Expressions Revise the following sentences to eliminate wordy phrases by substituting a single word wherever possible.

a. Push the red button in the event that you see any smoke rising from the cooking surface.
b. More than 40% of the people polled are of the opinion that government spending should be reduced.
c. Please send me more information pertaining to your new line of pesticides.
d. Due to the fact that two of the three highway lanes were closed for repairs, I was nearly 20 minutes late for my appointment.

8 Hidden Verbs Revise the following sentences to eliminate hidden verbs and convey the appropriate action.

a. After much deliberation, the group came to a decision about how to respond to the lawsuit.
b. Although Hugh wanted to offer an explanation of his actions, his boss refused to listen.
c. Nationwide Call Systems is performing an analysis of our calling patterns to determine how we can save money on long-distance telephone calls.

Writing Effective Sentences

9 Sentence Variety Rewrite the following paragraph by varying sentence types and sentence lengths to keep the writing interesting.

Health Foods was founded by Floyd Morales in 1994. The product was the first snack food to combine cheddar cheese and popcorn. Morales perfected the Health Foods recipe in his home kitchen after much trial and error. Health Foods sales were reportedly only $65,000 in 1995. During that time, the product was available only in the Midwest. By 1998, sales had soared to $12 million. This attracted the attention of Norton. The snack-food giant bought Health Foods in 1999 for $15 million. Since the purchase, Norton has not revised the popular Health Foods formula. It has used its marketing prowess to keep sales growing, despite the growing number of challengers crowding the market.

10 Sentence Length Write a long sentence (40 to 50 words) that attempts to make sense. Then revise the sentence so that it contains 10 or fewer words. Finally, rewrite the sentence so that it contains 16 to 22 words. Which sentence is the most effective? Why?

11 Active and Passive Voice For each of the following sentences, first identify whether the sentence is active or passive. Then, if necessary, revise the sentence to use the more effective verb voice.

a. We will begin using the new plant in 2003, and the old plant will be converted into a warehouse.
b. A very effective sales letter was written by Paul Mendleson. The letter will be mailed next week.
c. You failed to verify the figures on the quarterly report. As a result, $5,500 was lost by the company.

Developing Logical Paragraphs

12 Coherence Insert logical transitions in the blanks to give the following paragraph coherence.

Columbia is widening its lead over Kraft in the computer-magazine war. ———— its revenues increased 27% last year, whereas Kraft's increased 16%. ———— its audited paid circulation increased to 600,000, compared to 450,000 for Kraft. ———— Kraft was able to increase both the ad rate and the number of ad pages last year. One note of worry ———— is Kraft's decision to shut down its independent testing laboratory. Some industry leaders believe much of Kraft's success has been due to its reliable product reviews. ———— Columbia has just announced an agreement whereby Stanford University will perform product testing for Columbia.

13 Parallelism   Determine whether the following sentences use parallel structure. Revise sentences as needed to make the structure parallel.

   a. The store is planning to install a new cash-register system that is easier to operate, easier to repair, and cheaper to maintain than the current system.
   b. According to the survey, most employees prefer either holding the employee cafeteria open later or its hours to be kept the same.
   c. The quarterback is expert not only in calling plays but also in throwing passes.
   d. Our career-guidance book will cover
      1. Writing résumés
      2. Application letters
      3. Techniques for interviewing

14 Paragraph Length   Read the following paragraph and determine how it might be divided into two or more shorter paragraphs to help the reader follow the complex topic being discussed.

   Transforming a manuscript into a published book requires several steps. After the author submits the manuscript (in typewritten or computer-generated form), the copy editor makes any needed grammatical or spelling changes. The author reviews these changes to be sure that they haven't altered the meaning of any sentences or sections. Then the publisher sends the manuscript out for typesetting. Next, the author proofreads the typeset galleys and gives the publisher a list of any corrections. These corrections are incorporated into the page proofs, which show how the pages will look when printed. The author and publisher review these page proofs for any errors. Only after all corrections have been made does the book get published. From start to finish, this process can take as long as a year.

15 Writing with Style   Review this chapter briefly. What section was most difficult for you? Write a one-page double-spaced paper in which you explain that difficult material in your own words to someone who is having the same trouble you had. Your purpose is to make the section crystal clear to your reader.

16 Writing with Style   When Michael Sherman, founder of Sherman Assembly Systems in San Antonio, Texas, learned that one of his employees had been robbed after cashing a paycheck, he became concerned. Sherman Assembly makes electronic cable equipment, and some of its manufacturing employees are former welfare recipients who have little experience with financial institutions. Digging deeper, Sherman learned that many of these employees used check-cashing services on payday because they didn't understand how bank accounts worked. He decided to educate his employees by arranging for a local bank manager to visit the factory, explain how checking accounts work, and help employees fill out applications for special low-minimum-balance accounts. (Source: "In the Bank," *Inc.,* May 2001, p. 68.)

   As Sherman's assistant, you have volunteered to write an announcement about the bank manager's visit, explaining in simple and straightforward terms how employees will benefit from using checking accounts. Follow this chapter's principles of style as you draft this brief memo, making up any details you need to complete this assignment, such as the bank name, the manager's name, and the time and date of the visit.

   Finally, working in groups of three, read and comment on one another's memos. (Remember the techniques of giving effective feedback presented in Chapter 2.) Revise your papers, if necessary, and submit them to your instructor.

5

Writing with Style: Tone and Process

After you have finished this chapter, you should be able to:

- Write confidently.

- Use a courteous and sincere tone.

- Use appropriate emphasis and subordination.

- Use nondiscriminatory language.

- Stress the "you" attitude.

- Specify the purpose of your message and analyze your audience.

- Determine the content and organization of the message.

- Compose a first draft.

- Revise for content, style, and correctness.

- Format and proofread your document.

On the Job

NANCY EVANS
Cofounder,
Cochairperson, and
Editor-in-Chief, iVillage

Knowing that people can click away at any moment, Nancy Evans believes that connecting with the audience is as critical in cyberspace as it is in printed and oral messages. As cofounder, cochairperson, and editor-in-chief of iVillage, the leading women's online network, Evans is responsible for the editorial content of the company's Internet, print, and television products. Whether she is checking a Web page, developing a new feature, or lining up a new sponsor, Evans never forgets the differing needs of her online audience, the more than 7 million members (mostly women) who point their Web browsers to iVillage for practical ideas on parenting, relationships, and much more.

Evans initiates or responds to as many as 300 email messages as well as any number of traditional letters during an average business day. Despite this high volume of correspondence, she carefully plans what she will say in each message and customizes the content for each recipient, rather than falling back on generic language. "You might as well not even write a letter if it's going to be generic," says Evans. "Personalization shows that you've done your homework. I always think about what my goal is, how to connect with the audience, and what will get someone to read to the end."

What Do We Mean by *Tone?*

Having chosen the right words to construct effective sentences and then having combined these sentences into logical paragraphs, we now examine the tone of the complete message—the complete letter, memorandum, report, or the like. **Tone in writing refers to the writer's attitude toward both the reader and the subject of the message.** The overall tone of your written message affects your reader just as your tone of voice affects your listener in everyday exchanges. You also want to ensure the appropriateness of the overall tone of your electronic messages (see Spotlight 3, "Netiquette," on the next page).

The business writer should strive for an overall tone that is confident, courteous, and sincere; that uses emphasis and subordination appropriately; that contains nondiscriminatory language; and that stresses the "you" attitude. (Style Principles 1–10 were presented in Chapter 4.)

tone The writer's attitude toward the reader and the subject of the message

11. Write Confidently.

Your message should convey the confident attitude that you have done a competent job of communicating and that your reader will do as you ask or will accept your decision. If you believe that your explanation is complete, that your request is reasonable, or that your decision is based on sound logic, you are likely to write with confidence. Such confidence has a persuasive effect on your audience. Avoid using language that makes you sound unsure of yourself. Be especially wary of beginning sentences with "I hope," "If you agree," and similar self-conscious terms.

NOT: If you'd like to take advantage of this offer, call our toll-free number.

BUT: To take advantage of this offer, call our toll-free number.

NOT: I hope that you will agree that my qualifications match your job needs.

BUT: My qualifications match your job needs in the following respects.

If you believe in what you have written, write in such a way that your reader will, too.

In some situations, the best strategy is simply to omit information. For example, you should not provide the reader with excuses for denying your request, suggest that something might go wrong, or intimate that the reader might not be satisfied.

NOT: I know you are a busy person, but we would really enjoy hearing you speak.

BUT: The fact that you are involved in so many different enterprises makes your views on small business all the more relevant for our audience.

NOT: Let us know if you experience any other problems.

BUT: Your GrassMaster lawn mower should now give you many years of trouble-free service.

A word of caution: Do not appear *overconfident;* that is, avoid sounding presumptuous or arrogant. Be especially wary of using such strong phrases as "I know that" and "I am sure you will agree that."

Modest confidence is the best tactic.

NOT: I'm sure you'll agree our offer is reasonable.

BUT: This solution should enable you to collect the data you need while still protecting the privacy of our clients.

SPOTLIGHT ③ on technology

Netiquette[1]

"Netiquette" is network etiquette—a professional code of behavior for electronic communication. In other words, netiquette is a set of guidelines for behaving properly online. Follow these five guidelines to become (and remain) a welcomed member of the electronic community:

1. Remember That You're Communicating with Another Human Being.

Because of the lack of nonverbal clues, it's easy to misinterpret the other person's meaning. Remember that the recipient has feelings more or less like your own. Stand up for yourself and your beliefs but be sensitive to other people's feelings. Never write something to someone on email or in a discussion group that you would not say to that person in a face-to-face encounter. Avoid sending heated messages (called "flaming") even if you're provoked. As many users have learned to their dismay, email can be misaddressed or forwarded—sometimes with devastating consequences.

2. Behave Ethically.

Standards of online behavior are simply *different from*—but not lower than—those for personal behavior. Respect other people's privacy. Don't read other people's email, and get permission before copying or forwarding someone's message to another party. Before inserting a hyperlink from your Web page to someone else's site, notify that person (you don't *have* to ask permission, but it's the courteous thing to do). Similarly, don't copy another person's artwork (including cartoons and clipart) without securing permission.

3. Lurk Before You Leap.

When you enter a discussion group that's new to you, take time to look around. Read the messages for a few days to get a sense of how the people who are already there act. Then go ahead and participate. Read the FAQs (Frequently Asked Questions), a file that contains answers to commonly asked questions. Also, ensure the accuracy (and relevance) of anything you post. Bad information spreads like wildfire on the Internet.

4. Respect Other People's Time and Bandwidth.

When you send a message via email or a discussion group, you're taking up other people's time. Therefore, you should make sure the time they spend reading your message is time well spent. You're also taking up bandwidth—the information-carrying capacity of the telephone lines or networks used to transmit your message. Don't copy more people than necessary in an email note, don't include a copy of the original message in your reply unless necessary, and be careful about posting the same message to more than one newsgroup. Similarly, if you host a Web home page, avoid using large graphics.

5. Be Tolerant of Other People's Mistakes.

Electronic communication can be a scary place for novices, and we were all network newbies once. So when someone makes a mistake—whether it's a spelling error, a stupid question, an irrelevant comment, or an unnecessarily long answer—be kind. If you want to be helpful, point out errors by a private email message, not by public posting to a newsgroup. Give people the benefit of the doubt.

In short, netiquette, like good manners in all other situations, is based on adherence to the golden rule: Do unto others as you would have them do unto you. Communicate with others as you would like them to communicate with you.

NOT: I will schedule an interview with you next Thursday to discuss my qualifications further.

BUT: Please let me know when I may meet with you to discuss my qualifications further.

Competent communicators are *confident* communicators. They write with conviction, yet avoid appearing to be pushy or presumptuous.

No one understands the importance of a courteous and sincere tone better than Ali Kasikci, general manager of the Peninsula Beverly Hills hotel, the only hotel in Southern California to win both the Mobil Travel Guide Five-Star Award and the AAA Five-Diamond Award.

12. Use a Courteous and Sincere Tone.

A tone of courtesy and sincerity builds goodwill for you and your organization and increases the likelihood that your message will achieve its objective. For example, lecturing the reader or filling a letter with **platitudes** (trite, obvious statements) implies a condescending attitude. Likewise, readers are likely to find offensive such expressions as "you failed to," "we find it difficult to believe that," "you surely don't expect," or "your complaint."

platitude A trite, obvious statement

> **NOT:** Companies like ours cannot survive unless our customers pay their bills on time.
>
> **BUT:** By paying your bill before May 30, you will maintain your excellent credit history with our firm.
>
> **NOT:** You sent your complaint to the wrong department. We don't handle shipping problems.
>
> **BUT:** We have forwarded your letter to the shipping department. You should be hearing from them within the week.

Your reader is sophisticated enough to know when you're being sincere. To achieve a sincere tone, avoid exaggeration (especially using too many modifiers or too strong modifiers), obvious flattery, and expressions of surprise or disbelief.

> **NOT:** Your satisfaction means more to us than making a profit, and we shall work night and day to see that we earn it.
>
> **BUT:** We value your goodwill and have taken these specific steps to ensure your satisfaction.
>
> **NOT:** I'm surprised you would question your raise, considering your overall performance last year.
>
> **BUT:** Your raise was based on an objective evaluation of your performance last year.

Obvious flattery and exaggeration sound insincere.

Competent communicators use both verbal and nonverbal signals to convey courtesy and sincerity. However, it is difficult to fake these attitudes. The best way to achieve the desired tone is to truly assume a courteous and sincere outlook toward your reader.

13. Use Appropriate Emphasis and Subordination.

Not all ideas are created equal. Some are more important and more persuasive than others. Assume, for example, that you have been asked to evaluate and compare the Copy Cat and the Repro 100 photocopiers and then to write a memo report recommending one for purchase. Assume that the two brands are alike in all important respects except the following:

Feature	Copy Cat	Repro 100
Speed (copies per minute)	15	10
Cost	$2,750	$2,100
Enlargement/reduction?	Yes	No

As you can see, the Copy Cat has greater speed and more features. Thus, a casual observer might think you should recommend the Copy Cat on the basis of its additional advantages. Suppose, however, that most of your photocopying involves fewer than five copies of each original, all of them full-sized. Under these conditions, you might conclude that the Repro 100's lower cost outweighs the Copy Cat's higher speed and additional features; you therefore decide to recommend purchasing the Repro 100.

If you want your recommendation to be credible, you must make sure that your reader views the relative importance of each feature in the same way you do. To do so, use appropriate emphasis and subordination techniques.

Techniques of Emphasis   To emphasize an idea, use any of the following strategies (to subordinate an idea, simply use the opposite strategy):

1. Put the idea in a short, simple sentence. However, if you need a complex sentence to convey the needed information, put the more important idea in the independent clause. (The ideas communicated in each independent clause of a *compound* sentence receive *equal* emphasis.)

   SIMPLE: The Repro 100 is the better photocopier for our purposes.

   COMPLEX: Although the Copy Cat is faster, 98% of our copying requires fewer than five copies per original. (*emphasizes the fact that speed is not a crucial consideration for us*)

2. Place the major idea first or last. The first paragraph of a message receives the most emphasis, the last paragraph receives less emphasis, and the middle paragraphs receive the least emphasis. Similarly, the middle sentences within a paragraph receive less emphasis than the first sentence in a paragraph.

   The first criterion examined was cost. The Copy Cat sells for $2,750, and the Repro 100 sells for $2,100, or 24% less than the cost of the Copy Cat.

3. Make the noun you want to emphasize the subject of the sentence. In other words, use active voice to emphasize the doer of the action and passive voice to emphasize the receiver.

   ACTIVE: The Repro 100 costs 24% less than the Copy Cat. (*emphasizes the Repro 100 rather than the Copy Cat*)

   PASSIVE: The relative costs of the two models were compared first. (*emphasizes the relative costs rather than the two models*)

Let your reader know which ideas you consider most important.

Recall from Chapter 3 that a simple sentence contains one independent clause and no dependent clauses. A complex sentence contains one independent clause and one or more dependent clauses.

To subordinate an idea, put it in the dependent clause.

4. Devote more space to the idea.

   The two models were judged according to three criteria: cost, speed, and enlargement/reduction capabilities. Total cost is an important consideration for our firm because of the large number of copiers we use and our large volume of copying. Last year our firm used 358 photocopiers and duplicated more than 6.5 million pages. Thus, regardless of the speed or features of a particular model, if it is too expensive to operate, it will not serve our purposes.

5. Use language that directly implies importance, such as "most important," "major," or "primary."

   The most important factor for us is cost.

   (In contrast, use terms such as "least important" or "a minor point" to subordinate an idea.)

6. Use repetition (within reason).

   However, the Copy Cat is expensive—expensive to purchase and expensive to operate.

7. Use mechanical means (within reason)—enumeration, italics, solid capitals, second color, indenting from left and right margins, or other elements of design—to emphasize key ideas.

   But the most important criterion is cost, and the Repro 100 costs 24% less than the Copy Cat.

The Ethical Dimension　In using emphasis and subordination, your goal is to ensure a common frame of reference between you and your reader; you want your reader to see how important you consider each idea to be. Your goal is *not* to mislead the reader. For example, if you believe that the Repro 100 is a *slightly* better choice, you would not want to intentionally mislead your reader into concluding that it is a *clearly* better choice. Such a tactic would be not only unethical but also unwise. Use sound business judgment and a sense of fair play to help you achieve your communication objectives.

Use language that expresses your honest evaluation; do not mislead the reader.

CHECKPOINT 5.1

RECALL   Write a capital *T* for true or *F* for false before each statement.

1. _____ One effective way to emphasize an idea is to put it in a short, simple sentence.

2. _____ The last paragraph of a message receives the most emphasis.

3. _____ "If you agree, please return the enclosed order form today," would be an example of a confident style of writing.

4. _____ To achieve vigorous writing, you should use many strong adjectives and adverbs.

5. _____ Your objective in using emphasis and subordination should be to ensure that your reader understands the importance you placed on each aspect of the situation.

VOCABULARY   Define the following terms in your own words and give an original example of each.

6. platitude:

7. tone:

COMPREHENSION

8. Revise the following sentences to make them more effective:

   a. I think we should proceed with the expansion for three reasons.

   b. Why not take advantage of this offer?

9. List seven techniques for subordinating an idea.

CRITICAL THINKING

10. Assume you are giving a speech rather than writing a message. What are some ways you might emphasize an important idea orally?

14. Use Nondiscriminatory Language.

Nondiscriminatory language treats everyone equally, making no unwarranted assumptions about any group of people. Using nondiscriminatory language is smart business because it is the ethical thing to do and because we risk offending others if we do otherwise. Consider the types of bias in this report:

> The finishing plant was the scene of a confrontation today when two ladies from the morning shift accused a foreman of sexual harassment. Marta Maria Valdez, a Hispanic inspector, and Margaret Sawyer, an assembly-line worker, accused Mr. Engerrand of making suggestive comments. Mr. Engerrand, who is 62 years old and an epileptic, denied the charges and said he thought the girls were trying to cheat the company with their demand for a cash award.

Were you able to identify the following instances of bias or discriminatory language?

- The women were referred to as *ladies* and *girls*, although it is unlikely that the men in the company are referred to as *gentlemen* and *boys*.

- The term *foreman* (and all other *-man* occupational titles) has a sexist connotation.

- The two women were identified by their first and last names, without a personal title, whereas the man was identified by a personal title and last name only.

- Valdez's ethnicity, Engerrand's age, and Engerrand's disability were identified, although they were irrelevant to the situation.

Competent communicators make sure that their writing is free of sexist language and free of bias based on such factors as race, ethnicity, religion, age, sexual orientation, and disability.

Instead of	*Use*
chairman	chair, chairperson
best man for the job	best person for the job
using foul language around the ladies	using foul language
Lloyd, a broker, and his wife, a beautiful brunette	Lloyd, a broker, and his wife, a lawyer (*or* homemaker)
each manager and his assistant	all managers and their assistants
Dick McKenna, noted black legislator,	Dick McKenna, noted legislator,
Geraldine, an epileptic,	Geraldine, who has epilepsy, (*When the impairment is relevant, separate the impairment from the person.*)

Most of us like to think of ourselves as sensitive, caring people who do not wish to offend others. Our writing and speaking should reflect this attitude.

15. Stress the "You" Attitude.

Are you more interested in how well *you* perform in your courses or in how well your classmates perform? When you hear a television commercial, are you more

---

By the Numbers | WORD|wise

Shakespeare made up more than 1,700 words, including *accommodation, apostrophe, critic, generous, hurry, misplaced, obscene, road,* and *useless.*

To speak a word requires 72 muscles.

One No. 2 pencil can draw a line 70 miles long.

The letter string *ough* has 10 different sounds, as in *bough, bought, cough, dough, hiccough, lough, rough, thorough, through,* and *trough.*

---

nondiscriminatory language Language that treats everyone equally, without making any unwarranted assumptions

Use language that implies equality.

Males may also be the victims of sexist language.

Mention group membership only when it is clearly relevant.

Write from the reader's perspective.

Answer the reader's unspoken question, "What's in it for me?"

interested in how the product will benefit *you* or in how your purchase of the product will benefit the sponsor? If you're like most people reading or hearing a message, your conscious or unconscious reaction is likely to be "What's in it for *me?*" Recognizing this tendency provides you with a powerful strategy for structuring your messages to maximize their impact: Stress the "you" attitude, not the "me" attitude.

The **"you" attitude** emphasizes what the *receiver* (the listener or the reader) wants to know and how he or she will be affected by the message. It requires developing *empathy*—the ability to project yourself into another person's position and to understand that person's situation, feelings, motives, and needs. To avoid sounding selfish and uninterested, focus on the reader—adopt the "you" attitude.

"you" attitude A viewpoint that emphasizes what the reader wants to know and how the reader will be affected by the message

> **NOT:** I am shipping your order this afternoon.
>
> **BUT:** Your order should arrive by Friday.
>
> **NOT:** We will be open on Sundays from 1 to 5 P.M., beginning May 15.
>
> **BUT:** You will be able to shop on Sundays from 1 to 5 P.M., beginning May 15.

reader benefits The advantages a reader would derive from granting the writer's request or from accepting the writer's decision

Reader Benefits   An important component of the "you" attitude is the concept of **reader benefits**—emphasizing how the reader (or the listener) will benefit from doing as you ask. Sometimes, especially when asking a favor or refusing a request, the best we can do is to show how *someone* (not necessarily the reader) will benefit. Whenever possible, however, we should show how someone *other than ourselves* benefits from our request or from our decision.

> **NOT:** We cannot afford to purchase an ad in your organization's directory.
>
> **BUT:** Advertising exclusively on television allows us to offer consumers like you the lowest prices on their cosmetics.
>
> **NOT:** Our decorative fireplace has an oak mantel and is portable.
>
> **BUT:** Whether entertaining in your living room or den, you can still enjoy the ambience of a blazing fire because our decorative fireplace is portable. Simply take it with you from room to room.

Note that the revised sentences, which stress reader benefits, are longer than the original sentences—because they contain *more information*. Yet they are not verbose; that is, they do not contain unnecessary words. You can add information and still write concisely.

Exceptions   Stressing the "you" attitude focuses the attention on the reader, which is right where the attention should be—most of the time. In some situations, however, you may want to avoid focusing on the reader; these situations all involve conveying negative information. When you refuse someone's request, disagree with someone, or talk about someone's mistakes or shortcomings, avoid connecting the reader too closely with the negative information. In such situations, avoid second-person pronouns (*you* and *your*), and use passive sentences or other subordinating techniques to stress the receiver of the action rather than the doer.

In some situations you do not want to focus attention on the reader.

> **NOT:** You should have included more supporting evidence in your presentation.
>
> **BUT:** Including more supporting evidence would have made the presentation more convincing.

NOT: You failed to return the merchandise within the 10-day period.

BUT: We are happy to give a full refund on all merchandise that is returned within 10 days.

Note that neither of the revised sentences contains the word *you*. Thus, they help to separate the reader from the negative information, making the message more tactful and palatable.

Effective Business Writing

Writing style goes beyond *correctness*. Although a document that contains many grammatical, mechanical, or usage errors could hardly be considered effective, a document that contains no such errors might still be ineffective because it lacks style. Style involves choosing the right words, writing effective sentences, developing logical paragraphs, and setting an appropriate overall tone. Checklist 4 summarizes the 15 principles discussed in Chapters 4 and 5.

CHECKLIST 4

Writing with Style

Words

✓ *Write clearly.* Be accurate and complete; use familiar words; avoid dangling expressions and unnecessary jargon.

✓ *Prefer short, simple words.* They are less likely to be misused by the writer and more likely to be understood by the reader.

✓ *Write with vigor.* Use specific, concrete language; avoid clichés, slang, and buzz words.

✓ *Write concisely.* Avoid redundancy, wordy expressions, and hidden subjects and verbs.

✓ *Prefer positive language.* Stress what you *can* do or what *is* true rather than what you cannot do or what is not true.

Sentences

✓ *Use a variety of sentence types.* Use simple sentences for emphasis and variety, compound sentences for coordinate relationships, complex sentences for subordinate relationships, and compound-complex sentences for both coordinate and subordinate relationships. Most sentences should range from 16 to 22 words.

✓ *Use active and passive voice appropriately.* Use active voice in general and to emphasize the doer of the action; use passive voice to emphasize the receiver.

Paragraphs

✓ *Keep paragraphs unified and coherent.* Develop a single idea consistently and logically; use transitional words, pronouns, and repetition when appropriate.

✓ *Use parallel structure.* Match adjectives with adjectives, nouns with nouns, infinitives with infinitives, and so on.

✓ *Control paragraph length.* Use a variety of lengths, although most paragraphs should range from 60 to 80 words.

Overall Tone

✓ *Write confidently.* Avoid sounding self-conscious (by overusing such phrases as "I think" and "I hope"), but also avoid sounding arrogant or presumptuous.

✓ *Use a courteous and sincere tone.* Avoid platitudes, exaggeration, obvious flattery, and expressions of surprise or disbelief.

✓ *Use appropriate emphasis and subordination.* Emphasize and subordinate through the use of sentence structure, position, verb voice, amount of space, language, repetition, and mechanical means.

✓ *Use nondiscriminatory language.* Avoid bias about gender, race, ethnic background, religion, age, sexual orientation, and disabilities.

✓ *Stress the "you" attitude.* Emphasize what the receiver wants to know and how the receiver will be affected by the message; stress reader benefits.

These principles will help you communicate your ideas clearly and effectively. They provide a solid foundation for the higher-order communication skills you will be developing in later chapters. At first, you may find it somewhat difficult and time-consuming to constantly assess your writing according to these criteria. Their importance, however, merits the effort. Soon you will find that you are applying these principles automatically as you compose and revise messages.

CHECKPOINT 5.2

RECALL   Write a capital *T* for true or *F* for false before each statement.

1. ____ "Every nurse supplies her own uniform" would be an example of sexist language.

2. ____ The "you" attitude stresses how the reader is affected by the message.

3. ____ You should never mention a physical or mental disability in business writing.

4. ____ Sometimes you should *not* stress the "you" attitude in business writing.

5. ____ You should never refer to a female by her first name in business writing.

VOCABULARY   Define the following terms in your own words and give an original example of each.

6. reader benefits:

7. nondiscriminatory language:

8. "you" attitude:

COMPREHENSION

9. Revise the following sentences to make them more effective:
   a. The stewardesses served a light snack.

   b. We didn't have the manpower to handle the job.

   c. My girl will set up the appointment.

   d. William Barnwell and Helen attended the conference.

e. The company appeared to be an Indian giver in that deal.

10. Do you feel it is appropriate or inappropriate to use the pronoun *he* as a generic pronoun referring to both males and females (for example, "Each manager must ensure that *he* submits *his* reports on time"). If you feel it is inappropriate, what alternatives are available?

The Writing Process

When faced with a writing task, some people just start writing. They try to do everything at once, figuring out what to say and how to say it, visualizing an audience and a goal, keeping watch on spelling and grammar, and choosing their words and building sentences—all at the same time. It's not easy to keep switching back and forth from one of these distinct writing tasks to another and still make headway. In fact, unless you're an expert writer, it's harder and slower than breaking the job up into steps and completing each step in turn.

The idea of writing step by step may at first sound as if it will prolong the job, but it won't. The step of planning, for example, gives you a sense of where you want to go and that, in turn, makes getting there faster and easier. The clearer you are about your goals, the more likely your writing will accomplish those goals. If you save a separate step for proofreading, that job will also go more smoothly and efficiently. After all, it's difficult to spot a typo while you're still trying to think up the "big ending" for your report.

There is no single "best" writing process. In fact, all good writers develop their own process that suits their unique way of tackling a problem. But one way or another, competent communicators typically perform five steps when faced with a business situation that calls for a written response (see Figure 5.1):

> The writing process consists of planning, drafting, revising, formatting, and proofreading.

1. *Planning:* Determining what the purpose of the message is, who the reader will be, what information you need to give the reader to achieve your purpose, and in what order to present the information.
2. *Drafting:* Composing a first draft of the message.
3. *Revising:* Revising for content, style, and correctness.
4. *Formatting:* Arranging the document in an appropriate format.
5. *Proofreading:* Reviewing the document to check for content, typographical, and format errors.

The amount of time you will devote to each step depends on the complexity, length, and importance of the document. Not all steps may be needed for all writing tasks. Nevertheless, these steps represent a good starting point for completing a writing assignment—either in class or on the job.

Planning

Planning, the first step in writing, involves making conscious decisions about the purpose, audience, content, and organization of the message.

FIGURE 5.1 **The Five Steps in the Writing Process**

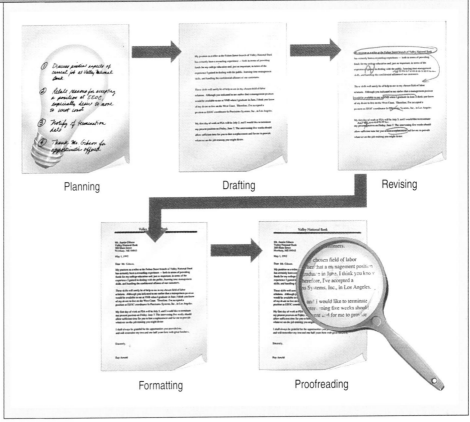

Planning   Drafting   Revising

Formatting   Proofreading

The purpose should be specific enough to serve as a yardstick for judging the success of the message.

Purpose   The first decision relates to the purpose of the message. If you don't know why you're writing the message (that is, if you don't know what you hope to accomplish), then later you'll have no way of knowing whether you've achieved your goal. In the end, what matters is not how well crafted your message was or how attractive it looked on the page; what matters is whether you achieved your communication objective. If you did, your communication was successful; if you did not, it was not.

Most writers find it easier to start with a general purpose and then refine the general purpose into a specific one. The specific purpose should indicate the response desired from the reader.

Assume, for example, that you are a marketing manager at Seaside Resorts, a small chain of hotels along the California, Oregon, and Washington coasts. You have noted that many of the larger hotel chains have instituted "frequent-stay" plans, which, like the frequent-flier programs on which they are modeled, reward repeat customers with free lodging, travel, or merchandise. You want to recommend a similar plan for Seaside Resorts. Your general purpose might be this:

General Purpose: To describe the benefits of a frequent-stay plan at Seaside Resorts.

Such a goal is a good starting point, but it is not specific enough. First, it doesn't identify the intended audience. Are you writing a memo to the vice president of marketing recommending this plan, or are you writing a letter to frequent business travelers recommending that they enroll in this plan? Assume, for the moment, that you're writing to the marketing vice president. What is she supposed to do as a result of reading your memo? Do you want her to simply understand what you've written? Agree with you? Commit resources for further research? Agree to implement the plan immediately? How will you know if your message achieves its objective? Perhaps you decide that your specific purpose is this:

Specific Purpose: To persuade Kiran to approve the development and implementation of a frequent-stay plan for a 12-month test period in Seaside's three Oregon resorts.

Now you have a purpose that's specific enough to guide you as you write the memo and to permit you to judge, in time, whether your message achieved its goal. Having a clear-cut statement of purpose lets you focus on the content and organization, eliminating any distracting information and incorporating all relevant information.

Audience Analysis   To maximize the effectiveness of your message, you should perform an **audience analysis;** that is, you should identify the interests, needs, and personality of your receiver. Recall our discussion of mental filters in Chapter 1. Each person perceives a message differently because of his or her unique mental filter. To reach our audience, we need to determine the level of detail, the language, and the overall tone that would be appropriate.

First, does your audience know you? If not, you must first establish your credibility by assuming a reasonable tone and giving enough evidence to support your claims. Are you writing to someone inside or outside the organization? If outside, your message will often be a little more formal and will contain more background information and less jargon than if you are writing to someone inside the organization.

What does the audience already know? Understanding the audience's present grasp of the topic is crucial to making decisions about content and writing style. You must decide how much background information is necessary, whether the use of jargon is acceptable, and what readability level is appropriate.

What is your status in the organization in relation to your audience? Communications to your superiors are obviously vital to your success in the organization. Such communications are typically somewhat more formal, less authoritarian in tone, and more information-filled than communications to peers or subordinates. In addition, such messages are generally "front-loaded"—that is, they use a direct organizational style and present the major idea in the first paragraph.

How will the audience react? If the reader's initial reaction to both you and your topic is likely to be positive, your job is relatively easy. You can use a direct

A clearly stated purpose helps you avoid including irrelevant and distracting information.

audience analysis The identification of the needs, interests, and personality of the receiver of a communication

Your relationship with the reader determines the tone and content of your message.

Determine how much information the reader needs.

The West Wing **creator and writer Aaron Sorkin completes the writing process week after week for 17 million viewers. "I just want to survive one episode at a time," he said, "so I'm trying to write better—and faster."**

approach—beginning with the most important information (for example, your conclusions or recommendations) and then supplying the needed details.

If the expected reader reaction is negative, present lots of evidence and expert testimony.

Some readers like a direct approach, regardless of the purpose of the message.

The purpose of this memo is to recommend implementing a frequent-stay plan for a 12-month test period in our three Oregon resorts. This recommendation is based on a review of the policies of our competitors and on an analysis of the costs and benefits of instituting such a program. The pertinent data is presented below.

Suppose, however, that you expect your reader's reaction—either to your topic or to you personally—to be negative. Now you have a real sales job to do. If the reader shows a personal dislike of you, your best strategy is to call on external evidence and expert opinion to bolster your position. Show that others, especially people whom the reader is likely to know and respect, share your opinions. Use courteous, conservative language, and suggest ways the reader can cooperate without appearing to "give in"—perhaps by reminding the reader that new circumstances and new information call for new strategies.

If you anticipate that your reader will oppose your proposal, your best strategy is to supply extra evidence. Instead of one example, give two or three. Instead of quoting one external source, quote several. Begin with the areas of agreement, stress reader benefits, and try to anticipate and answer any objections the reader might have. Through logic, evidence, and tone, build your case for the reasonableness of your position.

Establish credibility by showing the basis for your recommendations.

To gather the needed data, I studied published reports prepared by the Hotel and Restaurant Association. Then, I interviewed the person in charge of frequent-stay programs at three hotels. Finally, Dr. Kenneth Lowe, professor of hospitality services at Southern Cal, reviewed and commented on my first draft. Thus, this proposal is based on a large body of data collected over two months.

Do not start writing until you have planned what you want to say.

Content   Once you have determined the purpose of your message and identified the needs and interests of your audience, the next step is to decide what information to include. For some letters and simple memos, this step presents few problems. Other communication tasks require numerous decisions about what to include. How much background information is needed? What statistical data best support the conclusions? Is expert opinion needed? Would examples, anecdotes,

The need for audience analysis is nothing new to Marion Nestle, author of *Food Politics*. When she served on the commission that crafted the *Surgeon General's Report on Nutrition and Health*, she was told point-blank that the report could not recommend that Americans eat less meat, lest it upset the meat industy.

or graphics aid comprehension? Will research be necessary, or do you have what you need at hand?

The trick is to include enough information so that you don't lose or confuse the reader, yet avoid including irrelevant material that wastes the reader's time and obscures the important data. Different writers use different methods for identifying what information is needed. Some simply jot down notes on the points they plan to cover. For all but the simplest communications, the one thing you should *not* do is to start drafting immediately, deciding as you write what information to include. Instead, start with at least a rough outline of your message—whether it's in your head, in a well-developed typed outline, or in the form of notes on a piece of scratch paper.

Organization The final step in the planning process is to establish the **organization** of the message—that is, to determine in what order you will discuss each topic. After you have outlined your ideas around a main idea, you need to organize them into an outline that you can use to draft your message into its most effective form.

organization The sequence in which topics are discussed in a message

Classification (grouping related ideas) is the first step in organizing your message. Once you've grouped related ideas, you then need to differentiate between the major and minor points so that you can line up minor ideas and evidence to support the major ideas.

The most effective sequence for the major ideas often depends on the reaction you expect from your audience. If you expect a positive response, you may decide to use a direct approach, in which the conclusion or major idea is presented first, followed by the reasons. If you expect a negative response, you may decide to use an indirect approach, in which the reasons are presented first and the conclusion later.

To maintain good human relations, base your organization on the expected reader reaction.

Because of the importance of the sequence in which topics are discussed, the recommended organization of each specific type of communication is discussed in detail in the chapters that follow. (See also Chapter 4's extensive coverage of paragraph unity, coherence, and length—all of which are important elements of organization.)

Drafting

Having finished planning, you are finally ready to begin **drafting**—that is, composing a preliminary version of a message. The success of this second stage of the writing process depends on the attention you devoted to the first stage. The warning given earlier bears repeating: Don't begin writing too soon. Some people believe they have weak writing skills; when faced with a writing task, their first impulse is therefore to jump in and get it over with as quickly as possible. Avoid the rush. Go through each of the five steps of the writing process to ease the journey and improve the product.

drafting Composing a preliminary version of a document

Probably the most important thing to remember about drafting is to just let go—let your ideas flow as quickly as possible onto paper or computer screen, without worrying about style, correctness, or format. Separate the drafting stage from the revising stage. Although some people revise as they create, most find it easier to first get their ideas down on paper in rough-draft form, then revise. It's much easier to polish a page full of writing than a page full of *nothing*.

Do not combine drafting and revising. They involve two separate skills and two separate mind sets.

So avoid moving from author to editor too quickly. Your first draft is just that—a *draft*. Don't expect perfection, and don't strive for it. Concentrate, instead, on recording in narrative form all the points you identified in the planning stage. When you have finished drafting and then begin to revise your work, you will likely discover that a surprising amount of your first draft is usable and will be included in your final draft.

Revising

Revising is the process of modifying a document to increase its effectiveness. With the raw material—your first draft—in front of you, you can now refine it into the most effective document possible, considering its importance and the time constraints under which you are working. If possible, put your draft away for a period of time—the longer, the better. Leaving time between creation and revision helps distance you from your writing. If you revise your document immediately, the memory of what you "meant to say" rather than what you actually wrote may be so strong that it keeps you from spotting weaknesses in logic or diction.

If you're a typical writer, you will have made numerous minor revisions while you were composing; however, as noted earlier, you should save the major revisions until later. For important writing projects, you will probably want to solicit comments about your draft from colleagues as part of the revision process.

Although we have discussed revising as the third step of the writing process, it actually involves several separate steps. Most writers revise first for content, then for style, and finally for correctness. All types of revision are most efficiently done from a typed copy of the draft rather than from a handwritten copy.

Revising for Content   After an appropriate time interval, first reread your purpose statement and then the entire draft to get an overview of your message. Ask yourself such questions as the following:

- Is the content appropriate for the purpose I've identified?
- Will the purpose of the message be clear to the reader?
- Have I been sensitive to the needs of the reader?
- Is all the information necessary?
- Is any needed information missing?
- Is the order of presentation of the points effective?

Although it is natural to have a certain pride of authorship in your draft document, don't be afraid to make any changes necessary to strengthen your document—even if it means striking out whole sections and starting again from scratch. The aim is to produce a revised document in which you can take even more pride.

Revise for content, style, and correctness.

Revising for Style   Next, read each paragraph again (aloud, if possible), using the 15 criteria in Checklist 4 on page 121 as the basis for your evaluation. Reading aloud gives you a feel for the rhythm and flow of your writing. Long sentences that made sense as you wrote them may leave you out of breath when you read them aloud.

If time permits and the importance of the document merits it, try reading your message aloud to friends or colleagues, or have them read your revised draft. Ask them what is clear or unclear. Can they identify the purpose of your message? What kind of image do they get of the writer from reading the message? Adhering to Checklist 4 and securing feedback from colleagues will help you identify areas of your message that need revision.

Revising for Correctness   The final phase of revising is **editing,** the process of ensuring that writing conforms to standard English. Editing involves checking for correctness—that is, identifying problems with grammar, spelling, punctuation, word usage, and the like. You may want to use your word processor's grammar checker as a starting point for editing. The editing step should follow the revision step because there is no need to correct minor errors in passages that may later be modified or deleted. Writers who fail to check for grammar, mechanical, and usage errors risk losing credibility with their readers. Such errors may distract readers, delay comprehension, cause misunderstandings, and reflect negatively on the writer's abilities.

CHECKLIST 5

The Writing Process

Planning

✓ Determine the purpose of the message.
  a. Make it as specific as possible.
  b. Identify the type of response desired from the reader.

✓ Analyze the audience.
  a. Identify the audience and your relationship with this person.
  b. Determine how the audience will probably react.
  c. Determine how much the audience already knows about the topic.

✓ Determine what information to include in the message, given its purpose and your analysis of the audience.

✓ Organize the information in a logical sequence.

Drafting

✓ Let your ideas flow as quickly as possible, without worrying about style, correctness, or format. If helpful, write the easiest parts first.

✓ Do not expect a perfect first draft; avoid the urge to revise at this stage.

✓ If possible, leave a time gap between writing and revising the draft.

Revising

✓ Revise for content: determine whether all information is necessary, whether any needed information has been omitted, and whether the content has been presented in an appropriate sequence.

✓ Revise for style: follow the guidelines in Checklist 4 (see page 121).

✓ Revise for correctness: use correct grammar, mechanics, punctuation, and word choice.

Formatting

✓ Format the document according to commonly used standards (see the Style Manual).

Proofreading

✓ Proofread for content errors, typographical errors, and format errors.

All three types of revision—for content, style, and correctness—can be accomplished most efficiently on a computer.

You can write faster and revise much faster on a computer than in longhand.

Formatting

Letters are external documents that are sent to people outside the organization. Memos are internal documents that are sent to people inside the same organization as the writer. Today, most traditional paper-based memos have been replaced by email. Email messages and reports may be either internal or external. No one format for any type of business document is universally accepted as standard; a fair amount of variation is common in industry. Detailed guidelines for the most common formatting standards are presented in the Style Manual at the back of the book.

Regardless of who actually types your documents, *you* are the one who signs and submits them, so *you* must accept responsibility for not only the content but also the mechanics, format, and appearance of your documents. In addition, the increasing use of word processing means that executives now keyboard many of their own documents—without the help of an assistant.

Another advantage of standard formatting is simply that it is more efficient. Formatting documents the same way each time means that you do not need to make individual layout decisions for every document. Thus, a standard format not only saves time but also gives a consistent appearance to the organization's documents.

Finally, readers *expect* to find certain information in certain positions in a document. If the information is missing, the reader may be unnecessarily distracted. For all these reasons, you should become familiar with the standard conventions for formatting documents.

Proofreading

Proofreading is the final quality-control check for your document. Proofread for content, typographical, and format errors. Remember that a reader may not know whether an incorrect word resulted from a simple typo or from the writer's ignorance of correct usage. Being almost perfect is not good enough; for example, if your telephone directory were only 99% perfect, each page would contain about four wrong numbers!

Don't depend on an assistant to catch and correct every mistake; become a "super blooper snooper" yourself. After all, it's your reputation that is at stake. Take responsibility for ensuring the accuracy of your communications, just as you take responsibility for completing your other tasks.

Finally, after planning, drafting, revising, formatting, and proofreading your document (see Checklist 5 on page 129), transmit it—confident and satisfied that you have taken all reasonable steps to ensure that it achieves its objectives.

CHECKPOINT 5.3

RECALL   Write a capital *T* for true or *F* for false before each statement.

1. ____ Everyone should follow the same specific process when creating a written message.

2. ____ Editing is one stage of the revision step.

3. ____ The step of proofreading should come *after* the revision and formatting steps.

4. ____ Drafting and revising involve two separate skills and two separate mind sets.

5. ____ Email messages are internal documents sent to people inside the same organization as the writer.

VOCABULARY   Define the following terms in your own words.

6. audience analysis:

7. drafting:

8. editing:

9. organization:

10. revising:

COMPREHENSION

11. Write a general purpose and a specific purpose for a situation in which you complain about the poor condition of a FedEx package you received yesterday.

    a. General purpose:

    b. Specific purpose:

12. Assume that you have jotted down the following points you want to include in your letter to FedEx. Number the points in the order that you think will help you achieve your purpose.

    a. ____ Provide needed details about the problem

    b. ____ Tell what remedy you want

    c. ____ Identify the problem

    d. ____ Close on a positive note

    e. ____ Describe how you were inconvenienced

CRITICAL THINKING

13. Most word processing programs provide a grammar and spelling checker that flags many types of grammatical and mechanical errors. To what extent do you believe you can trust such tools?

Summary

Competent communicators achieve their objectives by writing with confidence, courtesy, and sincerity. They recognize that not all ideas are equally important, and they use techniques of emphasis and subordination to develop a common frame of reference between writer and reader. They use nondiscriminatory language in their writing by treating everyone equally and by not making unwarranted assumptions about any group of people. They also keep the emphasis on the reader—stressing what the reader needs to know and how the reader will be affected by the message.

The writing process consists of a series of steps designed to produce written messages in an effective and efficient manner. The five steps involve planning, drafting, revising, formatting, and proofreading the message (as summarized in Checklist 5 on page 129).

The amount of time devoted to each step depends on the complexity, length, and importance of the document. Not all steps may be needed for each document, the steps don't necessarily have to come in order, and one step doesn't always have to be completed before the next one begins. However, you would be well advised to follow each step conscientiously and carefully in the beginning. Then, after gaining experience and confidence, you can adapt the process to develop a writing routine that is most effective and efficient for you personally.

Writing an Unbiased Message

Problem

As chair of your company's employee grievance committee, you must approve the minutes of each meeting before they are distributed. Following is the draft of a paragraph from the minutes that the secretary has forwarded for your approval:

> Mr. Timmerman argued that the 62-year-old Kathy Bevier should be replaced because she doesn't dress appropriately for her seamstress position in the alteration department. However, the human resources director, who is female, countered that we don't pay any of the girls in the alteration department well enough for them to buy appropriate attire. Mr. Timmerman did acknowledge that the seamstress performs her job well, considering her age and the fact that she suffers from arthritis. He added that he just wished she would dress more businesslike instead of wearing the colorful clothes and makeup that reflect her immigrant background.

Process

1. List any examples of gender bias contained in this paragraph.

   - "Mr. Timmerman" versus "Kathy Bevier"
   - "seamstress"
   - "who is female"
   - "any of the girls"

2. Are there examples of age bias?

   - "62-year-old"
   - "considering her age"

3. Are there instances of other discriminatory biases that you would want to correct?

   - Disability bias: "suffers from arthritis"

   - Nationality bias: "colorful clothes and makeup that reflect her immigrant background"

The 3Ps
Problem, Process, Product

Ralph Timmerman argued that Kathy Bevier should be replaced because she doesn't dress appropriately for her sewing position in the alteration department. However, the human resources director countered that we don't pay these employees well enough for them to buy appropriate attire. Timmerman acknowledged that Bevier performs her job well. He added that he just wished she would dress more businesslike.

Product

Looking Ahead

Consider the effectiveness of the following sentence:

> Gerald Barak and Mercedes gave me this advice listen politely to his advice then follow your own well thought out plans.

This run-on sentence doesn't make much sense as it is written, does it? Or, to be more precise, it doesn't make much sense as it is *punctuated*. However, with the correct punctuation, the sentence makes perfectly good sense:

> Gerald, Barak, and Mercedes gave me this advice: Listen politely to his advice; then follow your own well-thought-out plans.

You'll learn how to punctuate your writing correctly in Chapter 6.

Key Terms

audience analysis
drafting
editing
nondiscriminatory language
organization

platitude
reader benefits
revising
tone
"you" attitude

Exercises

What Do We Mean by Style?

❶ Writing Confidently   Revise the following sentences and paragraph to convey an appropriately confident attitude.

a. Can you think of any reason not to buy a wristwatch for dressy occasions?
b. I hope you agree that my offer provides good value for the money.
c. Of course, I am confident that my offer provides good value for the money.
d. You might try to find a few minutes to visit our gallery on your next visit to galleries in this area.
e. If you believe my proposal has merit, I hope that you will allocate $50,000 for a pilot study. It's possible that this pilot study will bear out my profit estimates so that we can proceed on a permanent basis. Even though you have several other worthwhile projects to consider for funding, I know you will agree the proposal should be funded prior to January 1. Please call me before the end of the week to tell me that you've accepted my proposal.

❷ Using a Courteous and Sincere Tone   Revise the following paragraph to make it more courteous and sincere.

> You, our loyal and dedicated employees, have always been the most qualified and the most industrious in the industry. Because of your faithful and dependable service, I was quite surprised to learn yesterday that an organizational

meeting for union representation was recently held here. You must realize that a company like ours cannot survive unless we hold labor costs down. I cannot believe that you don't appreciate the many benefits of working at Allied. We will immediately have to declare bankruptcy if a union is voted in. Please don't be fooled by empty rhetoric.

3 Using Techniques of Emphasis Revise each sentence by applying the indicated technique of emphasis. In each case, emphasize the problems of cold weather.

a. Use one complex sentence.

Outdoor workers in White Butte, North Dakota, have to battle severe winter conditions. However, outdoor workers in Atlanta, Georgia, face mild winter conditions.

b. Choose the noun you want to emphasize as the subject of the sentence.

Telephone and utility repair personnel who work outdoors have to cope with dangerous working conditions created by subzero temperatures.

c. Use language that directly implies importance.

Outdoor workers generally face a range of weather conditions, but frigid temperatures can pose particularly severe problems.

d. Use repetition.

Utilities in the northern states frequently remind outdoor workers about the cold-weather dangers of frostbite and hypothermia.

4 Using Appropriate Emphasis and Subordination Assume that you have evaluated two candidates for the position of sales assistant. This is what you have learned:

a. Herbert Garcia has more sales experience.
b. Marcia Ford has more appropriate formal training (a college degree in marketing, attendance at several three-week sales seminars, and the like).
c. Marcia Ford's personality appears to mesh more closely with the prevailing corporate attitudes at your firm.

You must write a memo to Jordan Gardner, the company's vice president, recommending one of these candidates. First, assume that personality is the most important criterion and write a memo recommending Marcia Ford. Second, assume that experience is the most important criterion and write a memo recommending Herbert Garcia. Use appropriate emphasis and subordination in each message. You may make up any reasonable information needed to complete the assignment.

5 Using Nondiscriminatory Language Revise the following sentences to eliminate discriminatory language.

a. The mayor opened contract talks with the union representing local policemen.
b. While the salesmen are at the convention, their wives will be treated to a tour of the city's landmarks.
c. Our company gives each foreman the day off on his birthday.
d. Our public relations director, Aurelia Gordon, will ask her young secretary, Teresa Moretti, to take notes during the president's speech.
e. Both Dr. Marcos and his assistant, Terry Derek, attended the new-product seminar.

6 Stressing the "You" Attitude Revise the following paragraph to emphasize the "you" attitude.

> We are happy to announce that we are offering for sale an empty parcel of land at the corner of Mission and High Streets. We will be selling this parcel for $189,500, with a minimum down payment of $22,500. We have had the lot rezoned M-2 for student housing. We originally purchased this lot because of its proximity to the university and had planned to erect student housing, but our investment plans have changed. We still feel that our lot would make a profitable site for up to three 12-unit buildings.

7 Stressing Reader Benefits Revise the following sentences to emphasize reader benefits.

a. We have been in the business of repairing sewing machines for more than 40 years.
b. We need donations so we can expand the free-food program in this community.
c. Company policy requires us to impose a 2% late charge when customers don't pay their bills on time.
d. Although the refund department is open from 9 A.M. to 5 P.M., it is closed from 1 P.M. to 2 P.M. so our employees can take their lunch breaks.

The Writing Process

8 Communication Purpose Compose a specific goal for each of the following communication tasks:

a. An email to a professor asking him to change a grade
b. A letter to MasterCard about an incorrect charge
c. A letter to the president of a local bank thanking her for speaking at your student organization meeting
d. A memo of reprimand to a subordinate for leaving the warehouse unlocked overnight
e. A letter to a state senator about a proposed state surcharge on college tuition
f. An email to your payroll department head about an incorrect paycheck
g. A letter to the college newspaper discussing the quality of the cafeteria food in recent months
h. An email to your assistant asking about the status of an overdue report

9 Audience Analysis Assume you must write an email message to your current business communication professor, asking him or her to let you take your final examination one week early so that you can attend your cousin's wedding.

a. Perform an audience analysis of your professor. List everything you know about this professor that might help you compose an effective message.
b. Write two good opening sentences for this message, the first assuming that you are an A student who has missed class only once this term and the second assuming that you are a C student who has missed class six times this term.

10 Audience Analysis Revisited Now assume the role of the professor (see Exercise 9) who must reply to the request of the student with the C grade who has missed class six times. You'll tell the student that you are not willing to schedule an early exam.

a. Perform an audience analysis of yourself (as the student). What do you know about yourself that would help the professor write an effective message?
b. Should the professor use a direct or an indirect organization? Why?
c. Write the first sentence of the professor's message.

11 **Organizing**   Assume that you plan to write a letter to your state senator about a proposed state surcharge on college tuition fees. Determine a specific purpose, and then brainstorm at least six facts, ideas, and questions you might want to raise in your letter. Next, decide which are major points and which are minor points. Once you've selected either a direct or an indirect organization, arrange the items on your list in logical order.

12 **Drafting**   Building on the process of brainstorming and organizing in Exercise 11, draft the letter to your legislator.

a. Write the specific purpose at the top of your blank page.
b. Write the easiest part of the letter first. With which part did you start? Why?
c. Continue to draft the remaining sections of the letter. In what order did you complete your letter? Why?
d. Did you use every fact, question, or idea on your list? Explain your choices.

Submit your letter, along with your responses to the questions, to your instructor.

13 **Work-Team Communication**   You will work in groups of four for this assignment. Assume that a large shopping center is located next to your campus and that many day students park there for free while attending classes. The shopping center management is considering closing this lot to student use, citing the need for additional space for customer parking. The four members of your group represent four student organizations (a sorority, a fraternity, a business student organization, and a campus service organization), which have decided to write a joint letter to the manager of the shopping center, trying to convince him to maintain the status quo.

Following the five-step process outlined in this chapter, compose a one-page letter to the manager. Brainstorm to generate ideas for the content of the letter; have each member of the group call out possible points to include while one person writes down all the ideas. Don't evaluate the ideas until you have worked for 10 to 15 minutes. Then discuss each point and decide which ones to include and in what order.

Format your letter in block style (see the Style Manual at the back of this text). Address it to Mr. Marcos Harris, Executive Manager, Fairview Shopping Center, P.O. Box 1083, DeKalb, IL 60115.

14 **Revising**   Bring in a one-page composition you have written in the past—an essay exam response, business letter, one page of a report, or the like. Make sure your name is *not* on the paper. Exchange papers among several colleagues (so that you are not revising the paper of the person who is revising your own paper) and complete the following revision tasks:

a. Read the paper once, revising for content. Make sure that all needed information is included, no unneeded information is included, and the information is presented in a logical sequence.
b. Read the paper a second time, revising for style. Make sure that the words, sentences, paragraphs, and overall tone are appropriate.
c. Read the paper a third time, revising for correctness. Make sure that grammar, mechanics, punctuation, and word choice are error-free.

Return the paper to the writer. Then, using the revisions of your paper as a guide only (after all, *you* are the author), prepare a final version of the page. Submit both the marked-up version and the final version of your paper to your instructor.

⑮ Proofreading   Assume that you are Michael Land and you wrote and typed the following letter. Proofread the letter, using the line numbers to indicate the position of each error. Proofread for content, typographical errors, and format. For each error, indicate by a *yes* or *no* whether a computer's spelling checker would have identified the error. *(Hint:* Can you find 30 content, typographical, or format errors?)

1 April 31 2004

2 Mr. Thomas Johnson, Manger

3 JoAnn @ Friends, Inc.
4 1323 Charleston Avenue
5 Minneapolis, MI 55402

6 Dear Mr. Thomas:

7 As a writing consultant, I have often aksed aud-
8 iences to locate all teh errors in this letter.
9 I am allways surprized if the find all the errors.
10 The result being that we all need more practical
11 advise in how to proof read.
12 To aviod these types of error, you must ensure that
13 that you review your documents carefully. I have
14 prepared the enclosed exercises for each of you
15 to in your efforts at JoAnne & Freinds, Inc.

16 Would you be wiling to try this out on you own
17 workers and let me know the results.

18 Sincerly Yours

19 Mr. Michael Land,
20 Writing Consultant

Portfolio Project 1

Writing an Informational Message

This exercise is the first of eight portfolio projects that will provide you with actual evidence to demonstrate your communication competence to potential employers. The forms for these projects and blank letterheads are available on the Web at http://*business.college.hmco.com*. See the sample portfolio project shown in Figure 5.2. The project is shown at the left, and the student's finished document is shown at the right.

PROBLEM You are the head of the catalog sales department of Branford's, a large department store located in Albuquerque, New Mexico. Most of your 17 full-time employees are high school graduates, and many of them are female. For beginning workers, you pay $2.50 per hour over the minimum wage, plus fringe benefits. Send a message to your employees

---

FIGURE 5.2 Sample Portfolio Project

PORTFOLIO PROJECT

ROUTINE RESPONSE TO A REQUEST FOR PRODUCT INFORMATION

PROBLEM

As the assistant business manager for Maison Richard, a 200-seat restaurant in Seattle, you received an inquiry from Chris Shearing, 1926 Second Avenue, Seattle, WA 98101. She had several questions about the meat and fish served in your restaurant. Here are her questions and your answers.

  a. *Are the cattle from which your beef comes allowed to roam freely on an open range instead of being fattened in cramped feedlots?* No, allowing free-roaming would increase the muscle tissue in the beef, making it less tender.
  b. *Are the cattle fed antibiotics and hormones?* Yes, to ensure a healthy animal and to promote faster growth.
  c. *Do your trout come from lakes and streams?* No, they're farm-grown, which is more economical and results in less disease.

Ms. Shearing is a well-known animal-rights activist, and you want to present your case as positively as possible to avoid the loss of her goodwill and any negative publicity that might result. Respond to her letter, supplying whatever other appropriate information you feel is reasonable.

PROCESS

I decided to use a direct organizational plan for this letter because it was a routine reply to a routine request for product information. I used a descriptive subject line and direct opening paragraph to set the stage for my comments.

Most of the answers to Ms. Shearing's questions are probably not what she wanted to hear. Thus, I took pains to explain the reasons for our decisions and to avoid using negative language. The reasons show how people other than Maison Richard (for example, our customers and employees) benefit from our decision. The "you" approach is stressed throughout.

Finally, I closed on a positive, confident note, assuming that I had answered all of her questions in a satisfactory manner.

I formatted the letter in standard block style and did not include reference initials, because I typed my own letter.

PRODUCT

The document follows on the next page.

CERTIFICATION

I certify that this document was composed and formatted by this student.

Jorge Corey
Student   _April 10, 20—_
                                          Date
Virginia Perkins
Instructor   _April 15, 20_
                                          Date

OBER, FUNDAMENTALS OF CONTEMPORARY BUSINESS COMMUNICATION. COPYRIGHT © HOUGHTON MIFFLIN COMPANY. ALL RIGHTS RESERVED.   HANDOUT **5.0**

Maison Richard   WORLD TRADE CENTER, SEATTLE, WA 98100
                                          PHONE: 317-555-1083. WEB: HTTP://MAISONRICHARD

October 8, 20--

Ms. Chris Shearing
1926 Second Avenue
Seattle, WA 98101

Dear Ms. Shearing:

Subject: Your Inquiry of October 1, 20--

I am happy to provide you with the information you requested about our restaurant. You will be pleased to know that we purchase only top-quality government-inspected meat, fish, and fowl.

The U.S. Department of Agriculture provides strict guidelines for meat products. Most cattle today are raised in specially designed lots that are cleaned daily to ensure animal and human health. Also, to ensure healthy animals and promote faster growth, antibiotics and hormones that have been approved safe for both animals and humans are fed to the animals. The highest-quality beef, in demand by beef consumers in stores as well as by top restaurants such as ours, is produced this way.

The trout we serve in our restaurant is grown on a farm, where careful monitoring of water and other conditions results in less disease. This process provides a safer, higher-quality product for our customers.

I am pleased to answer your questions about the food we serve and look forward to seeing you soon at Maison Richard.

Sincerely,

Ima Student
Assistant Business Manager

OBER, FUNDAMENTALS OF CONTEMPORARY BUSINESS COMMUNICATION. COPYRIGHT © HOUGHTON MIFFLIN COMPANY. ALL RIGHTS RESERVED.   HANDOUT **5.0**

informing them that management has decided that no one can take vacation or personal days during the months of November and December. The reason, of course, is that the holiday season is your busiest sales period.

PROCESS   Compose a few paragraphs describing how you went about solving this problem. In narrative form, provide such information as the following:

1. What is the purpose of your message?

2. Describe your audience.

3. Will you use a direct or an indirect organizational plan? (What is your audience's likely reaction to this memo?)

4. What reasons can you give for your decision?

5. How can you stress the "you" attitude and use positive language to explain the reasons for this decision?

6. Will you format this document as a letter or memo? Why?

PRODUCT   Compose your document, following the five steps in the writing process (planning, drafting, revising, formatting, and proofreading). Format the final version on letterhead stationery (refer to the Style Manual at the back of the book for formatting guidelines).

6

Business-Style Punctuation

COMMUNICATION OBJECTIVES

After you have finished this chapter, you should be able to use correctly the following marks of punctuation:

- Commas
- Semicolons
- Colons
- Periods
- Parentheses
- Quotation marks
- Italics (underscores)
- Hyphens
- Apostrophes

On the Job

ALMA SANCHEZ
Administrative Assistant,
Recycled Paper Products

Alma hit the foot pedal of her dictation unit to rewind the last bit of dictation she heard from Mr. Yu. Here's what she heard—and it still made no sense:

> I then interviewed the director of public affairs Ms. Florence B. Glashan Mr. Michael McGinty the vice president for marketing Mr. Arch Davis and Mrs. Katie Hollister.

Alma wondered exactly how many people Mr. Yu interviewed. Four? Six? Who is the vice president for marketing—Mr. McGinty or Mr. Davis? Only Mr. Yu knew how many were interviewed and their titles. After conferring with her superior, Alma was able to transcribe the sentence with proper punctuation:

> I then interviewed the director of public affairs; Ms. Florence B. Glashan; Mr. Michael McGinty, the vice president for marketing; Mr. Arch Davis; and Mrs. Katie Hollister.

Now it was clear that Mr. Yu interviewed five people, one of whom was Mr. McGinty, the vice president for marketing. As this sentence illustrates, too many commas can put the reader in a comma coma—creating the need for the punctuation rules discussed in this chapter.

Why Punctuation?

Punctuation serves as a roadmap to help guide the reader through the twists and turns of your message—pointing out what is important (italics or underscores), subordinate (commas), copied from another source (quotation marks), explained further (colon), considered as a unit (hyphens), and the like.

Sometimes correct punctuation is absolutely essential for comprehension. Consider, for example, the different meanings of the following sentences, depending on the placement of the comma:

Our new model comes in red, green and brown, and white.
Our new model comes in red, green, and brown and white.

While he was walking his dog, Benjamin Franklin got lost.
While he was walking his dog Benjamin, Franklin got lost.

The award went to Maritza, and Carl and Uang protested.
The award went to Maritza and Carl, and Uang protested.

We must still play Michigan, which tied Ohio State, and Minnesota.
We must still play Michigan, which tied Ohio State and Minnesota.

You already know much about punctuation. For example, you already know to end a statement with a period and a question with a question mark. In this chapter, you will learn the most common uses of punctuation in narrative business writing. You should learn these punctuation rules thoroughly because you will use them frequently.

Commas

We start our discussion of punctuation with the comma—the most commonly used mark of punctuation. The punctuation rules presented in this chapter do not cover every possible situation. Comprehensive style manuals, for example, routinely give more than 100 rules for using the comma rather than just the 10 rules presented here (the use of commas with numbers is covered in Chapter 15). These 10 rules cover the most common uses of the comma.

Commas Used *Between* Expressions

Three types of expressions (words or groups of words) typically require commas between them: independent clauses, adjacent adjectives, and items in a series.

, ind

An independent clause can stand alone as a complete sentence.

Rule 1. Independent Clauses   Use a comma between two independent clauses joined by a coordinate conjunction.

Norma discussed last month's performance, and Rosa presented the sales projections.

The meeting was running late, but Ernesto was in no hurry to adjourn.

Recall from Chapter 3 that the major coordinate conjunctions are *and, but, or,* and *nor.* Also recall from Chapter 3 that an independent clause is a subject–predicate combination that can stand alone as a complete sentence.

Do not confuse two independent clauses joined by a coordinate conjunction and a comma with a compound predicate, whose verbs are *not* separated by a comma. *Hint:* Cover up the conjunction with your pencil. If what's on both sides of your pencil could stand alone as complete sentences, a comma is needed.

NO COMMA: Carla had read the report but had not discussed it with her colleagues. (*"Had not discussed it with her colleagues" is not an independent clause; it lacks a subject.*)

COMMA: Carla had read the report, but she had not discussed it with her colleagues.

Exception: If the sentence containing two independent clauses is quite short (say, 10 words or fewer) and no confusion results, omit the comma before the conjunctions *and* or *or* (but not before the conjunction *but*).

I typed_and she proofread.

BUT: I typed, but she proofread.

The firm hadn't paid_and John was angry.

Rule 2. Adjacent Adjectives   Use a comma between two adjacent adjectives   **, adj**
that modify the same noun.

He was an aggressive, unpleasant manager.

BUT: He was an aggressive_and unpleasant manager. (*The two adjectives are not adjacent; they are separated by the conjunction "and."*)

Do not use a comma if the first adjective modifies the combined idea of the second adjective plus the noun. *Hint:* Mentally insert the word "and" between the two consecutive adjectives. If it does not make sense, do not use a comma.

Please order a new bulletin board for the executive_conference room.

BUT: Please order a new, larger bulletin board for the executive conference room.

The Sounds of Silence   WORD|wise

All 26 letters of the alphabet are silent in at least one word:

a. bread
b. doubt
c. yacht
d. edge
e. height
f. halfpenny
g. reign
h. ghost
i. seize
j. marijuana
k. knob
l. would
m. mnemonic
n. column
o. tortoise
p. receipt
q. racquet
r. chevalier
s. debris
t. gourmet
u. dough
v. fivepence
w. answer
x. faux pas
y. crayon
z. rendezvous

Short compound sentences do not need a comma.

In the first sentence, *new* modifies *bulletin board*; you would not say "new and bulletin board." Similarly, *executive* modifies *conference room*; you would not say "executive and conference room.") In the second sentence, you could say "new and larger bulletin board"; hence, we use the comma.

, ser   **Rule 3. Items in a Series**   Use a comma between each item in a series of three or more. *(Do not use a comma after the last item in the series.)*

The committee may meet on Wednesday, Thursday, or Friday_of next week.

Carlota wrote the questionnaire, Vernon distributed the forms, and Louis tabulated the results_for our survey on employee satisfaction.

Planning the agenda, preparing the handouts, and appointing a secretary_are the three jobs left to complete.

Some style manuals indicate that the last comma before the conjunction is optional. However, to avoid ambiguity in business writing, insert this comma.

NOT: We were served salads, macaroni and cheese and crackers.

BUT: We were served salads, macaroni and cheese, and crackers.

OR: We were served salads, macaroni, and cheese and crackers.

Commas Used *After* Expressions

An introductory expression is a word, phrase, or clause that comes before the subject and verb of the independent clause. Introductory expressions typically require commas after them.

, intro   **Rule 4. Introductory Expressions**   Use a comma after an introductory expression. (When the same expression occurs at the end of the sentence, no comma is used.)

No, the status report is not ready. (*introductory word*)

Well, I'm not so sure of that.

Look, our company is as guilty as everyone else.

Of course, you are not required to sign the petition. (*introductory phrase*)

As a matter of fact, Carmela was instrumental in successfully defending the countersuit.

In the first place, we were not ready for the audit.

To do that, you will need the cooperation of the accounting department.

When the status report is ready, I shall call you. (*introductory clause*)

BUT: I shall call you when the status report is ready.

I'm happy to do that, but if you're not willing to do so, we will need to try something else. ("*If you're not willing to do so*" *is an introductory clause for the second independent clause.*)

James wanted us to know that if we insisted, he would attend the conference in Atlanta. ("*If we insisted*" *is an introductory clause for the dependent clause.*)

Do not use a comma between the subject and verb—no matter how long or complex the subject is.

To finish that boring and time-consuming task in time for the monthly sales meeting was a major challenge.

The effort to bring all of our products into compliance with ISO standards and to be eligible for sales in European Union countries required a full year of detailed planning.

COMPREHENSION   Insert any needed commas in the following sentences. In the space at the left of each sentence, indicate the reason for the comma (, *ind* or , *adj* or , *ser* or , *intro*). If the sentence needs no commas, write *C* in the space provided.

CHECKPOINT 6.1

1. At the sales manager's specific direction we are extending store hours until 7 P.M.

2. Ms. Long has prepared numerous reports news releases and sales presentations.

3. I will attend the conference in August and let you know what happens.

4. You may make the slides yourself or you may request assistance from audiovisual services.

5. Fernando hopes to get the figures to you soon but cannot promise delivery by a certain date.

6. Mr. Dunn gave a concise reasoned explanation of the process.

7. To do your job well will require a major time commitment.

8. Identifying prospects qualifying them and determining their preferences will consume most of the afternoon.

9. I agree with you but do not feel such drastic action is necessary.

10. A noun that comes before a nonrestrictive expression is followed by a comma but one that comes before a restrictive expression is not.

11. Arlene drove and I navigated.

12. Hart-Davis used compression bandages and so on to staunch the bleeding.

13. To end the quarter with a small surplus is the major goal for the division.

14. To end the quarter with a small surplus, we must reduce costs by at least 8%.

15. His attempt to conceal his role in the cover-up of the savings-and-loan scandal was not successful.

16. By working hard we gained approval to hold our conference in Phoenix.

17. We gained approval to hold our conference in Phoenix by working hard.

18. To do your job well you will require some assistance from another department.

Commas Used *Before* and *After* Expressions

restrictive expression An expression needed to complete the meaning of the sentence

Numerous types of expressions typically require commas before *and* after them. (Of course, if one of these expression comes at the beginning of a sentence, use a comma only after the expression; if it comes at the end of a sentence, use a comma only before.)

, nonr

nonrestrictive expression An expression not needed to complete the meaning of the sentence

Rule 5. Nonrestrictive Expressions   Use commas before and after a nonrestrictive expression. A **restrictive expression** is one that limits (restricts) the meaning of the noun or pronoun that it follows and is, therefore, essential to complete the basic meaning of the sentence. A **nonrestrictive expression**, in contrast, may be omitted without changing the basic meaning of the sentence.

> **RESTRICTIVE:** Anyone with some experience should apply for the position. (*"With some experience" restricts which "anyone" should apply.*)

> **NONRESTRICTIVE:** Bernardo Álvarez, a clerk with extensive experience, should apply for the position. (*Because Bernardo Álvarez can be only one person, the phrase "a clerk with extensive experience" does not serve to further restrict the noun and is, therefore, not essential to the meaning of the sentence.*)

> **RESTRICTIVE:** Only the papers left on the conference table are missing. (*identifies which papers are missing.*)

> **NONRESTRICTIVE:** Lever Brothers, one of our best customers, is expanding in Europe. (*"One of our best customers" could be omitted without changing the basic meaning of the sentence.*)

> **RESTRICTIVE:** Ms. Turner, using a great deal of tact, disagreed with her.

> **NONRESTRICTIVE:** The manager using a great deal of tact was Ms. Turner.

Examine the noun or pronoun that comes before the expression to determine whether the noun or pronoun needs the expression to complete its meaning. If it does, do *not* insert a comma.

Identifying expressions that follow a proper noun typically require commas before and after.

Whenever an identifying expression follows a proper noun, it is typically nonrestrictive because the proper noun already restricts the noun to one person, place, or thing. Thus, such expressions require commas before and after.

appositive A noun that identifies another noun or pronoun that precedes it

An **appositive** is a noun that identifies another noun or pronoun that comes immediately before it. If the appositive is nonrestrictive, insert commas before and after the appositive.

> **RESTRICTIVE:** The word *plagiarism* strikes fear into the heart of many. (*"Plagiarism" is an appositive that identifies which word; therefore, it is restrictive.*)

Nonrestrictive appositives require commas; restrictive appositives do not.

> **NONRESTRICTIVE:** Ms. Burns, president of the corporation, is planning to resign. (*"President of the corporation" is an appositive that provides additional, but nonessential, information about Ms. Burns.*)

, inter

Rule 6. Interrupting Expressions   Use commas before and after an interrupting expression. An interrupting expression breaks the normal flow of a sentence. Common examples of interrupting expressions are *in addition, as a result, therefore, in summary, on the other hand, however, unfortunately,* and *as a matter of fact.*

> You may, of course, cancel your subscription at any time.

> One suggestion, for example, was to undertake a leveraged buyout.

> I believe it was Carmen, not Jiro, who raised the question.

> It is still not too late to make the change, is it?

Mr. Kennedy's present salary, you must admit, is not in line with those of other network managers.

BUT: You must admit_Mr. Kennedy's present salary is not in line with those of other network managers.

If the expression does not interrupt the normal flow of the sentence, do not use a comma.

There is no doubt that you are qualified for the position.

BUT: There is, no doubt, a good explanation for his actions.

Be sure to insert the commas in the correct position when punctuating interrupting expressions. Make sure the sentence makes sense when you mentally omit the expression between the two commas.

NOT: That is the most convenient, but not the cheapest ticket, to purchase. (*"That is the most convenient to purchase" doesn't make sense; the noun is missing.*)

BUT: That is the most convenient, but not the cheapest, ticket to purchase.

NOT: Ms. Cerny has a great fondness for, as well as much expertise, in Web page development. (*You would not say, "Ms. Cerny has a great fondness for in Web page development."*)

BUT: Ms. Cerny has a great fondness for, as well as much expertise in, Web page development.

Rule 7. Date   Use commas before and after the year when it follows the month and day. Do not use comma after a partial date or when the date is formatted in day-month-year order. If the name of the day precedes the date, also use a comma *after* the name of the day.

The note is due on May 31, 2007, at 5 P.M.

BUT: The note is due on May 31 at 5 P.M.

BUT: The note is due in May 2007.

BUT: The note is due on 31 May 2007 at 5 P.M.

Let's plan to meet on Wednesday, December 15, 2007, for our year-end review.

Rule 8. Place   Use commas before and after a state or country that follows a city and between elements of an address in narrative writing.

The sales conference will be held in Phoenix, Arizona, in May.
Our business agent is located in Brussels, Belgium, in the P.O.M. Building.

You may contact her at 500 Beaufort Drive, LaCrosse, VA 23950. (*Note that no comma appears between the state abbreviation and the ZIP code.*)

Rule 9. Direct Address   Use commas before and after a name used in direct address. A name is used in **direct address** when the writer speaks directly to (that is, directly addresses) another person.

Thank you, Carol, for bringing the matter to our attention.
Ladies and gentlemen, we appreciate your attending our session today.

When you read the sentences aloud, notice how your voice tends to drop when you read the interrupting expression.

Do not forget the comma *after* the date.

, date

, place

Do not forget the comma *after* the state or country.

, dir ad

direct address A name used when the writer speaks directly to another person

, quote   **Rule 10. Direct Quotation**   Use commas before and after a direct quotation in a sentence.

> The president said, "You have nothing to fear," and then changed the subject.

> "I assure you," the human resources director said, "that no positions will be terminated."

If the quotation is a question, use a question mark instead of a comma.

> "How many have applied?" she asked.

CHECKPOINT 6.2

VOCABULARY   Define the following terms in your own words and give an original example of each.

1. appositive:

2. direct address:

3. nonrestrictive expression:

4. restrictive expression:

Always have a specific reason (that is, a *rule*) for inserting a comma.

COMPREHENSION   Insert any needed commas in the following sentences. In the space at the left of each sentence, indicate the reason for the comma (*, nonr* or *, inter* or *, date* or *, place* or *, dir ad* or *, quote*). If the sentence needs no commas, write *C* in the space provided.

_____   1. I assumed as a matter of fact that the project was finished.

_____   2. Portland Oregon is a lovely city.

_____   3. They must have your answer by the Monday before the board meeting.

_____   4. They must have your answer by April 5 which is when the board meets.

_____   5. Their catalog states "All merchandise is guaranteed for 90 days."

_____   6. That group of co-op students which was from Los Angeles visited our office today.

_____   7. The group of co-op students from Los Angeles visited our office today.

_____   8. Everyone please be seated.

_____   9. Their software-support department for example handles more than a thousand calls daily.

_____ 10. Our last mortgage which was at 7.85% will soon be paid off.

_____ 11. It is not too early I suspect to begin planning our tenth-anniversary sale.

_____ 12. The summer sales conference was held in Toronto not in Scottsdale.

_____ 13. We signed the original agreement on January 7 1999 in Gdansk.

_____ 14. You will note, Álvaro that your signature appears on the document.

_____ 15. The next computer expo will be held in Massachusetts sometime in November 2005.

Semicolons

Semicolons show where elements in a sentence are separated. The separation is stronger than a comma but not as strong as a period. When typing, leave one space after a semicolon and begin the following word with a lowercase letter.

Rule 11. Independent Clauses with Commas If a misreading might otherwise occur, use a semicolon (instead of a comma) to separate independent clauses that contain internal commas. Make sure that the semicolon is inserted *between* the independent clauses—not *within* one of the clauses.

; comma

CONFUSING: I ordered juice, toast, and bacon, and eggs, toast, and sausage were sent instead.

CLEAR: I ordered juice, toast, and bacon; and eggs, toast, and sausage were sent instead.

CONFUSING: I attended the meetings on October 29, 30, and 31, and on November 2 I returned home.

CLEAR: I attended the meetings on October 29, 30, and 31; and on November 2, I returned home.

BUT: Although high-quality paper was used, the photocopy machine still jammed, and neither of us knew how to repair it. (*No misreading is likely to occur*)

The reasons for the commas in the first four sentences are to separate items in a series (, ser). The reason for the first comma in the last sentence is to set off the introductory clause (, intro).

Rule 12. Independent Clauses Without a Conjunction Use a semicolon between independent clauses that are not connected by a coordinate conjunction (such as *and, but, or,* or *nor*). You have already learned to use a comma before coordinate conjunctions when they connect independent clauses. Rule 12 applies to independent clauses *not* connected by a conjunction.

; no conj

Recall that independent clauses can stand alone as complete sentences.

The president was eager to proceed with the plans; the board still had some reservations.

BUT: The president was eager to proceed with the plans, but the board still had some reservations. (*Use a comma instead of a semicolon if the clauses are joined by a coordinate conjunction.*)

I slept through my alarm; consequently, I was late for the meeting.

Bannon Corporation exceeded its sales goal this quarter; furthermore, it rang up its highest net profit ever.

BUT: Bannon Corporation exceeded its sales goal this quarter, and, furthermore, it rang up its highest net profit ever. (*Use a comma instead of a semicolon if the clauses are* joined *by a coordinate conjunction.*)

Rule 13. Series with Internal Commas Use a semicolon after each item in a series if any of the items already contain a comma. Normally, we separate items in a series with commas. However, if any of those items already contain a comma, we need a stronger mark (semicolon) between the items.

; ser

The human resources department will be interviewing in Dallas, Texas; Stillwater, Oklahoma; and Little Rock, Arkansas, for the new position.

Among the guests were Jerome Carpenter, our attorney; his wife, Veronica; and Carolyn Hart-Wilder, our new controller.

Separate the items in a series with a semicolon if even *one* of the items contains an internal comma.

Make sure the semicolon is inserted between (not within) the items in the series. Even if only one of the items contains an internal comma, separate all of them with semicolons.

NOT: That emergency procedure was assigned to Aaron, Hiroshi, who had just arrived from Osaka, and Lorraine.

BUT: That emergency procedure was assigned to Aaron; Hiroshi, who had just arrived from Osaka; and Lorraine.

Avoid beginning a sentence with items in a series separated by semicolons. Instead, reword the sentence to put the series at the end of the sentence.

AWKWARD: Norfolk, Virginia; Athens, Georgia; and Orlando, Florida, are being considered as sites for next year's convention.

BETTER: Sites being considered for next year's convention are Norfolk, Virginia; Athens, Georgia; and Orlando, Florida.

If commas do not occur within the series but do occur elsewhere in a sentence, use commas to separate the items within the series.

If it is convenient for you, you may schedule the appointment on Tuesday, Wednesday, or Thursday of next week. (*Not: "Tuesday; Wednesday; or Thursday"*)

Insert the semicolon between (not within) the items in a series.

Colons

Another title for this section could be "*Announcing* the Colon," because that is exactly what the colon does. It announces a list, rule, explanation, and the like. When typing, leave one space after a colon; do not begin the following word with a capital letter.

: exp

Rule 14. Explanatory Material   Use a colon to introduce explanatory material that is preceded by an independent clause. Expressions commonly used to introduce explanatory material are *the following, as follows, this,* and *these.*

His directions were as follows: turn right and proceed to the third house on the left.

I now have openings on the following dates: January 18, 19, and 20.

Just remember this: you may need a reference from her in the future.

The fall trade show offers the following advantages: inexpensive show space, abundant traffic, and free press publicity.

The new contract contains a number of improvements: one more personal day off, flexible work schedules, and cafeteria-type benefits.

There is only one word to describe Leroy's behavior: boorish. (*Use a colon even if what follows is a single word.*)

Make sure the clause preceding the explanatory material can stand alone as a complete sentence. Do not place a colon after a verb or a preposition that introduces a listing.

NOT: I now have openings on: January 18, 19, and 20.

BUT: I now have openings on January 18, 19, and 20.

NOT: My responsibilities were: opening the mail, sorting it, and delivering it to each department.

BUT: My responsibilities were opening the mail, sorting it, and delivering it to each department.

Do use a colon, however, if the items following a verb or preposition are listed on separate lines.

The members include:
1. Roger Axelrod
2. Wanda Hunicutt
3. Woody Slades

The menu consists of:
Caesar salad
Roast duckling
Vegetable medley
Key lime pie

Note that the first word of each item listed on a separate line is capitalized.

COMPREHENSION   Insert any needed punctuation in the following sentences. If a sentence is punctuated correctly, write a *C* before it.

1. Casey nominated Warren Jun and Carrie and Ronald Jerry and Larry seconded the nomination.

2. Lars gave the presentation Lauren operated the projector.

3. Ms. Murray finished the newsletter on time but in the meantime her other duties were left undone.

4. Drexell Training will hold desktop publishing seminars at the following locations in 2004 Reno Nevada Roswell New Mexico and Laramie Wyoming.

5. Drexell Training will hold desktop publishing seminars in 2003 at Reno Nevada Roswell New Mexico and Laramie Wyoming.

6. Drexell Training will hold desktop publishing seminars in 2003 at

   a. Reno Nevada

   b. Roswell New Mexico

   c. Laramie Wyoming

7. Mr. Torres wants to attend the trade show in Chicago but doesn't know whether he can fit it into his busy schedule.

8. It's never been easier to invest online and you can now do it for as little as $8 per transaction.

9. Kurt pried open the box and then decided to send it back to the storeroom.

10. Bertha showed signs of agitation that is she drummed her fingers on the table and frequently shifted her position in her seat.

CHECKPOINT 6.3

Periods

In addition to using a period at the end of a statement or command and in decimals (which you already know), there are several other frequent uses of periods in business writing.

The vast majority of the sentences you write will end in periods.

.req   **Rule 15. Polite Request**   Use a period after a polite request. Consider a statement a polite request if you expect the reader to respond by *acting* rather than by giving a yes-or-no answer.

> Would you please sign the form on page 2.
>
> May I please have the report by Friday.
>
> **BUT:**   Would you be willing to take on this assignment? (*This is a real question, because you expect the reader to respond by saying "yes" or "no."*)

.ind quest   **Rule 16. Indirect Question**   Use a period after an indirect question. (A question mark, of course, goes after a *direct* question.)

> We don't know why the machine broke.
>
> How to get it repaired promptly is our main concern.
>
> The question is what to do in the meantime.

.abb   **Rule 17. Abbreviation**   Use a period with certain abbreviations. Always consult your dictionary for the correct form of an abbreviation.

etc.	i.e.	e.g.	Mr.
Inc.	Mon.	Jr.	Oct.

Note: Many abbreviations follow the capitalization of the words as if written in full. In most lowercase abbreviations made up of single initials, use a period after each initial but no internal spaces.

a.m.	p.m.	i.e	c.o.d.
Exceptions:	mpg	mph	wpm

In most all-capital abbreviations made up of single initials, do not use periods or internal spaces.

WWW	OSHA	CEO	GPA
Exceptions:	P.O.	U.S.A.	B.S.

(Do not insert internal spaces in any of these abbreviations.)

.list   **Rule 18. Lists**   Use periods after clauses or long phrases displayed on separate lines in a list. Also use periods after short phrases that are needed to complete the meaning of the sentence that introduces the list.

Recall that a clause contains a subject and predicate; a phrase does not.

> Ms. Jordan wants to know the following:
> 1. When to replace the inventory.
> 2. Who will be assisting with the job.
> 3. How to write off damaged inventory.
> (*The items are clauses and therefore require a period at the end of each.*)

> His real estate requirements were:
> - Approximately one acre.
> - Underground utilities.
> - Convenient access to I-72.
> (*The items are short phrases that are needed to complete the meaning of the introductory statement and therefore require a period at the end of each.*)

> **BUT:**   His real estate requirements were these:
> a. Approximately one acre
> b. Underground utilities
> c. Convenient access to I-72
> (*The items are short phrases that do not complete the meaning of the introductory statement and therefore do not require periods.*)

Numbered, lettered, and bulleted lists are all treated the same way.

Parentheses

Use parentheses to enclose explanatory material, for items in a series, and for expressions that contain internal commas. (*Note:* Always use both an opening and a closing parenthesis—never just one.)

Rule 19. Explanatory Material   Use parentheses to enclose explanatory material that is not necessary to the grammatical structure of the sentence but that is too important to omit. (Often, but not always, such material could be enclosed by commas or dashes instead.)

() exp

Our Norfolk (Virginia) office will handle your recent claim.

The North American Free Trade Agreement (NAFTA) has dramatically increased our imports from Mexico.

The recommendations section (on page 34 of the report) caused quite a stir.

The recommendations section (see page 34 of the report) caused quite a stir.

The recommendations section caused quite a stir (see page 34 of the report).

The recommendations section caused quite a stir. (See page 34 of the report.)

Note the differences in capitalization and punctuation when a parenthetical statement comes within the sentence (sentence 4 above), comes at the end of the sentence (sentence 5 above), or serves as its own sentence (sentence 6 above). If the parenthetical statement comes after the sentence, capitalize and punctuate the sentence as you normally would.

> Do not capitalize the first word of an independent clause enclosed within parentheses within a sentence. If the clause is a statement or command, do not insert a period before the closing parenthesis. (Do, however, insert a question mark or exclamation point if needed.)

Rule 20. Series   Use parentheses to enclose numbers or letters that precede items in a series within a sentence.

() ser

NOT: We chose Bertille Harrison over Martin Garrett for the position because of her a. broader experience in production management, b. willingness to accept the position immediately, and c. wide range of contacts within the production operations community.

NOT: We chose Bertille Harrison over Martin Garrett for the position because of her a) broader experience in production management, b) willingness to accept the position immediately, and c) wide range of contacts within the production operations community.

BUT: We chose Bertille Harrison over Martin Garrett for the position because of her (a) broader experience in production management, (b) willingness to accept the position immediately, and (c) wide range of contacts within the production operations community.

Rule 21. Comma   Use parentheses instead of commas to set off an expression that already contains internal commas. (*Note:* Dashes instead of parentheses would also be correct.)

() comma

The nominees (Ms. Carillo, Mr. Porter, and Mr. Curtis) each made a short presentation.

Most of our employees (excluding Martha, Haruki, and Roy) would be available to help.

Some of the marked-down items (for example, the gold dinner ring, the pearl earrings, and the men's cufflinks) were really quite exquisite.

CHECKPOINT 6.4

COMPREHENSION

1. **PERIODS** Correct any errors in the use of periods in the following sentences. If a sentence is punctuated correctly, write a *C* before it.

   a. Would you be interested in attending that conference.
   b. We have not been able to determine why this happened so suddenly.
   c. Antonio submitted his résumé to J. C. Penney Company, Inc..
   d. The revised brochure (I really like it.) has been approved at all levels.
   e. My presentation will cover instructions for the following:
      - Requesting permission for a trip.
      - Applying for a cash advance.
      - Completing an expense report.

2. **PARENTHESES** Insert any needed parentheses (no other punctuation) to correctly punctuate the following sentences. If a sentence is correctly punctuated, write a *C* to the left of it.

   a. Maslow's hierarchy of needs includes 1 physiological needs, 2 safety needs, 3 social needs, 4 esteem needs, and 5 self-realization needs.
   b. Our Delhi India distribution center is completely automated.
   c. The corporate culture the rites, rituals, heroes, and values of a firm will greatly affect your job satisfaction.
   d. The National Endowment for the Humanities NEH awarded a small grant to our community theater group.
   e. US West experienced a small decline in revenue this past year see Table 14.5 .
   f. Three conditions the deadlines they establish, the kind of support they need, and their willingness to make modifications if needed will determine whether we accept their proposal.

Quotation Marks

> Recall (from Rule 10) that commas go before and after a direct quotation in a sentence.

Quotation marks are used for direct quotations, for expressions needing special attention, and for titles of certain publications. Commas and periods always go inside the closing quotation mark; colons and semicolons always go outside. Question marks and exclamation points go inside if they apply only to the quoted matter; they go outside if they apply to the entire sentence.

" quote **Rule 22. Direct Quotation** Use quotation marks before and after a direct quotation—that is, the *exact* words of a person.

> "When we return on Thursday," Akira said, "we need to meet with you."
> (*Note the placement of commas and periods inside quotation marks.*)

> **BUT:** Akira said that when we return on Thursday, we need to meet with you.
> (*no quotation marks needed in an indirect quotation*)

> Did Marvin say, "He will represent us"?
> Marvin asked, "Will he represent us?"

Note in the last two sentences above, when the quoted matter is itself a question, the question marks comes *before* the closing quotation mark; when the entire

question is a question, the question mark comes *after* the closing quotation mark. (The same is true for exclamation points.) Note also that one terminal mark of punctuation is sufficient. For example, in the last sentence above, a period does not follow the closing quotation mark—even though the entire sentence is a statement.

Rule 23. Special Attention   Use quotation marks around an expression that needs special attention.

> " attn

Net income after taxes is known as "the bottom line"; that's what's important around here. (*Semicolons and colons go outside the closing quotation mark.*)

The job title changed from "chairman" to "chief executive officer." (*Periods and commas go inside the closing quotation marks.*)

All items marked "hazardous" must be disposed of according to federal guidelines.

Please bring me the file folder labeled "Hudson Project."

Rule 24. Title   Use quotation marks around the title of a newspaper or magazine article, chapter in a book, report, conference, and similar items.

> " title

Read the article entitled "Wall Street Recovery."

Chapter 4, "Market Segmentation," of *Industrial Marketing* is of special interest.

The theme of this year's sales conference is "Quality Sells."

The report "Common Carriers" shows the extent of the transportation problems.

Note: The titles of *complete* published works are shown in italics. The titles of *parts* of published works and most other titles are enclosed in quotation marks.

If you need to use a quotation within another quotation, use single quotation marks for the internal quotation. (Use the apostrophe for the single quotation mark.)

Single quotation marks follow the same rules as double quotation marks in terms of placement with other marks of punctuation. Note the illustrations in the last two examples.

Gary replied, "I question your use of the word 'voluntary' in that memo."

The witness responded, "All Euridice said was 'not today.'"

Please read the article entitled "The President Asked, 'Why?'"

Italics (or Underlining)

Before the advent of word processing software, underlining was used to emphasize words or indicate certain titles. Although underlining is still correct, today, the use of italics is preferred for these functions.

word

Rule 25. Word Used as a Word   Italicize a word used as a word. Such expressions are used as nouns in the sentence and are often introduced by the expression *the word* or *the term*.

The word *angry* doesn't begin to explain the intensity of my reaction.

Are you aware of the real meaning of *edify*?

Should you capitalize the preposition *with* in the title of a book?

emp

Rule 26. Emphasis   Italicize a word or phrase for special emphasis. (To ensure that such italicized expressions do, in fact, receive special emphasis, employ this use of italics sparingly.)

For the hundredth time, I will *not* agree to chair that task force.

Place commas and periods *before* the closing quotation mark; place colons and semicolons *after* the closing quotation mark.

title

Rule 27. Title   Italicize the title of a book, magazine, newspaper, and other *complete* published works.

Irene's newest book, *All That Glitters*, was reviewed in *The New York Times* and in the *Atlantic Monthly*.

The cover story in last week's *Time* magazine was "Is the Economic Expansion Over?"

Hyphens

Use hyphens to form some compound adjectives and numbers and to divide words at the ends of lines. When typing, do not leave a space before or after a regular hyphen. Likewise, do not use a hyphen with a space before and after to substitute for a dash.

- adj

A compound word is made up of two or more words that express a single idea (for example, a "first-class" stamp).

Rule 28. Compound Adjectives   Hyphenate a compound adjective that comes *before* a noun (unless the adjective is a proper noun or unless the first word is an adverb ending in *-ly*).

We hired a first-class management team.

BUT: Our new management team is first class.

The long-term outlook for our investments is excellent.

BUT: We intend to hold our investments for the long term.

BUT: The General Motors warranty received high ratings.

BUT: Beryl presented a poorly conceived proposal.

Note: Don't confuse compound adjectives (which are generally temporary combinations) with compound nouns (which are generally well-established concepts). Compound nouns (such as *Social Security, life insurance, word processing,* and *high school)* are not hyphenated when used as adjectives that come before a noun.

income tax form   real estate agent
public relations firm   data processing center

Rule 29. Numbers   Hyphenate fractions and compound numbers 21 through 99 when they are spelled out.

- **num**

Nearly three-fourths of our new applicants were unqualified.

Seventy-two orders were processed incorrectly last week.

Apostrophes

Apostrophes are used to show that letters have been omitted (as in contractions) and to show possession. When typing, do not space before or after an apostrophe (unless a space after is needed before another word).

Remember this helpful hint: Whenever a noun ending in *s* is followed by another noun, the first noun is probably a possessive, requiring an apostrophe. However, if the first noun *describes* rather than establishes ownership, no apostrophe is used.

Wayne's department (*shows ownership; therefore, an apostrophe*)
the sales department (*describes; therefore, no apostrophe*)

Rule 30. Singular Nouns   To form the possessive of a singular noun, add an apostrophe plus *s.*

' sing

my accountant's fee   a child's toy
the company's stock   Ellen's choice
Alzheimer's disease   Mr. and Mrs. Dye's home
a year's time   the boss's contract
Ms. Morris's office   Liz's promotion
Gil Hodges's record   Carl Bissett, Jr.'s birthday

Rule 31. Plural Nouns Ending in S   To form the possessive of a plural noun that ends in *s* (that is, most plural nouns), add an apostrophe only.

' plur + s

our accountants' fees   both companies' stock
the Dyes' home   two years' time

Rule 32. Plural Nouns Not Ending in S   To form the possessive of a plural noun that does not end in *s*, add an apostrophe plus *s* (just as you would for singular nouns).

' plural – s

the children's hour   the men's room
The alumni's contribution   the mice's diet

Hint: To avoid confusion in forming the possessive of plural nouns, first form the plural; then apply the appropriate rule to the plural form.

Singular	*Plural*	*Plural Possessive*
employee	employees	employees' bonuses
hero	heroes	heroes' welcome
Mr. and Mrs. Lake	the Lakes	the Lakes' home
lady	ladies	ladies' clothing

'pro   **Rule 33. Indefinite Pronouns**   To form the possessive of an indefinite pronoun, add an apostrophe plus *s*. Do not use an apostrophe to form the possessive of a personal pronoun. Examples of indefinite possessive pronouns are *anybody's*, *everyone's*, *no one's*, *nobody's*, *one's*, and *somebody's*. Examples of personal possessive pronouns are *hers*, *his*, *its*, *ours*, *theirs*, and *yours*.

It is someone's responsibility

BUT: The responsibility is theirs.

I will review everybody's figures.

BUT: The bank will review its figures.

Note: Do not confuse the possessive pronouns *its*, *theirs*, and *whose* with the contractions *it's*, *there's*, and *who's*.

It's time to put litter in *its* place.

There's no reason to take *theirs*.

Who's determining *whose* jobs will be eliminated?

'ger   **Rule 34. Gerunds**   Use the possessive form for a noun or pronoun that comes before a gerund. (A gerund is the *-ing* form of a verb used as a noun.)

Garth questioned *Karen's* leaving so soon.

Stockholders' raising so many questions delayed the adjournment.

Mr. Matsumoto knew Karl and objected to *his* going to the meeting.

CHECKPOINT 6.5

COMPREHENSION

1. **QUOTATION MARKS**   Insert any needed quotation marks (no other punctuation) to correctly punctuate the following sentences. Be careful to place parentheses correctly in relation to other marks of punctuation. If a sentence is correctly punctuated, write a *C* to the left of it.

   a. Stick firmly to the topic of your raise, Rosales suggested, and do not let the boss change the direction of the discussion.
   b. Wasn't it our president who said, Generic products will never catch on,   asked Jonathan?
   c. After viewing the Christmas window display, Rose said, How wonderful!
   d. Doris's boss said that her position did not warrant a higher salary.
   e. Many firms are moving to Florida, better known as the Sunshine State.
   f. Please mark that contract Confidential.
   g. The title of my presentation is Why Not Now?
   h. You must read the article entitled New Trends in Marketing Techniques.

2. **ITALICS** Underline any words that should be shown in italics. If a sentence is correct, write a *C* to the left of it.

   a. The magazine Wired will help keep you up to date on new developments on the Internet.

   b. The term brand mark means the part of a brand that is a distinctive symbol or design.

   c. The text for the training program will be Who Moved My Cheese?

   d. Do not enter the laboratory until the light turns green!

3. **HYPHENS** Insert any needed hyphens in the following expressions. If an expression is correct, write a *C* to the left of it.

   a. a good looking actor

   b. agreed upon standards

   c. new mahogany desk

   d. fifty two weeks

   e. highly valued employee

   f. implications that were far reaching

   g. one third of a cup

4. **APOSTROPHES** Write the correct possessive form for each noun.

   a. agencies   _____

   b. attorneys   _____

   c. child   _____

   d. Congress   _____

   e. five minutes   _____

   f. man   _____

   g. mouse   _____

   h. Mr. and Mrs. Chambliss   _____

   i. the Foxes   _____

   j. everybody   _____

   k. it   _____

   l. one   _____

Summary

Here are the punctuation rules we have learned in this chapter. Would you be able to apply all of them correctly in your on-the-job writing?

Commas

1. Use a comma between two independent clauses joined by a coordinate conjunction.
2. Use a comma between two adjacent adjectives that modify the same noun.
3. Use a comma between each item in a series of three or more.
4. Use a comma after an introductory expression.
5. Use commas before and after a nonrestrictive expression.
6. Use commas before and after an interrupting expression.
7. Use commas before and after the year when it follows the month and day.
8. Use commas before and after a state or country that follows a city and between elements of an address in narrative writing.
9. Use commas before and after a name used in direct address.
10. Use commas before and after a direct quotation in a sentence.

Semicolons

11. If a misreading might otherwise occur, use a semicolon to separate independent clauses that contain internal commas.
12. Use a semicolon between two independent clauses that are not connected by a coordinate conjunction.
13. Use a semicolon after each item in a series if any of the items already contain a comma.

Colons

14. Use a colon to introduce explanatory material that is preceded by an independent clause.

Periods

15. Use a period after a polite request.
16. Use a period after an indirect question.
17. Use a period with certain abbreviations.
18. Use periods after clauses or long phrases displayed on separate lines in a list and after short phrases that are needed to complete the meaning of the sentence that introduces the list.

Parentheses

19. Use parentheses to enclose explanatory material that is not necessary to the grammatical structure of the sentence.
20. Use parentheses to enclose numbers or letters that precede items in a series within a sentence.
21. Use parentheses instead of commas to set off an expression that already contains internal commas.

Quotation Marks

22. Use quotation marks around a direct quotation.
23. Use quotation marks around an expression that needs special attention.
24. Use quotation marks around the title of a newspaper or magazine article, chapter in a book, report, conference, and similar items.

Italics (or Underlining)

25. Italicize a word used as a word.
26. Italicize a word or phrase for special emphasis.
27. Italicize the title of a book, magazine, newspaper, and other *complete* published works.

Hyphens

28. Hyphenate a compound adjective that comes *before* a noun (unless the adjective is a proper noun or unless the first word is an adverb ending in *-ly*).
29. Hyphenate fractions and compound numbers 21 through 99 when they are spelled out.

Apostrophes

30. To form the possessive of a singular noun, add an apostrophe plus *s*.
31. To form the possessive of a plural noun that ends in *s*, add an apostrophe only.
32. To form the possessive of a plural noun that does not end in *s*, add an apostrophe plus *s*.
33. To form the possessive of an indefinite pronoun, add an apostrophe plus *s*.
34. Use the possessive form for a noun or pronoun that comes before a gerund.

Looking Ahead

In the first two chapters of Part 2, you learned how to write with style. In this chapter, you learned how to punctuate correctly what you write. We're now ready to combine these two skills into writing routine business correspondence, which is introduced in the next chapter.

Key Terms

appositive   nonrestrictive expression
direct address   restrictive expression

Exercises

Commas

1 Insert any needed commas in the following sentences.

    a. Aldo had the time for as well as much interest in serving as program chairman.

    b. Any network administrator who speaks Spanish may attend the international conference.

    c. Drivers start your engines.

    d. Emerson Company plans to close 30 plants and move much of its production to Mexico.

    e. Huo was first in line but even so she did not get into the arena until noon.

    f. If you will do the research analyze the data and draft the report I'll edit proofread and format it.

    g. In the beginning we did not charge for this extra service.

    h. Ireland Scotland and Wales are on her agenda.

    i. Loretta's recipe which received the most votes won the bake-off.

    j. Lori's new address is 1323 Charleston Avenue Portsmouth Virginia.

    k. Margarita is scheduled to visit Ireland Scotland and Wales.

    l. Mr. Len signed the revision to the contract in Seattle in April 2005.

    m. Our president April Parker will address the conference.

    n. Please sign the revision to the contract in Bonn Germany on 3 April 2005.

    o. President April Parker will address the conference.

2 Insert any needed punctuation in the following sentences:

a. Running the marathon on that snowy day while still nursing a cold and suffering from an upset stomach was a real challenge.

b. Selling in Asia is a complex time-consuming task.

c. That was a startling development wouldn't you say?

d. The drive was exhausting but Jeremy enjoyed the scenery.

e. The new network administrator who speaks Spanish will attend the international conference.

f. The new personal computer replaces a four-year-old model.

g. "The new policy will start on May 1" Ms. Yang replied "and will continue for the remainder of the year."

h. The recipe that received the most votes won the bake-off.

i. The revision to the contract was signed on April 3 2005 in Seattle Washington.

j. The weather cooperated and we finished painting early.

k. This problem by the way was at least partially caused by the new tax laws.

l. We did not charge for this extra service in the beginning.

m. Welcome Class of 2009 to our orientation assembly; we hope you enjoy your stay here.

n. "Who will be transferred" Maria asked.

o. Yin was nevertheless still willing to cooperate.

Semicolons and Colons

3 Insert any needed punctuation in the following sentences.

a. Adriana reviewed the operations in South Carolina Tennessee and North Carolina and Virginia reviewed the operations in Pennsylvania.

b. Dario visited the Hertford Ahoskie and Windsor plants and Marilyn visited the Williamston and Greenville plants.

c. Here is what you will need 3 yards of fabric a staple gun and plenty of patience.

d. The dates under consideration are November 3 2005 November 27 2005 and January 13 2006.

e. The expectation was for a small profit by the end of the first year the reality was that we didn't make a profit for three years.

f. The point to remember is this all expenses must be accompanied by receipts.

g. We expected a small profit at the end of the first year but the reality was that we didn't make a profit for three years.

h. You will need 3 yards of fabric a staple gun and plenty of patience.

i. Your presentation was not just acceptable it was fantastic.

Periods and Parentheses

4 Insert any needed punctuation in the following sentences.

a. Mr. Enrique Hernández gave the luncheon speech at 12:30 pm at the NAFTA session

   b. My goals are to
     1. Finish my degree
     2. Get a good job
     3. Find a compatible mate
   c. My goals are these
     1. Finish my degree
     2. Get a good job
     3. Find a compatible mate
   d. The detailed specifications see Appendix C contain all of the backup information
   e. The only question I have is why we had to get involved in the first place
   f. The three leased automobiles a Ford Honda and Lexis will be auctioned off on Saturday
   g. Three colors blue green and yellow were used in the interior renovation
   h. Would you be interested in hearing my suggestion
   i. Would you please take your seats so that we can get started
   j. You should pack 1 overshoes 2 extra underwear and 3 a warm blanket

Quotation Marks, Italics, and Hyphens

5 Insert any needed punctuation in the following sentences. Underline an expression that should be shown in italics. (*Note:* Sentences a–c contain direct quotations.)

   a. A lot of the criticism is misguided Bill Ford said I don't know what tougher steps I could have taken
   b. Did Karina say I was unprepared for the fallout
   c. Karina said Were you prepared for the fallout
   d. All visitors must sign the register before being granted access into the building. (*Emphasize the third word in this sentence.*)
   e. President Reagan was known as the Great Communicator
   f. That rarely used parliamentary procedure caused a time consuming delay
   g. The article entitled Nice Guy, Knows Karate appeared in the April issue of Forbes magazine
   h. The Best Western hotel chain recently remodeled two thirds of its properties
   i. The word facetious contains all five vowels in order
   j. The word processing center is a well run operation

Apostrophes

6 Insert any needed apostrophes in the following sentences.

   a. After five minutes rest from painting my offices, they will paint yours.
   b. Doris Cermaks updating of the lobbies furnishings was hugely successful.
   c. Mens wallets and womens handbags are featured in this weeks sale.
   d. The Browns automobile is two weeks newer than the Wilsons.
   e. The inns guests complained about the geeses honking.

    f. The mayors voted to require three years experience for the new position.

    g. Those peoples reports were prepared on the secretaries computers.

Punctuation

7 Insert any needed punctuation in the following letter.

In accordance with the law I have enclosed twenty five copies of the Annual Report to Shareholders for the fiscal year ended December 31 2006. This report is being sent today by first class mail to shareholders of the above company and we are providing copies to the business press as well.

I am advised by the corporations accountants that the financial statements appearing in this annual report do not reflect a change from the preceding years report in any accounting principles or practices or in the method of applying any such principles or practices.

8 Insert any needed punctuation in the following memo.

In my opinion the Smith and Miller Company would be able to collect against our company for late delivery of its order for 45 desk lamps.

The terms of our agreement specified delivery to its client the Pine Cliff Inn on or before January 31. Delivery was made eight days late February 8. Although the opening date of the inn had been changed to February 11 the customers refusal to accept the shipment had far reaching implications. The fact that the opening date of the Pine Cliff Inn was changed is not grounds for a collection suit against Smith and Miller.

I think it would be worthwhile for you to go ahead with plans to secure acceptance of the order if you can reach a reasonable settlement. We may be forced to take a small loss on the transaction it would be quite difficult for us to sell these specially constructed lamps to our regular customers.

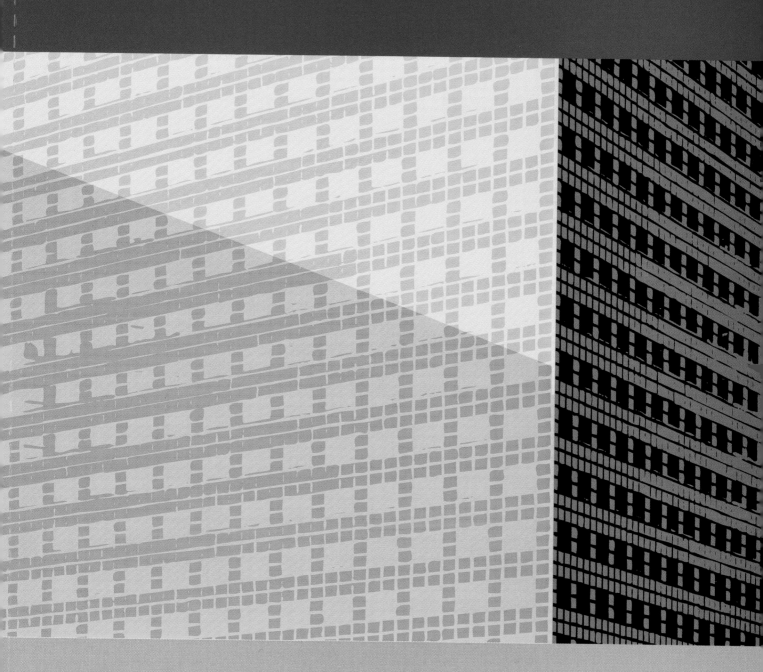

7

Routine and Negative Emails, Letters, and Memos

COMMUNICATION OBJECTIVES

After you have finished this chapter, you should be able to:

- Compose a routine request and reply.

- Compose a routine claim and adjustment letter.

- Decide when to use a direct or an indirect organizational plan for bad-news messages.

- Compose a message that rejects an idea.

- Compose a message that refuses a favor.

- Compose a message that refuses a claim.

On the Job

HOWARD HIGH
Strategic Communications Manager, Intel Corporation (Santa Clara, California)

Open disclosure is the way Howard High deals with messages about potential problems. High is strategic communications manager for Intel, the global leader in making microprocessors. As a company spokesperson, he shares information about the $21 billion company and its products with reporters from U.S. and foreign business publications. Intel products have a high profile, thanks to the "Intel Inside" brand-building campaign that has established the company's worldwide reputation for quality.

As Intel adds innovative features and more processing power to its new chips, the company faces the challenge of managing public perceptions and expectations of product performance. This endeavor is where insightful audience analysis and open disclosure pay off. "Chips are extremely complex," comments High. "Although they are becoming better and better, we try to communicate to the buying public that there are limitations, so that people do not expect absolute perfection."

Like most managers, High spends a great deal of his time communicating about routine (but necessary) matters. When he has to communicate a bad-news message about a problem that may affect a large number of customers, he will take additional steps to publicize the issue. "We would probably involve a senior-level manager as the spokesperson or the quoted source in the news release and, if necessary, hold a conference call with reporters to explain the situation," he says. Finally, High arranges for speedy replies to customers who write or email the company to express their views.

166

Planning the Routine Message

Most of the typical manager's correspondence involves communicating about routine matters. For example, a small-business owner asks for a catalog and credit application from a potential supplier; a manager at a large corporation sends an email informing employees of a change in policy; a consumer notifies a company that an ordered product arrived in damaged condition; or a government agency responds to a request for a brochure.

Although routine, such messages are of interest to the reader because the information contained in the message is necessary for day-to-day operations. For example, although no company is pleased when a customer is dissatisfied with one of its products, firms *are* interested in learning about such situations so that they can correct the problems and prevent their recurrence.

When the purpose of a message is to convey routine information and our analysis of the audience indicates that the reader will probably be interested in its contents, we use a **direct organizational plan.** The main idea is stated first, followed by any needed explanation, and then a friendly closing.

The advantage of using a direct organizational plan for routine correspondence is that it puts the major news first—where it stands out and gets the most attention. This strategy saves the reader time because he or she can quickly see what the message is about by scanning the first one or two sentences. The **indirect organizational plan,** in which the reasons are presented before the major idea, is often used for bad-news and persuasive messages and is covered later.

The direct style presents the major idea first, followed by needed details.

direct organizational plan A plan in which the major purpose of the message is communicated first, followed by any needed details

indirect organizational plan A plan in which the reasons or rationale are presented first, followed by the major idea

Routine Requests

A request is routine if you anticipate that the reader will readily do as you ask without having to be persuaded. For example, a request for specific information about an organization's product is routine because all organizations appreciate the opportunity to promote their products. However, a request for free samples of a company's product to distribute at your store's anniversary sale might not be routine because the company might have concluded that such promotion efforts are not cost-effective; thus, you would have to *persuade* the reader to grant the request.

Major Idea First

When making a routine request, present the major idea—your request—clearly and directly in the first sentence or two (see, however, Spotlight 4, "When in Rome . . . ," on page 168). You may use a direct question, a statement, or a polite request to present the main idea. Always pose your request clearly and politely, and give any background information needed to set the stage. All of the following are effective routine requests:

Use a direct question, statement, or polite request to present your request.

Direct Question: Does Black & Decker offer educational discounts for public institutions making quantity purchases of tools? Blair Junior High School will soon be replacing approximately 50 portable electric drills used by our industrial technology students.

Statement: Please let me know how I might invest in your deferred money-market fund. As an American currently working in Bangkok, Thailand, I cannot easily take advantage of your automatic monthly deposit plan.

SPOTLIGHT 4 across cultures

When in Rome . . .

The direct organizational style is suggested for routine messages. This style can be summarized in five words: *Present the major idea immediately.* American business executives have little time and patience for needless formalities and "beating around the bush."

Such is not always the case, however, when writing to someone whose culture and experiences are quite different from your own. Business people in some countries may find letters written in the direct style too harsh and abrupt, lacking in courtesy. You should therefore adapt your writing style to the expectations of the reader.

For example, an American manufacturer sent a form sales letter to many domestic and foreign retail stores inviting inquiries about stocking its line of fishing tackle. Note the differences in two of the responses the manufacturer received, shown below.

The moral is simple. Write as your receiver expects you to write. Take a cue from his or her own writing. If the letters you receive from an international associate are written in a direct style, you may safely respond in a similar style. However, if the letters you receive are similar to the Chinese response below, you might try a more formal, less-direct style when responding. Although you would not want to *adopt* the reader's style, you might need to *adapt* your own style, on the basis of your analysis of the audience.

Would you please send me a sample of the fishing tackle you advertised in your October 3 letter, along with price and shipping information. As a long-time retailer of fishing tackle, I would be especially interested in any items you might have for fly fishing.

Since the trout season starts in six weeks, I would appreciate having this information as soon as possible.

American Response

It was with great pleasure that we received your letter dated 3 October. We send our deepest respects and wish to inform you that Yoon Sung Fishing Tackle Company, Ltd., has been selling fishing items for 38 years.

We would be pleased to consider your merchandise. May we ask you to please send us samples, price, and shipping information. It will be a great pleasure to conduct business with your company.

Chinese Response

Polite Request: Would you please answer several questions about the work performance of Casandra Naser. She has applied for the position of industrial safety officer at Inland Steel and has given your name as a reference.

Decide in advance how much detail you are seeking. If you need only a one-sentence reply, it would be unfair to word your request in such a way as to prompt the writer to provide a three-page answer. Define clearly the type of response you want and phrase your request to elicit that response.

NOT: Please explain the features of your Interact word processing program.

BUT: Does your Interact word processing program automatically number lines and paragraphs?

Do not ask more questions than are necessary. Make the questions easy to answer.

Remember that you are imposing on the goodwill of the reader. Ask as few questions as possible—and never ask for any information that you can easily obtain on your own. If many questions *are* necessary, number them; most readers will answer questions in the order in which you pose them and will thus be less likely to skip one unintentionally. Yes-or-no questions or short-answer questions are easy for the reader to answer; but when you need more information, use open-ended questions.

Arrange your questions in logical order (for example, order of importance, chronological order, or simple-to-complex order), word each question clearly and objectively (to avoid bias), and limit the content to one topic per question. If appropriate, assure the reader that the information provided will be treated confidentially.

Explanation and Details

Most of the time you will need to give additional explanation or details about your initial request. Include any needed background information (such as the reason for asking) either immediately before or after making the request. For example, suppose you received the polite request given earlier asking about Casandra Naser's job performance. Unless you were also told that the request came from a potential employer and that Casandra Naser had given your name as a reference, you might be reluctant to provide such confidential information.

Or assume that you're writing to a former employer or professor asking for a letter of recommendation. You might need to give some background about yourself to jog the reader's memory. Also, you might need to justify or expand on your request. Put yourself in the reader's position. What information would you need to answer the request accurately and completely?

A reader is more likely to cooperate if you can show how he or she will benefit from agreeing to your request. In fact, it is often the communication of such benefits that makes the message routine rather than persuasive.

> Will you please help us serve you better by answering several questions about your banking needs. We're building a branch bank in your neighborhood and would like to make it as convenient for you as possible.

In general, you should identify reader benefits when they may not be obvious to the reader, but you need not belabor the point if such benefits are obvious. For example, a memo asking employees to recycle their paper and plastic trash would probably not need to discuss the value of recycling because most readers would already be familiar with the advantages of doing so.

Explain why you're making the request.

If possible, show how others benefit from your receiving the requested information.

WORD wise

Word Riddles

From what word can you take the whole and still have some left over? *Wholesome*

How do you learn the language in Athens? *Ab-zorba the Greek*

What do you call a petite fortune-teller who just broke out of prison? *A small medium at large*

What occurs once in every minute, twice in every moment, but not once in a thousand years? *the letter m*

What starts with T, ends with T, and is full of T? *A teapot*

What word becomes shorter when you add two letters to it? *Short*

Which letters are like a Roman emperor? *The C's are*

CATHY

by Cathy Guisewite

Friendly Closing

In your final paragraph, assume a friendly tone. Close by expressing appreciation for the assistance to be provided (but without seeming to take the recipient's cooperation for granted), by stating and justifying any deadlines, or by offering to reciprocate. Make your ending friendly, positive, and original, as illustrated by the following examples:

> Please let me know if I can return the favor.

> We appreciate your providing this information, which will help us make a fairer evaluation of Casandra Naser's qualifications for this position.

> May I please have the product information by October 1, when I place my Christmas wholesale orders. That way, I will be able to include Kodak products in my holiday sales.

> Model 1 illustrates the guidelines discussed previously for writing an effective routine request.

Routine Replies

Routine replies provide the information requested in the original message or otherwise comply with the writer's request. Like the original request letters, they are organized in a direct organizational style, putting the "good news"—the fact that you're responding favorably—up front.

Probably one of the most important guidelines to follow is to answer promptly. If a potential customer asks for product information, ensure that the information arrives before the customer must make a purchase decision. Otherwise, the time it took you to respond will have been wasted. Also, delaying

Sometimes it is not possible to provide the quickest reply by mail. In many cases, a prompt and courteous response by telephone is most welcome.

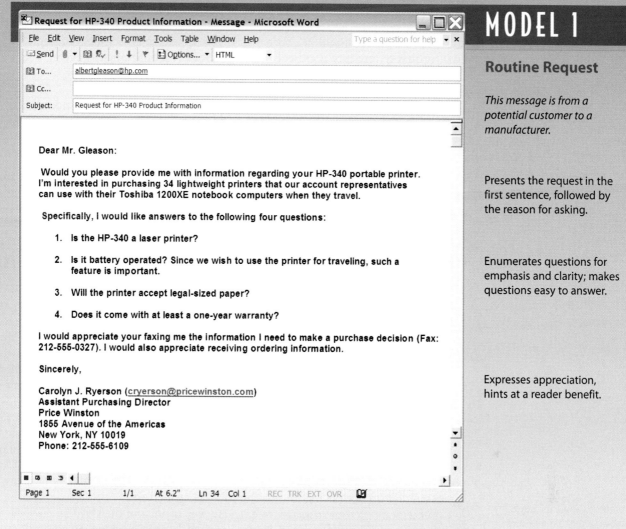

MODEL 1

Routine Request

This message is from a potential customer to a manufacturer.

Presents the request in the first sentence, followed by the reason for asking.

Enumerates questions for emphasis and clarity; makes questions easy to answer.

Expresses appreciation, hints at a reader benefit.

Grammar and Mechanics Notes

1 Format email messages for easy readability—and always proofread before sending.

2 *Your HP-340 portable printer.:* Use a period after a polite request.

3 *appreciate your faxing:* Use the possessive form of a pronoun *(your)* before a gerund *(faxing).*

a response might send the unintentional nonverbal message that you do not want to comply with the writer's request.

Your response should be courteous. If you appear to be acting grudgingly, you will probably lose any goodwill that a gracious response might have earned for you or your organization.

NOT: Although we do not generally provide the type of information you requested, we have decided to do so in this case.

BUT: We are happy to provide the information you requested.

Grant the request or give the requested information early in the message. Doing so not only saves the reader's time but also puts him or her in a good state of mind immediately. Although the reader may be pleased to hear that "We have received your letter of June 26," such news is not nearly so eagerly received as telling the reader that "I would be pleased to speak at your Engineering Society meeting on August 8; thanks for thinking of me." Put the good news up front—where it will receive the most emphasis.

Be sure to answer all the questions asked or implied, using objective and clearly understood language. Although it is often helpful to provide additional information or suggestions, you should never fail to at least address all the questions asked—even if your answers are not what the reader hopes to hear. Questions are usually answered in the order in which they were asked, but consider rearranging them if a different order makes more sense. Determining what your reader already knows about the topic should help you decide what information to include and how to phrase it.

The reader will probably be in a positive mood as the result of your letter, and you may consider either including some sales promotion if appropriate or building goodwill by implying such characteristics about your organization as public spiritedness, quality products, social responsibility, or concern for employees. To be effective, sales promotion and goodwill appeals should be subtle; avoid exaggeration and do not devote too much space to such efforts.

In the body of your message, refer to any enclosure and then add an enclosure notation at the bottom of the letter. Refer to a specific page of an enclosed brochure or to a particular paragraph of an enclosed document to help ensure that such enclosures will be read.

Close your letter on a positive, friendly note. Avoid such clichés as "If you have additional questions, please don't hesitate to let me know." Use original wording, personalized especially for the reader. After all, the reader might receive many letters like yours, and if he or she has already encountered "Thank you for your interest in our products" five times that day, the expression will sound trite and insincere.

Model 2 on page 173 is a routine reply to the request shown in Model 1 on page 171. The original request asked four questions about the printer, and the answers are as follows:

1. No, the HP-340 is not a laser printer.
2. No, it is not battery-operated.
3. Yes, it does accept legal-sized paper.
4. No, it does not come with a one-year warranty.

As you can see, only one of the four questions can be answered with an unqualified "yes," and that is the question the respondent chose to answer first. Positive language helps soften the impact of the negative responses to the other three questions. Also, reader benefits are stressed throughout the letter. Instead of just describing the features, the writer shows how the features can benefit the reader.

Checklist 6 summarizes the points you should consider when writing and responding to routine requests. Use this checklist as a guide in structuring your message and in evaluating the effectiveness of your first draft.

MODEL 2

Routine Reply

This letter responds to the request in Model 1 on page 171.

Albert Gleason
Sales Manager
Printers

650.456.7890 Tel
650.456.7890 Fax
albert_gleason@hp.com
albert_gleason hp e-cardfile

September 12, 20—

Ms. Carolyn J. Ryerson
Assistant Purchasing Director
PriceWinston
1855 Avenue of the Americas
New York, NY 10019

Hewlett-Packard Company
3000 Hanover Street
Palo Alto, CA 94304-1185
www.hp.com

1 Dear Ms. Ryerson:

Subject: Information You Requested About the HP-340

Yes, our popular HP-340 portable printer does accept legal-sized paper. Its 15-inch carriage will enable your representatives to print out even your most complex spreadsheets while on the road. Of course, the printer also adjusts easily to fit standard 8½-by 11-inch paper.

2 For quiet operation and easy portability, the HP uses ink-jet printing. This technology provides nearly the same quality output as a laser printer at less than half the cost. Plain paper may, of course, be used.

3 Although many travelers use their laptop computers on a plane or in their automobiles, they typically wait until reaching their destination to print out their documents. Thus, the HP-340 uses AC power only, thereby reducing its weight by nearly a pound. The extra-long 12-foot power cable will let you power up your printer easily no matter where the electrical outlet is hidden. And our six-month warranty, standard in the printer industry, ensures the reliability and trouble-free service that our customers have come to expect of all HP products.

4 To order or take the HP-340 for a test drive, call your local Computerland (Phone: 800-555-2189). It's representatives will show you how to increase your productivity while increasing your luggage weight by only about 4 pounds.

Sincerely yours,

Albert Gleason

Albert Gleason, Sales Manager

juc
5 By Fax

Begins by answering the "yes" question first.

Answers all questions, using positive language and pointing out the benefits of each feature.

Uses paragraphs instead of enumeration to answer each question because each answer requires elaboration.

Gives important purchase information; closes on a forward-looking note.

Grammar and Mechanics Notes

1 Always follow organizational preferences when formatting documents. This letter is formatted according to Hewlett-Packard's formatting style.

2 *ink-jet printing:* Hyphenate a compound adjective before a noun.

3 *its:* Do not confuse *its* (the possessive pronoun) with *it's* (the contraction for "it is").

4 *a test drive,:* Place a comma after an introductory expression.

5 *By Fax:* For reference purposes, include a delivery notation if appropriate.

CHECKLIST  6

Routine Requests and Replies

Routine Requests

✓ Present the major request in the first sentence or two, preceded or followed by reasons for making the request.

✓ Provide any needed explanation or details.

✓ Phrase each question so that it is clear, is easy to answer, and covers only one topic. Ask as few questions as possible, but if several questions are necessary, number them and arrange them in logical order.

✓ If appropriate, incorporate reader benefits and promise confidentiality.

✓ Close on a friendly note by expressing appreciation, justifying any necessary deadlines, offering to reciprocate, or otherwise making your ending personal and original.

Routine Replies

✓ Answer promptly and graciously.

✓ Grant the request or begin giving the requested information in the first sentence or two.

✓ Address all questions asked or implied; include additional information or suggestions if that would be helpful.

✓ Include subtle sales promotion if appropriate.

✓ Refer to any items you enclose with the letter, and insert an enclosure notation at the bottom.

✓ Close on a positive and friendly note, and use original wording.

CHECKPOINT 7.1

RECALL   Write a capital *T* for true or *F* for false before each statement.

1. ____ Most routine requests should be written using the direct organizational pattern.

2. ____ One of the most important guidelines in responding to a request is to grant the request.

3. ____ In responding to a request for information, you should always answer the questions in the order in which they were asked.

4. ____ If you enclose an item with your letter, you should refer to the enclosure in the body of your letter.

5. ____ Even for routine requests, you should generally tell the reader why you're making the request.

VOCABULARY   Define the following terms in your own words.

6. direct organizational plan:

7. indirect organizational plan:

COMPREHENSION

8. You're beginning your last year at school and are interested in securing a full-time paid internship in computer networking for the spring term. You decide to send an email inquiry to the human resources department at Dell Computers.

   a. Compose an appropriate subject line for your email.

b. Compose the first paragraph of your message.

c. Compose the last sentence of your message.

CRITICAL THINKING

9. Reconsider the situation in Exercise 8 regarding internship opportunities at Dell Computers. Do you think email or a telephone call would be the best medium for this inquiry? Why?

....

Routine Claim Letters

A **claim letter** is written by a buyer to a seller, seeking some type of action to correct a problem with the seller's product or service. The purchaser may be an individual or an organization. The desired adjustment might be nothing more than an explanation or apology, but the mere fact that you request some direct action will increase your chances of getting a satisfactory response.

A claim letter can be considered routine if you can reasonably anticipate that the reader will comply with your request. If, for example, you ordered a shipment of shoes for your store that were advertised at $23.50 each and the wholesaler charged you $32.50 instead, you would write a routine claim letter, asking the seller to correct the error. But suppose the wholesaler marked the price down to $19.50 two days after you placed your order. Then instead of writing a routine claim letter, you might want to write a persuasive letter, trying to convince the wholesaler to give you the lower price. (Persuasive letters are discussed in Chapter 8.)

Although you may be frustrated or angry as a result of the situation, remember that the person to whom you're writing was not *personally* responsible for your problem. Be courteous and avoid emotional language. Assume that the company is reasonable and will do as you reasonably ask. Avoid any hint of anger, sarcasm, threat, or exaggeration. A reader who becomes angry as a result of the strong language in your claim letter will be less likely to do as you ask. Instead, using factual and unemotional language, begin your routine claim letter directly, telling exactly what the problem is.

claim letter A letter from a buyer to a seller, seeking some type of action to correct a problem with the seller's product or service

NOT: You should be ashamed at your dishonest advertising for the videotape *Safety Is Job One.*

BUT: The videotape *Safety Is Job One* that I rented for $125 from your company last week lived up to our expectations in every way but one.

NOT: I am disgusted at the way United Express cheated me out of $17.50 last week. What a rip-off!

Assume a courteous tone; avoid emotionalism.

BUT: An overnight letter that I mailed on December 3 did not arrive the next day, as promised by United Express.

After you have identified the problem, begin your explanation. Provide as much background information as necessary—dates, model numbers, amounts, photocopies of canceled checks or correspondence, and the like. Use a confident tone and logic (rather than emotion) to present your case. Write in an impersonal style, avoiding the use of "you" pronouns so as not to link your reader too closely to the negative news.

Provide needed details.

NOT: I delivered this letter to you sometime in the early afternoon on December 3. Although you promised to deliver it by 3 P.M. the next day, you failed to do so.

BUT: As shown on the enclosed copy of my receipt, I delivered this letter to United Express at 3:30 P.M. on December 3. According to the sign prominently displayed in the office, any package received by 4 P.M. is guaranteed to arrive by 3 P.M. the following business day.

If possible, mention something positive about the product.

Tell exactly what went wrong and how you were inconvenienced. If it is true and relevant, mention something positive about the company or its products to make your letter appear reasonable.

According to the enclosed arrival receipt, my letter was not delivered until 8:30 A.M. on December 5. Because the letter contained material needed for a dinner meeting on December 4, it arrived too late to be of any use. This is not the type of on-time service I've routinely received from United Express during the eight years I've been using your delivery system.

Finally, tell what type of adjustment you expect. Do you want the company to replace the product, repair it, issue a refund, simply apologize, or what? End the letter on a confident note.

I would appreciate your refunding my $17.50, thereby reestablishing my confidence in United Express.

In some situations, you may not know what type of adjustment is reasonable; then, you would leave it up to the reader to suggest an appropriate course of action. This might be the situation when you suffered no monetary loss but simply wish to avoid an unpleasant situation in the future (such as discourteous service, long lines, or ordering the wrong model because of having received incomplete or misleading information).

Please let me know how I might avoid this problem in the future.

Model 3 on page 177 illustrates a routine claim letter about a defective product, asking for a specific remedy.

Routine Adjustment Letters

adjustment letter A letter written to inform a customer of the action taken in response to the customer's claim letter

An **adjustment letter** is written to inform a customer of the action taken in response to the customer's claim letter. Few people bother to write a claim letter unless they have a real problem, so most claims that companies receive are legitimate and are adjusted according to the individual situation. If the action taken is what the customer requested or expected, you should write a routine adjustment letter using the direct organizational plan.

MODEL 3

Routine Claim

This claim letter is about a defective product.

OTIS CANDY COMPANY   BOX 302, EDEN, NC 27932, 919-555-4022, FAX: 919-555-4031, WWW.OTISCANDY.COM

April 14, 20—

Customer Relations Representative
Sir Speedy, Inc.
26722 Plaza Drive
Mission Viejo, CA 92690-9077

1 Dear Customer Relations Representative:

Subject: Poor Quality of Photocopying from Invoice 4073

The poor quality of the 13-page full-color handout you duplicated for me on April 8 made the handouts unsuitable for use in my recent presentation to 65 marketing representatives. As a result, I had to use black-and-white copies duplicated in-house instead.

The enclosed copy of the handout is typical of all 75 handouts from this
2 order. As you can see, the colors often run together and the type is fuzzy. The photocopying is not equivalent in quality to that illustrated in Sir Speedy's
3 advertisement on page 154 of the April *Business Management.*

I have already given the presentation for which these handouts were made, so reduplicating them would not solve the problem. I placed my order online on April 3 at your home page using your "Print to Sir Speedy" service. Because I have not yet paid your Invoice 4073 for $438.75, dated April 12, would you please cancel this charge. If you would like me to return all 75 handouts, I shall be happy to do so.

4 I know that despite one's best efforts, mistakes will occasionally happen, and I am confident that you will correct this problem promptly.

Sincerely,

Claire D. Scriven

Claire D. Scriven
Marketing Manager

ric
Enclosure

Identifies the problem immediately and tells how the writer was inconvenienced.

Provides the needed details in a nonemotional, businesslike manner.

Identifies and justifies the specific remedy requested.

Closes on a confident note.

Grammar and Mechanics Notes

1 If an addressee's name is unknown, you may use a title in both the inside address and the salutation.

2 *run together and:* Do not insert any punctuation before the *and* separating the two independent clauses because the second clause, "the type is fuzzy," is so short.

3 April *Business Management:* Italicize magazine titles.

4 *occasionally:* Note that this word has two *c*'s and one *s*.

The customer service representatives at consumer-products companies spend much time handling customer questions and concerns. Simple claims can often be handled over the phone, but most claims (and adjustments) should be in writing—to provide a written trail for reference.

Note that *anyone* in an organization may be called upon to write claim and adjustment letters—not just those working in purchasing or sales or customer service. For example, an accounting manager may send (and receive) a letter complaining of poor service from an employee.

Overall Tone

A claim represents a possible loss of goodwill and confidence in your organization or its products. Because the customer is upset, the overall tone of your adjustment letter is crucial. As you have already decided to honor the claim, your best strategy is to adopt a gracious, trusting tone. Give your customer the benefit of the doubt. It does not make sense to adopt a grudging or resentful tone and risk losing whatever goodwill you might have gained from granting the adjustment.

Adopt a gracious, confident tone for your adjustment letter.

Avoid using negative language when describing the basis for the claim.

> **NOT:** Although our engineers do not understand how this problem could have occurred if the directions had been followed, we are nevertheless willing to repair your generator free of charge.

> **BUT:** We are happy to repair your generator free of charge. Within ten days, a factory representative will call you to schedule a convenient time to make the repair.

Your overall tone should show confidence both in the reader's honesty and in the essential worth of your own organization and its products. To the extent possible, use neutral or positive language in referring to the claim (for example, write "the situation" instead of "your complaint"). Also, avoid appearing to doubt the reader. Instead of saying "you claim that," use more neutral wording, such as "you state that."

Finally, respond promptly. Your customer is already upset; the longer this anger remains, the more difficult it will be to overcome.

Good News First

Nothing that you are likely to tell the reader will be more welcomed than the fact that you are granting the claim, so put this news up front—in the very first sentence if possible. The details and background information will come later, as illustrated by the following examples:

> A new copy of the *American World Dictionary* is on its way to your office, and I assure you that no pages are missing from this copy. I checked it myself!

> The enclosed $17.50 check reimburses you for your company's delayed overnight letter. Thank you for bringing this matter to my attention.

It is often appropriate to thank the reader for giving you an opportunity to resolve the situation, but what about apologizing? An apology, which tends to emphasize the negative aspects of the situation, is generally not advised for small, routine claims that are promptly resolved to the customer's satisfaction. Instead, emphasize the positive aspects and look forward to future transactions. If, however, the customer has been severely inconvenienced or embarrassed and the company is clearly at fault, a sincere apology would be in order. In such a situation, first give the good news and then apologize in a businesslike manner; avoid repeating the apology in the closing lines.

It is appropriate to apologize for serious problems.

> I have contracted with a local mason to rebuild your home's brick walkway, which our driver damaged on February 23. I am truly sorry for the inconvenience this situation has caused you and am grateful for your understanding.

Explanation

After presenting the "good news," you must educate your reader as to why the problem occurred and, if appropriate, what steps you've taken to make sure it doesn't recur. Explain the situation in sufficient detail to be believable, but don't belabor the reason for the problem. Emphasize the fact that you stand behind your products. Avoid using negative language, don't pass the buck, and don't hide behind a "mistakes-will-happen" attitude.

Explain specifically, but briefly, what went wrong.

> Let me explain what happened. On December 4, the plane that had your letter in its cargo bay could not land at O'Hare Airport because of a snowstorm and was diverted to Detroit. Although our Detroit personnel worked overtime to reload the mail onto a delivery truck, which was then driven to Chicago, the shipment did not arrive until early on December 5.

Because the reader's faith in your products has been shaken, you also have a sales job to do. You must build into your letter **resale**—that is, information that reestablishes the customer's confidence in the product purchased or in the company that sells the product. To be believable, do not promise that the problem will never happen again; that's unrealistic. Do, however, use specific language, including facts and figures when possible.

resale Information that reestablishes a customer's confidence in the product or company

Use resale to reassure the customer of the worth of your products.

> **NOT:** We can assure you that this situation will not happen again.

> **BUT:** Fortunately, such incidents are rare. For example, even considering bad weather, airline strikes, and the like, United Express has maintained an on-time delivery record of 97.6% during the past 12 months. No other delivery service even comes close to this record.

Positive, Forward-Looking Closing

End your letter on a positive note. Do not refer to the problem again, do not apologize again, do not suggest the possibility of future problems, and do not imply that the reader might still be upset. Instead, use strategies that imply a

Do not mention the claim in the closing. Instead, look to the future.

continuing relationship with the customer, such as including additional resale, a comment about the satisfaction the reader will receive from the repaired product or improved service, or appreciation for the reader's interest in your products.

Include sales promotion only if you are confident that your adjustment has restored the customer's confidence in your product or service; otherwise, it might backfire. If used, sales promotion should be subtle and should involve a new product or accessory rather than promoting a new or improved model of what the reader has already bought.

NOT: Again, I apologize for the delay in delivering your letter. If you experience such problems again, please don't hesitate to write.

BUT: We have enjoyed serving your delivery needs for the past eight years, Ms. Clarke, and look forward to many more years of service.

Model 4 on page 181 illustrates an adjustment letter, and Checklist 7 summarizes the guidelines for writing routine claim and adjustment letters.

CHECKLIST 7

Routine Claim and Adjustment Letters

Routine Claim Letters

✓ Write your claim letter promptly—as soon as you've identified a problem. Try to determine the name of the appropriate individual to whom to write; if that is not possible, address your letter to the customer relations department.

✓ Strive for an overall tone of courtesy and confidence; avoid anger, sarcasm, threats, and exaggeration. If true and relevant, mention something positive about the company or its products somewhere in the letter.

✓ Begin the letter directly, identifying the problem immediately.

✓ Provide as much detail as necessary. Using impersonal language, tell specifically what went wrong and how you were inconvenienced.

✓ If appropriate, tell what type of adjustment you expect—replacement, repair, refund, or apology. End on a confident note.

Routine Adjustment Letters

✓ Respond promptly; your customer is already upset.

✓ Begin the letter directly, telling the reader immediately what adjustment is being made.

✓ Adopt a courteous tone. Use neutral or positive language throughout.

✓ If appropriate, somewhere in the letter thank the reader for writing, and apologize if the customer has been severely inconvenienced or embarrassed because of your company's actions.

✓ In a forthright manner, explain the reason for the problem in sufficient detail to be believable, but don't belabor the point. If appropriate, briefly tell what steps you've taken to prevent a recurrence of the problem.

✓ Provide information that reestablishes your customer's confidence in the product or your company. Be specific enough to be believable.

✓ If the customer was at fault, explain in impersonal and tactful language the facts surrounding the case.

✓ Close on a positive note. Include additional resale, subtle sales promotion, appreciation for the reader's interest in your products, or some other strategy that implies customer satisfaction and the expectation of a continuing relationship.

MODEL 4

Routine Adjustment Letter

This adjustment letter responds to the claim letter in Model 3 on page 177.

Sir Speedy, Inc.

April 22, 20—

1 Ms. Claire Scriven
Marketing Manager
Otis Candy Company
Box 302
Eden, NC 27932

Dear Ms. Scriven:

Subject: Cancellation of Charge for Invoice 4073

2 Sir Speedy is, of course, happy to cancel the $438.75 charge for Invoice 4073. I appreciate your taking the time to write and send us a sample handout (you may simply discard the
3 other copies).

4 Upon receiving your letter, I immediately sent your handout to our quality-control personnel for closer examination. They agreed with you that the handouts should have been redone before they left our facilities. We have now revised our procedures to ensure that before each online order leaves our facilities, it is inspected by someone other than the person preparing it.

Corporate Offices

26722 Plaza Drive

To better serve the media needs of our corporate customers, we are installing the Xerox DocuCenter 480 copier, the most sophisticated industrial color copier system available. Thus, when you send us your next online order, you'll see that your handouts are of even higher quality than those in the *Business Management* advertisement that impressed you.

P.O. Box 9077

Mission Viejo, CA 92690-9077

Tel: (949) 348-5000

Fax: (949) 348-5010 Sincerely yours,

David Foster

www.sirspeedy.com

David Foster
Customer Relations

jed

Tells immediately that the adjustment is being made; thanks the reader.

Explains briefly, but specifically, what happened.

Looks forward to a continuing relationship with the customer; does not mention the problem again.

Grammar and Mechanics Notes

1 Type the position title either on the same line as the person's name or, as here, on a line by itself.

2 *Invoice 4073:* Capitalize a noun that precedes a number.

3 *copies).:* Place the period outside the closing parenthesis unless the entire sentence is in parentheses.

4 *personnel:* Do not confuse *personnel* (employees) with *personal* (private).

CHECKPOINT 7.2

RECALL Write a capital *T* for true or *F* for false before each statement.

1. ____ If your computer broke down during the 90-day warranty period, you would probably write a routine adjustment letter.

2. ____ You should avoid using "you" pronouns when describing the problem with the company's product.

3. ____ "Thank you for letting us know about your problem with our product" would be an effective way to begin a routine adjustment letter.

4. ____ In an adjustment letter, you should not promise that the problem will not recur.

5. ____ It is not advisable to apologize for small, routine claims.

VOCABULARY Define the following terms in your own words.

6. adjustment letter:

7. claim letter:

8. resale:

COMPREHENSION

9. The *Accounting Principles* textbook (ISBN: 0618191496) that you purchased online at textbooks.com arrived on time as advertised but in damaged condition. The front cover and several of the pages were torn—certainly not what you'd expect when you paid $45.99 for the used book. You complain via email.

   a. Compose an appropriate subject line for your email.

   b. Compose the first paragraph of your message.

   c. Compose the last sentence of your message.

CRITICAL THINKING

10. Some consumer advocates recommend addressing your claim letter directly to the company president instead of to the customer-service manager. Do you agree or disagree? Why?

Planning the Bad-News Message

At some point in our lives we have all probably been both the senders and the recipients of bad news. And just as most people find it difficult to accept bad news, they also find it difficult to convey bad news. How you write your messages won't change the news you have to deliver, but it may determine whether your reader accepts your decision as reasonable—or goes away mad.

Your purpose in writing a bad-news message is twofold: first, to say "no" or to convey bad news; and second, to retain the reader's goodwill. To accomplish these goals, you must communicate your message politely, clearly, and firmly. In addition, you must show the reader that you've seriously considered the request but that as a matter of fairness and good business practice, you must deny it.

Your objectives are to convey the bad news and to retain the reader's goodwill.

Organizing to Suit Your Audience

The reader's needs, expectations, and personality—as well as the writer's relationship with the reader—will largely determine the content and organization of a bad-news message. Thus you need to put yourself in the place of the reader.

To decide whether to use the direct or the indirect plan for refusing a request, check the sender's original message. If the original message was written in the direct style, the sender may have considered it a routine request, and you would be safe in answering in the direct style. If the original message was written in the indirect style, the sender probably considered it a persuasive request, and you should consider answering in the indirect style. (However, messages written to one's superior are typically written in the direct style, regardless of whether the reader considers the original request routine or persuasive.)

For example, an email message telling employees that the company cafeteria will be closed for one day to permit installation of new equipment can be written directly and in a paragraph or two. A message telling employees that the company cafeteria will be closed permanently and that employees will now have to go outside for lunch (and pay higher prices) would require more explanation and should probably be written in the indirect style.

Direct Plan—Present the Bad News Immediately   As discussed earlier, many requests are routine; the writer simply wants a yes-or-no decision and wants to

When Agilent Technologies had to cut pay and lay off 8,000 people, it handled the bad news in such a humane way that the company was named one of the "Best Companies to Work For" by *Fortune* magazine in 2002. After workers in this Agilent factory were told their plant was closing, they upped production higher than ever before.

hear it in a direct manner. Similarly, if an announcement of bad news is not likely to generate an emotional response from the reader, you should use a direct approach. The direct plan for bad-news messages is basically the same plan used for routine messages discussed earlier: present the major idea (the bad news) up front. To help readers accept your decision when using the direct plan, however, give a brief rationale along with the bad news in the first paragraph.

> **NOT:** The annual company picnic originally scheduled for August 3 at Riverside Park has been canceled.

> **BUT:** Because ongoing construction at Riverside Park might present safety hazards to our employees and their families, the annual company picnic originally scheduled for August 3 has been canceled.

As usual, state the message in language as positive as possible, while still maintaining honesty.

> **NOT:** Our departmental compliance report will be late next month.

> **BUT:** The extra time required to resolve the Baton Rouge refinery problem means that our departmental compliance report will be submitted on March 15 rather than on March 1.

Follow this information with any needed explanation and a friendly closing. Use the direct organizational plan in the following circumstances:

Prefer the direct organizational plan for communicating bad news to your superior.

- The bad news involves a small, insignificant matter and can be considered routine. If the reader is not likely to be emotionally involved and thus not seriously disappointed by the decision, use the direct approach.
- The reader prefers directness. Superiors typically prefer that *all* messages from subordinates be written in the direct style.

In rare situations, it is necessary to emphasize the bad news.

- The writer wants to emphasize the negative news. Suppose that you have already refused a request once and the reader writes a second time; under these circumstances, a forceful "no" might be in order. Or consider the situation where negative information will be included in a form letter—perhaps as an insert in a monthly statement. Because the reader might otherwise discard or merely skim an "unimportant-looking" message, you should consider placing the bad news up front—where it will be noticed.

Complex situations typically call for an indirect organizational pattern and require more explanation than simpler situations.

A message organized according to a direct plan is not necessarily any shorter than one organized according to an indirect plan. Both types of messages may contain the same basic information, albeit in a different order. Direct messages are often shorter than indirect messages only because the direct plan is often used for *simpler* situations, which require little explanation and background information.

Indirect Plan—Buffer the Bad News   Because the preceding conditions are *not* true for many bad-news situations, you will often want to use an indirect plan—especially when giving bad news to

- Subordinates
- Customers
- Readers who prefer the indirect approach
- Readers you don't know

With the indirect approach, you present the reasons first, then the negative news. This approach emphasizes the *reasons* for the bad news, rather than the bad news itself.

A buffer lessens the impact of the bad news.

Suppose, for example, a subordinate expects a "yes" answer upon receiving your email message. Putting the negative news in the first sentence might be too harsh and emphatic, and your decision might sound unreasonable until the reader has heard the rationale for it. In such a situation, you should begin with a neutral and relevant statement—one that helps establish or strengthen the reader–writer relationship. Such a statement serves as a *buffer* between the reader and the bad news that will follow.

An effective opening buffer for bad-news messages has these characteristics:

1. It is *neutral*. To serve as a true buffer, the opening must not convey the negative news immediately. At the same time, guard against implying that the request will be *granted*, thereby building up the reader for a big letdown.

2. It is *relevant*. The danger with starting *too* far from the topic is that the reader might not recognize that the letter is intended as a response to his or her request. In addition, an irrelevant opening seems to avoid the issue, thus sounding insincere or self-serving. To show relevance and to personalize the opening, you might include some reference to the reader's letter in your first sentence. A relevant opening provides a smooth transition to the reasons that follow.

3. It is *supportive*. The purpose of the opening is to help establish compatibility between reader and writer. If the opening is controversial or seems to lecture the reader, it will not achieve its purpose.

   An effective buffer is neutral, relevant, supportive, interesting, and short.

4. It is *interesting*. Buffer openings should motivate the recipient to continue reading. Therefore, avoid giving obvious information.

5. It is *short*. Readers become impatient if they have to wait too long to reach the major point of the message.

Assume that the owner of an appliance store has written you, one of his suppliers, asking you to provide an in-store demonstrator of your firm's products during his anniversary sale. For sound business reasons, you must refuse the request. Because you're writing to a good customer, you decide to use an indirect plan. You might effectively start your message by using any of the following types of buffers:

Buffer Type	*Example*
Agreement	We both recognize the promotional possibilities that often accompany big anniversary sales such as yours.
Appreciation	Thanks for letting us know of your success in selling Golden Microwaves. (*Avoid, however, thanking the reader for asking you to do something that you're going to refuse to do; such expressions of appreciation sound insincere.*)
Compliment	Congratulations on having served the community of Greenville for ten years.
Facts	Three-fourths of the Golden Microwaves distributors who held anniversary sales last year reported at least a 6% increase in annual sales of our home products.
General principle	We believe in furnishing Golden Microwaves distributors a wide range of support in promoting our products.
Good news	Golden Microwaves' upcoming 20%-off sale will be heavily advertised and will certainly provide increased traffic for your February anniversary sale.
Understanding	I wish to assure you of Golden Microwaves' desire to help make your anniversary sale successful.

Ethical communicators use a buffer *not* to manipulate or confuse the reader but rather to help the reader accept the disappointing information in an objective manner.

Justifying Your Decision

Focus on the reasons for the refusal—not on the refusal itself.

Presumably, you reached your negative decision by analyzing all the relevant information. Whether you began in a direct or an indirect manner, now explain your analysis to help convince the reader that your decision is reasonable. The major part of your message should, therefore, focus on the *reasons* rather than on the bad news itself.

For routine bad-news messages (that is, those written in a direct approach), the reasons can probably be stated concisely and matter-of-factly. Indirectly written messages, however, require more careful planning—because the stakes are typically higher.

Provide a smooth transition from the opening buffer and present the reasons honestly and convincingly. If possible, explain how the reasons benefit the reader or, at least, benefit someone other than your organization. For example, refusing to exchange a worn garment might enable you to offer better-quality merchandise to your customers, raising the price of your product might enable you to switch to nonpolluting energy in its manufacture, or refusing to provide copies of company documents might protect the confidentiality of customer transactions. Presenting reader benefits keeps your decision from sounding selfish.

Sometimes, of course, granting the request is simply not in the company's own best interests. In such situations, don't "manufacture" reader benefits; instead, just provide whatever short explanation you can and let it go at that.

> Because this data would be of strategic importance to our competitors, we treat the information as confidential. Similar information about our entire industry (SIC Code 1473), however, is collected in the annual *U.S. Census of Manufacturing*. These census reports are available in most public and university libraries and online.

Show the reader that your decision was a *business* decision, not a personal one. Indicate that the request was taken seriously, and don't hide behind company policy. If the policy is a sound one, it was established for good reasons; therefore, explain the rationale for the policy.

Don't rely on company policy. Instead, explain the rationale for the policy.

> **NOT:** Company policy prohibits our providing an in-store demonstrator for your tenth-anniversary sale.
>
> **BUT:** A survey of our dealers three years ago indicated they felt the space taken up by in-store demonstrators and the resulting traffic problems were not worth the effort; they were also concerned about the legal liability of having someone cooking in their stores.

The reasons justifying your decision should take up the major part of the message, but be concise or your reader may become impatient. Do not belabor a point and do not provide more background than is necessary. If you have several reasons for refusing a request, present the strongest one first—where it will receive the most emphasis. Avoid mentioning any weak reasons. If the reader feels he or she can effectively rebut even one of your arguments, you're simply raising false hopes and inviting needless correspondence.

Giving the Bad News

The bad news is communicated up front in directly written messages. Even in an indirectly written message, if you have done a convincing job of explaining the reasons, the bad news itself will come as no surprise; instead, the decision will appear logical and reasonable—indeed, the *only* logical and reasonable decision that could have been made under the circumstances.

To retain the reader's goodwill, state the bad news in positive or neutral language, stressing what you *are* able to do rather than what you are *not* able to do. Avoid, for example, such words and phrases as "cannot," "are not able to," "impossible," "unfortunately," "sorry," and "must refuse." To subordinate the bad news, put it in the middle of a paragraph, and include in the same sentence (or immediately afterward) additional discussion of reasons.

> In response to these dealer concerns, we eliminated in-store demonstrations and now advertise exclusively in the print media. Doing so has enabled us to begin featuring a two-page spread in each major Sunday newspaper, including your local paper, the *Greenville Courier*.

The reader should be able to infer the bad news before it is presented.

When using the indirect plan, phrase the bad news in impersonal language, avoiding the use of *you* and *your*. The objective is to distance the reader from the bad news so that it will not be perceived as a personal rejection. So as not to point out the bad news that lies ahead, avoid using "but" and "however" to introduce it. The fact is, most readers won't remember what was written before the "but"— only what was written after it.

Resist any temptation to apologize for your decision. You may reasonably assume that if the reader were faced with the same options and had the same information available, he or she would act in a similar way. There is no reason to apologize for any reasonable business decision.

You do not need to apologize for making a rational business decision.

In some situations, the refusal can be implied, making a direct statement of refusal unnecessary. But don't be evasive. If you think a positive, subordinated refusal might be misunderstood, go ahead and state it directly. Of course, even under these circumstances, you should use impersonal language and include reader benefits.

Closing on a Pleasant Note

Any refusal, even when handled skillfully, carries negative overtones. Therefore, you need to end your message on a more pleasant note. Avoid statements such as those listed here.

Do not refer to the bad news in the closing.

Problem to Avoid	*Example of Problem*
Apologizing	Again, I am sorry that we were unable to grant this request.
Anticipating problems	If you run into any problems, please write me directly.
Inviting needless communication	If you have any further questions, please let me know.
Referring again to bad news	Although we are unable to supply an in-store demonstrator, we do wish you much success in your tenth-anniversary sale.
Repeating a cliché	If we can be of any further help, please don't hesitate to call on us.
Revealing doubt	I trust that you now understand why we made this decision.
Sounding selfish	Don't forget to feature Golden Microwaves prominently in your anniversary display.

Make your closing original, friendly, and positive by using any of the following techniques. Avoid referring again to the bad news.

Technique	Example
Best wishes	Best wishes for success with your tenth-anniversary sale. We have certainly enjoyed our ten-year relationship with Parker Brothers and look forward to continuing to serve your needs in the future.
Counterproposal	To provide increased publicity for your tenth-anniversary sale, we would be happy to include a special 2-by-6-inch boxed notice of your sale in the *Greenville Courier* edition of our ad on Sunday, February 8. Just send us your camera-ready copy by January 26.
Other sources of help	A dealer in South Carolina switched from using in-store demonstrators to showing a video continuously during his microwave sale. He used the ten-minute film *Twenty-Minute Dinners with Pizzazz* (available for $45 from the Microwave Research Institute, P.O. Box 800, Chicago, IL 60625) and reported a favorable reaction from customers.
Resale or subtle sales	You can be sure that the new Golden promotion Mini-Micro we're introducing in January will draw many customers to your store during your anniversary sale.

Close the letter on a positive, friendly, helpful note.

To sound sincere and helpful, make your ending original. If you provide a counterproposal or offer other sources of help, provide all information the reader needs to follow through. If you include sales promotion, make it subtle and reader-oriented.

In short, the last idea the reader hears from you should be positive, friendly, and helpful. Checklist 8 on page 189 summarizes guidelines for writing bad-news letters. The rest of this chapter discusses strategies for writing bad-news replies and bad-news announcements.

Rejecting an Idea

One of the more challenging bad-news messages to write is one that rejects someone's idea or proposal. Put yourself in the role of the person making the suggestion. He or she has probably spent a considerable amount of time in developing the idea, studying its feasibility, perhaps doing some research, and, of course, writing the original persuasive message.

Take the reader's feelings into consideration when rejecting an idea.

Consider, for example, the situation faced by Elliott Lamborn of Newton Electrical Systems. He has just received a memo from Jenson Peterson, his marketing supervisor, proposing that the company restrict its close-in employee parking lots to use by drivers of Ford vehicles, because Ford Motor Company accounts for nearly half of the company's annual sales. Peterson obviously thought his idea had merit and likely expects Lamborn to approve it. If—or in this case *when*—his proposal is rejected, Peterson will be surprised and disappointed.

Because Lamborn is Peterson's superior, he could send Peterson a directly written memo saying in effect, "I have considered your proposal and must reject it."

CHECKLIST 8

Bad-News Messages

Determine How to Start the Message

✓ **Direct Plan**—Use a direct organizational plan when the bad news is insignificant, the reader prefers directness (such as your superior) or expects a "no" response, the writer wants to emphasize the bad news, or the reader–writer relationship is either extremely close or extremely poor. Present the bad news (see "Give the Bad News" at right), along with a brief rationale, in the first paragraph.

✓ **Indirect Plan**—Use an indirect organizational plan when writing to subordinates, customers, readers who prefer the indirect plan, or readers you don't know. Start by buffering the bad news, following these guidelines:

a. Remember the purpose: to establish a common ground with the reader.

b. Select an opening statement that is neutral, relevant, supportive, interesting, and short.

c. Consider establishing a point of agreement, expressing appreciation, giving a sincere compliment, presenting a fact or general principle, giving good news, or showing understanding.

d. Provide a smooth transition from the buffer to the reasons that follow.

Justify Your Decision

✓ If possible, stress reasons that benefit someone other than yourself.

✓ State reasons in positive language.

✓ Avoid relying on "company policy"; instead, explain the reason behind the policy.

✓ State reasons concisely to avoid reader impatience. Do not overexplain.

✓ Present the strongest reasons first; avoid discussing weak reasons.

Give the Bad News

✓ If using the indirect plan, subordinate the bad news by putting it in the middle of a paragraph and including additional discussion of reasons.

✓ Present the bad news as a logical outcome of the reasons given.

✓ State the bad news in positive and impersonal language. Avoid terms such as *cannot* and *your*.

✓ Do not apologize.

✓ Make the refusal definite—by implication if appropriate; otherwise, by stating it directly.

Close on a Positive Note

✓ Make your closing original, friendly, off the topic of the bad news, and positive.

✓ Consider expressing best wishes, offering a counterproposal, suggesting other sources of help, or building in resale or subtle sales promotion.

✓ Avoid anticipating problems, apologizing, inviting needless communication, referring to the bad news, repeating a cliché, revealing doubt, or sounding selfish.

But Peterson is obviously intelligent and enterprising, and Lamborn does not want to discourage future initiatives on his part. As with all such bad-news replies, then, Lamborn's twin objectives are to refuse the proposal and to retain Peterson's goodwill.

To be successful, Lamborn has an educating job to do. He must give Peterson the reasons for the rejection, reasons of which Peterson is probably unaware. He must also show that he recognizes Peterson's proposal as carefully considered and that the rejection is based on business—not personal—considerations.

Given the amount of effort Peterson has devoted to this project, Lamborn's response will be most effective if written in the indirect pattern. This pattern will let Lamborn move his subordinate gradually into agreeing that the proposal is not in the firm's best interests.

Model 5 shows Lamborn's memo rejecting Peterson's proposal. Although we label this memo a bad-news message, it is also a *persuasive* message. Like all bad-news messages, the memo seeks to persuade the reader that the writer's position is reasonable.

MODEL 5

Bad-News Reply— Rejecting an Idea

Uses a neutrally worded subject line.

Starts with a supportive buffer; the second sentence provides a smooth transition to the reason.

Begins discussing the reason.

Presents the refusal in the last sentence of the paragraph, using positive and impersonal language.

Closes on a forward-looking, off-the-topic note.

NEWTON
Electrical
Systems

1034 York Road
Baltimore, MD 21204
Phone: 301.555.1086
Fax: 301.555.3926
www.nes.com

+ — + — + — + — + — + — + — + — + — + — + — + — + — + — +
Serving the automotive industry for more than 50 years

MEMO TO: Jenson J. Peterson, Marketing Supervisor

FROM: Elliott Lamborn, Vice President EL

DATE: April 15, 20—

SUBJECT: Employee Parking Lot Proposal

Your April 3 memo certainly enlightened me regarding the automobile-buying habits of our employees. I had no idea that our workers drive such a variety of models.

The increasing popularity of foreign-made vehicles recently led management to conclude that we should consider extending our promotional thrust to take advantage of this expanding market. President Wrede has appointed a task force to determine how we might also promote our electrical systems to Japanese, German, and English automakers, as well as to Ford.

Our successful push into the international market will mean that many of the non-Ford vehicles our employees drive will, in fact, be supplied with Newton Electrical Systems components. Thus, our firm will benefit from the continuing presence of these cars in all our lots.

1   Your memo got me to thinking, Jenson, that we might be missing an opportunity to promote our products to headquarters visitors. Would you please develop some type of awareness campaign (perhaps a bumper sticker for employee cars that contain a Newton electrical system or some type of billboard) that shows our employees support the products we sell. I would appreciate having a memo from you with your ideas by November 3 so that I might include this project in next

2   year's marketing campaign.

amp

Grammar and Mechanics Notes

1 *thinking, Jenson, that:* Set off nouns of direct address (*Jenson*) with commas.
2 *year's:* Use apostrophe plus *s* to form the possessive of a singular noun (*year*).

Refusing a Claim

The indirect plan is almost always used when refusing an adjustment request because the reader (a dissatisfied customer) is emotionally involved in the situation. The customer is already upset by the failure of the product to live up to expectations. If you refuse the claim immediately, you risk losing the customer's goodwill.

The tone of your refusal must convey respect and consideration for the customer—even when the customer is at fault. To separate the reader from the refusal, begin with a buffer, using one of the techniques presented earlier (for example, showing understanding).

> Frequent travelers like you depend on luggage that "can take it"—luggage that will hold up for many years under normal use.

Use impersonal, neutral language to explain the basis for the refusal.

When explaining the reasons for denying the claim, do not accuse or lecture the reader. At the same time, don't appear to accept responsibility for the problem if the customer is at fault. In impersonal, neutral language, explain why the claim is being denied.

> **NOT:** The reason the handles ripped off your Sebastian luggage is that you overloaded it. The tag on the luggage clearly states that you should use the luggage only for clothing, with a maximum of 40 pounds. However, our engineers concluded that you had put at least 65 pounds of items in the luggage.

> **BUT:** On receiving your piece of Sebastian luggage, we sent it to our testing department. The engineers there found stretch marks on the leather and a frayed nylon stitching cord. They concluded that such wear could have been caused only by contents weighing substantially more than the 40-pound maximum weight that is stated on the luggage tag. Such use is beyond the "normal wear and tear" covered in our warranty.

Note that in the second example, the pronoun *you* is not used at all when discussing the bad news. By using third-person pronouns and the passive voice, the example avoids directly accusing the reader of misusing the product. The actual refusal, given in the last sentence, is conveyed in neutral language.

As with other bad-news messages, close on a friendly, forward-looking note. If you can offer a compromise, it will take the sting out of the rejection and show the customer that you are reasonable. It will also help the customer save face. Be careful, however, that your offer does not imply any assumption of responsibility on your part. The compromise can either come before or be a part of the closing.

An offer of a compromise, however small, helps retain the reader's goodwill.

> Although we replace luggage only when it is damaged in normal use, our repair shop tells me the damaged handle can easily be replaced. We would be happy to do so for $39.50, including return shipping. If you will simply initial this letter and return it to us in the enclosed, addressed envelope, we will return your repaired luggage within four weeks.

Somewhere in your letter you might also include a subtle pitch for resale. The customer has had a negative experience with your product. If you want your reader to continue to be a customer, you might restate some of the benefits that led him or her to buy the product in the first place. But use this technique carefully; a strong pitch may simply annoy an already unhappy customer.

Consider the situation in which a customer wrote to an airline company upset that his family's flight to Indianapolis was canceled and they were forced to make a six-hour drive instead. The customer wanted a refund of the $680 cost of his five nonrefundable tickets. For good business reasons, the company decided to refuse his claim. Model 6 on page 192 illustrates the guidelines discussed above for writing an effective bad-news message.

MODEL 6

Bad-News Reply— Refusing a Claim

Opens on an agreeable and relevant note.

Begins the explanation; presents the refusal in impersonal language.

Closes on a helpful note; assumes that the reader will continue to fly on Northern Airlines.

June 27, 20—

Mr. Oliver J. Arbin
518 Thompson Street
Saginaw, MI 48607

1   Dear Mr. Arbin

Subject: Further Information About Flight 126

We make no money when our customers are forced to take long trips by car rather than by flying Northern Airlines; and when that happens, we want to find out why.

2   A review of the June 2 log of the aborted Flight 126 shows that it was scheduled to depart at 8 p.m. and was canceled at 7:10 p.m. because of inclement weather. Passengers were asked to remain in the boarding area; those who did were rebooked on Flight 3321, which departed at 9:15 p.m. Flight 3321 arrived in Indianapolis at 10:40 p.m., just 75 minutes later than the scheduled arrival of Flight 126. Given these circumstances, Ms. Louise Nixon, the ticket agent, was correct in disallowing any refund on nonrefundable tickets.

Since you indicated that you're a frequent traveler on Northern, I've asked our Scheduling Department to add you to the mailing list to receive a complimentary subscription to our quarterly Saginaw flight schedule. A copy of the current schedule is enclosed. From now on, you'll be sure to know exactly when every Northern and Eagle flight arrives at and departs from Tri-Cities Airport.

Sincerely

Madelyn Masarani

Madelyn Masarani
Service Representative

eta
3   Enclosure

P.O. BOX 6001, DENVER, CO 80240 • (303) 555-3990 • FAX (303) 555-3992

Grammar and Mechanics Notes

1 Insert no punctuation after the salutation and complimentary closing when using open punctuation.
2 *boarding area;:* Use a semicolon to separate two closely related independent clauses not connected by a conjunction.
3 Use an enclosure notation to alert the recipient to look for some inserted material.

RECALL   Write a capital *T* for true or *F* for false before each statement.

1. ____ Bad-news messages should be written in the direct organizational pattern.
2. ____ The buffer opening of a bad-news letter should not indicate the topic of the letter.
3. ____ Most of the focus of the bad-news message should be on the reasons for the refusal.
4. ____ To establish good rapport with the reader, you should apologize for having to deliver bad news.
5. ____ Bad-news messages are also persuasive messages.

CHECKPOINT 7.3

COMPREHENSION

6. Now assume the role of the customer-service manager at textbooks.com (see Exercise 9 of Checkpoint 7.2 on page 182). The front cover and two of the pages of the textbook were torn when you shipped it. That's why you sold it as a used book at a deep discount. Customers must check a box on the online order form acknowledging their understanding that used books may have been marked up or show signs of wear and tear. The only thing you guarantee is that no pages are missing from the used books you sell. Decline the claim.

   a. Compose an appropriate subject line for your email.

   b. Compose the first sentence of your message.

   c. Compose the sentence in which you actually refuse the claim.

   d. Compose the final paragraph of your letter.

CRITICAL THINKING

7. What advice could you give to a friend who has to send a bad-news message to an Asian colleague?

A Bad-News Message

Problem

You are a facilities manager at General Mills. Your firm recently constructed a new administrative building on a five-acre lot, and you've landscaped the unused four acres with lighted walkways, fountains, and ponds for employees to enjoy during their lunch hours and before and after work. Your lovely campus-like site is one of the few such locations within the city limits.

Joan Bradley, the mayor of your city, is running for reelection. She has written to you asking permission to hold a campaign fund-raiser on your grounds on July 7 from 8 P.M. until midnight. This event will be for "heavy" contributors; as many as 150 people, each paying $500, are expected. Her reelection committee will take care of all catering, security, and cleanup.

You do not want to become involved in this event for numerous reasons. Write to the mayor (The Honorable Joan Bradley, Mayor of Clarkfield, Clarkfield, MN 56223) and decline her request.

Process

1. Describe your primary audience.

   ■ Very important person (Don't want to offend her)

   ■ Holds political views different from my own

   ■ Possibility of her losing the election (don't want to appear to be backing a loser)

2. Describe your secondary audience.

   ■ The 150 big contributors (What will be their reaction to my refusal?)

   ■ The other candidates (Do not wish to offend anyone who might become the next mayor)

3. Brainstorm: List as many reasons as you can think of why you might refuse the mayor's request. Then, after you've come up with several, determine which one will be most effective. Underline that reason.

   ■ Other sites in the city offering a more suitable environment for the event

   ■ Would have to provide the same favor for every other candidate

   ■ <u>Possible harm to lawn, plants, and animals</u>

   ■ Company policy that prohibits outside use

The **3P**s
Problem, Process, Product

4. Write your buffer opening—neutral, relevant, supportive, interesting, and short.

   Thank you for your kind comments about our lovely grounds. Our staff has been able to create an environment in which plants and animals not normally found in the Midwest are able to thrive.

5. Now skip to the actual refusal itself. Write the statement in which you refuse the request—making it positive, subordinated, and unselfish.

   To protect this delicate environment, we restrict the use of these grounds to company employees.

6. Write the closing for your letter—original, friendly, off the topic of the refusal, and positive. *Suggestions:* best wishes, counterproposal, other sources of help, or subtle resale.

   As an alternative, may I suggest the beautiful grounds at the Minnesota Educational Consortium on Lapeer Street. They were designed with a Minnesota motif by Larry Miller, the designer for our grounds.

195

Product

General Mills
General Offices

Post Office Box 1113
Minneapolis, Minnesota 55440

May 20, 20—

The Honorable Joan Bradley
Mayor of Clarkfield
Clarkfield, MN 56223

Dear Mayor Bradley:

Thank you for your kind comments about our lovely grounds. Our staff has been able to create an environment here in which plants and animals not normally found in the Midwest are able to thrive.

For example, after much effort, we have finally been able to attract a family of Eastern Bluebirds to our site. At this very moment, the female is sitting on three eggs, and various members of our staff unobtrusively check on her progress each day.

Similar efforts have resulted in the successful introduction of beautiful but sensitive flowers, shrubs, and marsh grasses. To protect this delicate environment, we restrict the use of these grounds to company employees, many of whom have contributed ideas, plants, and time in developing the grounds.

As an alternative, may I suggest the beautiful grounds at the Minnesota Educational Consortium on Lapeer Street. They were designed with a Minnesota motif by Larry Miller, the designer for our grounds. Various public events have been held there without damage to the environment. Susan Siebold, their executive director (555-9832), is the person to contact about using MEC's facilities.

Sincerely,

J.W. Hudson
Facilities Manager

tma

General Offices at Number One General Mills Boulevard

Summary

Most business writing tasks involve routine matters in which the writer conveys either positive or routine information that is of interest to the reader. Such situations call for a direct organizational plan in which the major purpose of the message is presented first. The major idea is followed by any needed background information or additional explanation, and the message ends on a friendly, forward-looking note.

When writing a bad-news message, your goal is to convey the bad news and, at the same time, keep the reader's goodwill. A direct organizational plan is recommended when you are writing to superiors, when the bad news involves a small, insignificant matter, or when you want to emphasize the bad news. When using the direct plan, state the bad news in positive language in the first paragraph, perhaps preceded or followed by a short buffer or a reason for the decision. Next, present the explanation or reasons for the decision. Finally, close on a friendly and positive note.

When writing to subordinates, customers, or people you don't know, you should generally use an indirect plan. This approach begins with a buffer—a neutral and relevant statement that helps establish or strengthen the reader–writer relationship. Next comes the explanation of or reasons for the bad news. The reasons should be logical and, when possible, should identify a reader benefit. The bad news should be subordinated, using positive and impersonal language; apologies are not necessary. The closing should be friendly, positive, and off the topic.

Use the three checklists presented on pages 174, 180, and 189 in composing routine and bad-news messages and in revising your drafts.

Key Terms

adjustment letter
claim letter
direct organizational plan

indirect organizational plan
resale

Looking Ahead

Think of the billions of dollars spent annually by companies on television and radio commercials and on magazine and newspaper advertisements. Their one purpose is to persuade you to buy their products. As a member of the business world, you will also have many opportunities to try to persuade others—perhaps not to buy a product but to accept your way of thinking. In Chapter 8 you will learn how to write effective persuasive emails, letters, and memos.

Exercises

Routine Requests and Replies

1 Routine Request—Membership Information Although your part-time job is only temporary (you plan to quit when you finish college), your boss wants you to gain more experience in public speaking and has suggested that you join Toastmasters International, an organization devoted to helping its members practice and improve their public-speaking skills. You are interested in determining whether your town has a local chapter and, if so, the time and place of meetings, the amount of annual dues, and the like.

Locate the Toastmasters International home page on the Internet and find an email address for the group. Compose an email message, asking several specific, pertinent questions. Email a copy of your message to your instructor. Follow your instructor's direction regarding whether to mail your message to Toastmasters.

2 **Routine Request—Letter of Recommendation**   As part of your application papers for a one-semester internship at American Express, you are asked to include a letter of recommendation from one of your business professors. You made a good grade in MGT 382: Wage and Salary Administration, which you took three semesters ago from Dr. Dennis Thavinet in the management department at your college. You liked the course so well that you missed class only twice (for good reasons). Although you were not one of the most vocal members in class, Dr. Thavinet did commend you for your group project. American Express (at 1850 East Camelback Road, Phoenix, AZ 85017) wants to know especially about your ability to work well with others.

Compose (but do not send) an email message to Dr. Thavinet (djthavinet @marsu.edu), asking for a letter of recommendation. You would like him to respond within one week.

3 **Routine Response—Student Information**   As the dean of admissions for Eastern State University, you have received a letter from Linda O'Kelly, a first-year student at the State University of New York, 665 Catskill Hall, Oswego, NY 13126. She is interested in transferring to your school, but she has a number of questions about the courses and the transfer requirements. Here are her questions and the answers:

a. Does the school offer an undergraduate degree in environmental engineering? *Yes, the school initiated this program two years ago.*
b. What are the requirements for transfer students? *Transfer students must have at least a 2.75 first-year GPA to be considered for admission as sophomores.*
c. Can all courses taken at another school be transferred for credit? *No, only courses for which Eastern State has an equivalent offering are accepted for credit.*

Your school accepts only a few transfer students each semester, but you don't want to discourage Ms. O'Kelly (who may be among the few accepted). Respond to her letter and mention that you are sending additional information (such as a college catalog) in a separate package.

4 **Work-Team Communication—Routine Response**   You are a member of the Presidents' Council, an organization made up of the presidents of each student organization on campus. You just received a memorandum from Dr. Robin H. Hill, dean of students, wanting to know the types of social projects in which the student organizations on campus have been engaged during the past year. The dean must report to the board of trustees on the important role played by student organizations—both in the life of the university and community and in the development of student leadership and social skills. She wants to include such information as student-run programs on drug and alcohol abuse, community service, and fund-raising.

Working in groups of four, identify and summarize the types of social projects that student organizations at your institution have completed this year. Then organize and synthesize your findings into a one-page memo to Dr. Hill.

After writing your first draft, have each member review and comment on the draft. Then revise as needed and submit it to your instructor. Use only factual data for this assignment.

Routine Claim and Adjustment Letters

5 **Claim Letter—Inaccurate Reporting**   As the assistant marketing manager for ReSolve, a basic computer spreadsheet program for Windows, you were pleased that your product was reviewed in the current issue of *Computing Trends*. The review praised your product for its "lightning-fast speed and convenient user interface." You were not pleased, however, that your product was downgraded because it lacked high-level graphics capability. The reviewer compared ReSolve with full-featured spreadsheet programs costing, on average, $200 more than your program. No wonder, then, that your program rated a 6.6 out of 10, coming in third out of the five programs reviewed. If it had been compared with similar low-level programs, you feel certain that ReSolve would have easily come out on top.

Although you do not want to get the magazine upset with your company (Software Entrepreneurs, Inc.), you do feel that it should compare apples with apples and should conduct another review of your program. Write to Roberta J. Horton, the magazine's review editor, at 200 Public Square in Cleveland, OH 44114, and tell her so.

6 **Routine Claim—Defective Product**   You are J. R. McCord, purchasing agent for People's Energy Company. On February 3, you ordered a box of four laser cartridges for your Sampson Model 25 printers at $69.35 each, plus $6.85 shipping and handling—total price of $284.25. The catalog description for this cartridge (Part No. 02-8R01656) stated, "Fits Epson and Xerox printers and most compatibles." As the Sampson is advertised as a Xerox clone printer, you assumed the cartridges would work with it. When the order arrived, you discovered that the cartridges didn't fit your Sampson printer. Although the cartridges are the same shape, the new cartridges are about $\frac{1}{4}$ inch thicker and won't seat properly on the spindles.

You believe that your supplier's misleading advertising caused you to order the wrong model cartridge. You'd like the company to either refund the $284.25 you paid on its Invoice 95-076 or replace the cartridges with ones that do work with your printers. You'll be happy to return all four cartridges if the company will give you instructions for doing so.

7 **Claim Letter—Poor Service**   As the owner of Parker Central, a small plumbing business, you try to instill in all your employees a *customer-first* attitude. Therefore, you were quite put off by your own treatment yesterday (July 13) at the hands of the receptionist at Englehard Investment Service (231 East 50 Street, Indianapolis, IN 46205). You showed up 20 minutes early for your 2:30 P.M. appointment with Jack Nutley, an investment counselor with the firm. You were meeting with him for the first time to discuss setting up a Simplified Employee Pension (SEP) plan for your 20 employees.

To begin with, the receptionist ignored you for at least five minutes until she finished the last paragraph of a document she was typing. Then, after finding out whom you wanted to see, she did not even call Jack's office to announce your arrival until 2:30 P.M. Finally, you learned that Jack had just become ill and had to go to the doctor. So you wasted half an afternoon and were also insulted by the receptionist's rude treatment.

You decide to write to Jack Nutley about the receptionist's office behavior. Your *claim* is for better service in the future. You want him to know that if you will continue to be treated in such a manner, you have no interest in doing business with his firm. Write the claim letter.

8 Adjustment Letter—Company at Fault   Assume the role of customer service representative at Nationwide Office Supply (see Exercise 6). You've received Mr. McCord's letter (People's Energy Company, Wheatley Road, Old Westbury, NY 11568). You've done some background investigation and have learned that what the customer said is true—the Sampson Model 25 *is* a Xerox clone and your catalog does state that this cartridge fits Xerox printers and most compatibles. The problem arose because the Model 25, Sampson's newest printer, was introduced shortly after your catalog went to press. This model's spindle is slightly shorter than previous Sampson models.

Unfortunately, you do not carry in your inventory a cartridge that will fit the Sampson Model 25. The customer should return the case COD, marking on the address label "Return Authorization 95-076R." In the meantime, you've authorized a refund of $284.25; Mr. McCord should receive the check within 10 days. Convey this information to Mr. McCord.

9 Adjustment Letter—Customer at Fault   Assume the role of customer service representative at Nationwide Office Supply (see Exercise 6). You've done some background investigation and have learned that Mr. McCord was somewhat mistaken in stating that the Sampson Model 25 is a Xerox clone. Sampson advertises that the Model 25 uses the same character set as Xerox printers; this means that all fonts available from Xerox can also be downloaded to the Model 25. The company neither states nor implies that Xerox-compatible cartridges or other supplies will fit its machines.

Because the customer made an innocent mistake and you will be able to resell the unused cartridges, you decide to honor his claim anyway. He should return the case prepaid, marking on the address label "Return Authorization 95-076R." In the meantime, you're shipping him four cartridges (Part No. 02-9R32732) that *will* work on the Model 25; he can expect to receive them within 10 days. You're also enclosing your summer catalog.

Bad-News Messages

10 Refusing an Application—McDonald's Franchise   As the director of franchise operations for McDonald's, Inc., you must evaluate the hundreds of applications for franchises you receive each month. Today you received an application from Maxine Denton, who is developing a large shopping-center complex in Austin, Texas. Her corporation wants to open a McDonald's restaurant in her shopping center. Of course, the company will have no trouble coming up with the initial investment. It will also select a qualified manager, who will then go through McDonald's extensive training and orientation course.

But McDonald's has a policy against granting franchises to corporations, real estate developers, and other absentee owners. The firm want its owners to manage their stores personally. McDonald's prefers high-energy types who will devote their careers to their restaurants and not be involved in numerous other business ventures. Write to Ms. Denton (she's the president of Lone Star Development Corporation, P.O. Box 1086, Houston, TX 77001), turning down her application.

11 Refusing a Claim—Direct Organization   You have just received a claim letter from John Stodel (306 Hyde Court, Kirkwood, MO 63122-4541). Mr. Stodel purchased a Clipper lawn mower (Model 306-B) from you two years ago. For the third time, he has written a claim letter requesting that you repair his $486 mower for free because its self-propelling mechanism stopped working after 15 months of use. Twice already, you've sent polite adjustment letters, denying the claim on the basis that the Model 306-B comes with a one-year warranty and the repair does not fall within the warranty period. You don't want to be rude, but you wish he would stop writing to you about a matter that you've already settled. Let him know.

12 Refusing a Favor—Summer Internship Assume the role of vice president of operations for Kolor Kosmetics, a small manufacturer in Biloxi, Mississippi. One of your colleagues from the local chamber of commerce, Dr. Andrea T. Mazzi, has written asking whether your firm can provide a summer internship in your department for her son Peter, a college sophomore who is interested in a manufacturing career. Kolor Kosmetics has no provisions for temporary summer employees and does not currently operate an internship program. Further, the factory shuts down for a two-week vacation every July.

Write Dr. Mazzi (at 3930 Lyman Turnpike, Biloxi, MS 39530) to let her know this information. Perhaps there are other ways that her son can gain firsthand experience in manufacturing during the summer.

13 Refusing Business—Hotel Reservation You are the manager of the Daytona 100, a 100-room hotel in Daytona, Florida, that caters to business people. You've received a reservation from Alpha Kappa Psi fraternity at Ball State University to rent 24 double rooms during the college's spring break (April 6–13). The fraternity has offered to send a $1,000 deposit to guarantee the rooms if necessary.

As a former AKPsi, you know that these fraternity members are responsible students who would cause no problems. You also recognize that when these students graduate and assume positions in industry, they are the very type of people you hope will stay at your hotel. However, because of previous bad experiences, you now have a strict policy against accepting reservations from student groups. Write to the AKPsi treasurer (Scott Rovan, 40 Cypress Grove Court, No. 25, Muncie, IN 47304), conveying this information.

14 Work-Team Communication—Dealing with AIDS Working in teams of three or four, assume the role of the grievance committee of your union. Your small company has its first known case of an employee with AIDS. The employee, an assistant manager (nonunion position), has indicated that she intends to continue working as long as she is physically able. The company has upheld her right to do so.

You've received a memo signed by six union members who work in her department, objecting to her continued presence at work. They are worried about the risks of contracting the disease from a coworker. Although they have compassion for the assistant manager, they want the union to step in and require that she either resign or be reassigned so that union members do not have to interact with her in the course of completing their own work.

Your committee does some Internet research on the topic and based on your findings decides not to intervene in this matter. Do the research and write a memo to Katherine Kellendorf, chair of the Committee of Concerned Workers, giving her your decision.

15 Declining an Invitation—Dinner You are the purchasing specialist at your firm and have received an email message from Barbara Sorrels, one of your firm's major suppliers. She will be in town on October 13 and would like to take you out to dinner that evening. However, you have an early morning flight on October 14 to Kansas City and will need to pack and make last-minute preparations on the evening of the 13th. Write to Ms. Sorrels (bsorrels@aol.com), declining her invitation.

Writing A Routine Adjustment Letter

PROBLEM   You are Kathryn Smith, a correspondent in the customer service department of Branford's Department Store. This morning (May 25, 20—), you received the following letter from Mrs. Henrietta Daniels, an angry customer:

> Dear Customer Service Manager:
>
> I am really upset at the poor-quality shades that you sell. Two months ago I purchased two pairs of your pleated fabric shades in Wedgwood Blue at $35.99 each for my two bathroom windows. A copy of my $74.32 bill is enclosed.
>
> The color has already begun to fade from these shades. I couldn't believe it when I checked and found that they now look tie-dyed! That is not the look I wish for my home.
>
> Since these shades did not provide the type of wear that I paid for, please refund my $74.32.
>
> Sincerely,

You take Mrs. Daniels' itemized bill down to the sales floor and find the model of shades she purchased. You conclude that Mrs. Daniels' home has large bathroom windows because the only size this particular shade comes in is 64 inches long by 32 inches wide. Printed right on the tag attached to the shade is this caution: "Warning: The imported fabric in this shade makes it unsuitable for use in areas of high humidity." Clearly, these shades were not made for bathroom use. You call up Mrs. Daniels' account on your computer and find that she has been a loyal customer for many years. You decide, therefore, to refund her $74.32, even though she misused the product. Write the adjustment letter (Mrs. Henrietta Daniels, 117 Pine Forest Drive, Atlanta, GA 30345).

PROCESS   Compose a few paragraphs describing how you went about solving this problem. In narrative form, provide such information as the following:

1. What is the purpose of your letter?

2. Describe your audience.

3. Will you use a direct or an indirect organizational plan?

4. How will you convey the information that Mrs. Daniels misused the product?

5. How can you promote your cotton and polyester bathroom curtains (which are appropriate for high-moisture environments)?

6. What is the purpose of your closing sentence?

PRODUCT   Compose your document, following the five steps in the writing process (planning, drafting, revising, formatting, and proofreading). Format the final version on letterhead stationery (refer to the Style Manual for formatting guidelines).

Writing a Bad-News Letter

PROBLEM You are Charles J. Redding, national sales manager for Midland Medical Supplies. You have received a memo from O. B. Presley, a sales representative, asking that the company purchase a new notebook computer with built-in printer (the Canon NoteJet) for all sales reps. You have, of course, considered all kinds of options to make the sales representatives more productive—notebook computers with built-in printers, cellular telephones for their cars, computerized answering and call-forwarding services, and the like. The fact is that your firm simply cannot afford these items for every sales representative. Also, some of the less energetic representatives clearly do not need them. Instead, your company's philosophy is to pay your representatives top salary and commission and then have them purchase out of their commission earnings whatever "extra" devices or services they deem worthwhile.

You have checked with your purchasing department and found that your corporate price for the Canon NoteJet is $1,350, instead of the retail price of $1,999 quoted by Presley. You would be happy to have the company purchase this machine for Presley and deduct the cost from his commission check. Even though Presley will be disappointed in what you have to say, send him a memo conveying this information.

PROCESS Compose a few paragraphs describing how you went about solving this problem. In narrative form, provide such information as the following:

1. What is the purpose of your letter?

2. Describe your audience.

3. Will you use a direct or an indirect organizational plan?

4. What attributes should your opening sentence have?

5. What attributes should the refusal sentence have?

6. When and how will you discuss your counteroffer?

7. What attributes should your closing paragraph have?

8. How can you use the "you" attitude and positive language throughout your letter?

PRODUCT Compose your document, following the five steps in the writing process (planning, drafting, revising, formatting, and proofreading). Format the final version on letterhead stationery (refer to the Style Manual for formatting guidelines).

8

Persuasive Emails, Letters, and Memos

COMMUNICATION OBJECTIVES

After you have finished this chapter, you should be able to:

- Decide when to use a direct or an indirect organizational plan for persuasive messages.

- Compose a persuasive message promoting an idea.

- Compose a persuasive message requesting a favor.

- Compose a persuasive claim.

- Compose a sales letter.

On the Job

JIM WALTMAN
Director of Refuges and Wildlife, The Wilderness Society

When Jim Waltman sits down to draft a persuasive message, a lot is riding on his words. As Director of Refuges and Wildlife for the nonprofit Wilderness Society, Waltman uses communication to promote the conservation of America's national wildlife refuges and endangered species.

Before writing a persuasive message, Waltman analyzes his audience to determine how much people know and how they feel about an issue. He can get a better idea of what might interest his readers by looking at demographic data (such as their ages) as well as social and cultural data (such as locally popular outdoor activities). "Understanding the needs and concerns of people in each part of the country helps us target messages by region," he says. "For example, knowing the favorite outdoor sport in an area allows us to write persuasively about how participants will be affected by an environmental issue in that region."

Waltman generally relies on a combination of logical and emotional appeals to create interest and add impact to his persuasive arguments. "We've learned to take a broader, more sophisticated approach," he says, "and we've become more skilled at explaining the economics as well as the ecology of an environmental issue." He cites expert opinions, statistics, and examples to support his arguments; he also includes photos to visually reinforce what may be lost if the audience doesn't act. To capture the reader's attention at the beginning of a persuasive letter, Waltman stresses the local angle on a particular issue. "The goal is to make readers understand that something they care about is at stake," he notes.

Planning the Persuasive Message

Persuasion is the process of motivating someone to take a specific action or to support a particular idea. Persuasion motivates someone to believe something or to do something that he or she would not otherwise have done. Every day many people try to persuade you to do certain things or to believe certain ideas. Likewise, you have many opportunities to persuade others each day.

As a businessperson, you will also need to persuade others to do as you want. You may need to persuade a superior to adopt a certain proposal, a supplier to refund the purchase price of a defective product, or a potential customer to buy your product or service. In a sense, *all* business communication involves persuasion. Even if your primary purpose is to inform, you still want your reader to accept your perspective and to believe the information you present.

The essence of persuasion is overcoming initial resistance. The reader may resist your efforts for any number of reasons. Your proposal may require the reader to spend time or money—at the very least, you're asking the reader to make the effort to *read* your message. Or perhaps the reader has had bad experiences in the past with similar requests or holds opinions that predispose him or her against your request.

Your job in writing a persuasive message, then, is to talk your readers into something, to convince them that your point of view is the most appropriate one. You'll have the best chance of succeeding if you tailor your message to your audience, provide your readers with reasons they will find convincing, and anticipate and deflect or disarm their objections. Such tailor-made writing requires careful planning; you need to define your purpose clearly and analyze your audience thoroughly.

> Persuasion is necessary when the other person initially resists your efforts.

Purpose

The purpose of a persuasive message is to motivate the reader to agree with you or to do as you ask. Unless you are clear about the specific results you wish to achieve, you won't be able to plan an effective strategy that will achieve your goals.

Suppose, for example, you want to convince your boss to adopt a complex proposal. The purpose of your memo might be to persuade your superior to either (1) adopt your proposal, (2) approve a pilot test of the proposal, or (3) schedule a meeting where you can present your proposal in person and answer any questions. Achieving any one of these three goals may require a different strategy.

Knowing your purpose lets you know what kind of information to include in your persuasive message. "Knowledge is power" and never is this saying truer than when you write persuasive messages. To write effectively about an idea or product, you must know the idea or product intimately. If you're promoting an idea, consider all of the ramifications of your proposal.

> Become thoroughly familiar with the idea or product you are promoting.

- Are there competing proposals that should be considered?
- What are the implications for the organization (and for you) if your proposal is adopted and it *fails?*
- How does your proposal fit in with the organization's existing plans and direction?

Audience Analysis

The more you're able to promote the features of your idea or product as satisfying a *specific* need of your audience, the more persuasive your message will be.

Suppose, for example, you're promoting a line of men's shoes; you should stress different features, depending on your audience.

Young executive:	stylish . . . comes in various shades of black and brown . . . a perfect accessory to your business wardrobe
Mid-career executive:	perfect detailing . . . 12-hour comfort . . . stays sharp-looking through days of travel
Retired executive:	economical . . . comfortable . . . a no-nonsense type of shoe

The point to remember is to know your audience and to personalize your message to best meet its needs and interests. Stress the "you" attitude to achieve the results you want.

Knowledge and Attitude of the Reader   What does the reader already know about the topic? Determining this level of understanding will tell you how much background information you should include. What is the reader's predisposition toward the topic? If it is negative, then where one or two reasons might ordinarily suffice, you will need to give more justifications. Initial resistance also calls for more objective, verifiable evidence than if the reader were initially neutral. You also need to learn *why* the reader is resistant so that you can tailor your arguments to overcome those specific objections.

Effect on the Reader   How will your proposal affect the reader? If the reader is being asked to commit resources (time or money), discuss the rewards for doing so. If the reader is being asked to endorse some proposal, provide enough specific information to enable the reader to make an informed decision. The reader wants to know "What's in it for me?" *You* are already convinced of the wisdom of your proposal. Your job is to let the reader know the benefits of doing as you ask.

> Show how the reader will be affected by your proposal.

To be persuasive, you must present *specific, believable* evidence. However, one of the worst mistakes you could make would be to simply describe the features of the product or list the advantages of doing as you ask. Instead, put yourself in the reader's place. Discuss how the reader will benefit from your proposal. Emphasize the *reader* rather than the product or idea you're promoting.

NOT: The San Diego Accounting Society would like you to speak to us on the topic of expensing versus capitalizing 401-C assets.

BUT: Speaking to the San Diego Accounting Society would enable you to present your firm's views on the controversial topic of expensing versus capitalizing 401-C assets.

Sometimes your readers won't benefit *directly* from doing as you ask. If you are trying to entice your employees to contribute to the United Way, for example, it would be difficult to discuss direct reader benefits. In such situations, discuss the *indirect* benefits of reader participation; for example, show how someone other than you, the solicitor of the funds, will benefit.

> Discussing indirect benefits prevents your request from sounding selfish.

Your contribution will enable inner-city youngsters, many of whom have never even been outside the city of Columbus, to see pandas living and thriving in their natural habitat.

Writer Credibility   What is your credibility with the reader? The more trustworthy you are, the more trustworthy your message will appear. Credibility comes from many sources. You may be perceived as being credible by virtue of the position you hold or by virtue of being a well-known authority. Or you may achieve credibility for your proposal by supplying convincing evidence, such as facts and statistics that can be verified.

> A reader who trusts you is more likely to trust your message.

Suppose, for example, you have worked in an advertising production department and have extensive experience with color reproduction. If you are writing a memo to a colleague suggesting that certain photos will not reproduce clearly and should therefore be replaced, you probably don't need to explain your expertise. Your colleague is likely to believe you. On the other hand, if you are writing a letter to the photographer, who does not know you, you would probably want to discuss past incidents that lead you to conclude the photos should be replaced.

Organizing a Persuasive Request

A persuasive request seeks to motivate the reader to accept your idea (rather than to buy your product). The purpose of your message and your knowledge of the reader will help determine the content of your message and the sequence in which you discuss each topic.

Determining How to Start the Message

In the past, it was common practice to organize *all* persuasive messages by using an indirect organizational plan—presenting the rationale first, followed by the major idea (the request for action). Many persuasive messages continue to follow this format. Nevertheless, writers today should determine which organizational plan (direct or indirect) will help them better achieve their objectives.

Direct Plan—Present the Major Idea First Most superiors prefer to have messages from their subordinates organized in the direct style introduced in Chapter 7. Thus, when writing persuasive memos that travel up the organization, you should generally present the main idea (your recommendation) first, followed by the supporting evidence. The direct organizational plan saves time and immediately satisfies the reader's curiosity about your purpose. To get readers to accept your proposal when using the direct plan, present your recommendation along with the criteria or brief rationale in the first paragraph.

Prefer the direct plan when writing persuasive messages to your superior.

Sister Patricia Daly, a Dominican nun and member of the Interfaith Center for Corporate Responsibility, spends her days meeting with corporate executives persuading them to be responsible citizens. Speaking with such high-level executives, she organizes her appeal in a direct plan, presenting the major idea first.

NOT: I recommend we hold our Pittsburgh sales meeting at the Mark-Congress Hotel.

BUT: I have evaluated three hotels as possible meeting sites for our Pittsburgh sales conference and recommend we meet at the Mark-Congress Hotel. As discussed below, the Mark-Congress is centrally located, has the best meeting facilities, and is moderately priced.

Destination Marks **WORD|wise**

Boise will be Boise.

Don't judge Dubuque by its cover.

Don't put Djakarta before the horse.

Go ahead; Mecca my day.

Have Van Nuys day.

I could have Gdansked all night.

The Morocco the merrier.

In general, prefer the direct organizational plan for persuasive messages when any of the following conditions apply:

- You are writing to superiors within the organization.
- Your audience is predisposed to listen objectively to your request.
- The proposal does not require strong persuasion (that is, no major obstacles to it exist).
- The proposal is long or complex. (Your reader may become impatient if you bury your main point in a long report.)
- You know that your reader prefers the direct approach.

Indirect Plan—Gain the Reader's Attention First Unfortunately, many times your readers will resist your suggestions—at least, initially. Your job then is to explain the merits of your proposal and show how the reader will benefit from doing as you ask. Because a reluctant reader is more likely to agree to an idea *after* he or she understands its merits, your plan of organization is to convince the reader before asking for action.

You should use the indirect organizational plan when writing to subordinates, when strong persuasion is needed, or when you know that your reader prefers the indirect plan. When using the indirect plan, delay asking for action until after you've presented your reasons. A subject line that does not disclose your recommendation should be used in persuasive letters. Don't announce your purpose immediately, but rather lead up to it gradually.

NOT: SUBJECT: Proposal to Purchase Color Copier

NOT: SUBJECT: Proposal (*too general*)

BUT: SUBJECT: Analysis of Color-Copy Needs

The first test of a good opening sentence in a persuasive request is whether it is interesting enough to catch and keep the reader's attention. It won't matter how much evidence you have marshaled to support your case if the recipient does not bother to continue reading carefully after the first sentence.

A **rhetorical question** often proves effective as an opening sentence. A rhetorical question is asked strictly to get the reader thinking about the topic of your message; a literal answer is not expected. Of course, questions with obvious answers are not effective motivators for further reading and, in fact, may insult the reader's intelligence. Similarly, yes-or-no questions rarely make good lead-ins because pondering an answer doesn't require much thought.

What is black and white and red (read) all over? Very few things, as a matter of fact!

Sometimes an unusual fact or unexpected statement will draw the reader into the message. At other times, you might want to select some statement about

rhetorical question
A question asked to encourage the reader to think about the topic; a literal answer is not expected

which the reader and writer will agree—to immediately establish some common ground.

> A study conducted by IBM showed that participants remembered almost twice as much of the information on color slides as on black-and-white slides.

> Almost 95% of the participants at our four seminars last month gave us an overall rating of "Outstanding."

Your opening statement must also relate to the purpose of your message. If it is too far off the topic or misleads the reader, you risk losing goodwill, and the reader may simply stop reading. At the very least, the reader will feel confused or deceived, making persuasion more difficult.

The opening statement must be relevant and short.

Keep your opening statement short. Often an opening paragraph of just one sentence will make the message inviting to read. Few readers have the patience to wade through a long introduction to figure out the purpose of the message. In summary, make the opening for a persuasive message written in the indirect organizational plan interesting, relevant, and short. The purpose is to make sure your reader is drawn into the body of your message.

Creating Interest and Justifying Your Request

Regardless of whether you write your opening in a direct or indirect style, you must now begin the process of convincing the reader that your request is reasonable. This effort may require several paragraphs of discussion, depending on how much evidence you think will be needed to convince the reader. Because it takes more space to state *why* something should be done than simply to state *that* it should be done, persuasive requests are typically longer than other types of messages.

Provide convincing evidence and use a reasonable tone.

To convince your reader, you must be objective, specific, logical, and reasonable. Avoid emotionalism, obvious flattery, insincerity, and exaggeration. Let your evidence carry the weight of your argument.

> **NOT:** Locating our plant in Suffolk instead of in Norfolk would result in considerable savings.

> **BUT:** Locating our plant in Suffolk instead of in Norfolk would result in annual savings of nearly $175,000, as shown in Table 3.

The type of evidence you present depends, of course, on the circumstances. The usual types of evidence are the following:

- *Facts and statistics:* Facts are objective statements whose truth can be verified; statistics are facts consisting of numbers. Both must be relevant and accurate. For example, statistics that were accurate five years ago may no longer hold true today. But avoid overwhelming the reader with statistical data. Instead, highlight a few key statistics—for emphasis.

  The Lexcraft prints a four-color transparency in 90 seconds at a cost of $1.80, including the transparency.

- *Expert opinion:* Testimony from authorities on the topic might be presented if their input is relevant and, if necessary, you can supply the experts' credentials. Expert opinion is especially persuasive to readers who don't recognize you as an authority on the subject.

  The Lexcraft rated a "Best-Buy" award in the February issue of *Personal Computing*.

- *Examples:* Specific cases or incidents used to illustrate the point under discussion should be relevant, representative, and complete.

We spent $162.50 to have Imagemaster develop the 32 transparencies we used in last month's purchasing managers' seminar. We could have printed them on the Lexcraft for less than $60—with same-day service.

Present the benefits (either direct or indirect) that will accompany the adoption of your proposal, and provide enough background and objective evidence to enable the reader to make an informed decision.

Dealing with Obstacles

Ignoring any obvious obstacles to granting your request would provide the reader with a ready excuse to refuse your request. Instead, your strategy should be to show that even considering such an obstacle, your request is still reasonable. Such a strategy is used in the following example:

Although the vice president has asked for a moratorium on equipment expenditures until June, if we purchase the $2,100 Lexcraft printer before December 31, we'll actually save that amount in printing costs by April—before our quarterly budget is due.

If you're asking someone to speak to a professional organization but cannot provide an honorarium, emphasize the free publicity the speaker will receive and the impact that the speaker's remarks will have on the audience. If you're asking for confidential information, discuss how you will treat it as such. If you're asking for a large donation, explain how payment can be made on the installment plan or by payroll deduction and point out the tax-deductible feature of the donation.

Even though you must address the major obstacles, do *not* emphasize them. Subordinate this discussion by devoting relatively little space to it, by dealing with obstacles in the same sentence that you highlight a reader benefit, or by putting the discussion in the middle of a paragraph. Regardless of how you do it, show the reader that you're aware of the obvious obstacles and that despite them, your proposal still has merit.

As general manager of Conoco's Rocky Mountain region, Carin Knickel motivates her managers to action by coaching. In regular meetings, they take turns in the "hot seat" by detailing goals for the next month and answering questions about results from the previous month.

Motivating Action

Although your request has been stated (direct organizational plan) or implied (indirect organizational plan) earlier, give a direct statement of the request late in the message—after most of the background information and reader benefits have been thoroughly covered. Make the specific action that you want clear and easy to take. For example, if the reader agrees to do as you ask, how should he or she let you know? Will a phone call suffice, or is a written reply necessary? If a phone call is adequate, have you provided a phone number? If you're asking for a favor that requires a written response, have you included a stamped, addressed envelope?

Ask for the desired action in a confident tone. If your request or proposal is reasonable, there is no need to apologize, and you surely do not want to supply the reader with excuses for refusing. Take whatever steps you can to ensure a prompt reply.

So that we can have this copier installed in time for us to use it at our January sales meeting, may I order this copier for $2,100 by December 1? Being able to update our charts right up to an hour before our presentation will mean that our figures are always the latest available.

Checklist 9 (on page 212) summarizes guidelines to use in writing persuasive requests. Although you will not be able to employ all of these suggestions in every persuasive request, you should consider them as an overall framework for structuring your persuasive message.

Ask for action in a confident tone.

CHECKLIST ⑨

Persuasive Requests

Determine How to Start the Message

✓ **Direct Plan**—Use a direct organizational plan when writing to superiors, when your audience is predisposed to listen objectively to your request, when the proposal does not require strong persuasion, when the proposal is long or complex, or when you know your reader prefers the direct approach. Present the recommendation, along with the criteria or brief rationale, in the first paragraph.

✓ **Indirect Plan**—Use an indirect organizational plan when writing to subordinates, when strong persuasion is needed, or when you know your reader prefers the indirect approach. Start by gaining the reader's attention.

a. Make the first sentence motivate the reader to continue reading. Use, for example, a rhetorical question, unusual fact, unexpected statement, or common-ground statement.

b. Keep the opening paragraph short (often just one sentence), relevant to the message, and, when appropriate, related to a reader benefit.

Create Interest and Justify Your Request

✓ Devote the major part of your message to justifying your request. Give enough background and evidence to enable the reader to make an informed decision.

✓ Use facts and statistics, expert opinion, and examples to support your proposal. Ensure that the evidence is accurate, relevant, representative, and complete.

✓ Use an objective, logical, reasonable, and sincere tone. Avoid obvious flattery, emotionalism, and exaggeration.

✓ Present the evidence in terms of either direct or indirect reader benefits.

Minimize Obstacles

✓ Do not ignore obstacles or any negative aspects of your request. Instead, show that even considering them, your request is still reasonable.

✓ Subordinate the discussion of obstacles by position and amount of space devoted to the topic.

Ask Confidently for Action

✓ State (or restate) the specific request late in the message—after most of the benefits have been discussed.

✓ Make the desired action clear and easy for the reader to take, use a confident tone, do not apologize, and do not supply excuses.

✓ End on a forward-looking note, continuing to stress reader benefits.

CHECKPOINT 8.1

RECALL   Write a capital *T* for true or *F* for false before each statement.

1. ____ Most persuasive messages to your superior should be written in the direct organizational style.

2. ____ Even when making your recommendation directly, you should also include your criteria or a brief rationale in the first paragraph.

3. ____ An important function of the rhetorical question is to get the reader to answer the question correctly and fully.

4. ____ To help you achieve your objective, it is often desirable to ignore major obstacles in your persuasive letter.

5. ____ In a persuasive letter written in the indirect style, the actual request should come early in the letter.

VOCABULARY Define the following term in your own words and give an original example.

6. rhetorical question:

COMPREHENSION

7. Assume you want to convince your fellow employees to volunteer one weekend (all day Saturday and Sunday) to help on a Habitat for Humanity construction project.

   a. Would you use a direct or an indirect plan of organization?

   b. Construct an appropriate subject line for your email message.

   c. Construct an effective opening attention-getter.

   d. Construct an effective closing sentence.

CRITICAL THINKING

8. In the body of your message, how much space should you devote to explaining what Habitat for Humanity is and how it helps others? What should you stress in your message?

Common Types of Persuasive Requests

In many ways, writing a persuasive request is more difficult than writing a sales letter because reader benefits are not always so obvious in persuasive requests. This section provides specific strategies and examples for selling an idea, requesting a favor, and writing a persuasive claim letter.

Persuasive messages are often more difficult to write than sales letters.

Selling an Idea

You will have many opportunities to use your education and experience to help solve problems faced by your organization. On the job you will frequently write messages proposing one alternative over another, suggesting a new procedure, or in some other way recommending some course of action. Organize such messages logically, showing what the problem is, how you intend to solve the problem, and

why your solution is sound. Write in an objective style and provide evidence to support your claims.

The memo in Model 7 on page 215 illustrates the selling of an idea.

Requesting a Favor

Favors require persuasion because the reader gets nothing tangible in return.

It has often been said that the wheels of industry are greased with favors. The giving and receiving of favors makes success more likely and makes life in general more agreeable.

A request for a favor differs from a routine request in that routine requests are granted almost automatically, whereas favors require persuasion. For example, asking a colleague to trade places with you on the program for the monthly managers' meeting might be considered a routine request. Asking the same colleague to prepare and give your presentation for you would more likely be a favor, requiring some persuasion.

Although friends and close colleagues often do each other favors as a matter of course, many times in business the granting of a favor might not be so automatic—especially if you don't know the person to whom you're writing. In such situations, you will want to begin your request with an attention-getter and stress the reader benefits from granting the favor.

Discuss at least one reader benefit before making your request. Explain why the favor is being asked and continue to show how the reader (or someone else) will benefit from the favor. Keep a positive, confident tone throughout, and make the action clear and easy to take.

For a sincere tone, make any complimentary comments unique to the reader.

Often the favor is requested because the reader is an expert on some topic. If that is the case, you may legitimately make a complimentary remark about the reader. Make sure, however, that your compliment sounds sincere. Readers are rightfully suspicious, for example, when they read in a form letter that they have been specifically chosen to participate in some project. ("Me and how many thousands of others?" they might wonder.) On the other hand, such a compliment in a letter that is obviously personally typed and signed has much more credibility.

The most important factor to remember in asking for a favor has to do with the favor itself rather than with the writing process: keep your request reasonable. Don't ask someone else to do something that you can or should do for yourself.

Model 8 on page 216 illustrates how to write an effective persuasive request. The reader and writer do not know each other, which makes persuasion a little

MODEL 7

Persuasive Request—Selling an Idea

Maxine's Fashions

Memo

1

To: Maxine Nordstrom, Executive Vice President

From: Robert Kilcline, Merchandising Manager

Date: April 24, 20–

Re: Proposal to Provide Oversized Dressing Rooms

As one means of reinforcing the superior customer service that Maxine's offers, I propose that we also provide oversized dressing rooms for our clients in our new Fashion Square Mall store.

We are noted, of course, for our commitment to customer service and already provide a liberal exchange policy, an abundant inventory, and a harpist who performs daily in the grand salon.

2 One area of concern to me, however, is the size of the dressing rooms that will be available in our new store. I recommend that we add 20 square feet per dressing room and that each room contain a comfortable chair, a garment rack, and an adjustable three-sided mirror. That would make it possible for our clients to make their selections in comfort.

The building contractor has estimated the initial cost of the additional space and furnishings to be approximately $18,500, and the monthly lease would thus be increased by $255. This small investment will make our dressing facilities comparable to the other two exclusive women's shops in this mall.

3 Ms. Nordstrom, I would appreciate receiving approval for increasing the size of the dressing rooms in our new store. Facility engineers are in the process of final floor design and layout and would need any changes approved by the end of next week.

This persuasive memo uses the direct plan because the memo travels up the organization.

Begins by introducing the recommendation, along with a brief rationale.

Provides a smooth transition to the necessary background information. Includes sufficient detail to enable the reader to make an informed decision.

Neutralizes an obvious obstacle (the cost of the project).

Closes on a confident note and motivates prompt action.

Grammar and Mechanics Notes

1 Because of its more readable format, writers often prefer a standard memo format for persuasive messages—even when email is available.

2 *three-sided mirror:* Hyphenate compound adjectives that come before a noun.

3 *Ms. Nordstrom, I:* Separate nouns of address by commas.

MODEL 8

Persuasive Request—Asking a Favor

This persuasive request uses the indirect plan because the writer does not know the reader personally and because strong persuasion is needed.

Opens by quoting the reader, thus complimenting her.

Intimates the request; provides the necessary background information.

Subordinates a potential obstacle by putting it in the dependent clause of a sentence.

Closes with a restatement of a reader benefit.

 NATIONAL
MULTIPLE SCLEROSIS
SOCIETY

National Multiple Sclerosis Society
733 Third Avenue
New York, NY 10017-3288

Tel 212 986 3240
1 800 FIGHT MS
Fax 212 986 7981
E-Mail: nat@nmss.org
www.nmss.org

January 21, 20—

1 Ms. Tanya Porrat, Editor
Autoimmune Diseases Monthly
1800 Ten Hills Road, Suite B
Boston, MA 02145

Dear Ms. Porrat

Subject: Program Planning for the Multiple Sclerosis Congress

2 "The average person in the United States has about 1 chance in 1,000 of developing MS." That comment of yours in a recent interview in the *Boston Globe* made me sit up and think.

Your knack for exploring little-known facts like that about autoimmune diseases would certainly be of keen interest to those attending our annual Multiple Sclerosis Congress in Washington, D.C., on April 23–25. As the keynote speaker at the closing banquet at the Mayflower Hotel on April 25, you would be able to present your ideas on current initiatives to the 200 people present. You would, of course, be our guest for the banquet, which begins at 7 p.m. Your 45-minute presentation would begin at about 8:30 p.m.

We will reimburse you for your air travel and hotel accommodations. Although our nonprofit association is unable to offer an honorarium, we do offer you an opportunity to introduce your journal and to present your ideas to representatives of major autoimmune groups in the country.

We would like to announce your presentation as the lead article in our next newsletter, which goes to press on March 3. Won't you please call me at 202-555-1036

3 to let me know that you can come. We'll have a large, enthusiastic audience of medical researchers waiting to hear you.

Cordially

May Lyon

May Lyon, Banquet Chair

rk

The National MS Society...One thing people with MS can count on.

Grammar and Mechanics Notes

1 To increase readability, do not italicize publication titles in addresses.
2 *Boston Globe:* Italicize the titles of separately published works, such as newspapers, magazines, and books.
3 *that you can come:* Use a period after a courteous request.

more challenging and which calls for an indirect organizational plan. Reader benefits (the opportunity to promote the reader's firm and the flattering prospect of being the center of attention) are included.

Writing a Persuasive Claim

As discussed in Chapter 7, most claim letters are routine letters and should be written using a direct plan of organization—stating the problem early in the letter. Because it is to the company's benefit to keep its clientele happy, most reasonable claims are settled to the customer's satisfaction. Therefore, persuasion is not ordinarily necessary.

Suppose, however, that you wrote a routine claim letter and the company, for some reason, denied your claim. If you still feel that your original claim is legitimate, you might then write a *persuasive* claim letter—using all the techniques discussed earlier in this chapter for writing persuasive requests. Or assume that your new photocopier broke three days after the warranty period expired. The company is not legally obligated to honor your claim, but you may decide to try to persuade it to do so anyway.

Showing anger in your persuasive claim letter would be counterproductive, even if the company turned down your original claim. The goal of your letter is not to vent your anger but rather to solve a problem. That is more likely to happen when a calm atmosphere prevails.

Avoid showing anger.

As in a routine claim letter, you will need to explain in sufficient detail precisely what the problem is, how it came about, and how you want the reader to solve the problem. Use a calm, objective, courteous tone, avoiding anger and exaggeration. Although similar in some respects to a routine claim letter, the persuasive claim differs in two important ways: it has an attention-getting opening and it presents more evidence.

Attention-Getting Opening Recall that you begin a routine claim letter by stating the problem. This type of opening would not be wise for a persuasive claim, because the reader may conclude the claim is unreasonable until he or she reads your rationale.

NOT: Would you please repair my Minolta 203 copier without charge, even though the 90-day warranty expired last week.

BUT: We took a chance and lost! We bet that the Minolta 203 we purchased from you 96 days ago would prove to be as reliable as the other ten Minoltas our firm uses.

The original opening is counterproductive, providing a ready excuse for denying the claim. The revised version holds off making the request until enough background information has been provided. Note also the personal relationship the writer is beginning to establish with the reader in the revised version—disclosing not only that the company owns ten other Minolta copiers but also that the other copiers have all been very reliable. Such an understanding tone will make the reader more likely to grant the request.

More Evidence Because your claim either is nonroutine or has been rejected once, you will need to present as much convincing evidence as possible. Explain fully the basis for your claim; then request a specific adjustment.

Provide convincing evidence.

Model 9 on page 218 illustrates these guidelines for writing a persuasive claim letter. Note that it is the original claim letter regarding a canceled airline flight that was subsequently rejected by the negative adjustment letter shown on page 192 in Chapter 7. This result demonstrates that sometimes even well-written claim letters might ultimately be rejected.

MODEL 9

Persuasive Claim

This persuasive claim letter uses the indirect plan.

Begins on a warm and relevant note.

Provides a smooth transition from the opening sentence.

Provides the necessary background information.

Tells exactly what the problem is in a neutral, courteous tone.

Provides a rationale for granting the claim; asks confidently for specific action; mentions the reader benefit of keeping a satisfied customer.

June 18, 20—

Customer Service Supervisor
Northern Airlines
P.O. Box 619616
Dallas/Fort Worth Airport, TX 75261-9616

Dear Customer Services Supervisor:

I think you will agree that a relaxing 90-minute flight on Northern Airlines is more enjoyable than a grueling six-hour automobile trip.

1 Yet, on June 2, my wife and I found ourselves doing just that—driving from Saginaw, Michigan, to Indianapolis—in the middle of the night and in the company of three tired children.

2 We had made reservations on Northern Flight 126 a month earlier. To obtain the cheapest fare ($136 per ticket), we had purchased nonrefundable tickets. When we arrived at the airport, we were told that Flight 126, scheduled to depart at 8 p.m., had been canceled. Your gate agent (Ms. Nixon) had graciously rebooked us on the next available flight, leaving at 9:45 the next morning.

Since the purpose of our trip was to attend a family wedding on June 3, we had no choice but to cancel our rebooked flight and to drive to Indianapolis instead. When we tried to turn in our tickets for a refund, Ms. Nixon informed us that because the flight had been canceled due to inclement weather, she would be unable to credit my American Express charge card.

3 As a frequent flier on Northern, I've experienced firsthand the "Welcome Aboard!" feeling that is the basis for your current advertising campaign; and I believe you will want to extend that same taken-care-of feeling to your ticket operations as well. Please credit my American Express charge card (Account No. 4102 817 171) for the $680 cost of the five tickets, thus putting out the welcome mat again for my family.

Sincerely,

Oliver J. Arbin

Oliver J. Arbin
4 518 Thompson Street
Saginaw, MI 48607

Grammar and Mechanics Notes

1 *just that—driving:* To insert a dash, type two hyphens (--) with no space before or after. The word processing program automatically converts two hyphens into a printed dash.

2 *nonrefundable:* Write most *non-* words solid—without a hyphen.

3 *taken-care-of feeling:* Hyphenate a compound adjective that comes before a noun.

4 For personal business letters printed on plain paper, type your address below your name.

RECALL   Write a capital *T* for true or *F* for false before each statement.

1. ___ You should avoid giving a compliment when asking for a favor.

2. ___ To sell an idea to your boss, you would probably not include an attention-getting opening.

3. ___ Regardless of whether you're using a direct or an indirect organizational plan, you should discuss at least one reader benefit before actually requesting the favor.

4. ___ Most claim letters are routine messages—not persuasive messages.

5. ___ A persuasive claim letter needs an attention-getting opening, whereas a routine claim letter does not.

CHECKPOINT 8.2

COMPREHENSION

6. When the beanbag chair that you purchased split after only four months' use, you immediately called the discount store where you purchased it to ask for either a replacement or a refund of your $49.95 purchase price. The store declined, stating that it had no way of knowing how heavy the person was who used the chair and that the chair was guaranteed to support only a maximum of 200 pounds. Now, you're really mad and decide to write a persuasive claim letter.

a. What is the purpose of your letter?

b. Should you hint at how angry you are at the store's refusal to honor the guarantee?

c. Construct an effective opening attention-getter.

d. Construct an effective closing sentence.

CRITICAL THINKING

7. Do you think that persuasive messages that attempt to sell an idea are more frequently written to one's superiors or to one's subordinates?

Writing a Sales Letter

The heart of most business is sales—selling a product or service. Much of a company's sales effort is accomplished through the writing of effective sales letters—either individual letters for individual sales or form letters for large-scale sales.

In large companies, the writing of sales letters is centered in the advertising department and is a highly specialized task performed by advertising copywriters

Small-business owners often write their own sales letters.

For Anny Wong, a sales rep for Caterpillar, selling the company's expensive building products in China is a challenge. According to her, "Right now the only thing most buyers look at is price. What they need to think about is productivity. Cat's products will last longer."

and marketing consultants. Within a few years after graduation, however, a growing number of college students opt to own their own businesses. These start-up companies are typically quite small, having only a few employees.

In such a situation, the company must mount an aggressive sales effort to develop business but is typically too small to hire a full-time copywriter or marketing consultant. Thus, the owner often ends up writing these sales letters, which are vital to the firm's ongoing health. So no matter where you intend to work, the chances are that at some point you will need to write sales letters.

Selecting a Central Selling Theme

central selling theme The major reader benefit that is introduced early and emphasized throughout a sales letter

Your first step is to become thoroughly familiar with your product, its competition, and your intended audience. Then, you must select a **central selling theme** for your letter. Most products have numerous features that you will want to introduce and discuss. For your letter to make a real impact, however, a single theme should run through it—a major reader benefit that you introduce early and emphasize throughout the letter.

It would be unrealistic to expect your reader to remember five different product features that you mention. In any case, you have only a short time to make a lasting impression on your reader. Use that time wisely to emphasize what you think is the most compelling benefit from owning your product. Two means of achieving this emphasis are *position* and *repetition*. Introduce your central selling theme early (in the opening sentence if possible), and keep referring to it throughout the letter.

Gaining the Reader's Attention

Review the earlier section on gaining the reader's attention when writing persuasive requests.

A reply to a request for product information from a potential customer is called a *solicited sales letter*. An *unsolicited sales letter*, on the other hand, is a letter promoting a firm's products that is mailed to potential customers who have not expressed any interest in the product. (Unsolicited sales letters are also called *prospecting letters*. Some recipients, of course, call them *junk mail*.)

Because most sales letters are unsolicited, you have only a line or two in which to grab the reader's attention. Unless a sales letter is addressed to the reader personally and is obviously not a form letter, the reader is likely just to skim it—either out of curiosity or because the opening sentence was especially intriguing.

Most readers will scan the opening even of a form letter, perhaps just to learn what product is being promoted. If you can capture their attention in these first few lines, they may continue reading. Otherwise, all your efforts will have been wasted. The following types of opening sentences have proven effective for sales letters.

Technique	*Example*
Rhetorical question	What is the difference between extravagance and luxury? (*promoting a high-priced car*)
Thought-provoking statement	Most of what we had to say about business this morning was unprintable! (*promoting an early-morning television news program*)
Unusual fact	If your family is typical, you will wash one ton of laundry this year. (*promoting a laundry detergent*)
Current event	The new Arrow assembly plant will bring 1,700 new families to White Rock within three years. (*promoting a real estate company*)
Anecdote	During six years of college, the one experience that helped me the most did not even occur in the classroom. (*promoting a weekly business magazine*)
Direct challenge	Drop the enclosed Pointer pen on the floor, writing tip first, and then sign your name with it. (*promoting a no-blot ballpoint pen*)

As in persuasive requests, the opening of a sales letter should be interesting, short, and original. When possible, incorporate the central selling theme into your opening; and avoid irrelevant, obvious, or timeworn statements.

Most attention-getting openings consist of a one-sentence paragraph.

Creating Interest and Building Desire

If your opening sentence is directly related to your product, the transition to the discussion of features and reader benefits will be smooth and logical. Make sure that the first sentence of the following paragraph relates directly to the idea introduced in your opening sentence. Unrelated ideas will make the reader pause and feel puzzled.

Interpreting Features   The major part of your letter (typically, several paragraphs) will probably be devoted to creating interest and building desire for your product. You should not only describe the product and its features but, more important, *interpret* these features by showing specifically how each will benefit the reader. Make the reader—not the product—the subject of most of your sentences.

NOT: The JT Laser II prints at the speed of 15 pages per minute.

BUT: After pressing the print key, you'll barely have time to reach over and retrieve the page from the bin. The JT Laser II's print speed of 15 pages per minute is twice that of the typical printer.

NOT: Masco binoculars zoom from 3 to 12 power.

BUT: With Masco binoculars, you can look a ruby-throated hummingbird squarely in the eye at 300 feet and see it blink.

Devote several paragraphs to interpreting the product's features.

Maintain credibility by providing specific facts and figures.

Using Objective, Ethical Language To be convincing, you must present specific, objective evidence. Simply saying that a product is great is not enough. You must provide evidence to show *why* or *how* the product is great. Here is where you'll use all the data you gathered before you started to write. Avoid generalities, unsupported superlatives and claims, and too many or too strong adjectives and adverbs.

NOT: At $595, the Sherwood moped is the best buy on the market.

BUT: The May *Independent Consumer* rated the $595 Sherwood moped the year's best buy.

Positive statements by independent agencies lend powerful support.

NOT: We know you will enjoy the convenience of our Bread Baker.

BUT: Our Bread Baker comes with one feature we don't think you'll ever use: a 30-day, no-questions-asked return policy.

Focus on the one feature that sets your product apart.

Focusing on the Central Selling Theme The recurring theme of your letter should be the one feature that sets your product apart from the competition. If your reader remembers nothing else about your product, this one feature is what you want him or her to remember. Whenever possible, unify the features under a single umbrella theme—whether that theme is convenience, ease of use, flexibility, price, or some other distinguishing characteristic around which you can build your case.

Discussing and fully interpreting these features may take a considerable amount of space, and some readers may be unwilling to read through a long sales letter. However, those who do will be more motivated to respond favorably. The test of an effective sales letter is the number of sales it generates—*not* the number of people who read the letter.

Mentioning Price If price is your central selling theme, introduce it early and emphasize it often. In most cases, however, price is not the central selling theme and should therefore be subordinated. Introduce the price late in the message, after you have discussed most of the advantages of owning the product. To subordinate price, state it in a long complex or compound sentence, perhaps in a sentence that also mentions a reader benefit.

Use subordination techniques when mentioning price.

You'll consider the $250 cost of this spreadsheet seminar repaid in full the very next time your boss asks you to revise the quarterly sales budget—on a Friday afternoon!

Sometimes it is helpful to present the price in terms of small units—for example, showing how subscribing to a weekly magazine costs less than $1 per week, rather than $50 per year. Or compare the price to that of a familiar object—"about what you'd pay for your morning newspaper or cup of coffee."

Motivating Action

Although the purpose of your letter should be apparent right from the start, delay making your specific request until late in the letter—after you have created interest and built desire for the product. Then state the specific action you want.

If the desired action is an actual sale, make the action easy to take by including a toll-free number, enclosing an order blank, accepting credit cards, and the like. For high-priced items, it would be unreasonable to expect to make an actual sale by mail. Probably no one has read a sales letter promoting a new automobile and then phoned in an order for the car. For such items, your goal is to get the reader to take just a small step toward purchasing—sending for more information, stopping by the dealer for a demonstration, or asking a sales representative to call. Again, make the step easy for the reader to take.

CHECKLIST (10)

Sales Letters

Prepare

✓ Learn as much as possible about the product, the competition, and the audience.

✓ Select a central selling theme—your product's most distinguishing feature.

Gain the Reader's Attention

✓ Make your opening brief, interesting, and original. Avoid obvious, misleading, and irrelevant statements.

✓ Use any of these openings: rhetorical question, thought-provoking statement, unusual fact, current event, anecdote, direct challenge, or some similar attention-getting device.

✓ Introduce (or at least lead up to) the central selling theme in the opening.

✓ If the letter is in response to a customer inquiry, begin by expressing appreciation for the inquiry and then introduce the central selling theme.

Create Interest and Build Desire

✓ Make the introduction of the product follow naturally from the attention-getter.

✓ Interpret the features of the product; instead of just describing the features, show how the reader will benefit from each feature. Let the reader picture owning, using, and enjoying the product.

✓ Use action-packed, positive, and objective language. Provide convincing evidence to support your claims—specific facts and figures, independent product reviews, endorsements, and so on.

✓ Continue to stress the central selling theme throughout.

✓ Subordinate price (unless price is the central selling theme). State price in small terms, in a long sentence, or in a sentence that also talks about benefits.

Motivate Action

✓ Make the desired action clear and easy to take.

✓ Ask confidently, avoiding the hesitant "if you'd like to" or "I hope you agree that."

✓ Encourage prompt action (but avoid a hard-sell approach).

✓ End your letter with a reminder of a reader benefit.

Provide an incentive for prompt action by, for example, offering a gift to the first 100 people who respond or stressing the need to buy early while a good selection remains, before the holiday rush begins, or while the three-day sale is in full swing. Make your push for action *gently*, however. Any tactic that smacks of high-pressure selling at this point is likely to increase reader resistance.

Use confident language when asking for action, avoiding such hesitant phrases as "If you want to save money" or "I hope you agree that this product will save you time." When asking the reader to part with money, it is always a good idea to mention a reader benefit in the same sentence.

NOT: Hurry! Hurry! Hurry! These sale prices won't be in effect long.

NOT: If you agree that this ice cream maker will make your summers more enjoyable, you can place your order by telephone.

BUT: To have your Jiffy Ice Cream Maker available for use during the upcoming July 4 weekend, simply call our toll-free number today.

These guidelines for writing an effective sales letter are illustrated in Model 10 and summarized in Checklist 10. As always, the test of the effectiveness of a message is whether it achieves its goal. Use whatever information you have available (especially in terms of audience analysis) to help your letter achieve its goal.

MODEL 10

Sales Letter

Starts with a rhetorical question.

Introduces need for safety and security as the central selling theme.

Presents specific evidence and discusses it in terms of reader benefits.

Emphasizes *you* instead of the product in most sentences.

Subordinates price in a long sentence that also discusses benefits.

Makes the desired action clear and easy to take; ends with a reader benefit.

2455 Paces Ferry Road, N.W. • Atlanta, GA 30339-4024
(770) 433-8211

1

2   Dear Homeowner:

Do you view your home as an investment or as your castle? Is it primarily a tax write-off or a place of refuge—where you can find comfort and respite from work-day stress?

Most of us view our homes as places where we can feel safe from outside intrusions. Thus, we feel threatened by government statistics showing that 5.3% of all U.S. households were burglarized last year. How can we protect ourselves?

Today, there's a simple and dependable alarm that protects as much as 2,500 square feet of your home. Just plug in the Safescan Home Alarm system, adjust the sensitivity to the size of your room, and turn the key. You then have 30 seconds to leave and 15 seconds to switch off the alarm once you return.

3   Worried that your dog might trigger the alarm? Safescan's microprocessor screens out normal sounds like crying babies, outside traffic, and rain. But hostile noises like breaking glass and splintering wood trigger the alarm. The 105-decibel siren is loud enough to alert neighbors and to drive away even the most determined burglar.

What if a smart burglar disconnects the electricity to your home or pulls the plug? Built-in batteries assure that Safescan operates through power failures lasting as long as 24 hours, and the batteries recharge automatically. Best of all, installation is easy. Simply mount the 4-pound unit on a wall (we supply the four screws), and plug it in. Nothing could be faster.

Finally, there is a $259 home alarm that you can trust; and the one-year warranty and ten-day return policy ensure your complete satisfaction.

Last year, 3.2 million burglaries occurred in the United States, but you can now tip the odds back in your favor. To order the Safescan Home Alarm System, stop by your nearest Home Depot. Within minutes, Safescan can be guarding your home, giving you peace of mind.

Sincerely yours,

Jeffrey Parret

Jeffrey Parret
National Sales Manager

USA
36 USC 380
Proud Sponsor

Grammar and Mechanics Notes

1 In general, omit the date and inside address in form sales letters. Subject lines are also frequently omitted.

2 *Dear Homeowner:* Note the generic salutation.

3 *crying babies, outside traffic, and:* Separate items in a series by commas.

RECALL   Write a capital *T* for true or *F* for false before each statement.

1. ____ Owners of small businesses often write their sales letters themselves.

2. ____ If your product or service has three major advantages over the competition, you should stress all of them in your letter.

3. ____ Unsolicited sales letters require more persuasion than solicited sales letters do.

4. ____ If price is your biggest advantage over the competition, you should stress price throughout your letter.

5. ____ You should devote most of the space in a sales letter to describing the features of your product or service.

CHECKPOINT 8.3

VOCABULARY   Define the following term in your own words and give an original example.

6. central selling theme:

COMPREHENSION

7. While studying for your bar exams, you decide to start a part-time business delivering singing telegrams throughout the Atlanta metropolitan area. For a flat fee of $150, you'll personally deliver a greeting card and sing any song (in good taste) of the customer's choice —using either the actual wording of the song or special lyrics composed by the customer. You promote your company (Musical Messages) as appropriate for birthdays, anniversaries, graduations, promotions, and other special occasions.

   a. What will be your central selling theme?

   b. Construct an appropriate attention-getter for your opening paragraph.

   c. Construct an effective sentence that mentions the price.

   d. Construct an effective closing sentence.

CRITICAL THINKING

8. Your boss has asked you to write a form sales letter advertising a new diet supplement for men that is "guaranteed to add at least 2 inches to your chest size or double your money back." Although the product is legal (and very popular), you personally feel that it is a sham and are hesitant to promote it. What do you tell your boss?

The 3Ps
*Problem, Process,
Product*

A Sales Letter

Problem

You are the marketing manager at Motorola for the C2K chip. This chip was designed for the Voice Note, a digital recorder that allows you to record messages to yourself rather than scribbling them on scraps of paper.

The recorder is $2\frac{1}{2} \times 1 \times \frac{1}{2}$ inches, weighs 3 ounces, and is made in Japan from sturdy plastic. It records messages that are a maximum of 3 minutes long and holds $4\frac{1}{2}$ hours of dictation. A lock button prevents recording over a message. After the message has been played back, the chip automatically resets for use the next time. The Voice Note is operated by pressing the Record button and speaking. It runs on two AAA batteries that are included and comes with a 90-day warranty and a 30-day full-refund policy.

To field-test this product, you decide to try a local direct-mail campaign directed at the business community. You purchase a mailing list containing the names and addresses of the 800 members of the Phoenix Athletic Club, a downtown facility used by business people for lunch, after-work drinks, exercise, and social affairs. The club has racquetball and tennis courts, an indoor pool, and exercise rooms. Its yearly membership fee is $3,000. You decide to send these 800 members a form letter promoting the Voice Note for $129.95. You'll include your local phone number (555-2394) for placing credit-card orders by phone, or the readers may stop by the store to purchase the recorder in person.

Process

1. Describe your audience.

   ■ Business men and women
   ■ Active (sports and exercise facilities)
   ■ Upscale (can afford $3,000 annual membership)
   ■ Probably very busy professionally and socially

2. What will be your central selling theme?

   Convenience/portability is the unique benefit of Voice Note.

3. Write an attention-getter that is original, interesting, and short; that is reader-oriented; that relates to the product; and, if possible, that introduces the central selling theme.

   You're driving home on the freeway in bumper-to-bumper traffic when the solution to a nagging problem facing you at work suddenly pops into your head. But by the time you get home 30 minutes later, your good idea has vanished.

4. Jot down the features you might discuss and the reader benefits associated with each feature.

   Size is $2\frac{1}{2} \times 1 \times \frac{1}{2}$ inches, weighs 3 ounces: *smaller and lighter than a microcassette recorder; fits in shirt pocket or purse; easy to use on the go.*

   Records 3-minute messages—a maximum of $4\frac{1}{2}$ hours, worth: *room enough for most "to-do" messages—90 different reminders.*

   Press Record button and then speak; lock function prevents overrecording: *easy to use, even in car; not a lot of buttons to fiddle with.*

   Powered by two AAA batteries (included): *real portability.*

226

Copyright © Houghton Mifflin Company. All rights reserved.

The 3Ps
Problem, Process,
Product

5. Write the sentence that mentions price. (Since price is not the central selling theme, it should be subordinated.)

The Voice Note's price of $129.95 is less than you'd pay for a bulky microcassette recorder that is much less convenient for on-the-go use.

6. What action are you seeking from the reader?

To purchase the Voice Note.

7. How can you motivate prompt action?

Make the action easy to take; offer warranty and guarantee satisfaction; stress that the sooner you buy, the sooner you'll enjoy using it.

 MOTOROLA

Dear Club Member:

You leave the Athletic Club and are heading home on the freeway in bumper-to-bumper traffic when the solution to a nagging problem at work suddenly pops into your head. But by the time you get home, your good idea has vanished.

Next time, carry Voice Note, the 3-ounce digital recorder with the new Motorola C2K chip that allows you to record reminders to yourself on the go. Now you can "jot" down your ideas as soon as they occur: while jogging, waiting at the bank, or lying in bed. As you know, inspiration often strikes far from a pad and pencil!

Much smaller than a microcassette ($2\frac{1}{2}$ x 1 x $\frac{1}{2}$ inches), Voice Note slips into your shirt pocket or purse. And there aren't a lot of buttons to fiddle with. Just press Record and speak. A lock button prevents overrecording your earlier messages.

You can record as many as 90 different messages of 37 minutes each—"to do" messages like "Call Richard about the Apple computer contract" or "Place order for 200 shares of SRP stock" or even "Pick up Jenny from soccer practice at 5:30." After playback, the tape automatically resets for immediate use.

For true portability, the Voice Note is powered by two AAA batteries (included). Your satisfaction is guaranteed by our 90-day warranty and 30-day refund policy.

The Voice Note's price of $129.95 is less than you'd pay for a bulky microcassette recorder that is much less convenient for on-the-go use. For credit-card orders, simply call us at 555-2394. Or stop by our retail store at Fiesta Mall for a personal demonstration. The next time you need to pick up a quart of milk on the way home, make a Voice Note. You won't come home empty-handed.

Sincerely,

Richard E. Lee

Richard E. Lee

Corporate Offices
1303 E. Algonquin Road, Schaumburg, IL 60196-1079 • (847) 576-5000

Summary

The ability to write persuasively is crucial for success in business. To write persuasively, you must overcome the reader's initial resistance, establish your own credibility, and develop an appeal that meets a need of the reader. You must also become thoroughly familiar with your reader so that you can translate the advantages of your idea or the features of your product into specific reader benefits.

When writing to superiors, use a direct writing style, giving the proposal or recommendation, along with the criteria or a brief rationale, in the first paragraph. For most other persuasive messages, prefer an indirect writing style. First gain the reader's attention by using an opening paragraph that is relevant, interesting, and short.

For persuasive requests, devote the majority of the message to discussing the merits of your proposal and showing specifically how it meets some need of the reader. Provide evidence that is accurate, relevant, representative, and complete. Discuss and minimize any obstacles to your proposal. For sales letters, introduce a central selling theme early and build on it throughout the message. Devote most of the message to showing how the reader will specifically benefit from owning the product. Subordinate the price, unless price is the central selling theme.

For all types of persuasive messages, end on a confident, positive note, making sure the reader knows what action is desired and making that action easy to take. Persuasive messages are often longer than other types of messages because of the need to present convincing evidence. By taking the space needed to support your statements with specific facts and figures, you'll increase your ability to persuade your readers.

Looking Ahead

Without a verb, you could not have a sentence because the verb makes a statement about the subject. It tells what the subject is doing or what is happening to the subject. Most verbs express action of some sort, but a small (but important) group of verbs simply link the subject with the words that describe it. We'll learn more about this important part of speech in Chapter 9.

Key Terms

central selling theme   rhetorical question

Exercises

Selling an Idea

1 **More Service at the Service Station**   You are the night manager for White Mountain Gas, a 24-hour, self-service gasoline station on a New Hampshire highway. The station owner, Adam Bream, has asked you to survey customers about the new credit-card–activated pumps that he is considering installing. This type of pump would authorize a sale and release the gasoline hose when the customer inserts a credit card; after the customer finishes using the hose, the pump would automatically shut off and print a receipt. Bream wants to know what customers think before he goes ahead with the pumps' installation.

You have talked with 300 customers over the course of two weeks, and more than three-quarters of them liked the idea: they don't like having to walk to the office to pay, and the new pump sounds as if it would be faster. But at least 35 people expressed concern over learning how to use the pump, and another 20 or so said they never pay by credit card. These people were worried that attendants might not be available for assistance and cash transactions after the new pumps were installed.

On the basis of your research, you want to recommend that the station install the pumps. To help reluctant customers, you think, extra attendants should be on hand for the first two months. You also want your boss to be aware that some people are worried about not being able to pay cash for their gas. Using a direct organizational plan, write a persuasive memo to Bream giving your recommendations.

2 **Writing Your Senator**   On January 29, the U.S. Senate will vote on funding for a wildlife refuge in Texas where several endangered animal species now flourish. In addition, the rare plants on this site are being tested by scientists in search of new medicines to treat burns and skin diseases, with promising results. Although there is some pressure to cut funding, you believe that more senators will support full funding for this refuge if they hear from their constituents. Write a letter to both of your senators urging the Senate to fully fund this refuge.

3 **Flying High**   Diana, Jean, and Larry were analyzing the quarterly expense report. "Look at line item 415," Diana said. "Air-travel expenses have increased 28% from last year. Is there any room for savings there?"

Larry said, "I think we should begin requiring our people to join all the frequent-flyer programs so that after they fly 20,000 to 30,000 miles on any one airline, they get a free ticket. Then we should require them to use that free ticket the next time they have to take a business trip for us. Company resources were used to purchase the original tickets, so logically the free tickets belong to the company. And why should our people who travel get free tickets, compliments of the company, when those who don't travel do not get free tickets?"

"I disagree," Jean said. "To begin with, there's no easy way to enforce the requirement. Who's going to keep track of how many miles each person flies on each airline and when a free flight coupon is due to that person? It would make us appear to be Big Brother, looking over their shoulders all the time. In addition, our people put in long hours on the road. If they can get a free ticket and occasionally are able to take their spouses along with them, what's the big deal? They're happier and probably end up doing a better job for us."

Diana put an end to the discussion. "Both of you think about the matter some more and let me have a memo giving me your position. Then I'll decide."

a. Assume the role of Larry. Write a memo to Diana trying to persuade her to begin requiring employees to use their frequent-flyer miles toward business travel. Knowing that Jean will be writing a memo arguing the opposing viewpoint—that employees should be able to use their free air-line tickets for personal use—try to counteract her possible arguments.

b. Now assume the role of Jean. Write a memo to Diana arguing for the status quo. Try to anticipate and counteract Larry's likely arguments.

4 **Sidestepping a Digital Ban**   The dean of your college recently read a news article describing how students can use pagers, cell phones, and handheld computers to share answers during classroom exams. According to the article, one-third of students in a recent survey said they had cheated during tests, and half said they had cheated on written assignments. As a result, the dean issued a statement forbidding students from having or using electronic hand-held devices in class when working on tests and projects.

Your sister is about to give birth to twins, and you've pleaded with your instructors to relax the ban on cell phones for the next three weeks so that you can take the call if it comes during a test. The instructors, however, need the dean's permission to make such an exception. Now you must submit a written request for the dean's consideration. Should you use a direct or an indirect organizational plan? Why? How can you justify your request? What obstacles can you anticipate—and how can you overcome them? Based on your knowledge of persuasive requests, write a letter to the dean (making up the details for this assignment).

5 **Internet Exercise**   Many businesses—on and off the Internet—use persuasive messages for both sales and nonsales purposes. Consider the situation at DoubleClick, a company that places advertisements for clients on various Web sites. Visit the firm's site (**http://www.doubleclick.com**) and follow the link to review its privacy policy, especially the section about cookies and how to prevent them from being placed on your computer. Next, find and follow the link that discusses how consumers can opt out of DoubleClick's customized advertising program. Now assume the role of DoubleClick's webmaster. Draft an email message intended to persuade consumers to reverse their opt-out decisions and continue allowing DoubleClick to send them customized advertising messages.

Requesting a Favor

6 **Field Trip**   You are David Pearson, owner and manager of Jack 'n Jill Preschool. During the next few weeks, you will be discussing food and nutrition with the youngsters; and you want to end the unit by having the children walk to the nearby Salad Haven, take a tour of the kitchens, and then make their own salads for lunch from the restaurant's popular salad bar. Of course, each family would pay for their child's meal. In fact, to help make the visit easier, you'll collect the money beforehand and pay the cashier for everyone at once. You will ask several parents to come with you to help supervise the 23 children, ages three through five, although they will probably need some extra help from the salad-bar attendants. You can come any day during the week of October 10–14. State regulations require that the children eat lunch between 11 a.m. and 12:30 p.m. Write to Donna Jo Luse (Manager, Salad Haven, 28 Grenvale Road, Westminster, MD 21157) asking for permission to make the field trip.

7 **Celebrity Donation**   Coming out of the movie theater after watching the Academy Award–winning movie *Rocky Mountain Adventure*, starring Robert Forte, you suddenly have an idea. As executive director of the Wilderness Fund, you've been searching for an unusual raffle prize for your upcoming fundraiser. You wonder whether you could persuade Robert Forte to donate some item used in this popular movie (perhaps a stage prop or costume item) for the raffle. The Wilderness Fund is an 8,000-member nonprofit agency dedicated to preserving forest lands—the very type of lands photographed so beautifully in Forte's latest movie. Write to the actor at Century Studios, 590 North Vermont Avenue, Los Angeles, CA 90004.

Writing a Persuasive Claim

8 Azaleas   You are Vera Malcolm, the facilities manager for Public Service Company of Arkansas. In preparation for the recent dedication of your new hydroelectric plant, you spruced up the grounds near the viewing stand. As part of the stage decorations, you ordered ten potted azaleas at $28.50 each (plus $10.50 shipping) from Jackson-Parsons Nurseries (410 Wick Avenue, Youngstown, OH 44555) on February 3. The bushes were guaranteed to arrive in show condition—ready to burst into bloom within three days—or your money would be cheerfully refunded.

The plants arrived in healthy condition but were in their final days (perhaps hours) of flowering—certainly in no shape to display at the dedication. You decided, instead, to plant the azaleas as part of your permanent landscaping. Because the plants arrived only three days before the dedication, you had to purchase substitute azaleas from the local florist—at a much higher price. In fact, you ended up paying $436 for the florist plants—$140.50 more than the Jackson-Parsons price. You feel that the nursery was responsible for your having to incur the additional expenditure. Write a letter asking Jackson-Parsons to reimburse your company for the $140.50.

9 Inaccurate Reporting   As the CEO of Software Entrepreneurs, Inc., you just received a memo from the marketing manager for your ReSolve spreadsheet program. The manager had written to the review editor at *Computing Trends* protesting inaccurate reporting; the reply (from Roberta J. Horton) was a form letter describing the magazine's policy on product reviews. Although you are glad to know that your product will be included in the yearly software review, you agree with your marketing manager that the editor made an error in downgrading your program. Apparently the reviewer worked with the original version of ReSolve and not with the improved version that was released one month before the review appeared. The new version is so powerful that it outperforms the competition on nearly every test used by the reviewer to determine product rankings.

Because magazine deadlines require that articles be completed well in advance of the printing date, you realize that the magazine could not possibly have included the improved version in its tests. However, you would like the review editor to print a small item noting the availability of the improved ReSolve in an upcoming issue. Write to Horton (*Computing Trends*, 200 Public Square, Cleveland, OH 44114) with this request.

10 Ripped Suit   After a hurried taxi ride from LaGuardia Airport to the Marriott Marquis Hotel on May 15, you barely made it to your 2 P.M. appointment. You did not realize until you sat down at the conference table that you had ripped the pants of your $450 suit on an exposed spring in the taxi seat. The next day, your tailor tells you there is no way to repair the rip invisibly, so the suit is, in effect, now useless. Because you've owned the suit for a year, you don't expect the taxi company to reimburse you for $450, but you do think reimbursement of $200 is reasonable. From your taxi receipt, you learn that you took Taxi 1145 belonging to Empire State Taxi (50 West 77th Street, New York, NY 10024). As this is a personal claim, write your letter on plain paper, using your own return address.

Writing a Sales Letter

11 Work Boots   As sales manager for Industrial Footwear, Inc., send a form sales letter advertising your Durham work boot to the 3,000 members of Local 147 of the Building Trades Union. Local 147 is made up primarily of construction workers on high-rise buildings in Houston, Texas.

The Durham is an 8-inch, waterproof, insulated boot, made of oil-tanned cowhide. It exceeds the guidelines for steel-toe protection issued by the American National Standards Institute (ANSI). The Durham has an all-rubber heel that provides firm footing, and its steel shanks provide additional support for arches and heels. It comes in whole sizes 7–13 in black or brown at a price of $79, plus $4.50 shipping. The price is guaranteed for the next 30 days. There is a one-year, no-questions-asked warranty.

Select a suitable salutation for your form letter, and omit the date and inside address. The purpose of the letter is to motivate readers to order the boot by using the enclosed order blank or by calling your toll-free order number, 800.555.2993.

12 Real Estate   As a Realtor in the local franchise of National Home Sales, you receive a letter from Ms. Edith Willis (667 Rising Hills Drive, Xenia, OH 45385). Her letter states, in part,

> I am a single mother of two young children who is being transferred to your town and wish to purchase a three-bedroom condominium in a nice area in the price range of $100,000 to $125,000. I would be able to make a maximum down payment of $25,000. Would you please write me, letting me know whether you have any property available that would fit my needs.

Although the housing market in your small town is tight, you do have a condominium available that might suit her needs. It has three bedrooms plus a finished basement, is air-conditioned (important in your part of the country), and is four years old. The neighborhood elementary school is considered the best in town; the only drawback is that the condominium is located next door to a large but attractive apartment building. The home is listed for $119,900.

Send Ms. Willis a photograph and fact sheet on the listing. The purpose of your letter is to encourage her to phone you at 602.555.3459 to make an appointment to visit your office so that you can personally show her this and perhaps other properties you have available.

13 Work-Team Communication   Select an ad from a newspaper or journal published within the past month. Working in groups of three or four, write an unsolicited form sales letter for the advertised product, to be signed by the sales manager. (You may need to gather additional information about the product, perhaps from the Internet.) The audience for your letter will be either the students or the faculty at your institution (you decide which). Include only actual data about the product and about the audience. Submit a copy of both the advertisement and your letter.

14 Selling for Charity   As the director of fund-raising for the Buckeye Bread Basket, a Cleveland, Ohio, charity that buys food for people in need, you are starting a new program. You plan to sell holiday greeting cards to raise money for your annual Thanksgiving Day dinner. This year, more than 400 needy people (including both single people and families) are expected to attend the dinner. An Ohio artist created the original watercolor scene on the cards, which come in boxes of ten, with green envelopes. People who buy the cards are able to take a tax deduction for their donations; the money from the sale of a single box can feed a hungry family of four on Thanksgiving. Write a form letter that will persuade people to order your cards. The price is $12 per box, plus $1 postage and handling, and orders can be placed using the enclosed form and return envelope.

Writing a Persuasive Message

PROBLEM   You are Cesar Gutiérrez, a claims adjuster for Statewide Insurance. Your job requires you to investigate automobile accident claims, negotiate settlements, and authorize payments. Customers are already distressed, of course, over their accidents and possible physical injury. The last thing they need is a delay in settling their insurance claims and getting their vehicles repaired.

Because you travel the entire eastern half of your state to physically examine the damaged vehicles and talk with those involved, you are constantly having to search maps and the Internet for directions to out-of-the-way places.

It occurs to you that you could be more productive and provide better customer service if you had an onboard automotive navigation system that relies on the federally operated Global Positioning System (GPS). The device in which you're interested is the Street Pilot III, which boasts a large color display as well as voice prompts (such as "turn right at the next intersection") and automatic routing capability. It's portable, so you can use it on any vehicle—which is particularly useful given that you sometimes have to fly to your destination and then rent an automobile. The cost is $699.99, but there is no monthly access charge.

Send a memo to your boss, Lisette Washington, vice president of operations, trying to sell her on the idea. She will be concerned, of course, about whether the other two adjusters will request the same device.

PROCESS   Compose a few paragraphs describing how you went about solving this problem. In narrative form, provide such information as the following:

1. What is the purpose of your letter?

2. Describe your audience.

3. Will you use a direct or an indirect organizational pattern?

4. List the reasons you might discuss for approving your proposal—including any reader benefits associated with each reason.

5. What is an obstacle that might prevent you from achieving your objective?

PRODUCT   Compose your document, following the five steps in the writing process (planning, drafting, revising, formatting, and proofreading). Format the final version on letterhead stationery (refer to the Style Manual for formatting guidelines).

9

Using Verbs in Business Communication

COMMUNICATION OBJECTIVES

After you have finished this chapter, you should be able to:

- Explain the difference in action, linking, and helping verbs.

- Distinguish between transitive and intransitive verbs.

- Describe the correct uses of the subjunctive mood.

- Explain the use of the three primary verb tenses.

- Identify the four parts of a verb.

- Use correct subject-verb agreement.

On the Job

ARVETTA COLEMAN
RPP Staff Accountant

Arvetta *laid* her computer printouts on the table and *sat* down for another scintillating meeting of the RPP finance committee. Paul Yu, who had been *lying* low as a result of a major disagreement with several other directors, called the meeting to order and reviewed the agenda. He then *raised* the issue of the upcoming bond program. Arvetta *raised* her hand, and after being recognized, *rose* to speak.

She wanted to *set* the record straight regarding the feasibility of issuing bonds at the present time. She *lay* out her arguments logically for delaying the bond issue and was just *setting* down when Peter raised an important point.

In this short scenario are nine occurrences (all italicized) of three troublesome pairs of irregular verbs (*lay/lie*, *raise/rise*, and *set/sit*). Was each verb used correctly? You'll know after studying this chapter that the last sentence contains errors. It should read "she *laid* out her arguments" and "was just *sitting* down."

Verb Functions and Mood

As we learned in Chapter 3, a verb expresses either physical or mental action (known, logically enough, as an *action* verb) or a state of being (known as a *linking* verb).

Do not confuse *action verbs*, discussed here, with *active voice*, discussed in Chapter 4. Action verbs may be in either active or passive voice.

Action Verbs

Action verbs may be either active or passive and either transitive or intransitive. A **transitive verb** requires a direct object to complete its meaning; that is, a transitive verb requires something (a noun or pronoun) to receive the action of the verb.

> Gail *typed* the medical report. (*"Medical report" receives the action of the transitive verb "typed."*)

> The board of directors gave the president a pay raise. (*"Pay raise" receives the action of the transitive verb "gave." Note that "president" is an indirect object.*)

transitive verb A verb that requires an object for the action it expresses

An **intransitive verb,** on the other hand, does not require an object. Thus, nothing receives the action of the verb. Although other words may follow the verb, they are used as complements or modifiers—not as objects.

> I *smiled.*

> I *smiled* weakly. (*"Weakly" is an adverb modifying the intransitive verb "smiled"; it does not receive the action of the verb.*)

> Greer *walked* into a room full of inquisitive reporters.

intransitive verb A verb that does not require an object

An intransitive verb may be followed by a complement but never by a direct object.

Some verbs are always transitive; other verbs are always intransitive. But, as is true for the parts of speech, whether a verb is transitive or intransitive often depends on how it is used in the sentence, as illustrated below.

> **TRANSITIVE:** The doctor *increased* my dosage of Celebrex.

> **INTRANSITIVE:** Interest rates *increased* rapidly.

> **TRANSITIVE:** Lena *grew* flowers on her patio.

> **INTRANSITIVE:** Lena *grew* increasingly anxious.

Why is it important to know the difference between transitive and intransitive verbs? First, you must understand the difference between transitive and intransitive verbs so as not to confuse frequently misused irregular verbs (such as *lie-lay, sit-set,* and *rise-raise,* which were discussed in the opening vignette in this chapter).

Second, when looking up a verb in the dictionary, you must know whether it is transitive or intransitive to be able to use the new word correctly. Note, for example, the definitions of *swoon* found in the third edition of the *American Heritage College Dictionary:*

> **swoon** (swo͞on) *intr. v.* **swooned, swoon•ing, swoons. 1.** To faint. **2.** To be overpowered by ecstatic joy. —*n.* **1.** a fainting spell; syncope. **2.** a state of ecstasy or rapture.

Note that the verb *swoon* is always intransitive (*intr. v.*) and thus may not be followed by an object. Therefore, to say, "the witness swooned" or "the witnesses swooned at the sight of the defendant" would be correct, but to say "the witness swooned the defendant" would be incorrect.

Linking Verbs

A linking verb *links* the subject with words in the predicate.

Recall from Chapter 3 that a small (but important) group of verbs do not express action but instead simply link the subject with words in the predicate. The most common linking verbs are forms of the verb *to be* and verbs involving the senses. Below is a list of the most common linking verbs. Keep in mind that some of these verbs may also function as action verbs, depending on their use in the sentence.

Common forms of the verb *to be* include *is, am, are, was, were,* and *will.*

am	appear	are	be
been	being	feel	is
look	seem	smell	sound
taste	was	were	

Linking verbs are neither active nor passive and are always intransitive.

Linking verbs do not have a voice (that is, they are neither active nor passive). Because they are always intransitive, they cannot take an object. Instead, they may be followed by a complement (either a noun or pronoun that renames the subject) or by an adjective that describes the subject. The linking verbs in the following sentences are italicized:

Catherine Nickersen *is* our new advertising director. (*"Our new advertising director" is a noun that renames the subject "Catherine Nickersen."*)

Today's weather *has been* cool. (*"Cool" is an adjective that describes the subject "weather."*)

Those new cookies *taste* great. (*"Great" is an adjective that describes the subject "cookies." Note, however, that in the sentence, "Did John taste the new cookies?" the verb "taste" is a transitive verb, with "cookies" serving as the direct object.*)

If you can substitute the = sign for the verb and the sentence makes sense, the verb is a linking verb.

If you have trouble deciding whether a verb is a linking verb or a transitive verb, try substituting an equals sign (=) for the verb. If it makes sense, the verb is linking. Applying this hint to the sentences above, we would have:

Catherine Nickersen = our new advertising director. (*makes sense, so the verb "is" is a linking verb*)

Today's weather = cool. (*makes sense, so the verb "has been" is a linking verb*)

Those new cookies = great. (*makes sense, so the verb "taste" is a linking verb*)

John = the new cookies. (*does not make sense, so the verb "taste" in this sentence is a transitive verb*)

Helping Verbs

helping verb A verb used before the main verb

A **helping verb** is used before the main verb to build a verb phrase so as to make the main verb more precise. For example, in the sentence "The pie has been eaten," the main verb is *eaten* and the helping verbs are *has been.* The helping verbs *has been* make the time of the action more precise (as compared to, for example, "The pie *will be* eaten").

A helping verb is always accompanied by another verb.

The most common helping verbs are these:

am	are	be	been	being
can	could	did	do	does
had	has	have	is	may
might	must	shall	should	was
were	will	would		

Verb Moods

The *mood* of a verb shows how the action of the verb is expressed. There are three moods. The *indicative mood* states a fact or asks a question ("The rent is due." "Have you written the check?"). The *imperative mood* issues a command or makes a request ("Do not leave early." "Please let me have your report.") These two moods rarely cause writers any problems and will not be discussed further. However, the **subjunctive mood** is a bit trickier and deserves fuller discussion.

The subjunctive mood of a verb expresses a demand, motion, or necessity or a condition that is improbable or contrary to fact. In such situations, always use the plural form of the verb (without the *s* or *es*). If the verb is some form of *to be*, you must use either *were* or *be*—never the singular *is, am, are,* or *was.* Study the following examples of the correct use of the subjunctive mood carefully.

> I demand that he *submit* to a drug test. (*not "submits"*)
>
> I recommend that everyone *be* tested for drugs. (*not "is tested"*)
>
> He insisted that he *be* allowed to finish my statement. (*not "was allowed" or "is allowed"*)
>
> I would do the same thing if I *were* John. (*not "was" because, obviously, I'm not John*)
>
> Sharon moved that the meeting *be* adjourned. (*not "is adjourned"*)
>
> I wish that I, rather than Rene, *were* going to receive the award. (*not "was"*)
>
> Donna acts as if she *were* the only one affected by the decision. (*not "was"*)

Do not, however, use the subjunctive mood if the statement might possibly be true.

> If I *am* nominated for the award, I will be quite happy. (*not "be nominated" because I might be nominated*)
>
> If Danny *was* at the meeting, I did not see him. (*not "were" because he might have been at the meeting*)

subjunctive mood The verb mood that expresses a demand, motion, or necessity or a condition that is unlikely or impossible

Do not use the verbs *is, am, are,* and *was* with verbs in the subjunctive mood.

WORD|wise

Mirror Reflections

Enthusiastic opera singer:	avid diva
Half of a double-boiler:	top pot
Indiana basketball review:	Pacer recap
Performing rodents:	star rats
Small weapons:	snug guns
Uninspired poet:	drab bard
Where the goodies are stored:	reward drawer
X-rated film:	leer reel

Verb Tenses

The **verb tense** indicates the time of the action expressed by the verb. The three primary tenses are present, past, and future tense.

verb tense The property of a verb that expresses time

Present Tense

Use the *present tense* to express action that is happening now or that continues to happen or continues to be true.

> Carlos coughs a lot. (*present action*)
>
> Raisa is staying home today. (*continuing action*)
>
> Mr. Bishop approves all purchase orders. (*continuing truth*)

Use the present tense to express "continuing truths" even if past-tense verbs are used elsewhere in the sentence.

He told me that you are efficient. (*not "were efficient"*)

Although Josephine received the promotion, you are the one for whom she rooted. (*not "you were"*)

Did the caller say he is an accountant? (*not "he was"*)

Past Tense

Use the past tense to express action that has been completed. Most verbs form the past tense by adding *d* or *ed* to the present tense. The past tense of the verb *to be* is *was* or *were*.

Casimir sorted his favorite sites in Internet Explorer. (*But he is now finished*)

Jesse was at his desk when I arrived. (*Both actions are now finished*)

When Hoshi finished her report, she submitted it to the council. (*Both actions are now finished*)

Do not confuse the present tense with the past tense.

NOT: Yesterday, I say to him, "Don't even think about it."

BUT: Yesterday, I said to him, "Don't even think about it."

NOT: Last month, I get this notice from personnel.

BUT: Last month, I got this notice from personnel.

Future Tense

Use the future tense to express action that has not yet taken place. The future tense is typically formed by adding the helping verb *will* before the present tense of the verb.

Mr. Wang will address the stockholders.

Mr. Wang will be addressing the stockholders.

Do not confuse the present tense with the future tense.

NOT: Next week, José begins his new job.

BUT: Next week, José will begin his new job.

NOT: I fly to Atlanta next Thursday.

BUT: I will fly to Atlanta next Thursday.

VOCABULARY Define these terms in your own words and give an original example of each.

1. helping verb:

2. intransitive verb:

3. subjunctive mood:

4. transitive verb:

5. verb tense:

CHECKPOINT 9.1

COMPREHENSION

6. Write a capital *T* if the italicized verb in the sentence is transitive and a capital *I* if the verb is intransitive. If the verb is transitive, underline the direct object.

   a. ___ Rosario felt sick the day of the meeting.
   b. ___ Ilsa felt her forehead to see if she had a fever.
   c. ___ Our computer repair service provides us excellent service.
   d. ___ Did Joseph actually snore during the conference call?
   e. ___ Nishi lay down for a quick rest before the cross-examination.
   f. ___ Please lay down your packages and rest for a moment.

7. In the following sentences, underline each linking verb once and underline each helping verb twice.

   a. Elsie is a caring pediatrician who always helps others.
   b. She is working at the clinic this afternoon to inoculate the children.
   c. Jason, I heard that you were leaving our company for a job overseas. Is that true?
   d. Honestly, I have not felt secure since he was released from prison.
   e. I tasted the new recipe and it tasted good. In fact, it was great.

8. Underline the correct verb in parentheses in the following sentences.

   a. If I (was, were) you, I'd forget about it.
   b. If I (was, were) the one who tipped off the media, I've completely forgotten about it.
   c. I demand that I (am, be) elected chair of this group.

    d. If I (am, be) chosen, I will do my best.

    e. It is my desire that Pat (attend, attends) the technology conference.

9. Underline the correct verb in parentheses.

    a. Christmas (is, was) celebrated on December 25 each year.

    b. Tomorrow, I (give, will give) him a physical examination.

    c. Did she say her name (is, was) Doris?

    d. Bert (was, is) talking to me when you arrived.

    e. Yesterday, I (gave, give) him some help on the project.

Principal Parts of Verbs

The four parts of a verb, upon which all verb tenses are formed, are the present, past, past participle, and present participle.

Regular Verbs

A regular verb adds d or ed to form the past tense and past participle.

A *regular verb* forms the past tense and past participle by adding *d* or *ed* to the present tense. The present participle of all verbs (regular or irregular) is formed by adding *ing* to the present tense. Most verbs are regular.

Present	*Past*	*Past Participle*	*Present Participle*
follow	followed	(has) followed	(is) following
occur	occurred	(has) occurred	(is) occurring

The present and past tenses never take a helping verb. The past participle and present participle always take a helping verb.

Note that the terms *present* and *past* each comprise one word, and all verbs in the present and past tenses comprise one word. The terms *past participle* and *present participle* each comprise more than one word, and all past participle and present participle verbs comprise more than one word. The helping verbs for the past participle are either *have, has,* or *had.* The helping verbs for the present participle are either *is, am, are, was, were, be,* or *been.*

To choose the correct present-tense verb, say to yourself, "Today, I ____" and then fill in the blank. To choose the correct past-tense verb, say, "Yesterday, I ____." To choose the correct past participle, say, "I have ____;" and to choose the correct present participle, say "I am ____." For example:

Today, I *try.* (*present*)
Yesterday, I *tried.* (*past*)
I have *tried.* (*past participle*)
I am *trying.* (*present participle*)

This simple memory device works for both regular and irregular verbs.

Irregular Verbs

Most people (whether native English speakers or English-as-second-language [ESL] speakers) have little difficulty using regular verbs correctly. Fortunately, most verbs are regular. A number of verbs (called *irregular verbs*), however, do not form the past tense and past participle by adding *d* or *ed.* Because irregular verbs do not form their past tense and past participles in any consistent fashion, you will simply need to study and learn the different forms of these verbs.

Do not confuse the past participle with the past tense of irregular verbs.

NOT: Her blouse *shrunk* when she washed it.

BUT: Her blouse *shrank* when she washed it.

NOT: Mr. Vasilev *begun* to read aloud his statement.

BUT: Mr. Vasilev *began* to read aloud his statement.

Similarly, do not confuse the past tense with the past participle.

NOT: Jessica had already *broke* the rules by arriving late.

BUT: Jessica had already *broken* the rules by arriving late.

NOT: I have *sank* that putt numerous times.

BUT: I have *sunk* that putt numerous times.

Three pairs of irregular verbs deserve special consideration because of their frequent misuse. Here are their principal parts:

Present	*Past*	*Past Participle*	*Present Participle*
lay (to place)	laid	laid	laying
lie (to recline)	lay	lain	lying
raise (to lift)	raised	raised	raising
rise (to ascend)	rose	risen	rising
set (to place)	set	set	setting
sit (to rest)	sat	sat	sitting

The verb pair *lie/lay* is especially troublesome because the present tense of *lay* is the same as the past tense of *lie*.

The first verb in each group (*lay, raise, set*) is transitive, meaning that it will always require a direct object. The second verb in each group (*lie, rise, sit*) is intransitive and is not followed by a direct object. Here is a memory aid: The three intransitive verbs all contain the letter *i*; associate that *i* with *intransitive*.

The direct objects in the following sentences are italicized.

Remember: l**i**e, r**i**se, and s**i**t are all **i**ntransitive and thus do not take a direct object.

Please <u>lay</u> your *books* on the table and <u>lie</u> down to relax.

<u>Raise</u> your *hand* and <u>rise</u> when you take the oath of office.

I will <u>set</u> the *report* on the table and then <u>sit</u> for awhile.

She <u>laid</u> her *books* on the table and <u>lay</u> down to relax.

He <u>raised</u> his *hand* and <u>rose</u> when he took the oath of office.

I <u>set</u> the *report* on the table and then <u>sat</u> for awhile.

She had <u>laid</u> her *books* on the table and was <u>lying</u> down to relax when the doorbell rang.

He had <u>raised</u> his *hand* and was <u>rising</u> when the judged walked in.

I had <u>set</u> the *report* on the table and was now <u>sitting</u> in the audience.

CHECKPOINT 9.2

COMPREHENSION

1. Write the correct form of the verb in the space provided. Remember to think:

Past:	"Yesterday, I ___"
Past participle:	"I have ___"
Present participle:	"I am ___"

Present	Past	Past Participle	Present Participle
become	_____	_____	_____
blow	_____	_____	_____
die	_____	_____	_____
drop	_____	_____	_____
fall	_____	_____	_____
forgive	_____	_____	_____
grow	_____	_____	_____
keep	_____	_____	_____
run	_____	_____	_____
sell	_____	_____	_____
think	_____	_____	_____

2. Underline the correct verb in each sentence.

   a (Lay, Lie) down here for a few minutes.
   b. The unused Dell Inspiron computer was just (setting, sitting) there.
   c. Please (raise, rise) that question at the press conference tomorrow.
   d. She (sat, set) the papers on the desk before leaving for the day.
   e. Monica had just (laid, lain) her coat down when the telephone rang.

Subject and Verb Agreement

Use singular verbs with singular subjects and plural verbs with plural subjects.

The basic rule of subject-verb agreement is this: Use a singular verb with a singular subject and a plural verb with a plural subject. (Your subject and verb will then *agree.*) To make the subject and verb agree, you must, of course, first be able to identify the subject and verb. In many sentences, doing so is easy:

> *Toshi* <u>needs</u> the contract for the new lease.
> The *accountants* <u>want</u> to verify the financial terms of the lease.

In the first sentence, *Larry* is the subject; *needs* is the verb. Both are singular; that is, they agree. In the second sentence, *accountants* is the subject; *want* is the verb. Both are plural, meaning that they also agree. Note that most nouns become plural by adding *s*; however, most verbs become plural by omitting *s*. Thus, one *s* in the subject-verb combination is usually *just right:* "Larry need<u>s</u>" or "accountants want."

Compound Subjects

When two subjects are joined by *and*, the subject is plural and requires a plural verb.

> Ms. Qasim *and* Ms. Olson <u>make</u> this presentation every quarter.
> The driver of the bus *and* two passengers <u>were</u> injured in the accident.
> The paralegal *and* his supervisor <u>are</u> proofreading the deposition.

"No, Jimmy, it's not 'I sawed a chair'-- it's
'I have seen a chair' or 'I saw a chair'."

Note: To focus attention on subject-verb agreement, only the part of the verb that changes is underlined in these examples. For example, in the last example, the complete verb is *are proofreading.* Because *proofreading* remains the same whether the verb is singular or plural, however, only *are* is underlined.

Here is one exception to our rule (Aren't there exceptions to all rules?): If the two subjects connected by *and* are preceded by the word *each* or *every,* the subject is singular and requires a singular verb.

Each lease and purchase agreement <u>is</u> reviewed for tax purposes.

Every man, woman, and child <u>is</u> eligible for medical coverage.

BUT: The *man, woman, and child* <u>are</u> eligible for medical coverage.

When two subjects are joined by *or, either/or, nor, neither/nor,* or *not only/but also,* the verb must agree with the subject closer to it. In other words, it doesn't matter whether the other subject (the one farther from the verb) is singular or plural.

Monday or *Tuesday* <u>is</u> a good day for the conference.

Mondays or *Tuesdays* <u>are</u> good days for the conference.

The managers or their *assistant* <u>is</u> required to attend.

Not only the computer but also the *printers* <u>are</u> to be upgraded.

Not only the computer but also the *printer* <u>is</u> to be upgraded.

Not only the computers but also the *printer* <u>is</u> to be upgraded.

Indefinite Pronouns as Subjects

An **indefinite pronoun** is a word that stands for a noun but that does not refer to a *specific* noun. Examples are *all, somebody, one, several,* and *everything.* When used as subjects or as adjectives that modify subjects, some indefinite pronouns are always singular, some are always plural, and some may be either singular or plural, depending on how they are used in the sentence.

These indefinite pronouns are always singular and require a singular verb:

another	each	either	every
much	neither	one	

Plus: all pronouns ending with *body, one,* or *thing.*

Each <u>is</u> required to notify the agency within two days. (*"Each" is the subject.*)

indefinite pronoun A pronoun that does not refer to a specific noun

Indefinite pronouns may always be singular, always be plural, or be either singular or plural.

Each company is required to notify the lease agency within two days. (*"Each" modifies the subject "company."*)

Much remains to be done.

Everybody has to contribute to the effort.

Neither is correct.

Neither of the offices was large enough for our purposes.

Note in the last two sentences above that when *neither* appears by itself as the subject, it is always singular; but when it appears in a *neither/nor* combination, it may be singular or plural, depending on the noun closer to the verb. The same is true, of course, for *either* and *either/or*.

These indefinite pronouns are always plural and require a plural verb:

both   few   many   others   several

Many are called but *few* are chosen.

A few were chosen.

The *others* are awaiting our decision.

Several files are missing.

Several of the files are missing.

These indefinite pronouns may be singular or plural, depending on the noun they refer to:

all   none   any   some   more   most

All of the *report* has to be retyped. (*all of one thing*)

All of the *reports* have to be retyped. (*all of several things*)

Some *effort* was spent on reading her handwriting. (*some of one thing*)

Some *grievances* were referred to the arbitrator. (*some of several things*)

Measurements

Expressions of time, money, and quantity generally refer to *total amounts* and are singular. Only when emphasizing the *individual units* of time, money, and quantity would you use a plural verb.

Three weeks was too long to spend on this project. (*refers to a total amount*)

For me, *$15* was a high price to pay for admission. (*refers to a total amount*)

BUT: *Two full days* were required to update the financial information. (*emphasizes the individual units*)

Fractions and portions may be singular or plural, depending on the noun they refer to.

Half of the *time* was spent in updating the financial information.

Three-fourths of the *reports* are still in need of updating.

A minimum of *effort* is needed for the project.

A large percentage of the *voters* were uninformed on the issue.

The expression *the number* refers to one thing and is singular; the expression *a number* refers to more than one thing and is plural.

The number of complaints has decreased dramatically.

A number of these complaints have involved the packaging of the napkins.

When either or neither appears by itself, it is singular. If it appears in an either/or or neither/nor combination, it may be singular or plural.

Because we think of a measurement as a total unit, measurements are treated as singular.

The number is singular; a number is plural.

VOCABULARY Define the following term in your own words and give an original example.

1. indefinite pronoun:

CHECKPOINT 9.3

COMPREHENSION

2. Underline the simple subject in each sentence.

   a. Each of the accountants must verify the numbers.
   b. At this table sat the three witnesses.
   c. McDonald's should be pleased with the new design of the napkins.
   d. In the case of a tie, the judges may determine the winner.
   e. Yasmin, not her accountants, will interview the candidates.
   f. The vice president of development and financial affairs can speak at our banquet.
   g. Three of the workers stayed late to finish the job.
   h. Where should I put the new computer?

3. Underline the correct verb in parentheses.

   a. Neither the supervisor nor the managers (are, is) responsible.
   b. The secretary and treasurer of our credit union (was, were) both at the board meeting.
   c. The texture and absorbency of the napkin (appear, appears) to be important.
   d. Not only Ms. Perry and Mr. Morris but also Mr. Austin (expect, expects) to attend.
   e. Every policy and procedure (are, is) to be reviewed.
   f. The contract and cover letter (remain, remains) in the office safe.

4. Underline the correct verb in parentheses.

   a. Both employees (was, were) required to pass the physical examination.
   b. Most of the time (was, were) spent on defining the problem.
   c. Everyone (has, have) to attend the toxic-substance training session.
   d. None of the programmers (has, have) written a single line of code.
   e. Several of the third-shift runs (need, needs) to be checked for imperfections.
   f. Either of the alternatives (require, requires) more personnel than we can spare.
   g. Everything (seem, seems) to be in order for his visit.
   h. Few (was, were) expected to sign up for the insurance.
   i. None of the report (has, have) been cleared for release by legal.

5. Underline the correct verb in parentheses.

   a. The number of compliance statements required by the federal and state governments (are, is) increasing.
   b. One-third of the hepatitis tests (was, were) negative.
   c. Hussein stated that 30 minutes (was, were) all the time he needed.
   d. A number of revisions (are, is) necessary before Mr. Russo will okay the contract.
   e. The majority of L. J.'s time (are, is) spent in developing new marketing plans.
   f. Fifteen gallons (are, is) the capacity of my gas tank.
   g. Two-thirds of the orientation (discuss, discusses) employee benefits.
   h. A large portion of the raise (was, were) designated as a merit increase.

Special Types of Subjects

Proper nouns (such as company names, names of products, and titles of publications), collective nouns, and clauses beginning with *who*, *which*, or *that* require special consideration when determining subject-verb agreement.

Company Names, Products, and Publication Titles   Company and product names and publication titles are considered singular, even though they may look like they are plural in form. It helps to remember that in each case we're talking about just one thing.

Standard & Poor's <u>is</u> a financial information company. (*one company*)
Shake 'n Bake <u>is</u> what I will prepare for dinner tonight. (*one product*)

Consumer Reports <u>is</u> on my required reading list each month. (*one magazine*)

The Agony and the Ecstasy <u>is</u> my all-time favorite novel. (*one book*)

collective noun A noun that refers to a group of people, places, or things

Collective nouns are treated as singular. It may help to remember that they do not end in *s*.

Mentally delete the *who, which,* or *that.*

Collective Nouns   A **collective noun** is a word that is singular in form (such as *committee, company, department, group,* and *team*) but that represents a group of people or things. In general, consider collective nouns as singular.

The *committee* <u>is</u> finishing up its assignments this afternoon.
Our *board of directors* <u>meets</u> on the first Friday of each quarter.

***Who, Which,* and *That* Clauses**   Verbs that follow *who, which,* or *that* clauses must agree with the word these pronouns refer to. Most of the time this word comes immediately before the pronoun. *Hint:* For purposes of determining which verb to use after these pronouns, mentally delete the pronoun.

Hester, who <u>is</u> one of our best employees, won the "I Care" award last month. (*Hester* <u>is</u> *one of our best employees.*)

Hoshiko and Lester, who <u>are</u> also excellent employees, were the runners-up. (*Hoshiko and Lester* <u>are</u> *also excellent employees.*)

The *idea* that <u>bothers</u> me most is that I was not told earlier of this problem. (*The idea* <u>bothers</u> *me most.*)

Problems in Subject-Verb Agreement

Before finishing our discussion of subject-verb agreement, let's look at two special situations to make sure they do not cause any problems: sentences in which the subject and verb are separated by other expressions and sentences in which the subject comes after the verb.

Ignore any words that come between the subject and verb.

Words Coming Between the Subject and Verb   When establishing agreement between the subject and verb, disregard any words that come between them. (Remember: To find the subject, ask *who* or *what* before the verb. Then make the verb agree with the subject.)

Yasuo's *motion,* including both amendments, <u>was</u> defeated.

The *contents* of the annual report, not its format, <u>determine</u> investor reaction.

Alma's *experience* with three software programs <u>was</u> invaluable.

In the first sentence, *what* was defeated? A *motion* was defeated; *motion* is singular and requires the singular verb *was.* In the second sentence, *what* determines investor reactions? The *contents* determine investor reaction; *contents* is plural and requires the plural verb *determine.* (Remember: One *s* in the subject-verb combination is "just right.")

Subjects Coming After the Verb   As you know, the normal order of sentences is *subject-verb.* In some sentences, however, the order is *verb-subject.* In that case, you must look for the subject after the verb. As always, the subject and verb must agree. It sometimes helps to rephrase the sentence so that the subject comes first.

Among the list of deadlines <u>was</u> the due *date* for the performance appraisals. (*the due date <u>was</u>*)

Where <u>were</u> *you* when the lights went out? (*you <u>were</u> where*)

How difficult <u>are</u> those *forms* to complete? (*those forms <u>are</u>*)

Another situation in which you will find the subject coming after the verb is in sentences beginning with *here* or *there*. These words are adverbs, and adverbs cannot serve as the subject (only nouns and pronouns can serve this function). In these sentences, look beyond the verb to find the true subject.

There <u>was</u> *no one* available to help me complete the project. (*The verb <u>was</u> must agree with the subject "no one."*)

Here *are* the tax *receipts* for our sales-recognition dinner last evening. (*The verb <u>are</u> must agree with the subject "receipts."*)

> In sentences beginning with *here* or *there,* the subject appears *after* the verb.

VOCABULARY   Define the following term in your own words and give an original example.

1. collective noun:

CHECKPOINT 9.4

COMPREHENSION

2. Underline the correct verb in parentheses.

   a. (Are, Is) Proctor & Gamble interested in our new wrapping paper?
   b. The quality-control team (are, is) planning to survey all users.
   c. Yushino's estimates, which (was, were) the largest, were finally accepted.
   d. Mr. West's statement, which (was, were) printed in our newsletter, drew many critical comments.
   e. Peter, Paul, and Mary (was, were) a popular folk trio in the 1960s.
   f. Their customers who (has, have) complaints are now getting some answers.
   g. The steps that (take, takes) the most time should be simplified.

3. Underline the correct verb in parentheses.

   a. What (are, is) the names of the prospective customers you are visiting?
   b. My best estimate of how many will attend the three training sessions (are, is) at least 75.
   c. Dustin, as well as Gustavo and Marie, (are, is) on the new task force.
   d. Among the exhibits submitted (was, were) a testimonial letter from MCL Cafeteria.
   e. Our new bag design, in addition to the new wrapping paper, (are, is) to be evaluated by a focus group.
   f. The format of the report, as well as its contents, (are, is) sure to be evaluated.
   g. There (was, were) too many unanswered questions for the board to make a decision.

Summary

Action verbs may be either transitive or intransitive. A transitive verb requires a direct object to complete its meaning; an intransitive verb does not. Linking verbs do not express action but instead simply link the subject with words that rename or describe it. Linking verbs are neither active nor passive and are always intransitive. A helping verb (such as "has been" or "is") is used before the main verb to build a verb phrase to make the main verb more precise.

The subjunctive mood of a verb expresses a demand, motion, or necessity or a condition that is improbable or contrary to fact. The tense of the verb indicates the time of the action; the three primary tenses are present, past, and future. The four parts of a verb, upon which all verb tenses are formed, are the present, past, past participle, and present participle.

A regular verb forms the past tense and past participle by adding *d* or *ed* to the present tense. Irregular verbs form these tenses in a variety of ways, but the present participle of all verbs is formed by adding *ing* to the present tense.

The basic rule of agreement is to use singular verbs with singular subjects and plural verbs with plural subjects. Subjects joined by *and* require a plural verb; those joined by *or, either/or, neither/nor,* or *not only/but also* require that the verb agree with the subject closer to the verb.

The pronouns *another, each, either, every, much, neither,* and *one,* plus pronouns ending with *body, one,* or *thing* require singular verbs. The pronouns *both, few, many, others,* and *several* require plural verbs. The pronouns *all, none, any, some, more,* and *most* may be singular or plural, depending on the noun they refer to.

Most expressions of time, money, and quantity require singular verbs. The verbs for fractions and portions must agree with the nouns they refer to. The expression *the number* is singular; *a number* is plural.   Company names, products, publication titles, and collective nouns take a singular verb. In *who, which,* and *that* clauses, the verb agrees with the word the pronoun refers to. When establishing agreement, you should ignore words that come between the subject and verb and should make the subject and verb agree, even if the subject comes after the verb.

Key Terms

collective noun	helping verb
indefinite pronoun	intransitive verb
subjunctive mood	transitive verb
verb tense	

Looking Ahead

In Part 3 (Chapters 7, 8, and 9), we have studied effective communication through letters, email, and memorandums, as well as the correct use of verbs. We now turn to longer and more formal documents—the business report. In Chapter 10, you will learn about the characteristics of a business report and how to collect and analyze the data needed to solve the report problem.

Exercises

Verb Functions, Mood, and Tense

1 Action Verbs   Complete the following sentences and then indicate whether the verb is transitive or intransitive.

<table>
<tr><td></td><td>Transitive or
Intransitive</td></tr>
<tr><td>a. Ruth threw _____</td><td>_____</td></tr>
<tr><td>b. Jesús will speak _____</td><td>_____</td></tr>
<tr><td>c. Today is _____</td><td>_____</td></tr>
<tr><td>d. This past week has been _____</td><td>_____</td></tr>
<tr><td>e. Rita has taken _____</td><td>_____</td></tr>
<tr><td>f. Your plan sounds _____</td><td>_____</td></tr>
<tr><td>g. Beth read _____</td><td>_____</td></tr>
<tr><td>h. I gave _____</td><td>_____</td></tr>
</table>

2 Linking and Helping Verbs   Underline each linking verb once and each helping verb twice in the following sentences.

a. Catherine will be able to pay for the refreshments from petty cash.

b. I am at a loss for words.

c. I am going to pursue that lead tomorrow.

d. Ms. Ortega could not have been thinking when she made that remark.

e. That seems like a tremendous amount of work.

f. We can still get there on time if we hurry.

3 Subjunctive Mood   Circle the correct verb in parentheses in the following sentences.

a. I wish he (was, were) here to help me figure it out.

b. It is important that this project (be, is) finished on time.

c. I insist that I (am, be) allowed to speak.

d. Nathan spoke as if he (was, were) actually present at the scene.

e. If I (was, were) Estela, I'd quit right now.

4 Verb Tenses   Circle the correct verb in parentheses in the following sentences.

a. I found out yesterday that you (are, were) twenty-five years old.

b. I (talked, have talked) on the phone last night.

c. Did you say you (are, were) an uncle?

d. Our records (show, showed) an unpaid balance of $350.

e. Anthony (is, was) the type of person everyone instantly liked.

f. On Thursday, I (think, thought) to myself that the project was in trouble.

g. I (begin, will begin) my internship next week.

Principal Parts of Verbs

5 Circle the correct verb in parentheses in the following sentences.

  a. Don't just (sit, set) there; do something.

  b. Dr. Hashimoto has (wore, worn) out his welcome with us.

  c. He (sat, set) down at the head chair.

  d. He (sat, set) down his books and began playing the piano.

  e. I (am, be) fascinated by the whole field of phlebotomy.

  f. I felt like I have (ate, eaten) enough for three people.

  g. I have already (broke, broken) in my new baseball glove.

  h. I'm glad you have (chose, chosen) to continue your education here.

  i. Just (lay, lie) down until the nausea subsides.

  j. Kathryn (began, begun) work on the inventory project immediately.

  k. Please (rise, raise) your hand before asking a question.

  l. She (been, was) thinking of starting something similar in this office.

  m. They had (lay, laid, lain) the folders on the file cabinet.

  n. We (saw, seen) the intersection where the accident occurred.

  o. We (see, seen) several opportunities to cut costs.

Subject-Verb Agreement

Directions: Circle the correct verb in parentheses in the following sentences.

6 **Basic Rule of Agreement**

  a. One of the companies (need, needs) an effective turnaround strategy.

  b. I (has, have) seriously considered the consequences of this action.

  c. She (has, have) seriously considered the consequences of this action.

  d. They (has, have) seriously considered the consequences of this action.

  e. I (was, were) not aware that the federal regulations had changed.

  f. He (was, were) not aware that the federal regulations had changed.

  g. They (was, were) not aware that the federal regulations had changed.

  h. The coated bags (offer, offers) environmental advantages.

  i. The coated bag (offer, offers) environmental advantages.

  j. The man (was, were) asked to wear a tie at the restaurant.

  k. The men (was, were) asked to wear a tie at the restaurant.

  l. They (do, does) want me to work the second shift.

  m. She (do, does) want me to work the second shift.

  n. Only you (has, have) been selected to work on the project.

  o. You both (has, have) been selected to work on the project.

  p. The most important issue (are, is) taxes.

  q. Taxes (are, is) the most important issue.

  r. The backup file (are, is) on the shelf behind all those plants.

  s. On the shelf behind all those plants (are, is) the backup file.

  t. The box (was, were) stored in Warehouse 3.

  u. The box of ribbons and cartridges (was, were) stored in Warehouse 3.

7 **Compound Subjects**

  a. Both September and October (are, is) good months for the trial run.

  b. Each hamburger and hotdog (require, requires) a different type of wrapper.

  c. Either the Chamber of Commerce or the Federal Reserve (are, is) predicting a low rate of inflation next quarter.

  d. Every Monday, Wednesday, and Friday (are, is) considered a file-backup day.

e. Expenses or salaries (has, have) to be adjusted.

f. James and Arvetta (has, have) to prepare the quarterly FICA statements.

g. Neither personal checks nor money orders (are, is) acceptable for payment.

h. Not only the marketing division but also the manufacturing division (has, have) to come into compliance.

i. The two tables and one wide chair (need, needs) to be moved to the conference room.

8 Indefinite Pronouns

a. All of the agenda items (was, were) covered during the meeting.

b. All of the cake (was, were) eaten before the meeting ended.

c. Any one of the computer manuals (are, is) sure to contain the solution.

d. Both (are, is) eligible to apply for the position.

e. Both employees (want, wants) to apply for the position.

f. Each (has, have) to be considered on its own merits.

g. Each grievance (has, have) to be addressed in our response.

h. Either of the two alternatives (satisfies, satisfy) the diversity objective.

i. Everybody (has, have) to contribute to the refreshment fund.

j. Few (has, have) been successful using that innovation.

k. Many of the new employees in the accounting area (need, needs) to be tested.

l. More than one customer (has, have) complimented us on the design of our logo.

m. Most of the problem (was, were) due to poor communication.

n. Much (has, have) been accomplished in the past few weeks.

o. Neither of the alternatives (are, is) acceptable.

p. Neither one of the secretaries (take, takes) shorthand.

q. Several new vendors (was, were) considered for the contract.

r. Some of the assemblers (has, have) already met their quotas.

s. Something (seem, seems) suspicious about the low bid.

t. Two temporaries reported yesterday; another (are, is) due to report tomorrow.

9 Measurements

a. A majority of the committee members (agree, agrees) with our proposal.

b. A number of trials (was, were) necessary before we got it right.

c. A small percentage of the budget (was, were) spent on entertainment.

d. I thought that $100 (was, were) too much to spend on a going-away gift.

e. Nearly two-thirds of the workers (are, is) also covered by their spouses' insurance.

f. That $5,000 (was, were) spent within two weeks.

g. The five corner lots (are, is) to be auctioned at noon.

h. The number of team members (depend, depends) on the complexity of the task.

i. Three-fourths of the document (refer, refers) to OSHA requirements.

10 Special Types of Subjects

a. *Bob and Tom* (are, is) my favorite radio talk show.

b. Brooks Brothers (are, is) having a sale on men's lightweight suits.

c. Microsoft (has, have) been sued by the federal government as well as several states.

    d. Our department (are, is) extremely angry about the change in coverage.

    e. *Pride and Prejudice* (was, were) an alternate selection for the company-sponsored play.

    f. The AlphaSmart is a basic word processing device that (cost, costs) only $250.

    g. The evaluators, who (was, were) present for the demonstration, are still deliberating.

    h. The ISO 9000 team (are, is) scheduled to report next month.

    i. The pieces of evidence, which (are, is) still in custody, are not challenged by our counsel.

    j. The team players (are, is) scheduled to have a dress rehearsal Friday evening.

11 Problems in Subject-Verb Agreement

    a. All of the budget except for the sales and tax projections (has, have) been finalized.

    b. Here (are, is) the report that you requested yesterday.

    c. In the lobby of their new headquarters (sit, sits) a bronze bust of their founder.

    d. Included in his lists of demands (was, were) the use of a company car.

    e. Only one of our marketing representatives (are, is) going to attend.

    f. Our order for two color photocopiers (was, were) shipped last week.

    g. The cost for conference registration, hotel, and supplies (are, is) $1,500.

    h. The cost of tuition, not including room and board, (are, is) $500 for each module.

    i. The wholesale price of the no-leak wrapper, plus tax, (are, is) $18.33 per thousand.

    j. There (are, is) several ways to approach this problem.

    k. Under these piles of papers (are, is) the most recent draft.

    l. Who (was, were) the ones responsible for the flawed production run?

    m. Why (aren't, isn't) the medical department monitoring this situation?

PART FOUR
BUSINESS REPORT WRITING

■ **CHAPTER 10**
**Planning the Business Report
and Collecting Data**

■ **CHAPTER 11**
Writing the Business Report

■ **CHAPTER 12**
**Using Pronouns, Adjectives, and
Adverbs in Business Communication**

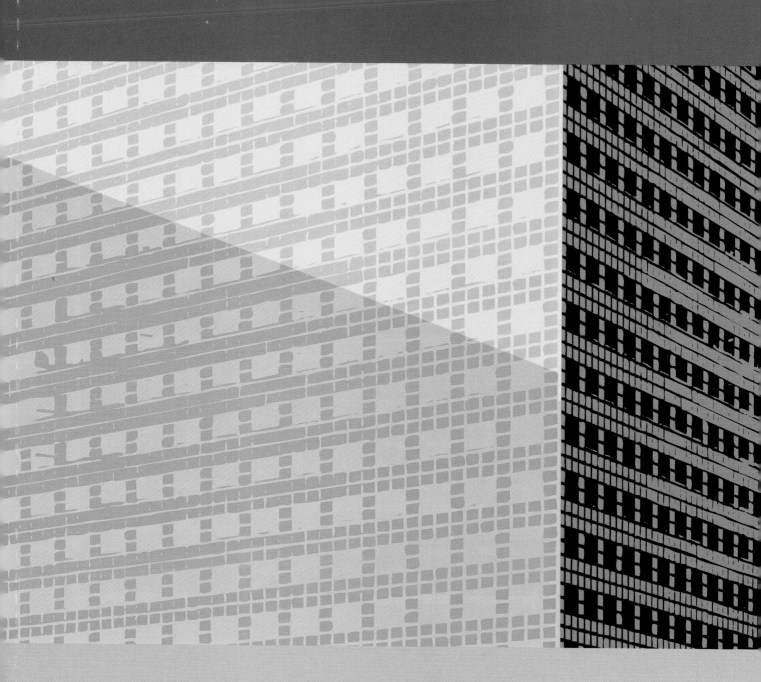

10

Planning the Business Report and Collecting Data

COMMUNICATION OBJECTIVES

After you have finished this chapter, you should be able to:

■ Identify the three major purposes of business reports.

■ Analyze the audience for business reports.

■ Evaluate the quality of data already available.

■ Develop an effective questionnaire and cover letter.

■ Construct effective tables and charts.

On the Job

JANIS LAMAR
Director of External Communications, Experian

Talking with reporters from CNN, the *Los Angeles Times*, and *Newsweek* is all in a day's work for Janis Lamar. As director of external communications for Experian, an international supplier of information about consumer and business credit, direct marketing, and real estate, it is Lamar's role to help top management communicate the company's positions to the press.

Lamar and her team continuously track how many times the company is mentioned in the media—as many as 2,000 mentions per year—and examine the context as well as the content of each mention. Then, every six months, she prepares an analytical report for an internal audience of 70 top executives, discussing both the details of Experian's media exposure and the meaning of that exposure for the company and its competitive situation.

In planning and writing this report, Lamar takes into consideration her audience's level of knowledge and interest in the subject. "Our executives are not media experts, so I try to keep jargon to a minimum," she says. To speed busy readers through the main points of the 10-page report, she presents the major findings in a one-page executive summary, written after she completes the body of the report. "This media analysis report serves as a measure of the return on investment of our company's media relations efforts," explains Lamar. "It's also a way to benchmark our media coverage against that of our competitors."

Report Accuracy

Any organization needs comprehensive, up-to-date, accurate, and understandable information to achieve its goals. Much of this information is communicated in the form of reports—such as progress reports, proposals, and policies and procedures. Also, in any organization, unique problems and opportunities appear that require one-time-only reports. Many of these situations call for information to be gathered and analyzed and for recommendations to be made. These so-called *situational reports* are perhaps the most challenging for the report writer. Because they involve a unique event, the writer has no previous reports to use as a guide; he or she must decide what types of information and how much information are needed and how best to organize and present the findings. Model 11 shows a sample situational report.

No report weakness—including making major grammatical mistakes, misspelling the name of the report reader, or missing the deadline for submitting the report—is as serious as communicating inaccurate information. It's a basic tenet of management that bad information leads to bad decisions. In such situations, the bearer of the "bad" news will surely suffer the consequences. To achieve accuracy, follow these guidelines:

1. *Report all relevant facts.* Errors of *omission* are just as serious as errors of *commission*. Don't mislead the reader by reporting just those facts that tend to support your position.

   > Your most important job is to ensure that the information you transmit is correct.

   NOT: During the two-year period of 1999–2000, our return on investment averaged 13%.

   BUT: Our return on investment was 34% in 1999 but –8% in 2000, for an average of 13%.

2. *Use emphasis and subordination appropriately.* Your goal is to help the reader see the relative importance of the points you discuss. If you honestly think a certain idea is of minor importance, subordinate it—regardless of whether it reinforces or weakens your ultimate conclusion. Don't emphasize a point simply because it reinforces your position, and don't subordinate a point simply because it weakens your position.

3. *Give enough evidence to support your conclusions.* Make sure that your sources are accurate, reliable, and objective and that enough evidence exists to support your position. Sometimes your evidence (the data you gather) may be so sparse or of such questionable quality that you cannot draw a valid conclusion. If so, simply present the findings and don't draw a conclusion. To give the reader confidence in your statements, discuss your procedures thoroughly and cite all your sources.

   > Back up your conclusions with evidence.

4. *Avoid letting personal biases and unfounded opinions influence your interpretation and presentation of the data.* Sometimes you will be asked to draw conclusions and to make recommendations; such judgments inevitably involve a certain amount of subjectivity. You must make a special effort to look at the data objectively and to base your conclusions solely on the data. Avoid letting your personal feelings influence the outcomes. Sometimes the use of a single word can unintentionally convey bias.

   NOT: The accounting supervisor *claimed* the error was unintentional.

   BUT: The accounting supervisor *stated* the error was unintentional.

MODEL 11

Situational Report

Begins by introducing the topic and discussing the procedures used. This report uses the indirect pattern, saving the recommendations until the end.

Is organized according to the criteria used to solve the problem.

Uses the author-date format for citing references (see Style Manual).

Closes by making a recommendation based on the findings presented.

THE FEASIBILITY OF AN MXD IN PHOENIX
David M. Beall

1 Mixed-use development (MXD) integrates three or more land uses (e.g., office, retail, hotel, residential, and recreation) in a high-density configuration with uninterrupted circulation from one component to another. Interviews with seven local real estate developers and bankers and secondary sources provided information on the feasibility of constructing a mixed-use development in Phoenix.

Low Land Prices and Low-Density Population Weaken MXD Potential

2 Land prices are a key economic factor in real estate development. High prices force developers to develop land with intensive uses to justify land costs. The much more expensive cost of an MXD makes economic sense only when high land prices justify the investment. Land prices in Phoenix, however, are relatively low compared to prices in other U.S. cities. The Galleria in Houston and Metrocenter in Phoenix are similar-sized developments that offer an excellent comparison of how land prices dictate development intensity. The Galleria site cost $85,000 per acre; six years later, the Metrocenter site cost only $10,000 per acre (Rogers, 1997, p. 148).

Successful MXDs tend to be located in high-density urban cores. The Phoenix market, however, is a low-density environment. Approximately 67% of the Phoenix housing stock is single-family homes, and relatively few commercial buildings reach more than six stories high ("Inside Phoenix," 2001).

3 Financing Would Be Difficult

The area bankers interviewed are reluctant to become involved with a new type of large-scale commercial development. Instead, they prefer to sponsor projects with which they have had experience. According to one banker, "A bank is only as successful as its last loan" (Weiss, 2002). The bankers believe the economic risks associated with developing an MXD outweigh the rewards. They cite such adverse factors as high development costs, complexity, and lack of expertise (Allen, 2001).

Davenport Should Delay MXD Project

Because of Phoenix's relatively low land costs and low-density population and the difficulty of securing financing, Davenport should not pursue a mixed-use development in the Phoenix area now. However, because the Southwest is growing so rapidly, we should reevaluate the Phoenix market in three years.

Grammar and Mechanics Notes

1 *real estate developers:* Do not hyphenate a compound noun (*real estate*) that comes before another noun (*developers*).
2 *site:* location (*cite:* "to quote"; *sight:* "to view").
3 Be consistent in formatting report side headings; there is no one standard format (other than consistency). This report uses "talking" headings, which identify both the topic and the major conclusion of each section.

Purposes of Reports

At the outset, you need to determine why you are writing the report. Business reports generally aim to inform, analyze, or recommend.

Informing

Informational reports relate objectively the facts and events about a particular situation. No attempt is made to analyze and interpret the data, draw conclusions, or recommend a course of action. Most progress reports, as well as policies and procedures, are examples of informational reports. In most cases, these types of reports are the easiest to complete. The report writer's major interest is in presenting all of the relevant information objectively, accurately, and clearly, while refraining from including unsolicited analysis and recommendations.

Informational reports present data without analyzing it.

Analyzing

One step in complexity above the informational report is the analytical report, which not only presents information but also analyzes it. Data by itself may be meaningless; the information must be put into some context before readers can make use of it. As social forecaster John Naisbitt has remarked, "We are drowning in information, but starved for knowledge."[1]

Consider, for example, this informational statement: "Sales for the quarter ending June 30 were $780,000." Was this performance good or bad? We cannot possibly know unless the writer *analyzes* the information for us. Here are two possible interpretations of this statement:

Analytical reports interpret data.

> **EITHER:** Sales for the quarter ending June 30 were $780,000, up 7% from the previous quarter. This strong showing was achieved despite an industry-wide slump and may be attributed to the new "Tell One—Sell One" campaign we introduced in January.

> **OR:** Sales for the quarter ending June 30 were $780,000, a decline of 5.5% from the same quarter last year. All regions experienced a 3% to 5% *increase* except for the western region, which experienced an 18% decrease in sales. John Manilow, western regional manager, attributes his area's sharp drop in sales to the budgetary problems now being experienced by the state governments in California and Arizona.

The report writer must ensure that any conclusions drawn are reasonable, valid, and fully supported by the data presented. Although the writer must attempt to avoid inserting his or her own biases or preexisting opinions into the report, analysis and interpretation can never be completely objective. The report writer makes numerous decisions that call for subjective evaluations. Note the difference in effect of the following two statements, which contain the same information but in reversed order:

> **ORIGINAL:** Although it is too early to determine the effectiveness of Mundrake's efforts, he believes the steps he is taking will bring Limerick's absentee rate down to the industry average of 3.6% by December.

> **REVERSED:** Although Mundrake believes the steps he is taking will bring Limerick's absentee rate down to the industry average of 3.6%

by December, it is too early to determine the effectiveness of his efforts.

The original order leaves a confident impression of the probable success of the steps taken, whereas the reversed order leaves a much more skeptical impression. Only the report writer can determine which version leaves the more accurate impression.

Recommending

Recommendation reports add the element of endorsing a specific course of action. The writer presents the relevant information, interprets it, and then suggests a plan of attack. The important point is that you must let the *data* form the basis for any conclusions you draw and any recommendations you make. You want to analyze and present your data so that the truth, the whole truth, and nothing but the truth emerges. In other words, avoid the temptation of beginning with a pre-conceived idea and then marshaling evidence and manipulating data to support it.

In a sense, your final recommendation represents only the tip of the iceberg, but it is a very visible tip. The logic, clarity, and strength of your recommendation can have major implications for your career and for your organization's well-being.

Recommendation reports propose a course of action.

Audience Analysis

The audience for a report—the reader or readers—is typically homogeneous. Many times, of course, the audience includes only one person; but even when it does not, the audience usually consists of people with similar levels of expertise, background knowledge, and the like. Thus, you can, and should, develop your report to take into account the needs of your reader. In doing so, you will need to consider the following elements.

Internal Versus External Audiences

Internal reports are written for readers within the organization and are usually less formal than external reports, for which the reader might be a customer, potential customer, or government agency. Internal reports also typically require less background information and can safely use more technical vocabulary than external reports, which are often more sensitive to public relations issues. Internal reports are also directional and are aimed at the writer's superiors, peers, or subordinates. The strategy used must be appropriate for the audience's position.

Internal reports are generally less formal and contain less background information than external reports.

Level of Knowledge and Interest

Is the reader already familiar with your topic? Will he or she understand the terms used, or will you need to define them? If you have a heterogeneous audience for your report, striking an appropriate balance in level of detail given will require careful planning.

Most reports are written in the direct pattern, with the major conclusions and recommendations given up front. This situation is especially true when you know the reader is interested in your project or is likely to agree with your opinions and judgments. In contrast, reports that make a recommendation with which the

Gear the amount of information presented and the order in which it is presented to the needs of the reader.

reader may disagree are often written in the indirect pattern because you want the reader to study the reasons first. The reader will be more likely to accept or at least consider the recommendation if he or she has first had an opportunity to study the underlying rationale.

What Data Is Already Available?

Before collecting any data, you must define the report purpose and analyze the intended audience. Then you must determine what data is needed to solve the problem. (*Note:* The word *data* is the plural form of *datum* and technically requires a plural verb when referring to several individual items of data. In most cases in this text, however, the term is used in the sense of a collective noun and takes a singular verb. The Usage Panel for the *American Heritage Dictionary* endorses this position.) Sometimes the data you need will be in your mind or in documents you already have in hand, sometimes it will be in documents located elsewhere, and sometimes the data is not available at all but must be generated by you.

Start the data-collection phase by breaking your problem down into its component parts so that you will know what data you need to collect. The easiest way to do so is to think about what questions you need to answer before you can solve the problem. The answers to these questions will ultimately provide the solution to the overall problem under investigation, and the question topics may, in fact, ultimately serve as the major divisions of your report.

Determine what questions must be answered to solve your report problem.

WORD|wise

Deft Definitions

Cannibal:	Someone who is fed up with people
Chicken:	The only animal you eat before it is born and after it is dead
Committee:	A body that keeps minutes and wastes hours
Handkerchief:	Cold storage
Inflation:	Cutting money in half without damaging the paper
Nonorganic gardener:	Herbicidal maniac
Politician:	Hot-air buffoon
Short-order cook:	Frequent fryer

Common Types of Data

The two major types of data you will collect are secondary and primary data. **Secondary data** consists of data collected by someone else for some other purpose; it may be published or unpublished. Published data includes any material that is widely disseminated, including the following:

secondary data Data collected by someone else for some other purpose

- World Wide Web and other Internet resources
- Journal, magazine, and newspaper articles; these articles may be located in print format or retrieved from an electronic database (see Spotlight 5, "Finding Printed Sources on the Internet")
- Books
- Brochures and pamphlets
- Technical reports

Unpublished secondary data includes any material that is not widely disseminated, including the following:

- Company records (such as financial records, personnel data, and minutes of previous correspondence and reports)
- Legal documents (such as court records and minutes of regulatory hearings)
- Personal records (such as diaries, receipts, and checkbook registers)
- Medical records

SPOTLIGHT ⑤ on technology

Finding Printed Sources on the Internet

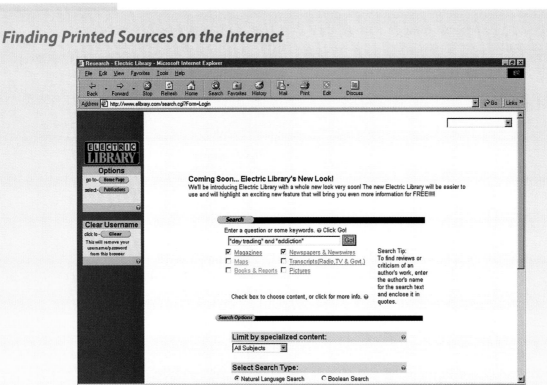

Mmoja has been assigned a term paper in his finance class on the topic of day-trading addiction. Because he wants to locate the full text of published articles, he decides to use a full-text search service such as *The Wall Street Journal Interactive, New York Times Online, Lexis-Nexis,* or, in this case, *Electric Library*. Using Boolean operators, he types in the following in the search line: "day trading" and "addiction."

---

primary data Data collected by the researcher to solve the specific problem at hand

Nearly all reporting tasks use secondary data.

Primary data consists of data collected by the researcher to solve the specific problem at hand. Because you are collecting the data yourself, you have more control over its accuracy, completeness, objectivity, and relevance.

Although secondary and primary data both serve as important sources for business reports, we usually start our data collection by reviewing the data that is already available. Not all report situations require collecting new (primary) data, but it would be unusual to write a report that did not use some type of secondary data.

Studying what is already known about a topic and what remains to be learned makes the reporting process more efficient because the report writer can then concentrate scarce resources on generating new information rather than rediscovering existing information. Also, studying secondary data can highlight sources for additional information, suggest methods of primary research, or give clues for questionnaire items—that is, provide guidance for primary research. For these reasons, our discussion of data collection first focuses on secondary sources.

Secondary data is neither better than nor worse than primary data; it's simply *different*. The source of the data is not as important as its quality and its relevance for your particular purpose. The major advantages of using secondary data are economic: using secondary data is less costly and time-consuming than collecting primary data. Its disadvantages relate not only to the availability of sufficient secondary data but also to the quality of the data that is available. Never use any data before you have evaluated its appropriateness for the intended purpose.

SPOTLIGHT ⑤ on technology

Continued from previous page

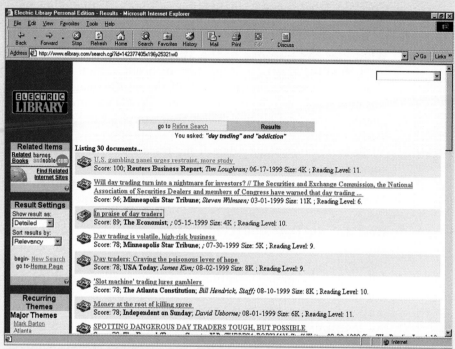

Electric Library displays the titles of the first 30 hits. Note that all articles are from traditional published sources—not Web pages or discussion-group entries. Because Mmoja knows that *The Economist* is a well-respected periodical, he clicks on the article "In praise of day traders."

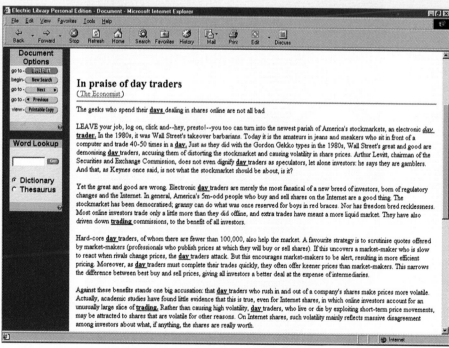

Electric Library displays the full text of the entire article—not just an abstract. For ease in scanning the article to determine its appropriateness, each occurrence of a search term is highlighted in the document. If Mmoja decides that he may use the article, he can either print it out or save it as a word processing file.

Evaluating Secondary Data

By definition, secondary data was gathered for some purpose other than your particular report needs. Therefore, the categories used, the population sampled, and the analyses reported might not be appropriate for your use. In Chapter 2 we discussed guidelines for evaluating the quality of data gathered from the Internet (see Checklist 1 on page 43). In addition, ask yourself the following questions about any secondary sources you're considering incorporating into your report.

What Was the Purpose of the Study?

If the study was undertaken to genuinely find the answer to a question or problem, you can have more confidence about the accuracy and objectivity of the results than if, for example, the study was undertaken merely to prove a point. People seeking honest answers to honest questions are more likely to select their samples carefully, to ask clear and unbiased questions, and to analyze the data appropriately.

Be wary of secondary data if the researcher had a vested interest in the outcome of the study. For example, you would probably have more faith in a study extolling the merits of the Toyota Camry automobile that had been conducted by *Consumer Reports* than one conducted by Toyota, Inc.

> Avoid using biased data in your report.

How Was the Data Collected?

Were appropriate procedures used? Although you may not be an experienced researcher yourself, your reading of secondary data will likely alert you to certain standard research procedures that should be followed. For example, common sense should tell you that if you are interested in learning the reactions of all factory workers in your organization to a particular proposal, you would not gather data from just the newly hired workers. Likewise, if a questionnaire was sent to all the factory workers and only 10% responded, you probably would not conclude that the opinions of these few respondents represented the views of all workers.

Researching his comparable value guided the New York Jets in signing tackle Jason Fabini to a multiyear contract. Their salary-cap analysts constructed charts listing the contracts of 15–20 comparable players and detailed the financial and performance statistics for each player.

How Was the Data Analyzed?   As we shall see later, different types of data lend themselves to different types of analyses. Sometimes the low number of responses to a particular question or ambiguity in the question itself prevents us from drawing any valid conclusions.

In some situations, even though the analysis was appropriate for the original study, it may not be appropriate for your particular purposes. For example, suppose you're interested in the reactions of teenagers and the only available secondary data used the category "younger than 21 years of age." You would not know whether the responses came mostly from those younger than 13 years old, those 13 to 19 years old (your target group), or those older than 19 years old.

How Consistent Is the Data with That from Other Studies?   When you find the same general conclusions drawn in several independent sources, you can have greater confidence in the data. On the other hand, if four studies on a particular topic reached one conclusion and a fifth study reached the opposite conclusion, you would need to scrutinize the fifth study carefully before accepting its findings.

Avoid accepting something as true simply because you read it in print or saw it on the Internet. Because the reader of your report will be making decisions based on the data you present, take care to include only accurate data in your report.

> Generally, the more consensus you find in secondary data, the more trustworthy the data.

How Old Is the Data?   Data that was true at the time it was collected might or might not be true today. A job-satisfaction study completed at your organization last year may have yielded accurate data at the time. If your organization has since merged with another company, moved its headquarters, or been torn by a strike, however, the job-satisfaction data may have no relevance today. On the other hand, some data may remain accurate years after its collection. For example, a thorough study of the origins of the labor movement in the United States may have almost permanent validity.

Your data must pass these five tests, whether it comes from company records or printed sources on the Internet. Data that fails even one of the tests should probably be discarded and not used in your report. At the very least, such data requires extra scrutiny and perhaps extra explanation in the report itself if you do choose to use it.

RECALL   Write a capital *T* for true or *F* for false before each statement.

1. ____   Reports written in response to a one-time-only, unique situation are called situational reports.

2. ____   The most important trait of a report is that it be formatted in an easy-to-read manner.

3. ____   Recommendations typically involve a certain degree of subjectivity on the part of the report writer.

4. ____   Most reports require the use of secondary data.

5. ____   Secondary data has been published; primary data has not been published.

CHECKPOINT 10.1

VOCABULARY   Define the following terms in your own words and give an original example.

6. primary data:

7. secondary data:

COMPREHENSION

8. What are four guidelines for ensuring report accuracy?

9. What are three major purposes of reports?

10. What five questions should you answer before relying on secondary data?

CRITICAL THINKING

11. What does this statement by John Naisbett mean: "We are drowning in information but starved for knowledge"?

Collecting Data Through Questionnaires

Despite your best efforts, you will sometimes find that not enough high-quality secondary data is available to solve your problem. In such a situation, you will probably need to collect primary data.

survey   A data-collection method that gathers data through questionnaires, telephone or email inquiries, or interviews

questionnaire   The document containing questions designed to obtain information from the individual being surveyed

The main disadvantage of surveys is a low response rate.

A **survey** is a data-collection method that gathers information through questionnaires, telephone or email inquiries, or interviews. The **questionnaire** (a written instrument containing questions designed to obtain information from the individual being surveyed) is the most frequently used method in business research. The researcher can economically get a representative sampling over a large geographical area. After all, it costs no more to mail a questionnaire across the country than across the street.

Also, the anonymity of a questionnaire increases the validity of some responses. Certain personal and economic data may be given more completely and honestly when the respondent remains unidentified. In addition, no interviewer is present to possibly bias the results. Finally, respondents can answer at a time convenient for them, which is not always the case with telephone or interview studies. The big disadvantage of mail questionnaires is the low response rate; also, those individuals who do respond may not be representative (typical) of the population.

Constructing the Questionnaire

Because the target audience's time is valuable, make sure that every question you ask is necessary—that it is essential to help you solve your problem and that you cannot acquire the information from other sources (such as through library or online research). Checklist 11 on page 266 provides guidelines for constructing a questionnaire. Some of the more important points are highlighted in the following paragraphs.

Your language must be clear, precise, and understandable so that the questionnaire yields valid and reliable data. Moreover, each question must be neutral (unbiased).

NOT: Do you think our company should open an on-site child-care center as a means of ensuring the welfare of our employees' small children?

_____ yes
_____ no

BUT: Which one of the following possible additional fringe benefits would you most prefer?

_____ a dental insurance plan
_____ an on-site child-care center
_____ three personal-leave days annually
_____ other (please specify: _____)

CHECKLIST 11

Questionnaires

Content

✓ Do not ask for information that is easily available elsewhere.

✓ Have a purpose for each question. Make sure that all questions directly help you to solve your problem. Avoid asking for unimportant or merely "interesting" information.

✓ Use precise wording so that no question can possibly be misunderstood. Use clear, simple language, and define any term that may be unfamiliar to the respondent or that you are using in a special way.

✓ Use neutrally worded questions and deal with only one topic per question. Avoid loaded, leading, or multifaceted questions.

✓ Ensure that the response choices are both exhaustive and mutually exclusive (that is, that there is an appropriate response for every one and that there are no overlapping categories).

✓ Be especially careful about asking sensitive questions, such as information about age, salary, or morals. Consider using broad categories for such questions (instead of narrow, more specific categories).

✓ Pilot-test your questionnaire on a few people to ensure that all questions function as intended. Revise as needed.

Organization

✓ Arrange the questions in some logical order. Group together all questions that deal with a particular topic. If your questionnaire is long, divide it into sections.

✓ Arrange the alternatives for each question in some logical order—such as numerical, chronological, or alphabetical.

✓ Give the questionnaire a descriptive title, provide whatever directions are necessary, and include your name and return address somewhere on the questionnaire.

Format

✓ Use an easy-to-answer format. Check-off questions draw the most responses and are easiest to answer and tabulate. Use free-response items only when absolutely necessary.

✓ To increase the likelihood that your target audience will cooperate and take your study seriously, ensure that your questionnaire has a professional appearance:

- Use a simple and attractive format, allowing for plenty of white (blank) space.

- Ensure that the questionnaire is free from errors in grammar, spelling, and style.

- Use a high-quality printer and make high-quality photocopies.

The wording of the original question obviously favors the "pro" side, thereby biasing the responses. A more neutral question is needed if valid responses are to result. Note several things about the revised question. First, it is more neutral than the original version; no "right" answer is apparent. Second, the alternatives are arranged in alphabetical order. To avoid possibly biasing the responses, always present the alternatives in some logical order—alphabetical, numerical, chronological, or the like.

Finally, note that the question provides an "other" category; this option always goes last and is accompanied by the request to "please specify." Suppose the one fringe benefit that the vast majority of employees really wanted most was for the company to increase its pension contributions. If the "other" category were missing, the researcher would never learn that important information. Ensure that your categories are *exhaustive* (that is, that they include all possible alternatives) by including an "other" category if necessary.

Also, be certain that each question contains a single idea. Note the following question:

NOT: Our company should spend less money on advertising and more money on research and development.

___ agree
___ disagree

Ask only one question in each item.

Suppose the respondent believes that the company should spend more (or less) money on advertising *and* on research and development? How is he or she supposed to answer? The solution is to put each of the two ideas in a separate question.

Finally, ensure that your categories are *mutually exclusive*—that is, that no categories overlap.

NOT: In your opinion, what is the major cause of high employee turnover?

___ lack of air-conditioning
___ noncompetitive financial package
___ poor fringe benefits
___ poor working conditions
___ weak management

The problem with this item is that the "lack of air-conditioning" category overlaps with the "poor working conditions" category, and "noncompetitive financial package" overlaps with "poor fringe benefits." And all four of these probably overlap with "weak management." Such intermingling of categories will thoroughly confuse the respondent and yield unreliable survey results.

Recognize that respondents may hesitate to answer sensitive questions (regarding age, salary, morals, and the like). Even worse, they may deliberately provide *inaccurate* responses. When it is necessary to gather such data, ensure that the respondent understands that the questionnaire is anonymous (by prominently discussing that fact in the cover letter). Respondents tend to be more cooperative in answering such questions when the survey uses broad categories. Accurate estimates provided by broad categories are preferable to precise but incorrect data.

NOT: What is your annual gross salary? $_____

BUT: Please check the category that best describes your annual salary:

___ Less than $15,000
___ $15,000–$30,000
___ $30,001–$60,000
___ More than $60,000

The use of the number "$30,001" in the third category is necessary to avoid overlap with the figure "$30,000" in the second category; remember that the categories must be mutually exclusive.

Even experienced researchers find it difficult to spot ambiguities or other problems in their own questionnaires. If time permits, administer the draft questionnaire to a small sample of potential respondents and then revise it as necessary. At a minimum, ask a colleague to edit your instrument with a critical eye. The sample questionnaire shown in Model 12 (on pages 268–269) illustrates a variety of question types, along with clear directions and efficient format.

Simply checking a broad range of figures might be less threatening than having to write in an exact figure.

Writing the Cover Letter

Unless you intend to distribute the questionnaires personally (in which case, you would be able to explain the purpose and procedures in person), include a cover letter like the one shown in Model 13 on page 270) with your questionnaire. The cover letter should be written as a regular persuasive letter (see Chapter 8). Your

MODEL 12

Questionnaire

Uses a descriptive title.

Provides clear directions.

Uses check-off responses for Questions 1–3.

Uses fill-in-the-blank responses for Question 4.

Uses a qualification (branching) response for Question 6.

---

1 **STUDENT USE OF COMPUTERS AT CMU**

This survey is being conducted as part of a class research project. Please complete this questionnaire only if you (a) are a full-time junior or senior student at CMU, (b) attended CMU last semester, and (c) have declared a major.

A. DESCRIPTIVE INFORMATION

2 1. Grade level: 2. Sex: 3. Age:
        ___ junior   ___ female   ___ 20 or younger
        ___ senior   ___ male   ___ 21–24
                                                    ___ 25 or older

   4. Are you pursuing a teaching or nonteaching major?
       ___ teaching *(Please write in the name of your major: _____)*
       ___ nonteaching *(Please write in the name of your major: _____)*

   5. College where major is located:
       ___ Arts and Sciences
       ___ Education
       ___ Business
       ___ Other *(Please specify: _____)*

   6. Did you use a computer in a CMU computer lab last semester?
       ___ yes *(Please continue with Question 7.)*
       ___ no   *(Please disregard the following questions and return the questionnaire to the researcher in the enclosed campus envelope.)*

B. EXTENT OF COMPUTER USE

   7. Which on-campus computer labs were most convenient for completing your computer assignments? Please rank the labs from 1 *(most convenient)* to 4 *(least convenient)* by writing in the appropriate number in each blank.
       ___ business lab   ___ library lab
       ___ dormitory lab   ___ student center lab

3 8. Listed on the next page are different types of software. For each, first check the type of use you made of this software at any time during the previous semester.

Grammar and Mechanics Notes

1 Make the title and section heading stand out through the use of bold type and perhaps a larger font size.

2 If space is at a premium, you may group shorter questions on the same line (as in Questions 1–3).

3 Although not always possible (as illustrated here), try to avoid splitting a question between two pages.

MODEL 12

(Continued)

You may check both *Required* and *Personal* if appropriate. An example of personal use would be using a spreadsheet in a business term paper—if such use were not required. Then, if you used this software, check the total number of hours of use during the semester, including both in-class and out-of-class use.

Software	Type of Use			Hrs Used Per Sem		
	None	Req'd	Pers'l	<5	5–15	>15
Example: Games	___	___	✔	___	___	✗
Accounting/Financial	___	___	___	___	___	___
Educational/Tutorial	___	___	___	___	___	___
Email	___	___	___	___	___	___
Graphics/Presentation	___	___	___	___	___	___
Internet	___	___	___	___	___	___
Programming	___	___	___	___	___	___
Spreadsheet	___	___	___	___	___	___
Word Processing	___	___	___	___	___	___

4   **C. OPINIONS**

> Provides clear directions and an example for the complex response in Question 8.

> Lists alternatives in alphabetical order.

9. Please check whether you agree with, have no opinion about, or disagree with each of the following statements.

	Agree	No Opin	Disagree
a. I am receiving adequate training in the use of computers.	___	___	___
b. I have to wait an unreasonable length of time to get onto a computer in the lab.	___	___	___
c. The computer labs at CMU are current.	___	___	___
d. Lab attendants are not very helpful.	___	___	___

> Uses attitude-scale responses for Question 9, with both positive and negative statements.

D. IMPROVEMENTS NEEDED

10. How could the university administration improve computer services at CMU?

5   _____

_____

_____

> Places the open-ended question last.

Thanks for your help. Please return the completed questionnaire in the enclosed campus envelope to Matt Jones, 105 Woldt Hall.

> Provides name and address of the researcher.

Grammar and Mechanics Notes

4 Label different sections if the questionnaire is more than one or two pages long.

5 Provide sufficient space for the respondent to answer open-ended questions.

MODEL 13

Questionnaire Cover Letter

This cover letter would accompany the questionnaire shown in Model 12.

Begins with a short attention-getter.

Provides a smooth transition to the purpose of the letter.

Provides reasons for cooperating.

Makes the requested action easy to take.

CENTRAL METROPOLITAN UNIVERSITY

P.O. Box 0049 • Fairbanks, Alaska 99701

February 8, 20—

1 Dear Fellow Student:

"Oh no—not another computer project!"

Have you ever felt this way during the first day of class when the instructor makes the course assignments? Or, instead, do you sometimes wonder, "Why is the instructor

2 making us do this project manually when it would be so much easier to do on a computer?"

Either way, here is your chance to provide the CMU administration with your views on student computer use at Central Metropolitan University. This research project is a class project for BEOA 249 (Business Communication), and the results will be shared with Dr. Dan Rulong, vice president for academic computing.

If you are a full-time junior or senior student, attended CMU last semester, and have

3 declared a major, please take five minutes to complete this questionnaire. Then simply return it by February 19 in the enclosed envelope. You'll be doing yourself and your fellow students a big favor.

Sincerely,

Matt Jones, Project Leader
105 Woldt Hall

Enclosures

Grammar and Mechanics Notes

1 *Dear Fellow Student:* Use a generic salutation for form letters that are not individually prepared.
2 *on a computer?":* Position the question mark *inside* the closing quotation mark if the entire quoted matter is a question.
3 The word *questionnaire* contains two *n*'s and one *r*.

job is to convince the reader that it's worth taking the time to complete the questionnaire.

Constructing Tables

A **table** is an orderly arrangement of data into columns and rows (see Model 14 on page 272). It represents the most basic form of statistical analysis and is useful for showing a large amount of numerical data in a small space. A table presents numerical data more efficiently and more interestingly than narrative text and provides more information than a graph, albeit with less visual impact. Because of its orderly arrangement of information into vertical columns and horizontal rows, a table also permits easy comparison of figures. However, trends are more obvious when presented in graphs.

Your reader must be able to understand each table on its own, without having to read the surrounding text. Thus, at a minimum, each table should contain a table number, a descriptive but concise title, column headings, and body (the items under each column heading). If you need footnotes to explain individual items within the table, put them immediately below the body of the table, not at the bottom of the page. Similarly, if the table is based on secondary data, type a source note below the body, giving the appropriate citation. Common abbreviations and symbols are acceptable in tables.

As discussed earlier, the check-off alternatives in your questionnaire items should be arranged in some logical order, most often either numerical or alphabetical, to avoid biasing the responses. Once you have the data in hand, however, it is often helpful to the reader if you rearrange the data from high to low.

In Figure 10.1 on page 273, for example, the categories have been rearranged from their original *alphabetical* order in the questionnaire into *descending* order in the report table. Note also that the four smallest categories have been combined into a miscellaneous category, which always goes last, regardless of its size. Finally, note the position and format of the table footnote, which explains an entry in the table.

> **table** An orderly arrangement of data into columns and rows
>
> Tables are often the most economical way of presenting numerical data.
>
> The reader should be able to understand the table without having to refer to the text.
>
> Arrange the data in logical format—usually from high to low.

Preparing Charts

The appropriate use of well-designed charts can aid in reader comprehension, emphasize certain data, create interest, and save time and space because the reader can perceive immediately the essential meaning of large masses of statistical data.

Because of their visual impact, charts receive more emphasis than tables or narrative text. Therefore, you should save them for presenting information that is important and that can best be grasped visually—for example, when the overall picture is more important than the individual numbers. Also, recognize that the more charts your report contains, the less impact each individual chart will have.

The cardinal rule for designing charts is this: keep them simple. Trying to cram too much information into one chart will merely confuse the reader and lessen the effectiveness of the graphic. Well-designed charts have only one interpretation, and that interpretation should be clear immediately; the reader shouldn't have to study the chart at length or refer to the surrounding text to figure out its meaning.

Regardless of their type, label all your charts as *figures,* and assign them consecutive numbers, separate from table numbers. Although tables are captioned at the top, charts may be captioned at the top or the bottom. Charts used alone (for example, as an overhead transparency or slide) typically have a caption at the top.

> Keep charts simple. Immediate comprehension is the goal.

MODEL 14

Table

Use tables to present a large amount of data clearly and concisely.

Table number
Title
Subtitle (optional)

Column Heading

Body

Source (optional)

Footnote (optional)

the market leader for all of 2002 and for the first two quarters of 2003 as well, based primarily on governmental sales. As it has for the past three years, the Eastern Region led the company's sales force, as shown in Table 14.

1

Table 14
2003 APEX SALES LEADERS BY REGION
As of December 15

Region	Sales Leader	Sales*	Yearly Change
Eastern	Ronald Miller	$17.5	13.4%
Western			
Continental	Dorothy Cheung	13.6	−2.1
Hawaii/Alaska	David Kane	3.2	4.0
Midwestern	C. J. Peri-Watts	9.7	4.6
Southern	Rita Rosales	8.2	−5.2
Plains	B. B. Cody	6.0	15.8
Average		$9.7	5.1%

2

3

Source: *Insurance Leaders DataQuest* (New York: Insurance Institute of North America, 2003), pp. 143–179.

*In millions.

4

The sales leaders in two of the regions (Western and Southern) experienced decreased sales, even though they remained the top producers in their respective regions. The reason

Grammar and Mechanics Notes

1 Position the table below the first paragraph that makes reference to the table. A variety of table formats are appropriate, but be consistent throughout the report.

2 Unless the column heading clearly indicates that the amounts represent dollars or percentages, insert the dollar sign before or the percent sign after the first number and before or after a total or average amount.

3 Align word columns at the left; align number columns either at the right (for whole numbers) or on the decimal point.

4 Leave the same amount of space (2–3 blank lines) before and after the table.

FIGURE 10.1 Arranging Data in Tables

From This Survey Response:

6. In which of the following categories of clerical workers do you expect to hire additional workers within the next three years? (Check all that apply.)

_211_ bookkeepers and accounting clerks
_31_ computer operators
_30_ data-entry keyers
_24_ file clerks
_247_ general office clerks
_78_ receptionists and information clerks
_323_ secretaries/administrative assistants
_7_ statistical clerks
_107_ typists and word processors

To This Report Table:

TABLE 2.   COMPANIES PLANNING TO HIRE ADDITIONAL CLERICAL WORKERS, BY CATEGORY ($N = 326$)

Category	Pct.*
Secretaries/administrative assistants	99
General office clerks	76
Bookkeepers and accounting clerks	65
Typists and word processors	33
Receptionists and information clerks	24
Miscellaneous	28

*Answers total more than 100% because of multiple responses.

Charts preceded or followed by text or containing an explanatory paragraph typically have a caption at the bottom. As with tables, you may use commonly understood abbreviations.

Today, many microcomputer software programs can generate special charts automatically from data contained in spreadsheets or from data entered at the keyboard. The professional appearance and ready availability of such charts often make up for the loss of flexibility in designing graphics that precisely match your wishes.

The main types of charts used in business reports and presentations are line charts, bar charts, and pie charts, as illustrated in Model 15 on page 274.

Line Charts

A **line chart** is a graph based on a grid of uniformly spaced horizontal and vertical lines. The vertical dimension represents values; the horizontal dimension represents time. Line charts are useful for showing changes in data over long periods of time and for emphasizing the movement of the data—that is, trends. Both axes should be marked off at equal intervals and clearly labeled. The vertical axis should begin with zero, even when all the amounts are quite large (in some situations, it may be desirable to show a break in the intervals by drawing in slash marks). Fluctuations of the line over time indicate variations in the trend; the distance of the line from the horizontal axis indicates quantity.

line chart A graph based on a grid, with the vertical axis representing values and the horizontal axis representing time

MODEL 15

Charts

1 Line Chart

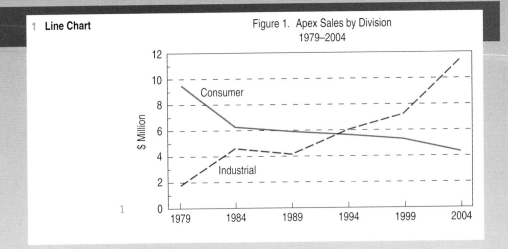

Figure 1. Apex Sales by Division
1979–2004

1

2 Bar Chart

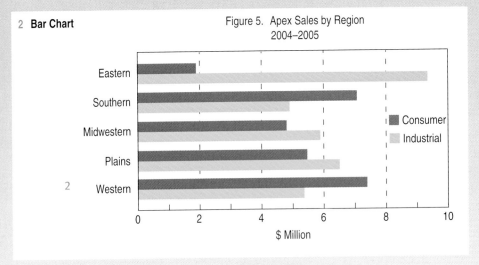

Figure 5. Apex Sales by Region
2004–2005

2

3 Pie Chart

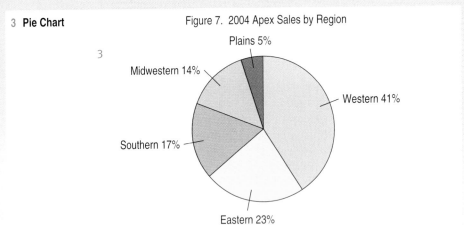

Figure 7. 2004 Apex Sales by Region

3

Grammar and Mechanics Notes

1 Start the vertical axis at the zero point. Clearly differentiate between the two trend
lines, and label each.

2 Make all bars be the same width; show value differences by varying the length or
height. Position the bars either vertically or horizontally.

3 Begin slicing the pie at the 12 o'clock position and move clockwise in a logical

Bar Charts

A **bar chart** is a graph whose horizontal or vertical bars represent values. Bar charts are one of the most useful, simple, and popular graphic techniques. They are particularly appropriate for comparing the magnitude or size of items, either at a specified time or over a period of time. The bars may be vertical or horizontal. The vertical bar chart (sometimes called a *column chart*) is typically used for portraying a time series when the goal is to emphasize the individual amounts rather than the trends.

All of the bars should be the same width, with the length changing to reflect the value of each item. The spacing between the bars should generally be about half the width of the bars themselves. As with tables, you should arrange the bars in some logical order. If space permits, include the actual value of each bar for quicker comprehension.

bar chart A graph with horizontal or vertical bars representing values

Pie Charts

A **pie chart** is a circle graph whose area is divided into component wedges. It compares the relative parts that make up a whole. Some software charting programs permit you to "drag out" a particular wedge of the pie chart to give it special emphasis.

Although pie charts rank very high in popular appeal, graphics specialists hold them in somewhat lower esteem because of their lack of precision and because of the difficulty in differentiating more than a few categories and in comparing component values across several pie charts. However, pie charts are useful for showing how component parts add up to make a total when the whole contains three to five component parts. On the one hand, a chart is rarely needed for presenting only two component parts; on the other hand, more than five components can present visual difficulties in perceiving the relative value of each wedge.

It is customary to begin "slicing" the pie at the 12 o'clock position and move clockwise in some logical order (often in order of descending size). When used, a miscellaneous category goes last, regardless of its size. The labels should be placed either inside each wedge, directly opposite the wedge but outside the pie, or in a legend or key.

It is also customary to include the percentages or other values represented by each wedge and to distinguish each wedge by shading, cross-hatched lines, different colors, or some similar device.

Three-dimensional graphics, although attention grabbing, are difficult to interpret because they typically display only two-dimensional data (horizontal and vertical), with the third dimension (depth) having no significance. Similarly, three-dimensional pie charts, which are shown slanted away from the viewer rather than vertically, can prove misleading because of perspective—the slices farthest away appear smaller than they actually are. Such graphics are effective for gaining attention and providing a general impression but are less effective for conveying the precise meanings needed in business communications. One laboratory experiment found that two-dimensional graphs communicated information more quickly and accurately than corresponding three-dimensional graphs.[2]

Checklist 12 on page 276 summarizes the most important points to consider when constructing tables and charts.

pie chart A circle graph whose area is divided into component wedges

A Word of Caution

As the name *visual aids* implies, charts act as a *help*—not a substitute—for the narrative presentation and interpretation. Never use visual aids simply to make your report "look prettier."

Do not overuse visual aids; they will detract from your message.

CHECKLIST 12

Visual Aids

Tables

✓ Use tables to present a large amount of numerical data in a small space and to permit easy comparisons of figures.

✓ Number tables consecutively and use concise but descriptive table titles and column headings.

✓ Ensure that the table is understandable by itself—without reference to the accompanying narrative.

✓ Arrange the rows of the table in some logical order (most often, in descending order).

✓ Combine smaller, less important categories into a miscellaneous category and put it last.

✓ Use only as much detail as necessary; for example, rounding figures off to the nearest whole increases comprehension. Align decimals (if used) vertically on the decimal point.

✓ Use easily understood abbreviations and symbols as needed.

✓ Ensure that the units (dollars, percentages, or tons, for example) are identified clearly.

Charts

✓ Use charts only when they will help the reader interpret the data better—never just to make the report "look prettier."

✓ Label all charts as *figures,* and assign them consecutive numbers (separate from table numbers).

✓ Keep charts simple. Strive for a single, immediate, correct interpretation, and keep the reader's attention on the *data* in the chart rather than on the chart itself.

✓ Prefer two-dimensional charts; use three-dimensional charts only when generating interest is more important than precision.

✓ Use the most appropriate type of chart to achieve your objectives. Three of the most popular types of business charts are line, bar, and pie charts.

Line Charts: Use line charts to show changes in data over a period of time and to emphasize the movement of the data—the trends.

■ Use the vertical axis to represent amount and the horizontal axis to represent time.

■ Mark off both axes at equal intervals and clearly label them.

■ Begin the vertical axis at zero; if necessary, use slash marks (//) to show a break in the interval.

■ If you plot more than one variable on a chart, clearly distinguish between the lines and label each clearly.

Bar Charts: Use bar charts to compare the magnitude or relative size of items (rather than the trend over time), either at a specified time or over a period of time.

■ Make all bars the same width; vary the length to reflect the value of each item.

■ Arrange the bars in a logical order and clearly label each.

Pie Charts: Use pie charts to compare the relative parts that make up a whole.

■ Begin slicing the pie at the 12 o'clock position, moving clockwise in a logical order.

■ Label each wedge of the pie, indicate its value, and clearly differentiate the wedges.

Research indicates that the format of the data (tables versus graphs) has little effect on the quality of the decisions made when the task requires a thorough analysis of financial data; both formats are judged to be equally effective. Managers appear to have more confidence in their decisions when such decisions are based on data from tables alone as opposed to data from graphs alone, but they have the most confidence when both formats are used.[3]

These research findings suggest that you should use graphic devices as an *adjunct* to your textual and tabular presentations. Although most numerical data can be presented more efficiently in tables, the competent business communicator uses charts to call attention to particular findings. Rarely should the same data be presented in both tabular and graphic formats.

In *The Visual Display of Quantitative Information,* Edward Tufte warns against *chartjunk*—charts that call attention to themselves instead of to the information they contain.[4] With the ready availability and ease of use of computer graphics, the temptation might be to "overvisualize" your report. Avoid using too many, too large, too garish, or too complicated charts. If the impact is not immediate or if interpretations vary, the chart loses its effectiveness. As with all other aspects of the report project, the visual aids must contribute directly to telling your story more effectively. Avoid chartjunk; strive to *express*—not to *impress*.

CHECKPOINT 10.2

RECALL   Write a capital T for *true* or F for *false* before each statement.

1. ____ The terms "questionnaire" and "survey" may be used interchangeably.

2. ____ Questionnaire categories should be either exhaustive or mutually exclusive.

3. ____ The cover letter for a questionnaire is basically a persuasive letter.

4. ____ You should not use abbreviations or symbols in a table or chart.

5. ____ Line charts are typically used to show changes in data over a period of time.

VOCABULARY   Define the following terms in your own words.

6. bar chart:

7. line chart:

8. pie chart:

9. table:

COMPREHENSION

10. As president of the Marketing Club on campus, you want to know how much money students spend on off-campus entertainment during a typical week.

    a. How would you define the term "entertainment" for the students?

    b. Write an appropriate questionnaire item, including check-off responses.

11. Assume that you surveyed 50 students in each grade on campus and found that 42 freshmen purchased at least one musical CD each week; the corresponding numbers for other students

were 39 for sophomores, 29 for juniors, and 17 for seniors. Construct an appropriate table summarizing this information.

CRITICAL THINKING

12. Suppose the importance of the data contained in the table in Question 11 merited a single sentence of interpretation. What is the most important thing you could tell the reader?

Summary

Accuracy is the most important trait of all reports. The purpose of a particular report may be either to inform, to analyze, or to recommend. Because the audience for a specific report is typically homogeneous, you should develop your report to take into account the reader's needs—in terms of his or her level of knowledge and interest as well as the issue of internal versus external readers.

All reports rely on some type of data. Secondary data is collected by others for their own specific purposes. Therefore, the researcher who wants to use secondary data for his or her own study must first evaluate it in terms of why and how the data was collected, how the data was analyzed, how consistent the data is with that found in other studies, and how old the data is.

Primary data is collected by various survey methods—primarily questionnaires, telephone inquiries, and interviews. Mail questionnaires are an economical and convenient way to gather primary data when the desired information can be supplied easily and quickly. Take care to ensure that all questions are necessary, clearly worded, complete, and unbiased. Organize the questions and their alternatives in a logical order, provide clear directions, and use an attractive and efficient overall format. The cover letter for the questionnaire should be a persuasive letter explaining why it is in the reader's interest to answer the survey.

Each table you construct from the data should be interpretable by itself, without reference to the text. Include only as much data in a table as is helpful, keeping the table as simple as possible. Arrange the data in logical order, most often in order of descending value. Use well-designed line, bar, and pie charts to aid in reader comprehension, emphasize certain data, create interest, and save time and space. Avoid using too many, too large, too garish, or too complicated charts.

The 3Ps
Problem, Process, Product

A Questionnaire

You are Martha Halpern, assistant store manager for Just Pool Supplies, a small firm in San Antonio, Texas. You have been asked by Joe Cox, store owner, to determine the feasibility of expanding into the spa supply business. To help yourself determine whether there is a sufficient demand for spa (hot tub) supplies, you decide to develop and administer a short questionnaire to potential customers.

Problem

Process

1. What is the purpose of your questionnaire?

   To determine whether there are enough potential customers to make it profitable for us to expand into the spa supply business.

2. Who is your audience?

   The theoretical population for my study would be all spa owners in the San Antonio area. However, because our major business will still be pool supplies, I'll assume that most of my spa supply business would come from my present pool supply customers.

   Thus, the real population for my survey will be the approximately 1,500 existing customers that I have on my mailing list. I don't need to contact every customer, only a representative sample. I'll have my database program generate address labels for every fifth customer.

3. What information do you need from these customers?

   a. Whether they presently own a spa or intend to purchase one in the near future

   b. Where they typically purchase their spa supplies

   c. How much money they typically spend on spa supplies each year

   d. How satisfied they are with their suppliers

   e. What the likelihood is that they'd switch their spa supply business to us

   f. How many spa supply firms are located in the area

4. Is all this information necessary? Can any of it be secured elsewhere?

   I can probably determine the number of spa supply firms and their volume of business from secondary data or from the local chamber of commerce, so I won't need to address that question (3f) in my survey. All of the other information is needed and none of it can be obtained elsewhere.

The 3Ps
Problem, Process, Product

5. Do any of these questions ask for sensitive information, or are any of them difficult to answer?

No. The question asking about the amount of money spent on spa supplies depends a little on memory; because most people buy spa supplies only four or five times a year, however, respondents should be able to provide a fairly accurate estimate.

6. Is there any logical order to the questions in Item 3?

The question about spa ownership must come first, because respondents cannot answer the other questions unless they own a spa. In reviewing the other questions, I think the logical order appears to be a, c, b, d, and e.

7. Will the questionnaire require a cover letter?

Yes, because it will be mailed to the respondents, instead of being administered personally. I'll use my word processing program to generate a personalized form letter to each of the customers selected.

Product   **Cover Letter**

 **POOL SUPPLIES**

P.O. Box 2277 San Antonio, TX 78298
Phone: (512) 555-0083 Fax: (512) 555-2994

February 22, 20—

Mr. Frederic J. Diehl
Rio Rancho Estates
1876 Anderson Road
San Antonio, TX 79299

Dear Mr. Diehl:

We miss you during the winter!

Although you're a frequent shopper at Just Pool Supplies during the summer months when you're using your pool, we miss having the opportunity to serve you during the rest of the year. Therefore, we're considering adding a complete line of spa supplies to our inventory.

Would you please help us make this decision by answering the enclosed five questions and then returning this form to us in the enclosed stamped envelope.

Thanks for sharing your views with us. We look forward to seeing you during our traditional Pool Party Sale in March.

Sincerely,

Martha Halpern

Martha Halpern
Assistant Manager

swm
Enclosures

The 3Ps
Problem, Process, Product

Questionnaire

SPA SUPPLIES

1. Do you presently own a spa?
   ___ yes
   ___ no (Please skip the remaining questions and return this form to us in the enclosed envelope.)

2. Considering the number of times you purchased spa supplies last year and the average amount of each purchase, how much do you estimate you spent on spa supplies last year (include all types of purchases—chemicals, accessories, decorative items, and the like).
   ___ less than $100
   ___ $100–$300
   ___ $301–$500
   ___ more than $500

3. Where did you purchase <u>most</u> of your spa supplies last year? (Please check only one.)
   ___ at a general-merchandise store (e.g., Kmart or Sears)
   ___ at a pool- or spa-supply store
   ___ from a mail-order firm
   ___ other (please specify: _____)

4. How satisfied were you with each of these factors at the store where you purchased most of your spa supplies?

Factor	Very Satisfied	Satisfied	Very Dissatisfied
Customer service	___	___	___
Hours of operation	___	___	___
Location of store	___	___	___
Prices	___	___	___
Quality of products	___	___	___
Quantity of products	___	___	___

5. If Just Pool Supplies were to sell spa supplies, how likely would you be to purchase most of your spa supplies there, assuming that the quality, selection, and pricing would be similar to those for its pool supplies?
   ___ very likely
   ___ somewhat likely
   ___ don't know
   ___ somewhat unlikely
   ___ very unlikely

Thanks for your cooperation. Please return the completed questionnaire in the enclosed envelope to Martha Halpern, Just Pool Supplies, P.O. Box 2277, San Antonio, TX 78298.

Looking Ahead

As you have just seen, reports are a much more complex form of written communication than are letters, email, and memos. They are typically longer, involve more complex situations, and require more planning and execution time. In this chapter, you learned how to plan the report and gather the data needed to write it. It is only logical, then, that the next chapter concentrate on how to analyze the data you've gathered and present it in an accurate, understandable, and attractive format.

Key Terms

bar chart	questionnaire
line chart	secondary data
pie chart	survey
primary data	table

Exercises

Planning the Report

1 **Planning a Questionnaire**   You are the president of the Hospitality Services Association (HAS), a campus organization made up of students planning careers in hotel and motel management, tourism, and the like. You've just received a memo from the vice president at your institution addressed to the presidents of all campus organizations. The school is seeking proposals from student organizations to run a part-time business, tentatively named College Hosts (CH), that would provide local services and organize various events for campus visitors.

For example, when the admissions office lets CH know that a prospective student and his or her family plan to visit the campus, CH would immediately contact the family and offer to provide any reasonable service to help the campus visitors enjoy their stay and receive a favorable impression of the institution. The service would be aimed at potential students and their families, alumni, donors, prospective faculty and staff members, and visiting legislators.

You believe that HSA would be the most logical organization to run this enterprise for the school. Your organization has authorized you to submit a proposal to the provost. Personnel time (to be supplied by student members of HSA) would be billed at $12 per hour; a 10% surcharge would be added to the actual cost of all services provided (for example, tickets to campus or local events); automobile expenses would be billed at 28 cents per mile; and other charges would be billed at actual cost. Depending on the purpose of the campus visits, costs of the services would be billed either to the university or to the actual clients.

a. What is the purpose of your report?

b. Describe your audience.

c. Is this a solicited or an unsolicited proposal?

d. List the major advantages of this project and indicate how someone other than HSA will benefit from each advantage.

e. What costs are involved?

f. What qualifies HSA members to operate this business?

g. Will you request approval for this project at the beginning or the end of your proposal? Why?

h. Compose an effective first sentence for your proposal.

i. What topics will you cover and in what order? Compose the specific headings for each topic.

2 **Small Business Reporting Needs** Interview the owner/operator of a small business (10 to 50 employees) in your area. Determine the extent and types of reports written and received by employees in this firm. Write a memo to your instructor summarizing your findings.

3 **Work-Team Communication** You are one member of a four-student team that has volunteered to look into the advantages and disadvantages of extending the college library's hours the week before each long break and the final week of each term or semester. You have heard some students complain that the evening hours are too short; they would especially like to see the library remain open later during periods when most students are working on research papers, examinations, and projects. Of course, longer hours would affect payroll, staff scheduling, and other aspects of the library's operation. Your team will examine the issues, report your findings, and suggest how the administration might proceed.

Team up with three other students to plan a report for your school's head of administrative services. Prepare a one- to two-page memo to your instructor indicating the purpose of your report, the audience, and the data that you will gather. Also list the issues you expect to examine. Will this situational report include recommendations? Why or why not?

Collecting Data

4 **Preparing a Questionnaire** The placement director at your institution has asked you, her assistant, to survey typical businesses in your state that have hired your business graduates within the past five years. The purpose of the survey is to determine whether your business graduates have competent communication skills. Draft, revise, format, and proofread a one-page questionnaire designed to elicit the needed information. Use the questionnaire model on page 268 as a formatting guide.

5 **Gathering Secondary Data** You have been asked to write a report on the feasibility of opening a frozen yogurt store in Akron, Ohio. (Your instructor may substitute a different product or different city for these assignments.) Do some research on the Internet and using printed sources. Identify at least eight published sources of information on the topic. Evaluate the quality of these sources using the five questions presented on page 262–263. Now prepare a memo to your instructor listing the good and poor qualities of your articles. Would you use them all in your report?

6 **Preparing a Questionnaire** Because the student body at the University of Akron would provide a major source of potential customers for your yogurt store (see Exercise 5), you decide to survey the students to gather relevant data. Working in a group of four or five, develop a two-page questionnaire and a cover letter that you will mail to a sample of these students. Ensure that the content and appearance of the questionnaire follow the guidelines given in Checklist 11. Pilot-test your questionnaire and cover letter on a small sample of students; then revise it as necessary and submit it to your instructor.

Constructing Visual Aids

The following exercises are based on the survey results shown in Figure 10.2 on page 285. Next year Broadway Productions will move its headquarters from Manhattan to Stamford, Connecticut, in the building where Tri-City Bank occupies the first floor. The bank hopes to secure many Broadway Productions employees as customers and has conducted a survey to determine their banking habits. The handwritten figures on the questionnaire show the number of respondents who checked each alternative.

7 Constructing Tables

 a. Is a table needed to present the information in Question 1?

 b. Construct a table that presents the important information from Question 4 of the questionnaire in a logical, helpful, and efficient manner. Give the table an appropriate title and arrange it in final report format.

8 Constructing Charts You decide to use a chart rather than a table to convey the data in Question 4 of the questionnaire shown in Figure 10.2.

 a. Can you use a line chart to present the data? Why or why not? If a line chart is appropriate, construct it and label the vertical and horizontal axes.

 b. Can you use a bar chart to present the data? Why or why not? If a bar chart is appropriate, construct it, arranging the bars in a logical order and clearly labeling each bar as well as the vertical axis.

 c. Can you use a pie chart to present the data? Why or why not? If a pie chart is appropriate, construct it, label each wedge, and clearly differentiate the wedges.

 d. You want to construct a visual aid to emphasize the proportion of respondents who have changed banks within the past three years. Calculate this percentage using the survey results. Decide which type of chart would most effectively convey this information. Then construct the chart, using appropriate values and helpful labels.

FIGURE 10.2 Survey Results

BROADWAY PRODUCTIONS SURVEY

1. Do you currently have an account at Tri-City Bank?
    58 yes
    170 no

2. At which of the following institutions do you currently have an account?
    (Please check all that apply.)
    201 commercial bank
    52 employee credit union
    75 savings and loan association
    6 other (please specify: _____)
    18 none

3. In terms of convenience, which one of the following bank locations do you consider
    most important in selecting your main bank?
    70 near home
    102 near office
    12 near shopping
    31 on way to and from work
    13 other (please specify: _____)

4. How important do you consider each of the following banking services?

	Very Important	Somewhat Important	Not Important
Bank credit card	88	132	8
Check-guarantee card	74	32	122
Convenient ATM machines	143	56	29
Drive-in service	148	47	33
Free checking	219	9	0
Overdraft privileges	20	187	21
Personal banker	40	32	156
Telephone transfer	6	20	202
Trust department	13	45	170

5. If you have changed banks within the past three years, what was the major reason
    for the change?
    33 relocation of residence
    4 relocation of bank
    18 dissatisfaction with bank service
    7 other (please specify: _____)

    Thank you so much for your cooperation. Please return this questionnaire in the enclosed envelope to Customer
    Service Department, Tri-City Bank, P.O. Box 1086, Stamford, CT 06902.

11

Writing the Business Report

After you have finished this chapter, you should be able to:

- Interpret data for the report reader.

- Determine an appropriate report structure.

- Organize a report in a logical manner.

- Develop an effective report outline.

- Write each part of the report body using an effective writing style.

- Provide appropriate documentation.

- Revise, format, and proofread the report.

On the Job

STEVE MESSINETTI
Director, Campus Chapters and Youth Programs, Habitat for Humanity International

When Steve Messinetti writes a report, he wants to do more than simply inform, analyze, or recommend—he also wants to touch his readers in a very personal way. Messinetti is the director of campus chapters and youth programs at the Americus, Georgia, headquarters of Habitat for Humanity International, a nonprofit, ecumenical organization dedicated to eliminating poverty housing throughout the world.

Messinetti writes a variety of reports, including periodical management reports, progress reports, proposals for new programs, and one-time reports about special events. Whether writing for internal or external audiences, he brings his reports to life by including photos and quotes that capture the feelings of program participants.

One of Messinetti's longer reports summarizes the results of Habitat's Spring Break Collegiate Challenge. This 15-page report opens with a transmittal document bound directly into the report. "We use the letter to introduce the report, summarize the program, recognize the participants, and catch the reader's attention by mentioning a few highlights," Messinetti says. Next comes the table of contents, comprising the report's generic headings, which helps readers quickly locate sections of particular interest. Throughout the report, graphs and charts interspersed with the narrative offer a visual snapshot of the program's success.

When Messinetti quotes from other documents, he is careful to provide a complete citation on the same page. "The documentation gives proper credit to the source and confirms the validity of the information, so readers don't wonder where it came from," he says.

Interpreting the Data

At some point in the reporting process, you will have gathered enough data from your secondary and primary sources to enable you to solve your problem. (It is always possible, of course, that during data analysis and report writing you may find that you need additional information on a topic.)

Your job at this point, then, is to convert your raw data, which might be represented by your notes, photocopies of journal articles, completed questionnaires, audiotapes of interviews, Internet and computer printouts, and the like, into information—meaningful facts, statistics, and conclusions—that will help the reader of your report make a decision.

Data analysis is not a step that can be accomplished at one sitting. The more familiar you become with the data and the more you pore over it, the more different things you will see. Data analysis is usually the part of the report process that requires the most time as well as the most skill. The more insight you can provide the reader about the meaning of the data you've collected and presented, the more helpful your report will be.

Analysis and interpretation turn data *into* information.

The Three-Step Process of Analysis

When analyzing the data, you must first determine whether the data does, in fact, solve your problem. It would make no sense to prepare elaborate tables and other visual aids if your data is irrelevant, incomplete, or inaccurate. To help yourself make this initial evaluation of your data, assume for the sake of simplicity that you have gathered only three bits of information—a paraphrase from a secondary source, a chart you developed, and a computer printout, labeled Findings A, B, and C, respectively (see Figure 11.1). Now, you are ready to analyze this data.

First, look at each piece of data in isolation (Step 1). If Finding A were the only piece of data you collected, what would it mean in terms of solving the problem? What conclusions, if any, could you draw from this one bit of data? Follow the same process for Findings B and C, examining each in isolation, without considering any other data.

Next, look at each piece of data in combination with the other bits (Step 2). For example, by itself Finding A might lead to one conclusion, but when viewed in conjunction with B and C, it might take on a different shade of meaning. In other words, does adding Findings B and C to your data pool reinforce your initial

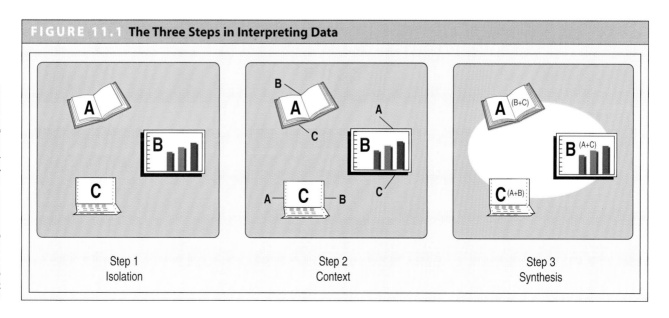

FIGURE 11.1   The Three Steps in Interpreting Data

Step 1	Step 2	Step 3
Isolation	Context	Synthesis

conclusion? If so, you can use stronger language in drawing your conclusion. Or does it weaken your initial conclusion? If so, you might want to qualify your conclusion with less certain language or refrain from drawing any conclusion at all.

Finally, synthesize all of the information you've collected (Step 3). When you consider all facts and their relationships together, what do they mean? For example, if Findings A, B, and C all point in the same direction, you might be able to define a trend. More important, you must determine whether all the data taken together provide an accurate and complete answer to your problem statement. If so, then you're ready to begin the detailed analysis and presentation that will help the reader understand your findings. If not, you must backtrack and start the research process again.

Determine the meaning of each finding by itself, in conjunction with each other finding, and in conjunction with all other findings.

Making Sense of the Data

As a report writer, you cannot simply present the raw data without interpreting it. The data in your tables and charts helps to solve a problem, and the report writer must make the connection between that data and the solution to the problem. In the report narrative, you need not discuss all data in the tables and charts; that would be boring and insulting to the reader's intelligence. But you must determine what you think the important implications of your data are, and then you must identify and discuss them for the reader.

Don't just present tables and figures. Interpret their important points.

What types of important points do you look for? Almost always, the most important finding is the overall response to a question (rather than the responses of the subgroups). And almost always the category within the question that receives the largest response is the most important point. So discuss this question and this category first. Let's look at Apex Company's Table 4, as shown in Figure 11.2.

In Table 4, the major finding is this: four-fifths of the respondents believe that Apex Company is an asset to their community. Note that if you give the exact figure in the table (here, 80%), you can use less precise language in the narrative— "four-fifths" in this case, or in other cases "one in four," "a slight majority," and the like. Doing so helps you avoid presenting facts and figures too quickly. Pace your analysis because the reader will not be able to comprehend data that is presented too quickly or in too concentrated a format.

At a minimum, discuss the overall response and any important subgroup findings.

Once you've discussed the overall finding, begin discussing the data from the subgroups as necessary. Look for any of these features:

- Trends
- Unexpected findings
- Data that reinforces or contradicts other data
- Extreme values
- Data that raises questions

FIGURE 11.2 Table for Analysis

Table 4.   Response to Statement, "Apex Company is an asset to our community."
(*N* = 271; all figures in %)

	Total	Marital Status		Sex		Age		
		Married	Single	Male	Female	Under 21	21–50	Over 50
Agree	80	82	77	83	57	69	77	90
No opinion	12	11	15	12	21	18	14	9
Disagree	8	7	8	5	22	13	9	1
Total	100	100	100	100	100	100	100	100

If these features are important, discuss them. In our example, there were no major differences in the responses by marital status, so you would probably not need to discuss them. However, you would need to discuss the big difference in responses between males and females. If possible, present data or draw any valid conclusions regarding the reasons for these differences.

Finally, point out the trend that is evident with regard to age: the older the respondent, the more positive the response. If it's important enough, you might illustrate this trend in a graph to achieve a more powerful visual effect.

By now, you probably know more about the topic on which you're writing than the reader knows. Assist the reader, then, by pointing out the important implications, findings, and relationships of your data. Help your reader reach the same conclusions you have reached.

What's in a Name?	**WORD**|wise
Adam and Eve	dad, even a ma
Clint Eastwood	Old West action
Madam Curie	radium came
Ralph Waldo Emerson	person whom all read
Tom Cruise	so I'm cuter
Woodrow Wilson	O Lord, so now WWI

Planning the Writing

As we have seen throughout our study of business communication, the writing process consists of planning, drafting, revising, formatting, and proofreading. You follow this same process when writing a report.

Although much of the planning in the report process is, of necessity, done even before data collection begins, the written presentation of the results requires its own stage of planning. You need to make decisions about the structure of the report, the organization of the content, and the framework of the headings before and while you write.

Determining the Report Structure

The physical structure of the report and such general traits as complexity, degree of formality, and length depend on the audience for the report and the nature of the problem that the report addresses. The three most common formats for a report are *manuscript, memorandum,* and *letter* format.

Manuscript reports, the most formal of the three, are formatted in narrative (paragraph) style, with headings and subheadings separating the different sections. If the report addresses a complex problem that has serious consequences, it will likely follow a manuscript format and a formal writing style. A formal writing style typically avoids the use of first- and second-person pronouns, such as *I* and *you*. In addition, the more formal the report, the more supplementary parts are included (such as a table of contents, executive summary, and appendix) and, therefore, the longer the report.

Memorandum and letter reports contain the standard correspondence parts (for example, lines identifying the names of the sender and receiver). They use a more informal writing style and may or may not contain headings and subheadings. Compare the informal, simple, and short report in memo format shown in Model 16 on page 290 with the formal, complex, and long report (only the first page is shown) in manuscript format shown in Model 17 on page 291.

Most reports are formatted as manuscripts, memos, or letters.

MODEL 16

Informal Memorandum Report

The memo format indicates the reader is someone from within the firm.

Uses a direct organizational style: the recommendation and conclusions are given first, followed by the supporting evidence.

Uses informal language; makes extensive use of first- and second-person pronouns such as *I, me, we,* and *you.*

Uses talking headings to reinforce the direct plan.

Does not include the detailed statistical information but makes it available if needed.

Weight Watchers International, Inc.
175 Crossways Park West
Woodbury, New York 11797-2055
516 390-1400

FAX 516 390-1445

MEMO TO:	Marketing Manager
FROM:	Barbara Novak, Sales Assistant
DATE:	August 9, 20—
SUBJECT:	Yellow Pages Advertising

I recommend we continue purchasing a quarter-page ad in the Yellow Pages. My recommendation is based on the fact that Yellow Pages advertising has produced more inquiries than any other method of advertising and has increased net profits.

A Pilot Test Was Set Up

On March 1, you asked me to conduct a three-month test of the effectiveness of Yellow Pages advertising. I subsequently purchased a quarter-page ad for the edition of the Yellow Pages that was distributed the week of June 2–6. For six weeks thereafter, we queried all telephone and walk-in customers to determine how they had learned about our company. I also compared the percentage of signed contracts resulting from each source. Precise before-and-after sales data could not be generated because of other factors that affected sales for each period (for example, time of year and other promotional campaigns).

Results Were Positive

My analysis of the data shows that 38% of the callers after June 2–6 first learned about our company from the Yellow Pages. The next highest source was referrals and repeat business, which accounted for 26% of the calls. In addition, 21% of the Yellow Pages inquiries resulted in signed contracts.

We Should Continue Advertising

Based on the $358 monthly cost of our quarter-page ad, each dollar of ad cost is producing $3.77 in sales revenue and $0.983 toward profit margin. These results clearly support the continuation of our Yellow Pages advertising. I would be happy to discuss the results of this research with you in more detail and to provide the supporting statistical data if you wish.

jeo

Grammar and Mechanics Note

See the Style Manual at the end of the text for guidance on how to format memorandums.

THE EFFECTIVENESS OF YELLOW PAGES ADVERTISING FOR WEIGHT WATCHERS INTERNATIONAL

Barbara Novak, Sales Assistant

According to Mountain Bell, display advertising typically accounts for 55% of total sales for a firm in the moving business.[1] Thus, Hiram Cooper, director of marketing, requested a three-month test be conducted of the effectiveness of Yellow Pages advertising for our organization. This report describes the procedures used to gather the data and the results obtained. Based on the data, a recommendation is made regarding the continuation of Yellow Pages advertising.

A quarter-page ad was purchased in the edition of the Mountain Bell Yellow Pages that was distributed the week of June 2–6. For the six-week period encompassing June 9 through July 17, all telephone and walk-in customers were queried to determine how they had learned about the company. One delimitation of this study was that precise before-and-after sales data could not be generated because of other factors that affected sales for each period.

Findings

The findings of this study are reported in terms of the sources of information for learning about our company, the amount of new business generated, and a cost-benefits comparison for Yellow Pages advertising.

Sources of Information

As shown in Table 1, 38% of the callers during the test period first learned about Weight Watchers from the Yellow Pages display. The second highest source was referrals and repeat business, which together accounted for 26% of the calls. In addition, 21% of the Yellow Pages inquiries resulted in signed contracts, when

---

[1] Joseph L. Dye <jldye@aol.com>, "Answers to Your Questions," May 18, 2007, personal e-mail (May 18, 2007).

Manuscript Report

The first page of a formal manuscript report is shown.

Uses an indirect organizational style: the conclusions and recommendations will be given after the supporting data is presented.

Uses formal language; avoids first- and second-person pronouns.

Uses visual aids (such as tables and charts) and multilevel headings, which are typical of formal reports.

Grammar and Mechanics Note

See the Style Manual at the end of the text for guidance on how to format manuscript reports.

So that your written presentation will have an overall sense of proportion and unity, decide beforehand on the complexity, formality, length, and format of the report. The "right" decision depends on the needs and desires of the reader.

Organizing the Report

A sculptor creating a statue of someone doesn't necessarily start at the head and work down to the feet in lock-step fashion. Instead, he or she may first create part of the torso, then part of the head, then another part of the torso, and so on. Likewise, a movie director may film segments of the movie out of narrative order. In the end, both creations are put together in such a way as to show unity, order, logic, and beauty.

Similarly, you may have organized the collection and analysis of data in a way that suited the investigation of various subtopics of the problem. Now that it is time to put the results of your work together into a coherent written presentation, however, you may need a *new* organization, one that integrates the whole and takes into account what you have learned through your research.

Planning your written presentation to show unity, order, logic, and yes, even beauty, involves selecting an organizational basis for the *findings* (the data you've collected and analyzed) and developing an outline. You must decide in what order to present each piece of the puzzle and when to "spill the beans"—that is, when to present your overall *conclusions* (the answers to the research questions raised in the introduction) and any recommendations you may wish to make.

Most reports are organized by time, location, importance, or criteria.

As shown in Figure 11.3, the four most common bases for organizing your findings are *time, location, importance,* and *criteria.* The purpose of the report (information, analysis, or recommendation), the nature of the problem, and your knowledge of the reader will help you select the most useful organizational framework.

Organize your report by time only when it is important for the reader to know the sequence of events.

Time   The use of chronology, or time sequence, is appropriate for agendas, minutes of meetings, programs, many status reports, and similar projects. Discussing events in the order in which they occurred or in the order in which they will or should occur is an efficient way to organize many informational reports—those whose purpose is simply to inform.

Despite its usefulness and simplicity, time sequence should not be overused. Because events *occur* one after another, chronology is often the most efficient way to *record* data, but it may not be the most efficient way to *present* that data to your readers. Assume, for example, that you are writing a progress report on a recruiting trip you made to four college campuses. Each day you interviewed candidates for the three positions you have open. The first passage, given in time sequence, requires too much work of the reader. The second version saves the reader time.

> **NOT:** On Monday morning, I interviewed one candidate for the budget-analyst position and two candidates for the junior-accountant position. Then, in the afternoon, I interviewed two candidates for the asset-manager position and another for the budget-analyst position. Finally, on Tuesday, I interviewed another candidate for budget analyst and two for junior accountant.

> **BUT:** On Monday and Tuesday, I interviewed three candidates for the budget-analyst position, four for the junior-accountant position, and two for the asset-manager position.

Obviously, a blow-by-blow description is not necessarily the most efficient means of communicating information to the reader—sometimes it forces the

FIGURE 11.3 Organizing the Data

Topic	Basis	Format	Heading
A. Eastern Electronics: A Case Study 1. Start-up of Firm: 1997 2. Rapid Expansion: 1997–2000 3. Industrywide Slowdown: 2001 4. Retrenchment: 2001–2003 5. Return to Profitability: 2004	Time	Noun phrases	Generic
B. Renovation Needs 1. Expanding the Mailroom 2. Modernizing the Reception Area 3. Installing a Humidity System in Warehouse C 4. Repaving the North Parking Lot	Location	Participial phrases	Generic
C. Progress on Automation Project 1. Conversion on Budget 2. Time Schedule Slipped One Month 3. Branch Offices Added to Project 4. Software Programs Upgraded	Importance	Partial statements	Talking
D. Evaluation of Applicants for Communications Director 1. Sefcick Has Higher Professional Training. 2. Jenson Has More Relevant Work Experience. 3. Jenson's Written Work Samples Are More Effective.	Criteria	Statements	Talking
E. Establishing a Policy on AIDS in the Workplace 1. What Are the Firm's Legal and Social Obligations? 2. What Policies Have Other Firms Established? 3. What Policies Are Needed to Deal with the Needs of AIDS-Infected Employees? 4. What Policies Are Needed to Deal with the Concerns of Noninfected Employees? 5. How Should These Policies Be Implemented?	Criteria	Questions	Generic

reader to do too much work. Organize your information chronologically only when it is important for the reader to know the sequence in which events occurred.

Location   Like the use of time sequence, the use of location as the basis for organizing a report is often appropriate for simple informational reports. Discussing topics according to their geographical or physical location (for example, describing an office layout) may be the most efficient way to present the data. Again, be sure that such an organizational plan helps the reader process the information most efficiently and that it is not merely the easiest way for you to report the data. Decisions should be based on reader needs rather than on writer convenience.

Importance   For the busy reader, the most efficient organizational plan may discuss the most important topic first, followed in order by topics of decreasing importance. The reader then gets the major idea up front and can skim the less important information as desired or needed. This organizational plan is routinely used by newspapers, where the most important points are discussed in the lead paragraph.

For some types of reports, especially recommendation reports, the opposite plan might be used effectively. If you've analyzed four alternatives and will recommend the implementation of Alternative 4, you might first present each of the other alternatives in turn (starting with the least-viable solution) and show why they're *not* feasible. Then, you save your "trump card" until last, thus making the alternative you're recommending the freshest in the reader's mind because it is the last one read. If you use this option, make sure that you effectively "slay all the dragons" except your own, so that the reader will agree that your recommendation is the most logical one.

The most logical organization for most analytical and recommendation reports is by criteria.

Criteria   For most analytical and recommendation reports, where the purpose is to analyze the data and possibly recommend a solution, the most logical arrangement is to organize the data by criteria. One of the important steps in the reporting process is to develop hypotheses regarding causes of or solutions for the problem you're exploring. This process requires breaking down your problem into its component subproblems. These factors, or criteria, then, become the basis for organizing the report.

In Example D in Figure 11.3, for instance, the three factors presented—professional training, work experience, and written work samples—are the bases on which you will evaluate each candidate. Thus, they should also form the bases for presenting the data. By focusing attention on the criteria, you help lead the reader to the same conclusion you reached. For this reason, organizing data by criteria is an especially effective organizational plan when the reader might initially resist your recommendations.

If you're evaluating three sites for a new facility, for example, avoid the temptation to use the *locations* of these sites as the report headings. Such an organizational plan focuses attention on the sites themselves instead of on the criteria by which you evaluated them and on which you based your recommendations. Instead, use the criteria as the headings. Similarly, avoid using "Advantages" and "Disadvantages" as headings. Keep your reader in step with you by helping the reader focus on the same topics—the criteria—that you highlighted during the research and analysis phases of your project.

In actual practice, you might use a combination of these organizational plans. For instance, you might organize your first-level (major) headings by criteria but your second-level headings in simple-to-complex order. Or you might organize your first-level headings by criteria but present these criteria in their order of importance. Competent communicators select an organizational plan with a view toward helping the reader comprehend and appreciate the information and viewpoints being presented in the most efficient manner possible.

In general, prefer the direct plan (conclusions and recommendations first) for most business reports.

Presenting Conclusions and Recommendations   Once you've decided how to organize the findings of your study, you must decide where to present the conclusions and any recommendations that have resulted from these findings. The differences among findings, conclusions, and recommendations can be illustrated by the following examples:

Finding:	The computer monitor sometimes goes blank during operation.
Finding:	Nonsense data sometimes appears on the screen for no reason.
Conclusion:	The computer is broken.

Recommendation:	We should repair the computer before May 3, when payroll processing begins.
Finding:	Our Statesville branch has lost money four out of the past five years.
Conclusion:	Our Statesville branch is not profitable.
Recommendation:	We should close our Statesville branch.

Academic reports and many business reports have traditionally presented the conclusions and recommendations of a study at the end of the report, with the rationale being that conclusions cannot logically be drawn until the data has been presented and analyzed; similarly, recommendations cannot be made until conclusions have been drawn.

Models 16 and 17, presented earlier, illustrate these two approaches. The informal memo report presents the conclusions and recommendations in the first paragraph; the manuscript report delays such presentation until after the findings have been presented and analyzed.

Although no hard-and-fast rules exist regarding when to use the direct and indirect organizational plans in reports, some guidance can be given. Generally, it is better to use the direct organizational plan (in which the conclusions and recommendations are presented at the beginning of the report) when

- The reader prefers the direct plan for reports (as is typically the case when preparing a business report for your superior).
- The reader will be receptive to your conclusions and recommendations.
- The reader can evaluate the information in the report more efficiently if the conclusions and recommendations are given up front.
- You have no specific reason to prefer the indirect pattern.

Similarly, the indirect plan (in which the evidence is presented first, followed by conclusions and recommendations) is more appropriate when

- The reader prefers the indirect plan for reports.
- The reader will be initially uninterested in or resistant to the conclusions and recommendations.
- The topic is so complex that detailed explanations and discussions are needed for the conclusions and recommendations to be understood and accepted.

The decision isn't necessarily an either/or situation. Instead of putting all the conclusions and recommendations either first or last, you may choose to split them up, discussing each in the appropriate subsection of your report. Similarly, even though you write a report using an indirect plan, you may add an executive summary or letter of transmittal that communicates the conclusions and recommendations to the reader before the report itself has been read.

Outlining the Report

Although we have not used the term *outlining* thus far, whenever we've talked about organizing, we've actually been talking about outlining as well. For example, early in the report process you broke your problem statement into its logical component subproblems. Thus, your problem statement and subproblems served as your first working outline.

Many business writers find it useful at this point in the report process to construct a more formal outline. A formal outline provides an orderly visual representation of the report, showing clearly which points will be covered, in what order they will be covered, and how each relates to the rest of the report. The purpose of the

The outline provides a concise visual picture of the structure of your report.

outline is to guide you, the writer, in structuring your report logically and efficiently. Consider it a working draft, subject to being revised as you compose the report.

Use the working title of your report as the title of your outline. Use uppercase roman numerals for the major headings, uppercase letters for first-level subheadings, arabic numerals for second-level subheadings, and lowercase letters for third-level subheadings. Only rarely will you need to use all four levels of headings. Model 18 on page 297 shows an outline for a formal report.

As part of the process of developing a formal outline, you should compose the actual wording for your headings and decide how many headings you will need. Headings play an important role in focusing the reader's attention and in helping your report achieve unity and coherence, so plan them carefully, and revise them as needed as you work toward a final version of your report.

Talking Versus Generic Headings   Talking headings identify not only the topic of the section but also the major conclusion. For instance, Example C in Figure 11.3 on page 293 uses talking headings to indicate not only that the first section of the report is about the budget for the conversion but also that the conversion is actually proceeding on budget.

Talking headings, which are typically used in newspapers and magazines, are often useful for business reports as well. For example, they can serve as a preview or executive summary of the entire report. They are especially useful when directness is desired—the reader can simply skim the headings in the report (or in the table of contents) and get an overview of the topics covered and each topic's conclusions.

Generic headings, on the other hand, identify only the topic of the section, without giving the conclusion. Most formal reports and any report written in an indirect pattern would use generic headings, similar to the headings used for Examples A and B in Figure 11.3 and used throughout Model 18 on page 297.

Parallelism   As illustrated in Figure 11.3, you have wide leeway in selecting the formats of headings used in your report. Noun phrases are probably the most common form of heading, but you may also choose participial phrases, partial statements (in which a verb is missing—the kind often used in newspaper headlines), statements, or questions. Perhaps there are other forms you might choose as well.

Regardless of the form of heading you select, be consistent within each level of heading. If the first major heading (a first-level heading) is a noun phrase, all first-level headings should be noun phrases. If the first major heading is a talking heading, the others should be, too. As you move from level to level, you may switch to another form of heading if it would be more appropriate. Again, however, the headings within the same level must be parallel.

Length and Number of Headings   Four to eight words is about the right length for most headings. Headings that are too long lose some of their effectiveness; the shorter the heading, the more emphasis it receives. Yet headings that are too short are ineffective because they do not convey enough meaning.

Similarly, choose an appropriate *number* of headings. Having too many headings weakens the unity of a report—they chop the report up too much, making it look more like an outline than a reasoned analysis. Having too few headings, however, confronts the reader with page after page of solid copy, without the chance to stop periodically and refocus attention on the topic.

In general, consider having at least one heading or visual aid to break up each single-spaced page or each two consecutive, double-spaced pages. Make your report inviting to read.

Balance   Maintain a sense of balance within and among sections. It would be unusual to give one section of a report eight subsections (eight second-level headings) and give the following section none. Similarly, it would be unusual to have

MODEL 18

Report Outline

This report uses generic, not talking, headings.

STAFF EMPLOYEES' EVALUATION OF THE BENEFIT PROGRAM AT ATLANTIC STATE UNIVERSITY
David Riggins

1   **I.   INTRODUCTION**

    A. Purpose and Scope
    B. Procedures

Uses the working title of the report as the outline title.

  II.   FINDINGS

Organizes the findings by criteria.

2   A. Knowledge of Benefits
        1. Familiarity with Benefits
        2. Present Methods of Communication
           a. Formal Channels
           b. Informal Channels
        3. Preferred Methods of Communication
    B. Opinions of Present Benefits
        1. Importance of Benefits
        2. Satisfaction with Benefits
    C. Desirability of Additional Benefits

Contains at least two items in each level of subdivision.

  III.   SUMMARY, CONCLUSIONS, AND RECOMMENDATIONS

    A. Summary of the Problem and Procedures
    B. Summary of the Findings
    C. Conclusions and Recommendations

Uses parallel structure (noun phrases are used for each heading and subheading).

  APPENDIX

3   A. Cover Letter
    B. Questionnaire

Grammar and Mechanics Notes

1 Align the Roman numerals vertically on the periods.
2 Type each entry in upper- and lowercase letters.
3 Identify each appendix item by letter.

one section be ten pages long and another section be only half a page long. Also, ensure that the most important ideas appear in the highest levels of headings. If you're discussing four criteria for a topic, for example, all four should be in the same level of heading—presumably in first-level headings.

When you divide a section into subsections, it must have at least two subsections. You cannot logically have just one second-level heading within a section because when you divide something, it divides into more than one "piece."

Drafting

The final product—the written report—is the only evidence the reader has of your efforts.

Although it is the last step of a long and sometimes complex process, the written presentation of your research is the only evidence your reader has of the effort you have invested in the project. The success or failure of your hard work depends on this physical evidence. Prepare the written report carefully to bring out the full significance of your data and to help the reader reach a decision and solve a problem.

The report body consists of the introduction; the findings; and the summary, conclusions, and recommendations. As stated earlier, the conclusions may go first or last in the report. Each part may be a separate chapter in long reports or a major section in shorter reports.

CHECKPOINT 11.1

RECALL   Write a capital *T* for true or *F* for false before each statement.

1. ____ Conclusions are always based on the findings of a report.

2. ____ In the report narrative, you should discuss all of the data from a table or chart.

3. ____ The most logical basis for organizing the data in most analytical and recommendation reports is by the criteria you used to solve the problem.

4. ____ Conclusions and recommendations may be presented either at the beginning or at the end of the report, depending on the situation.

5. ____ Formal reports should use talking headings.

VOCABULARY   Define the following terms in your own words.

6. generic headings:

7. talking headings:

COMPREHENSION

8. Consider the three report headings in Section D of Figure 11.3 on page 293. Recast these headings into generic headings.

9. Compose a report title for which it would be appropriate to use location as the basis for organizing the body of the report.

10. Assume that in a survey of community residents, 212 out of 314 respondents indicated that the local police had been rude to them on at least one occasion. Compose a statement of finding, conclusion, and recommendation based on this data.

   Finding:

   Conclusion:

   Recommendation:

CRITICAL THINKING

11. The section on data analysis stresses the importance of accurately and completely interpreting your data. Can a report writer be guilty of biased reporting even though all the data he or she discusses is accurately and completely interpreted?

....

Introduction

The introduction sets the stage for understanding the findings that follow. In this section, present such information as the following:

- Background of the problem
- Need for the study
- Authorization for the report

The introduction presents the information the reader needs to make sense of the findings.

© 1998 Randy Glasbergen. www.glasbergen.com

"I used a $3,000 computer, a $1200 laser printer and a $300 word-processing program—and I still got a <u>D</u> on my term paper!"

- Hypotheses or problem statement and subproblems
- Purpose and scope (including definition of terms, if needed)
- Procedures used to gather and analyze the data

The actual topics and amount of detail presented in the introductory section will depend on the complexity of the report and the needs of the reader. For example, if the procedures are extensive, you may want to place them in a separate section, with their own first-level heading. Model 19 on page 301 is an example of an introductory section for a formal report.

Findings

The findings of the study represent the major contribution of the report and make up the largest section of the report. Discuss and interpret any relevant primary and secondary data you gathered. Organize this section using one of the plans discussed earlier (for example, by time, location, importance, or, more frequently, criteria). Using objective language, present the information clearly, concisely, and accurately.

Many reports will display numerical information in tables and figures (such as bar, line, or pie charts). The information in such displays should be self-explanatory; that is, readers should understand it without having to refer to the text. Nevertheless, all tables and figures must be mentioned and explained in the text so that the text, too, is self-explanatory. All text references should be by number (for example, "as shown in Table 4")—never by a phrase such as "as shown below," because the table or figure might actually appear at the top of the following page.

Summarize the important information from the display (see Model 20 on page 302). Give enough interpretation to help the reader comprehend the table or figure, but don't repeat all the information it contains. Discussing displayed information in the narrative *emphasizes* that information, so discuss only what merits such emphasis.

The table or figure should appear immediately *below* the first paragraph of text in which the reference to it occurs. Avoid splitting a table or figure between two pages. If not enough space is available on the page for the display, continue with the text to the bottom of the page and then place the table or figure at the very top of the following page.

For all primary and secondary data, point out important items, implications, trends, contradictions, unexpected findings, similarities and differences, and the like. Use emphasis, subordination, preview, summary, and transition to make the report read clearly and smoothly. Avoid presenting facts and figures so fast that the reader becomes overwhelmed with data. Always keep the reader's needs and desires uppermost in mind as you organize, present, and discuss the information.

Summary, Conclusions, and Recommendations

A one- or two-page report may need only a one-sentence or one-paragraph summary. Longer or more complex reports, however, should include a more extensive summary. Briefly review the problem and the procedures used to solve the problem, and provide an overview of the major findings. Repeating the main points or arguments immediately before presenting the conclusions and recommendations reinforces the reasonableness of those conclusions and recommendations. To avoid monotony when summarizing, use wording that differs from the original presentation.

If your report merely analyzes the information presented but does not make recommendations, you might label the final section of the report "Summary" or

MODEL 19

Report Introduction

1   **INTRODUCTION**

Employee benefits are a rapidly growing and an increasingly important form of employee compensation for both for-profit and nonprofit organizations. According to a recent U.S. Chamber of Commerce survey, benefits now constitute 37% of all payroll costs, averaging $10,732 yearly for each employee (Berelson, 2004, p. 183). Thus, on the basis of cost alone, an organization's benefit program must be carefully monitored and evaluated.

Provides a citation for statistics, direct quotations, or paraphrases.

To ensure that the benefit program for Atlantic State University's 2,500 staff personnel is operating as effectively as possible, David Riggins, director of personnel, authorized this report on October 15, 2005.

Identifies who authorized the report.

Purpose and Scope

Specifically, the following problem was addressed in this study: What are the opinions of staff employees at Atlantic State University regarding their employee benefits? To answer this question, the following subproblems were addressed:

Provides the problem statement in the form of a question to be answered.

2   1. How knowledgeable are the employees about the benefit program?
2. What are the employees' opinions of the value of the benefits already available?
3. What benefits, if any, would the employees like to have added to the program?

Identifies the subproblems that must be answered to resolve the problem statement.

This study attempted to determine employee preferences only. Whether employee preferences are economically feasible is not within the scope of this study.

As used in this study, employee benefits (also called fringe benefits) means an employment benefit given in addition to one's wages or salary.

Defines terms, as needed.

Procedures

A list of the 2,489 staff employees eligible for benefits was generated from the
3   October 15 payroll run. Using a 10% systematic sample, 250 employees were selected for the survey. On November 3, each of the selected employees was sent the cover letter and questionnaire shown in Appendixes A and B via campus mail. A total of 206 employees completed usable questionnaires, for a response rate of 82%.

Provides concise, but complete, discussion of the procedures used to answer the problem statement.

In addition to the questionnaire data, personal interviews were held with three benefits managers. The primary data provided by the survey and personal interviews was then analyzed and compared with findings from secondary sources to determine the staff employees' opinions of the benefit program at ASU.

Ends with an appropriate sense of closure for this section.

Grammar and Mechanics Notes

1 Because the heading *Introduction* immediately follows another report heading (the report title), its use is optional.
2 In a single-spaced report, single-space numbered and bulleted lists if every item comprises a single line. Otherwise, single-space lines within an item but double-space between items.
3 Be consistent in using either the percent sign (%) or the word *percent.* Regardless, use figures for the actual percentage.

MODEL 20

Report Findings

Refers to tables and charts by number.

Discusses only the most important data from the table.

Subordinates the reference to tables and charts by placing it in a dependent clause ("As shown in Figure 1").

Recent studies (Egan, 1995; Ignatio, 1996) have shown that employees' satisfaction with benefits is directly correlated with their knowledge of such benefits. Thus, the ASU staff employees were asked to rate their level of familiarity with each benefit. As shown in Table 2, most staff employees believe that most benefits have been adequately communicated to them.

1

TABLE 2. LEVEL OF FAMILIARITY WITH BENEFIT PROGRAM

| Benefit | Level of Familiarity | | | | |
	Familiar	Unfamiliar	Undecided	No Resp.	Total
Sick leave	94%	4%	1%	1%	100%
Vacation	94%	4%	1%	1%	100%
Paid holidays	92%	4%	3%	1%	100%
Hospital/medical ins.	90%	7%	2%	0%	100%
Life insurance	84%	10%	5%	1%	100%
Retirement	84%	11%	4%	1%	100%
Long-term disability ins.	55%	33%	12%	1%	100%
Auto insurance	36%	57%	6%	15%	100%

In general, benefit familiarity is not related to length of employment at ASU. Most employees are familiar with most benefits regardless of their length of employment. However, as shown in Figure 1, the only benefit for which this is not true is life insurance. The longer a person has been employed at ASU, the more likely he or she is to know about this benefit.

2

FIGURE 1. KNOWLEDGE OF LIFE INSURANCE BENEFIT

3

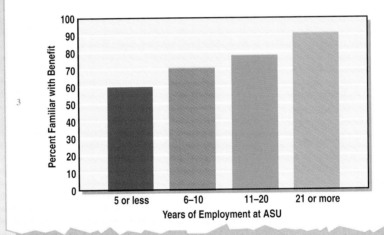

Grammar and Mechanics Notes

1 Position tables and charts immediately below the paragraph that introduces them.
2 Label charts as "figures" and number them independently of table numbers.
3 If a display does not fit completely at the bottom of the page, continue with the text to the bottom of the page and then place the display at the top of the following page.

"Summary and Conclusions," as appropriate. If your report includes both conclusions and recommendations, ensure that the conclusions stem directly from your findings and that the recommendations stem directly from the conclusions. Provide ample evidence to support all your conclusions and recommendations. Model 21 on page 304 shows an example of a closing section of a report.

As shown in Model 21, you should end your report with an overall concluding statement that provides a definite sense of project completion. Don't leave your reader wondering if additional pages will follow.

Developing an Effective Writing Style

You can enhance the effectiveness of your written reports by paying attention to your writing style.

Tone   Regardless of the structure of your report, the writing style used is typically more objective and less conversational than, for example, the style of an informal memorandum. Avoid colloquial expressions, attempts at humor, subjectivity, bias, and exaggeration.

NOT: The company *hit the jackpot* with its new system.

BUT: The new system saved the company $125,000 the first year.

NOT: He *claimed* that half of his projects involved name-brand advertising.

BUT: He stated that half of his projects involved name-brand advertising.

Pronouns   For most business reports, the use of first- and second-person pronouns is not only acceptable but also quite helpful for achieving an effective writing style. Formal language, however, focuses attention on the information being conveyed instead of on the writer; reports written in the formal style should use third-person pronouns and avoid using *I*, *we*, and *you*.

First- and second-person pronouns can be used appropriately in most business reports.

You can avoid the awkward substitute "the writer" by revising the sentence. Most often, it is evident that the writer is the person doing the action communicated.

Informal: I recommend that the project be canceled.
Awkward: The writer recommends that the project be canceled.
Formal: The project should be canceled.

Using the passive voice is a common device for avoiding the use of *I* in formal reports, but doing so weakens the impact. Instead, revise the sentence to avoid undue use of the passive voice.

Informal: I interviewed Jan Smith.
Passive: Jan Smith was interviewed.
Formal: In a personal interview, Jan Smith stated . . .

You will probably also want to avoid using *he* as a generic pronoun when referring to an unidentified person. Chapter 5 discusses many ways to avoid such discriminatory language.

Verb Tense   Use the verb tense (past, present, or future) that is appropriate at the time the reader *reads* the report—not necessarily at the time that you *wrote* the report. Use past tense to describe procedures (because they have already been completed at the time the reader reads the report) and to describe the findings of other studies already completed, but use present tense for conclusions from those studies (because we assume they continue to be true).

MODEL 21

Report Summary, Conclusions, and Recommendations

Quickly summarizes the need for the study.

Summarizes the problem and procedures used to solve the problem.

Summarizes the findings.

Presents the recommendations based on the findings and conclusions.

Provides an appropriate concluding statement.

1

SUMMARY, CONCLUSIONS, AND RECOMMENDATIONS

Nationwide, employee benefits now account for more than a third of all payroll costs. Thus, on the basis of cost alone, an organization's benefit program nust be carefully monitored and evaluated.

The problem in this study was to determine the opinions of the nearly 2,500 staff employees at Atlantic State University regarding the employee benefit program. Specifically, the investigation included determining the employees' present level of knowledge about the program, their opinions of the benefits presently offered, and their preferences for additional benefits. A survey of 206 staff employees and interviews with three managers familiar with the ASU employee benefit program provided the primary data for this study.

2   The findings show that staff employees at Atlantic State University are extremely knowledgeable about all benefits except long-term disability and automobile insurance; however, a majority would prefer to have an individualized benefit statement instead of the brochures now used to explain the benefit program. They consider paid time off the most important benefit and automobile insurance the least important. A majority are satisfied with all benefits, although retirement benefits generated substantial dissatisfaction. The only additional benefit desired by a majority of the employees is compensation for unused sick leave.

The following recommendations are based on these conclusions:

3   1. Determine the feasibility of generating an annual individualized benefit statement for each staff employee.

2. Reevaluate the attractiveness of the automobile insurance benefit in one year to determine staff employees' knowledge about, use of, and desire for this benefit. Consider the feasibility of substituting compensation for unused sick leave for the automobile insurance benefit.

3. Conduct a follow-up study of the retirement benefits at ASU to determine how competitive they are with those offered by comparable public and private institutions.

These recommendations, as well as the findings of this study, should help the university administration ensure that its benefit program is accomplishing its stated objectives of attracting and retaining high-quality employees and meeting their needs once employed.

Grammar and Mechanics Notes

1 If necessary, break a long heading at a logical point and single-space the lines of the heading. Try to make the second line shorter than the first.
2 Note the use of the present tense when summarizing the findings.
3 Leave a blank line between multiline numbered items.

When possible, use the stronger present tense to present the data from your study. The rationale for doing so is that we assume our findings continue to be true; thus, the use of the present tense is justified. (If we cannot assume the continuing truth of any findings, we should probably not use them in the study.)

NOT: These findings *will be discussed* later in this report.

BUT: These findings *are discussed* later in the report. (*But:* These findings *were discussed* earlier in this report.)

NOT: Three-fourths of the managers *believed* quality circles *were* effective at the plant.

BUT: Three-fourths of the managers *believe* that quality circles *are* effective at the plant.

Procedure: Nearly 500 people *responded* to this survey.

Finding: Only 11% of the managers *received* any specific training on any new procedure.

Conclusion: Most managers *do not receive* any specific training on any new procedure.

Emphasis and Subordination   Only rarely does all of the data consistently point to one conclusion. More likely, you will have a mixed bag of data from which you will have to evaluate the relative merits of each point. For your report to achieve its objective, the reader must evaluate the importance of each point in the same way that you did. At the very least, your reader must be *aware* of the importance you attached to each point. To ensure this outcome, employ the emphasis and subordination techniques you learned in Chapter 5 when discussing your findings.

By (a) making sure that the amount of space devoted to a topic reflects the importance of that topic, (b) carefully positioning your major ideas, and (c) using language that directly tells what is more and less important, you can help ensure that you and your reader share the same perspective when your reader analyzes the data.

Use emphasis and subordination to let the reader know what you consider most and least important—but *not* to unduly sway the reader. If the data honestly leads to a strong, definite conclusion, then by all means make your conclusion strong and definite. But if the data permits only a tentative conclusion, then say so.

Coherence   One difficulty in writing any long document—especially when the document is drafted in sections and then put together—is making the finished product read smoothly and coherently, like a unified presentation rather than a cut-and-paste job. This problem is even more challenging for team-written reports (see "Team Writing" on page 30 of Chapter 2).

One effective way to achieve coherence in a report is to use previews, summaries, and transitions regularly. At the beginning of each major section, preview what is discussed in that section. At the conclusion of each section, summarize what was presented and provide a smooth transition to the next topic. For long sections, the preview, summary, and transition might each be a separate paragraph; for short sections, a single sentence might suffice.

Note how preview, summary, and transition are used in the following example of a report section opening and closing.

Training of System Users

The training program can be evaluated in terms of the opinions of the users and in terms of the cost of training in proportion to the cost of the system itself. . . . (*After this topic preview, several paragraphs follow that discuss the opinions of the users and the cost of the training program.*)

Team writing is quite prevalent in organizations because the increasing quantity and complexity of the workplace make it difficult for any one person to have either the time or the expertise to solve many of the problems that arise and prepare a written report. Regardless of who prepares each individual part of the report, the final document must look and sound as though it were prepared by one writer. Here members of a work team are shown reviewing their report for errors in content, gaps or repetition, and effective writing style.

Even though a slight majority of users now feel competent in using the system, the training provided falls far short of the 20% of total system cost recommended by experts. This low level of training may have affected the precision of the data generated by the system. (*The first sentence contains the summary of this section; the second sentence provides the transition to the next section.*)

Always introduce a topic before dividing it into subtopics. Thus, you should never have one heading following another without some intervening text. (The exception to this guideline is that the heading "Introduction" may be used immediately after the report title or subtitle.) Preview for the reader how the topic will be divided before you actually make the division.

Paraphrasing Versus Direct Quotation

Use direct quotations sparingly.

When including the ideas of another person in your report, avoid the temptation to become lazy and simply repeat everything in the author's exact words. It is unlikely that the problem you're trying to solve and the problem discussed by the author mesh exactly. More than likely, you'll need to take bits and pieces of information from numerous sources and integrate them into a context appropriate for your specific purposes.

paraphrase A summary or restatement of a passage in one's own words

direct quotation The exact words of another

A **paraphrase** is a summary or restatement of a passage in your own words. A **direct quotation,** on the other hand, contains the exact words of another. Use direct quotations (always enclosed in quotation marks) only for definitions or for text that is so precise, clear, or otherwise noteworthy that it cannot be improved upon. Most of your references to secondary data should take the form of paraphrases. Paraphrasing involves more than just rearranging the words or leaving out a word or two, however. It requires that you understand the writer's idea and then restate it in your own language.

Documenting Your Sources

documentation Giving credit to another person for his or her words or ideas that are used in a report

Documentation is the identification of sources by giving credit to another person, either in the text or in the reference list, for using his or her words or ideas. You may, of course, use the words and ideas of others, provided such use is properly documented; in fact, for many business reports such secondary information may be the *only* data you use. You must, however, provide appropriate documentation whenever you quote, paraphrase, or summarize someone else's work.

Plagiarism is the use of another person's words or ideas without giving proper credit. Writings are considered the writer's legal property; someone else who wrongfully uses such property is guilty of theft. Plagiarism, therefore, carries stiff penalties. In the classroom, the penalty ranges from failure in a course to expulsion from school. On the job, the penalty for plagiarism ranges from loss of credibility to loss of employment.

You must document all material in your report that comes from secondary sources; that is, you must give enough information about the original source to enable the reader to locate the source if he or she so desires. If the secondary source is published (for example, a journal article), the documentation should appear as a reference citation. If the source is unpublished, sufficient documentation can generally be given in the narrative, making a formal citation unnecessary, as illustrated here:

> According to Board Policy 91-18b, all position vacancies above the level of C-3 must be posted internally at least two weeks prior to being advertised.

> The contractor's letter of May 23, 2003, stated, "We agree to modify Blueprint 3884 by widening the southeast entrance from 10 feet to 12 feet 6 inches for a total additional charge of $273.50."

Once a study has been cited once, it may be mentioned again in continuous discussion on the same page or even on the next pages without further citation if no ambiguity results. If several pages intervene or if ambiguity might result, give the citation again.

The three major forms for documenting the ideas, information, and quotations of other people in a report are endnotes, footnotes, and author–date references (see the Style Manual at the back of this text for examples and formatting conventions). Let the nature of the report and the needs of the reader dictate the documentation method used. Regardless of which method you select, ensure that the citations are accurate, complete, and consistently formatted and that your bibliography format is consistent with your documentation format.

- *Footnotes:* For years, footnotes have been the traditional method of citing sources. A bibliographic footnote provides the complete reference at the bottom of the page on which the citation occurs in the text. Thus, a reader interested in exploring the source does not have to turn to the back of the report. Today's word processors can format footnotes almost painlessly—automatically numbering and positioning each note correctly. Some readers, however, find the presence of footnotes on the text page distracting.

- *Endnotes:* The endnote format uses superscript (raised) numbers to identify secondary sources in the text and then provides the actual citations in a numbered list entitled "Notes" at the end of the report. The endnotes are numbered consecutively throughout the report. Some readers prefer the endnote format because it avoids the clutter of footnotes and because it's easy to use.

- *Author–Date Format:* Some report readers prefer the author–date format of documentation, regarding the method as a reasonable compromise between endnotes (which provide *no* reference information on the text page) and footnotes (which provide *all* the reference information on the text page). In the author–date format, the writer inserts at an appropriate point in the text the last name of the author and the year of publication in parentheses. Complete bibliographic information is then included in the Notes or References section at the end of the report.

plagiarism Using another person's words or ideas without giving proper credit

Standard citation formats are footnotes, endnotes, and author–year citations.

Word processing has simplified the generation of endnotes and footnotes.

Refining Your Draft

Once you have produced a first draft of your report, put it away for a few days. Doing so will enable you to view the draft with a fresh perspective and perhaps find a more effective means of communicating your ideas to the reader. Don't try to correct all problems in one review. Instead, look at this process as having three steps—revising first for content, then for style, and finally for correctness.

Revising

Revise first for content. Make sure you've included sufficient information to support each point, that you've included no extraneous information (regardless of how interesting it might be or how hard you worked to gather the information), that all information is accurate, and that the information is presented in an efficient and logical sequence. Keep the purpose of the report and the reader's needs and desires in mind as you review for content.

Once you're satisfied with the content of the report, revise for style. Ensure that your writing is clear and that you have used short, simple, vigorous, and concise words. Check whether you have used a variety of sentence types and have relied on active and passive voice appropriately. Do your paragraphs have unity and coherence, and are they of reasonable length? Have you maintained an overall tone of confidence, courtesy, sincerity, and objectivity? Finally, review your draft to ensure that you have used nondiscriminatory language and appropriate emphasis and subordination.

After you're confident about the content and style of your draft, revise once more for correctness. This revision step, known as *editing*, identifies and resolves any problems with grammar, spelling, punctuation, and word usage. Do not risk losing credibility with the reader by careless English usage. If possible, have a colleague review your draft to catch any errors you may have overlooked.

Formatting

Adopt a consistent, logical format, keeping the needs of the reader in mind.

The physical format of your report (margins, spacing, and the like) depends to a certain extent on the length and complexity of the report and the format preferred by either the organization or the reader.

Consistency and readability are the hallmarks of an effective format. For example, be sure that all of your first-level headings are formatted consistently; if they are not, the reader may not be able to tell which headings are superior or subordinate to other headings. Regardless of the format used, make sure the reader can instantly tell which are major headings and which are minor headings. You can differentiate the different levels of headings by using different fonts, font sizes, styles (such as bold or italic), and horizontal alignment.

If the organization or reader has a preferred format style, use it. Otherwise, follow the report formatting guidelines provided in the Style Manual at the back of this text.

Proofreading

First impressions are important. Even before reading the first line of your report, the reader will have formed an initial impression of the report—and of *you*. Make

CHECKLIST  13

Reviewing Your Report Draft

Introduction

✓ Is the report title accurate, descriptive, and honest?

✓ Is the research problem or the purpose of the study stated clearly and accurately?

✓ Is the scope of the study identified?

✓ Are all technical terms, or any terms used in a special way, defined?

✓ Are the procedures discussed in sufficient detail?

✓ Are any questionable decisions justified?

Findings

✓ Is the data analyzed completely, accurately, and appropriately?

✓ Is the analysis free of bias and misrepresentation?

✓ Is the data *interpreted* (its importance and implications discussed) rather than just presented?

✓ Are all calculations correct?

✓ Is all relevant data included and all irrelevant data excluded?

✓ Are visual aids correct, needed, clear, appropriately sized and positioned, and correctly labeled?

Summary, Conclusions, and Recommendations

✓ Is the wording used in the summary different from that used earlier to present the data initially?

✓ Are the conclusions supported by ample, credible evidence?

✓ Do the conclusions answer the questions or issues raised in the introduction?

✓ Are the recommendations reasonable in light of the conclusions?

✓ Does the report end with a sense of completion and convey an impression that the project is important?

Writing Style and Format

✓ Does the overall report take into account the needs and desires of the reader?

✓ Is the material appropriately organized?

✓ Are the headings descriptive, parallel, and appropriate in number?

✓ Are emphasis and subordination used effectively?

✓ Does each major section contain a preview, summary, and transition?

✓ Has proper verb tense been used throughout?

✓ Has an appropriate level of formality been used?

✓ Are all references to secondary sources properly documented?

✓ Is each needed report part included and in an appropriate format?

✓ Is the length of the report appropriate?

✓ Are the paragraphs of an appropriate length?

✓ Is the report free from spelling, grammar, and punctuation errors?

✓ Does the overall report provide a positive first impression and reflect care, neatness, and scholarship?

this impression a positive one by ensuring that the report bears a professional appearance.

After making all your revisions and formatting the various pages, give each page one final proofreading. Check closely for typographical errors. Assess the page's appearance. Have you arranged the pages in correct order and stapled them neatly? If you're submitting a photocopy, are all copies legible and of even darkness? Is each page free of wrinkles and smudges?

In short, let your pride of authorship shine through in every facet of your report. Appearances and details count. Review your entire document to ensure that you can answer "yes" to every question found in Checklist 13.

CHECKPOINT 11.2

RECALL   Write a capital T for *true* or F for *false* before each statement.

1. ____ The procedures used to gather the data represent the major contribution of the report.

2. ____ Conclusions must stem directly from the findings, and recommendations must stem directly from the conclusions.

3. ____ Most business reports should not use first- or second-person pronouns.

4. ____ You should prefer the present tense when discussing findings and conclusions from your study.

5. ____ You do not need to provide reference citations for using another person's statements if you paraphrase the statements in your own words.

VOCABULARY   Define the following terms in your own words.

6. direct quotation:

7. documentation:

8. paraphrase:

9. plagiarism:

COMPREHENSION

10. Refer to Section E of Figure 11.3 on page 293. Assume that you have just discussed the fourth topic and are now ready to begin discussing the fifth and last topic. Write an appropriate transition sentence that will move you smoothly from one topic to the next.

11. In Section D of Figure 11.3, assume that you consider the applicant's work experience to be the most important criterion. List five methods you might use to emphasize this idea.

CRITICAL THINKING

12. This chapter emphasizes the importance of documenting sources of data that are not your own words or ideas. Can you think of any instances in which documentation of such sources would *not* be necessary—or even appropriate?

Summary

Data is converted into information by careful analysis and is interpreted in the report in narrative form and by visual aids. Each table you construct from the data should be interpretable by itself, without reference to the text. Include only as much data in a table as is helpful, keeping the table as simple as possible. Arrange the data in logical order, most often in order of descending value. Do not analyze every figure from the table in your narrative. Instead, interpret the important points from the table, pointing out the major findings, trends, contradictions, and the like.

The most common report formats are manuscript (for formal reports) and letter or memorandum (for informal reports). The most common plans for organizing the findings of a study are by time, location, importance, and especially, criteria. Present conclusions at the beginning of the report unless the reader prefers the indirect plan, the reader will not be receptive toward the conclusions, or the topic is complex. Compose report headings carefully—in terms of their type, parallelism, length, and number.

The body of the report consists of the introduction, findings (the major part of the report), and, as needed, the summary, conclusions, and recommendations. Use an objective writing style, appropriate pronouns, and verb tenses that reflect the reader's time frame (rather than the writer's). Use emphasis and subordination techniques to help alert the reader to what you consider important; and use preview, summary, and transitional devices to help maintain coherence.

Use direct quotations sparingly; most references to secondary data should take the form of paraphrases. Provide appropriate documentation whenever you quote, paraphrase, or summarize someone else's work by using endnotes, footnotes, or the author–date method of citation. Do not omit important, relevant information from the report.

Revise the report in three distinct steps: first for content, then for style, and finally for correctness. The format selected should enhance the report's appearance and readability and should be based on the organization's and reader's preferences. Unless directed otherwise, follow generally accepted formatting guidelines for margins, report headings, and pagination. Use a simple, consistent design and make generous use of white space.

After all revisions and formatting have been completed, give each page one final proofreading. Make sure the final report reflects the highest standards of scholarship, critical thinking, and pride of authorship.

A Section of a Report

Problem

You are a manager at a software-development house that publishes communication software for the HAL and Pear microcomputers. Together, these two computers account for about 90% of the business market. In 2004, you were asked to survey users of communication software—a repeat of a similar study you undertook in 1999.

You conducted the survey using the same questionnaire and same procedures from the 1999 study. Now you've gathered the data, along with the comparable data collected in 1999, and have organized it roughly into draft tables, one of which is shown in Figure 11.4. You're now ready to put this table into final report format and analyze its contents.

FIGURE 11.4 Draft Table

Q. From what source did you obtain your last software program?

Source	1999						2004					
	Total		HAL		Pear		Total		HAL		Pear	
	N	%	N	%	N	%	N	%	N	%	N	%
Mail-order company	28	21.2	24	26.1	4	10.0	60	41.1	25	30.9	35	53.9
Online bulletin board	3	2.3	2	2.2	1	2.5	4	2.7	2	2.5	2	3.1
Retail outlet	70	53.0	46	50.0	24	60.0	63	43.2	44	54.3	19	29.2
Software publisher	9	6.8	4	4.3	5	12.5	10	6.8	4	4.9	6	9.2
Unauthorized copy	21	15.9	15	16.3	6	15.0	6	4.1	3	3.7	3	4.6
Other	1	.8	1	1.1	0	0.0	3	2.1	3	3.7	0	0.0
Total	132	100.0	92	100.0	40	100.0	146	100.0	81	100.0	65	100.0

Process

1. **Table Format**

   a. Examine the format of your draft table—the arrangement of columns and rows. Should you change anything for the final table?

   First, the year columns (1999 and 2004) should be reversed. The new data is more important than the old data, so putting it first will emphasize it.
   Second, the rows need to be rearranged. They're now in alphabetical order but should be rearranged in descending order according to the first amount column—the 2004 total column. Doing this will put the most important data first in the table.

   b. Assuming that you will have many tables in your final report, is there some way to condense the information in this table without undue loss of precision or detail?

   Although the number of respondents is important, the readers of my report will be much more interested in the percentages. Therefore, I'll give only the

The 3Ps
Problem, Process,
Product

Writing a Concise Message

total number of respondents for each column and put that figure immediately under each column heading.

Also, I see immediately that very few people obtained their software from online bulletin boards either in 1999 or 2004, so I'll combine that category with the "Other" category.

These changes are shown in Figure 11.5.

FIGURE 11.5 Revised Table

	2004			1999		
Source	Total (*N* = 146)	HAL (*N* = 81)	Pear (*N* = 65)	Total (*N* = 132)	HAL (*N* = 92)	Pear (*N* = 40)
Retail outlet	43	54	29	53	50	60
Mail-order company	41	31	54	21	26	10
Software publisher	7	5	9	7	4	13
Unauthorized copy	4	3	5	16	17	15
Other	5	7	3	3	3	2
Total	100	100	100	100	100	100

2. Table Interpretation

a. Study the table in Figure 11.5. If you had space to make only one statement about this table, what would it be?

Retail outlets and mail-order companies are equally important sources for obtaining software, together accounting for more than four-fifths of all sources.

b. What other 2004 data should you discuss in your narrative?

HAL and Pear users obtain their software in different ways: the majority of HAL users obtain theirs from retail outlets whereas the majority of Pear users obtain theirs from mail-order firms.

c. What should you point out in comparing 2004 data with 1999 data?

The market share for retail outlets decreased by almost 20% from 1999 to 2004 while the market share for mail-order companies almost doubled.

Also, the use of unauthorized copies appears to be decreasing (although the actual figures for both years are probably somewhat higher than these self-reported figures).

3. Report Writing

a. Develop an effective generic heading and an effective talking heading for this section of the report. Which one will you use?

313

Generic Heading: **SOURCES OF SOFTWARE PURCHASES**
Talking Heading: **MAIL ORDERS CATCHING UP WITH RETAIL SALES**

Because I do not know personally the readers of the report and their preferences, I'll make the conservative choice and use a generic heading.

b. Compose an effective topic (preview) sentence for this section.

Respondents were asked to indicate the source of the last software program they purchased.

c. Where will you position the table for this section?

At the end of the first paragraph that refers to the table.

d. What verb tense will you use in this section?

Past tense for the procedures; present tense for the findings.

e. Assume that the next report section discusses the cost of software. Compose an effective summary/transition sentence for this section of the report.

Perhaps the increasing reliance on mail-order purchases is one reason that the cost of communication software has decreased since 1999.

Product

SOURCES OF SOFTWARE PURCHASES

Respondents were asked to indicate the source of the last software program they purchased. As shown in Table 8, retail outlets and mail-order companies are now equally important sources for obtaining software, together accounting for more than four-fifths of all sources. HAL and Pear users obtain their software in different ways: the majority of HAL users obtain theirs from retail outlets whereas the majority of Pear users obtain theirs from mail-order firms.

TABLE 8. SOURCE OF LAST SOFTWARE PROGRAM
(In Percentages)

	2004			1999		
Source	Total (N = 146)	HAL (N = 81)	Pear (N = 65)	Total (N = 132)	HAL (N = 92)	Pear (N = 40)
Retail outlet	43	54	29	53	50	60
Mail-order co.	41	31	54	21	26	10
Software pub.	7	5	9	7	4	13
Unauthor. copy	4	3	5	16	17	15
Other	5	7	3	3	3	2
Total	100	100	100	100	100	100

Retail outlets have decreased in popularity (down 10%) since 1998, while mail-order companies have dramatically increased in popularity (up 20%). Also, the use of unauthorized copies appears to be decreasing (although the actual figure is probably somewhat higher than these self-reported figures).

Perhaps the increasing reliance on mail-order purchases is one reason that the cost of communication software has declined since 1998.

COST OF SOFTWARE

. . .

Looking Ahead

Kathryn Butler arrived at Kathryn Butler's desk early because Kathryn Butler had an early morning meeting with Kathryn Butler's staff. Kathryn Butler brought Kathryn Butler's latest spreadsheet with Kathryn Butler because Kathryn Butler needed Kathryn Butler's staff to help Kathryn Butler with Kathryn Butler's quarterly report.

Let's stop right there. What a boring, choppy, and dull paragraph. The problem, of course, is that the paragraph does not use pronouns. The correct use of pronouns avoids needless repetition and makes writing flow more smoothly. We'll learn about the correct use of pronouns—and adjectives and adverbs as well—in the next chapter.

Key Terms

direct quotation	paraphrase
documentation	plagiarism
generic headings	talking headings

Exercises

Interpreting the Data

1 Interpreting a Table   The following sentences interpret the table in Figure 11.2 on page 288. Analyze each sentence to determine whether it represents the data in the table accurately.

a. Males and females alike believe Apex is an asset to the community.

b. More than one-fifth of the females (22%) did not respond.

c. Age and the generation gap bring about different beliefs.

d. Married males over age 50 had the most positive opinions.

e. Females disagree more than males—probably because most of the workers at Apex are male.

f. Female respondents tend to disagree with the statement.

g. Apex should be proud of the fact that four-fifths of the residents believe the company is an asset to the community.

h. Thirteen percent of the younger residents have doubts about whether Apex is an asset to the community.

i. More single than married residents didn't care or had no opinion about the topic.

j. Overall, the residents believe that 8% of the company is not an asset to the community.

2 Interpreting Charts   Examine the following interpretations of the data shown in Model 15 on page 274. Indicate whether each statement accurately represents the data in those charts.

a. The industrial sector has provided most of Apex's sales and profits since 1999.
b. The average age of Apex customers has increased since 1979.
c. The average age of Apex customers reached a peak of 45 in 1994.
d. Nearly half of Apex's sales in 2004 were to the industrial sector.
e. More than half of Apex's sales in 1999 were to the industrial sector.
f. Nearly half of Apex's sales in 1979 were to the consumer sector.
g. The decline in Apex's consumer sales is due to the increase in the average age of the firm's consumer customers.
h. Sales to the industrial sector have risen steadily since 1979.
i. Sales to the consumer sector have fallen steadily since 1979.

Short Report—Data Furnished

3 Caller ID   You are the research assistant for Congresswoman Anna Murray. A constituent has written her asking that she introduce legislation to ban telephone call identification. Congresswoman Murray sent you the letter with this handwritten message attached: "I really don't know much about this telephone service. Please research it and prepare a short informal report (no tables, charts, or footnotes, please) so that I can make an informed decision about this matter. Should I or should I not introduce legislation to ban this type of telephone service?"

You've talked to numerous people at the telephone company and have read brochures, magazine articles, and editorials about this topic. You've jotted down the following notes—in no particular order:

a. Caller ID: A telephone service that displays the phone number of the person calling you.
b. You can use Caller ID to decide which calls you want to answer and simply ignore the others.
c. It can threaten the privacy and personal safety of users.
d. Every caller's number would be displayed—even those with unpublished numbers who have paid extra for their privacy.
e. Delivery businesses (taxis and pizzerias, for example) can use Caller ID to ensure that telephone orders are legitimate.
f. The device that displays the callers' numbers costs up to $80.
g. Emergency services can use the number to dispatch help quickly for people who may be too panicky to give an address.
h. Customer service agents at your local utility or your stockbroker can immediately call up your file when you call to serve you more efficiently. A computer can even be programmed to do this automatically as soon as your call goes through.
i. Caller ID allows businesses to record the number of every caller—and perhaps even to sell your number to telemarketers.
j. New Jersey Bell Telephone Co. began the service after learning that a whopping 1.2 million of its customers had received threatening or obscene calls.
k. If you receive a threatening, obscene, or harassing call, you can record the number to notify the police or phone company without their having to tap your phone. (You can even call the person back yourself, although that might not be wise.)
l. People who make calls from their homes may have legitimate reasons for not wanting their private numbers revealed—law enforcement officers, doctors, psychiatrists, or social workers, for example.
m. New Jersey Bell reported that phone-trace requests in Hudson County dropped 49% after Caller ID was established—even though only 2.3% of its customers used it.
n. It's now available in a growing number of states.

o. You can even program Caller ID to prevent your phone from receiving calls from a specified number, thus preventing harassers from repeatedly calling your number from the same phone.

p. Runaway children might be scared to call home for fear of being traced.

q. Only a few states require a feature that lets callers prevent their numbers from being displayed (which defeats the whole purpose of the service).

r. New Jersey Bell says complaints about obscene or harassing phone calls have dropped nearly 50% since it began offering Caller ID.

s. You can refuse to answer telephone sales pitches that come in the middle of dinner.

t. It threatens the privacy of individuals who call suicide-prevention, drug-treatment, AIDS, and abortion-counseling hotlines.

u. It took 23 years to catch and convict Bobby Gene Stice, who used the telephone for two decades to terrorize thousands of California women. Caller ID could have stopped him in a day.

v. The service charge for the Caller ID feature is as much as $8.50 monthly.

Organize and analyze the data, and then write the requested recommendation report. Use whatever report headings would be helpful.

4 **Generic Products**   North Star is a producer of consumer products with annual sales of $847.2 million. It has 4.5% of the consumer market for its six consumer products (soap, deodorant, ammonia, chili, canned ham, and frozen vegetables).

On July 8 of this year, Paul Gettisfield, sales manager, asked you, a product manager, to study the feasibility of North Star's entering the generic-products market. Generic products are products that do not have brand names but instead carry a plain generic label, such as "Paper Towels." Generic products are typically not advertised; they involve less packaging, less processing, and cheaper ingredients than brand names; and they compete both with private brands (those distributed solely by individual store chains such as A&P and Kroger) and with national brands (those available for sale at all grocery stores and advertised nationally). At the present time, North Star produces only national brands.

Paul specifically asked you *not* to explore whether North Star had the necessary plant capacity. He wanted you only to provide up-to-date information on the generic market in general and to explore likely consumer acceptance of generic brands for the products that North Star produces. He is quite interested in learning the results of your research.

In August you conducted a mail survey of 1,500 consumers in the three states (California, Texas, and Arizona) that constitute your largest market. Responses were received from 832 consumers to the following questions; responses are provided for all 832 consumers and for the 237 largest consumers (those who indicated that they did 51% to 100% of their household shopping):

Have you purchased a food generic product (such as canned fruit or vegetables) in the last month?

> All consumers: 36% yes, 64% no
> Largest consumers: 29% yes, 71% no

Was this the first time you had purchased a food generic product?

> All consumers: 18% yes, 82% no
> Largest consumers: 20% yes, 80% no

Have you purchased a nonfood generic product (such as paper towels or soap) in the last month?

All consumers: 60% yes, 40% no
Largest consumers: 59% yes, 41% no

Was this the first time you had purchased a nonfood generic product?

All consumers: 5% yes, 95% no
Largest consumers: 7% yes, 93% no

If you could save at least 30% by purchasing a generic brand rather than a national brand, would you purchase a generic brand of any of the following products?

Bar of soap: 43% yes, 57% no, 0% don't use this product
Deodorant: 31% yes, 67% no, 2% don't use this product
Ammonia: 80% yes, 10% no, 10% don't use this product
Chili: 34% yes, 52% no, 14% don't use this product
Canned ham: 19% yes, 44% no, 37% don't use this product
Frozen vegetables: 54% yes, 30% no, 16% don't use this product

You also asked the local North Star sales representatives to audit 20 randomly selected chain supermarkets in each of these three states in August. Personal observation showed that 39 of the stores stocked generic brands, 37 of these 39 stocked 100 or more generic items, and 15 had separate generic-product sections. All but 3 of the 60 stores stocked all six products that North Star now produces.

In gathering your data, you also made the following notes from three secondary sources:

1. *Hammond's Market Reports,* Gary, IN, 2004, pp. 1027–1030: This annual index lists various information for more than 2,000 consumer products. The percentages of market share for the six products North Star produces are as follows:

	1997	2000	2003
Generic brands	1.5%	2.6%	7.3%
Private labels	31.6%	30.7%	27.8%
National brands	66.9%	66.7%	64.9%

2. H. R. Nolan, "No-Name Brands: An Update," *Supermarket Management,* April 2003, pp. 31–37.

   a. Generic brands are typically priced 30% to 50% below national brands. (p. 31)
   b. Consumers require a 36% saving on a bar of soap and 40% savings on deodorant to motivate them to switch to a generic. (p. 32)
   c. Consumer awareness of generics has tripled since 1979. (p. 33)
   d. "The easiest way to become a no-name store is to ignore no-name brands." (direct quotation from p. 33)
   e. Many leading brand manufacturers feel compelled to produce the lower-profit generic brands because either the market has grown too big to ignore or the inroads generic brands have made on their own brands have left them with idle capacity. (p. 35)

3. Edward J. Rauch and Pamela G. McCleary, "National Brands to Play a Bit Part in the Future," *Grocery Business,* Fall 2002, pp. 118–120.

   a. Eight out of ten food-chains believe their costs will rise more than their prices this year. (p. 118)
   b. Generics are now available in 84% of the stores nationwide and account for about 4% of the store space. (p. 118)
   c. "Supermarket executives foresee a drop in shelf space allocated to brand products and an increase in the space allocated to generics and private labels. Many experts predict that supermarkets will ultimately carry no

more than the top two brands in a category plus a private label and a generic label." (p. 119)

d. Today, 37% of the grocery stores have switched from paper bags to the less expensive plastic bags for packaging customer purchases, even though the plastic bags are nonbiodegradable. (p. 119)

e. Starting from nearly zero in 1979, generics have acquired 7% of the $275 billion grocery market. Many observers predict they will go up to 25% within the next five years. (p. 120)

Analyze the data, prepare whatever visual aids would by helpful, and then write a formal report for Gettisfield.

Short Report—Secondary Data Needed

5 The Female Manager Using the appropriate business indexes (print or online), identify three women who are presidents or CEOs of companies listed on the New York Stock Exchange. Provide information on their backgrounds. Did they make it to the top by rising through the ranks, by starting the firm, by taking over from another family member, or by following some other path?

Analyze the effectiveness of these three individuals. How profitable are the firms they head in relation to others in the industry? Are their firms more or less profitable now than when they assumed the top job? Finally, try to uncover data regarding their management styles—how they see their role, how they relate to their employees, what problems they've experienced, and the like.

From your study of these three individuals, are there any valid conclusions you can draw? Write a report objectively presenting and analyzing the information you've gathered.

6 Keyboarding Skills You are the director of training for an aerospace firm located in Seattle, Washington. Your superior, Charles R. Underwood, personnel manager, is concerned that so many of the firm's 2,000 white-collar employees use their computers for hours each day but still do not know how to touch-type. He believes the hunt-and-peck method is inefficient and increases the possibility of making errors when inputting data, thus lowering its reliability.

Underwood has asked you to recommend a software program that teaches the user how to touch-type. He is specifically interested in a program that is IBM-compatible, is geared toward adults, is educationally sound, and can be learned on an individual basis without an instructor present.

Identify and evaluate three to five keyboarding software programs that meet these criteria, and write a report recommending the best one to Underwood. Justify your choice.

Short Report—Primary Data Needed

7 Career Choices Explore a career in which you are interested. Determine the job outlook, present level of employment, salary trends, typical duties, working conditions, educational or experience requirements, and the like. Interview someone holding this position to gain firsthand impressions. Then write up your findings in a report to your instructor. Include at least five secondary sources and at least one table or visual aid in your report.

8 Intercultural Dimensions To what extent does network and cable television accurately portray members of cultural, ethnic, and racial minorities? To what extent are they portrayed at all during prime time (8 P.M. to 11 P.M.)? In what types of roles are they shown, and what is their relationship with nonminority characters? As assistant to the director of public relations of the National Minority Alliance, you are interested in such questions.

Locate and review at least three journal articles on this topic. Then develop a definition of the term *minority*. Randomly select and view at least ten prime-time television shows, and develop a form for recording the needed data on minority representation in these shows. As part of your research, compare the proportion of minority members in this country with their representation on prime-time television. Integrate your primary and secondary data into a report. Use objective language, being careful to present ample data to support any conclusions or recommendations you may make.

Long Report—Primary Data Needed

9 Frozen Yogurt   Assume that you have been asked by Jim Miller, executive vice president of Jefferson Industries, to write an exploratory report on the feasibility of Jefferson opening a frozen yogurt store in Akron, Ohio. If the preliminary data you gather warrants further exploration of this project, a professional venture-consultant group will be hired to conduct an in-depth, "dollars-and-cents" study. Your job, then, is to recommend whether such an expensive follow-up study is justified. Assume that Jefferson has the financial resources to support such a venture if it looks promising.

You can immediately think of several areas you'll want to explore: the general market outlook for frozen yogurt stores, the demographic makeup of Akron (home of the University of Akron), the local economic climate, franchise opportunities in the industry, and the like. Undoubtedly, other topics (or criteria) will surface as you brainstorm the problem.

Carry through the entire research process for this project—planning the study, collecting the data, organizing and analyzing the data, and writing the report. Write the body of the report using formal language, organize the study by criteria, and place the conclusions and recommendations at the end. (*Note:* If you gathered any data by completing the exercises at the end of Chapter 10, integrate that data into your study as needed.)

10 Student Living Arrangements   Darlene Anderson, a real estate developer and president of Anderson and Associates, is exploring the feasibility of building a large student-apartment complex on a lot her firm owns two blocks from campus. Even though the city planning commission believes there is already enough student housing, Anderson thinks she can succeed if she addresses specific problems of present housing. She has asked you, her executive assistant, to survey students to determine their views of off-campus living. Specifically, she wants you to develop a ranked listing of the most important attributes of student housing. How important to students are such criteria as price, location (access to campus, shopping, public transportation, and the like), space and layout, furnishings (furnished versus unfurnished), social activities, parking, pets policy, and the like?

In addition, the architect has drawn a plan that features the following options: private hotel-like rooms (sleeping and sitting area and private bath but no kitchen); private one-room efficiency apartments; one-bedroom two-person apartments; and four-bedroom four-person apartments. Which of these arrangements would students most likely rent, given their present economic situation? Would another alternative be more appealing to them?

Develop a questionnaire and administer it to a sample of students. Then analyze the data and write a report for Anderson.

Writing a Business Report

PROBLEM The manufacturing facility where you work employs three data-entry operators who work full-time keyboarding production, personnel, and inventory data into a computer. This data is then sent via secure Internet connection to the headquarters minicomputer, where it becomes part of the corporate database for financial, production, and personnel management.

Last year, one of the operators was absent from work for two weeks for a condition diagnosed as carpal tunnel syndrome, a neuromuscular disorder of the tendons and tissue in the wrists caused by repeated hand motions. Her symptoms included a dull ache in the wrist and excruciating pain in the shoulder and neck. Her doctor treated her with anti-inflammatory medicine and a cortisone injection, and she has had no further problems. However, just last week a second data-entry operator experienced similar symptoms; her doctor diagnosed her ailment as "repeated-motion illness" or RSI (repetitive stress injury).

Because the company anticipates further automation in the future, with more data-entry operators to be hired, your boss has asked you to gather additional information on this condition. Once the extent of the problem is known, she wants you to make any appropriate recommendations regarding the work environment—posture, furniture, work habits, rest breaks, and the like—that will alleviate this problem.

PROCESS Compose a few paragraphs describing how you went about solving this problem. In narrative form, provide such information as the following:

1. The problem statement and subproblems for your report

2. How you went about gathering the needed secondary data

3. How you evaluated the quality and relevance of any data you collected from online searching

4. How you decided whether to use a direct or indirect organizational plan

5. The degree of formality you decided to use

6. Factors you use to determine whether to include any visual aids

PRODUCT Compose your five- to seven-page double-spaced report, following the five steps in the writing process (planning, drafting, revising, formatting, and proofreading). Include a title page and bibliography or reference list. Format the final version in appropriate style (refer to the Style Manual for formatting guidelines).

12

Using Pronouns, Adjectives, and Adverbs in Business Communication

On the Job

GAIL HART-DAVIS
RPP Medical Assistant

Gail Hart-Davis was transcribing a medical consulta-tion report that Dr. Ruiz had dictated that morning. Here is what she had transcribed so far:

> Adrian Shoemaker was seen for an emergency consultation early this morning concerning her increasing health problems with both of her lower extremities but primarily her left knee. Shoemaker is a young female employee who is grossly overweight and is now an assistant manager in our administrative area. Her severe knee problems started with her right knee soon after she hit it sharply on a computer desk about five years ago, resulting in an immediate arthroscopic procedure to her right knee.

At the end of Chapter 11, we mentioned the importance of pronouns in business writing (the preceding passage includes eight pronouns). To get an idea of the important role that modifiers (adjectives and adverbs) also play in our writing, read through Gail's first paragraph and circle each adjective and adverb. You will find that more than half of the words (41 out of 80) are modifiers. Read on to learn how to use these important parts of speech correctly.

Pronouns

As noted earlier, pronouns are little words that can cause big problems—until, that is, you study this chapter. Although many thousands of nouns (*millions*, if you include proper nouns) exist, the English language includes fewer than 100 pronouns. The most common ones are listed below:

all	another	any	anybody	anyone
anything	both	each	each one	each other
either	everybody	everyone	everything	few
he	her	hers	him	his
I	it	its	many	me
mine	my	neither	no one	nobody
none	nothing	one	one another	ones
other	our	ours	several	she
some	somebody	someone	something	that
their	theirs	them	these	they
this	those	us	we	what
whatever	which	whichever	who	whoever
whom	whomever	whose	whosoever	you
your	yours			

Learn these 67 most common pronouns. (The important point is to recognize that these words are, in fact, pronouns and therefore follow special rules of grammar.)

Because pronouns take the place of nouns, your first job is to ensure that the noun the pronoun replaces is clear. Consider, for example, the following sentence:

Robin explained the proposal to Joy, but *she* was not happy with it.

Who was not happy with the proposal—Robin or Joy? It is not clear from the sentence. This error of writing is called a *vague pronoun reference*. In such a situation, you have no choice but to rename the noun instead of using a pronoun.

Robin explained the proposal to Joy, but *Robin* was not happy with it.

OR: Robin explained the proposal to Joy, but *Joy* was not happy with it.

Remember also that a pronoun replaces a noun—and the noun it replaces must be clear, which generally means that it must be stated either in the same sentence or in a previous sentence.

THE FAR SIDE BY GARY LARSON

"So, then ... would that be 'us the people' or 'we the people'?"

NOT: *They* make *you* attend these orientation sessions.

BUT: *Management* makes all *new employees* attend these orientation sessions.

The Case of Personal Pronouns

Personal pronouns include the pronouns *I, you, he, she, it,* and *they* and their related forms (such as *my, mine, your, yours, her,* and *us*). The **case** of a personal pronoun indicates how it is used in the sentence (either *nominative, objective,* or *possessive,* which we will explain shortly).

Nominative Case   The nominative-case pronouns are *I, we, you, he, she, it,* and *they.* In Table 12.1, **person** is the characteristic of a pronoun that indicates whether a person is speaking (first person), being spoken to (second person), or being spoken about (third person). **Gender** refers to the sex of a pronoun—that is, masculine (*he*), feminine (*she*), or neuter (*it*). A pronoun that can refer to either a male or female (such as *child* or *employee*) is considered to be of *common* gender.

Study Table 12.1 to avoid errors in using personal pronouns in the nominative case. Work through this table by inserting each listed pronoun into the sentence "___ smelled like a rose."

Whenever a pronoun is used as the subject of a verb, it must be in the nominative case.

She manually counted the votes from the first and second precincts. (*"She" is the subject of the sentence.*)

Arthur agreed, but *he* failed to give convincing reasons. (*"He" is the subject of the second independent clause.*)

Cathy wanted to know whether *I* had finished my assignments. (*"I" is the subject of the dependent clause.*)

Nominative pronouns are also used as subject complements. Thus, when a pronoun follows a linking verb (such as *am, are, was, were, is,* or *has been*) and renames the subject, it must be in the nominative case.

It could have been *he* who inadvertently gave away the secret. (*it = he*)

This is *she.* (*this = she*)

If Earl were *he,* he would have acted differently. (*Earl = he*)

The nominee was expected to be *she.* (*nominee = she*)

When a telephone caller asks for you by name, how do you respond? Do you say, "This is him" or "This is her"? Such a response might be tolerated in

case The form of a pronoun that indicates how it is used in the sentence

I, we, you, he, she, it, and *they* are the nominative pronouns.

person The characteristic of a pronoun that indicates whether a person is speaking, is spoken to, or is spoken about

gender The characteristic of a pronoun that indicates whether it is masculine, feminine, or neuter

A complement renames the subject.

TABLE 12.1

To remember that "I" is first person, think of the "I" as a "1"—for *first.*

Nominative Case

	Singular	Plural
First person	I	we
Second person	you	you
Third person: Masculine gender Feminine gender Neuter gender	 he she it	 they they they

TABLE 12.2

Objective Case

	Singular	Plural
First person	me	us
Second person	you	you
Third person:		
Masculine gender	him	them
Feminine gender	her	them
Neuter gender	it	them

informal oral communication because it sounds so natural, but it would not be acceptable in writing. Grammatically, of course, you should respond, "This is *he*" or "This is *she*." However, to avoid sounding pompous, you might opt for the more graceful "This is Johnny" or "This is Jenny."

Objective Case   The objective-case pronouns are *me, us, you, him, her, it,* and *them.* Logically enough, objective-case pronouns serve as *objects*—direct objects, indirect objects, or objects of prepositions. Study Table 12.2 to avoid errors in using personal pronouns in the objective case. Work through the table by inserting each listed pronoun into the sentence "She thanked ___."

- **Direct Object** A pronoun serves as a direct object when it receives the action of the verb.

    Katie asked *me* for help on the project.

    The training director asked *them* to complete the exercise.

- **Indirect Object** A pronoun serves as an indirect object when it tells to whom or for whom the action of the verb was done.

    Please give *her* your response by tomorrow afternoon.

    Did Fatima hand *him* the papers he needed?

- **Object of a Preposition** The pronoun following the preposition is its object.

    Ms. Batista worked with *me* to complete the examination on time. (*"With me" is the prepositional phrase.*)

    The monthly revision was handled by *him.* (*"By him" is the prepositional phrase.*)

Possessive Case   Possessive-case pronouns show ownership. Most (but not all) personal pronouns have two possessive forms. Work through Table 12.3 by

You can often avoid sounding stuffy or unnatural by rewording the sentence.

Me, us, you, him, her, it, and *them* are the objective pronouns.

Note that the pronoun *you* can be both singular and plural and both nominative and objective.

Both direct and indirect objects must be in the objective case.

Remember that a sentence with an indirect object must also contain a direct object.

Most possessive pronouns have two forms.

TABLE 12.3

Possessive Case

	Singular	Plural
First person	my/mine	our/ours
Second person	your/yours	your/yours
Third person:		
Masculine gender	his	their/theirs
Feminine gender	her/hers	their/theirs
Neuter gender	its	their/theirs

inserting the listed pronoun into either the sentence "This is ___ report" or the sentence "This report is ___."

Use *my, our, your, his, her, its,* or *their* when the pronoun comes *before* the noun it modifies. Use *mine, ours, yours, his, hers, its,* or *theirs* when the pronoun comes *after* the noun it modifies.

This is *my* report.	This report is *mine.*
Mr. Ortiz was *her* colleague.	Mr. Ortiz was a colleague of *hers.*
It is *their* decision.	The decision is *theirs.*

Do not confuse possessive pronouns ending in *s* with contractions. Possessive personal pronouns *never* contain an apostrophe; contractions *always* do.

> **Contractions contain apostrophes; possessive personal pronouns do not.**

- *its/it's: Its* is a possessive pronoun; *it's* is a contraction for "it is" or "it has."

  It's time to let the department increase *its* budget.

- *their/they're: Their* is a possessive pronoun; *they're* is a contraction for "they are."

  They're too busy with *their* work to attend the conference.

- *theirs/there's: Theirs* is a possessive pronoun; *there's* is a contraction for "there is."

  We finished our meal, but *there's* no time for them to finish *theirs.*

- *whose/who's: Whose* is a possessive pronoun; *who's* is a contraction for "who is" or "who has."

  Who's going to let us know *whose* turn it is to make coffee?

> *Whose* is not a personal pronoun but is included here because of its frequent confusion with the contraction *who's.*

- *your/you're: Your* is a possessive pronoun; *you're* is a contraction for "you are."

  You're going to present *your* report first.

To test for the correct form (possessive pronoun or contraction), mentally substitute the full term for the contraction. If the substitution does not make sense, use the possessive form. For instance, in the first example above:

It is time to let the department increase *it is* budget.

"It is time" makes sense, so the contraction (with the apostrophe) is correct. "It is budget" does not make sense, so the possessive pronoun (without the apostrophe) is correct.

A **gerund** is the *-ing* form of a verb used as a noun. Use the possessive case for a pronoun that modifies a gerund.

> **gerund** The *-ing* form of a verb used as a noun

Antonia questioned *my leaving* so soon. (*not "me leaving"*)

Their raising so many questions delayed the adjournment. (*not "them raising" or "they raising"*)

Art objected to *his going* to the meeting. (*not "him going"*)

Remember that gerunds are nouns. If you have trouble with pronouns that modify a gerund, simply substitute another noun for the gerund. For example, revising the sentences above makes clear that the possessive pronoun is the correct form.

Antonia questioned *my* decision to leave so soon.

Their questions delayed the adjournment.

Art objected to *his* presence at the meeting.

VOCABULARY   Define the following terms in your own words.

1. case:

2. gender:

3. gerund:

4. person:

COMPREHENSION

5. Underline the correct pronoun in the following sentences, and in the space at the left, indicate whether it functions as a subject (S) or complement (C).

   a. ⎯⎯ Estralita became a manager when (he, him) transferred to the Tulsa office.

   b. ⎯⎯ I don't want to point fingers, but it was (them, they) who leaked the results.

   c. ⎯⎯ Matsu asked if (I, me) were responsible.

   d. ⎯⎯ If I were (her, she), I would have handled matters differently.

   e. ⎯⎯ Could it have been (he, him) who lost the combination to the safe?

6. Underline the correct pronoun in the following sentences, and in the space at the left, indicate whether it functions as a direct object (DO), an indirect object (IO), or an object of a preposition (OP).

   a. ⎯⎯ Mr. Patterson gave (I, me) the keys to the safe.

   b. ⎯⎯ Mr. Patterson gave the keys to the safe to (I, me).

   c. ⎯⎯ Mr. Patterson asked (I, me) to take the keys to the safe.

   d. ⎯⎯ The president asked (them, they) if they would critique her draft of the announcement.

   e. ⎯⎯ For (them, they), the solution to the problem was as simple as determining the expected rate of return.

7. Underline the correct pronoun in the following sentences.

   a. I appreciated (you/your) handling that complex question.

   b. (It's, Its) a shame that the company lost (it's, its) lease.

   c. (Their/They're) jobs are finished so (their/they're) going home.

   d. (Theirs/There's) no way this extra computer could be (theirs/there's).

   e. (Whose/Who's) going to decide (whose/who's) project will be funded?

   f. (Your/You're) vacation request was granted because (your/you're) the senior manager.

Problems in Determining Pronoun Case

Discussed below are situations that sometimes cause problems in determining the correct case of pronouns.

To determine the correct form of the pronoun, ignore the first noun in compound expressions.

Compound Subjects and Objects Pay special attention to the correct use of pronouns in compound subjects and objects. No one (we hope) would say, "Me is having fun." However, you occasionally hear people say, "Mitzi and me are having fun." To avoid problems like this, mentally omit the first noun. You can then generally "hear" the correct form of the pronoun.

NOT: Betty and *me* are having fun.

BUT: Betty and *I* are having fun. (*I am having fun.*)

NOT: Are L. J. and *them* finished with their audit?

BUT: Are L. J. and *they* finished with their audit? (*Are they finished?*)

NOT: Mr. Matthews asked Ms. Little and *I* for help.

BUT: Mr. Mathews asked Ms. Little and *me* for help. (*Jill asked me for help.*)

NOT: To Betty and *I*, the solution was obvious.

BUT: To Betty and *me*, the solution was obvious. (*To me, the solution was obvious.*)

Be especially careful with compound objects preceded by *between*. Because *between* is a preposition, the pronoun must be in the objective case.

NOT: Between Arturo and *I*, we could answer all of the questions.

BUT: Between Arturo and *me*, we could answer all of the questions.

An appositive identifies another noun or pronoun that comes directly before it.

Appositives When a pronoun is used with an appositive, mentally omit the noun to determine the correct case of the pronoun.

We employees need to speak with one voice. (*We need to speak with one voice.*)

The union wants *us* employees to speak with one voice. (*The union wants us to speak with one voice.*)

Comparisons When a pronoun follows *than* or *as* in a statement of comparison, sometimes you need to mentally supply any missing words to select the correct form of pronoun.

NOT: Mr. Liu works harder than *me*.

BUT: Mr. Liu works harder than *I*. (*Mr. Liu works harder than I* "do.")

NOT: Eduardo is not as creative as *her*.

BUT: Eduardo is not as creative as *she*. (*Eduardo "is" not as creative as she* is.)

NOT: Uncertainty worries the new employees more than *I*.

BUT: Uncertainty worries the new employees more than *me*. (*Uncertainty worries the new employees more than "it worries" me.*)

***Self* Pronouns**   The *-self* pronouns are shown in Table 12.4.

Pronouns ending in *-self* either emphasize the noun or pronoun already expressed or reflect the action to the subject.

> I will tell her myself. (*emphasizes the pronoun "I"*)

> Armando himself was confused by her statement. (*emphasizes the noun "Armando"*)

> Ms. Zhu disappointed herself by her inaction to challenge the decision. (*reflects the action to "Ms. Zhu"*)

Never use the words *hisself, ourself, themself,* or *theirselves.* Also, do not use a *-self* pronoun unless the noun or pronoun to which it refers appears in the same sentence.

> **NOT:** Bruce did the work *hisself.*

> **BUT:** Bruce did the work *himself.*

> **NOT:** The award went to Douglas and *myself.*

> **BUT:** The award went to Douglas and *me.*

Who/Whom   *Who* (or *whoever*) is the nominative form and *whom* (or *whomever*) is the objective form. Here's a hint: if *he* or *she* can be substituted, *who* is the correct choice; if *him* or *her* can be substituted, *whom* is the correct choice.

Remember: *who* = *he; whom* = *him.*

> *Who* is chairing the meeting? (*He is chairing the meeting.*)
> Mr. Aguirre wanted to know *who* was responsible. (*He was responsible.*)

> To *whom* shall we mail the specifications? (*Mail them to him.*)

> Louise is the type of person *who* can be depended upon. (*She can be depended upon.*)

> Louise is the type of person *whom* we can depend upon. (*We can depend upon her.*)

What's for Dinner?   WORD|wise

Lawyers: Split-Fee Soup, Claim Chowder, Squid Pro Quo, Porpoise Delecti, and Shysters Rockefeller

Writers: Stephen à la King, Spuds Terkel, and Truman Compote with Robert Frosting

Actors: Beauty and the Beets, Salad of the Lambs, Dead Pullets Society, and Butch Cassoulet and the Sun-Dried Tomatoes

---

TABLE 12.4

Self Pronouns	Singular	Plural
First person	myself	ourselves
Second person	yourself	yourselves
Third person:		
Masculine gender	himself	themselves
Feminine gender	herself	themselves
Neuter gender	itself	themselves

CHECKPOINT 12.2

COMPREHENSION

1. Underline the correct pronoun in the following sentences.

   a. (Us/We) single workers complained about the cost of our health benefits.
   b. Louise and (her/she) will be at the sales booth all afternoon.
   c. Ral asked (us/we) part-time employees to reconsider our action.
   d. Just between you and (I/me), I have real doubts about that decision.
   e. Mr. Friesen wanted Paula and (I/me) to attend the court hearing.
   f. Why were Ms. Young and (he/him) standing in line to register?

2. Underline the correct pronoun in the following sentences.

   a. (Who/Whom) do you know on the FTC staff?
   b. (Whoever/Whomever) you select must begin work immediately.
   c. It was Pauline (who/whom) made the original concession.
   d. Ms. Bruno was more concerned than (I/me) about the new developments.
   e. Laura and (I/me/myself) invested in high-tech stocks.
   f. Unfortunately, Kun is not as productive as (her/she).
   g. We (ourself/ourselves) were confused by the ballot.

Adjective or Adverb?

Recall from Chapter 3 that adjectives modify nouns or pronouns and adverbs modify verbs, adjectives, or other adverbs. Modifiers are present in most sentences. Even as short a sentence as "Sit down" contains a modifier.

> I tend to be *quiet* when I'm around *assertive* people.
> Maurice spoke *very excitedly* about the option that was *less* popular.

In the first sentence, *quiet* is an adjective modifying the pronoun *I*, and *assertive* is an adjective modifying the noun *people*. In the second sentence, *excitedly* is an adverb modifying the verb *spoke*, *very* is an adverb modifying the adverb *excitedly*, and *less* is an adverb modifying the adjective *popular*.

Which of the following two sentences is correct?

> The operation runs *smoother* now than it did before.

> The operation runs *more smoothly* now than it did before.

[margin note] Learn the difference between adjectives and adverbs.

To benefit from the instruction that follows, you must, first of all, know the difference between adjectives and adverbs. Because they both modify other words, writers sometimes confuse one with the other. To avoid problems, always identify the word that the adjective or adverb is modifying. If that word is a noun or pronoun, the modifier is an adjective. If it is a verb, an adjective, or another adverb, the modifier is an adverb.

A modifier that follows an action verb is an adverb. A modifier that follows a linking verb is an adjective—not an adverb. Remember that adjectives tend to answer the questions *what kind?*, *how many?*, or *which one?* Adverbs tend to answer the questions *when?*, *how?*, *where?*, or *to what extent?*

[margin note] The most common linking verbs are forms of the verb *to be*, such as *is, am, are, was, were,* and *will*. Other forms of linking verbs involve the senses, such as *feel, look, smell, sound,* and *taste*.

> The surface of the refinished counter is *smooth*. ("Was" is a linking verb, which requires an adjective)

> The entire operation ran *smoothly*. (not "smooth" because "ran" is an action verb, which requires an adverb)

The surface of the refinished counter felt *smoother* than the one it replaced. (*not "more smoothly," because "felt" is a linking verb, which requires an adjective*)

The entire operation runs *more smoothly* now than it did before we installed the new system. (*not "smoother," which is an adjective*)

Our new variety of yogurt tastes *sweet*. (*not "sweetly" because "tastes" is a linking verb, which requires an adjective*)

NOT: Giuseppe was *sure* glad that the meeting ended on time. (*"Sure" is an adjective and thus cannot modify another adjective.*)

BUT: Giuseppe was *surely* glad that the meeting ended on time. (*The adverb "surely" modifies the adjective "glad."*)

Some words (such as *fast, long, hard, early,* and *better*) can serve as both adjectives or adverbs, depending upon how they are used in the sentence.

I read the *first* [adjective telling what kind] draft *first* [adverb telling when], before reading the revisions.

I am *better* [adverb telling to what extent] at math than most people, but it still took me the *better* [adjective telling how much] part of the day to complete the assignment.

Most adverbs end in *-ly.* Most adjectives do not.

Noun	Adjective	Adverb
intention	intentional	intentionally
interest	more interested	interestingly
theory	theoretical	theoretically
truth	truthful	truthfully

However, some adverbs do *not* end in *-ly,* and, to confuse the situation even more, some adjectives *do* end in *-ly.* Shown below are some common examples:

Adverbs Not Ending in -ly		*Adjectives Ending in -ly*	
almost	quite	earthly	lonely
around	soon	fatherly	lovely
down	then	friendly	neighborly
here	very	homely	orderly
now	when	lively	worldly
often			

Make sure you understand why each italicized word in each example sentence is an adjective or adverb.

Most adverbs end in *-ly,* but most adjectives do not. However, some adverbs do not end in *-ly,* and some adjectives do end in *-ly.*

He drove *around* the circle and *then down* the block before he got *here.*

In this sentence, even though they do not end in *-ly,* the words *around, down,* and *here* serve as adverbs because they answer the question "where"; *then* is also an adverb because it answers the question "when."

The *lively* discussion of alternatives resulted in a *friendly* debate.
Mr. Alvarado spoke in a *fatherly* manner when addressing the *lonely* teenager.

In the preceding two sentences, even though they end in *-ly,* the words *lively, friendly, fatherly,* and *lonely* serve as adjectives because they modify nouns and answer the question "what kind."

CHECKPOINT 12.3

COMPREHENSION

1. Look up each of these words in the dictionary and indicate whether it can be used only as an adjective, only as an adverb, or as either. (Ignore parts of speech other than adjectives and adverbs.)

	Adjective	Adverb	Either
around	——	——	——
close	——	——	——
cowardly	——	——	——
funny	——	——	——
good	——	——	——
often	——	——	——
quickly	——	——	——
short	——	——	——
unique	——	——	——
very	——	——	——

2. Underline each adjective once and each adverb twice in the following sentences.

   a. I was really tired from that long workout.

   b. Navarro almost forgot about his lonely dog.

   c. Ravi looked suspicious when asked directly about his involvement.

   d. Please call us direct if you have any questions.

   e. Lately, I have been sleeping late because of my late hours at work.

Comparison of Adjectives and Adverbs

comparison The manner by which adjectives and adverbs express greater or lesser degrees of the same quality

When we talk about **comparison** of adjectives and adverbs, we simply mean the manner by which an adjective or adverb expresses a greater or lesser degree of the same quality. The three degrees (or *forms)* of an adjective or adverb are *positive, comparative,* and *superlative.*

Regular Comparisons

The positive degree is the basic adjective or adverb; it doesn't compare one with another. Use the comparative degree (*-er, more,* or *less*) to refer to two persons, places, or things and the superlative degree (*-est, most,* or *least*) to refer to more than two.

> I talked *fast.* (*positive degree of the adverb "fast"*)

> I talked *faster* than Rivero. (*comparative degree of the adverb "fast"*)

> I talked the *fastest* of the three speakers. (*superlative degree of the adverb "fast"*)

> Ms. Rivas is *competent.* (*positive degree of the adjective "competent"*)

> Ms. Rivas is *more competent* than Rachael. (*comparative degree of the adjective "competent"*)

> Ms. Rivas is the *most competent* of the five court reporters. (*superlative degree of the adjective "competent"*)

For one-syllable adjectives and adverbs, use *-er* or *-est* to form the comparative and superlative degrees, as in *fast, faster,* and *fastest.* For three- (or more) syllable adjectives and adverbs, use *more/less* or *most/least,* as in *competent, more competent,* and *most competent.*

But how do we form the comparative and superlative forms of two-syllable adjectives and adverbs? The "safe" answer (as it is to so many questions about business English) is to "look it up." For example, if you look up *funny* and *recent* in the *American Heritage College Dictionary,* you will find the entries shown in Figure 12.1.

If an adjective or adverb can be compared by adding *-er* or *-est* to the positive form, those forms will be shown immediately after the part of speech of the root word (see the entry for *funny* in Figure 12.1). If these forms are not shown, compare these words by inserting *more/less* or *most/least* (see the entry for *recent* in Figure 12.1). Most of the time, however, your ear will tell you which is correct. For example, you can probably "hear" that *most fun* does not sound as natural as *funniest* and that *recenter* does not sound as natural as *more recent.*

> His *more recent* routines are *funnier* than his earlier ones.

The important point is to use one or the other forms of comparison—not both. Do not combine two comparatives or two superlatives.

> **NOT:** Quitting college was the *most stupidest* thing I ever did.

> **BUT:** Quitting college was the *stupidest* thing I ever did.

The positive degree describes—it doesn't compare. The comparative degree compares two things. The superlative degree compares three or more things.

If your ear doesn't tell you which form is correct, take the time to look up the word in your dictionary.

FIGURE 12.1 Dictionary Entries for *Funny* and *Recent*

fun·ny (fŭn′ē) *adj.* **-ni·er, -ni·est. 1.a.** Causing laughter or amusement. **b.** Intended or designed to amuse. **2.** Strangely or suspiciously odd; curious. **3.** Tricky or deceitful. *—n., pl.* **-nies.** *Informal.* **1.** A joke; a witticism. **2. funnies. a.** Comic strips. **b.** The section of a newspaper containing comic strips. [<FUN.] **–fun′ni·ly** *adv.* **–fun′ni·ness** *n.*

re·cent (rē′sənt) *adj.* **1.** Of, belonging to, or occurring at a time immediately before the present. **2.** Modern; new. **3. Recent.** *Geol.* Of, belonging to, or being the Holocene Epoch. See table at **geologic time.** [ME, new, fresh <Lat. *recēns, recent-,* See ken-*.] **–re′cen·cy, re′cent·ness** *n.* **–re′-cent·ly** *adv.*

NOT: Ms. Rivera was *more friendlier* to me after the contest ended.

BUT: Ms. Rivera was *more friendly* to me after the contest ended.

Irregular Comparisons

A few adjectives and adverbs have irregular comparisons.

Positive	Comparative	Superlative
bad/ill	worse	worst
far	farther/further	farthest/furthest
good/well	better	best
little	littler/less	littlest/least
many/much	more	most

Memorize the irregular comparisons of these adjectives and adverbs.

Absolute Modifiers

Some adjectives and adverbs are *absolute;* that is, either you have the quality or you don't. These modifiers state the ultimate or perfect degree of something and thus cannot be compared. For example, you cannot be *deader* than someone who is merely *dead.* Here are some common absolute modifiers that cannot be compared: *square, round, complete, unique, perfect, dead, unanimous, true,* and *infinite.*

Avoid using such modifiers as very or quite with absolutes. You may, however, use modifiers such as nearly or almost with absolutes.

NOT: Vivian is a *very unique* individual.

BUT: Vivian is a *unique* individual.

NOT: The final vote was *quite unanimous.*

BUT: The final vote was *unanimous.*

These words can, however, be *qualified*, as in "The accident victim was *nearly dead* when the ambulance arrived." or "The highway reconstruction is *almost complete*."

Comparisons Within a Group

Use other or else when making comparisons within a group.

When comparing a person or thing to a group, use the phrase "other" or "else" to make clear that the person or thing you're comparing is a member of the group.

NOT: Javier is a faster typist than any typist in our department. (*implies that Javier is not in our department*)

BUT: Javier is a faster typist than any *other* typist in our department.

NOT: Alvin is more sensitive to the political situation than anyone on the staff. (*implies that Alvin is not on the staff*)

BUT: Alvin is more sensitive to the political situation than anyone *else* on the staff.

VOCABULARY   Define the following term in your own words.

1. comparison:

CHECKPOINT 12.4

COMPREHENSION

2. Write in the comparative and superlative forms of the adjectives and adverbs shown below. If needed, use *more* or *most* with these modifiers.

Positive	Comparative	Superlative
bad	_____	_____
badly	_____	_____
careful	_____	_____
direct	_____	_____
efficient	_____	_____
funny	_____	_____
many	_____	_____
thoughtful	_____	_____
warm	_____	_____
warmly	_____	_____

3. Strike through any unnecessary words and add any needed words in the following sentences. If a sentence is correct, write *C* before it.

   a. The new shipping cartons are very square.

   b. His office is larger than any office in his building.

   c. Xavier was more embarrassed than anyone about the situation.

   d. His office is the largest one in his building.

   e. The accident victim was very dead.

Special Problems with Adjectives and Adverbs

Be alert to the proper use of articles as adjectives and of *this/that* and *these/those*. Avoid double negatives, position adverbs correctly, and do not use unnecessary adverbs.

Articles as Adjectives

The adjectives *a, an,* and *the* are called *articles. A* and *an* are considered indefinite articles; *the* is considered the definite article. For example, "*a* book" does not identify a definite book whereas "*the* book" does.

In choosing between using *a* or *an,* be guided by the initial *sound* (not necessarily the spelling) of the word that follows. Use the article *a* before consonant sounds, including words beginning with a pronounced *h* (as in *has*) and long *u* (as in *use*). Use the article *an* before all vowel sounds except the long *u* (which is sounded as *yu).*

The articles *a, an,* and *the* are adjectives.

a stamp

BUT: an envelope

a house (*The* h *is pronounced.*)

BUT: an honor (*The* h *is silent; the initial sound is* o.)

a uniform (*The initial sound is* y.)

BUT: an umbrella (*The initial sound is* u.)

a one-day sale (*The initial sound is* w.)

BUT: an opening

a B.A. degree

BUT: an M.B.A. degree (*The initial sound is* m, *which is pronounced* em.)

a SWAT team (*The abbreviation is pronounced as a word.*)

BUT: an S.P.C.A. open house (*The abbreviation is pronounced letter by letter.*)

a two-hour delay

BUT: an 11 A.M. meeting

For abbreviations pronounced letter by letter, the following letters begin with a vowel sound and therefore require the article an: *a, e, f, h, i, l, m, n, o, r, s,* and *x.*

Avoid the following common errors in the use of articles.

■ Do not insert the definite article *the* before the word *both.*

NOT: We should hire *the both* of them.

BUT: We should hire *both* of them.

■ Do not insert the indefinite article *a* or *an* after phrases such as "kind of" or "sort of."

NOT: Kevin is the *sort of a* person you can trust.

BUT: Kevin is the *sort of* person you can trust.

■ Do not use one indefinite article to stand for two different ones.

NOT: I need *an* envelope and stamp.

BUT: I need *an* envelope and *a* stamp.

This/That and *These/Those*

The adjectives *this* and *that* are singular, and the adjectives *these* and *those* are plural. Match the singular adjectives to singular antecedents and the plural adjectives to plural antecedents.

NOT: *This kind* of filters should be used in the new equipment.

BUT: *These kinds* of filters should be used in the new equipment.

NOT: *Those type* of assignment do not occur very often.

BUT: *Those types* of assignments do not occur very often.

OR: *That type* of assignment does not occur very often.

Double Negatives

To express a negative idea, use only one negative expression. The incorrect addition of a second negative word (such as *not, never, none, no, nothing, barely, hardly,* or *scarcely*) in an expression that is already negative is known as a *double negative.* The first sentence below doesn't make sense because, logically, if you *don't* know *nothing,* then you *must* know *something.* In other words, two negatives make a positive.

NOT: You don't know nothing. (*"Don't"*—meaning *"do not"*—and *"nothing" are both negative.*)

BUT: You know nothing.

OR: You don't know anything.

Remember that all contractions (such as *hasn't* and *doesn't*) are negative.

Placement of Adverbs

Where you place an adverb affects the meaning of the sentence. Be sure to place the adverb as close as possible to the word you want it to modify. Most of the time, the adverb should come directly before the word modified. Note, for example, the three different meanings of the sentence below, depending upon where the word "only" is placed.

Only I like you. (*meaning that no one else likes you*)

I *only* like you. (*meaning that "like" is the extent of my feelings; for example, I do not "love" you*)

I like *only* you. (*meaning that I like no one else*)

In addition to *only,* other adverbs that require care in placement include *almost, also, ever, merely, nearly,* and *too.*

NOT: They were almost married for seven years.

BUT: They were married for almost seven years.

EITHER: I nearly slept through the entire presentation. (*Meaning I nodded but didn't really fall asleep*)

OR: I slept through nearly the entire presentation. (*Meaning I slept through most, but not all, of the presentation*)

Which of these three sentences would a special friend most likely prefer to hear?

Unnecessary Adverbs

Do not use an adverb to express an idea that is already expressed or implied by the verb. For example, *assemble* means "to come together," so do not write "assemble *together.*" As we learned in Chapter 4, repeating an idea that has already been expressed or implied is called a *redundancy.* Here are other examples:

combine (*Not: combine together*)	continue (*Not: continue on*)
cooperate (*Not: cooperate together*)	divide (*Not: divide up*)
drop (*Not: drop down*)	finish (*Not: finish up*)
follow (*Not: follow after*)	over (*Not: over again*)
plan (*Not: plan ahead*)	recline (*Not: recline back*)
refer (*Not: refer back*)	repeat (*Not: repeat again*)
return (*Not: return back*)	separate (*Not: separate apart*)

CHECKPOINT 12.5

COMPREHENSION

1. Underline the correct expression in parentheses.

   a. (A, An) youthful-looking woman purchased (a, an) uniform at (a, an) undisclosed price.

   b. Casey is the (type of, type of a) person whom you can trust.

   c. Please recycle (this, these) (sort, sorts) of items.

   d. I can interview (both, the both) of them at the same time.

   e. (A, An) scientist removed (a, an) X-chromosome from each specimen.

   f. It was (a, an) honor to stay in (a, an) hotel on the secluded island.

   g. These (kind, kinds) of mistakes should be avoided.

   h. (A, An) NBC news anchor discussed (a, an) NATO meeting being held in Belgium.

   i. We worked (a, an) 8-hour day and (a, an) 40-hour week.

2. Correct any errors in the following sentences. If a sentence is correct, write a *C* before it.

   a. Mr. Novotny hardly never finishes his projects on time.

   b. Regardless, I can't do nothing about the situation now.

   c. I only took the empty seat in the packed conference room.

   d. The newborn nearly weighed 10 pounds.

   e. Please type that report over again.

   f. You should plan ahead to ensure sufficient inventory for the holidays.

Summary

Nominative-case pronouns serve as subjects or complements in a sentence. Objective-case pronouns serve as direct objects, indirect objects, or objects of prepositions. Possessive-case pronouns show ownership; most pronouns have two possessive forms. Pronouns that modify a gerund must also be in the possessive case.

To avoid problems in using the correct case with compound subjects and objects, mentally omit the first noun; you can then generally "hear" the correct form of the pronoun. Similarly, mentally omit the noun when a pronoun is used with an appositive to determine the correct case of the pronoun. When a pronoun follows *than* or *as* in a statement of comparison, you may need to mentally supply any missing words to select the correct form of the pronoun. A pronoun that ends in *-self* should be used in sentences only when the noun or pronoun to which it refers appears in the same sentence. *Who* is the nominative form of the pronoun, and *whom* is the objective form.

Adjectives modify nouns or pronouns and tend to answer the questions *what kind?, how many?,* or *which one?* Adverbs modify verbs, adjectives, or other adverbs and tend to answer the questions *when?, how?, where?,* or *to what extent?* Some words can be used as either adjectives or adverbs.

Most adverbs end in *-ly;* most adjectives do not. However, some adverbs do *not* end in *-ly,* and some adjectives *do.* In addition, some adverbs have two forms—one ending in *-ly* and one not. In some cases, the different forms have different meanings; in other cases, the difference is largely a matter of traditional usage or formality.

Use comparative adjectives and adverbs (-er or *more/less*) to refer to two persons, places, or things, and use superlative adjectives and adverbs (-est or *most/least*) to refer to more than two. A few adjectives and adverbs have irregular comparisons. Some modifiers are absolute and cannot be compared (although they can be qualified). When comparing a person or thing within a group, use the expression "other" or "else" to make clear that the person or thing is a member of that group.

The indefinite article *a* is used before consonant sounds and *an* is used before vowel sounds. The adjectives *this* and *that* are singular and should be used with singular antecedents; *these* and *those* are plural and should be used with plural antecedents. Avoid using double negatives when expressing a negative idea, place adverbs close to the words they modify, and avoid including unnecessary adverbs.

Looking Ahead

To this point in the text, we have concentrated mostly on written communication in business. Recognize, however, that much of what you have learned about written communication applies to oral communication as well. This spillover should not be surprising, of course, inasmuch as we communicate by words whether orally or in writing. Chapter 13 covers issues specific to oral communication in business.

Key Terms

case	gerund
comparison	person
gender	

Exercises

The Case of Personal Pronouns

1 Circle the correct pronoun in the following sentences.

a. All members of the department gave (their, theirs, there, they're) views on the new proposal.

b. Although Howard had taken his qualifying test, Lawrence and Máximo had not taken (theirs, their's, theres, there's).

c. Anwar tried but (he, him) was unable to unlock the safe.

d. Did (her, she) work overtime to complete the project?

e. Did you offer (he, him) the job of chief legal assistant yet?

f. Edward asked if (I, me) would help him repaint the office.

g. For (her, she), it was a simple job to rewire the computer.

h. Here is (mine, my) plan of action for the coming quarter.

i. Howard sat directly behind (I, me) at the press briefing.

j. I agree, but it is (her, hers, her's) reputation that is at stake.

k. I want to know (whos, who's, whose) Ms. Howell supposed to see once she gets there.

l. I was annoyed by (he, him, his) continuing to make so many demands.

m. I was told (theirs, their's, theres, there's) no time to apply a second coat of paint.

n. It might have been (he, him) who gave the original order.

o. It will soon be (you're, your) turn to speak to the new employees.

2 Circle the correct pronoun in the following sentences.

a. Ms. Vásquez instructed (I, me) on the new procedures.

b. My task was simplified immensely by (their, there, they're, they) offering to help.

c. Please give (I, me) directions to the branch office.

d. The director asked (them, they) to wait outside until called.

e. The dog was crying because (its, it's) collar was too tight.

f. The final judgment regarding the matter is (their, theirs, there, they're) to make.

g. The manager thought (its, it's) a shame that the deadline passed unnoticed.

h. The network administrators shouldn't quit when (their, there, they're) so close to finding a solution.

i. The new energy czar is expected to be (he, him).

j. The observer asked, "(You're, Your) sure you know what you're doing?"

k. The original idea for the reconstruction was (mine, my).

l. The press asked (whos, who's, whose) idea it was in the first place.

m. The stranger gruffly answered, "This is (he, him) speaking."

n. They quickly gave (their, there, they're) approval for the increased expenditures for the investigation.

o. They were bluntly told that it really was no one's business but (her, hers).

Problems in Determining Pronoun Case

3 Circle the correct pronoun in the following sentences.

a. (Who, Whom) do you know on the staff of the review committee?

b. Because of the strike, they had to do the work (themself, themselves).

c. Between Joyce and (he, him), they were able to piece together what had actually happened.

d. Clyde finished his design project faster than (I, me).

e. For Mr. Bryant and (her, she), the decision meant rescheduling their planned vacations.

f. Have Mr. Hawkins and (them, they) read the X rays and made a decision?

g. I think (whoever, whomever) is responsible should fix the problem.

h. It is generally the clerical workers (who, whom) favor the flexible shifts the most.

i. It was Ms. Hayes (who, whom) made the original offer.

j. Management wanted (us, we) clerks to use the same style manual.

k. Mr. Dixon asked Amy and (I, me) to lock up the office when we left.

l. Mr. Myer mailed off the package (himself, hisself).

m. Mr. Snyder is not as happy about the matter as (her, she).

n. Ms. Powell and (I, me) are having trouble grasping the concept.

o. Should (us, we) court reporters ask for a raise in transcription fees?

p. Tell me (who, whom) you will ask to draw up the documents.

q. The job of cleaning up afterwards went to (me, myself).

Adjective or Adverb?

4 Circle the correct adjective or adverb in the following sentences.

a. Although lunch smelled (delicious, deliciously), I decided not to eat until later.

b. I am (sure, surely) glad that you decided to join our company.

c. I am convinced that the mistake was not (intentional, intentionally).

d. I feel (bad, badly) that you were inconvenienced.

e. Please try to finish the job (quick, quickly).

f. Raymond feels (good, well) when he argues a case successfully.

g. The doctor's (father, fatherly) manner soothed the patient.

h. The lemon pie tasted (bitter, bitterly).

i. The new president tends to dress very (conservative, conservatively).

j. When repairs became so (frequent, frequently), we traded in the copier for a newer model.

Comparison of Adjectives and Adverbs

5 Circle the correct alternative in parentheses in the following sentences.

a. Because she is (decenter, more decent) than her opponent, Hazel refused to retaliate.

b. Crystal is a more efficient technician than (anyone, anyone else) in her department.

c. Miyoko received (a perfect, the most perfect) score on the entrance exam.

d. Mr. Payne was the (carefulest, most careful) proofreader I've ever worked with.

e. Ms. Lawson is the (more, most) impatient of the two clients waiting to see you.

f. My kitten was the (littlest, most little) of the entire litter.

g. Of the three choices, the one involving doing nothing is the (baddest, worse, worst).

h. Suzanne is (happier, happy, more happier, more happy) now than she was five days ago.

i. The session on benefits was (more short, shorter) than the one on safe work practices.

j. This stew tastes (badder, worse, worst) now that you've added salt to it.

Special Problems with Adjectives and Adverbs

6 Circle the correct alternative in parentheses in the following sentences.

a. First, (combine, combine together) the eggs and milk.

b. I can't (ever, never) remember the correct combination for the lock.

c. I soon developed (a, an) understanding of the seriousness of the situation.

d. Mr. Suzuki wanted us to (plan, plan ahead) for any possible contingencies.

e. Razi hasn't heard (anything, nothing) from the colleges to which she applied.

f. This is the (type of, type of a) choice that you look forward to.

g. Those (sort of, sorts of) errors could have been prevented.

h. We have deleted (both, the both) offensive references from our manuals.

i. We requested a microphone and (amplifier, an amplifier).

j. Would you please (repeat that, repeat that again).

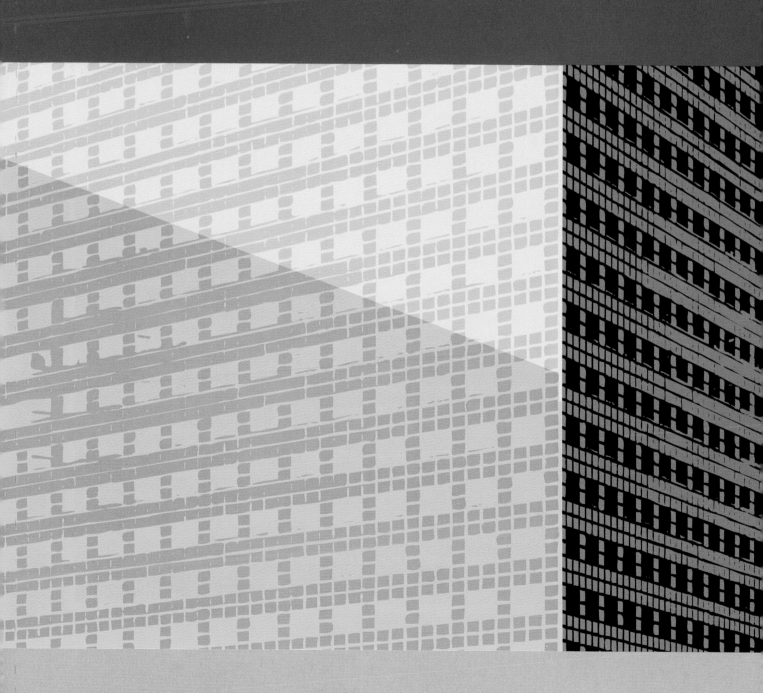

Business Presentations

COMMUNICATION OBJECTIVES

After you have finished this chapter, you should be able to:

- Plan and organize a presentation.

- Plan and deliver a team presentation.

- Plan and deliver a video presentation.

- Develop effective visual aids for a presentation.

- Practice and deliver a presentation in a clear, confident, and effective manner.

- Critique your performance as a presenter.

- Listen effectively.

On the Job

DAVID HANCOCK
Director of Sales,
Southeast Region, Royal
Caribbean International

David Hancock wants to add a cruise vacation to every traveler's itinerary. As director of sales, Southeast Region, for Royal Caribbean International, Hancock works with sales managers and telemarketing representatives who provide travel agents with the information they need to sell Royal Caribbean cruises.

Before Hancock speaks to a travel agent group, he sets aside time to analyze the audience and plan the presentation. "By finding out about the size of the audience, their level of knowledge, and their objectives, I can tailor my presentation to fit their needs," he says.

In addition, by analyzing his audience, he can determine whether industry-specific terms will be understood. "When I used to talk about an 'outside cabin,' there was a chance that some people in the audience might think the cabin was literally outside on the deck somewhere," Hancock notes. As a result, he now uses the term "ocean-view cabin" to describe a cabin with a porthole or balcony.

The way Hancock handles questions depends on the size of the audience. When he speaks to large groups, he invites questions only at the end, which helps him stay on schedule and avoid interrupting the flow of the talk. However, when addressing a smaller audience, he will often take questions at any time during the presentation.

Hancock's methods must be successful. Royal Caribbean's ships are now busier than ever.

The Role of Business Presentations

Anyone who plans a career in sales, training, or education expects to make many oral presentations to customers, employees, or students each week. What you may not realize, though, is that almost *everyone* in business will give at least one major presentation and many smaller ones each year, to customers, superiors, subordinates, or colleagues—not to mention presentations at PTA meetings, homeowners' association meetings, civic clubs, and the like.

The costs of ineffective presentations are immense. With many managers earning six-figure salaries, a presentation that discusses ideas incompletely and inefficiently wastes time and money. Sales are lost, vital information is not communicated, training programs fail, policies are not implemented, and profits fall.

Technology is undoubtedly changing the physical characteristics of oral presentations in business—for example, by making possible presenting via videotape or interactive television rather than in person. Competent communicators recognize, however, that the compelling effects of verbal and nonverbal communication strategies that are possible in oral presentations will continue to make them a critical communication competency in the contemporary business organization.

> Almost everyone in business is required to give a presentation occasionally.

Planning the Presentation

When assigned the task of making a business presentation, your first impulse might be to sit down at your desk or computer and begin writing. Resist the temptation. As in written communications, several important steps precede the actual writing. These steps involve determining the purpose of the presentation, analyzing the audience, and selecting a delivery method.

Purpose

Keeping your purpose uppermost in mind helps you decide what information to include and what to omit, in what order to present this information, and which points to emphasize and which to subordinate. Most business presentations have one of these four purposes:

> Most presentations seek either to report, explain, persuade, or motivate.

- *Reporting:* Updating the audience on some project or event
- *Explaining:* Detailing how to carry out a procedure or how to operate a new piece of equipment
- *Persuading:* Convincing the listeners to purchase something or to accept an idea you're presenting
- *Motivating:* Inspiring the listeners to take some action

After your presentation is over, your purpose provides a criterion—the *only* important criterion—by which to judge the success of your presentation. No matter how well or how poorly you spoke and no matter how impressive or ineffective your visual aids were, the most important question remains whether you accomplished your purpose.

Audience Analysis

In addition to identifying such demographic factors as the size, age, and organizational status of your audience, you will need to determine the audience members' level of knowledge about your topic and their psychological needs (values, attitudes, and beliefs). These factors provide clues about everything from the overall content, tone, and types of examples you should use to the types of questions to expect and even the way you should dress.

The principles by which you analyze your audience are the same as those discussed in the chapters on writing letters, memos, and reports. Consider the effect of your message on your audience and your credibility with them. The key is to put yourself in your audience's place so that you can anticipate their questions and reactions. The "you" attitude applies to oral as well as to written communication.

The larger your audience, the more formal your presentation will be. When you speak to a large group, you should speak more loudly and more slowly and use more emphatic gestures and larger visuals. Usually, you should allow questions only at the end of your talk. If you're speaking to a small group, you can be more flexible about questions, and your tone and gestures will be more like those used in normal conversation. Furthermore, when presenting to small groups, your options in terms of visual aids increase.

If your audience is unfamiliar with your topic, you will need to use clear, easy-to-understand language, with extensive visual aids and many examples. If the audience is more knowledgeable, you can proceed at a faster pace.

The audience's psychological needs will also affect your presentation. If, for example, you think your listeners will be hostile—either to you personally or to your message—then you'll have to oversell yourself or your idea. Instead of giving one or two examples, you'll need to give several. In addition to establishing your own credibility, you may need to quote other experts to bolster your case.

Delivery Method

By far the most common (and generally the most effective) method for business presentations is speaking from prepared notes, such as an outline. The notes contain key phrases rather than complete sentences, and you compose the exact wording as you speak. Although you may occasionally stumble in choosing a word, the spontaneous, conversational quality and the close audience rapport that follow are generally superior to the results of other presentation methods. The notes help ensure that you cover all the material and in a logical order; yet this method provides enough flexibility that you can adapt your remarks in reaction to verbal and nonverbal cues from the audience.

The specific content and format of the notes is not important; choose whatever works best for you. Some people use a formal outline on full sheets of paper; others prefer notes jotted on index cards. Some use complete sentences; others, short phrases. If desirable, include notes to yourself, such as when to pause, which phrases to emphasize, and when to change a slide or transparency.

Whether you use full sheets or index cards, be sure to number each page (in case you drop the pages). For ease in moving from sheet to sheet or from card to card, write on just one side and do not staple. Typed copy is better than hand-written copy and large type is better than small type. Type your notes in standard upper- and lowercase letters rather than in all capitals, which are more difficult to read because all the letters are the same size.

Figure 13.1 shows examples of excerpts from a written report and outline notes for an oral presentation. Note that the outline notes are typed in larger type for ease of reading, and that they contain prompts indicating when to display each visual aid (slide). The outline notes also consist of mostly phrases, with each subtopic indented to show its relationship to the main idea.

Of course, you can tailor this approach to suit your needs. Some speakers insert delivery cues, indicating when to pause, smile, make a gesture, display a visual aid, slow down, and the like. Some start off by writing out the entire speech

FIGURE 13.1 **Outline Notes**

Outline Notes for
an Oral Presentation

FAMILIARITY WITH BENEFITS—SLIDE 1

- Most know about most benefits
- + 3/4 know about all but 2 benefits:
  - —Long-term disability = slight majority
  - —Auto insur = +1/3 (begun 6 wks before survey)

- No correlation between employment length & familiarity
  - —Not true for life insur—SLIDE 2
  - —Life insur: Longer employment = more familiarity

Note the incomplete sentences and abbreviations used in these notes.

and then practice extensively from the prepared script. Only after they are thoroughly familiar with their verbatim script do they condense it into an outline and then speak from the outline. Whichever method you use, the key to a successful delivery is practice, practice, practice.

Organizing the Presentation

For most presentations, the best way to begin is simply to brainstorm: write down every point you can think of that might be included in your presentation. Don't worry about the order or format—just get it all down. During the next several days, carry a pen and paper with you so that you can jot down random thoughts as they occur—during a meeting, at lunch, going to and from work, or in the evening at home.

Later, separate your notes into three categories: opening, body, and ending. As you begin to analyze and organize your material, you may find that you need additional information. You may need to retrieve records from files, consult with a colleague, visit your corporate or local library to fill in the gaps, or perhaps go online to retrieve data from the World Wide Web.

The Opening

The purpose of the opening is to capture the interest of your audience, and the first 90 seconds of your presentation are crucial in that regard. The audience will be observing every detail about you—your dress, posture, facial features, and voice qualities, as well as what you're actually saying—for clues about you and your topic, and they will be making preliminary judgments accordingly.

Begin immediately to establish rapport and build a relationship with your audience—not just for the duration of your presentation but for the long term. Because the opening is so crucial, some speakers write out the entire opening and practice it word for word until they know it by heart.

The kind of opening that will be effective depends on what your topic is, how well you know the audience, and how well they know you. If, for example, you're giving a status report on a project about which you've reported before, you can immediately announce your main points (for example, that the project is on schedule and proceeding as planned) and go immediately to the body of your

Your opening should introduce the topic, identify the purpose, and preview the presentation.

Effective openings include a quotation, question, hypothetical situation, story, startling fact, or visual aid.

remarks. If, however, you're presenting a new proposal to your superiors, you'll first have to introduce the topic and provide background information.

If most of the listeners don't know you, you'll need to gain their attention with a creative opening. The following types of attention-getting openings have proven successful for business presentations. The examples given are for a presentation to union employees whose purpose is to motivate them to decrease absenteeism.

- *Quote a well-known person:* "Comedian Woody Allen once noted that 90% of the job is just showing up."
- *Ask a question:* "If we were able to cut our absenteeism rate by half during the coming six months, exactly how much do you think that would mean for each of us in our end-of-year bonus checks?"
- *Present a hypothetical situation:* "Suppose, that as you were leaving home this morning to put in a full day at work, your son came up to you and said he was too tired to go to school because he had stayed up late last night watching 'Wrestle Mania.' What would be your reaction?"
- *Relate an appropriate anecdote, story, joke, or personal experience:* "George, a friend of mine who had recently changed jobs, happened to meet his former boss on the street and asked her whom she had hired to fill his vacancy. 'George,' his former boss said, 'when you left, you didn't *leave* any vacancy!' Perhaps the reason George didn't leave any vacancy was that. . . ."
- *Give a startling fact:* "During the next 24 hours, American industry will lose $136 million because of absenteeism."
- *Use a dramatic prop or visual aid:* (holding up a paper clip) "What do you think is the true cost of this paper clip to our company?"

Don't apologize or make excuses (for example, "I wish I had had more time to prepare my remarks today" or "I'm not really much of a speaker"). The audience may agree with you! At any rate, you'll turn them off immediately and weaken your credibility.

Your opening should lead into the body of your presentation by previewing your remarks: "Today, I'll cover four main points. First, . . . " For most business presentations, let the audience know up front what you expect of them. Are you simply presenting information for them to absorb, or will audience members be expected to react to your remarks? Are you asking for their endorsement, their resources, their help, or what? Let the audience know what their role will be so that they can then place your remarks in perspective.

The Body

The body of your presentation conveys the real content. Here you'll develop the points you introduced in the opening, giving background information, specific evidence, examples, implications, consequences, and other needed information.

Organize the body logically, according to your topic and audience needs.

Choose a Logical Sequence   Just as you do when writing a letter or report, choose an organizational plan that suits your purpose and your audience's needs. The most commonly used organizational plans are the following:

- *Criteria:* Introduce each criterion in turn and show how well each alternative meets that criterion (typically used for presenting proposals).
- *Direct sequence:* Give the major conclusions first, followed by the supporting details (typically used for presenting routine information).
- *Indirect sequence:* Present the reasons first, followed by the major conclusion (typically used for persuasive presentations).

- *Chronology:* Present the points in the order in which they occurred (typically used in status reports or when reporting on some event).
- *Cause/effect/solution:* Present the sources and consequences of some problem and then propose a solution.
- *Order of importance:* Arrange the points in order of importance and then pose each point as a question and answer it (an effective way of ensuring that the audience can follow your arguments).
- *Elimination of alternatives:* List all alternatives and then gradually eliminate each one until only one option remains—the one you're recommending.

Words Are Made from Letters	**WORD|wise**
anemone (NMNE)	enemy (NME)
any (NE)	escapee (SKP)
arcadian (RKDN)	essay (SA)
decay (DK)	excellency (XLNC)
devious (DVS)	expediency (XPDNC)
empty (MT)	opium (OPM)

Whatever organizational plan you choose, make sure that your audience knows at the outset where you're going and can follow your organization. In a written document, signposts such as headings tell the reader how the parts fit together. In an oral presentation, you must compensate for the lack of such aids by using frequent and clear transitions that tell your listeners where you are. Pace your presentation of data so that you do not lose your audience.

Establish Your Credibility   Convince the listener that you've done a thorough job of collecting and analyzing the data and that your points are reasonable. Support your arguments with credible evidence—statistics, actual experiences, examples, and support from experts. Use objective language; let the data—not exaggeration or emotion—persuade the audience. Be guided by the same principles you use when writing a persuasive letter or report.

Avoid saturating your presentation with so many facts and figures that your audience won't be able to absorb them. Regardless of their relevance, statistics will not strengthen your presentation if the audience cannot digest all the data. A more effective tactic is to prepare handouts of detailed statistical data to distribute for review at a later time.

Deal with Negative Information   It would be unusual if *all* the data you've collected and analyzed support your proposal. (If that were the case, persuasion would not be necessary.) What should you do, then, about negative information, which, if presented, might weaken your argument? You cannot simply ignore it. To do so would surely open up a host of questions and subsequent doubts that would seriously undermine your position.

Do not ignore negative information.

Think about your own analysis of the data. Despite the negative information, you still concluded that your solution has merit. Your tactic, then, is to present the important information—both pro and con—and to show through your analysis and discussion that your recommendations are still valid, despite the disadvantages and drawbacks. Use the techniques you learned in Chapter 5 about emphasis and subordination to let your listeners know which points you considered major and which you considered minor.

Although you should discuss the important negative points, you may safely omit discussing minor ones. You must, however, be prepared to discuss these issues if any questions about them arise at the conclusion of your presentation.

The Ending

The ending of your presentation is your last opportunity to achieve your objective. Don't waste it. A presentation without a strong ending is like a joke without a punch line.

Finish on a strong, upbeat note, leaving your audience with a clear and simple message.

Summarize the important points in your closing.

Your closing should summarize the main points of your presentation, especially if it has been a long one. Even if the members of your audience have had an easy time following the structure of your talk, they won't necessarily remember all your important points. Let them know the significance of what you've said. Draw conclusions, make recommendations, or outline the next steps to take. Leave the audience with a clear and simple message.

To add punch to your ending, you may want to use one of the same techniques discussed for opening a presentation. You might tell a story, make a personal appeal, or issue a challenge. However, resist the temptation to end with a quotation. It won't sound dramatic enough. Besides, you want your listeners to remember *your* words and thoughts—not someone else's. Also avoid fading out with a weak "That's about all I have to say" or "I see that our time is running out."

After you've developed some experience in giving presentations, you will be able to judge fairly accurately how long to spend on each point so as to finish on time. Until then, practice your presentation with a stopwatch. If necessary, insert reminders at critical points in your notes indicating where you should be at what point in time. Avoid having to drop important sections or rush through the conclusion of your presentation because you misjudged your timing.

Your audience will remember best what they hear last, so think of your ending as one of the most important parts of your presentation. Finish on a strong, upbeat note. If you've used a projector during your presentation, turn it off and turn the room lights on so that *you* are the center of attention. Also remember that no one ever lost any friends by finishing a minute or two ahead of schedule. As Toastmasters International puts it, "Get up, speak up, shut up, and sit down."

CHECKPOINT 13.1

RECALL   Write a capital *T* for true or *F* for false before each statement.

1. ____ Audience analysis for oral presentations is similar to that used for written presentations.

2. ____ The most effective method of presentation for most business presentations is to speak from brief prepared notes.

3. ____ Your speech notes should consist of a formal outline using phrases rather than complete sentences.

4. ____ All business presentations should begin with an attention-getting opening.

5. ____ You should avoid discussing negative aspects of your oral proposal.

COMPREHENSION

6. Give an original example of a presentation whose purpose is:

   a. Reporting:

   b. Explaining:

   c. Persuading:

   d. Motivating:

7. Assume you are preparing a motivational presentation to your classmates on the importance of drinking responsibly (or not at all). Create an attention-getting opening for your presentation.

CRITICAL THINKING

8. Assume that because of your so-so grades, you were initially denied admission to graduate school at your institution. You have been given the chance, however, to formally present your case to the graduate council. What are some ways that you might establish your personal credibility with them?

The Use of Humor in Business Presentations

Memory research indicates that when ideas are presented with humor, the audience is able not only to recall more details of the presentation but also to retain the information longer.[1]

If you know you do not tell humorous stories well, the moment you're in front of an audience is not the time to try to rectify that situation. Both you and your audience will suffer. If, however, you feel that you can use humor effectively, doing so might add just the appropriate touch to your presentation.

Jokes, puns, satire, and especially amusing real-life incidents are just a few examples of humor, all of which serve to form a bond between speaker and audience. Humor can be used anywhere in a presentation—in the opening to get attention, in the body to add interest, or in the closing to drive home a point. Humor should, of course, be avoided if the topic is very serious or has negative consequences for the audience.

If you tell an amusing story, it must always be appropriate to the situation and in good taste. Never tell an off-color or sexist joke; never use offensive language; never single out an ethnic, racial, or religious group; and never use a dialect or foreign accent in telling a story. Such tactics are always in bad taste. The best stories are directed at yourself; they show that you are human and can laugh at yourself.

Before telling a humorous story, make sure you understand it and think it's funny. Then personalize it for your own style of speaking and for the particular situation. Avoid beginning jokes by saying, "I heard a funny story the other day about . . . . " A major element of humor is surprise, so don't warn the audience a joke is coming. If you do, they're mentally preparing for a funny punch line, and you may disappoint them. If, on the other hand, you're already halfway into the story before the audience even realizes it's a joke, your chances of success are greater.

Resist the temptation to laugh at your own stories. A slight smile is more effective. Wait for the (hoped-for) laughter to subside; then continue your presentation by relating the punch line to the topic at hand.

Regardless of your expertise as a joke teller, do not use humor too frequently. Humor is a means to an end—not an end in itself. When all is said and done, you don't want your audience to remember that you were funny. You want them to remember that what you had to say was important and made sense.

Use humor if it is appropriate and if you are adept at telling humorous stories.

Personalize humorous stories to fit your specific purpose and situation.

When addressing North American audiences, always stand to the left of your visual aids. Because most people read from left to right, the eyes of the audience can move easily from you to the audiovisual aid.

Work-Team Presentations

Work-team presentations are common strategies for communicating about complex projects. Such presentations require extensive planning, close coordination, and a measure of maturity and goodwill. If you are responsible for coordinating such efforts, allow enough time and assign responsibilities on the basis of individual talents and time constraints.

Your major criterion for making assignments is the division of duties that will result in the most effective presentation. Tap into each team member's strengths. Some individuals may be better at collecting and analyzing the information to be presented, others may be better at developing the visual aids, and still others may be better at delivering the presentation. Does any work-team member have a knack for telling good stories or connecting with strangers? Perhaps he or she should begin the presentation. Consider picking a "diplomat" to moderate the question-and-answer session.

Everyone need not share equally in each aspect of the project. As coordinator, ensure that all efforts are recognized publicly and equally during the actual presentation, regardless of how much "podium time" is assigned to each person.

> Make individual assignments for a team presentation based on individual strengths and preferences.

Achieving Coherence

Just as people have different writing styles, so they have different speaking styles. You must ensure that your overall presentation has coherence and unity—that is, that it sounds as if it were prepared and given by one individual. Thus, the group members should decide beforehand the most appropriate tone, format, organization, style for visual aids, manner of dress, method of handling questions, and similar factors that will help the presentation flow smoothly from topic to topic and from speaker to speaker.

> Make your team presentation look and sound as though it were prepared and given by a single person.

Use one of the presentation templates that came with your software presentation program to maintain a consistent "look-and-feel" across everyone's slides. These templates define backgrounds and colors, slide heading formats, and font styles and sizes. Someone must also monitor the presentation for semantic consistency—both in the visual aids and in the verbal portion. Do you refer to people by first and last names, last names only, or a personal title and last name? Do you refer to your visual aids as charts, slides, overheads, graphics, or something else? If an unfamiliar term is used, ensure that the first person using the term (and only the first person) defines it.

Practicing the Team Presentation

At least one full-scale rehearsal—in the room where the presentation will take place and using all visual aids—is crucial for work-team presentations. If possible, videotape this rehearsal for later analysis by the entire group. Schedule your final practice session early enough that you will have time to make any changes needed—and then to run through the presentation once more, if necessary.

Critiquing the performance of a colleague requires tact, empathy, and goodwill; accepting such feedback requires grace and maturity. For the entire presentation to succeed, each individual element must succeed. If it does, each contributor shares in the success and any rewards that may result.

The failure to plan and coordinate introductions and transitions is a frequently encountered dilemma. Will the first speaker introduce all team members at the beginning, or will each one introduce himself or herself as he or she gets up to speak?

> Present a professional appearance—regardless of which team member is actually speaking.

Finally, consider yourself to be on stage during the entire team presentation—no matter who is presenting. If you're on the sidelines for the moment, stand erect, pay attention to the presenter (even though you may heard the content a dozen times), and try to read the audience for nonverbal signs of confusion, boredom, disagreement, and the like.

Video Presentations

If you are taking this course online, your instructor may ask you to videotape your class presentation. Increasingly, organizations are also videotaping presentations, which can then be shown on a television monitor using a video cassette recorder (VCR), CD-ROM, computer projection, or even the Internet.

Most of the same principles mentioned earlier apply equally to video presentations. In addition, unique effects may result when the presenter faces the camera, because gazing into the eye of the camera for a long time is such an unnatural, artificial situation. The only solution is to practice. Fortunately, handheld videocameras and VCRs are now so common that you can practice easily in the comfort of your own home or office.

The best colors to wear when participating in a video presentation are shades of blue; a light blue shirt or blouse with a blue jacket or blazer is ideal. Avoid contrasting colors and stripes. Makeup is recommended for both men and women to reduce sweat and even out skin tone. When recording, sit or stand straight and look into the camera as long as possible while talking. Always focus your eyes on one of two places—either directly at the camera or at your notes; never gaze off to the side or over the camera. Because television exaggerates movements, stand or sit as still as possible and keep gestures to a minimum. Also, stay within an established area of movement (determined beforehand with the person who will be doing the videotaping).

If possible, use actual color printouts of your visuals instead of an overhead or computer projection; the camera will pick up the image much better. Use at least one-inch lettering, printed on a light blue or pastel background rather than white. Try to group your visuals so that the camera is not zooming in and out too much, as it can be distracting to the audience.

The increasing use of video presentations also means that you may be called upon to operate the video camera. As a camera operator:

Learn how to operate a video camera effectively.

- Control the noise level in the room; even an air-conditioner can add distracting background noise. Also, make sure that the room has good overall lighting, although it does not have to be "spotlights."

- Check your camera batteries beforehand and perhaps have a spare on hand.

- Use a tripod for stability. If you do not have access to a tripod, use your body as a brace for the camera, tucking it in against your body to steady it.

- Zoom in on the visual when the speaker mentions it.

- Minimize camera movement, but don't be afraid to move the camera. Use smooth, slow movement rather than fast, jerky movement.

- Try to "frame" or block the person in the camera (waist up, for example); don't get a shot that is too wide, covering too much area. A good rule of thumb is to provide a one-inch border around the subject. If the presenter plans to move around, establish the area for movement with him or her before filming. Then let the person move within this frame, instead of always following the person with the camera.

- Think in terms of what will be viewed by the audience rather than what will be filmed by the camera operator (that is, think in terms of showing, not shooting). Rarely will you use all of the footage shot; consider it the raw material from which to select and organize an effective presentation.

Contemporary business people need to become not only "computer literate," but also "video literate." If you're unfamiliar with videotaping procedures, visit a local video studio and observe a shoot to see how the process is handled and how directors and camera crews work with the presenter.

Visual Aids for Business Presentations

Today's audiences are accustomed to multimedia events that bombard the senses with information. They often assume that any formal presentation must be accompanied by some visual element, whether it is a flipchart, overhead transparency, slide, film, videotape, or actual model.

Visual aids are relatively simple to create and help the audience understand the presentation, especially if it includes complex or statistical material. A University of Pennsylvania study found that presenters who used visual aids successfully persuaded 67% of their audience, whereas those who did not use such aids persuaded only 50% of their audience. In addition, meetings in which visual aids were used were 28% shorter than those that lacked such aids. Similarly, a University of Minnesota study found that the use of graphics increased a presenter's persuasiveness by 43%. Presenters who used visual aids were also perceived as being more professional, better prepared, and more interesting than those who didn't use visual aids.[2]

Transparencies and Electronic Presentations

Inexpensive, easy to produce, and simple to update, transparencies for overhead projection can be used without darkening the room and while you face the audience. Thus, your audience can see to take notes, and you can maintain eye contact with them. Thanks to presentation software, overhead transparencies can readily take advantage of color, designed fonts, charts, artwork, and preplanned layouts (called *templates*). Despite their convenience and ease of use, the availability and low cost of computer projectors, combined with growing sales of notebook computers, has caused the use of transparencies to drop significantly in recent years.

Electronic presentations are the newest medium for visual aids. They consist of slides or video shown directly from a computer and projected onto a screen via a projector. Because the slide images come directly from the computer file, actual transparencies do not have to be made. Electronic presentations enable you to easily add multimedia effects to your presentation—if doing so helps you tell your story more effectively. You could, for example, show a short video, move text across the screen, or play background sound effects. Electronic slide presentations offer greater flexibility than traditional slide presentations do, but they require the use of high-powered projectors to obtain the best results.

When giving an electronic presentation, follow these guidelines:

- Check colors for accuracy. If precise color matching is important (for example, with the color of your corporate logo), ensure that the color projected on the computer on which you designed the presentation matches the color shown on the projection system on which you will display it.

- Keep special effects simple. Elaborate or random transition effects, for example, are distracting. Nevertheless, consider using builds to reveal one bullet point at a time; doing so helps focus the audience's attention. Avoid sound effects unless absolutely essential for understanding.

- Disable any screen savers and energy-saving automatic shutdown features of your computer. You don't want your screen to begin displaying a screen saver or to go blank in the middle of your presentation.

- Be seen and heard. Stand on the left side of the screen from the audience's point of view—in the light and away from the computer—using a remote mouse if necessary. Make sure that you're still clearly visible when the projection screen is dark.

Preparing Visual Aids

Avoid using too many visual aids. Novice presenters sometimes employ them as a crutch. Such overuse keeps the emphasis on the visual aid rather than on the presenter. Instead, use visual aids only when they will help the audience grasp an important point, and remove them when they're no longer needed. One or two relevant, helpful visual aids are better than an entire armload of irrelevant ones—no matter how attractive they are.

If you do not keep your visual aids clear and simple, your audience can easily become overwhelmed, with their attention being drawn to the technology rather than to the content. As always, seek to *express*—not to *impress*. With visual aids, less is more.

According to Joan Detz, speaker, trainer, and author of *How to Write and Give a Speech*,

> A successful presentation has little to do with technical wizardry. The single biggest mistake I see is overusing technology. Most of the time, visuals are used as a security blanket for people who haven't thought through a presentation. It's easier to have an audience look at a slide or other visual rather than at you.[3]

Do not simply photocopy tables or illustrations from reports, printouts, or journals and project them on a screen. Print graphics usually contain far too much information to serve effectively as presentation graphics. Using such graphics in a presentation will often do more to hinder your presentation than to help it.

As a general rule, each slide or transparency should contain no more than 40 characters per line, no more than six or seven lines per visual, and no more than three columns of data (think of your slide as a highway billboard rather than a memo). Use upper- and lowercase letters (rather than all capitals) in a large, simple typeface and plenty of white (empty) space. Use bulleted lists to show a group of related items that have no specific order and numbered lists to show related items in a specific order. Establish a color scheme and stick with it for all your visual aids; that is, use the same background color for each slide or transparency. Ensure that your visual aids are readable by testing them beforehand; look at them from the back seat of the room in which you will be presenting.

The quality of your visual aids sends a nonverbal message about your competence and your respect for your audience. Just as you don't want your audience's attention distracted by the razzle-dazzle of your slides, neither do you want their attention distracted by poor quality. If the visual aid isn't readable or attractive, don't use it.

Using Visual Aids

Even the best visual aid will not be effective if it is used improperly during the presentation or if the equipment doesn't work. Operating equipment smoothly does not come naturally; it takes practice and a keen awareness of audience needs, especially when using a slide or overhead projector.

Confirm that your equipment is in top working order and that you know how to operate it and how to secure a spare bulb or spare machine quickly if one becomes necessary. Adjust the projector and focus the image so that it is clearly readable from the farthest seat. However, do not make the image larger than necessary; the presenter should be the center of attention. The image should be a square or rectangle. Avoid the common keystoning effect (where the top of the image is wider than the bottom) by tilting the top of the screen forward slightly toward the projector. Also, avoid walking in front of the projected image.

Prepare for potential problems. Number your transparencies so that they can be reorganized quickly if dropped; clean the overhead projector glass before using it; have an extra bulb handy (and know how to insert it). Finally, be

Margin notes

Visual aids should be used only when needed and should be simple, readable, and of high quality.

Simplify and enlarge printed graphics before using them as a visual aid.

Practice using your visual aids smoothly and effectively.

Be prepared to give your presentation without visual aids if necessary.

prepared to give your presentation without visual aids if that should become necessary.

With practice, you can learn to stand to the side of the screen, facing the audience with your feet pointed toward them. Then, when you need to refer to an item on the screen, point with either a finger, pointer, or pen. (Many people find the use of laser pointers distracting.) Turn your body from the waist, keeping your feet pointed toward the audience. Doing so enables you to maintain better eye contact with the audience as well as better control of the presentation.

CHECKPOINT 13.2

RECALL   Write a capital T for *true* or F for *false* before each statement.

1. ____ It is inappropriate to use humor in most business presentations.

2. ____ Each member of a work-team presentation should use the same software template to format his or her slides.

3. ____ The best colors to wear when giving a video presentation are shades of blue.

4. ____ Generally, the more visual aids you use, the more effective your presentation.

5. ____ The screen should be on the speaker's left as he or she faces the audience.

COMPREHENSION

6. Assume you're giving a 15-minute presentation on the effective use of email to a campus group. Do research to locate a humorous story you might use in your presentation. Then personalize it for your particular situation. Relate the story below.

CRITICAL THINKING

7. What has been the major problem in work-team presentations (or other group projects) in which you have personally participated? How did your group solve it?

Practicing the Presentation

Use appropriate language, voice qualities, gestures, and posture.

The language of oral presentations must be simple. Because the listener has only one chance to comprehend the information presented, shorter sentences and simpler vocabulary should be used for oral presentations than for written presentations. Presenters have trouble articulating long, involved sentences with complex vocabulary, and listeners have trouble understanding them. A long sentence that reads easily on paper may leave the speaker breathless when he or she says it aloud. Avoid such traps. Use short, simple sentences and a conversational style. Use contractions freely, and avoid using words that you may have trouble pronouncing.

Begin practicing by simulating the conditions of the meeting room as closely as possible. Always practice standing, with your notes at the same level and angle as at a podium, and use any visual aids that will be a part of your presentation.

Videotaping your rehearsal can help you review and modify your voice qualities, gestures, and speech content. If videotaping is not possible, two good substitutes are a large mirror and a tape recorder. The mirror can help you judge the appropriateness of your posture, facial expressions, and gestures. Remember that 55% of your credibility with an audience comes from your body language, 38% comes from your voice qualities, and only 7% comes from the actual words you use.[4] Play back the tape several times, paying attention to your voice qualities (especially speed and pitch), pauses, grouping of words and phrases, and pronunciation.

For important presentations, plan on a minimum of three run-throughs. Record how much time it takes on each section of your outline. If necessary, cut out a key point so that you have time for a solid, well-rehearsed, and unrushed summary and conclusion. Schedule your practice sessions far enough ahead of time to allow you to make any needed changes.

Become familiar enough with your message that a few notes or a graphic will keep you on track. Practice the most important parts (introduction, summary of key points, conclusion) the most number of times.

Speak in a conversational tone, but at a slightly slower rate than normally used in conversation. For interest and to fit the situation, vary both your volume and your rate of speaking, slowing down when presenting important or complex information and speeding up when summarizing. Use periodic pauses to emphasize important points. Use correct diction, avoid slurring or dropping off the endings of words, and practice pronouncing difficult names.

Occasional hand and arm gestures are important for adding interest and emphasis, but only if they are appropriate and appear natural. If you never "talk with your hands" in normal conversation, it is unlikely you will do so naturally while presenting. Generally, one-handed gestures are more effective and less distracting than two-handed ones.

Avoid annoying and distracting mannerisms and gestures, such as jingling coins or keys in your pocket; coughing or clearing your throat excessively; wildly waving your hands; gripping the lectern tightly; nervously swaying or pacing; playing with jewelry, pens, or paper clips; or peppering your remarks with "and uh" or "you know."

Practice smiling occasionally, standing tall and naturally, with the body balanced on both feet. Rest your hands on the podium, by your side, or in any natural, quiet position. Your voice and demeanor should reflect professionalism, enthusiasm, and self-confidence.

Delivering the Presentation

Your clothing is a part of the message you communicate to your audience, so dress appropriately—in comfortable and businesslike attire. Different clothes give us different energy levels; if you can feel the difference, so can your audience. Follow these guidelines:[5]

- Dress just slightly better than the audience; the audience will be complimented by your efforts.

- Make sure that your shoes are the same color or darker than the hemline of your pants or skirt.

- Always wear long sleeves when presenting. They project authority and a higher level of professionalism and respect. Short sleeves create a more casual appearance.

Videotape your practice sessions and study the tape carefully for verbal and nonverbal cues.

Use appropriate hand and arm gestures.

Dress comfortably—just slightly dressier than your audience.

- Ensure that the tip of a man's tie hits the middle of his belt buckle.
- Be aware that the higher the stage, the shorter a woman's skirt will appear. The best skirt length is mid-knee for women of short or medium height and a few inches below mid-knee for taller women.

If you're speaking after a meal, eat lightly, avoiding heavy sauces, desserts, and alcoholic beverages. As you're being introduced, take several deep breaths to clear your mind, walk confidently to the front of the room, take enough time to arrange yourself and your notes, look slowly around you, establish eye contact with several members of the audience, and then, in a loud, clear voice, begin your presentation.

Maintain eye contact with all members of the audience.

You should know your presentation well enough that you can maintain eye contact easily with your audience, taking care to include members in all corners of the room. Lock in on one person and maintain eye contact for at least three seconds—or until you have completed a thought.

If you lose your place in your notes, relax and take as much time as you need to regroup. If your mind actually does go blank, try to keep talking—even if you repeat what you've just said. The audience will probably think you intentionally repeated the information for emphasis, and the extra time may jog your memory. If this trick doesn't work, simply skip ahead to another part of your presentation that you do remember; then come back later to the part you omitted.

Stage Fright

According to author Mark Twain, "There are two types of speakers—those who are nervous and those who are liars." If you've ever experienced stage fright, take comfort in the fact that you're not alone. Fear of giving a speech is the number 1 fear of most Americans. In a national poll of 3,000 people, 42% said the one thing they're most afraid of in life—even more than having cancer or a heart attack—is giving a speech.[6] Fortunately, behavior-modification experts have found that of the full range of anxiety disorders, people can most predictably overcome their fear of public speaking.[7]

Recognize that you have been asked to make a presentation because someone obviously thinks you have something important to say. You should feel complimented by the request. Unless you are an exceptionally good or exceptionally bad speaker, the audience will more likely remember *what* you say rather than *how* you say it. Most of us fall somewhere between these two extremes as presenters. Recognize also that some nervousness, of course, is good. It gets the adrenaline flowing and gives your speech an edge.

To avoid anxiety, practice, develop a positive attitude, and concentrate on friendly faces.

The best way to minimize any lingering anxiety is to overprepare. For the anxious presenter, there is no such thing as overpractice. The more familiar you are with the content of your speech and the more trial runs you've made, the better you'll be able to concentrate on your delivery once you're actually in front of the group. You may want to memorize the first several sentences of your presentation just so you can approach those critical first moments (when anxiety is highest) with more confidence.

Practice mental imagery. Several times before your big presentation, sit in a comfortable position, close your eyes, and visualize yourself giving your speech. Picture yourself speaking confidently, loudly, and clearly in an assured voice. If you can imagine yourself giving a successful speech, you will be able to do so.

Before your presentation, take a short walk to relax your body. While waiting for your presentation to begin, let your arms drop loosely by your sides and shake your wrists gently, all the while breathing deeply several times. As you begin to speak, look for friendly faces in the crowd, and concentrate on them initially.

Finally, business people who are anxious about speaking in public should consider taking a public speaking course or joining Toastmasters International, the world's oldest and largest nonprofit educational organization. The purpose of

Toastmasters is to improve the speaking skills of its members. Members meet weekly or monthly and deliver prepared speeches, evaluate one another's oral presentations, give impromptu talks, develop their listening skills, conduct meetings, and learn parliamentary procedure.

Answering Questions

One advantage that oral presentations have over written reports is the opportunity to engage in two-way communication. The question-and-answer session is a vital part of your presentation, and you should plan for it accordingly.

Normally, you should announce at the beginning of your presentation that you will be happy to answer any questions when you're through. Holding questions until the end prevents you from being interrupted and losing your train of thought or possibly running out of time and not being able to complete your prepared remarks. Also, there is always the possibility that the listener's question will be answered later in the course of your presentation.

The exception to a questions-at-the-end policy occurs when your topic is so complex that a listener's question must be answered immediately if he or she is to follow the rest of the presentation. Another exception is informal (and generally small) meetings, where questions and comments naturally occur throughout the presentation.

Always listen carefully to the question; repeat it, if necessary, for the benefit of the entire audience; and look at the entire audience as you answer—not just at the questioner. Treat each questioner with unfailing courtesy. If the question is antagonistic, be firm but fair and polite.

If you don't know the answer to a question, freely say so and promise to have the answer within a specific period. Then write down the question (and the name of the questioner) to remind yourself to find the answer later. Do not risk embarrassing another member of the audience by referring the question to him or her.

Plan your answers to possible questions ahead of time.

Post-Presentation Activities

After the presentation ends and you're back in your office, evaluate your performance using the guidelines presented in Checklist 14 so that you can benefit from the experience. What seemed to work well and what not so well? Analyze each aspect of your performance—from initial research through delivery. Regardless of how well the presentation went, vow to improve your performance next time.

Listening

Effective communication—whether across continents or across a conference table—requires both sending and receiving messages; that is, it involves both transmission and reception. Whether you are making a formal presentation to 500 people or conversing with one person over lunch, your efforts will be in vain if your audience does not listen.

There is a difference between hearing and listening.

CHECKLIST 14

The Oral Presentation Process

Planning

✓ Determine your purpose: What response do you want from your audience?

✓ Analyze your audience in terms of demographic factors, level of knowledge, and psychological needs.

✓ Select an appropriate delivery method.

Organizing

✓ Brainstorm. Write down every point you think you might cover in the presentation.

✓ Separate your notes into the opening, body, and ending. Gather additional data if needed.

✓ Write an effective opening that introduces the topic, discusses the points you'll cover, and tells the audience what you hope will happen as a result of your presentation.

✓ In the body, develop the points fully, giving background data, evidence, and examples.

   a. Organize the points logically.

   b. To maintain credibility, discuss any major negative points and be prepared to discuss any minor ones.

   c. Pace the presentation of data to avoid presenting facts and figures too quickly.

✓ Finish on a strong, upbeat note by summarizing your main points, adding a personal appeal, drawing conclusions and making recommendations, discussing what needs to be done next, or using some other logical closing.

✓ Use humor only when appropriate and only if you are effective at telling amusing stories.

✓ Ensure that your visual aids are needed, simple, easily readable, and of the highest quality.

Practicing

✓ Rehearse your presentation extensively, simulating the actual speaking conditions as much as possible and using your visual aids.

✓ Use simple language and short sentences, with frequent preview, summary, transition, and repetition.

✓ Stand tall and naturally, and speak in a loud, clear, enthusiastic, and friendly voice. Vary the rate and volume of your voice.

✓ Use correct diction and appropriate gestures.

Delivering

✓ Dress appropriately—in comfortable, businesslike, conservative clothing.

✓ Maintain eye contact with the audience, including all corners of the room in your gaze.

✓ To avoid anxiety, practice extensively, develop a positive attitude, and concentrate on the friendly faces in the audience.

✓ Plan your answers to possible questions ahead of time. Listen to each question carefully and address your answer to the entire audience.

Listening involves much more than just hearing. You can hear and not listen (just as you can listen and not understand). Hearing is simply perceiving sound; sound waves strike the eardrum, sending impulses to the brain. It is a passive process, whereas listening is an active process. When you *perceive* a sound, you're merely aware of it; you don't necessarily comprehend it. When you *listen*, you interpret and assign meaning to the sounds.

Consider the automobile you drive. When the car is operating normally, even though you *hear* the sound of the engine as you're driving, you're barely aware of it because you tend to tune it out. But the minute the engine begins to make a strange sound—not necessarily louder or harsher, but just *different*—you immediately tune back in, listening intently to try to discern the nature of the problem. You *heard* the normal hum of the engine but *listened* to the strange noise.

The good news is that you can improve your listening skills. Tests at the University of Minnesota show that individuals who receive training in listening improve their listening skills by 25% to 42%.[8] To learn to listen more effectively, whether you're involved in a one-on-one dialogue or are part of a mass audience, give the speaker your undivided attention, stay open-minded, avoid interrupting, and involve yourself in the communication.

Give the Speaker Your Undivided Attention

During a business presentation, a member of the audience may hear certain familiar themes, think, "Oh no, not again," and proceed to tune the speaker out. Or during a conference with a subordinate, an executive may make or take phone calls, doodle, play around with a pen or pencil, or do other distracting things that give the speaker the impression that what he or she has to say is unimportant or uninteresting.

Physical distractions are the easiest to eliminate. Simply shutting the door or asking your assistant to hold all calls will eliminate many interruptions during personal conferences. If you're in a meeting where the environment is noisy, the temperature too cold or hot, or the chairs uncomfortable, try to block out the distractions rather than the speaker. Learn to ignore those annoyances over which you have no control and concentrate instead on the speaker and what he or she is saying.

Mental distractions are more difficult to eliminate. With practice and effort, however, you can discipline yourself—for example, to temporarily forget about your fatigue or to put competing thoughts out of your mind—so that you can give the speaker your full attention.

Just as it is important for the speaker to maintain eye contact with the whole audience, it is also important for the *listener* to maintain eye contact with the speaker. Doing so sends the message that you're interested in what the speaker has to say, and the speaker will be more likely to open up to you and provide the information you need.

We talk about giving the speaker your undivided attention. Actually, it would be more accurate to say that you give the speaker's *comments* your undivided attention; that is, focus on the content of the talk and don't be overly concerned about how the talk is delivered. It is true, of course, that nonverbal clues do provide important information. However, do not be put off by the fact that the speaker may have dressed inappropriately, spoken too fast or in an unfamiliar accent, or appeared nervous. Almost always, *what* is said is more important than *how* it is said.

Likewise, avoid dismissing a topic simply because it is uninteresting or is presented in an uninteresting manner. "Boring" does not mean unimportant. Some information that may be boring or difficult to follow may, in fact, prove to be quite useful to you and thus well worth your effort in giving it your full attention.

Stay Open-Minded

Regardless of whom you're listening to or what the topic is, keep your emotions in check. Listen objectively and empathetically. Be willing to accept new information and new points of view, regardless of whether they mesh with your existing beliefs. Concentrate on the content of the message rather than on its source.

Don't look at the situation as a win/lose proposition—that is, that the speaker wins and you lose if you concede the merits of his or her position. Instead, think of it as a win/win situation—that is, that the speaker wins by convincing you of the merits of his or her position, and you win by gaining new information and insights that will help you perform your duties more effectively.

> Physical distractions are easier to eliminate than mental distractions.

> Pay more attention to what the speaker says than to how he or she says it.

> Keeping an open mind results in a win/win situation.

Maintain neutrality as long as possible, and don't jump to conclusions too quickly. Instead, try to understand *why* the speaker is arguing a particular point of view and what facts or experience convinced the speaker to adopt this position.

When you assume this empathetic frame of reference, you will likely find that you neither completely agree with nor completely disagree with every point the speaker makes. This ability to evaluate the message objectively will help you gain the most from the exchange.

Don't Interrupt

Perhaps because of time pressures, we sometimes become impatient. As soon as we've figured out what a person is going to say, we tend to interrupt to finish the sentence for the speaker; this practice is especially a problem when listening to a slow speaker. Or as soon as we can think of a counterargument, we tend to rush right in—regardless of whether the speaker has finished or even paused for a breath.

Such interruptions have many negative consequences. First, they are rude. Second, instead of speeding up the exchange, such interruptions actually tend to drag it out because they often interfere with the speaker's train of thought, causing backtracking. The most serious negative consequence, however, is the nonverbal message such an interruption sends: "I have the right to interrupt you because what I have to say is more important than what you have to say!" Is it any wonder, then, that such a message hinders effective communication?

There is a difference between listening and simply waiting to speak. Even if you're too polite to interrupt, don't simply lie in wait for the first available opportunity to barge in with your version of the truth. If you're constantly planning what you'll say next, you can hardly listen attentively to what the other person is saying.

Americans tend to have low tolerance for silence. Yet waiting a moment or two after someone has finished before you respond has several positive effects—especially in an emotional exchange. It gives the person speaking a chance to elaborate on his or her remarks, thereby drawing out further insights. It also helps create a quieter, calmer, more respectful atmosphere, one that is more conducive to solving the problem at hand.

Involve Yourself

As we have said, hearing is passive whereas listening is active. You should be *doing* something while the other person is speaking (and we don't mean doodling, staring out the window, or planning your afternoon activities).

Much of what you should be doing is mental. Summarize to yourself what the speaker is saying; create what experts call an *internal paraphrase* of the speaker's comments. We can process information much faster than the speaker can present it, so use that extra time for active listening—ensuring that you really are hearing not only what the person is saying but his or her motives and implications as well.

Some listeners find it helpful to jot down points, translating their mental notes into written notes. If you do so, keep your notes brief; don't become so busy writing down the facts that you miss the message. Concentrate on the main ideas; if you get them, you'll be much more likely to remember the supporting details later. Recognize also that even if a detail or two of the speaker's message might be inaccurate or irrelevant, the major points may still be valid. Evaluate the validity of the overall argument; don't get bogged down in trivia.

Be selfish in your listening. Constantly ask yourself, How does this point affect *me*? How can I use this information to further my goals or to help me perform my job more effectively? Personalizing the information will help you to concentrate more easily and to weigh the evidence more objectively—even if the topic is difficult to follow or uninteresting and even if the speaker has some annoying mannerisms or an unpleasant personality.

Encourage the speaker by letting him or her know that you're actively involved in the exchange. Maintain eye contact, nod in agreement, lean forward, utter encouraging phrases such as "Uh huh" or "I see." In a conversation, ensure that your mental paraphrases are on target by summarizing aloud for the speaker what you think you're hearing. You can give such feedback as "So you believe . . . , is that true?" or "Do you mean that . . . ?" which in turn enables the speaker to clarify remarks, add new information, or clear up any misconceptions. In addition, it tells the speaker that you're paying attention to the exchange.

RECALL Write a capital T for *true* or F for *false* before each statement.

1. ____ Behavior modification experts have found that fear of public speaking is almost impossible to overcome.

2. ____ Unless you're talking about a rather complex topic or speaking to a small group, it is generally better to hold questions until the end of your presentation.

3. ____ You can hear and still not listen.

4. ____ Mental distractions are easier to eliminate than physical distractions.

5. ____ You should take extensive notes as an aid to remembering what the speaker said.

CHECKPOINT 13.3

COMPREHENSION

6. What are some ways in which effective spoken language differs from written language?

7. Use the Internet to locate the nearest Toastmasters International chapter **(www.toastmasters.org).** Give the name of the chapter and tell when and where it meets.

CRITICAL THINKING

8. What does the guideline "Be selfish in your listening" mean?

The 3Ps
Problem, Process, Product

Visual Aids for a Business Presentation

Problem

You are Matt Kromer, an administrative assistant at Lewis & Smith. Your company publishes three major external documents—a quarterly customer newsletter, a semiannual catalog, and an annual report. All three are currently prepared by an outside printing company. However, the company recently decided to switch to some form of in-house publishing to produce these publications.

Your superior asked you to research the question of whether your firm should use word processing or desktop publishing software to create these documents. You have completed your research and drafted a formal 20-minute presentation of your findings and recommendations to the firm's administrative committee. You are now ready to develop some visual aids.

Process

1. What types of visual aids will you use?

   Slides (in the form of an electronic presentation)

   a. Two slides at the beginning—to preview the topic and to illustrate our three publications

   b. Two in the middle—to compare the costs and features of the two programs

   c. Two at the end—to give my recommendations and to show what needs to be done next

2. Will you develop an audience handout?

   I could, of course, easily develop a one-page handout showing miniature copies of the six slides—as a summary of my important points and for future reference. Because the purpose of my presentation is to get a decision made today and I have no supplementary information to present, however, a handout isn't necessary.

3. How will you practice your presentation?

   I'll do a dry run in the conference room where I'll be speaking, standing where I'll actually be giving the presentation and using my computer and projector. I'll also set up a cassette recorder at the far end of the conference table to tape my practice presentation to ensure that I can be heard, to check for clarity and voice qualities, and to time my presentation. In addition, I'll practice answering any questions I think the managers might ask.

4. Afterward, how will you determine whether your presentation was a success?

   If the administrative committee votes to accept my recommendation and schedule, I will have achieved my purpose and the presentation will have been successful.

364

Product

Actual document can be scanned into the computer, sized to fit, and positioned as desired.

Tables and charts are created easily using presentation software.

During the presentation, each bulleted point and each schedule line is projected one at a time—for emphasis.

Slide 1

Slide 2

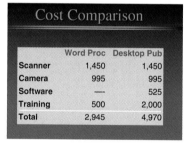

Slide 3

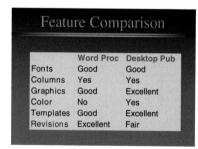

Slide 4

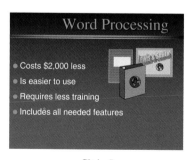

Slide 5

Slide 6

Grammar and Mechanics Notes

This presentation uses the Double Lines template in Microsoft PowerPoint. All font faces, sizes, and locations are preselected for you. Do not try to crowd too much information on each slide.

365

Summary

Oral presentations are a vital part of the contemporary business organization. Planning a presentation requires determining the purpose, analyzing the audience, and planning the method of presentation appropriate for the situation. Organizing the presentation requires developing an effective opening, developing each point logically in the middle, and ending on a strong, confident note.

When making a work-team presentation, allow enough time to prepare, assign responsibilities on the basis of individual talents, and rehearse sufficiently to ensure that the overall presentation has coherence and unity. When giving a video presentation, wear appropriate clothing, look directly into the camera, avoid exaggerated movements, and stay within an established area of movement.

Visual aids are an important component of most business presentations. Although overhead transparencies were traditionally the format of choice, increasingly presenters are making electronic presentations, with the slides or video being shown directly from a computer connected to a projector. Regardless of the format used, your visual aids should be relevant, simple, easily readable, and of high quality.

Practice your presentation until you know it well and feel comfortable presenting it. If needed, follow the recommended techniques for dealing with stage fright. When actually delivering your presentation, dress appropriately, speak in a clear and confident manner, and maintain eye contact with the audience. Finally, evaluate your performance afterward to ensure that your presentation skills improve with each opportunity to speak.

Listening is the most used but least developed of the verbal communication skills. Whether listening to a formal presentation or conversing with others, you can learn to listen more effectively by giving the speaker your undivided attention, staying open-minded about the speaker and the topic, avoiding interrupting the speaker, and involving yourself actively in the communication process.

Looking Ahead

For many students, one of the prime skills they hope to develop in this course is the ability to conduct a successful job campaign at the conclusion of their education. Learning effective employment communication skills—including preparing a professional résumé and cover letter and conducting a successful job interview—are the focus of Chapter 14.

Exercises

Planning and Organizing the Presentation

1 **Understanding the Role of Business Presentations**   Interview two business people in your community who hold positions in your area of career interest to learn more about their experiences in making oral presentations. Write a memorandum to your instructor summarizing what you've learned. You may want to ask such questions as the following:

a. How important has the ability to make effective oral presentations been to your career?
b. What kinds of oral presentations do you make in and out of the office, and how often do you make them?
c. How do you typically prepare for such presentations?

2 Internet Exercise General Electric executives are much in demand as speakers to internal and external audiences. Select and analyze one of the speeches posted on the company's Web site (**http://www.ge.com/news/podium _speech.html**). How does the executive open this speech? Does the speaker use the opening to preview the points he or she will make? How does the speaker organize the body of the speech? How does the speaker deal with any negative points? Looking at the ending, does the speaker summarize the main points? How does he or she add punch to the ending? What can you suggest to improve this speech? Along with your responses to these questions, submit a copy of the speech you analyzed.

3 Planning a Presentation You decided at the last minute to apply to the graduate school at your institution to work toward an MBA degree. Even though you have a 3.4 GPA (on a 4.0 scale), you were denied admission because you had not taken the GMAT, which is a prerequisite for admission. You have, however, been given ten minutes to appear before the Graduate Council to try to convince them to grant you a temporary waiver of this requirement and permit you to enroll in MBA classes next term, during which time you will take the GMAT. The Graduate Council consists of the director of the MBA program and two senior faculty members, one of whom is your business communication professor.

a. What is the purpose of your presentation?
b. What do you know or what can you surmise about your audience that might help you prepare a more effective presentation?
c. What considerations affect the timing of your presentation?
d. What method of delivery should you use?

Work-Team and Video Presentations and Visual Aids

4 Presenting Research Data Review the analytical or recommendation report you prepared in Chapter 12. Assume that you have been given 15 minutes to present the important information from your written report to a committee of your superiors who will not have an opportunity to read the written report. Write out your presentation notes, using either full sheets of paper or note cards. Also, develop at least four visual aids using Microsoft PowerPoint or some other software presentation program. Submit your notes along with a handout (four to a page) of your visual aids.

5 Work-Team Presentation Divide into teams of four or five students. Your instructor will assign you to either the pro or the con side of one of the following topics:

■ Drug testing should/should not be mandatory for all employees.

■ All forms of smoking should/should not be banned completely from the workplace—including outside the building.

■ Employers should/should not provide flextime (flexible working hours) for all office employees.

■ Employers should/should not provide on-site child-care facilities for the preschool children of their employees.

■ Employees who deal extensively with the public should/should not be required to wear a company uniform.

■ Employers should/should not have the right to hire the most qualified employees without regard to affirmative action guidelines.

Assume that your employee group has been asked to present its views to a management committee that will make the final decision regarding your topic. The presentations will be given as follows:

a. Each side (beginning with the pro side) will have eight minutes to present its views.
b. Each side will then have three minutes to confer.
c. Each side (beginning with the con side) will deliver a two-minute rebuttal—to refute the arguments and answer the issues raised by the other side.
d. Each side (beginning with the pro side) will give a one-minute summary of its argument.
e. The management committee (the rest of the class) will then vote by secret ballot regarding which side (pro or con) presented its case more effectively.

Gather whatever data you think will be helpful to your case, organize it, divide up the speaking roles as you deem best, and prepare speaker notes. (*Hint:* It might be helpful to gather information on both the pro and the con sides of the issue in preparation for the rebuttal session, which will be given impromptu.)

6 Video Presentation   Locate two journal articles on some aspect of business communication (the topics in this book's table of contents will provide clues for searching). The two articles should be about the same topic. Integrate the important information from both articles, and present your findings to the class in a five-minute videotaped presentation.

7 Planning the Visual Element   You are the trainer for an in-house survey course in effective advertising techniques that is being offered to franchise owners of your Mexican fast-food chain. As part of the course, you are scheduled to present a 30-minute session on writing effective bad-news letters. You decide to use the bad-news letter section of Chapter 8 in this text as the basis for your presentation. Prepare four to six slides that you might use for your presentation to the 25 participants in the course. Submit full-sized color copies of the transparencies to your instructor.

Practicing and Delivering the Presentation and Listening

8 Presenting Research Data   Review the analytical or recommendation report that you prepared in Chapter 12 and the presentation notes and visual aids that you prepared for this 15-minute oral presentation in Exercise 4 of this chapter. Practice your presentation several times—including at least once in the classroom where you will actually give it. Give your presentation to the class. (Your instructor may ask the audience to evaluate each presentation in terms of the effectiveness of its content, use of visual aids, and delivery.)

9 Providing Feedback Make copies of the presentation feedback form shown below. As required by your instructor:

a. Provide a self-evaluation of your performance in a classroom presentation.
b. Evaluate the performance of other classroom presenters.
c. Evaluate the performance of another speaker assigned by your instructor.

Presentation Feedback Form

Directions: Circle the score you believe most accurately reflects the performance of the presenter(s) on each criterion. Fill in the ID information, including the score (total number of points circled, ranging from 8 to 40). Finally, write in specific comments that will aid the presenter in improving his or her performance in future presentations. (*Note:* If this form is returned to the presenter, the rater identification will be cut off from this form.)

Presenter _____   Rater _____   Score ____

Criteria	Extremely Effective	Effective	Average	Ineffective	Extremely Ineffective
CONTENT: Relevant, accurate, complete, understandable, well organized, interesting, at an appropriate level of complexity	10	8	6	4	2
DELIVERY: Clear and pleasant articulation, confident demeanor, good eye contact with audience, appropriate length, extemporaneous presentation (not read or memorized)	10	8	6	4	2
VISUAL AIDS: Helpful, informative, easily readable, attractive, consistent, and error-free transparencies, handouts, and other aids; smooth and unobtrusive use of visual aids	10	8	6	4	2
OVERALL RATING: Considering the above criteria (as well as any other relevant criteria), how effective was the presentation?	10	8	6	4	2

Strong point(s) of presentation:

Area(s) for improvement:

10 Petition for Entry into Graduate School Review Exercise 3 regarding your petition to be accepted into graduate school at your institution. Prepare your presentation notes, any needed visual aids, and make this ten-minute presentation to the Graduate Council.

11 Listening Your instructor will assign you a television show to watch this week—a news program, talk show, or documentary. Using the listening techniques you learned in this chapter, take notes on the important points covered in the presentation. Listen for the major themes, not the details. Write a one-page memo to your instructor summarizing the important information you heard. Should every student's paper contain basically the same information? Explain your answer.

Making a Business Presentation

Problem   You are a legal assistant in the corporate law department of a large business firm. The five attorneys for whom you work are interested in learning more about the topic of speech-recognition software and which is the best program. Use the Internet and any printed resources available to locate at least five articles on speech-recognition software. Use these articles to develop a ten-minute videotaped presentation to an audience comprising these five attorneys.

Process   Compose a few paragraphs describing how you went about solving this problem. In narrative form, provide such information as the following:

1. What is the purpose of your presentation?

2. Describe your audience.

3. What kind of presentation notes will you prepare?

4. How will you organize your presentation?

5. What kind of visual aids will you prepare?

6. What kind of opening and closing will you use?

7. Describe how you decided what to wear for this videotaped presentation.

8. How will you secure a video camera and operator? Will you act as operator for another person's presentation?

9. How many times did you videotape your presentation?

Product   Have your presentation videotaped as many times as you feel necessary to ensure a competent and professional presentation.

14 Employment Communications

COMMUNICATION OBJECTIVES

After you have finished this chapter, you should be able to:

- Determine the appropriate length, format, and content for your résumé.

- Compose job-application letters.

- Prepare for an employment interview and conduct yourself appropriately during the interview.

- Complete the communication tasks needed after the employment interview.

On the Job

PAUL ORVOS
Corporate Manager of Employment, Computer Sciences Corporation

Before electronic résumés became available, Paul Orvos, the corporate manager of employment for Computer Sciences Corporation (CSC), used to receive mailbags full of résumés and job-application letters. CSC is growing so fast that Orvos and his colleagues can no longer read each of the résumés they receive every year—many from college graduates starting their careers. Instead, CSC has gone paperless, requesting that applicants submit electronic résumés directly to the company's database, which stores tens of thousands of résumés for screening and consideration when openings arise.

Although CSC indicates in its employment ads and on its World Wide Web site that electronic résumés in ASCII (text) format are preferred, it will scan paper résumés so they can be entered into the database. Because no one actually reads the résumés before they are stored in the database, the look of the résumé is far less important than the content. "The days of fancy fonts, underscoring, and bold type are gone," says Orvos. "Content is what counts today." Grammar and mechanics remain important, however: "Double- and triple-check your grammar, spelling, and punctuation, because employers view résumés as samples of the quality of work they can expect from you," advises Orvos.

Planning Your Career

Although we've stressed throughout this book the importance of communication skills for success on the job, one of your first professional applications of what you've learned will likely be in securing a job. Think for a moment about some of the important communication skills you've developed thus far—how to analyze your audience, write effective letters, research and analyze data, speak persuasively, and use nonverbal communication to achieve your objectives.

These communication skills will serve you well when you apply for an internship or begin your job-getting campaign. To refine these skills further, in this chapter you will learn how to develop a résumé, write application letters, conduct yourself during an interview, and write post-interview letters.

You must put considerable time, effort, and thought into getting a job if you want to have a rewarding and fulfilling work life. The process is the same whether you're applying for an internship, beginning your first job, changing careers, or returning to the workplace after an extended absence.

Communication skills play an important role in the job campaign.

Preparing Your Résumé

résumé A brief record of one's personal history and qualifications usually prepared by a job applicant

A **résumé** is a brief record of one's personal history and qualifications that is typically prepared by an applicant for a job. Although recruiters sometimes refer to the résumé as a *wilawid* ("What I've learned and what I've done"), the emphasis in the résumé should be on the future rather than on the past: you must show how your education and work experience prepared you for future jobs—specifically, the job for which you are applying.

The purpose of a résumé is to get you a job interview—not to get you a job.

Right from the start, be realistic about the purpose of your résumé. Few people are hired on the basis of their résumés alone. (On the other hand, many people are *not hired* because of their poorly written or poorly presented résumés.) Instead, applicants are generally hired on the basis of their performance during one or more job interviews.

Thus, the purpose of the résumé is to get you an interview, and the purpose of the interview is to get you a job. Remember, however, that the résumé and accompanying application letter (cover letter) are crucial in advancing you beyond the mass of initial applicants and into the much smaller group of potential candidates invited to an interview.

Résumé Length

Most recruiters prefer a one-page résumé for entry-level positions.

Decisions about résumé length become much easier when you consider what happens on the receiving end: recruiters typically spend no more than 35 seconds looking at each résumé during their initial screening to pare down the perhaps hundreds of applications for a position into a manageable number to study in more detail.[1] How much information can the recruiter be expected to read in less than a minute? It won't matter how well qualified you are if no one ever reviews those qualifications.

How much is too much? Surveys of employment and human resources executives consistently show that most managers prefer a one-page résumé for the entry-level positions typically sought by recent college graduates, with a two-page résumé being reserved for unusual circumstances or for higher-level positions.[2] True or not, take note of the old placement-office adage, "The thicker the résumé, the thicker the applicant."

(Note, however, that a recent survey of personnel recruiters from Big Five accounting firms found that recruiters ranked candidates with two-page résumés more favorably than candidates with one-page résumés. The researchers recommended that graduating seniors with accounting majors *and outstanding credentials* consider writing two-page résumés when applying for entry-level Big Five accounting positions.)[3]

According to one survey of 200 executives from major U.S. firms, the most serious mistake job candidates make is including too much information in their résumés. Their ranking (in percentages of the whole) of the most serious résumé errors is as follows:[4]

A too-long résumé is one of the most serious weaknesses, according to one study.

Too long	32%
Typographical or grammatical errors	25%
No description of job functions	18%
Unprofessional appearance	15%
Achievements omitted	10%
	100%

A one-page résumé is *not* the same as a two-page résumé crammed onto one page by means of small type and narrow margins. Your résumé must be attractive and easy to read. Shorten it by making judicious decisions about what to include and then by using concise language to communicate what is important.

But do not make your résumé *too* short, either. A résumé that does not fill one page may tell the prospective employer that you have little to offer. It has been estimated that one page is ideal for 85% of all résumés, and that is the length you should target.[5]

Résumé Format

Although the content of your résumé is obviously more important than its format, remember that first impressions are lasting. As pointed out earlier, those first impressions are formed during the half-minute that is typically devoted to the initial screening of each résumé. For this reason, even before you begin writing your résumé, think about the format, because some format decisions will affect the amount of space available to discuss your qualifications and background.

Use a clear, simple design, with plenty of white space.

Choose a simple, easy-to-read typeface, and avoid the temptation to use a lot of "special effects" just because they're available on your computer. One or two typefaces in one or two different sizes should be enough. Use a simple format, with lots of white space, short paragraphs, and a logical organization. Through the use of type size and style, indentation, bullets, and the like, make clear which parts are subordinate to main features. One of your word processor's built-in résumé templates is a good place to start.

Format your résumé on standard-sized paper (8½ by 11 inches) so that it can be filed easily. Also, avoid brightly colored papers: they'll get attention but perhaps the wrong kind. Dark colors do not photocopy well, and you want photocopies of your résumé (whether made by you or by the potential employer) to look professional. Choose white or an off-white (cream or ivory) paper of good quality—at least 20-pound bond.

Unless you're applying for a creative position (such as a copywriter of advertising material) and know your intended audience well, avoid being too artistic and original in formatting your résumé. If you are applying for the typical business position, the overall appearance of your résumé should present a professional, conservative appearance—one that adds to your credibility. Don't scare off your readers before they have a chance to meet you.

Finally, your résumé and application letter must be 100% free from error—in content, spelling, grammar, and format. Ninety-nine percent accuracy is simply not good enough when seeking a job. One survey of large-company executives showed that fully 80% of them had decided against interviewing a job seeker simply because of poor grammar, spelling, or punctuation in his or her résumé.[6] Don't write, as one job applicant did, "Education: Advanced Curses in Accounting," or as another did, "I have an obsession for detail; I make sure that I cross my i's and dot my t's." Show right from the start that you're the type of person who takes pride in your work.

Résumé Content

Fortunately, perhaps, there is no such thing as a standard résumé; each is as individual as the person it represents. There are, however, standard parts of the résumé—those parts recruiters expect and need to see to make valid judgments. For example, one survey of 152 *Fortune* 500 company personnel indicated that 90% or more wanted the following information on a résumé:[7]

- Name, address, and telephone number
- Job objective
- College major, degree, name of college, and date of graduation
- Jobs held, employing company or companies (but not complete mailing address or the names of your supervisors), dates of employment, and job duties
- Special aptitudes and skills

Similarly, items *not* wanted on the résumé (items rated unimportant by more than 90% of those surveyed) related primarily to bases for possible discrimination: religion, ethnicity, age, gender, photograph, and marital status. Additionally, most of the employers questioned thought high school activities should not be included on the résumés of college graduates.

The standard and optional parts of the résumé are discussed here in the order in which they typically appear on the résumé of a recent (or soon-to-be) college graduate.

Identifying Information   It doesn't do any good to impress a recruiter if he or she cannot locate you easily to schedule an interview; as a consequence, your name and complete address (including phone number) are crucial.

Your name should appear as the very first item on the résumé, arranged attractively at the top. Use whatever form you typically use for signing your name (for example, with or without initials). Give your complete name, avoiding nicknames, and do not use a personal title such as *Mr.* or *Ms.*

It is not necessary to include the heading "Résumé" at the top (any more than it is necessary to use the heading "Letter" at the top of a business letter). The purpose of the document will be evident to the recruiter. Besides, you want your name to be the main heading—where it will stand out in the recruiter's mind.

If you will soon be changing your address (for example, from a college address to a home address), include both, along with the relevant dates for each. If you are away from your telephone most of the day and no one is at home to answer it and take a message, you would be wise to secure phone company voice mail, invest in an answering machine, or get permission to use the telephone number where you work as an alternate phone listing. The important point is to be available for contact.

Increasingly, employers also expect the résumé to list an email address. An email address not only provides another means of contact but also sends a nonverbal message that you are computer savvy. And, of course, if you have a personal Web page that highlights your accomplishments in a positive and professional manner, include that address as well.

Job Objective   The job objective is a short summary of your area of expertise and career interest. Most recruiters want the objective stated so that they will know where you might fit into their organization. Don't force the employer to guess about your career goals.

Include the information employers want; exclude the information they do not want.

Furthermore, don't waste the objective's prominent spot at the top of your résumé by giving a weak, over-general goal like these:

NOT: "A position that offers both a challenge and an opportunity for growth."

"Challenging position in a progressive organization."

"A responsible position that lets me use my education and experience and that provides opportunities for increased responsibilities."

The problem with such goals is not that they're unworthy objectives; they are *very* worthwhile. That is why everyone—including the recruiter presumably—wants such positions. The problem is that such vague, high-flown goals don't help the recruiter find a suitable position for *you*. They waste valuable space on your résumé.

For your objective to help you, it must be personalized—both for you and for the position you're seeking. Also, it must be specific enough to be useful to the prospective employer but not so specific as to exclude you from many types of similar positions. The following job objectives meet these criteria:

BUT: "A paid, one-semester internship in marketing or advertising."

"Position in personal sales in a medium-sized manufacturing firm."

"Opportunity to apply my accounting education and Spanish-language skills outside the United States."

"A public relations position requiring well-developed communication, administrative, and computer skills."

After reading these objectives, you feel you know a little about each candidate, a feeling you did not get from reading the earlier, too-general objectives. If your goals are so broad that you have difficulty specifying a job objective, consider either eliminating this section of your résumé or developing several résumés, each with a different job objective and emphasis.

Include a job objective if you have specific requirements.

You should be aware that most large corporations now scan the résumés they receive into their computer systems and then search this computerized database by keyword (see "On the Job" on page 371). For this reason, make certain that your résumé includes the title of the actual position you desire and other relevant terms. (Later in this chapter, we discuss electronic résumés.)

Education Unless your work experience has been extensive, fairly high level, and directly related to your job objective, your education is probably a stronger job qualification than your work experience and should therefore come first on the résumé.

Most traditional students will list their education before their work experience.

List the title of your degree, the name of your college and its location if needed, your major and (if applicable) minor, and your expected date of graduation (month and year).

List your grade-point average if it will set you apart from the competition (generally, at least a 3.0 on a 4.0 scale). If you've made the dean's list or have financed any substantial portion of your college expenses through part-time work, savings, or scholarships, mention that fact. Unless your course of study provided distinctive experiences that uniquely qualify you for the job, avoid including a lengthy list of college courses.

Work Experience Today, almost half of all full-time college students are employed, with most of them working between 15 and 29 hours per week.[8]

Most other students have had at least some work experience—for example, summer jobs. Thus, most students will have some work experience to bring to their future jobs.

Work experience—*any* work experience—is a definite plus. It shows the employer that you've had experience in satisfying a superior, following directions, accomplishing objectives through team effort, and being rewarded for your labors. If your work experience has been directly related to your job objectives, consider putting it ahead of the education section, where it will receive more emphasis.

In relating your work experience, use either a chronological or a functional organizational pattern.

■ *Chronological:* In a chronological arrangement, you organize your experience by date, describing your most recent job first and working backward. This format is most appropriate when you have had a strong continuing work history and much of your work has been related to your job objective (see Model 22 on page 377). Approximately 95% of all résumés are chronological, beginning with the most recent information and working backward.[9]

■ *Functional:* In a functional arrangement, you organize your experience by type of function performed (such as *supervision* or *budgeting*) or by type of skill developed (such as *human relations* or *communication skills*). Then, under each, you list specific examples (evidence) as illustrated in Model 23 on page 378. Functional résumés are most appropriate when you're changing industries, moving into an entirely different line of work, or reentering the work force after a long period of unemployment, because they emphasize your skills rather than your employment history and let you show how these skills have broad applicability to other jobs.

Regardless of which type of organizational pattern you use, provide complete information about your work history.

In actual practice, these patterns are not mutually exclusive; you can use a combination of the two. And regardless of which arrangement you ultimately select, remember that more than 90% of the employers in the survey cited earlier indicated they want to see on a résumé the jobs held, employing company or companies, dates of employment, and job duties.

Recall that the purpose of describing your work history is to show the prospective employer what you've learned *that will benefit the organization*. No matter what your previous work, you've developed certain traits or had certain experiences that can be transferred to the new position. On the basis of your research into the duties of the job you are seeking, highlight those transferable skills.

Use concrete, achievement-oriented words to describe your work experience.

If you can honestly do so, show in your résumé that you have developed as many of the following characteristics as possible:

■ Ability to work well with others
■ Communication skills
■ Competence and good judgment
■ Innovation
■ High-level computer proficiency
■ Reliability and trustworthiness
■ Enthusiasm
■ Honest and moral character
■ Increasing responsibility

Complete sentences are not necessary. Instead, start your descriptions with action verbs, using present tense for current duties and past tense for previous job duties or accomplishments. Concrete words such as those shown on page 379 make your work experience come alive:

MODEL 22

Résumé in Chronological Format

225 West 70 Street
New York, NY 10023
Phone: 212-555-3821
Email: agomez@nyu.edu

1
2

Aurelia Gomez

Objective	Entry-level staff accounting position with a public accounting firm	

Provides specific enough objective to be useful.

3 **Experience** | Summer 2003 | ***Accounting Intern:*** Coopers & Lybrand, NYC
• Assisted in preparing corporate tax returns
• Attended meetings with clients
• Conducted research in corporate tax library and wrote research reports

Places work experience before education because applicant considers it to be her stronger qualification.

4 | Nov. 1999 – Aug. 2001 | ***Payroll Specialist:*** City of New York
• Worked in a full-time civil service position in the Department of Administration
• Used payroll and other accounting software on both DEC 1034 minicomputer and Pentium III
• Represented 28-person work unit on the department's management–labor committee
• Left job to pursue college degree full-time

Uses action words like *assisted* and *conducted;* uses incomplete sentences to emphasize the action words and to conserve space.

Education | Jan. 1997 – Present | Pursuing a 5-year bachelor of business administration degree (major in accounting) from NYU
• Expected graduation date: June 2004
• Attended part-time from 1997 until 2002 while holding down a full-time job
• Have financed 100% of all college expenses through savings, work, and student loans
• Plan to sit for the CPA exam in May 2005

Provides degree, institution, major, and graduation date.

Personal Data | • Helped start the Minority Business Student Association at NYU and served as program director for two years; secured the publisher of *Black Enterprise* magazine as a banquet speaker
• Have traveled extensively throughout South America
• Am a member of the Accounting Society
• Am willing to relocate

Provides additional data to enhance her credentials.

References | Available upon request

Omits actual names and addresses of references.

Grammar and Mechanical Notes

1 The name is formatted in larger type for emphasis.
2 Horizontal and vertical rules separate the heading information from the body of the résumé.
3 The major section headings are parallel in format and in wording.
4 The side headings for the dates are formatted in a column for ease of reading. Note that abbreviations may be used.

MODEL 23

Résumé in Functional Format

Objective introduces three skill areas and expands on each with bulleted examples.

Relates each listed item directly to the desired job.

Provides specific evidence to support each skill.

Weaves work experiences, education, and extracurricular activities into the skill statements.

Avoids repeating the duties given earlier.

RAYMOND J. ARNOLD

1 **OBJECTIVE**

Labor relations position in a large multinational firm that requires well-developed labor relations, management, and communication skills

SKILLS

LABOR RELATIONS

2
- Majored in labor relations; minored in psychology
- Belong to Local 463 of International Office Workers Union
- Was crew chief for the second-shift work team at Wainwright Bank

MANAGEMENT
- Learned time-management skills by working 30 hours per week while attending school full-time
- Was promoted twice in three years at Wainwright Bank
- Practiced discretion while dealing with the financial affairs of others; treated all transactions confidentially

COMMUNICATION

3
- Developed a Web page for Alpha Kappa Psi business fraternity
- Ran for senior class vice president, making frequent campaign speeches and impromptu remarks
- Took elective classes in report writing and business research
- Am competent in Microsoft Office XP and Internet research

4 **EDUCATION**

B.S. Degree from Boston University to be awarded June 2004
Major: Labor Relations; Minor: Psychology

EXPERIENCE

Bank teller, Wainwright Bank, Boston, Massachusetts: 2001–Present
Salesperson, JC Penney, Norfolk, Nebraska: Summer 1999

REFERENCES

Available from the Career Information Center
Boston University, Boston, MA 02215; phone: 617-555-2000

15 TURNER HALL, BOSTON UNIVERSITY, BOSTON, MA 02215 PHONE: 617-555-9833 • E-MAIL: RJARNOLD@BU.EDU

Grammar and Mechanical Notes

1 Putting the headings along the side and indenting the copy opens up the résumé, providing more white space. (This document is based on the "Elegant" résumé template in Microsoft Word.)

2 Bullets are used to highlight the individual skills; asterisks would have worked just as well.

3 All items are in parallel format.

4 More space is left *between* the different sections than *within* sections (to clearly separate each section).

accomplished	constructed	increased	produced
achieved	contracted	instituted	purchased
administered	controlled	interviewed	recommended
analyzed	coordinated	introduced	reported
applied	created	investigated	researched
approved	delegated	led	revised
arranged	designed	maintained	scheduled
assisted	determined	managed	screened
authorized	developed	marketed	secured
balanced	diagnosed	modified	simplified
budgeted	directed	motivated	sold
built	edited	negotiated	studied
changed	established	operated	supervised
collected	evaluated	ordered	taught
communicated	forecast	organized	trained
completed	generated	oversaw	transformed
conceived	guided	planned	updated
concluded	handled	prepared	wrote
conducted	hired	presented	
consolidated	implemented	presided	

Avoid weak verbs such as *attempted, endeavored, hoped,* and *tried,* and avoid sexist language such as *manpower* and *chairman.* When possible, ensure credibility by listing specific accomplishments, giving numbers or dollar amounts. Highlight especially those accomplishments that have direct relevance to the desired job. Here are some examples:

NOT: I was responsible for a large sales territory.

BUT: Managed a six-county sales territory; increased sales 13% during first full year.

NOT: I worked as a clerk in the cashier's office.

BUT: Balanced the cash register every day; was the only part-time employee entrusted to make nightly cash deposits.

NOT: Worked as a bouncer at a local bar.

BUT: Maintained order at Nick's Side-Door Saloon; learned firsthand the importance of compromise and negotiation in solving problems.

NOT: Worked as a volunteer for Art Reach.

BUT: Personally sold more than $1,000 worth of tickets to annual benefit dance; introduced an "Each one, reach one" membership drive that increased membership every year during my three-year term as membership chairperson.

As illustrated in the last example, if you have little or no actual work experience, show how your involvement with professional, social, or civic organizations has helped you develop skills that are transferable to the workplace. Volunteer work, for example, can help develop valuable skills in time management, working with groups, handling money, public speaking, accepting responsibility, and the like. In addition, most schools offer internships in which a student receives course credit and close supervision while holding down a temporary job.

It has been said that the closest any of us comes to perfection is when we develop our résumé, which has also been called "a balance sheet without any liabilities." Employers recognize your right to put your best foot forward in your résumé—that is, to highlight your strengths and minimize your weaknesses. However, you must never lie about anything and must never take credit for

Work experience need not be restricted to paid positions.

Be ethical in all aspects of your résumé.

anything you did not do. A simple telephone call can verify any statement on your résumé. A recent study by Automatic Data Processing found that more than 40 percent of applicants misrepresented their education or employment history.[10]

Don't risk destroying your credibility before being hired, and don't risk the possibility of being dismissed later for misrepresenting your qualifications.

Other Relevant Information   If you have special skills that might give you an edge over the competition (such as knowledge of a foreign language or Web-page–creation competence), list them on your résumé. Although employers assume that college graduates today have competence in word processing, you should specify any other particular software skills you possess.

Include any honors or recognitions that have relevance to the job you're seeking. Memberships in business-related organizations demonstrate your commitment to your profession, and you should list them if space permits. Likewise, involvement in volunteer, civic, and other extracurricular activities gives evidence of a well-rounded individual and reflects your values and commitment.

Avoid including any data that can become grounds for a discrimination suit—such as information about age, gender, race, religion, handicaps, marital status, and the like. Do not include a photograph with your application papers. Some employers like to have the applicant's Social Security number included as an aid in verifying college or military information. If you have military experience, include it. If your name stereotypes you as a possible noncitizen and citizenship is important for the job you want, you may want to explicitly state your citizenship.

Other optional information includes hobbies and special interests, travel experiences, willingness to travel, and health status. (However, because it is unlikely that anyone has ever written "Health—Poor" on a résumé, a health statement may be meaningless.) Such information may be included if it has direct relevance to your desired job and if you have room for it, but it may be safely omitted if you need space for more important information.

References   A **reference** is a person who has agreed to provide information to a prospective employer regarding a job applicant's fitness for a job. As a general rule, the names and addresses of references need not be included on the résumé itself. Instead, give a general statement that references are available. This policy ensures that you will be contacted before your references are called. The exception to this practice occurs when the person reading the résumé is likely to know your references; in this case, list their names.

Your references should be professional references rather than character references. The best ones are employers, especially your present employer. College professors with whom you have had a close and successful relationship are also valuable references. When asking for references, be prepared to sign a waiver stating that you forgo your right to see the recommendation or that you won't claim that a reference prevented you from getting a job. Many firms are becoming reluctant to authorize their managers to provide reference letters because of the possibility of being sued.

As space permits, include other information that uniquely qualifies you for the type of position for which you're applying.

reference A person who provides information to a prospective employer about an applicant's qualifications

The names of references are generally not included on the résumé.

Study the two résumés shown earlier in Models 22 and 23. Note the different formats that can be used to present the data. As stated earlier, there is no standard résumé format. Use these résumés or others to which you have access (available from your college career-center office or from job-hunting books) to glean ideas for formatting your own.

Note also the different organizational patterns used to convey work experience. The résumé in Model 22 is arranged in a chronological pattern (with the most recent work experience listed first), whereas the one in Model 23 is arranged in a functional pattern that stresses the skills learned rather than the jobs held. Note how job descriptions and skills are all geared to support the applicant's qualifications for the desired job. Note also the concise, concrete language used and the overall tone of quiet confidence.

Electronic Résumé

An **electronic résumé** is a résumé that is stored in a computer database designed to help manage and initially screen job applicants. These résumés come from a variety of sources: applicants may simply mail or fax a paper copy of their standard résumé, which is then scanned into a database; they may fill out (type in) an online résumé form and submit it; they may send the résumé as an email message; or they may post their résumé on the Internet, using a bulletin board system, a newsgroup, or a personal home page on the World Wide Web. (Note, for example, the directions provided by Eli Lilly and Company for copying and pasting a résumé directly into an online form, shown in Figure 14.1.)

Electronic résumés provide benefits to the recruiter and to the job seeker:

- The job seeker's résumé is potentially available to many employers.
- The job seeker may be considered for positions of which he or she wasn't even aware.
- The initial screening is done by a bias-free computer.
- Employers are relieved of the drudgery of having to manually screen and acknowledge résumés.

electronic résumé
A résumé stored in a computer database

An electronic résumé provides broader and longer exposure for the job applicant.

FIGURE 14.1 **Directions for Submitting an Electronic Résumé**

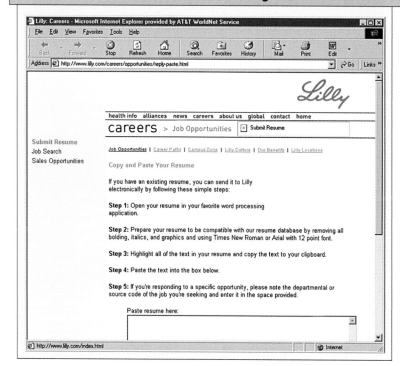

- A focused search can be conducted quickly.
- Information is always available until the individual résumé is purged from the system (often in six months).

When jobs need to be filled, company personnel feed the computer a list of keywords and phrases. The computer then looks through the database and prints out a list of candidates with the most keyword matches. A person picks the process up from there, manually studying each selected résumé to determine whom to invite for an interview. (So far, electronic tools alter only the screening—not the selection—process. People are still hired by people.)

Building appropriate keywords into your résumé is essential to successfully using automated résumé systems. Keywords are the descriptive terms for which employers search when trying to fill a position. They are the words and phrases employers believe best summarize the characteristics that they are seeking in candidates for particular jobs, such as college degree, foreign language skills, job titles, specific job skills, software packages, or names of competitors for whom applicants may have worked. Examples of key terms include *human resources manager, Hughes Aircraft, Windows XP, teamwork,* and *ISO 9000.*

Electronic résumés must be picked up by a computer search before they are seen by human eyes. Optical character recognition (OCR) software creates an ASCII (text) file of your résumé, and artificial intelligence software then "reads" the text and extracts important information about you. Thus, your first hurdle is to be selected by the computer.

Because you can never be sure how your résumé will be treated, you should prepare two résumés—one for the computer to read and one for people to read. When mailing a résumé, you may wish to include both versions, making note of that fact in your cover letter. Differences between the two versions concern both content and format.

Content Guidelines for Electronic Résumés   Using your standard résumé as a starting point, make these modifications to ensure that your résumé is "computer-friendly" and to maximize the chance that your résumé will be picked by the computer for further review by humans.

1. Think "nouns" instead of "verbs" (users rarely search for verbs). Use concrete words rather than vague descriptions. Include industry-specific descriptive nouns that characterize your skills accurately and that people in your field use and commonly look for. (Browse other online résumés, newspaper ads, and industry publications to see what terms are currently being used.)
2. Put keywords in proper context, weaving them throughout your résumé. (This strategy is considered a more polished and sophisticated approach than listing them in a block at the beginning of the résumé.)
3. Use a variety of different words to describe your skills, and don't overuse important words. In most searches, each word counts once, no matter how many times it is used.

4. Because your résumé will look very bland in plain ASCII text, stripped of all formatting, consider adding a sentence such as this to the end of your posted résumé: "An attractive and fully formatted hard-copy version of this résumé is available upon request."

These guidelines are illustrated in Model 24, which is an electronic version of the standard résumé shown in Model 22. The savvy job seeker would probably send both versions to a prospective employer.

Format Guidelines for Electronic Résumés   The following guidelines will ensure that your résumé is in a format that can be scanned accurately and transmitted accurately as an email message.

MODEL 24

Electronic Résumé

```
PERSONAL DATA
    * Helped start the Minority Business Student
      Association at New York University and served as
      program director for two years; secured the
      publisher of BLACK ENTERPRISE magazine as a banquet
      speaker
    * Have traveled extensively throughout South America
    * Am a member of the Accounting Society
    * Am willing to relocate

REFERENCES
    Available upon request

NOTE
    An attractive and fully formatted hard-copy version
    of this resume is available upon request.
```

Runs longer than one page (acceptable with electronic résumés).

Includes notice of availability of a fully formatted version.

Begins with name at the top, followed immediately by addresses (both an email address and a home page address).

```
AURELIA GOMEZ

    225 West 70 Street
    New York, NY 10023
    Phone: 212-555-3821
    Email: agomez@nyu.edu

OBJECTIVE

    Entry-level staff accounting position with a public
    accounting firm

EXPERIENCE
    Summer 2003
    Accounting Intern: Coopers & Lybrand, NYC
    * Assisted in preparing corporate tax returns
    * Attended meetings with clients
    * Conducted research in corporate tax library and
      wrote research reports

    Nov. 1999-Aug. 2002
    Payroll Specialist: City of New York
    * Full-time civil service position in the Department of
      Administration
    * Proficiency in payroll and other accounting
      software on DEC 1034 minicomputer and Pentium III
    * Representative for a 28-person work unit on the
      department's management-labor committee
    * Reason for leaving job: To pursue college degree
      full-time

EDUCATION

    Jan. 1997-Present
    Pursuing a 5-year bachelor of business
    administration degree (major in accounting) from NYU
    * Expected graduation date: June 2003
    * Attended part-time from 1996 until 2001 while
      holding down a full-time job
    * Have financed 100% of all college expenses through
      savings, work, and student loans
    * Plan to sit for the CPA exam in May 2004
```

Emphasizes, where possible, nouns as keywords.

Grammar and Mechanics Notes

Only ASCII characters are used; all text is one size with no special formatting; no rules, graphics, columns, tables, and the like are used. Vertical line spaces (Enter key) and horizontal spacing (space bar) show relationship of parts. Lists are formatted with asterisks instead of bullets.

5. Create a traditionally formatted résumé following the guidelines discussed earlier in this chapter, and save it as you normally would (so that you will always have the formatted version available).

6. Save the résumé a second time as a text-only file. Most word processors allow you to save a file as an ASCII or DOS file, which has a file name with a .txt extension. Special formatting, fonts, tabs, margin changes, and the like are lost in a text file. By saving your scannable résumé as a text file, you can view a printout of your résumé pretty much as it will look after it has been scanned by the prospective employer.

7. Reopen the text file and make any needed changes to your résumé (see the remaining guidelines). Make sure you always save the document as a text file—not as a word processing document.

8. To ensure accurate reading by computer software, make the format as plain as possible. Do not change typefaces, justification, margins, tabs, font sizes, and the like; do not insert underlines, bold, or italic; and do not use horizontal or vertical rules, graphics, boxes, tables, or columns. None of these items will show up in a printout or scan of a text file. (If necessary for clarity, you can insert a row of hyphens to simulate a horizontal rule.)

9. Use a line length of no more than 70 characters. Because you can't change margins in a text file, press Enter at the ends of lines if necessary.

10. Do not divide (hyphenate) words at the end of a line.

11. Change bullets to * (asterisks) or + (plus) signs at the beginning of the line; then insert spaces at the beginning of runover lines to make all lines of a bulleted paragraph begin at the same point.

FIGURE 14.2 **An Electronic Résumé in an Email Message**

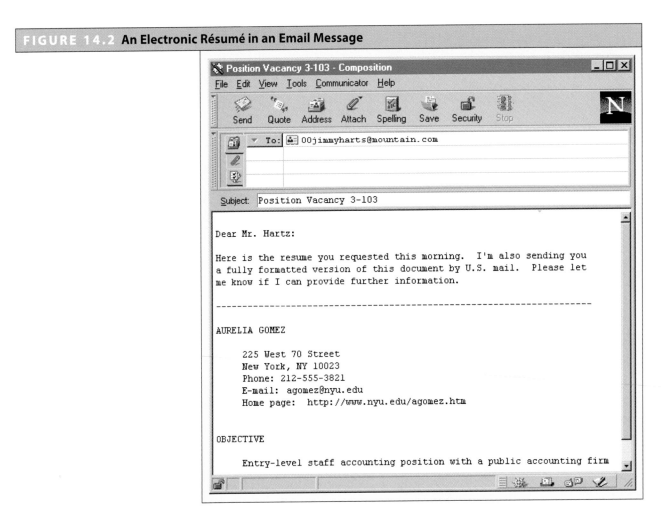

12. Press the space bar (instead of the tab) to show any needed indentions.

13. Type your name on the first line by itself, use a standard address format below your name, and type each phone number on its own line. Include an email address if possible.

14. Make the résumé as long as necessary (most database résumés average 2–3 pages).

15. After making all needed changes, as a test, mail your text file in the body of an email message to yourself or to a friend to see how it looks after being mailed. This step will help you identify any formatting problems before you send it out to possible employers.

16. Use white 8½-by-11-inch paper, printed on one side only. Do not use textured paper.

17. Submit a clean, laser-printed original copy; do not fold or staple it.

18. If responding to an employment advertisement via email, use the job title or noted reference number as the subject of your message. Always send the résumé in the body of the email message. Don't assume that you can attach a word-processed document to an email message; it may or may not be readable.

19. Whenever you update your résumé, remember to update both versions.

As illustrated in Figure 14.2, when formatted in plain ASCII text, an electronic résumé can be sent as an email message with the assurance that it will arrive in readable format.

Because your résumé is about you, it is perhaps the most personal business document you'll ever write. Use everything you know about successful communication techniques to ensure that you tell your story in the most effective manner possible. After you're satisfied with the content and arrangement of your résumé, proofread the document carefully and have several others proofread it as well. Then have your résumé printed on high-quality white or off-white 8½-by-11-inch paper, and turn your attention to your cover letters.

Checklist 15 summarizes the guidelines for developing a résumé.

> Follow the suggested steps carefully to ensure that your résumé is machine-readable.

RECALL Write a capital T for *true* or F for *false* before each statement.

1. _____ The purpose of a well-written résumé is to get you a good job.

2. _____ There is no such thing as a standard format for résumés.

3. _____ Most traditional college graduates should use a chronological arrangement for their work experience.

4. _____ Electronic résumés for most graduates should be no longer than one page.

5. _____ You should send your electronic résumé in the body of an email message instead of as a separate attachment.

CHECKPOINT 14.1

VOCABULARY Define the following terms in your own words.

6. electronic résumé:

7. reference:

CHECKLIST 15

Résumés

Length and Format

✓ Use a one-page résumé when applying for most entry-level positions.

✓ Use a simple format, with lots of white space and short blocks of text. By means of type size, indenting, bullets, boldface, and the like, show which parts are subordinate to other parts.

✓ Print your résumé on standard-sized (8½ × 11 inches), good-quality, white or off-white paper.

✓ Make sure the finished document looks professional, and attractive and that it is 100% error-free.

Content

✓ Type your complete name without a personal title at the top of the document (omit the word *résumé*), followed by an address, a daytime phone number, and an email address.

✓ Include a short job objective that is specific enough to be useful to the employer but not so specific as to preclude consideration for similar jobs.

✓ Decide whether your education or work experience is your stronger qualification, and list it first. For education, list the title of your degree, the name of your college and its location, your major and minor, and your expected date of graduation (month and year). List your grade-point average if it is impressive and any academic honors. Avoid listing college courses that are part of the normal preparation for your desired position.

✓ For work experience, determine whether to use a chronological (most recent job first) or a functional (list of competencies and skills developed) organizational pattern. For either, stress those duties or skills that are transferable to the new position. Use short phrases and action verbs, and provide specific evidence of the results you achieved.

✓ Include any additional information that will help to distinguish you from the competition. Avoid including such personal information as age, gender, ethnicity, religion, disabilities, or marital status.

✓ Provide a statement that references are available on request.

✓ Throughout, highlight your strengths and minimize any weaknesses, but always tell the truth.

Electronic Résumés

✓ In general, describe your qualifications and experiences in terms of nouns rather than verbs. Weave these keywords throughout your résumé.

✓ Save the electronic résumé in plain ASCII text. Do not include any special formatting.

✓ Use a line length of no more than 70 characters—manually press the Enter key if necessary.

✓ Include a note at the end of your electronic résumé that a fully formatted version is available upon request.

✓ Print your résumé on plain 8½-by-11-inch smooth white paper (print on one side only) and mail it unfolded and unstapled.

8. résumé

COMPREHENSION

9. For your own personal situation, will you use a chronological or functional arrangement for your work experience? Why?

10. For your own résumé, will you list your education or work experience first? Why?

11. Why is it important to make your electronic résumé attractive as well as machine-readable?

CRITICAL THINKING

12. Think about a specific volunteer job you have held. Identify that job and list the skills you learned that can transfer to a professional career.

Writing Job-Application Letters

A résumé itself is all that is generally needed to secure an interview with an on-campus recruiter. However, you will likely not want to limit your job search to those employers that interview on campus. Campus recruiters typically represent large organizations or regional employers. Thus, if you want to work in a smaller organization or in a distant location, you will need to contact those organizations by writing application letters.

An **application letter** communicates to the prospective employer your interest in and qualifications for a position within the organization. The letter is also called a *cover letter,* because it introduces (or "covers") the major points in your résumé, which you should include with the application letter. A *solicited application letter* is written in response to an advertised vacancy, whereas an *unsolicited application letter* (also called a *prospecting letter*) is written to an organization that has not advertised a vacancy.

Most job applicants use the same résumé when applying for numerous positions and then use their application letters to personalize their qualifications for the specific job for which they are applying.

Because the application letter is the first thing the employer will read about you, it is of crucial importance. Make sure the letter is formatted appropriately, looks attractive, and is free from typographical, spelling, and grammatical errors. Don't forget to sign the letter and enclose a copy of your résumé (or perhaps both versions—formatted and plain-text).

Your cover letter is a sales letter—you're selling your qualifications to the prospective employer. You should use the same persuasive techniques you learned earlier: provide specific evidence, stress reader benefits, avoid exaggeration, and show confidence in the quality of your product.

An application letter should be no longer than one page. Let's examine each part of a typical letter. Model 25 shows a solicited application letter, written to accompany the résumé presented in Model 22. (An unsolicited application letter appears in the 3Ps model on page 403.)

Use the application letter to personalize your qualifications for one specific job.

application letter A letter that communicates an applicant's interest in and qualifications for a position to a prospective employer

Address and Salutation

Your letter should be addressed to an individual rather than to an organization or department. Remember, the more hands your letter must go through before it

MODEL 25

Job-Application Letter

This model is an example of a solicited application letter; it accompanies the résumé in Model 22 on page 377.

Begins by identifying the job position and the source of advertising.

Emphasizes a qualification that might distinguish her from other applicants.

Relates her work experience to the specific needs of the employer.

Provides a telephone number (may be done either in the body of the letter or in the last line of the address block).

March 13, 20—

Mr. David Norman, Partner
Ross, Russell & Weston
452 Fifth Avenue
New York, NY 10018

1   Dear Mr. Norman:

Subject: EDP Specialist Position (Reference No. 103-G)

My varied work experience in accounting and payroll services, coupled with my accounting degree, has prepared me for the position of EDP specialist that you
2   advertised in the March 9 *New York Times*.

3   In addition to taking required courses in accounting and management information systems as part of my accounting major at New York University, I took an elective course in EDP auditing and control. The training I received in this course in applications, software, systems, and service-center records would enable me to immediately become a productive member of your EDP consulting staff.

My college training has been supplemented by an internship in a large accounting firm. In addition, my two and one-half years of experience as a payroll specialist for the city of New York have given me firsthand knowledge of the operation and needs of nonprofit agencies. This experience should help me to contribute to your large consulting practice with governmental agencies.

4   After you have reviewed my enclosed résumé, I would appreciate having the opportunity to discuss with you why I believe I have the right qualifications and personality to serve you and your clients. I can be reached by phone after 3 p.m. daily.

Sincerely,

Aurelia Gomez

5   Aurelia Gomez
225 West 70 Street
New York, NY 10023
Phone: 212-555-3821
Email: agomez@nyu.edu

Enclosure

Grammar and Mechanics Notes

1 This letter is formatted in modified-block style with standard punctuation (colon after the salutation and comma after the complimentary closing).
2 *New York Times:* Italicize the names of newspapers.
3 *accounting and management information systems:* Do not capitalize the names of college courses unless they include a proper noun.
4 *résumé:* This word may also properly be written without the accent marks: *resume.*
5 Putting the writer's name and address together at the bottom of the letter makes it convenient for the reader to respond.

reaches the right person, the more chance for something to go wrong. Ideally, your letter should be addressed to the person who will actually interview you and who will likely be your supervisor if you get the job.

If you do not know enough about the prospective employer to know the name of the appropriate person (the decision maker), you have probably not gathered enough data. If necessary, call the organization to make sure you have the right name—including the correct spelling—and position title. In your salutation, use a courtesy title (such as *Mr.* or *Ms.*) along with the person's last name.

Some job-vacancy ads are blind ads; they do not identify the hiring company by name and provide only a box number address, often in care of the newspaper or magazine that contains the ad. In such a situation, you (and all others responding to that ad) have no choice but to address your letter to the newspaper and to use a generic salutation, such as "Dear Human Resources Manager." Insert a subject line to identify immediately the purpose of this important message.

Opening

The opening paragraph of a solicited application letter is fairly straightforward. Because the organization has advertised an opening, it is eager to receive quality applications, so use a direct organization: state (or imply) the reason for your letter, identify the particular position for which you're applying, and indicate how you learned about the opening.

Gear your opening to the job and to the specific organization. For positions that are widely perceived to be somewhat conservative (such as in finance, accounting, and banking), use a restrained opening. For more creative work (such as sales, advertising, and public relations), you might start out on a more imaginative note. Here are two examples:

Use the direct organizational plan for writing a solicited application letter.

Conservative:

Mr. Adam Storkel, manager of your Fleet Street branch, has suggested that I submit my qualifications for the position of assistant loan officer that was advertised in last week's *Indianapolis Business.*

Creative:

If quality is Job 1 at Ford, then Job 2 must surely be communicating that message effectively to the public. My degree in journalism and work experience at the Kintzell agency will enable me to help you achieve that objective. The enclosed résumé further describes my qualifications for the position of advertising copywriter posted in the June issue of *Automotive Age.*

For unsolicited application letters, you must first get the reader's attention. You can gain that attention most easily by talking about the company rather than about yourself. One effective strategy is to show that you know something about the organization—its recent projects, awards, changes in personnel, and the like—and then show how you can contribute to the corporate effort.

Now that Russell Industries has expanded operations to Central America, can you use a marketing graduate who speaks fluent Spanish and who knows the culture of the region?

Your opening should be short, interesting, and reader-oriented. Avoid tired openings such as "This is to apply for . . ." or "Please consider this letter my application for . . ." Maintain an air of formality by using a personal title and last name when addressing the reader.

Body

Don't repeat all the information from the résumé.

In a paragraph or two, highlight your strongest qualifications and show how they can benefit the employer. Show—don't tell; that is, provide specific, credible evidence to support your statements, using wording different from that used in the résumé. Tell an anecdote about yourself ("For example, recently I . . . "). Your discussion should reflect modest confidence rather than a hard-sell approach. Avoid starting too many sentences with *I.*

> **NOT:** I am an effective supervisor.
>
> **BUT:** Supervising a staff of five counter clerks taught me . . . .

> **NOT:** I am an accurate person.
>
> **BUT:** In my two years of experience as a student secretary, none of the letters, memorandums, and reports I typed were ever returned with a typographical error marked.

> **NOT:** I took a course in business communication.
>
> **BUT:** The communication strategies I learned in my business communication course will enable me to solve customer problems as a customer-service representative at Allegheny Industries.

Refer the reader to the enclosed résumé. Subordinate the reference to the résumé, and emphasize instead what the résumé contains.

> **NOT:** I am enclosing a copy of my résumé for your review.
>
> **BUT:** As detailed in the enclosed résumé, my extensive work experience in records management has prepared me to help you "take charge of this paperwork jungle," as headlined in your classified ad.

Closing

Politely ask for an interview.

You are not likely to get what you do not ask for, so close by asking for a personal interview. Indicate flexibility regarding scheduling and location. Provide your phone number and email address, either in the last paragraph or immediately below your name and address in the closing lines.

> After you have reviewed my qualifications, I would appreciate your letting me know when we can meet to discuss further my employment with Connecticut Power and Light. I will be in the Hartford area from December 16 through January 4 and could come to your office at any time that is convenient for you.
>
> **OR:** I will call your office next week to see if we can arrange a meeting at your convenience to discuss my qualifications for working as a paralegal with your firm.

Use a standard complimentary closing (such as "Sincerely"), leave enough space to sign the letter, and then type your name, address, phone number, and email address. Even though you may be sending out many application letters at the same time, take care with each individual letter. You never know which one will be the letter that actually gets you an interview. Sign your name neatly in blue or black ink, fold each letter and accompanying résumé neatly, and mail them.

Checklist 16 summarizes the guidelines for writing an application letter.

CHECKLIST 16

Job-Application Letters

✓ Use your job-application letter to show how the qualifications listed in your résumé have prepared you for the specific job for which you're applying.

✓ If possible, address your letter to the individual in the organization who will interview you if you're successful.

✓ When applying for an advertised opening, begin by stating (or implying) the reason for the letter, identify the position for which you're applying, and tell how you learned about the opening.

✓ When writing an unsolicited application letter, first gain the reader's attention by showing that you are familiar with the company and can make a unique contribution to its efforts.

✓ In one or two paragraphs, highlight your strongest qualifications and relate them directly to the needs of the specific position for which you're applying. Refer the reader to the enclosed résumé.

✓ Treat your letter as a persuasive sales letter: provide specific evidence, stress reader benefits, avoid exaggeration, and show confidence in the quality of your product.

✓ Close by tactfully asking for an interview.

✓ Maintain an air of formality throughout the letter. Avoid cuteness.

✓ Make sure the finished document presents a professional, attractive, and conservative appearance and that it is 100% error-free.

RECALL Write a capital *T* for true or *F* for false before each statement.

1. ＿＿ All advertised job vacancies require the applicant to write a job-application letter.

2. ＿＿ Most applicants will submit a unique application letter for every job for which they apply.

3. ＿＿ "Please consider this letter my application for ..." would be an appropriate opening for an unsolicited letter of application.

4. ＿＿ In the body of your application letter, you should highlight all of your qualifications for the job.

5. ＿＿ You should not directly ask for a personal interview in your first application letter.

CHECKPOINT 14.2

VOCABULARY Define the following term in your own words.

6. application letter:

COMPREHENSION

7. Rewrite the following sentences of an application letter to make them more effective.

a. I am a hard worker.

b. I am good at sales.

c. I can be trusted.

8. Assume that you are applying for a full-time position as an admissions representative at your institution upon graduation. Compose an effective opening sentence for your unsolicited application letter.

CRITICAL THINKING

9. Do you think it is savvy to include an attention-grabbing gimmick in your application letter, such as sending a worn, once-white running shoe with the note "Now that I have one foot in the door, I hope you'll let me get the other one in" or writing the application letter beginning at the bottom of the page and working upward (to indicate a willingness to start at the bottom and work one's way up)?

Preparing for a Job Interview

Ninety-five percent of all employers require one or more employment interviews before extending a job offer, resulting in as many as 150 million employment interviews being conducted annually.[11] The employer's purpose in these interviews is to verify information on the résumé, explore any issues raised by the résumé, and get some indication of the probable chemistry between the applicant and the organization. (It is estimated that 90% of all job failures result from personality clashes or conflicts—not incompetence.[12]) The job applicant will use the interview to glean important information about the organization and to decide whether the culture of the organization meshes with his or her personality (see Spotlight 6, "The Ethical Dimensions of the Job Campaign").

Consider the employment interview to be a sales presentation. Just as any good sales representative would never walk into a potential customer's office without having a thorough knowledge of the product, neither should you. You are both the product and the product promoter, so do your homework—both on yourself and on the potential customer.

Researching the Organization

Learn as much as you can about the organization—your possible future employer.

As a result of having developed your résumé and written your application letters, you have probably done enough general homework on yourself. You are likely to have a reasonably accurate picture of who you are and what you want out of your career. Now is the time to zero in on the organization.

It is no exaggeration to say that you should learn everything you possibly can about the organization. Research the specific organization in depth. Search the current business periodical indexes and go online to learn what has been

SPOTLIGHT on law and ethics

The Ethical Dimensions of the Job Campaign[13]

Most recruiters have heard the story about the job applicant who, when told that he was overqualified for a position, pleaded in vain, "But I lied about my credentials." When constructing your résumé and application letter, when completing an application form, and when answering questions during an interview, you will constantly have to make judgments about what to divulge and what to omit. Everyone would agree that outright lying is unethical (and clearly illegal as well). But when is hedging or omitting negative information about yourself simply being smart, and when is it unethical?

The Ethics of Constructing a Résumé

Recruiters believe that the problem they call "résumé inflation" has increased in recent years, and plenty of research backs them up. One survey of executives found that 26% of them reported hiring employees during the previous year who had misrepresented their qualifications, education, or salary history. By far, the most frequent transgression is misrepresenting one's qualifications.

Acting ethically does not, of course, require that you emphasize every little problem that has occurred in your past. Indeed, one study showed that the majority of Fortune 500 human resources directors agree with the statement "Interviewees should stress their strengths and not mention their weaknesses unless the interviewer asks for information in an area of weakness."

Recognize, however, that some employers have a standard policy of terminating all employees who are found to have falsely represented their qualifications on

their résumés. Generally, the employer must show evidence that the employee intentionally misrepresented his or her qualifications so as to fraudulently secure a job. Claiming to have a college degree when, in fact, one does not would likely be grounds for termination, whereas an unintentional mistake in the dates of previous employment would probably not be.

The Ethics of Accepting a Position

For some applicants, another ethical dilemma occurs when they receive a second, perhaps more attractive, job offer after having already accepted a prior offer. Most professionals believe that such a situation should not present a dilemma. A job acceptance is a promise that the applicant is expected to keep. The hiring organization has made many decisions based on the applicant's acceptance, not the least of which was to notify all other candidates that the job had been filled. Reneging on the commitment to the employer not only puts the applicant in a bad light (and don't underestimate the power of the network in spreading such information) but also puts the applicant's school in a bad light.

If you're unsure about whether to accept a job offer, ask for a time extension. Once you've made your decision, however, stick to it and have no regrets. If you decide to accept the job, immediately notify all other employers that you are withdrawing from further consideration. If you decide to decline the job, move on to your next interviews without looking back. Learn to live with your decisions.

happening recently with the company. Many libraries maintain copies of the annual reports from large companies. Study these or other sources for current product information, profitability, plans for the future, and the like. Learn about the company's products and services, its history, the names of its officers, what the business press has to say about the organization, its recent stock activity, financial health, corporate structure, and the like.

Relate what you discover about the individual company to what you've learned about competing companies and about the industry in general. By trying to fit what you've learned into the broader perspective of the industry, you will be able to discuss matters more intelligently during your interview instead of just having a bunch of jumbled facts at your disposal.

If you're interviewing at a governmental agency, determine its role, recent funding levels, recent activities, spending legislation affecting the agency, and the extent to which being on the "right" side (that is, the official side) of a political question matters. If you're interviewing for a teaching position at an educational institution, determine the range of course offerings, types of students, conditions of the facilities and equipment, professionalism of the staff, and funding levels. In short, every tidbit of information you can gather about your prospective employer will help you make the most appropriate career decision.

You will use this information as a resource to help you understand and discuss topics with some familiarity during the interview. No one is impressed by the interviewee who, out of the blue, spouts, "I see your stock went up 5½ points last week." However, in response to the interviewer's comment about the company's recent announcement of a new product line, it would be quite appropriate to respond, "That must have been the reason your stock jumped so high last week."

In short, bring up such information only if it flows naturally into the conversation. Even if you're never able to discuss some of the information you've gathered, the knowledge itself will still provide perspective in helping you to make a reasonable decision if a job offer is extended.

Practicing Interview Questions

Following is a sample of typical questions that are often asked during an employment interview. Questions such as these provide the interviewer with important clues about the applicant's qualifications, personality, poise, and communication skills. The interviewer is interested not only in the content of your responses but also in *how* you react to the questions themselves and *how* you communicate your thoughts and ideas.

Before going for your interview, practice dictating a response to each of these questions into a cassette recorder. Then assume the role of the interviewer and play back your responses. How acceptable and appropriate was each response?

- Tell me about yourself.
- How would you describe yourself?
- Tell me something about yourself that I won't find on your résumé.
- What do you take real pride in?
- Why would you like to work for our organization?
- Why should we hire you?
- What are your long-range career objectives?
- What types of work do you enjoy doing most? Least?
- What accomplishment has given you the greatest satisfaction?
- What would you like to change in your past?
- What courses did you like best and least in college?
- Specifically, how does your education or experience relate to this job?

These questions are fairly straightforward and not especially difficult to answer if you have practiced them. Not infrequently, however, interviewers may pose more difficult questions—ones that seemingly have no "right" answer. Examples of such questions are "What do you consider your major weakness?" or "What aspect of your present job do you like least?" Sometimes they even try to create a stressful situation by asking pointed questions, interrupting, or feigning disbelief in an attempt to gauge your behavior under stress.

The strategy to use in such a circumstance is to keep the desired job firmly in mind and to formulate each answer—no matter what the question—so as to highlight your ability to perform the desired job competently. You don't have to accept each question as asked. You can ask the interviewer to be more specific or to rephrase the question. Doing so not only will provide guidance for answering the question but will give you a few additional moments to prepare your response.

Preparing Your Own Questions

During the course of the interview, many of the questions you may have about the organization or the job will probably be answered. However, an interview is a two-way conversation, so it is legitimate for you to pose relevant questions at appropriate moments, and you should prepare those questions beforehand.

Questions such as the following will provide useful information on which to base a decision if a job is offered:

- How would you describe a typical day on the job?
- How is an employee evaluated and promoted?
- What types of training are available?
- What are your expectations of new employees?
- What are the organization's plans for the future?
- To whom would I report? Would anyone report to me?
- What are the advancement opportunities for this position?

Each of these questions not only secures needed information to help you make a decision but also sends a positive nonverbal message to the interviewer that you are interested in this position as a long-term commitment. Do not, however, ask so many questions that the roles of the interviewer and the interviewee become blurred, and avoid putting the interviewer on the spot.

Avoid asking about salary and fringe benefits during the initial interview. There will be plenty of time for such questions later, after you've convinced the organization that you're the person it wants. In terms of planning, you should know ahead of time the market value of the position for which you're applying. Check the classified ads, reports collected by your college career service, and library and Internet sources to learn what a reasonable salary figure for your position would be.

> Ask relevant, important, and appropriate questions of your own.

> Avoid appearing to be overly concerned about salary.

Dressing for Success

The importance of making a good first impression during the interview can hardly be overstated. One study has shown that 75% of the interviewees who made a good impression during the first five minutes of the interview received a job offer, whereas only 10% of the interviewees who made a bad impression during the first five minutes received a job offer.[13]

The most effective strategy for making a good impression is to pay careful attention to your dress, grooming, and posture. Dress in a manner that flatters your appearance while conforming to the office norm. The employment interview is not the place for a fashion statement. You want the interviewer to remember what you had to say and not what you wore. Although different positions, different companies, different industries, and different parts of the country and world have different norms, in general prefer well-tailored, clean, conservative clothing for the interview.

> Prefer a well-tailored, clean, conservative outfit for the interview.

> **A job interview is a two-way conversation. Be prepared to ask relevant questions of your own—but avoid asking about salary or fringe benefits during the initial interview.**

For most business interviews, men should dress in a blue or gray suit and a white or pale blue shirt with a subtle tie, dark socks, and black shoes. Women should dress in a blue or gray tailored suit with a light-colored blouse and medium-height heels. Avoid excessive or distracting jewelry, heavy perfumes or after-shave lotions, and elaborate hairstyles. Impeccable grooming is a must, including clothing clean and free of wrinkles, shoes shined, teeth brushed, nails clean, and hair neatly styled and combed. Blend in; you will have plenty of opportunity to express your individual style once you've been hired.

Conducting Yourself During the Interview

Observe the organizational environment very carefully and treat everyone you meet, including the receptionist and the interviewer's assistant or secretary, with scrupulous courtesy. Maintain an air of formality. When shown into the interview room, greet the interviewer by name, with a firm handshake, direct eye contact, and a smile.

Assume a confident, courteous, and conservative attitude during the interview.

At the beginning, address the interviewer as "Mr." or "Ms.," switching to a first-name basis only if specifically requested to do so. If you're not asked to be seated immediately, wait until the interviewer is seated and then take your seat. Sit with both feet planted firmly on the floor, lean forward a bit in your seat, and maintain comfortable eye contact with the interviewer. Avoid taking notes, except perhaps for a specific name, date, or telephone number.

Recognize that certain parts of the office are off-limits—especially the interviewer's desk and any area behind the desk. Do not rest your hands, purse, or notes on the desk and never wander around the office. Show interest in everything the interviewer is saying; don't concentrate so hard on formulating your response that you miss the last part of any question. Answer each question in a positive, confident, forthright manner. Recognize that more than yes-or-no answers are expected.

Overpreparation is the best way to control nervousness.

Control nervousness during the interview the same way you control it when making an oral presentation; that is, practice until you're confident you can face whatever the interviewer throws your way. The career centers at many colleges conduct mock interviews to prepare prospective interviewees. If yours does not, ask a professor or even another student to interview you. Practice answering lists of common questions.

Throughout the interview, your attitude should be one of confidence and courtesy. Assume a role that is appropriate for you. Don't go in with the attitude that "You're lucky to have me here." The interviewer might not agree. Likewise, you needn't fawn or grovel. You're *applying*—not begging—for a job. If the match works, both you and the employer will benefit. Finally, don't try to take charge of the interview. Follow the interviewer's lead, letting him or her determine which questions to ask, when to move to a new area of discussion, and when to end the interview.

Answer each question put to you as honestly as you can. Keep your mind on the desired job and how you can show that you are qualified for that job. Don't try to oversell yourself, or you may end up in a job for which you're unprepared. However, if the interviewer doesn't address an area in which you believe you have strong qualifications, be ready to volunteer such information at the appropriate time, working it into your answer to one of the interviewer's questions.

If asked about your salary expectations, try to avoid giving a salary figure, indicating that you would expect to be paid in line with other employees at your level of expertise and experience. If pressed, however, be prepared to reveal your salary expectations, preferably using a broad range.

When discussing salary, talk in terms of what you think the position and responsibilities are worth rather than what you think *you* are worth. If salary is not discussed, be patient. Few people have ever been offered a job in industry without first being told what they would be paid.

It is also likely that you will be interviewed more than once—having either multiple interviews the same day or, if you survive the initial interview, a more intense set of interviews to be scheduled for some later date. Be on the alert for clues you can pick up from your early interviews that might be of use to you in later interviews and be sure to provide consistent responses to the same questions asked by different interviewers. The different interviewers will typically get together later to discuss their reactions to you and your responses.

When the interview ends, if you've not been told, you have a right to ask the interviewer when you might expect to hear from him or her. You will likely be evaluated on these four criteria:

- *Education and experience:* Your accomplishments as they relate to the job requirements, evidence of growth, breadth and depth of your experiences, leadership qualities, and evidence of your willingness to assume responsibility
- *Mental qualities:* Intelligence, alertness, judgment, logic, perception, creativity, organization, and depth
- *Manner and personal traits:* Social poise, sense of humor, mannerisms, warmth, confidence, courtesy, aggressiveness, listening ability, manner of oral expression, emotional balance, enthusiasm, initiative, energy, ambition, maturity, stability, and interests
- *Appearance:* Grooming, dress, posture, cleanliness, and apparent health

> You will likely be evaluated on your education and experience, mental qualities, manner and personal traits, and appearance.

Communicating After the Interview

Immediately after the interview, conduct a self-appraisal of your performance. Try to recall each question that was asked and evaluate your response. If you're not satisfied with one of your responses, take the time to formulate a more effective answer. Chances are that you will be asked a similar question in the future.

> After the interview, critique your performance, your résumé, and your application letter.

Also reevaluate your résumé. Were any questions asked during the interview that indicated some confusion about your qualifications? Does some section need to be revised or some information added or deleted?

In addition, determine whether you can improve your application letter on the basis of your interview experience. Were the qualifications you discussed in your letter the ones that seemed to impress the interviewers the most? Were these qualifications discussed in terms of how they would benefit the organization? Did you provide specific evidence to support your claims?

You should also take the time to send the interviewer (or interviewers) a short thank-you note or email message as a gesture of courtesy and to reaffirm your interest in the job. The interviewer, who probably devoted quite a bit of time to you before, during, and after the interview session, deserves to have his or her efforts on your behalf acknowledged.

Recognize, however, that your thank-you note may or may not have any effect on the hiring decision. Most decisions to offer the candidate a job or to invite him or her back for another round of interviewing are made the day of the interview, often during the interview itself. Thus, your thank-you note may arrive after the decision, good or bad, has been made.

The real purpose of a thank-you note is to express genuine appreciation for some courtesy extended to you; you do not write to earn points. Also, avoid trying to resell yourself. You've already made your case through your résumé, cover letter, and interview.

Your thank-you note should be short and may be either typed or handwritten. Consider it a routine message that should be written in a direct organizational pattern. Begin by expressing appreciation for the interview; then achieve credibility by mentioning some specific incident or insight gained from the interview.

MODEL 26

Interview Follow-Up Letter

The interview follow-up letter should be written within a day or two of the job interview.

Addresses the person in the salutation as he or she was addressed during the interview.

Begins directly, with a sincere expression of appreciation.

Mentions a specific incident that occurred and relates it to the writer's background.

Closes on a confident, forward-looking note.

April 15, 20—

1 Mr. David Norman, Partner
   Ross, Russell & Weston
   452 Fifth Avenue
   New York, NY 10018

2 Dear Mr. Norman:

Thank you for the opportunity to interview for the position of EDP specialist yesterday. I very much enjoyed meeting you and Arlene Worthington and learning more about the position and about Ross, Russell & Weston.

3 I especially appreciated the opportunity to observe the long-range planning meeting yesterday afternoon and to learn of your firm's plans for increasing your consulting practice with nonprofit agencies. My experience working in city government leads me to believe that nonprofit agencies can benefit greatly from your expertise.

4 Again, thank you for taking the time to visit with me yesterday. I look forward to hearing from you.

Sincerely,

Aurelia Gomez

Aurelia Gomez
225 West 70 Street
New York, NY 10023
Phone: 212-555-3821
Email: agomez@nyu.edu

Grammar and Mechanics Notes

1 Use the ampersand (&) in a firm name only if it is used by the firm itself.
2 Use a colon (not a comma) even if the salutation uses the reader's first name.
3 *nonprofit:* Write most words beginning with *non* solid—without a hyphen.
4 *Again,:* Use a comma after an introductory expression.

CHECKLIST 17

Employment Interviews

Preparing for an Employment Interview

✓ Before going on an employment interview, learn everything you can about the organization.

✓ Practice answering common interview questions and prepare questions of your own to ask.

✓ Select appropriate clothing to wear.

✓ Control your nervousness by being well prepared, well equipped, and on time.

Conducting Yourself During the Interview

✓ Throughout the interview, be aware of the nonverbal signals you are communicating through your body language.

✓ Answer each question completely and accurately, always trying to relate your qualifications to the specific needs of the desired job.

✓ Whether you are interviewed by one person or a group of people, you will be evaluated on your education and experience, mental qualities, manner and personal traits, and general appearance.

Communicating After the Interview

✓ Immediately following the interview, critique your performance and also send a thank-you note or email message to the interviewer.

Close on a hopeful, forward-looking note. The thank-you note in Model 26 (page 399) corresponds to the résumé and application letter presented in Model 22 (page 377) and Model 25 (page 389).

If you have not heard from the interviewer by the deadline date he or she gave you for making a decision, telephone or email the interviewer for a status report. If no decision has been made, your inquiry will keep your name and your interest in the position in the interviewer's mind. If someone else has been selected, you need to know so that you can continue your job search. Checklist 17 summarizes the steps in the interview process.

RECALL Write a capital T for *true* or F for *false* before each statement.

1. ____ Most job failures result from incompetence on the job.

2. ____ It is appropriate for you to ask questions of your own during the interview.

3. ____ You should avoid asking about salary and fringe benefits during the initial interview.

4. ____ Most applicants who make a good impression during the first five minutes of the interview receive a job offer.

5. ____ The purpose of a thank-you note following the interview is to reiterate your interest in and qualifications for the position

CHECKPOINT 14.3

COMPREHENSION

6. Go online to the U.S. government's *Occupational Outlook Handbook* home page **(www.bls.gov/oco).** What is the median annual income for each of the following occupations:

   a. Administrative assistant/secretary:

   b. Computer programmer:

   c. Medical assistant:

   d. Paralegal:

   e. *Your occupational choice:*

7. Why should you write a thank-you note after the interview? And why should you *not?*

CRITICAL THINKING

8. Assume during your job interview, you're asked, "What do you like most or least about your present job?" How might you answer?

Summary

One of the most important communication tasks you will ever tackle is securing a rewarding and worthwhile job. The job-seeking campaign thus requires considerable time, effort, and thought.

The purpose of your résumé is to get you a job interview. Strive for a one-page document, preferably typed in a simple, readable format on a computer and output on a laser printer. Include your name, address, phone number, job objective, information about your education and work experience, and special aptitudes and skills. Include other information only if it will help distinguish you favorably from the other applicants. Use either a chronological or a functional organization for your work experience, and stress those skills and experiences that can be transferred to the job you want. Consider formatting an electronic version of your résumé for emailing or computer scanning. This version should be in plain text, with no special formatting, printed on standard white paper (one side only), and mailed unfolded and unstapled.

You will typically use the same résumé when applying for numerous positions and then compose an application letter that discusses how your education and work experience qualify you for the specific job at hand. If possible, address your letter to the person who will interview you for the job. When writing a solicited application letter, begin by stating the reason for your letter, identify the position for which you're applying, and tell how you learned about the position. When writing an unsolicited letter, first gain the reader's attention. Then use the body of your letter to highlight one or two of your strongest qualifications, relating them to the needs of the position for which you're applying. Close by politely asking for an interview.

If your application efforts are successful, you will be invited to come for an interview. To succeed at the interview phase of the job campaign, prepare for the interview, conduct yourself appropriately during the interview, and complete the communication tasks needed after the interview.

An Application Letter

Problem

You are Ray Arnold, a senior and labor relations major at Boston University. You have analyzed your interests, strengths and weaknesses, and preferred lifestyle and have decided you would like to work in some area of labor relations for a large multinational firm in southern California. Because you attend a school in the East, you decide not to limit your job search to on-campus interviewing.

In your research you learned that Precision Systems, Inc. (PSI), has recently been awarded a $23 million contract by the U.S. Department of State to develop a high-level computerized message system to provide fast and secure communications among U.S. government installations throughout Europe. PSI, which is headquartered in Los Angeles, will build a new automated factory in Ciudad Juárez, Mexico, to assemble the electronic components for the new system.

You decide to write to PSI to see whether it might have an opening for someone with your qualifications. You will, of course, include a copy of your résumé with your letter. (See Model 23 for the résumé.) Send your letter to Ms. Phyllis Morrison, Assistant Director of Human Resources, Precision Systems, Inc., P.O. Box 18734, Los Angeles, CA 90018.

Process

1. Will this letter be a solicited or unsolicited (prospecting) letter?

   Unsolicited—I don't know whether PSI has an opening.

2. Write an opening paragraph for your letter that gets attention and that relates your skills to PSI's needs. Make sure the purpose of your letter is made clear in your opening paragraph.

   PSI's recently accepted proposal to the State Department estimated that you would be adding as many as 3,000 new staff for the Ciudad Juárez project. With this dramatic increase in personnel, do you have an opening in your human resources department for a college graduate with a major in labor relations and a minor in psychology?

3. Compare your education with PSI's likely requirements. What will help you stand out from the competition?

   ■ It's somewhat unusual for a labor relations major to have a psychology minor.

   ■ My course work in my major and minor were pretty standard, so there's no need to list individual courses.

The 3Ps
Problem, Process, Product

4. Compare your work experiences with PSI's likely requirements. What qualifications from your résumé should you highlight in your letter?

 ■ The interpersonal and human relations skills developed as a teller will be an important asset in labor management.

 ■ Written and oral communications skills developed through work and extracurricular activities will enable me to communicate effectively with a widely dispersed work force.

5. What other qualifications should you mention?

 My degree in labor relations, combined with my union membership, will help me look at each issue from the perspective of both management and labor.

6. Write the sentence in which you request the interview.

 I would welcome the opportunity to come to Los Angeles to discuss with you the role I might play in helping PSI manage its human resources in an efficient and humane manner.

The 3P's
Problem, Process, Product

Product

1 15 Turner Hall
Boston University
Boston, MA 02215
February 7, 20—

Ms. Phyllis Morrison
Assistant Human Resources Director
Precision Systems, Inc.
P.O. Box 18734
Los Angeles, CA 90018

2 Dear Ms. Morrison

PSI's recent proposal to the State Department estimated that you would be adding as many as 3,000 new positions for the Ciudad Juárez project. With this increase in person-
3 nel, will you have an opening in your human resources department for a recent college graduate with a major in labor relations and a minor in psychology?

My combination of course work in business and liberal arts will enable me to approach each issue from both a management and a behavioral point of view. Further, my degree in labor relations along with my experience as a union member will help me consider each issue from the perspective of both management and labor.

During my term as webmaster for a student association, the Scholastic Internet
4 Association recognized our site for its "original, balanced, and refreshingly candid writ-ing style and format." On the job, dealing successfully with customers' overdrawn accounts, bank computer errors, and delayed-deposit recording has taught me the value of active listening and has provided me experience in explaining and justifying the com-pany's position. As detailed on the enclosed résumé, these communication and human relations skills will help me to interact and communicate effectively with PSI employees at all levels and at widely dispersed locations.

I would welcome the opportunity to come to Los Angeles at your convenience to discuss with you the role I might play in helping PSI manage its human resources in an efficient and humane manner. I will call your office on February 15, or you may call me at any time after 2 p.m. daily at 617-555-9833.

Sincerely

Raymond J. Arnold

Raymond J. Arnold

Enclosure

This prospecting letter accompanies the résumé in Model 23 on page 378.

Begins with an attention-getting opening that relates the writer's skills to the needs of the company.

Shows how the writer's unique qualifications will benefit the company.

Provides specific evidence to support his claims: *shows* rather than *tells.*

Gives the reader the option of phoning the applicant or having him phone her.

Grammar and Mechanics Notes

1 In a personal business letter, the writer's return address may be typed above the date (as shown here) or below the sender's name in the closing.
2 This letter is formatted in block style, with all lines beginning at the left margin, and in open punctuation style, with no punctuation after the salutation and complimentary closing.
3 *major in labor relations:* Do not capitalize the names of college majors and minors.
4 *writing style and format.":* A period goes inside the closing quotation marks.

403

Key Terms

application letter   reference
electronic résumé   résumé

Looking Ahead

We have devoted 14 chapters of this book to helping you develop and refine your strategic business communication skills by focusing on how to write not only correctly but also effectively. We now have one more finishing touch to polish off your skills, by introducing the elements of mechanics—those aspects of your writing that show up only on the printed page. Chapter 15 discusses such aspects as capitalization, abbreviations, number expression, and, of course, spelling. Read on.

Exercises

Résumés

1 **Who Am I?**   Assume that you are beginning your last term of college before graduating. Using factual data from your own education, work experience, and so on (include any data that you expect to be true at the time of your graduation), answer the following questions (you will use this information to prepare a traditional résumé for your job portfolio).

a.   How will you word your name at the top of your résumé—for example, with or without any initials? (Remember *not* to include a personal title before your name.)

b.   What is your mailing address? If you will be changing addresses during the job search, include both addresses, along with the effective dates of each.

c.   What is your daytime phone number? When can you typically be reached at this number? What is your email address?

d.   For what type of position are you searching? Prepare an effective one-sentence job objective—one that is neither too general nor too specific.

e.   What is the title of your degree? The name of your college? The location of the college? Your major and minor? Your expected date of graduation (month and year)?

f.   What is your grade-point average overall and in your major? Is either one high enough to be considered a personal selling point?

g.   Have you received any academic honors throughout your collegiate years, such as scholarships or inclusion on the dean's list? If so, list them.

h.   Did you take any elective courses (courses that most applicants for this position probably did *not* take) that might be especially helpful in this position? If so, list them.

i. List in reverse chronological order (most recent job first) the following information for each job you've held during your college years: job title, organizational name, location (city and state), inclusive dates of employment, and full- or part-time status. Describe your specific duties in each position, stressing those duties that helped prepare you for your job objective. Use short phrases, beginning each duty or responsibility with one of the action verbs on page 379 and showing, where possible, specific evidence of the results you achieved.

j. Will your education or your work experience be more likely to impress the recruiter?

k. What additional information might you include, such as special skills, professional affiliations, offices held, or willingness to relocate or travel?

l. Are your reference letters on file at your school's placement office? If so, provide the office name, address, and phone number. (If not, include a statement such as "References available on request" at the bottom of your résumé.)

2 **Your Electronic Résumé** After you have prepared your résumé in traditional format for your job portfolio at the end of this chapter, reformat your résumé for accurate scanning into a computer.

3 **Career Planning Online** Select a career in which you might be interested. Using at least four online references (one of which should be the latest edition of the *Occupational Outlook Handbook*), write a two- or three-page memo report to your instructor with the following sections:

- *Job description:* Include in this section a description of the job, including perhaps a definition of the job, typical duties, working conditions, and the kinds of knowledge, skills, and education needed.

- *Employment levels:* Nationally, how many people are employed in this type of job? Are employment levels increasing or decreasing? Why? What industries or what parts of the country are experiencing the greatest and the least demand for this job? What are the projected employment levels in the future?

- *Salary:* Discuss the latest salary statistics for this job—actual salaries, changes, trends, and projections.

- *Expected changes:* What changes are expected in this career within the next ten years or so? Discuss both the expected changes and the factors causing such changes. For example, will technology have any impact on this job? Will international business competition affect it? Federal or state regulations?

  Provide a concluding paragraph for your memo report that summarizes the career information you've discussed; then indicate whether your initial opinion about the job has changed as a result of your research. Be sure to cite your sources accurately.

Job-Application Letters

4 **Application Letter Project** This project consists of writing both a solicited and an unsolicited application letter. Prepare each letter in an appropriate format and on appropriate paper. Include a copy of your résumé with each letter. Submit each letter to your instructor folded and inserted into a correctly addressed envelope (don't forget to sign your letter).

a. Identify a large prospective employer—one that has not advertised for an opening in your field. Write an unsolicited application letter.

b. For various reasons, you might not secure a position directly related to your college major. In such a situation, it is especially important to be able to show how your qualifications (no matter what they are) match the needs of the employer. Using your own background, apply for the following position, which was advertised in last Sunday's *New York Tribune:*

> Manager-Trainee Position. Philip Morris is looking for recent college graduates to enter its management-trainee program in preparation for an exciting career in one of the diversified companies that make up Philip Morris. Excellent beginning salary and benefits, good working conditions, and a company that cares about you. (Reply to Box 385-G in care of this newspaper.)

The Job Interview and Follow-up

5 Researching the Organization   Assume you're interested in a job with Computer Sciences Corporation (CSC) (see "On the Job" on page 371). Go online (**http://www.csc.com**) to find answers to the following questions and write a short memo to your instructor containing your findings.

a. What industry is CSC in? What does the company do? What types of customers does it serve? Where are its offices located?

b. How do your skills and personal interests match up with CSC's industry, operations, and locations?

c. Browse through CSC's online job listings. What types of positions does CSC recruit for? Are your education and work experience appropriate for the positions that sound interesting? What other qualifications do you need to apply for the jobs that interest you?

6 Preparing for the Interview   Page 394 lists some commonly asked interview questions. Prepare a written answer for each question based on your own qualifications and experience. Type each question and then your answer.

7 Tell Me About Yourself   One of the most common strategies an interviewer uses to start an interview is to ask you to tell him or her something about yourself. Of course, you need to think about this question much earlier than the interview. In approximately 250 words (i.e., a one-page double-spaced report), respond to the interviewer's request to "tell me about yourself." Keep in mind your job objective.

8 Work-Team Communication—Mock Interviews   This project uses information collected as part of Exercise 4. Divide into groups of six students. Draw straws to determine which three members will be interviewers and which three will be job applicants. Both groups now have homework to do. The interviewers must get together to plan their interview strategy (10 to 12 minutes for each candidate); the applicants, working individually, must prepare for this interview; and both groups must learn more about Philip Morris.

The interviews will be conducted in front of the entire class, with each participant dressed appropriately. On the designated day, the three interviewers as a group will interview each of the three job applicants in turn (while the other two are out of the room). Given the short length of each interview, the applicant should refrain from asking any questions of his or her own, except to clarify the meaning of an interviewer's question.

After each round of interviews, the class as a whole will vote for the most effective interviewer and interviewee.

Résumé, Cover Letter, and Videotape of Practice Interview

Problem   You are finally in your last term of college before graduating and are searching for the perfect full-time post-college job. Using the information gleaned from this chapter and end-of-chapter exercises, from your campus career center, and from other sources:

1. Prepare a factual résumé in traditional format.

2. Go online to locate an advertised position in which you might be interested. Online suggestions include the following Web sites:

   America's Job Bank (**http://www.ajb.dni.us**),
   CareerMosaic (**http://www.careermosaic.com**),
   Careerpath.Com (**http://www.careerpath.com**),
   Monster Board (**http://www.monster.com**).

   Print out the job description for which (for this assignment) you're going to apply.

3. Compose and format an application letter for this position.

4. In preparation for a job interview, learn as much about your prospective employer as you can.

5. Ask someone to tape a 15-minute practice job interview, with your instructor or a career center representative playing the role of the prospective employer.

Process   Compose a few paragraphs describing how you went about solving this problem. In narrative form, provide such information as the following:

1. What factors entered into your description of your job objective?

2. How did you decide whether to place your education or job experience first?

3. How did you determine which optional information to include (and which to *exclude*)?

5. Did you use a chronological or a functional arrangement for your job experience? Why?

6. How did you decide which of your qualifications to stress in your application letter?

7. How did you prepare for your practice interview?

8. How did you decide how to dress for your interview?

Product Compose your résumé and application letter and make a video-tape of your practice interview.

15

Mechanics in Business Writing

COMMUNICATION OBJECTIVES

After you have finished this chapter, you should be able to:

- Use correct capitalization.
- Use abbreviations appropriately.
- Express numbers correctly.
- Use correct spelling.

LARRY SIMON
RPP Paralegal

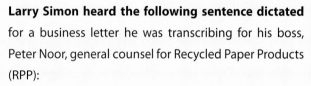

On the Job

Larry Simon heard the following sentence dictated for a business letter he was transcribing for his boss, Peter Noor, general counsel for Recycled Paper Products (RPP):

on or about august thirtieth two thousand and four the two plaintiffs george and trudy mason phone eight one seven five five five three seven zero five purchased a twenty-six inch bicycle manufactured by the defendant, speedway bikes inc fifteen thirty seven west fourth street northwest, providence rhode island zero two nine zero eight the said bicycle costing five hundred thirty seven dollars and fifty eight cents and bearing the serial number two zero eight one five.

This sentence contains seven sets of numbers: a date, general number, phone number, measurement, address, amount of money, and serial number. Do you know how to express these numbers—in words or in figures? Do you know which words in the paragraph to capitalize and which ones to abbreviate? Finally, can you spell all of the words correctly?

Mechanics refers to those elements in communication that appear only in written form—including capitalization, number expression, abbreviations, spelling, and, of course, punctuation, which we already discussed in Chapter 6.

Capitalization

Did you know that English is the only language to capitalize the first-person singular pronoun *I*? Why? There is no logical reason—only custom. As we shall see, the function of capitalization is usually to emphasize words and make them stand out. Some of the rules that follow will already be familiar to you; others may not be. Some of the rules are absolutes—you *always* capitalize that type of expression. Others require more careful judgment or knowledge of the writer's intention. In any event, it would be a capital idea for you to learn these rules.

First Words

We have already mentioned that in English you should capitalize the first-person pronoun *I*. In addition, capitalize the first word of:

- A sentence or partial sentence. (*Exception:* Do not capitalize the first word of a sentence following a colon.)

  Capitalize the first word of a sentence. Even a partial sentence. Why? Because standard usage requires it!

  One more job remains: we need to replace the furnace filter.

- A quoted sentence.

  Francis replied, "She would rather be right than rich."

  BUT: Francis replied that Ilsa would rather "be right than rich."

Capitalize the first word of each line in a listing.

- Each item in a list or outline.

  Please bring to the meeting:
  1. Your agenda.
  2. The draft budget.
  3. A list of questions or concerns you have.

**"I make in the seven figures.
Unfortunately there's a decimal point involved."**

People

Capitalize the name of a particular person, race, nationality, language, and religion. Also capitalize nicknames or other designations for people. Be sure to treat a person's name exactly as he or she prefers—in terms of spelling, capitalization, punctuation, and spacing.

John F. Kennedy, Jr.	African American
F. W. Woolworth	Italian
Madonna	Sioux
F. Scott Fitzgerald	Catholic
Elizabeth II	Amish
the Great Emancipator	William the Conqueror

Capitalize proper nouns and adjectives derived from proper nouns.

Titles with Names

Capitalize personal and official titles when they precede personal names. Do not capitalize titles when they follow or replace a person's name or when they are followed by an appositive.

Ms. Ida Ryan	Vice President Anthony
Professor J. Randall Scott	Colonel Wright
J. Randall Scott, professor of law,	Dr. Lian Yuan
Senator Ashley	Mayors York and Lindsey
My professor, J. Randall Scott,	the professor

Capitalize titles before names—but not after them.

An appositive is a noun that identifies another noun that comes immediately before it.

Capitalize a title used in direct address (but not terms such as *sir, madam,* and *miss*).

I want to know, Doctor, if there are other options available.

Please answer the question, sir, if you can.

Do not capitalize *ex-, -elect, late,* or *former* when used with official titles.

Governor-elect Johnson   ex-President Clinton

Direct address is an expression in which the writer speaks directly to another person.

Capitalize family titles when they stand alone or are followed by a personal name. Do not capitalize them when they are preceded by possessive pronouns.

Let me ask Dad and Uncle Chad for their help.

Let me ask my dad and my uncle, Chad Vaughan, for their help.

Places

Capitalize the official names of places: continents, countries, states, cities, streets, regions, rivers, oceans, mountains, parks, squares, monuments, statues, buildings, houses of worship, colleges, and the like. Also capitalize names that substitute for these places and adjectives derived from these place names.

Capitalize the official names of places.

Asia	Canada
Florida, the Sunshine State	Smithsonian Institution
Great Lakes	Rocky Mountains
Statue of Liberty	Sears Tower
University of Phoenix	Japanese cherry tree
German-made automobile	North Carolinian

Capitalize a common noun (and its plural form) if it is part of the official name. Do not capitalize a common noun that is not part of the official name or that serves as a short form for the official name. Capitalize *the* (or its foreign-language equivalent) only if it is part of the official name. Do not capitalize *state* unless it follows the official name of the state.

Stapleton Airport	the airport in Denver
Kansas City	the city of Charlotte
Fifth Avenue	the avenue
the Federal Bureau of Investigation	the federal government
Georgia State University	the state of Georgia
Hamilton County	the county of Hamilton
the Atlantic Ocean	the Atlantic and Pacific Oceans
St. Patrick's Cathedral	the cathedral in New York City
the United States of America	The Hague
New York State	the state of New York

Capitalize a compass point that designates a definite region or that is part of an official name. Do not capitalize compass points used as directions.

Do not capitalize a compass point used as a direction.

Margot lives in the South.

Our display window faces west.

Northern State University is in northern South Dakota.

Organization and Brand Names

Do not capitalize unimportant words in proper names.

Capitalize the names of companies, organizations, associations, clubs, teams, and the like. In general, do not capitalize articles (*the, a, an*), conjunctions, or prepositions containing three or fewer letters. However, treat the organization's name exactly as the organization prefers—in terms of spelling, capitalization, punctuation, and spacing. Do not capitalize shortened forms of the name.

United Airlines	Delta Air Lines
Disney World	Disneyland
the Elks	the Republican Party
the Centers for Disease Control	**BUT:** the centers
BankAmerica Corp.	**BUT:** the corporation
the U. S. Army	**BUT:** the army

Capitalize brand names (exactly as the owner of the brand name does), but do not capitalize a generic name that follows.

Do not capitalize a common noun following a brand name.

IBM computer	Kleenex tissues
Air Jordan sneakers	Lincoln sedan

Capitalize the name of a department or division within an organization if it is preceded by the word *the* and is the official name of the department or division. In all other circumstances, use lowercase letters.

Capitalize the full name of a department if it is preceded by the word the.

the Department of Administrative Services

BUT: our administrative services department

the Finance Committee of your firm

BUT: your finance committee

the Board of Directors of Honeywell Inc.

BUT: our board of directors

Publications and Creative Works

Capitalize the important words in titles of books, magazines, newspapers, television programs, speeches, and other important literary or creative works. Also capitalize the first and last words, the first word after a colon or dash, and all other words except articles, conjunctions, and prepositions containing three or fewer letters.

> the article "A Word to the Wise"
> *Pricing Strategies: The Link With Reality*
> Archie Bunker from *All in the Family*

Recall that titles of complete published works are italicized, whereas titles of parts of published works are enclosed in quotation marks.

Miscellaneous

Nouns Followed by a Number   Capitalize a noun followed by a number or letter (except for page, size, line, and paragraph numbers).

Capitalize most nouns followed by a number.

Table 3	page 79
Flight 107	size 12D
Route 95	line 13

Days, Months, and Holidays   Capitalize the names of days, months, and holidays, but do not capitalize the names of seasons.

Do not capitalize the names of the seasons.

> St. Patrick's Day occurred in the spring on Friday, March 17.

Academic Courses and Degrees   Capitalize the names of specific course titles; do not capitalize the names of general areas of study. Capitalize the name of a degree (whether written in full or abbreviated) when it follows a person's name.

Degrees following a name are capitalized; titles following a name are not.

> I took Management 301, accounting, and business English last term.
> She received a master's degree in international business.
> Margot Spencer, Ph.D. (*Or "Margot Spencer, Doctor of Philosophy"*)

COMPREHENSION

1. Use the standard proofreaders' mark for capitalization (≡) under a letter to indicate which words should be capitalized.

   a. who is going?

   b. really!

   c. there is one other option: you can resign.

   d. the president said, "we must persevere."

   e. The late president richard m. nixon was a republican.

   f. please submit a hiring requisition for:

      ▪ an accounting clerk.

      ▪ a part-time file clerk.

      ▪ two receptionists.

2. Use the standard proofreaders' mark for capitalization (≡) under a letter to indicate which words should be capitalized.

   a. My doctor, Clifford Fetters, was present.

   b. Clifford Fetters, my doctor, was present.

   c. Ask vice president Bradley Adams.

   d. May I please have $10, dad?

   e. I visited cousin Isabela and my grandmother during the holidays.

CHECKPOINT 15.1

    f. Does the snake river run through yosemite national park?

    g. The european and asian continents border four oceans.

    h. We visited washington state and then drove south to carson city.

    i. The federal communications commission is a branch of the federal government in washington, d.c.

    j. The northern part of the state of michigan is known as the upper peninsula.

3. Use the standard proofreaders' mark for capitalization (≡) under a letter to indicate which words should be capitalized.

    a. The topeka board of education met briefly, but the board did not take a vote.

    b. Please take a bic ballpoint pin with you to the committee meeting.

    c. The department of corporate communications is the only department at r. h. macy & co., inc., that is authorized to respond to the newspaper item.

    d. The head of our accounting department came from dow chemical company.

    e. The title of the newspaper article was "the real crisis in housing: no home to go home to," and it appeared in thursday's edition of the raleigh *news and observer*.

    f. Please order model 17-C shown on page 117 of our spring catalog.

    g. The fourth of july was celebrated in my american history class.

Number Expression

Business writing would not be business writing without numbers. Think how often you find dates, amounts of money, identification numbers, sizes, and the like in letters, email, memos, and business reports. Because figures are easier (and faster) to comprehend than words, we use them for most business numbers. Nevertheless, figures interrupt the flow of the sentence more than words do (after all, the rest of the sentence is also composed of words), so words are typically used for small and isolated references to numbers.

Authorities do not always agree on a single style for expressing numbers—whether to spell out a number in words or to write it in figures. The following guidelines apply to typical business writing.

"I'll have the misspelled 'Ceasar' salad and the improperly hyphenated veal osso-buco."

General Rules

General Business Writing   Spell out the numbers zero through ten and use figures for 11 and higher. Separate thousands by commas.

the first three pages	ten complaints
18 photocopies	5,376 stockholders

At the Beginning of a Sentence   Spell out a number that begins a sentence. If the number requires more than two words when spelled out, reword the sentence instead.

Eight temporary employees lost their jobs.
Fifteen people attended the seminar.
One hundred homes were damaged in the flood.

Spell out the numbers zero through ten; use figures for 11 and higher.

Adjacent Numbers   When adjacent numbers are expressed both in figures or both in words, separate them with a comma. If one of the adjacent numbers is a compound modifier, express the number with fewer letters in words and the other number in figures.

In *2004, 18* people showed up to testify. (*Both numbers are in figures.*)

At *nine, three* people showed up to testify. (*Both numbers are in words.*)

I examined *8 two*-room office suites and *two 8*-room suites. (*"Eight" contains more letters than "two."*)

Grace printed *500 four*-page flyers and *four 500*-page catalogs.

Related Numbers   Within the same sentence, express related numbers in the same way. If both numbers are ten or lower, use words. If *either* is greater than ten, use figures (unless the number begins a sentence). If the numbers in the same sentence are not related, follow the general rules for number expression.

Express related numbers in a parallel format.

Either *nine or ten* of the test results were positive. (*Both related numbers are ten or lower.*)

Only *6 men and 13 women* chose that life insurance option. (*One of the related numbers is greater than ten.*)

Fifteen to twenty people attended the seminar. (*The first related number begins a sentence.*)

BUT: I administered *two* of the hemoglobin tests to the *47* patients. (*The numbers are not related.*)

Indefinite Numbers   Spell out indefinite numbers.

a few hundred complaints	thousands of dollars
tens of thousands of people	more than a million acres

Ordinal Numbers   With the exception of numbered street names and certain dates (discussed later), spell out ordinal numbers (such as *first, second, thirtieth*) that can be expressed in one or two words.

Hyphenate the numbers 21–99, whether they are cardinal or ordinal numbers.

the twenty-second century	her fifty-third birthday
thirty-second-floor apartment	our one hundredth anniversary
our one millionth visitor	**BUT:** our 117th anniversary

Best Palindromes

A man. A plan. A canal. Panama.
Oh, who was it I saw? Oh, who?
Able was I ere I saw Elba. droop.
Desserts I stressed.
I prefer Pi.

WORD|wise

Mix a maxim.
Never odd or even.
Poor Dan is in a
Madam, I'm Adam.
Sir, I'm Iris.

Fractions, Decimals, and Percentages

Fractions   Spell out and hyphenate a fraction that stands alone, unless it requires more than two words or is used in a calculation. Use figures for a mixed number (a whole number plus a fraction).

a two-thirds majority	one-fourth of the population
nine-tenths of the vote	one-third smaller than before
multiply by 3/5	13/42 of the time (*not "13/42nds"*)
interest rate of 7 5/8	adding 1½ cups of sugar

When constructing fractions that do not appear on the keyboard (see *7 5/8* above), use a diagonal and leave a space (not a hyphen) between the whole number and the fraction. Do not leave a space between a whole number and a *formatted* fraction (such as *1½* above).

Decimals   Write decimals in figures. If a whole number does not precede the decimal, insert a zero before the decimal point (to avoid misreading).

4.21	98.6	0.16	14,876.38

Percentages   Write percentages in figures and spell out the word *percent*. (Use the % symbol only in tables, business forms, technical writing, or other situations in which space is at a premium or percentages occur frequently.)

8 percent	15.5 percent	7½ percent	0.5 percent

Dates

Your word processor may automatically convert a manual ordinal (1st, 2nd) to a printed ordinal (1st, 2nd) for a more professional appearance. Either form is correct—so long as you are consistent.

Use figures for dates. When the day follows the month, use cardinal figures (such as *1*, *2*, and *30*). When the day precedes the month or stands alone, use ordinal figures (such as *1st*, *2nd*, and *30th*).

January 25	March 1, 2004
the 8th of August	going to trial on the 23rd

Use a comma before and after the year in a complete date unless some other punctuation mark is needed after the year. Do not use a comma with incomplete dates.

We had to sign the contract before April 15, 2004, and wanted to sign on

April 10, 2004; we actually signed on April 11, 2004 (because of the rolling electrical blackout on April 10).

The April 11, 2004, signing was attended by 35 members from management and labor.

We notarized the signatures on April 11 for legal reasons.

We notarized the signatures in April 2004 for legal reasons.

Money

Use figures for definite amounts of money and words for indefinite amounts of money.

$5	$18.53	Nearly $50,000
$500 worth	a $10 bill	a $67,500-a-year opening

BUT:

a few thousand dollars	millions of dollars	nearly a hundred dollars

Do not add a decimal point and zeros to a whole-dollar amount that occurs by itself or with other whole-dollar amounts. Do add a decimal point and zeros if the whole-dollar amount appears in the same context as a fractional-dollar amount.

My check for $78 is enclosed.

The amount of your order is $32.50, plus $3.00 shipping and handling, for a total of $35.50.

Express related amounts of money in parallel format.

Express round large amounts of money (a million dollars or more) partly in words.

$57 million	$6.7 billion
$5½ million	a $5 million-plus mansion

In general, use figures and the word *cents* for amounts less than a dollar. Use the dollar sign only if related amounts of money require it.

Phaedra paid me the *5 cents* I was owed. (*not* "*five cents*" *or* "*$.05*" *or* "*5¢*")

The price was *$2.97* plus *$.12* tax, for a total of *$3.09*.

Measurements

Express measurements that serve as significant statistics in figures. Within sentences, spell out the unit of measurement.

You must be less than *6 feet* tall to apply for that position.

The express package weighed *2 pounds 8 ounces*. (*No comma between elements of a measurement because it is thought of as a single unit*)

The first lab test required *5 hours 30 minutes* to complete.

Our sedan got *32 miles per gallon* on the *375-mile* trip.

A *9-foot-6-inch* rug was placed in the room that was *12 by 14 feet*.

Follow the rules for general number expression for an isolated, nontechnical reference to a measurement within a sentence.

I've lost five pounds since June.	I've lost 17 pounds since June.
Olaf drove ten miles farther.	Olaf drove 11 miles farther.

Street Addresses

Write house and building numbers in figures. (*Exception:* For clarity, use words for the number *one*.) Do not insert commas.

Differentiate between house or building numbers (which come *before* the street name) and numbered street names.

9 Loblolly Lane	536 Mission Street
10378 Glendale Road	One Park Avenue

Spell out street numbers one through ten and use figures for street numbers greater than ten. Do not abbreviate a compass direction before a street name or a one-word compass direction after a street name. Abbreviate a compound compass direction after a street name, and insert a comma but no periods.

8 East Second Avenue	148-B North 102nd Street
750 Clarion Street, South	1800 Tenth Avenue, SW

Time

Use figures with A.M. or P.M. and words with *o'clock*. Do not insert zeros with time on the hour unless a related time in the same sentence requires the expression of minutes.

Type *A.M.* and *P.M.* in lower-case letters with no internal space—but do space between the number and the abbreviation.

My flight arrives at *8:05 P.M.*

The meeting is at *three o'clock.*

We're open from *9 A.M.* until *6 P.M.*

We're open from *9:00 A.M.* until *6:30 P.M.*

Follow the rules for general number expression for general references to clock time without *A.M.*, *P.M.*, or *o'clock.* Spell out hours one through ten (and related minutes) and use figures for hours 11 and 12.

We started at *eight* in the morning and worked until *midnight.*

I arrived at *quarter to eight* and stayed until *half past nine.*

The tea begins at *two-thirty* and ends at *four forty-five.* (*A hyphen is used between hours and minutes unless the minutes themselves are hyphenated.*)

We started at 11 in the morning and worked until 2 in the afternoon. (*Express related numbers in a consistent format.*)

In general, follow the rules for general number expression for time periods other than clock time. Use figures only if the time period represents a significant statistic.

I worked there for only *six months.* Stacy worked there for only *13 months.*

Almost *five years* ago, I assumed a *30-year* mortgage.

Ages

Follow the general rules for numbers to express most references to ages.

Write ages in figures when they serve as significant statistics and spell out indefinite ages. Otherwise, follow the general rules for numbers.

Students must get this vaccination before the age of *8.*

You may retire at age *62½* with at least *20* years of service.

Her dependent is 18 years 7 months old. (*no comma between the years and months*)

Even a *five-year-old* can understand these directions.

Evan is in his early *forties*, and Samantha is in her *mid-thirties.*

Serial Numbers

Express serial numbers in figures. Capitalize the noun preceding the figure (except for *page*, *size*, *line*, and *paragraph*). Do not separate thousands with commas.

page 4	Flight 8701	Route 75
size 3	line 48	Table 4

CHECKPOINT 15.2

COMPREHENSION

1. Underline the correct alternatives in each sentence.

   a. Of the (3, three), (2, two) have related experience.

   b. Please put (7, seven) (5, five)-cent stamps on that package.

   c. (79, Seventy-nine) cases were investigated.

   d. A total of (4, four) men and (5, five) women took the test.

   e. (60, Sixty) men and (48, forty-eight) women took the test.

   f. I ordered several (100, hundred) vacation brochures.

g. My (53rd, fifty-third) birthday fell on the day of our company's (150th, one hundred fiftieth) anniversary.

h. A (¾, three-fourths) majority overruled the chair.

i. More than (⅓, one-third) of the computers need repairs.

j. Then divide the numerator by (⅓ one-third).

k. A cut-off date in (April 2004 was chosen; April, 2004, was chosen).

2. Circle the correct alternatives in each sentence.

a. Let's try to finish by the (⅕, 5th, fifth) of next month.

b. The envelope indicated that (13¢, $.13, 13 cents, thirteen cents) was owed for postage.

c. We left on the (18, 18th, eighteenth) of May.

d. Your total is ($75, $75.00) plus $3.75 tax, for a total of $78.75.

e. Please deliver the contract to (18773, 18,773) (10th, Tenth) Street, (NE, N.E., Northeast).

f. The (18′, 18-feet, 18-foot) timber began to sway in the wind.

g. Iram moved from (1, One) Trump (Ave., Avenue) to (8, Eight) Wall Street.

h. I checked into the hotel at (8 P.M., 8:00 P.M., eight P.M.)

i. Please be here by (9:30, nine thirty, nine-thirty).

j. Please refer to Table (2, Two) on (page, Page) (1273, 1,273).

k. The session lasted from (8, 8:00) A.M. until 9:30 P.M.

Abbreviations

An abbreviation is a shortened form of a word or phrase. You should use abbreviations sparingly in narrative writing. Many are appropriate only in technical writing, statistical material, tables, and other situations where space is at a premium.

Consult a dictionary for the correct form for abbreviations, and follow the rule "When in doubt, write it out." If there is any possibility of confusion, spell out the word the first time it is used and follow it with the abbreviation in parentheses. For example, does *CD* stand for "compact disk" or "certificate of deposit" (or even "Civil Defense")? Be consistent in the way you treat abbreviations within a document. Is it *C.D.* or *CD?*

Do not follow an abbreviation with a word that is part of the abbreviation itself. Also, do not precede a name with a courtesy title if an academic degree or designation follows the name. Thus, do not write "PIN (personal identification number) number" or "ATM (automated teller machine) machine." Also, do not write "Dr. Alan London, Ph.D." or "Ms. Lana Vawdry, Esq."

Do not repeat a word that is part of the abbreviation itself.

Abbreviations Not Used

In narrative writing, do not abbreviate common nouns (such as *acct., assoc., bldg., dept. misc.,* and *pkg.),* measurements, or the names of cities, states (except in addresses), months, and days of the week.

NOT: Please see Thos. in our accounting dept. before Mon., Dec. 13.

BUT: Please see Thomas in our accounting department before Monday, December 13.

Do not abbreviate common nouns in normal business writing.

NOT: The new security officer is more than 6 ft tall and weighs 250 lbs.

BUT: The new security officer is more than 6 feet tall and weighs 250 pounds.

Abbreviations Always Used

An acronym is an abbreviation pronounced as a word.

Some abbreviations are always appropriate: *Mr., Ms., Mrs., Dr.,* A.M., P.M., and those that are official parts of company names, such as *Co., Inc.,* or *Ltd.* Follow an individual's preference for using initials or spelling out his or her first or middle names. Well-established acronyms (abbreviations pronounced as words, such as *NATO*—for the North Atlantic Treaty Organization) are also always appropriate. Many times, these acronyms are more familiar to the reader than their spelled-out counterparts.

NOT: Doctor Allumbaugh worked for the National Association of Security Dealers Automated Quotations but volunteered for the United Nations International Children's Emergency Fund at Halloween.

BUT: Dr. Allumbaugh worked for NASDAQ but volunteered for UNICEF at Halloween.

Punctuation and Spacing

Use periods but no internal spaces with most lowercase abbreviations. Omit periods and spaces with most all-capital abbreviations.

Many abbreviations follow the capitalization of the words as if written in full. In most lowercase abbreviations made up of single initials, use a period after each initial but no internal spaces.

a.m.	p.m.	i.e.	e.g.	c.o.d.
Exceptions:	mpg	mph	wpm	

In most all-capital abbreviations made up of single initials, do not use periods or internal spaces.

WWW	OSHA	PBS	AMA	ASAP	CEO	EST	GPA
Exceptions:	P.O.	U.S.A.	A.A.	B.S.	Ph.D.	B.C.	A.D

(*Do not insert internal spaces in any of these abbreviations.*)

Measurements

As discussed and illustrated on page 417, in normal business writing, you should spell out isolated measurements. Abbreviate units of measure only when they occur frequently—for example, in technical and scientific writing, on forms, and in tables. Type them in the following format:

- Use lowercase letters without periods.
- Leave one space between the number and the abbreviation and between abbreviations.
- Use figures for all numbers.
- Do not insert a comma between the parts of a single measurement.
- Use the same abbreviation for singular and plural forms.

6 lb 7 oz   5 ft 10 in   10 sq yd   3 gal   34 mpg   50 km

COMPREHENSION

1. Underline any abbreviation that should not be used in general business writing. Draw a line through any term that would normally be abbreviated, and write the correct form of the abbreviation above it.

   a. OPEC set the price of oil to $27.65 bbl. at its Dec. meeting.

   b. Please R.S.V.P. to the invitation we rec'd. from the TX Alamo Comm.

   c. Doctor Wainwright received his B.S. degree from Indiana U.

   d. My ETA at Douglas Airport is 10:30 ante meridiem.

   e. The next high-tech expo will be held in Boston, Mass.

2. In the space provided, write the correct form of the abbreviation for each term listed.

Mistress	_____
miles per hour	_____
grade point average	_____
associate in arts degree	_____
compact disk-read-only memory	_____
6 feet and 3 inches	_____
650 megahertz	_____
merchandise	_____
Enclosure	_____
World Wide Web	_____

CHECKPOINT 15.3

Spelling

Correct spelling is essential to effective communication. A misspelled word can distract the reader, cause misunderstanding, and send a negative message about the writer's competence. No doubt you already use your computer spell checker to proofread your spelling. As helpful as these devices are, they do have limitations. Most spell checkers will not, for example, catch the misuse of *their* for *there*, will not identify an erroneous addition or omission of an *-s* to a word, and can play havoc with proper names. In short, you must still proofread carefully.

Because of the many variations in the spelling of English words, no spelling guidelines are foolproof; there are exceptions to every spelling rule. The five rules that follow, however, may be safely applied in most business writing situations. Learning them will save you the time of looking up many words in a dictionary.

Doubling a Final Consonant   If the last syllable of a root word is stressed, double the final consonant when adding a suffix.

Last Syllable Stressed		*Last Syllable Not Stressed*	
prefer	preferring	happen	happening
control	controlling	total	totaling
occur	occurrence	differ	differed

One-Syllable Words   If a one-syllable word ends in a consonant preceded by a single vowel, double the final consonant before a suffix starting with a vowel.

Suffix Starting with a Vowel		*Suffix Starting with a Consonant*	
ship	shipper	ship	shipment
drop	dropped	glad	gladness
bag	baggage	bad	badly

Final E   If a final -e is preceded by a consonant, drop the e before a suffix starting with a vowel.

Suffix Starting With a Vowel		*Suffix Starting With a Consonant*	
come	coming	hope	hopeful
use	usable	manage	management
sincere	sincerity	sincere	sincerely

Note: Words ending in -ce or -ge usually retain the e before a suffix starting with a vowel: noticeable, advantageous.

Final Y   If a final -y is preceded by a consonant, change the y to i before any suffix except one starting with i.

Most Suffixes		*Suffixes Starting With an i*	
company	companies	try	trying
ordinary	ordinarily	forty	fortyish
hurry	hurried	baby	babyish

EI and IE Words   Remember the rhyme:

Use i before e:	believe	yield
Except after c:	receive	deceit
Or when sounded as a:	freight	their
As in *neighbor* and *weigh*.		

CHECKPOINT 15.4

COMPREHENSION

Underline the misspelled word and write it correctly.

1. phenomenon	hypocricy	assistance	_____
2. liaison	precedant	miniature	_____
3. surprise	harrass	nickel	_____
4. similiar	occasionally	embarrassing	_____
5. concensus	innovate	irresistible	_____
6. benefited	exhaustible	parallell	_____
7. seperately	inadvertent	exhilarated	_____
8. efficiency	insistance	disapproval	_____
9. accidentally	camouflage	alloted	_____
10. criticize	innocence	indispensible	_____
11. accommodate	perserverance	plausible	_____
12. apparent	deterrant	license	_____
13. category	occurrence	wierd	_____
14. recommend	changeable	hairbrained	_____
15. argument	boundry	deceive	_____

Summary

Follow these guidelines for capitalization. Capitalize the following items:

- The first-person pronoun *I* and the first word of a sentence or partial sentence, quoted sentence, and each item in a list or outline.

- The name of a particular person, race, nationality, language, and religion.

- A title that precedes a person's name but not one that follows a name or that is followed by an appositive.

- A noun used in direct address.

- The official names of places.

- Organization and brand names but not common nouns following them.

- The official names of departments and divisions within an organization if they are preceded by *the*.

- The important words in publications and creative works.

- The first word of a compound at the beginning of a sentence, and all important words in a title or heading.

- Most nouns followed by a number; days, months, and holidays; official names of academic courses; and degrees.

Follow these guidelines for writing numbers in typical business writing:

- Unless special rules apply, spell out the numbers zero through ten and use figures for 11 and higher. Separate thousands by commas.

- When adjacent numbers are both in figures or both in words, separate them with a comma. If one of the adjacent numbers is a compound modifier, express the number with fewer letters in words and the other number in figures.

- Within the same sentence, express related numbers the same way.

- Spell out a number that begins a sentence; indefinite numbers, amounts of money, and ages; ordinal numbers (except for dates and street addresses); a fraction that stands alone; street numbers one through ten; and time expressed with "o'clock."

- Write in figures mixed numbers; decimals; percentages; dates; definite amounts of money; measurements and ages that serve as significant statistics; house and building numbers greater than one and street numbers greater than ten; time expressed with *a.m.* or *p.m.*; and serial numbers.

Use abbreviations sparingly in general business writing. Do not abbreviate common nouns, measurements, or the names of cities, states, months, and days of the week in narrative writing. Some abbreviations, however, are always acceptable, as are shortened forms of many words. Consult a dictionary for the correct capitalization, punctuation, and spacing of abbreviations. Measurements may be abbreviated whenever they occur frequently.

Follow these rules for correct spelling:

- If the last syllable of a root word is stressed, double the final consonant when adding a suffix.

- If a one-syllable word ends in a consonant preceded by a single vowel, double the final consonant before a suffix starting with a vowel.

- If a final -*e* is preceded by a consonant, drop the *e* before a suffix starting with a vowel.

- If a final -*y* is preceded by a consonant, change the *y* to *i* before any suffix except one starting with *i*.

- Use *i* before *e*, except after *c*, or when sounded as *a*, as in *neighbor* and *weigh*.

Exercises

Capitalization

1 Correct any errors in capitalization in the following sentences.

a. As you did last Fall, you may park in the visitor's parking lot on Canyon drive in front of the Riverside medical center.

b. Please report to the admitting department of Riverside hospital, where you will be directed to see Dr. Raymond Shield, chief of staff, who will administer the Exam.

c. Your Doctor, Guadalupe Suárez, should be returning to her office on Monday; She finishes her Lecture at the Mayo Clinic on Sunday and will be taking flight 307 back to east Orange, New Jersey.

d. The west Indian ambassador met Ex-president Bush at the LBJ ranch.

e. Chowan county is not as large as the county of Perquimans; both are located in eastern North Carolina.

f. I purchased some Starbucks Coffee for the vice president and for each member of the board of directors.

Number Expression

2 Circle the correct alternatives in each sentence.

a. On May 7, (50, fifty) new members were initiated.

b. Please put (7, seven) (37, thirty-seven)-cent stamps on that package.

c. Please retype the first (10, ten) pages.

d. We ordered (100, one hundred) invitations for the reception.

e. A total of (4, four) men and (12, twelve) women took the test.

f. A total of (15, fifteen) men took the (3, three)-hour test.

g. Please make (3, three) (1st, first)-class plane reservations.

h. The incumbent received nearly a (1,000, thousand) votes more than her challenger.

i. Last year our profit rose to (4, four) (%, percent) of net sales.

j. The overtime rate was ($1\frac{1}{2}$, $1\frac{1}{2}$, one and one-half) times the normal rate.

k. We replaced (19/25, 19/25th, nineteen twenty-fifths) of the solution.

l. I wrote a ($500, five-hundred-dollar) check for the deposit.

m. The date of April 3, (2004 was chosen; 2004, was chosen).

n. We left on May (18, 18th, eighteen).

o. We spent ($1,000s, thousands of dollars) to refurbish the studio.

p. By the way, our grandson weighed nearly (9, nine) pounds at birth.

q. Please purchase a credenza that is (4′ 8″, 4 ft 8 in, 4 feet 8 inches) wide.

r. Their showroom is located at (7, Seven) (E., East) (7th, Seventh) Boulevard.

s. His first appointment is at (9, nine) o'clock.

t. In our city, children can begin school only after they have reached the age of (5, five).

u. Please ensure that the package arrives by (one, 1) p.m. (EST, E.S.T.) tomorrow.

v. The meeting will last from (8, 8:00, eight) until (12:30, twelve thirty, twelve-thirty).

Abbreviations

3 Circle any abbreviations that should not be used in general business writing. Draw a line through any term that would normally be abbreviated, and write the correct form of the abbreviation above it. Correct any abbreviations that are shown in incorrect format. If necessary, use your dictionary.

a. Doctor R. Jason Gage, Jr., sent Angélica Blanco, Esquire, a bill for the amt. she still owed from her visit on Mon.

b. Their address in NYC is 183 W. 53rd St., Northwest.

c. The Federal Bureau of Investigation set up an appointment on Thurs. at 9 a.m. Eastern Standard Time to talk to me.

d. The NASCAR races in Indy are always held on a Sunday.

e. How many lbs. and ozs. did the FedEx package weigh?

f. The bank's home loan dept. will let you know how much is left in your escrow acct.

g. The Y.M.C.A. is less than 300 ft. from Mister Smith's cement co.

h. I received my BS degree in lib. sci. from the U. of Virginia.

i. I accessed Amazon.com on the W.W.W. to learn whether my package would arrive c.o.d.

j. Please let me know ASAP if the C.E.O. will be able to see Geo. & me about the N.A.S.A. account.

Spelling

4 Correct any misspellings in the following lines:

a. ecstasy	milennium	supercede
b. accidently	minuscule	accomodate
c. iresistible	liaison	harras
d. definitely	ocurence	embarass
e. cemetary	innoculate	sacrilegious
f. confidance	disappoint	defendent
g. occassionally	calendar	merchendise
h. apparant	abreviate	peculiar
i. absence	mayonnaise	commitment
j. acordance	tarrif	phisycian
k. alotted	miniscule	amateurish
l. renumeration	auxiliary	catastrophy
m. changeable	carbueretor	clientele
n. beneficial	milage	techniciality
o. celophane	questionaire	wierd
p. persuasive	unanimiously	caffeine
q. benafactor	subtle	consensus

Credits

Grateful acknowledgment is made to the following companies for allowing their letterheads to be included in this book. These letters are for text examples only; they were not written by employees of the companies.

Chapter 7: Courtesy of Hewlett-Packard Company; courtesy of Sir Speedy, Inc.; courtesy of General Mills. *Chapter 8:* Courtesy of National MS Society; courtesy of The Home Depot; M and Motorola are registered trademarks of Motorola, Inc. © 1999 Motorola, Inc.

Text Credits

All Microsoft Internet Explorer screen shots reproduced courtesy of Microsoft.

All AltaVista screen shots reproduced with the permission of AltaVista Company. All rights reserved.

Handout 2.1 from RACE MANNERS by Bruce A. Jacobs (Arcade Publishing: 1999).

"Evaluating the Quality of Internet Resources" adapted from Jan Alexander and Marsha Ann Tate, "Evaluating Web Resources," July 25, 2001. From http://muse.widener.edu/Woflgram-Memorial-Library/webevaluation.

"Netiquette" from Virginia Shea, "The Core Rules of Etiquette," ALBION.COM (January 16, 2002).

List of Irregular Verbs from L. Scot Ober, "The Basic Vocabulary of Written Business Communication," DELTA PI EPSILON JOURNAL, Vol. 24, January 1982, pp. 13–27. Reprinted by permission of Delta Pi Epsilon Journal.

Electric Library screen shots © 1999 The Economist Newspaper Group, Inc. Reprinted with permission of The Economist Newspaper, Inc. and Electric Library. Further reproduction prohibited. www.economist.com; www.infonautics.com.

Eli Lilly web page reprinted with permission of Eli Lilly and Company.

Definitions of "funny" and "recent": Copyright © 2000 by Houghton Mifflin Company. Reproduced by permission from THE AMERICAN HERITAGE COLLEGE DICTIONARY, THIRD EDITION.

Photo and Cartoon Credits

page 2: Courtesy of Nissan North America; *page 9:* ©Katie Murray; *page 13:* AP/Wide World/Gene Puskar; *page 16:* Dilbert reprinted by permission of United Feature Syndicate, Inc.; *page 27:* Courtesy of 3M Corporate Marketing and Public Affairs; *page 28:* Ki Ho Park/Kistone Photography; *page 33:* Stoddart/IPG/Matrix; *page 40:* ©Joseph Kohl; *page 51:* ©Francisco Rangel; *page 61:* Rachel Epstein/PhotoEdit; *page 65:* Cathy©1983 Cathy Guisewite. Reprinted with permission of Universal Press Syndicate. All rights reserved; *page 74:* Dilbert reprinted by permission of United Feature Syndicate, Inc.; *page 84:* Courtesy of Bank of Montreal; *page 89:* ©Kate Swan; *page 93:* AP/Wide World; *page 95:* Non Sequitur © 2001 Wiley Miller. Reprinted with permission of Universal Press Syndicate. All rights reserved; *page 98:* Robert Houser; *page 112:* Courtesy of iVillage; *page 115:* Misha Gravenor; *page 117:* Wizard of Id reproduced by permission of Johnny Hart and Creators Syndicate, Inc.; *page 125:* Michael Lewis; *page 126:* Kristine Larsen; *page 141:* David Young-Wolff/PhotoEdit; *page 143:* B.C. reproduced by permission of Johnny Hart and Creators Syndicate, Inc.; *page 155:* Dilbert reprinted by permission of United Feature Syndicate, Inc.; *page 166:* Media Relations Manager/Intel Corporation; *page 169:* Cathy©1982 Cathy Guisewite. Reprinted with permission of Universal Press Syndicate. All rights reserved; *pages 170, 178:* Index Stock Photography; *page 183:* Elena Dorfman/Matrix; *page 205:* Courtesy of the Wilderness Society; *page 208:* Michael Nagle/New York Times; *page 214:* Dilbert reprinted by permission of United Feature Syndicate, Inc.; *page 220:* Fritz Hoffmann/Document China; *page 221:* Gail Albert Halaban/Corbis SABA; *page 234:* Michael Newman/PhotoEdit; 238: Calvin and Hobbes © 1993 Watterson. Reprinted with permission of Universal Press Syndicate. All rights reserved; *page 243:* ©Glenn Bernhardt; *page 254:* Courtesy of Janis Lamar; *page 261* © John Dunn; *page 265:* Dilbert reprinted by permission of United Feature Syndicate, Inc.; *page 286:* Courtesy of Habitat for Humanity; *page 299:* © Randy Glasbergen; *page 306:* Index Stock Photography; *page 322:* Bonnie Kamin/PhotoEdit; *page 323:* Far Side cartoon reproduced courtesy of Creators Syndicate 331: Beetle Bailey cartoon reprinted with special permission of King Features Syndicate; *page 344:* Courtesy of Royal Caribbean International; *page 351:* Susan Van Etten/PhotoEdit; *page 363:* Dilbert reprinted by permission of United Feature Syndicate, Inc.; *page 371:* Courtesy Paul Orvos Computer Sciences Corporation; *page 380:* Dilbert reprinted by permission of United Feature Syndicate, Inc.; *pages 395, 409:* David Young-Wolff/PhotoEdit; *page 410:* © 2002 Peter Steiner from cartoonbank.com. All Rights Reserved; *page 414:* © The New Yorker Collection 2002 Jack Ziegler from cartoonbank.com. All Rights Reserved.

Appendix

Correspondence Formats

November 1, 20—

Ms. Ella Shore, Professor
Department of Journalism
Burlington College
South Burlington, VT 05403

Dear Professor Shore:

Subject: Newspaper Advertising

Thank you for thinking of Ben & Jerry's when you were planning the advertising for the back-to-school edition of your campus newspaper at Mountainside College. We appreciate the wide acceptance your students and faculty give our products, and we are proud to be represented in the *Mountain Lark*. We are happy to provide a quarter-page ad as follows:

• The ad should include our standard logo and the words "Welcome to Ben & Jerry's."

• We would prefer that our ad appear in the top-right corner of a right-facing page, if possible.

Our logo is enclosed for you to duplicate. I am also enclosing a check for $375 to cover the cost of the ad. Best wishes as you publish this special edition of your newspaper.

Sincerely,

Joseph W. Dye
Sales Manager

rmt
Enclosures
c: Advertising Supervisor

Block Style Letter

November 1, 20—

Ms. Ella Shore, Professor
Department of Journalism
Burlington College
South Burlington, VT 05403

Dear Professor Shore:

Subject: Newspaper Advertising

Thank you for thinking of Ben & Jerry's when you were planning the advertising for the back-to-school edition of your campus newspaper at Mountainside College. We appreciate the wide acceptance your students and faculty give our products, and we are proud to be represented in the *Mountain Lark*. We are happy to provide a quarter-page ad as follows:

• The ad should include our standard logo and the words "Welcome to Ben & Jerry's."

• We would prefer that our ad appear in the top-right corner of a right-facing page, if possible.

Our logo is enclosed for you to duplicate. I am also enclosing a check for $375 to cover the cost of the ad. Best wishes as you publish this special edition of your newspaper.

Sincerely,

Joseph W. Dye
Sales Manager

rmt
Enclosures
c: Advertising Supervisor

Modified Block Style Letter

MEMO TO: Max Dillon, Sales Manager

FROM: Andrea J. Hayes

DATE: February 25, 20—

SUBJECT: New-Venture Proposal

I propose the purchase or lease of a van to be used as a mobile bookstore. We could then use this van to generate sales in the outlying towns and villages throughout the state.

We have been aware for quite some time that many small towns around the state do not have adequate bookstore facilities, but the economics of the situation are such that we would not be able to open a comprehensive branch and operate it profitably. However, we could afford to stock a van with books and operate it for a few days at a time in various small towns throughout the state. As you are probably aware, the laws of this state would permit us to acquire a statewide business license fairly easily and inexpensively.

With the proper advance advertising (see attached sample), we should be able to generate much interest in this endeavor. It seems to me that this idea has much merit because of the flexibility it offers us. For example, we could tailor the length of our stay to the size of the town and the amount of business generated. Also, we could customize our inventory to the needs and interests of the particular locales.

The driver of the van would act as the salesperson, and we would, of course, have copies of our complete catalog so that mail orders could be taken as well. Please let me have your reactions to this proposal. If you wish, I can explore the matter further and generate cost and sales estimates in time for your next manager's meeting.

jmc
Attachments

Interoffice Memorandum

Email Message

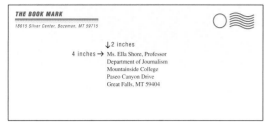

Large (No. 10) Envelopes

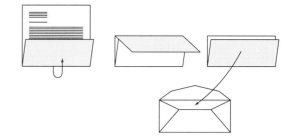

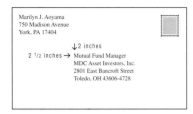

Small (No. 6³/₄) Envelopes

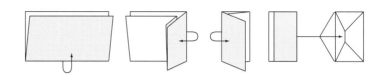

POSTAL SERVICE ABBREVIATIONS

U.S. POSTAL SERVICE ABBREVIATIONS
FOR STATES, TERRITORIES, AND CANADIAN PROVINCES

States and Territories			
Alabama . . . . AL	Kansas . . . . KS	North Dakota . . . . ND	Wyoming . . . . WY
Alaska . . . . AK	Kentucky . . . . KY	Ohio . . . . OH	
Arizona . . . . AZ	Louisiana . . . . LA	Oklahoma . . . . OK	
Arkansas . . . . AR	Maine . . . . ME	Oregon . . . . OR	
California . . . . CA	Maryland . . . . MD	Pennsylvania . . . . PA	Canadian Provinces
Colorado . . . . CO	Massachusetts . . . . MA	Puerto Rico . . . . PR	Alberta . . . . AB
Connecticut . . . . CT	Michigan . . . . MI	Rhode Island . . . . RI	British Columbia . . . . . BC
Delaware . . . . DE	Minnesota . . . . MN	South Carolina . . . . SC	Labrador . . . . LB
District of Columbia . . DC	Mississippi . . . . MS	South Dakota . . . . SD	Manitoba . . . . MB
Florida . . . . FL	Missouri . . . . MO	Tennessee . . . . TN	New Brunswick . . . . . . NB
Georgia . . . . GA	Montana . . . . MT	Texas . . . . TX	Newfoundland . . . . . . NF
Guam . . . . GU	Nebraska . . . . NE	Utah . . . . UT	Northwest Territories . NT
Hawaii . . . . HI	Nevada . . . . NV	Vermont . . . . VT	Nova Scotia . . . . NS
Idaho . . . . ID	New Hampshire . . . . NH	Virgin Islands VI	Ontario . . . . ON
Illinois IL	New Jersey . . . . NJ	Virginia . . . . VA	Prince Edward Island . . PE
Indiana . . . . IN	New Mexico . . . . NM	Washington . . . . WA	Quebec . . . . PQ
Iowa . . . . IA	New York . . . . NY	West Virginia . . . . WV	Saskatchewan . . . . SK
	North Carolina . . . . NC	Wisconsin . . . . WI	Yukon Territory . . . . . . YT

Sample Report in Business Style

EVALUATION OF THE STAFF BENEFIT PROGRAM

AT ATLANTIC STATE UNIVERSITY

David Riggins

I. INTRODUCTION
    A. Purpose and Scope
    B. Procedures

II. FINDINGS
    A. Knowledge of Benefits
        1. Familiarity with Benefits
        2. Present Methods of Communication
            a. Formal Channels
            b. Informal Channels
        3. Preferred Methods of Communication
    B. Opinions of Present Benefits
        1. Importance of Benefits
        2. Satisfaction with Benefits
    C. Desirability of Additional Benefits

III. SUMMARY, CONCLUSIONS, AND RECOMMENDATIONS
    A. Summary of the Problem and Procedures
    B. Summary of the Findings
    C. Conclusions and Recommendations

APPENDIX
    A. Cover Letter
    B. Questionnaire

Outline

EVALUATION OF THE STAFF BENEFIT PROGRAM

AT ATLANTIC STATE UNIVERSITY

Prepared for

David Riggins
Director of Human Resources
Atlantic State University

Prepared by

Loretta J. Santorini
Assistant Director of Human Resources
Atlantic State University

December 8, 20—

Title Page

MEMO TO: David Riggins, Director of Human Resources

FROM: Loretta J. Santorini, Assistant Director of Human Resources

DATE: December 8, 20—

SUBJECT: Evaluation of the Staff Benefit Program at Atlantic State University

Here is the report evaluating our staff benefit program that you requested on October 15.

The report shows that overall the staff is familiar with and values most of the benefits we offer. At the end of the report, I've made several recommendations regarding the possibility of issuing individualized benefit statements annually and determining the usefulness of the automobile insurance benefit, the feasibility of offering compensation for unused sick leave, and the competitiveness of our retirement program.

I enjoyed working on this assignment, Dave, and learned quite a bit from my analysis of the situation that will help me during the upcoming labor negotiations. Please let me know if I can provide further information.

emc
Attachment

Transmittal Document

CONTENTS

Table of Contents

EVALUATION OF THE STAFF BENEFIT PROGRAM AT ATLANTIC STATE UNIVERSITY

Loretta J. Santorini

INTRODUCTION

Employee benefits are a rapidly growing and increasingly important form of employee compensation for both for profit and nonprofit organizations. According to a recent U.S. Chamber of Commerce survey, benefits now constitute 37% of all payroll cost, averaging $11,857 per year for each full-time employee.[1] Thus, on the basis of cost alone, an organization's employee benefit program must be carefully monitored and evaluated.

Atlantic State University employs nearly 2,500 staff personnel, and they have not received a cost-of-living increase in two years. As a result, staff salaries may not have kept pace with private industry, and the university's employee benefit program may become more important in attracting and retaining good workers. In addition, the contracts of three of the four staff unions expire next year, and the benefit program is typically a major area of bargaining.

PURPOSE AND SCOPE OF THE STUDY

To help ensure that the staff benefit program at ASU operates as effectively as possible, the director of personnel authorized this report on October 15, 20—. Specifically, this problem was addressed in this study: What are the opinions of staff employees at Atlantic State University regarding their employee benefits? To answer this question, the following subproblems were addressed:

1. How knowledgeable are the employees about the benefit program?

2. What are the employees' opinions of the value of the benefits that are presently available to them?

[1]Sarah Berelson et al., *Managing Your Benefit Program*, 13th ed., Novak-Siebold, Chicago, 2002, p. 183.

First Page

FINDINGS

For a benefit program to achieve its goals, employees must be aware of the benefits provided. Thus, the first section that follows discusses the employees' familiarity with their benefits as well as the effectiveness of the university's present method of communicating benefits and those methods that employees would prefer. An effective benefit package must also include benefits that are relevant to employee needs. Thus, the employees' opinions of the importance of and their satisfaction with each benefit offered are discussed next. The section concludes with a discussion of those benefits employees would like to see added to the benefit program at ASU.

KNOWLEDGE OF BENEFITS

One study[3] has shown that employees' satisfaction with benefits is directly correlated with their knowledge of such benefits. Thus, an indication of the staff employees' level of familiarity with their benefits and suggestions for improving communication were solicited.

Familiarity with Benefits. Numerous methods are presently being used to communicate the fringe benefits to employees. According to Lewis Rigby, director of the State Personnel Board, every new state employee views a 30-minute video entitled "In Addition to Your Salary" as part of the new-employee orientation. Also, the major benefits are explained during one-on-one counseling during the first day of the orientation session.

The staff employees were asked to rate their level of familiarity with each benefit. As shown in Table 1, most staff employees believe that most benefits have been adequately communicated to them. At least three-fourths of the employees are familiar with all major benefits except for long-term disability insurance, which is familiar to only a slight majority, and auto insurance, which is familiar to only one-third of the respondents. This low level of knowledge is

[3]Donna Jean Egan and Annette Kantelzoglou (eds.), *Human Resources*, Varsity Books, 2001

New-Section Page

TABLE 1. LEVEL OF FAMILIARITY WITH THE BENEFIT PROGRAM

Employee Benefit	Level of Familiarity			
	Familiar	Unfamiliar	Undecided	Total
Sick leave	94%	4%	2%	100%
Vacation/paid holidays	93%	4%	3%	100%
Hospital/medical insurance	90%	7%	3%	100%
Life insurance	84%	10%	6%	100%
Long-term disability insurance	53%	33%	14%	100%
Retirement	76%	14%	10%	100%
Auto insurance*	34%	58%	8%	100%

*This benefit started six weeks before the survey was taken.

In general, benefit familiarity is not related to length of employment. Most employees are familiar with most benefits regardless of their length of employment. As shown in Figure 1, however, the longer a person has been employed at ASU, the more likely he or she is to know about the life insurance benefit.

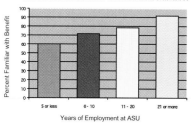

FIGURE 1. KNOWLEDGE OF LIFE INSURANCE BENEFIT

Page with Audiovisual Aids

BIBLIOGRAPHY

Abbey Petroleum Industries, *2004 Annual Report*, API, Inc., San Francisco, 2005.

Adams, Josiah B., *Compensation Systems*, Brunswick Press, Boston, 2003.

Berelson, Sarah, et al., *Managing Your Benefit Program*, 13th ed., Novak-Siebold, Chicago, 2002.

Directory of Business and Financial Services, Corporate Libraries Assoc., New York, 2001.

Ignatio, Enar, "Can Flexible Benefits Promote Your Company?" *Personnel Quarterly*, Vol. 20, September 2004, pp. 804–816.

"Let Employees Determine Their Own Benefits," *Manhattan Times*, January 12, 2004, p. C17, col. 2.

"Market Research," *Encyclopedia of Business*, 2d ed., 2004.

National Institute of Mental Health, *Who Pays the Piper? Ten Years of Passing the Buck*, DHHS Publication No. ADM 82-1195, U.S. Government Printing Office, Washington, 2001.

Preminger, Larry (Executive Producer), *The WKVX-TV Evening News*, Valhalla Broadcasting Co., Los Angeles, August 5, 2002.

Quincy, Dinah J., "Maxwell Announces New Health Benefit," *Maxwell Corp. Home Page*, November 13, 2002, <http://www.max...corp.com/NEWS/2001/193500.html> (January 14, 2003).

Young, Laurel <lyoung2@express.com>, "Training Doesn't Always Last," June 3, 2002, <http://groups.yahoo.com/group/personnel/message151> (April 20, 2003).

Bibliography

Sample Report in APA and MLA Styles

Staff Benefit Program 2

Evaluation of the Staff Benefit Program

at Atlantic State University

Loretta J. Santorini

Introduction

Employee benefits are a rapidly growing and increasingly important form of employee compensation for both for-profit and nonprofit organizations. According to a recent U.S. Chamber of Commerce survey, benefits now constitute 37% of all payroll cost, costing an average of $11,857 per year for each full-time employee (Adhams & Stevens, 2000, p. 183). Thus, on the basis of cost alone, an organization's employee benefit program must be carefully monitored and evaluated.

Atlantic State University employs nearly 2,500 staff personnel, and they have not received a cost-of-living increase in two years. As a result, staff salaries may not have kept pace with private industry, and the university's employee benefit program may become more important in attracting and retaining good workers. In addition, the contracts of three of the four staff unions expire next year, and the benefit program is typically a major area of bargaining (Ignatio, 2001, p. 28). Purpose and Scope of the Study

As has been noted by J. B. Adams (2002), a management consultant, "The success of employee benefit programs depends directly on whether employees need, understand, and appreciate the value of the benefits provided" (p. 220). Thus, to ensure that the benefit program is operating as effectively as possible, David Riggins, director of personnel, authorized this report on October 15, 20—. Specifically, the following problem was addressed in this study: What are the opinions of staff employees at Atlantic State University regarding their

Report Page in APA Style

Staff Benefit Program 18

References

Abbey Petroleum Industries. (2005). *2004 annual report*. San Francisco: Author.

Adams, J. B. (2003). *Compensation systems*. Boston: Brunswick Press.

Adhams, R., & Stevens, S. (2000). *Personnel management*. Cambridge, MA: All-State.

Directory of business and financial services. (2001). New York: Corporate Libraries Association.

Ivarson, A., Jr. (2001, September 29). Creating your benefit plan: A primer. *Business Month, 75,* 19–31.

Let employees determine their own benefits. (2004, January 12). *Manhattan Times*, p. C17.

Market research. (2004). In *The encyclopedia of business* (Vol. 2, pp. 436–441). Cleveland, OH: Collins.

National Institute of Mental Health. (2001). *Who pays the piper? Ten years of passing the buck* (DHHS Publication No. ADM 82-1195). Washington, DC: U.S. Government Printing Office.

Preminger, L. (Executive Producer). (2002, August 5). *The WKVX-TV evening news* [Television Broadcast]. Los Angeles: Valhalla Broadcasting Co.

Quincy, D. J. (2002, November 13). Maxwell announces new health benefit. New York: Maxwell. Retrieved January 14, 2003, from http://www.max_corp.com /NEWS/2001/f93500.html

Salary survey of service industries. (n.d.). Retrieved July 8, 2002, from http://www.bizinfo.com/census.gov/ind.lib/tab-0315.html

Young, L. (2002, June 3). Training doesn't always last. Message posted to http://groups.yahoo.com/group/personne1/message/51

References in APA Style

Santorini 2

Loretta J. Santorini

Professor Riggins

Management 348

8 December 20—

Evaluation of the Staff Benefit Program

at Atlantic State University

Employee benefits are a rapidly growing and increasingly important form of employee compensation for both for-profit and nonprofit organizations. According to a recent U.S. Chamber of Commerce survey, benefits now constitute 37% of all payroll cost, costing an average of $11,857 per year for each full-time employee (Adhams and Stevens 183). Thus, on the basis of cost alone, an organization's employee benefit program must be carefully monitored and evaluated.

Atlantic State University employs nearly 2,500 staff personnel, and they have not received a cost-of-living increase in two years. As a result, staff salaries may not have kept pace with private industry, meaning the university's employee benefit program may become more important in attracting and retaining good workers. In addition, the contracts of three of the four staff unions expire next year, and the benefit program is typically a major area of bargaining (Ivarson 28).

As has been noted by Berelson, a management consultant, "The success of employee benefit programs depends directly on whether the employees need, understand, and appreciate the value of the benefits provided" (220). Thus, to ensure that the benefit program is operating as effectively as possible, David Riggins, director of personnel, authorized this report on 15 October 20—.

Report Page in MLA Style

Santorini 18

Works Cited

Abbey Petroleum Industries. *2004 Annual Report*. San Francisco: Abbey Petroleum Industries, 2005.

Adams, Josiah B. *Compensation Systems*. Boston: Brunswick Press, 2003.

Adhams, Ramon, and Seymour Stevens. *Personnel Management*. Cambridge, MA: All-State, 2000.

Corporate Libraries Association. *Directory of Business and Financial Services*. New York: Corporate Libraries Association, 2001.

Ivarson, Andrew, Jr. "Creating Your Benefit Plan: A Primer." *Business Month*, 29 Sep. 2001: 19–31.

"Let Employees Determine Their Own Benefits." *Manhattan Times*, 12 Jan. 2004: C17.

"Market Research." *Encyclopedia of Business*, 2nd ed., Cleveland: Collins, 2004.

National Institute of Mental Health. *Who Pays the Piper? Ten Years of Passing the Buck*. DHHS Publication No. ADM 82-1195. Washington, DC: GPO, 2001.

O'Brian, Douglas, Personal interview. 13 May 2004.

Preminger, Larry (Executive Producer). *The WKVX-TV Evening News*. Los Angeles: Valhalla Broadcasting Co., 5 Aug. 2002.

Quincy, Dinah J. "Maxwell Announces New Health Benefit." *Maxwell Corp. Home Page*. 13 Nov. 2002. 14 Jan. 2002 <http://www.maxcorp.com/2002 /193500.html>.

Waerov, Denis V. "Reaction to Management's Offer." E-mail to the author. 18 Aug. 2004.

Works Cited Page in MLA Style

Citation Styles

Shown below is a representative list of different types of citations formtted in the three most common citation styles—business styloe (also appropriate for most academic reports, APA style, and MLA style. Although the list is quite extensive, you may occasionally encounter a type of citation not illustrated here. In that case, simply find a similar type of citation and adapt it to your specific source.

Within Document

	Business Style
One author—not named in text	In fact, fringe benefits are growing in importance as a part of an overall salary package.[1]
One author—named in text	Adams argues that health insurance is the most important benefit of all.[2]
Multiple authors—not named in text	The personalized benefit statement shown in Figure 3 contains all necessary legal information.[3]
Multiple authors—named in text	According to Berelson, Lazarsfield, and Connell,[4] the personalized benefit statement shown in Figure 3 contains all necessary legal information.
Multiple sources	Numerous research studies[5] have shown that white-collar employees prefer an increase in benefits to an increase in salary.
Author not identified	Another variation that is growing in popularity is the cafeteria-style program.[6]
Direct quotation	According to Ivarson, "There is no such creature as a 'fringe benefit' anymore."[7]

End of Report

	Business Style—Bibliography
Annual report	Abbey Petroleum Industries, *2003 Annual Report*, API, Inc., San Francisco, 2004.
Book—one author	Adams, Josiah B., *Compensation Systems*, Brunswick Press, Boston, 2002.
Book—two authors	Adhams, Ramon, and Seymour Stevens, *Personnel Administration*, All-State, Cambridge, Mass., 1999.
Book—three or more authors	Berelson, Sarah, et al., *Managing Your Benefit Program*, 13th ed., Novak-Siebold, Chicago, 2001.
Book—organization as author	*Directory of Business and Financial Services,* Corporate Libraries Assoc., New York, 2000.

References

Businesss Style: William A. Sabin, *The Gregg Reference Manual*, 9th ed., Westerville, Ohio, Glencoe/McGraw-Hill, 2001.

APA Style: *Publication Manual of the American Psychological Association*, 5th ed., Washington, D.C., American Psychological Association, 2001.

MLA Style: Joseph Gibaldi, *MLA Handbook for Writers of Research Papers*, 5th ed. New York, Modern Language Association of America, 1999; "MLA Style," *MLA Home Page*, September 20, 2000, ,http://www.mla.org. (October 30, 2001).

APA Style	MLA Style
In fact, fringe benefits are growing in importance as a part of an overall salary package (Ignatio, 2003).	In fact, fringe benefits are growing in importance as a part of an overall salary package (Ignatio 813).
Adams (2002) argues that health insurance is the most important benefit of all.	Adams argues that health insurance is the most important benefit of all (386–387).
The personalized benefit statement shown in Figure 3 contains all necessary legal information (Berelson, Lazarsfield, & Connell, 2001).	The personalized benefit statement shown in Figure 3 contains all necessary legal information (Berelson, Lazarsfield, & Connell 563).
According to Berelson, Lazarsfield, and Connell (2001, p. 563), the personalized benefit statement shown in Figure 3 contains all necessary legal information.	According to Berelson, Lazarsfield, and Connell, the personalized benefit statement shown in Figure 3 contains all necessary legal information (563).
Numerous research studies have shown that white-collar employees prefer an increase in benefits to an increase in salary (Adhams & Stevens, 1999; Ivarson, 2003; White, 2002).	Numerous research studies have shown that white-collar employees prefer an increase in benefits to an increase in salary (Adhams & Stevens 76, Ivarson 29; White).
Another variation that is growing in popularity is the cafeteria-style program ("Let Employees," 2003).	Another variation that is growing in popularity is the cafeteria-style program ("Let Employees" C17).
According to Ivarson (2003), "There is no such creature as a 'fringe benefit' anymore" (p. 27).	According to Ivarson, "There is no such creature as a 'fringe benefit' anymore" (27).

APA Style—References	MLA Style—Works Cited
Abbey Petroleum Industries. (2004). *2001 annual report*. San Francisco: API, Inc.	Abbey Petroleum Industries. *2003 Annual Report,* San Francisco: API, Inc., 2004.
Adams, J. B. (2002). *Compensation systems*. Boston: Brunswick Press.	Adams, Josiah B. *Compensation Systems*. Boston: Brunswick Press, 2002.
Adhams, R., & Stevens, S. (1999). *Personnel administration*. Cambridge, MA: All-State.	Adhams, Ramon, and Seymour Stevens. *Personnel Administration*. Cambridge, MA: All-State, 1999.
Berelson, S., Lazarsfield, P. F., & Connell, W., Jr. (2001). *Managing your benefit program* (13th ed.). Chicago: Novak-Siebold.	Berelson, Sarah, Paul Lazarsfield, and Will Connell, Jr. *Managing Your Benefit Program,* 13th ed. Chicago: Novak-Siebold, 2001.
Directory of business and financial services. (2000). New York: Corporate Libraries Association.	Corporate Libraries Association. *Directory of Business and Financial Services*. New York: Corporate Libraries Association, 2000.

End of Report (*continued*)

	Business Style—Bibliography
Journal article—paged continuously throughout the year	Ignatio, Enar, "Can Flexible Benefits Promote Your Company?" *Personnel Quarterly,* Vol. 20, September 2003, pp. 804–816.
Magazine article—paged starting anew with each issue	Ivarson, Andrew, Jr., "Creating Your Benefit Plan: A Primer," *Business Month,* September 29, 2000, pp. 19–31.
Newspaper article—unsigned	"Let Employees Determine Their Own Benefits," *Manhattan Times,* January 12, 2003, p. C17, col. 2.
Reference work article	"Market Research," *Encyclopedia of Business,* 2d ed., 2003.
Government document	National Institute of Mental Health, *Who Pays the Piper? Ten Years of Passing the Buck,* DHHS Publication No. ADM 82-1195, U.S. Government Printing Office, Washington, 2000.
Interview	O'Brian, Douglas, Interview by author, May 13, 2003.
Paper presented at a meeting	Patts, Regina. *Tuition Reimbursement,* paper presented at the meeting of the National Mayors' Conference, Trenton, N.J., August 5, 2003.
Television/radio broadcast	Preminger, Larry (Executive Producer), *The WKVX-TV Evening News,* Valhalla Broadcasting Co., Los Angeles, August 5, 2001.
CD-ROM article	Petelin, Rosana, "Wage Administration," *Martindale Interactive Business Encyclopedia* (CD-ROM), Martindale, Inc., Pompton Lakes, N.J., 2001.
World Wide Web page	Quincy, Dinah J., "Maxwell Announces New Health Benefit," *Maxwell Corp. Home Page,* November 13, 2001, <http://www.max_corp.com/NEWS/2001/f93500.html> (January 14, 2002).
Online database article	"Salary Survey of Service Industries," *BizInfo,* n.d., <http://www.bizinfo.com/census.gov/ind.lib/tab-0315.html> (July 8, 2001).
Email	Waerov, Denis V. <dvwaerov@aol.com>, "Reaction to Management's Offer," August 18, 2003, personal email (August 19, 2003).
Electronic discussion message (including listservs and newsgroups)	Young, Laurel <lyoung2@express.com>, "Training Doesn't Always Last," June 3, 2001, <http://groups.yahoo.com/group/personnel/message/51> (April 20, 2002).

APA Style—References	MLA Style—Works Cited
Ignatio, E. (2003). Can flexible benefits promote your company?" *Personnel Quarterly, 20,* 804–816.	Ignatio, Enar. "Can Flexible Benefits Promote Your Company?" *Personnel Quarterly* 20 (2003): 804–816.
Ivarson, A., Jr. (2000, September 29). Creating your benefit plan: A primer. *Business Month, 75,* 19–31.	Ivarson, Andrew, Jr. "Creating Your Benefit Plan: A Primer." *Business Month* 29 Sep. 2000: 19–31.
Let employees determine their own benefits. (2003, January 12). *Manhattan Times,* p. C17.	"Let Employees Determine Their Own Benefits." *Manhattan Times,* 12 Jan. 2003: C17.
Market research. (2003). In *The encyclopedia of business* (Vol. 2, pp. 436–441). Cleveland, OH: Collins.	"Market Research." *Encyclopedia of Business,* 2nd ed., Cleveland: Collins, 2003.
National Institute of Mental Health. (2000). *Who pays the piper? Ten years of passing the buck* (DHHS Publication No. ADM 82-1195). Washington, DC: U.S. Government Printing Office.	National Institute of Mental Health. *Who Pays the Piper? Ten Years of Passing the Buck.* DHHS Publication No. ADM 82-1195. Washington, DC: GPO, 2000.
O'Brian, D. (2003, May). Personal interview.	O'Brian, Douglas, Personal interview, 10 May 2003.
Patts, R. (2003, August). Tuition reimbursement. Paper presented at the meeting of the National Mayors' Conference, Trenton, NJ.	Patts, Regina. *Tuition Reimbursement.* Paper presented at the meeting of the National Mayors' Conference. Trenton, NJ, 5 Aug. 2003.
Preminger, L. (Executive Producer). (2001, August). *The WKVX-TV Evening News.* Los Angeles: Valhalla Broadcasting Co.	Preminger, Larry (Executive Producer). *The WKVX-TV Evening News.* Los Angeles: Valhalla Broadcasting Co., 5 Aug. 2001.
Petelin, R. (2001). *Wage administration.* Pompton Lakes, NJ: Martindale, Inc. Retrieved from Martindale database (Martindale Interactive Business Encyclopedia, CD-ROM).	Petelin, Rosana. "Wage Administration," *Martindale Interactive Business Encyclopedia.* CD-ROM. Pompton Lakes, NJ: Martindale, Inc., 1999.
Quincy, D. J. (2001, November 13). Maxwell announces new health benefit. New York: Maxwell. Retrieved January 14, 2002 from the World Wide Web: http://www.max_corp.com/NEWS/2001/f93500.html	Quincy, Dinah J. "Maxwell Announces New Health Benefit." *Maxwell Corp. Home Page.* 13 Nov. 1999. 14 Jan. 2000 <http://www.max_corp.com/NEWS/2001/f93500.html>.
Salary survey of service industries. (n.d.). Retrieved July 8, 2001, from BizInfo database on the World Wide Web: http://www.bizinfo.com/census.gov/ind.lib/tab-0315.html	"Salary Survey of Service Industries." *BizInfo.* n.d. 8 Jul. 2001 <http://www.bizinfo.com/census.gov/ind.lib/tab-0315.html>.
[Not cited in reference list. Cited in text as "D. V. Waerov (personal communication, August 18, 2003) proposes that . . . ."]	Waerov, Denis V. "Reaction to Management's Offer." Email to the author. 18 Aug. 2003.
Young, L. (2001, June 3). Training doesn't always last. Message posted to http://groups.yahoo.com/group/personnel/message/51	Young, Laurel. <lyoung2@express.com> "Training Doesn't Always Last." Online posting. 3 Jun. 2001. 20 Apr. 2002 <http://groups.yahoo.com/group/personnel/message/51>.

BUSINESS STYLE POINTERS

❑ The major differences between footnote and bibliographic entries are that (a) footnotes use the normal order for author names (e.g., "Raymond Stevens and Seymour Adams"), whereas bibliographies invert the order of the first author (e.g., "Stevens, Raymond, and Seymour Adams"); and (b) page numbers are included in bibliographic entries only when the material being cited is part of a larger work (for example, a journal or newspaper article).

❑ Type the authors' names exactly as they appear in print. For publications by two authors, arrange only the first name in last-name/first-name order. With three or more authors, type only the first name followed by *et al.* (not in italics). Arrange publications by the same author in alphabetical order, according to the publication title.

❑ Include page numbers only when the material being cited is part of a larger work. Do not italicize edition numbers. Be consistent in formatting the ordinal in raised position (13th) or in normal position (13th).

❑ Include the two-letter state name (using the USPS abbreviation) only if confusion might result. Use a shortened form of the publisher's name; e.g., *McGraw-Hill* rather than *McGraw-Hill Book Company,* and use common abbreviations (such as *Assoc.* or *Co.).*

❑ For online citations:

• For email, insert the type of email (e.g., "office communication" or "personal email").

• If the date of an online posting cannot be determined, insert the abbreviation *n.d.* (no date)—not in italics.

• Enclose in parentheses as the last section of the citation the date you accessed the site, followed by a period.

• Follow the capitalization, punctuation, and spacing exactly as given in the original online address.

• You may break an online citation *before* (but never after) a dot (.), single slash (/), double slash (//), hyphen (-), underscore (_), at symbol (@), or any other mark of punctuation. Do *not* insert a hyphen within an online address to signify an end-of-line break.

End Notes

Chapter 1

1. Watson Wyatt Worldwide, *Linking Communications with Strategy to Achieve Business Goals*, Bethesda, MD, 1999, p. 6.
2. Kathleen Driscoll, "Your Voice Can Make or Break You," *Democrat and Chronicle*, August 26, 1993, p. 10B.
3. David Shenk, *Data Smog: Surviving the Information Glut*, HarperCollins, San Francisco, 1997.
4. Peter Drucker, quoted by Bill Moyers in *A World of Ideas*, Doubleday, Garden City, NY, 1990.
5. Richard Saul Wurman, *Information Anxiety 2*, Que Publishers, Indianapolis, IN, 2001.
6. Albert Mehrabian, "Communicating Without Words," *Psychology Today*, September 1968, pp. 53–55.
7. Edward T. Hall, *The Hidden Dimension*, Doubleday, Garden City, NY, 1966, pp. 107–122.
8. Stephen Karel, "Learning Culture the Hard Way," *Consumer Markets Abroad*, May 1988, pp. 1, 15.
9. Judi Sanders, "Top 20 College Slang Terms," *California State Polytechnic University, Pomona Home Page*, May 1, 2001 <http://www.intranet.csupomona.edu/~jasanders/slang/top20.html> (January 17, 2003).
8. Stephen Karel, "Learning Culture the Hard Way," *Consumer Markets Abroad*, May 1988, pp. 1, 15.
10. This case was adapted from Brenda R. Sims, "Linking Ethics and Language in the Technical Communication Classroom," Technical Communication Quarterly, Vol. 2, No. 3, Summer 1993, p. 285.

Chapter 2

1. John R. Pierce, "Communication," *Scientific American*, vol. 227, September 1972, p. 36.
2. Irving R. Janis, *Victims of Groupthink*, Houghton Mifflin, Boston, 1972.
3. These guidelines are based on principles contained in Peter R. Scholtes, *The Team Handbook: How to Use Teams to Improve Quality*, Madison, WI, Joiner Associates, 1988, pp. 6.23–6.28.
4. *2000 Statistical Abstract of the United States*, Washington, DC, U.S. Government Printing Office, 2000, Table 16.
5. Ibid.
6. Sondra Thiederman, "The Diverse Workplace: Strategies for Getting 'Culture Smart,'" *The Secretary*, March 1996, p. 8.
7. Alice Sargeant, *The Androgeneous Manager*, American Management Association, New York, 1983, p. 37.
8. Beth Belton, "U.S. Brings Economy into Information Age," *USA Today*, March 17, 1999, p. 1B.
9. "Reaching Out with Email," *PC Week*, May 4, 1998, p. 100.
10. Charles McGoon, "Speed versus Accuracy in Cyberspace," *Communication World*, January/February 1996, p. 23.

11. "Number of Telephones per 100 People," n.d., <http://www.american.edu/MOGIT/li1116a/no_tel.html> (February 12, 2002).
12. Tina Brown, "The Dress-Down Debate," *Industry Week*, June 20, 1994, p. 43.
13. *Casual Clothing in the Workplace*, San Francisco, Levi Strauss & Co., 1995.

Chapter 4

1. Marilyn vos Savant, "Ask Marilyn," *Parade Magazine*, November 3, 1996, p. 8.
2. Richard Lederer, "Strength of a Single Syllable," *Reader's Digest*, June 1991, p. 157.

Chapter 5

1. "Netiquette" from Virginia Shea, "The Core Rules of Netiquette," Albion.com (January 16, 2002).

Chapter 11

1. John Naisbitt, *Megatrends: Ten New Directions Shaping Our Lives*, Warner Books, New York, 1984, p. 17.
2. Theophilus B. A. Aldo, "The Effects of Dimensionality in Computer Graphics," *Journal of Business Communication*, vol. 31, December 1994, pp. 253—265.
3. See, for example, "Tabling the Move to Computer Graphics," *Wall Street Journal*, January 30, 1991, p. B1; Jerimiah J. Sullivan, "Financial Presentation Format and Managerial Decision Making: Tables Versus Graphs," *Management Communication Quarterly*, vol. 2, November 1988, pp. 194—216.
4. Edward Tufte, *The Visual Display of Quantitative Information*, Graphics Press, Cheshire, CT, 1983.

Chapter 13

1. Kerry L. Johnson, "You Were Saying," *Managers Magazine*, February 1989, p. 19.
2. Wharton Applied Research Center, "A Study of the Effects of the Use of Overhead Transparencies on Business Meetings, Final Report," Philadelphia: University of Pennsylvania, September 14, 1981; Tad Simons, "Study Shows Just How Much Visuals Increase Persuasiveness," *Presentations Magazine*, March 1998, p. 20.
3. Betty A. Marton, "How to Construct a Winning Presentation," *Harvard Management Communication Letter*, April 2000, p. 5.
4. Albert Mehrabian, "Communicating Without Words," *Psychology Today*, September 1968, pp. 53–55.

5. Dawn E. Waldrop, "What You Wear Is Almost as Important as What You Say," *Presentations*, July 2000, p. 74.

6. David Wallechinsky, Irving Wallace, and Amy Wallace, *The Book of Lists*, William Morrow, New York, 1977, pp. 469–470.

7. Jolie Solomon, "Executives Who Dread Public Speaking Learn to Keep Their Cool in the Spotlight," *Wall Street Journal*, May 4, 1990, p. B1.

8. *Clear Communication*, vol. 1, no. 2, Fall 1993, p. 2.

Chapter 14

1. Sandra L. Latimer, "First Impressions," *Mt. Pleasant (MI) Morning Sun*, May 8, 1989, p. 6.

2. See, for example, Jules Harcourt and A. C. "Buddy" Krizan, "A Comparison of Résumé Content Preferences of *Fortune 500* Personnel Administrators and Business Communication Instructors," *Journal of Business Communication*, Spring 1989, pp. 177–190; Rod Little, "Keep Your Résumé Short," *USA Today*, July 28, 1989, p. B1; Darlene C. Pibal, "Criteria for Effective Résumés as Perceived by Personnel Directors," *Personnel Administrator*, May 1985, pp. 119–123.

3. Elizabeth Blackburn-Brockman and Kelly Belanger, "One Page or Two? A National Study of CPA Recruiters' Preferences for Résumé Length," *Journal of Business Communication*, January 2001, pp. 29–57.

4. "Most Serious Résumé Gaffes," *Communication Briefings*, March 1991, p. 6.

5. "To Be or Not to Be," *The Secretary*, April 1991, p. 6.

6. Albert P. Karr, "Labor Letter," *Wall Street Journal*, September 1, 1992, p. A1.

7. Harcourt and Krizan, pp. 177–190.

8. "Flashcard," *Education Life* (supplement to *New York Times*), November 5, 1989, p. 21.

9. Therese Droste, "Executive Résumés: The Ultimate Calling Card," *Hospitals*, March 5, 1989, p. 72.

10. Stephanie Armour, "Security Checks Worry Workers," *USA Today*, June 19, 2002, p. B1.

11. Lynn Ulrich and Don Trumbo, "The Selection Interview Since 1949," *Psychological Bulletin*, vol. 43, 1956, p. 100.

12. Shelly Liles, "Wrong Hire Might Prove Costly," *USA Today*, June 6, 1989, p. 6B.

13. "Creative Résumés," *Dun's Business Month*, June 1985, p. 20; Nelda Spinks and Barron Wells, "Employment Interviews: Trends in the *Fortune 500* Companies—1980–1988, *ABC Bulletin*, December 1988, p. 17; "Will Ethical Conflicts Undo Your Career?" *Mt. Pleasant (MI) Morning Sun*, May 12, 1988, p. 9.

Index

I-1